# LEADING FROM THE NORTH

RETHINKING NORTHERN
AUSTRALIA DEVELOPMENT

# LEADING FROM THE NORTH

RETHINKING NORTHERN
AUSTRALIA DEVELOPMENT

EDITED BY RUTH WALLACE,
SHARON HARWOOD, ROLF GERRITSEN,
BRUCE PRIDEAUX, TOM BREWER,
LINDA ROSENMAN AND ALLAN DALE

PRESS

Published by ANU Press
The Australian National University
Acton ACT 2601, Australia
Email: anupress@anu.edu.au

Available to download for free at press.anu.edu.au

ISBN (print): 9781760464424
ISBN (online): 9781760464431

WorldCat (print): 1262904233
WorldCat (online): 1262903656

DOI: 10.22459/LN.2021

This title is published under a Creative Commons Attribution-NonCommercial-NoDerivatives 4.0 International (CC BY-NC-ND 4.0).

The full licence terms are available at
creativecommons.org/licenses/by-nc-nd/4.0/legalcode

Cover design and layout by ANU Press

This edition © 2021 ANU Press

# Contents

| | |
|---|---|
| Preface | ix |
| Acknowledgements | xiii |
| Contributors | xv |

**Section 1: Rethinking Regional Development and Social Infrastructure in Northern Australia**
Sharon Harwood

1. Place-Based Land Use Planning and Development in Northern Australia: Cape York Peninsula, Queensland — 5
   Sharon Harwood and Benjamin Christie-Johnston
2. Place-Based Agricultural Development: A New Way of Thinking about an Old Idea in Northern Australia — 25
   Jim Turnour, Kate Andrews, Allan P. Dale, Connar McShane, Michelle Thompson and Bruce Prideaux
3. Investing in the Future: Human and Social Service Development in Northern Australia — 45
   Hurriyet Babacan and Narayan Gopalkrishnan
4. Underpinning Development: Health and Health Workforce in Northern Australia — 81
   Scott R. Davis, Felicity Croker and Alexandra Edelman

**Section 2: Economic and Business Development in the North**
Rolf Gerritsen

5. Pulse and Pause: Researching the Economic Future of Northern and Remote Australia — 109
   Rolf Gerritsen
6. Issues in the Future Directions of Tourism in Northern Australia — 125
   Bruce Prideaux, Benxiang Zeng and Sharon Harwood

7. Economic Equity and Major Development  143
Natalie Stoeckl

8. Other Views of Northern Australian Aspirations: Pre-Notions, Ideologies and Remoteness  159
Judith Lovell and Don Zoellner

9. National Data: Reflecting Northern Australian Aspirations?  183
Don Zoellner and Judith Lovell

## Section 3: Demographic Trends and Migration: Key Issues Facing Further Development in Northern Australia
Bruce Prideaux

10. The Demography of Developing Northern Australia  219
Andrew Taylor and Pawinee Yuhun

11. Attracting and Retaining International Migrants: A Key Issue in Developing Northern Australia  243
Linda Rosenman, Kate Golebiowska, Andrew Taylor, Petra T. Buergelt, Hannah Payer, Huw Brokensha, Jan Salmon, Alicia Boyle, Kerstin K. Zander and Pawinee Yuhun

## Section 4: Water, Land and Energy in the North
Tom D. Brewer

12. A Case-Based Discussion on the Disjuncture between Local Values and Federal, State and Territory Development Policy in Northern Australia  273
Tom D. Brewer, Sharon Harwood, Ainsley Archer, David Williams and Allan P. Dale

13. Land Tenure and Development in Northern Australia  293
Allan P. Dale, Bruce Taylor and Marcus B. Lane

14. Governing the Community-Based Natural Resource Management System in Northern Australia: Challenges and Opportunities  309
Allan P. Dale, Gabriel Crowley, Tom D. Brewer, Kate Andrews, Brian Warren, Karen Vella and Ruth Potts

15. Comparing Roles and Rights of Indigenous Groups in Local Governance of Trepang Fisheries in Northern Australia and Eastern Indonesia  329
Dirk J. Steenbergen, Gemma Wickens and Jackie Gould

16. Dry Thinking, Wet Places: Conceptualising Fluid States  353
Paul Carter

## Section 5: Thriving in Northern Climates
Linda Rosenman

17. Timing and Climate: Rainfall Variability in Northern Australia 373
    Chris O'Brien, Sara Beavis, Andrew Campbell and Tom Griffiths
18. Killing Two Birds with One Stone: Developing Northern Australian Adaptive Capabilities to Sustainably Develop Competent and Thriving Communities Capable of Responding Effectively to Natural Hazards 391
    Petra T. Buergelt, Douglas Paton, Andrew Campbell, Helen James and Alison Cottrell
19. Perceptions About Climate Change Impacts and Adaptation — Case Studies from Indigenous Communities in Northern and Central Australia 419
    Kerstin K. Zander, Yiheyis T. Maru, Digby Race, Supriya Mathew and John Rainbird
20. Design for Liveability in Tropical Australia 435
    Lisa Law, Shokhida Safarova, Andrew Campbell and Edward Halawa

## Section 6: Governance Systems in Northern Australia
Allan P. Dale

21. New Pathways for the Governance of Northern Development 455
    Allan P. Dale, Andrew Campbell, Michael Douglas, Alistar Robertson, Ruth Wallace and Peter Davies
22. Collaborative Research into Contemporary Indigenous Governance 479
    Linda Ford, Michael Christie, Catherine Bow, Tanyah Nasir, Michaela Spencer, Matt Campbell, Helen Verran and John Prior
23. Local Knowledge and the Challenge of Regional Governance 493
    Paul Carter
24. Revisiting Governance Systems Analysis in Northern Australia: Exploring Critical Systems Thinking as a Framework for Engaging with Multiplicity and Incommensurability 509
    Anne Stephens, Elspeth Oppermann and Allan P. Dale
25. Building Regional Research Capacity: The Northern Research Futures Collaborative Research Network 541
    Lawrence Cram

# Preface

Northern Australia, as defined in the 2015 Australian Government' report *Our north, our future: White paper on developing Northern Australia*, consists of the Northern Territory and parts of Western Australia and Queensland above the Tropic of Capricorn. The region, covering 40 per cent of Australia's land mass, has abundant minerals and energy resources as well as vast potentials in agriculture and tourism.

As outlined in the 2015 white paper, a series of large-scale projects are set to drive population growth, urbanisation and infrastructure development in Northern Australia. To achieve these goals, it is important to capture and analyse existing knowledge of the economic, social and environmental impacts of existing policies and explore the potential impacts of these factors on any plans for development.

*Leading from the North. Rethinking Northern Australia Development* originated from a multi-disciplinary research collaboration that helped establish important research essential to meet the national challenges associated with living sustainably in the remote tropic zone and the interfaces between community and environments. It consists of place-based research focused on and in Northern Australia. The research considers the implications of these realities for development and the differential impact of development on communities and environments. Each chapter is based on research by northern-based researchers and practitioners that provide evidence-based analysis of the secondary costs and effects of development, including for Indigenous citizens and communities. Policies and funding to encourage development of Northern Australia need to consider the social, environmental, climatic and economic realities of Northern Australia to understand and minimise unanticipated and often perverse outcomes.

Several topics are addressed throughout this book, including social infrastructure; governance systems; economic, business and regional development; climates and adaptations; natural resources policies; and trends in demography and migration in the region.

Section 1 of this book analyses the impact of the one-size-fits-all approach to policy development and implementation in Northern Australia. Each chapter examines the specific attributes that define the socioeconomic characteristics of Northern Australian residents to describe how the application of current policy affects the health and wellbeing of these residents and makes a series of recommendations for reform. The four chapters in this section address these seemingly opposing views, but from a pragmatic northern-held view.

Section 2 of this book comprises five chapters that contribute to but do not define northern economic development. The chapters offer insights into the history and theory of northern economic development, a perspective on the northern tourism industry and its failure of demand creation and an interpretation of inequity issues in Northern Australia's economic development, and the final two interlinked chapters on a 'ground-up' approach to Aboriginal economic development use micro-level statistics to delineate a mixed-market economy in central Australian Aboriginal settlements.

Section 3 of this book outlines a number of the key demographic and migration challenges that need to be addressed if the ambitious population targets contained in the 2015 white paper are to be achieved. The two chapters in this section discuss population as a key factor in determining development pathways for regions, with the small resident population of Northern Australia being one of the principle limitations hampering future economic and social development of the region.

Section 4 of this book contains five chapters that offer a rich set of ideas portraying northern development in a different light. The chapters range from critical reflections on and possible solutions to the northern development dilemma, to governance of natural resource management. Connecting themes include the fluid and intertwined nature of northern people, places and policy; the emergence of the north as a place with a past and present able to speak for its future; and the north as a place of undervalued uniqueness and potential for innovation.

Climatic conditions are widely viewed as having negative implications for the development of Northern Australia. Against a backdrop of predictions of major climate changes, the chapters in Section 5 of this book consider the region's climate and its implications for human living and working conditions and the future economic development of Northern Australia.

The authors identify adaptive strategies to reduce the impacts and mitigate the negative effects of climatic extremes to facilitate people living and working healthily in Northern Australia. These present a starting point for providing regionally specific analyses of climate to support appropriate measures to enable populations to thrive in Northern Australia.

Overall, charting a clear pathway for the future of Northern Australia will rise or fall based on the health of our overall system of governance and decision-making related to the north, inclusive of national, pan-northern, jurisdictional (Western Australian, Northern Territory and Queensland), regional and local scales. The final collection of chapters in Section 6 of this book provide overviews of some of the key governance challenges and opportunities essential to building a stronger future for Northern Australia and its communities. These opportunities and challenges include wide exploration of the need for greater engagement and evidence-building in governance at all scales. They also include the need to focus on supporting strong Indigenous governance as an important feature of the wider system. Particular attention is also paid to supporting improved regional and local governance. The importance of building the endemic research and development capacity of Northern Australia is also explored, reminding us of the importance of independent academic critique in strengthening Northern Australian governance and decision-making.

This book aims to improve public dialogue around the future of Northern Australia to underpin robust and flexible planning and policy frameworks and provide opportunities for growth in the face of changing economies and technologies. Due to its collaborative nature, this book has taken a few years in the making and experienced delays during the COVID-19 pandemic. The issues and challenges mentioned in each chapter, faced by the people living in Northern Australia, continue to be relevant and crucial to Northern Australia development. I hope that the research and discussions presented in this book will help guide the policies associated with Northern Australia development based on the unique viewpoints of those who have worked and lived in the north.

Professor Ruth Wallace
Dean, College of Indigenous Futures, Education & the Arts
Director, Northern Institute
Charles Darwin University

# Acknowledgements

We would like to thank the editors, authors and other contributors who assisted in the production of this book and their patience as the publication was brought to press.

This book was initially developed and funded through the Australian Government's Collaborative Research Networks program. The multi-disciplinary collaboration titled *Northern Research Futures* was a collaboration between Charles Darwin University, The Australian National University, James Cook University and the Australian Institute of Marine Science. The alliance between four partner institutions built on existing strengths and research relationships to establish a long-anticipated focus on research on issues of national importance facing Northern Australia and its immediate regional neighbours.

The research resulting from this collaboration addressed the social impacts and processes of change in Northern Australia related to infrastructure development, public policy, climate change, migration and security.

# Contributors[1]

**Kate Andrews**, Fenner School for Environment and Society, The Australian National University, Canberra, ACT, Australia.

**Ainsley Archer**, Australian Institute of Marine Science, Townsville, Qld, Australia.

**Hurriyet Babacan**, The Cairns Institute, James Cook University, Cairns, Qld, Australia.

**Sara Beavis**, Fenner School for Environment and Society, The Australian National University, Canberra, ACT, Australia.

**Catherine Bow**, Northern Institute, Charles Darwin University, Darwin, NT, Australia.

**Alicia Boyle**, Northern Institute, Charles Darwin University, Darwin, NT, Australia.

**Tom D. Brewer**, Australian National Centre for Ocean Resources and Security, University of Wollongong, Wollongong, NSW, and Northern Institute, Charles Darwin University, Darwin, NT, and Arafura Timor Research Facility, Australian Institute of Marine Science, Darwin, NT, Australia.

**Huw Brokensha**, Northern Institute, Charles Darwin University, Darwin, NT, Australia.

**Petra T. Buergelt**, Faculty of Health, University of Canberra, Canberra, ACT, and College of Health and Human Sciences, Charles Darwin University, Darwin, NT, Australia.

**Andrew Campbell**, Research Institute for the Environment and Livelihoods, Charles Darwin University, Darwin, NT, and Australian Centre for International Agricultural Research, Canberra, ACT, Australia.

---

1   Affiliations are at the time of writing.

**Matt Campbell**, Northern Institute, Charles Darwin University, Darwin, NT, Australia.

**Paul Carter**, School of Architecture and Urban Design, RMIT University, Melbourne, Vic., Australia.

**Michael Christie**, Northern Institute, Charles Darwin University, Darwin, NT, Australia.

**Benjamin Christie-Johnston**, Centre for Tropical Urban and Regional Planning, James Cook University, Cairns, Qld, Australia.

**Alison Cottrell**, College of Marine and Environmental Sciences, Centre for Disaster Studies, James Cook University, Townsville, Qld, Australia.

**Lawrence Cram**, Charles Darwin University, Darwin, NT, and Research School of Physics, The Australian National University, Canberra, ACT, Australia.

**Felicity Croker**, College of Medicine and Dentistry, James Cook University, Qld, Australia.

**Gabriel Crowley**, The Cairns Institute, James Cook University, Cairns, Qld, and Research Institute for the Environment and Livelihoods, Charles Darwin University, Darwin, NT, Australia.

**Allan P. Dale**, The Cairns Institute, James Cook University, Cairns, Qld, Australia.

**Peter Davies**, Food Futures Institute, Murdoch University, Murdoch, WA, and The University of Western Australia, Perth, WA, Australia.

**Scott R. Davis**, The Cairns Institute, James Cook University, Cairns, Qld, Australia.

**Michael Douglas**, NESP Resilient Landscape Hub, University of Western Australia, Perth, WA, Australia.

**Alexandra Edelman**, Australian Institute of Tropical Health and Medicine, James Cook University, Townsville, Qld, Australia.

**Linda Ford**, Northern Institute, Charles Darwin University, Darwin, NT, Australia.

**Rolf Gerritsen**, Northern Institute, Charles Darwin University, Darwin, NT, Australia.

**Kate Golebiowska**, Northern Institute, Charles Darwin University, Darwin, NT, Australia.

**Narayan Gopalkrishnan**, College of Arts, Society and Education, James Cook University, Cairns, Qld, Australia.

**Jackie Gould**, Northern Institute, Charles Darwin University, Darwin, NT, Australia.

**Tom Griffiths**, Centre for Environmental History, The Australian National University, Canberra, ACT, Australia.

**Edward Halawa**, Charles Darwin University, Darwin, NT, Australia.

**Sharon Harwood**, Centre for Tropical Urban and Regional Planning, James Cook University, Cairns, Qld, Australia.

**Helen James**, School of Culture, History and Language, Asian Disasters Research Network, The Australian National University, Canberra, ACT, Australia.

**Marcus B. Lane**, Division of Tropical Environments and Societies, James Cook University, Townsville, Qld, Australia.

**Lisa Law**, Tropical Urbanism and Design Lab, College of Science and Engineering, James Cook University, Cairns, Qld, Australia.

**Judith Lovell**, Northern Institute, Charles Darwin University, Darwin, NT, Australia.

**Yiheyis T. Maru**, CSIRO, Canberra, ACT, and CSIRO Land and Water Flagship, Alice Springs, NT, Australia.

**Supriya Mathew**, Centre for Remote Health, Menzies School of Health Research, and Northern Institute, Charles Darwin University, and Cooperative Research Centre for Remote Economic Participation, Alice Springs, NT, Australia.

**Connar McShane**, College of Healthcare Sciences, James Cook University, Townsville, Qld, Australia.

**Tanyah Nasir**, Tanya Nasir Consulting Services, Darwin, NT, Australia.

**Chris O'Brien**, Research Institute for the Environment and Livelihoods, Charles Darwin University, Darwin, NT, Australia.

**Elspeth Oppermann**, Rachel Carson Center for Environment and Society, Ludwig Maximilian University, Munich, Germany, and National University of Singapore, Singapore, and Northern Institute, Charles Darwin University, Darwin, NT, Australia.

**Douglas Paton**, College of Health and Human Sciences, Charles Darwin University, Darwin, NT, and Faculty of Health, University of Canberra, Canberra, ACT, Australia.

**Hannah Payer**, Northern Institute, Charles Darwin University, Darwin, NT, Australia.

**Ruth Potts**, School of Geography and Planning, Cardiff University, Cardiff, UK, and School of Civil Engineering and Built Environment, Science and Engineering Faculty, Queensland University of Technology, Brisbane, Qld, Australia.

**Bruce Prideaux**, School of Business and Law, Centre for Tourism and Regional Opportunities, Central Queensland University, Qld, Australia.

**John Prior**, Northern Institute, Charles Darwin University, Darwin, NT, Australia.

**Digby Race**, University of the Sunshine Coast, Qld, and CSIRO Land and Water Flagship, and Cooperative Research Centre for Remote Economic Participation, Alice Springs, NT, Australia.

**John Rainbird**, Torres Strait Regional Authority, Cairns, Qld, Australia.

**Alistar Robertson**, School of Biological Sciences, University of Western Australia, Perth, WA, Australia.

**Linda Rosenman**, Northern Institute, Charles Darwin University, Darwin, NT, and The University of Queensland, Brisbane, Qld, Australia.

**Shokhida Safarova**, Charles Darwin University, Darwin, NT, Australia.

**Jan Salmon**, Northern Institute, Charles Darwin University, Darwin, NT, Australia.

**Michaela Spencer**, Northern Institute, Charles Darwin University, Darwin, NT, Australia.

**Dirk J. Steenbergen**, Australian National Centre for Ocean Resources and Security, University of Wollongong, NSW, and Research Institute for Environment and Livelihoods, Charles Darwin University, NT, Australia.

**Anne Stephens**, The Cairns Institute, James Cook University, Cairns, Qld, Australia.

**Natalie Stoeckl**, College of Business and Economics, University of Tasmania, Hobart, TAS, and (Adjunct) James Cook University, Townsville, Qld, Australia.

**Andrew Taylor**, Northern Institute, Charles Darwin University, Darwin, NT, Australia.

**Bruce Taylor**, CSIRO, Brisbane, Qld, Australia.

**Michelle Thompson**, School of Business and Law, Centre for Tourism and Regional Opportunities, Central Queensland University, Qld, Australia.

**Jim Turnour**, The Cairns Institute, James Cook University, Cairns, Qld, Australia.

**Karen Vella**, School of Civil Engineering and Built Environment, Science and Engineering Faculty, Queensland University of Technology, Brisbane, Qld, Australia.

**Helen Verran**, Northern Institute, Charles Darwin University, Darwin, NT, Australia.

**Ruth Wallace**, Northern Institute, Charles Darwin University, Darwin, NT, Australia.

**Brian Warren**, Rangelands NRM Pty Ltd, Perth, WA, and Independent Consultant, Margaret River, WA, Australia.

**Gemma Wickens**, Northern Institute, Charles Darwin University, Darwin, NT, Australia.

**David Williams**, Arafura Timor Research Facility, Australian Institute of Marine Science, Darwin, NT, Australia.

**Pawinee Yuhun**, Northern Institute, Charles Darwin University, Darwin, NT, Australia.

**Kerstin K. Zander**, Northern Institute, Charles Darwin University, Darwin, NT, Australia.

**Benxiang Zeng**, Northern Institute, Charles Darwin University, Darwin, NT, Australia.

**Don Zoellner**, Northern Institute, Charles Darwin University, Darwin, NT, Australia.

# Section 1

# Rethinking Regional Development and Social Infrastructure in Northern Australia

Sharon Harwood

There has never been a political or intellectual consensus about how or why to develop the north (Megarrity, 2018). Therefore, service provision, infrastructure investment and government policy has been subject to a series of fads and fashions. Megarrity (2018) suggests that these fads and fashions are underpinned by opposing fears and perceptions held by southern Australians about the large tracts of vacant and unused lands and, conversely, the belief of those in the north that underdevelopment should be righted by Commonwealth investment to increase access to basic services and a minimum standard of living.

The four chapters included in this section address these seemingly opposing views but from a pragmatic northern-held view. By this it is inferred that the authors are northerners and apply evidence to suggest a middle ground, whereby policy allows the north to prosper and develop but in accordance with the culture, needs and aspirations of those who are most affected by the outcomes of decision-making.

This section analyses the impact of the prevailing one-size-fits-all approach to policy development and implementation in Northern Australia. Each chapter examines the specific attributes that define the socioeconomic characteristics of Northern Australian residents to describe how the application of current policy affects the health and wellbeing of its these residents and makes a series of recommendations for reform.

The first two chapters describe the disjunct between land use as a planning system and as the use of the land for agriculture, and the ability of the policy system to reflect the capacity of the land to respond to and supply externally bound expectations. The following two chapters describe how the social wellbeing and health of Northern Australia residents can be enhanced by policy that responds to and applies an evidence-based approach to guide service delivery and decision-making.

Harwood and Christie-Johnston apply the analogy of the 'have and have-nots' to describe the impact of southern-based decisions on northern-based residents. This chapter describes how the industrialised planning and development system exacerbates Indigenous disadvantage. The authors recommend the creation of a separate Indigenous planning system for lands owned by Aboriginal entities to reflect landowner and native title aspirations, as opposed to the top-down state-based constraints model to planning that focuses on developing large city centres.

Turnour et al. describe how the enduring productivist models of agriculture pervade because of the need to do something with the empty and unused lands in the north. The authors describe the impact of policies' circular conundrum (from failure to high expectations) that impairs the capacity to learn and adapt from past mistakes. This creates a perception of failure that is attributed to location such as being remote and north. The authors propose a move to a post-productivist model of agriculture that focuses on the relationship between the farmer, the wider community, landscape values and environmental protection, referred to as a place-based framework. The authors argue that the place-based framework provides a new narrative for northern agriculture that involves a deeper understanding of the physical, environmental and sociocultural assets of the region.

The chapters by Babacan and Gopalkrishnan and Davis et al. describe how Commonwealth investment can be directed more efficiently to gain more effective outcomes for northerners.

Babacan and Gopalkrishnan describe the effects of spatial disadvantage in Northern Australia that leads to social disadvantage and marginalisation. The authors argue that ineffective investment in the social and human services sector exacerbates Northern Australia's lack of competitiveness, reinforces the persistence of weak human capital and increases the cost of service provision. The focus of this chapter is on the creation of policy to support a sustainable model of rural and remote human service delivery that includes sustained service funding, policy coordination, community involvement in planning and delivery, and adoption of place-based approaches, creating a Northern Australian evidence base and building the capacity of the sector's workforce.

Davis et al. describe the critical health challenges experienced in Northern Australia, including poor health status, shorter lives, higher rates of accident and injury, greater levels of illness and lower rates of certain medical treatment. This is significantly worse for Indigenous Australians living in the north. The authors describe the range of reforms to service provisions such as integrated telehealth, a move to prevention to manage health and lifestyle and a focus on connected primary health care as opposed to reactionary acute care models. These reforms in service delivery necessitate changes to the way in which health care professionals are educated, trained and supported after graduation. The health service delivery and workforce training models continue to suffer from the circular conundrum described by Turnour et al. and require strategic collaboration across the north to deliver place-based responses, but these continue to be hampered by legislative and regulatory discord between jurisdictions.

All the chapters in this section highlight the fundamental principles underpinning a competitive region. These include place-based policy responses, explicit recognition of the impact the circular conundrum has on the capacity of northern residents to design and respond to appropriate models of land use and service delivery, and a fundamental need to support Northern Australia in developing policy in and with the north, by the north and for the north.

# Reference

Megarrity, L. (2018). *Northern dreams: The politics of northern development in Australia*. Melbourne, Vic.: Australian Scholarly Publishing.

# 1

# Place-Based Land Use Planning and Development in Northern Australia: Cape York Peninsula, Queensland

Sharon Harwood and Benjamin Christie-Johnston

The purpose of this chapter is to describe how urban and regional planning practice applied to the creation of development plans reinforce social and economic dislocation in remote settlements in Northern Australia. This chapter examines the range of planning policies that affect regional planning and development in remote Queensland using the Cape York region as a case study. The planning literature readily acknowledges that regional economies and land use planning are inter-related, yet little is known about how a change in land use regulation may affect the performance of local and regional economies (Kim, 2011). In urban and regional planning the interaction between regional economies and land use have traditionally been considered through a top-down approach (Kim, 2011). The literature regarding planning for economic development in remote regions in Australia (Harwood et al., 2011) and Canada (Markey et al., 2006, 2008, 2012) highlight the inadequacies of top-down and industry sector–based approaches in favour of a place-based approach, yet the practice of place-based planning remains elusive. This chapter analyses the implications of contemporary planning practice on development opportunities for the Aboriginal people of Cape York in Queensland and provides a conceptual framework for a place-based approach to land use planning for future application.

## Introduction

This chapter applies the 'haves' (decision-makers in the urban core) and 'have-nots' (affected communities in the periphery) analogy created by Taylor et al. (2011) to illustrate the need for alternative approaches to planning and development in remote townships and communities in Northern Australia using Cape York as an example. Taylor et al. (2011, p. 14) argued there is a high risk of the continuation of a bifurcated society in Northern Australia between the 'haves' and 'have-nots' from current policies and proposals to develop the north. Bifurcated in this context infers that development is concentrated in the urban centres, while rural and remote populations become vulnerable from a lack of development. This vulnerability is exacerbated from the export of social and natural capital from rural and remote regions that is only partially compensated by return flows of financial capital from national beneficiaries (e.g. welfare transfers). Taylor et al. (2011) suggested that larger development projects in the north have fallen well short of their stated intentions and benefited a small but elite group of 'haves' (e.g. owners and operators associated with the resource sector), while many of the local long-term residents, including the Indigenous residents, are relegated to a group of 'have-nots'.

Northern Australia is not a homogenous region. Rather, it is a collection of regions and local communities north of the Tropic of Capricorn, each with their own set of unique characteristics. Development should logically follow on from planning activities; however, there are varied and at times opposing views on development that obscure the realisation of community aspirations for the way in which their settlements are spatially arranged and economies are transformed. Altman (2013, p. 13) maintained there is a tendency to interchange the words 'development' and 'growth' and that they connote very different concepts. Development is generally associated with production and wealth creation, but it can also connote improvements in social wellbeing, living standards and opportunities. Altman also argued that often the real social and cultural costs of development are borne by the 'poorest and least powerful'.

Australian Indigenous people own much of Northern Australia under land rights and native title laws that account for 48 per cent of the 3 million km$^2$ of land north of the Tropic of Capricorn (Altman, 2014). In the Cape York Peninsula, this rate is much higher at 98 per cent (Shannon Burns, Cape York Land Council, personal communication, 22 January 2018).

This suggests that all future development in Northern Australia and Cape York specifically will need to be carefully negotiated with Indigenous landowners. Despite their significant ownership, government policy continues to apply (albeit unsuccessfully) urban-centric and 'western industrialised' standards upon the people who inhabit these mostly remote locales (Harwood et al., 2011). There is a plethora of federal government policy (e.g. COAG, 2008, 2009) aimed at reducing the inequality in social wellbeing and economic conditions experienced by Indigenous Australians living in remote communities. However, none of this policy has addressed the role of statutory planning initiatives, rather, the focus has been on securing local economic development in remote communities via home ownership. To this end, the COAG, through the National Partnership on Remote Indigenous Housing, has focused on supporting the states and territories of Australia to implement changes to their land legislation that would resolve tenure issues on community-titled land. The COAG (2014) also agreed to implement mainstream land planning and administration systems and comparable local government services in remote areas.

In the absence of any policy or intellectual thought on how planning in remote regions should consider the residents of the region under investigation, the planning profession tends to apply one of two theoretical approaches to regional planning practice. One approach is to gain economic efficiencies through the spatial organisation of predominantly urban areas and the other is to address problems associated with backward areas in industrially advanced nations (Harwood et al., 2011).

Northern Australia has experienced a combination of both of these approaches. For instance, the Far North Queensland Regional Plan (State of Queensland, 2009) applies the smart growth model (Duany et al., 2011) to its region to identify infrastructure efficiencies through the spatial organisation of its urban areas. Those lands outside the urban footprint are zoned for one of two purposes—rural production or environmental protection. The Kimberley Regional Planning and Infrastructure Framework (Western Australian Planning Commission, 2015) primarily identifies critical physical infrastructure (utility and transport) required to support the region's resource economy and its associated settlements. Surprisingly, little attention is paid to the quality and quantity of the community infrastructure required to sustain the liveability of the settlements in this region. An analysis by Harwood et al. (2016) of the 2014 Cape York Regional Plan found that instead of addressing the goals and aspirations of the Indigenous people of the Cape York region, the plan focused on how the state government would manage its economic intentions for the region. The plan was silent on the needs and aspirations of the Aboriginal landowners and residents. Moreover, the zoning contained within the plan focused on large-scale resource developments and the locking up of land from resource development by making these national parks and conservation zones or wilderness areas. This is not to say that environmental protection is not warranted; however, this form of 'exclusionary zoning' focuses on what cannot be developed as opposed to addressing the long-term sustainability of the townships or communities themselves. Planning in this context fails to identify and promote a balanced approach to economic development (location, type, scale and intensity) and environmental protection.

The approaches taken by both the West Australian and the Queensland governments to development planning has been to achieve infrastructure efficiencies for their respective governments. What appears to be missing is a focus on increasing the liveability of these regions. It appears that the purpose of these development plans is to create a strategic investment plan for government relative to economic returns from private sector development contributions, rather than support the development of self-sustaining communities.

## Planning in Remote Regions

Harwood et al. (2016) maintained that the spatial territory of a remote region is typically defined by the range of 'problems' they share. For instance, the regional plans for the Cape York Peninsula region in northern Queensland and the Nunavut Territory in northern Canada identify their limitations to realising economic development opportunities as being a combination of:

- small population and local market base
- remoteness of the location and limited infrastructure
- limited financial and technical capacity and capability of the population
- climatic conditions (that is, extremes that impair all-weather access)
- increasing global demand for goods and/or services and the high cost of transporting goods to market (State of Queensland, 2014; Nunavut Planning Commission, 2014).

It would appear that simply being included in a remote sparse region with a challenging climate is an impediment to stimulating economic development. By this it is inferred that economic development in remote regions is constrained due to a range of locational factors including a highly dispersed population—except, of course, where mining is concerned. This form of development is dependent on private sector investment, as opposed to government, to facilitate. However, as Harwood et al. (2016) and Dale (2014) asserted, the narrative of any story depends on who is telling the story. Therefore, it is crucial that the narrative of any plan reflects the lived experiences of the community that the plan is intended to serve (as opposed to the urban cores or industrial resource firms), especially in remote locations.

There is a significant disjuncture between planning and development for remote regions. Moreover, there is no literature to describe the relationship between development, planning and the circumstances that some communities face in remote settlements (Dillon Consulting, 2012) and in Northern Australia (Harwood et al., 2011). The current approach, while described as top down by some, is known in land use planning literature as the core–periphery model (Harwood et al., 2011). The core–periphery model describes the spatial economic organisation of the leading urbanised core and the lagging rural periphery (Moore, 1994). Peripheral areas often experience lagging growth or stagnation and rely on the growth driven by the urban core in the form of increased demand for unprocessed resources located in the periphery (Friedmann, 1966) and provide capital to support growth opportunities (Harwood, 2010). The core areas are industry and knowledge-driven, as opposed to resource dependent, for growth (Smith & Steel, 1995). The application of the core–periphery model exacerbates the gap between the 'haves' and the 'have-nots', which in turn supports the bifurcation of societies in Northern Australia.

The core–periphery model is premised upon the possibility that a mature regional economic system may eventually bridge the development gap between the urban and peripheral regions (Moore, 1994); however, the reality is very different. Resource peripheries tend to remain on the economic (and social) margin as their development paths become locked in and the periphery remains dependent on demand, investment and decision-making from the core (Carson et al., 2010; Harwood et al., 2011).

Government offices located in Australia's periphery (i.e. Cairns, Townsville, Darwin and Broome) often become the executive arms of the external investing core as they seek continued investment from the core (see, for example, how Darwin responds to resource development proposals in Carson et al., 2010). As a result, decision-makers are inclined to favour decisions that may lead to fast economic growth in the core but not necessarily sustainable development in the periphery (Barnes et al., 2001). Taylor et al. (2011) concluded that improving quality of life for the 'have-nots' (including those located within and beyond the resource periphery) will require large investments and a substantial reconsideration of the way in which economic development is envisaged. Current regional development practices indicate that neither is occurring as most investment is market-driven and involves large government-funded projects that derive large rents received from resource extraction that are not matched by investments in human capital by those industries (Taylor et al., 2011).

Spatial planning theory and practice within the urban centre is essentially related to and has evolved from the management of change within complex urban and industrial systems and the political and legislative processes that govern the change in land uses (Selman, 1995). By comparison, remote areas have been neglected in relation to planning theory and practice. This may be attributed to a perception by planners that non-metropolitan areas possess less complex and competitive economic structures associated with primary industries and the mining sector. Planning practice in remote areas continues to unsuccessfully apply urban planning models and approaches (Markey et al., 2006; Harwood et al., 2011; Harwood et al., 2016).

Markey et al. (2006) maintained that the application or misapplication of development notions from urban settings is particularly problematic for remote areas. This misapplication creates development strategies for remote areas that reinforces the existing urban-based industrial resource economy and dependence on external capital and business opportunities for remote communities (Markey et al., 2006). This is particularly evident in Cape York and, as a consequence, has created a bifurcated society where mining development has created significant wealth for some (e.g. Weipa) and minimal benefits for the people living in Aboriginal settlements such as Mapoon, Aurukun and Napranum. Table 1.1 shows a comparison of Aboriginal settlements and the mining town of Weipa in the western region of Cape York.

**Table 1.1: Comparison of western Cape York settlements.**

| Settlement | Total population | Indigenous % | Unemployed % | Attained year 11/12 % | Non-school qualification % |
|---|---|---|---|---|---|
| Weipa | 3,951 | 18.6 | 2.9 | 52.7 | 62.5 |
| Aurukun | 1,435 | 92.2 | 84.8 | 16 | 29 |
| Napranum | 993 | 95.9 | 30 | 31.7 | 17.8 |
| Mapoon | 312 | 89.1 | 29.6 | 25.2 | 33.7 |
| Queensland | 4,853,048 | 3.6 | 6.1 | 55.3 | 54.2 |

Source: State of Queensland (2017b).

The 'haves' of Weipa are employed, mostly non-Indigenous and have attained a higher level of education and/or non-school qualification. The benefits from mining have not positively affected the neighbouring Aboriginal settlements of Mapoon, Napranum and Aurukun.

Remote settlements are less connected to the urban and rural sectors, possess diverse histories and are incredibly complex due to the interface with cultural, land tenure, environmental values and land management issues that do not fit easily into an urban-based planning system. Therefore, a new remote-planning paradigm based on the concept of place must be created that addresses the unique characteristics of Northern Australia.

# Cape York Region

This chapter examines the Cape York Peninsula region to describe how the various planning outcomes have attempted to reduce the disparities between the urban core and the residents and communities in Cape York Peninsula.

LEADING FROM THE NORTH

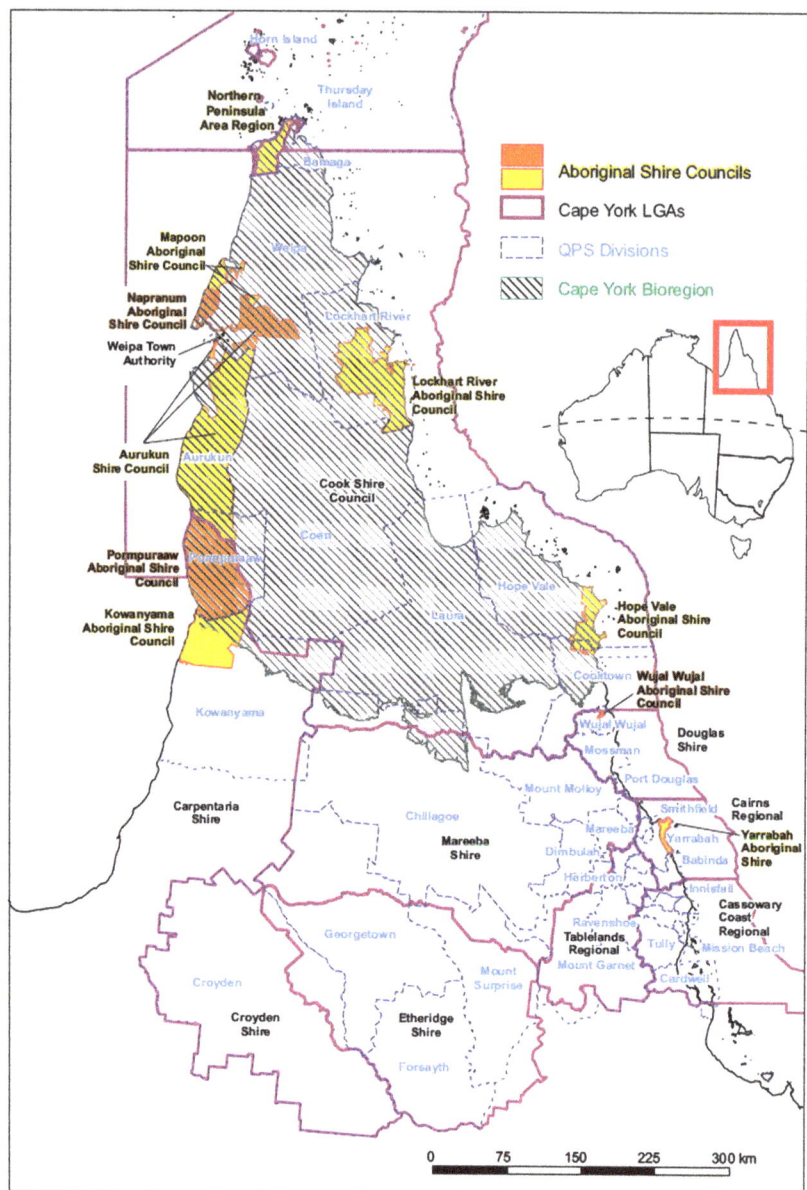

**Figure 1.1: Cape York.**
Source: Map created by Adella Edwards of Connect Spatial, Townsville, Queensland.

The site characteristics of the Cape York Peninsula are highly contestable because of the way each entity conceptualises the values within. The spatial extent of the region defined as Cape York varies significantly (see Figure 1.1) and this in and of itself creates confusion for the people who live in the region. The land use regional plans in Queensland have entirely separate sets of boundaries to the state government departments (e.g. Police) and their associated service delivery. Exacerbating this disconnect in regional planning is a different spatial extent of the Cape York Peninsula Bioregion, which identifies the various land cover attributes, to the Cape York Regional Plan, which regulates how these land cover attributes can be used. The Torres Strait continues to be excluded from regional planning altogether and as a consequence is subjected to a series of local government plans.

Despite the various ways of conceptualising a region and spatially mapping its boundaries, the Cape York region is treated as a homogenous area when viewed from a southern urban perspective. This means a common feature of the entire region (with the exception of Weipa Township Area) is that it is an economically underperforming region—that is, dependent on welfare transfers from the core (see Appendix 1 for Socio-Economic Indexes for Areas [SEIFA] scores for each of the local government areas).

## Land Use Planning and Cape York Peninsula

Land use planning policy and legislation in Australia is designed and controlled by each of the state/territory governments, with each possessing its own sets of legislation, policies and procedures that are a result of their own unique histories and types of developable resources. Typically each of the states/territories planning legislation has evolved from the regulation of the inner-city urban development and over time has been applied to areas outside of the city, for instance suburbs, rural lands and, more recently, remote areas.

There are three levels of planning affecting development in Queensland: state planning policies, regional plans and local government planning schemes. The state planning policy is a set of principles that describe the state's interests that must be considered in plan making and development assessment. There are 17 state interests (as of July 2017) arranged under five themes (State of Queensland, 2017a), some of which are mapped as constraints (e.g. natural hazards, coastal environment and vegetation) and some of which are not (e.g. tourism and mining). These 17 state interests and their relative locations cannot be ignored at either a regional or local level, and in some instances a potential development site can impact on multiple state interests, which means that the proposed development is essentially prohibited even where it may be locally appropriate. These state interests are mapped at a small scale and, therefore, are prone to be incorrect. To rectify or amend the relative location of a state interest involves specialist consultants to undertake extensive site analysis to determine whether the interest applies to the proposed development site and, if so, where and to what spatial extent. Moreover, the state interests are typically mapped as constraints, while development (tourism and mining) does not have a location on a map with statutory protection. While this is not to imply that development should be undertaken in an unsafe or environmentally irresponsible way, there does need to be some flexibility in the way in which a local community can decide how land could be used that first meet the aspirations of the local residents as opposed to the expectations of urban-based populations.

Regional planning in Queensland is undertaken at a jurisdictional level and, as a consequence, is a series of local government authorities sharing a common feature—for example, the North West Queensland region experiences low population density but high-intensity hard rock mining activities. The Cape York region is comprised of 11 local governments and is bounded as a region by the highly contestable environmental values of state significance (Dale et al., 2017), with a high Indigenous population and 10 of the 11 local governments referred to as Indigenous Local Governments (ILGs). These were once Aboriginal mission settlements that have over time become local government authorities in their own right. Over the past 20 or so years since the introduction of *Native Title Act 1993* (Cth), ongoing Aboriginal connections to and with significant tracts of government-owned land in Cape York have been legally acknowledged in the Federal Court system. In many instances, the Queensland Government has assigned the ownership and title to lands that have been subject to exclusive native title determinations to the relevant Aboriginal corporate entity (e.g. a Prescribed Body Corporate or Land Trust).

At the same time, another government policy was implemented to transition Aboriginal Community Councils to ILGs, and in Queensland this included mainstreaming land planning and administration systems. Those areas within the ILG jurisdiction that had native title extinguished were typically retained by the relevant local government, whereas the balance of the shire became owned and controlled by one or more Aboriginal corporate entities. For example, in Hope Vale Aboriginal Shire Council area, 99.5 per cent of the shire is owned, managed and controlled by the Hope Vale Congress Aboriginal Corporation (combined Land Trust and Prescribed Body Corporate), and 0.5 per cent of the shire is owned, managed and controlled by the local government. However, in this instance, the Council create plans for 100 per cent of the shire jurisdiction and are required to implement state planning policies as part of the statutory land use planning system.

## Local Government Planning

Since the application of the COAG agreement to implement mainstream land planning and administrations systems in Queensland, most ILGs in Queensland have a statutory land use plan. At the time of making these plans, the *Sustainable Planning Act 2009* (Qld) required a template approach (referred to as the Queensland Planning Provisions) be applied to plan making. These plans focused on infrastructure efficiencies and surveying existing house lots within the township zone, with the balance of the shire being designated as either Environmental Management and Conservation or Rural. There was scant attention or opportunity to undertake a comprehensive land cover assessment outside of the township zone. What has emerged from this concentration on the township is a comprehensive infrastructure plan (i.e. trunk water and sewerage) at the expense of considering future economic development options. It is also worth noting that while these plans were being developed, the land administration system was also transferring lands from the state to the relevant native title corporate entities. Stephenson (2009, p. 547) referred to this system as 'land rights legislation', whereby a statutory system is established for the transfer of inalienable freehold land to Indigenous people. A variety of systems exist in Australia (see Stephenson, 2009, for a comprehensive assessment), but in Queensland the land is transferred to an Aboriginal corporate entity that in turn holds the land in perpetuity on behalf of Indigenous people specifically concerned with the land. Native title rights and interests continue to be held and managed by the relevant Prescribed Body Corporate.

These two policy approaches inadvertently culminated to create two types of land holders in any given ILG area in Queensland. The local government typically assumes ownership of land and infrastructure within the township and the Aboriginal corporate entity (one or more) owns the lands zoned Rural or Environmental Management and Conservation as the balance of the shire territory. This has created angst for the Aboriginal landowning entities as they not only have to deal with the restrictions of a one-size-fits-all statutory land use plan (including land use definitions) but must also deal with the state planning policy that maps land for environmental values (e.g. vegetation) and hazards (e.g. coastal, flooding, etc.) that invariably constrain future development (see Harwood, 2014, for detailed analysis). This implies that lands within the township zone have been considered for future development, whereas the balance is owned by an Aboriginal corporate entity and contains highly constrained lands.

If the Aboriginal corporate entity has development aspirations, for example, creating an economic platform via a housing and construction industry on their own lands, then they are required to undertake a costly development application process associated with the mainstream planning system. This is, of course, after they have applied their own internal cultural governance protocols to identify a range of 'appropriate' land uses and the Prescribed Body Corporate administrative roles (including the granting of an Indigenous Land Use Agreement pursuant to the *Native Title Act*).

This process is financially prohibitive and involves lengthy timeframes that are not funded by government. The Aboriginal corporate entity as the 'developer' must also bear the costs of trying to amend the statutory system to better reflect their own aspirations for the use and management of their own lands. In essence, the Aboriginal corporate entity must repeat the planning role of the local government by undertaking an additional planning process for their own lands. An alternative system is required to enable development that allows the Aboriginal corporate entity's aspirations to be realised.

## Place-Based Planning

Land use planning is about how communities make decisions about the spatial allocation of resources and prioritise action strategies to meet predetermined objectives and outcomes. More specifically, Indigenous planning in a Northern Australia context has not yet been conceptualised from an Indigenous lens; rather, the urban-centric focus pervades, which perpetuates flawed planning outcomes for remote Indigenous communities. It would seem logical to align land use planning outcomes with the aspirations of the Indigenous landowners as opposed to mainstreaming the system to be comparable with predominantly non-Indigenous urban areas.

Place-based planning explicitly acknowledges the relationship between the people and the attributes of the space that they inhabit. People identify with a space, the parameters of which may transcend geopolitical boundaries and may be the result of an ongoing and enduring association with those geographical features. Associated with the place-based approach is a departure from the focus on industry sector development associated with economics and a move towards the delineation of a place as a spatial unit and the subsequently appropriate forms of development.

The concept of place is associated with the relationship between individuals, the space that they inhabit and the subsequent value that individuals associate with the attributes of that space. Tuan (1977) maintained that what begins as a space when imbued with value becomes a place. The concept of place reinforces that decision-making in planning for spatial transformation is value laden and reflects the values and beliefs of its inhabitants. Planning in remote locations as both a land use and decision-making process must consider the complex relationship between the physical environment and the manner in which the affected community perceives both themselves as individuals and as a community.

Therefore, spatial planning requires an understanding of the assets that an area possesses and whether these can be used to create a better future for its inhabitants and, if so, then how. Malczewski (2004) drew a distinction between the land cover attributes and the subsequent uses of these attributes. This distinction allows for two very important and often overlooked aspects of land use planning in remote regions. An inventory of the land cover attributes is necessary to understand how the local people value those attributes and how they may be used to improve their overall wellbeing. It is the values of the people who are connected to the space that should be respected in land use planning and decision-making.

More often than not, planning for remote areas starts with the extent of the geopolitical jurisdiction and then proceeds on the basis of how the region's natural resources can be exploited with little regard for how the local inhabitants may value those assets (Harwood et al., 2016). A place-based approach to planning would start with the local inhabitants, a land cover assessment, an overview of how the locals identify with the region as their place, how they value the land cover attributes and other natural assets, and the land uses that they may see as being vital for their long-term wellbeing.

Matunga (2013) described Indigenous planning as inherently place based because it links specific Indigenous communities to defined ancestral places, environments and resources and uses Indigenous (and other) knowledge to make decisions highly contextual to that community and how a community sees its own future. Indigenous planning is also place based because it implies a long and close association of the people with their traditional lands and, therefore, knowledge of the specific environment and what it can sustain (Matunga, 2013).

The Queensland division of the Planning Institute of Australia (2017) recently published an Indigenous planning policy that defines why a place-based approach that is embedded within a rights-based framework is required for application to the planning of the Indigenous estate in Queensland. More specifically, that Aboriginal and Torres Strait Islander peoples' knowledge, culture and tradition is held by them and that undertaking functions under the new *Planning Act 2016* (Qld) will require developing a working relationship with Aboriginal and Torres Strait Islander peoples based on mutual trust and respect.

Figure 1.2 provides a schematic overview of the procedure that place-based planning should take and compares this to the way in which planning is currently undertaken in Queensland.

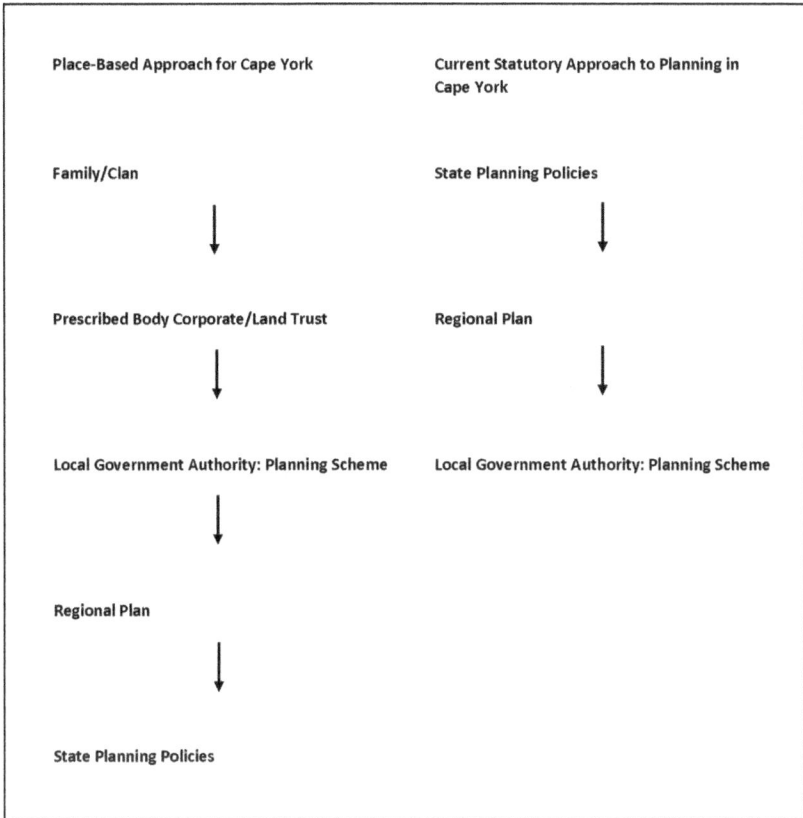

**Figure 1.2: Proposed place-based planning procedure in Cape York versus the current statutory approach.**
Source: Authors' research.

The place-based approach, as represented in Figure 1.2, acknowledges the social organisation and knowledge holders of the place that is being considered. This process also acknowledges that only the rightful owners of the native title rights are able to speak on behalf of the area being planned. This implies that local government planning approaches are not only ignorant of the cultural protocols about using land, but also the ways in which decisions are made by Indigenous families and their clan groups about using the land cover attributes (see Harwood, 2015, for an overview of how this system could work at a family/clan level).

## Conclusion

Referring back to the 'haves' and 'have-nots' analogy by Taylor et al. (2011), it becomes evident why the 'have-nots' are excluded from accessing the benefits of development. There is no consideration of both the social organisation and cultural obligations governing the Indigenous-owned lands, nor is planning focused on what is an appropriate and inappropriate use of the land and land cover attributes. A fundamental shift in the way that planning is conceptualised in Northern Australia is required to ensure that statutory land use planning can transform the lives and environments of remotely located communities and, in particular, for Indigenous landowners and their associated corporate entities.

Harwood et al. (2016) found from their review of the Cape York Regional Plan that top-down sectoral-based approaches to planning do not necessarily work very well because they tend to be more externally driven rather than being internally driven. This is consistent with Taylor et al.'s (2011) findings regarding large resource developments and the benefit flows from these developments. It is critical to amend the planning system across Northern Australia to include place-based approaches that are bottom up to ensure that they are internally driven and reflect the values of the people that inhabit these locales. This new approach may necessitate the creation of a separate Indigenous planning statute for lands owned by Aboriginal corporate entities to enable development to reflect the landowner and native title holder aspirations. It would appear that Northern Australia and Cape York in particular will continue to experience a south ('haves') and north ('have-nots') bifurcation if they are unable to control the way in which Aboriginal corporate entities can use and protect their land estates.

## Appendix 1.1

SEIFA is a measure of the social and economic conditions of areas across Australia. The SEIFA score is a composite score generated by the Australian Bureau of Statistics that ranks geographic areas according to socioeconomic disadvantage. The score considers low-income earners, education attainment, unemployment and dwellings without a motor vehicle.

The results presented in Table A.1 indicate that all ILG areas experience 100 per cent disadvantage, whereas the mining town of Weipa experiences a disproportionate percentage of its population in the more advantaged quintiles (4 and 5).

Table A.1: SEIFA scores for Indigenous Local Government Areas in Cape York region.

| Local Government Area | Quintile 1 (most disadvantaged) | Quintile 2 | Quintile 3 | Quintile 4 | Quintile 5 (least disadvantaged) |
|---|---|---|---|---|---|
| Aurukun | 100 | 0.0 | 0.0 | 0.0 | 0.0 |
| Cooktown | 70.2 | 26 | 3.8 | 0.0 | 0.0 |
| Hope Vale | 100 | 0.0 | 0.0 | 0.0 | 0.0 |
| Kowanyama | 100 | 0.0 | 0.0 | 0.0 | 0.0 |
| Lockhart River | 100 | 0.0 | 0.0 | 0.0 | 0.0 |
| Mapoon | 100 | 0.0 | 0.0 | 0.0 | 0.0 |
| Mornington | 100 | 0.0 | 0.0 | 0.0 | 0.0 |
| Napranum | 100 | 0.0 | 0.0 | 0.0 | 0.0 |
| Northern Peninsula Area | 100 | 0.0 | 0.0 | 0.0 | 0.0 |
| Pompuraaw | 100 | 0.0 | 0.0 | 0.0 | 0.0 |
| Weipa | 0.0 | 0.0 | 0.0 | 85.4 | 14.6 |
| Wujal | 100 | 0.0 | 0.0 | 0.0 | 0.0 |
| QUEENSLAND | 20 | 20 | 20 | 20 | 20 |

Source: State of Queensland (2017b).

# References

Altman, J. (2013). Land rights and development in Australia: Caring for, benefiting from and governing the Indigenous estate. In T. Rowse & L. Ford (Eds), *Between Indigenous and settler governance* (pp. 121–134). London, England: Routledge.

Altman, J. (2014, March). The political ecology and political economy of the Indigenous land titling 'revolution' in Australia. *Maori Law Review*, 1–17.

Barnes, T. J., Hayter, R. & Hay, E. (2001). Stormy weather: Cyclones, Harold Innis and Port Alberni, BC. *Environment and Planning A*, *33*(12), 2127–2147.

Carson, D., Schmallegger, D. & Harwood, S. (2010). A city for the temporary: Political economy and urban planning in Darwin, Australia. *Urban Policy and Research*, *28*(3), 293–310.

Council of Australian Governments (COAG). (2008). *National Indigenous reform agreement*. Canberra, ACT: Commonwealth of Australia.

Council of Australian Governments (COAG). (2009). *National Indigenous reform agreement*. Canberra, ACT: Commonwealth of Australia.

Council of Australian Governments (COAG). (2014). *National partnership on remote Indigenous housing—progress review (2008–2013)*. Canberra, ACT: Commonwealth of Australia.

Dale, A. (2014). *Beyond the north-south culture wars: Reconciling Northern Australia's recent past with its future*. Springer.

Dale, A., Potts, R. & Harwood, S. (2017). Northern Australia: A contested landscape. In N. Sipes & K. Vella (Eds), *Australian handbook of urban and regional planning* (pp. 86–97). Milton Park, England: Routledge.

Dillon Consulting. (2012, 15 June). *Independent review: Draft Nunavut land use plan*. Retrieved from assembly.nu.ca/library/Edocs/2012/000710-e.pdf

Duany, A., Speck, J., Lydon, M. & Goffman, E. (2011). The smart growth manual. *Sustainability: Science, Practice and Policy*, *7*(2), 89–90.

Friedmann, J. (1966). *Regional development policy: A case study of Venezuela*. Cambridge, MA: MIT Press.

Harwood, S. (2010). Planning for community based tourism in remote areas: Bird watching in Arfak Mountains West Papua (Unpublished doctoral thesis). Charles Darwin University, Darwin, NT.

Harwood, S. (2014, 16 June). *Submission to the Aboriginal and Torres Strait Islander Land (Providing Freehold) and Other Legislation Amendment Bill 2014*. Agriculture, Resources and Environment Parliamentary Committee.

Harwood, S. (2015). *Submissions – COAG land investigation*. Retrieved from pmc.gov.au/indigenous-affairs/land/coag-investigation-indigenous-land-administration-and-use/submissions

Harwood, S., Schmallegger, D. & Prideaux, B. (2011). Social equity in regional development planning: Who plans for remote communities? *Journal of Contemporary Issues in Business and Government*, *17*(1), 13–30.

Harwood, S., Wensing, E & Ensign, S. (2016). Place based planning for economic development in remote Aboriginal settlements. In A. Taylor, D. Carson, P. Ensign, L. Husky, G. Eilmsteiner-Saxinger & R. Rasmussen (Eds), *Settlements at the edge: Remote human settlements in developed nations* (pp. 124–149). Cheltenham, England: Edward Elgar Publishing.

Kim, J. H. (2011). Linking land use planning and regulation to economic development: A literature review. *CPL Bibliography*, *26*(1), 35–47.

Malczewski, J. (2004). GIS-based land use suitability analysis: A critical overview. *Progress in Planning*, *62*, 3–65.

Markey, S., Halseth, G. & Manson, D. (2006). The struggle to compete: From comparative to competitive advantage in Northern British Columbia. *International Planning Studies*, *11*(1), 19–39.

Markey, S., Halseth, G. & Manson, D. (2008). Challenging the inevitability of rural decline: Advancing the policy of place in northern British Columbia. *Journal of Rural Studies*, *24*(4), 409–421.

Markey, S., Halseth, G. & Manson, D. (2012). *Investing in place: Economic renewal in northern British Columbia*. UBC Press.

Matunga, H. (2013). Theorising Indigenous planning. In R. Walker, T. Jojola & D. Natcher (Eds), *Reclaiming Indigenous planning* (pp. 3–32). Montreal, Canada: McGill-Queens University Press.

Moore, T. (1994). Core-periphery models, regional planning theory and Appalachian development. *The Professional Geographer*, *46*(3), 316–331.

Nunavut Planning Commission. (2014). *Draft Nunavut land use plan*. Retrieved from www.nunavut.ca/land-use-plans/draft-nunavut-land-use-plan

Planning Institute Australia. (2017). *PIA Queensland position statement—Aboriginal and Torres Strait Islander planning policy*. Retrieved from www.planning.org.au/documents/item/8606

Selman, P. (1995). Theories for rural environmental planning. *Planning Practice and Research*, *10*(1), 5–13.

Smith, C. & Steel, B. (1995). Core-periphery relationships of resource-based communities. *Community Development*, *26*(1), 52–70.

State of Queensland. (2009). *Far North Queensland regional plan 2009–2031*. Brisbane, Qld: Department of Infrastructure and Planning.

State of Queensland. (2014). *Cape York regional plan*, Department of State Development, Infrastructure and Planning. Retrieved from dsdmipprd.blob.core.windows.net/general/cape-york-regional-plan.pdf

State of Queensland. (2017a, July). *State planning policy*. Department of Infrastructure, Local Government and Planning. Retrieved from dilgpprd.blob.core.windows.net/general/spp-july-2017.pdf

State of Queensland. (2017b). *Queensland regional profile for Cape York region*. Queensland Government Statistician's Office, Queensland Treasury.

Stephenson, M. (2009). To lease or not to lease? The leasing of Indigenous statutory lands in Australia: Lessons from Canada. *Commonwealth Law Bulletin*, *35*(3), 545–570.

Taylor, A., Larson, S., Stoeckl, N. & Carson, D. (2011). The *haves* and *have nots* in Australia's Tropical North—new perspectives on a persisting problem. *Geographical Research*, *49*(1), 13–22.

Tuan, Y. (1977). *Space and place: The perspective of experience*. London, England: Edward Arnold.

Western Australian Planning Commission. (2015). *Kimberley regional planning and infrastructure framework*. Perth, WA: Department of Planning.

# 2

# Place-Based Agricultural Development: A New Way of Thinking about an Old Idea in Northern Australia

Jim Turnour, Kate Andrews, Allan P. Dale, Connar McShane, Michelle Thompson and Bruce Prideaux

## Introduction

The establishment of a northern food bowl has been a central theme in discussions about the development of Australia north of the Tropic of Capricorn (Australian Government, 2014; Australian Labor Party, 2013; Liberal Party of Australia, 2013). This policy drive has remained despite over a century of failed attempts to develop broad-scale cropping in the north beyond central and coastal North Queensland. This cycle of publicly expressed expectation for Northern Australia to produce food and fibre through broad-acre cropping is discussed as a 'circular conundrum' (Andrews, 2014, p. 2). This circular conundrum begins with the setting of high expectations, moves to cropping attempts, then usually to project failure, and back around to high expectations (Andrews, 2014).

This chapter argues that we must learn from these past mistakes by building on this experience to embrace new models of agriculture grounded in place-based approaches. Place-based approaches emphasise the importance of local context including sociocultural, physical and institutional factors in development (Barca, et al., 2012; Hildreth & Bailcy, 2014; Tomaney, 2010). Australia has traditionally relied on agri-industrial models of agriculture characterised by a focus on production and marketing of bulk commodities (Lawrence et al., 2013). Internationally, however, new models have emerged that characterise agriculture as being multifunctional, contributing not only through production but to the environmental and social sustainability of a region (Renting et al., 2009). Marsden (2003) defined a post-productivist model of agriculture that leveraged the importance of environmental sustainability and amenity and a rural development model that leveraged the links between agriculture and local communities to support development that reflected more broadly the needs for economic, environmental and social sustainability.

In an Australian context, post-productivist models of agriculture provide an opportunity to leverage Northern Australia's unique environmental values through branding for food safety, sustainability and ecosystems services. Similarly, rural development approaches to agriculture are more inclusive of the broader community. This inclusiveness is achieved, for example, through supporting diversification, value adding and creating jobs via links to regional supply chains for agricultural products. These supply chains can be centred on local communities and/or linked to new high-value markets in Asia and Southern Australia.

In Australia, the idea that agriculture is multifunctional has been resisted by policymakers because it has been used as an argument for protectionist trade policies, particularly in Europe (Cocklin et al., 2006; Renting et al., 2009). Increasingly, however, the multifunctionality of the landscape of Northern Australia is emerging in research and needs to be considered in the development of agriculture (see Bohnet & Smith, 2007; Holmes, 2006, 2012; Turnour et al., 2015).

Case study research in the Wet Tropics of North Queensland focused on developing a theoretical framework that enables consideration of agriculture's broader contributions to place-based regional development. The theoretical framework that emerged combined the traditional agri-industrial model of agriculture with emerging post-productivist and rural development models (Turnour et al., 2015). The place-based agricultural development framework developed provides a new perspective for considering agricultural development in Northern Australia based on well-contextualised regional competitive advantage. This chapter details this framework and through case studies highlights the opportunities and benefits of place-based approaches to the development of agriculture across Northern Australia.

## The 'circular conundrum': Learning from Past Experiences of Cropping in Northern Australia

Despite over a century of attempts at cropping in Northern Australia, cropping makes only a minor contribution to overall economic activity outside of central and coastal North Queensland. Approximately 88 per cent of the total agriculture production from Northern Australia is produced in Queensland, where more than 70 per cent of the region's population resides (BITRE, 2011). However, it is in these more remote regions dominated by pastoralism where high expectations are again being built around irrigated agriculture. In these regions, traditional approaches to agricultural development have produced disappointing results. In 2009, the value of irrigated agriculture production in this part of Northern Australia was worth about A$160 million, 0.8 per cent of total regional economic activity. The total irrigated area was 34,000 hectares, less than 0.03 per cent of Northern Australia. Horticulture was the highest-value crop with sandalwood (a forestry product valued at A$60 million) being of increasing importance. These cropping industries are dwarfed by the contribution of the beef industry at approximately A$1 billion (Webster et al., 2009). Understanding the circular conundrum can help us to break the cycle of failed attempts at agricultural cropping development in Northern Australia. We can learn from the variables that lead to failed attempts and hindered learning, enabling expectations to be raised again and again.

Diverse and multiple variables have impacted on cropping attempts in Northern Australia over the last 150 years, contributing to their subsequent failure (Andrews, 2014). From the poor soils at sites of the Northern Territory sugar plantations of the 1880s to a lack of sufficient scale of production for the sugar industry on the Ord in the early 2000s. Or the lack of a profitable rotation crop for peanuts noted in the early 1920s and still recognised as a problem for Territory peanut growers in the 2000s. From overcapitalisation and lack of managerial capacity in the Territory Rice saga of the 1950s (magpie geese scapegoated) to the lack of willingness to learn from available knowledge exhibited most egregiously by the Northern Australia Development Corporation on Willeroo Station in the 1970s (and still exhibited in less dramatic ways today). This can-do frontier culture was also exhibited in the heady days of Northern Development Pty Ltd at Camballin in Western Australia. These are only a few of the many examples (Andrews, 2014).

Where agriculture has been successfully developed, including in central and coastal North Queensland, it has been important to start at a manageable scale and to learn and adapt to the environment. Establishing enabling infrastructure and supply chains have been as important as overcoming the agronomic challenges. This has generally required significant government investment in irrigation infrastructure and research and development for which farmers have not had to pay a return on the sunk costs (Ash, 2014).

The relationship between these impacting variables contributes further to the complexity and vulnerability of cropping attempts. This complex socio-ecological system can be reframed and conceptualised as five assets—social, human, natural, physical and financial. It is these five assets that are required for successful development, yet we find a lack of each as required for broad-scale cropping in most of the north. Examples include:

- Social and institutional—government legislation and policy (such as access to water resources) and access to skilled and unskilled labour
- Human—lack of agronomic knowledge and personality (such as willingness to learn from local sources and experience)
- Natural—climate (extreme temperatures, pattern of rainfall, high evaporation rates, variability and unpredictability) and soil suitability (nutrients, water holding/shedding, structure and erodibility)
- Physical/manufactured—suitable crop varieties and rotation crops and agricultural infrastructure (such as processing and storage facilities)
- Financial—high price of inputs and low and/or fluctuating price of outputs, capacity to raise or access finance.

There has been improvement in some assets over time, particularly assisting small-scale success in horticulture and pastoralism. History shows, however, that attempts to address any of these assets in isolation from the others has generally not been sufficient to ensure success. Millions of dollars of both government and private investment have been lost in efforts to do just that.

The final step in the circular conundrum is from failure back to continuing high expectations—the mystery of the persistence of the cycle. This relationship is perpetuated by 'hindered learning' (Andrews, 2014, p. 336), including the gap between 'rhetoric and reality' (Powell,

1977, p. 83) and 'a reprehensible aversion to learning by experience' (Bauer, 1985, p. 27). This is something Ash (2014) emphasised as being critically important where agriculture has been successfully developed in the north. Other parts of the cycle contribute to hindering learning, whether the powerful cultural drivers or the very variables that contribute to failure such as remoteness. The circular conundrum reflects settler Australia's slow journey to develop landscape literacy of the north, and our even slower journey to develop complex systems literacy including a capacity to deal with variability and complexity. It demonstrates how, to break this stubborn cycle, we need to understand the place and learn to manage complex socio-ecological systems rather than continuing with a disaggregated approach.

## Models of Agriculture Development and Influences on Northern Australia

Agriculture is traditionally understood in Australia as providing food and fibre to be sold within bulk commodity markets. This approach to agriculture has been described as an agri-industrial model of production (Marsden, 2003). It underpinned the founding of the wool, beef, grain and sugar industries and the early economic development of Australia and our national identity. Agri-industrial agriculture continues to dominate Australian agricultural production and continues to influence our understanding of how agricultural development in Northern Australia should occur (Lawrence et al., 2013).

Globalisation and economic reforms that began in the 1970s, however, have changed the relative competitiveness of agri-industrial agriculture in many regions. Industry deregulation has seen a reduction in farmgate prices for commodities while costs of production have continued to rise. New business, production and transport technologies have enabled the scale of production to increase and supply chains to be consolidated. These factors have combined to see an increasing corporatisation of Australian agriculture and contributed to a decline in smaller family farms on which the agri-industrial model was founded (Productivity Commission, 2005; Turnour et al., 2015).

During the 1980s and 1990s, environmentalism also emerged as a social movement that began to call into question the sustainability of many agricultural practices. These movements began changing consumer preferences and farm practices. The National Landcare and Property Management Planning programs began to encourage farmers to take responsibility for the sustainable management of their natural resources and environment (Lockie & Higgins, 2007). Today, regional natural resource management (NRM) bodies have been established across the country and significant investments are being made to improve agricultural sustainability (Dale et al., 2013). Climate change has also emerged as a major environmental risk and opportunity for Australian agriculture. Consequently, governments, industry and the community are much more aware of the risks of inappropriate agricultural development on the environment.

More recently, the re-emergence of Indigenous interests in land in Northern Australia is similarly challenging the sustainability of the agri-industrial model of agriculture. The forced removal of Indigenous people from their land and the introduction of sheep, cattle and new crops during colonial settlement significantly changed the Australian landscape (Gammage, 2011). As a result of native title, Indigenous people are now reasserting their legal rights and interests in the majority of land in Northern Australia (Hill et al., 2013; Dale, 2014). Aboriginal people must now be engaged in decision-making about any new developments. They are major landowners in their own right and there are opportunities to increase production and profitability from Indigenous-owned lands (NAILSMA, 2014). So, although the idea of agricultural development in Northern Australia continues to draw on the imagery of Australia's agri-industrial pioneering past, opportunities for agricultural development have changed significantly. Recognising and learning from this past is important if we are to break out of the circular conundrum (Andrews, 2014; Turnour, 2014).

Different visions for agricultural development in the north are emerging. The seemingly more populist approach reflected in the bipartisan Coalition and Labor policies would see significant new government investment in irrigation infrastructure and research and development (Australian Labor Party, 2013; Liberal Party of Australia, 2013). This populist vision of the north as a food bowl draws on this historical imagery rather than being based in evidence of the opportunities for agricultural development in Northern Australia. Economic analysis of large-scale irrigation developments demonstrate that they do not provide a return to the private sector without significant government investment in the water infrastructure (CSIRO, 2013; Webster et al., 2009).

A more modest vision for agriculture development in the north was recently set out in the 2009 Northern Australia Land and Water Taskforce report. This vision, developed by industry, Indigenous and conservation interests and underpinned by a CSIRO Science Review, would rely on governments improving the investment environment for smaller-scale agricultural development through, for example, research, development and extension (RD&E) and regulatory and tenure reform. The Australian Government *White paper on developing Northern Australia* similarly focused on the importance of creating the right investment environment, although large-scale irrigation development remained a central objective (Australian Government, 2015).

The diversity of the north and the competing visions and narratives of vested interests can make untangling fact from fiction difficult. As such, there is a need to maximise the contribution of established industries like the beef industry while also looking to new development opportunities. This requires an assessment of not only the physical and economic constraints and opportunities but a consideration of development proposals in the context of evolving social and environmental values and changes in the global demand pattern of food.

Considering the multiple contributions that agriculture can make to Northern Australia requires a consideration of new models of development. Two new models of agricultural development, referred to as post-productivist and rural development, have been identified internationally and were found to be operating in the Wet Tropics of Northern Australia (Turnour et al., 2015). These models provide new ways of looking at the opportunities available for agricultural development in Northern Australia. They reflect a growing recognition that agriculture can be multifunctional in its contributions to regional development (Cocklin et al., 2006; Marsden & Farioli, 2015; Renting et al., 2009).

The post-productivist model emphasises the role of agriculture in contributing to and capitalising on the aesthetic beauty of the surrounding environment and adopting environmentally friendly farming practices (Marsden, 2003; Marsden & Sonnino, 2008). Post-productivist agriculture is a more complex model that moves from a solely production focus to engaging not only the farmer but the wider community in NRM and environmental protection. The model recognises the increasing value being placed on agricultural lifestyles and landscape amenity reflected in rural property prices, particularly around major urban centres (Bohnet, 2008; Turnour et al., 2015).

The rural development model makes a distinct move away from sector- or industry-focused agricultural development towards regionally focused, place-based agricultural and rural sustainability (Marsden, 2003; Marsden & Sonnino, 2008). Some strategies of a rural development approach would include place/regional branding, value adding, agri-tourism and niche marketing. The rural development model, therefore, has the capacity to leverage established agri-industrial and post-productivist models to create new markets and supply chains from Northern Australia linked to Asia, a region increasingly prepared to pay a premium for safe sustainable food (The Economist Intelligence Unit, 2013).

Each of these models provides a different approach to agricultural development. When integrated through and combined within a place-based development framework, they provide a practical tool to assist in planning and development of agriculture in Northern Australia.

## Place-Based Development: A New Framework for Decision-Making about Agriculture in Northern Australia

Place-based approaches provide a new way of engaging in agricultural development that moves beyond the grand visions and narratives of northern development intrinsic to the circular conundrum. They encourage collaboration between industry, community, business and government to tackle complex social, economic and environmental problems within a defined geographic location. Properly implemented, they respect local knowledge and values while keeping communities open to outside values (Barca et al., 2012; Tomaney, 2010). This creates an environment where competing visions of agricultural development underpinned by different values are more likely to be constructively resolved. In this way, place-based approaches can provide a framework for recognising and respecting the different physical and sociocultural environments present in the regions of Northern Australia and the range of opportunities these present.

They have been adopted as a framework for NRM in Australia and form part of the Australian Government's Indigenous Advancement Strategy (Department of the Prime Minister and Cabinet, 2014). Internationally, they have been identified as providing an alternative approach to tackling entrenched agriculture and rural community decline as a result of globalisation and economic reforms by supporting regions to leverage their innate competitive advantages (OECD, 2006).

Recognising the strengths of place-based approaches and the emerging alternative models of agriculture provided the catalyst for the development of a new agricultural development tool in North Queensland. The place-based agricultural development framework combines the three models—agri-industrial, post-productivist and rural development—with eight critical factors important to maximising agriculture's contribution to regional development. The three models provide different lenses to explore how agriculture can contribute to regional development. The eight factors include five assets (social capital, human capital, natural resources, infrastructure/technology and environment/amenity) that provide the foundation for agricultural development and three factors (balancing needs, strong regionalism and governance and institutions) that influence whether the different opportunities presented by the models are realised (see Figure 2.1) (Turnour et al., 2015). The frameworks' combination of assets, governance and institutional environment and models of agriculture provides a new structured way of relooking at agricultural development. This expanded vision demonstrates how agriculture can contribute to regional development building on the traditional agri-industrial model of development.

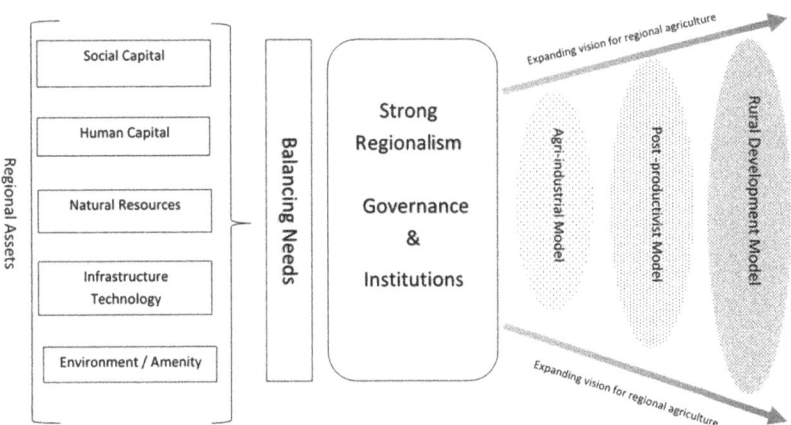

**Figure 2.1: Place-based agriculture development framework.**
Source: Turnour et al. (2015).

The eight factors are elaborated on below.

Social capital is the level of connectedness and trust of people and organisations within and between local communities (Cocklin & Alston, 2002; Onyx & Bullen, 2000; Woodhouse, 2006). Social capital reflects an ability to work together in a cooperative and coordinated way to tackle problems. It is important to have a cohesive approach to development within a region (bonding social capital) and strong links beyond the region (bridging social capital).

Human capital is important as it is individual farmers, businesses and industry leaders who must be entrepreneurial and take the risks to identify new markets and develop new enterprises and supply chains. This requires new knowledge and skills to be developed by individuals and businesses and provides opportunities for new and younger farmers to enter into agriculture.

Natural resources including soils, water, topography and climate underpin the type of agriculture that is possible within a region.

Infrastructure/technology are critically important as combining infrastructure and technology (transport, information and communication technologies and energy) with security of access to natural resources (land and water) can change the relative competitiveness of agriculture within a region.

Environment/amenity can underpin new industries and regional supply chains based on food safety and sustainability and regional tourism. They can also underpin increasing land values as rural amenity and lifestyle are increasingly sought-after commodities.

Balancing needs emphasises that different agriculture businesses balance a range of needs according to their varying economic, environmental and social values. Businesses may be focused on different models or have income streams outside of agriculture. The capacity within a region to recognise and enable agricultural businesses to manage what can be competing needs can influence a business's ability to engage in development.

Strong regionalism reflects the need for industry and regional self-reliance post-deregulation. It also stresses the need for regions to speak with a strategic and coordinated voice and for development to be controlled and driven regionally.

Effective governance and institutions are critical to creating the right environment for expanding agriculture's contribution within a region. This includes the values and norms reflected through community and industry-based organisations and governments' and corporations' policies and regulations that mediate agricultural production and associated markets and supply chains (Turnour et al., 2015).

## Applying Place-Based Agricultural Development in Northern Australia

Applying the place-based agricultural development framework to Northern Australia would enable a wider range of agricultural development opportunities to be considered and supported. As the framework details, development is dependent on a range of factors (see Figure 2.1) and there are unique challenges to agricultural development in Northern Australia that need to be considered. Some of these are fixed assets, such as natural resources and environment/amenity, while other factors are evolving and changing, such as human and social capital and infrastructure/technology. These changes are influenced by the governance and institutional environment that regulate land use, export opportunities and a range of operational matters such as occupational health and safety.

Government policy, not always in obvious ways, plays an important role in establishing the governance and institutional environment that has shaped agricultural development. Trade, immigration and Indigenous policies have been important, as have economic investments in infrastructure and RD&E (Turnour, 2014). Breaking out of the circular conundrum, therefore, particularly involves understanding and creating a governance and institutional environment that can support a range of different models of agricultural development. As these cases demonstrate, there are new and emerging opportunities for agriculture in the north.

Growing food and fibre is still central to agriculture; too often, however, governments overlook investments in rural development that can produce additional returns and employment from agriculture. The environment and a rural lifestyle similarly provide opportunities for additional returns for agriculture that should not be overlooked. The following two case studies are examples of post-productivist and rural development approaches to agriculture in Northern Australia. They emerged out of research in the Wet Tropics of North Queensland including focus groups, interviews and literature reviews (Turnour et al., 2015). They are examples of how agri-industrial agriculture is being built on to generate multiple contributions to regional development. They represent examples of how wider views of agriculture are emerging in a place-based context across Northern Australia.

# Ecosystem Services and Carbon in Northern Australia

If we are to create a place-oriented multifunctional approach to agriculture inclusive of a functioning ecosystem services economy, a simple and understandable national stewardship-oriented policy framework needs to emerge. A new national framework could establish in-principle agreement on the need for society to pay for those ecosystem services delivered by land managers over and above their current duty of care responsibilities. The Australian Government would also need to, through the development of cohesive national partnerships with key stakeholder sectors, secure an appropriate policy and delivery framework for managing these ecosystem service payments (see, for example, Van Oosterzee et al., 2010). Without a cohesive policy framework of this kind, urban and rural Australia will struggle to reconcile their cultural divide. This is the current situation as governments continue to take a simplistic approach to regulating away the economic opportunities of land managers to deliver the ecosystem services desired and needed by those living in Australia's cities (Dale, 2014).

There are already some emerging market-based approaches within a broader policy-based stewardship framework that could fund a range of ecosystems services (e.g. carbon trading). In the Wet Tropics region of North Queensland, for example, from 2005 to 2010, Terrain NRM (the regional NRM body for Queensland's Wet Tropics) partnered with a private sector entity (Biocarbon) to work towards establishing the Wet Tropics region as an international supplier of quality ecosystems service credits (see Van Oosterzee et al., 2012, for details). The alliance sought to pool (or aggregate) a range of carbon products arising from improved land use activities that delivered on the region's NRM plan. In addition to carbon sequestration or abatement, these activities would deliver other measurable biodiversity and community benefits. At the time, market brokers heavily involved in the world's emerging ecosystem services markets were buoyant that the region's high forest growth rates, high endemic biodiversity, localised scientific capacity and institutional stability would make the region's potential biosequestration products a jewel in the crown among what the world has to offer.

It is also important to note that the northern savanna also similarly provides opportunities for such emerging markets. Recently, the Tipperary Group of Stations were issued over 26,000 credits in 2013 for early season burning under the savanna burning carbon farming methodology (Brann, 2012). Getting the policy and institutional environment right is critical to securing these opportunities. A cohesive policy response to the development of ecosystem service markets, however, should never just continue to be about reducing carbon emissions alone. Indeed, it must, in parallel, encourage global efforts towards the protection and enhancement of biodiversity, cultural diversity and food security (see Dale, 2014, pp. 113–122). This means:

- setting up a wider policy framework for combining good landscape-scale regulation with balanced efforts to enhance landholder contributions to environmental or land stewardship
- establishing trading systems that enable society to offset the impact of its consumption on biodiversity, agricultural sustainability and water quality.

We need both a wider policy framework that embeds a place-oriented, integrated approach to landscape-scale management and a clear national framework for the development of ecosystems services trading products and services delivered in alignment with this system.

# Regional Food Network Tropical North Queensland

The Regional Food Network (RFN) is an example of how farmers building on established agri-industrial industries have adopted what could be described as a rural development approach to remain viable. Reconnecting communities with regional or local food is a key component to implementing place-based agricultural development (Kneafsey, 2010). The network is made up of mostly family-owned businesses that have set themselves apart through value adding, niche marketing and diversification. The network has developed its own brand, 'Taste Paradise' making the most of tropical North Queensland's clean green image and its tourism industry to generate additional value for farm-based products (see www.tasteparadise.com.au).

Established in 2011, the success of the RFN can be attributed to leveraging the region's competitive advantages. It capitalises on the region's assets, facilitating a greater connectivity between existing businesses and producers, addressing one of the major challenges of successful development at a regional level (Iyer et al., 2005; Marsden & Smith, 2005; Sharp & Smith, 2003). The RFN facilitated this greater connectivity in a number of ways. It capitalised on tourists' behaviours through promoting the natural aesthetics of the region and existing value-added farm businesses. In turn, community businesses and organisations have supported the RFN by promoting product origin. Further, the network also built a relationship of trust with consumers through brand development, whereby members of the supply chain need to become accredited. Accreditation assures the consumer that the product is grown, sourced, distributed and sold locally. In doing so, the network demonstrates an understanding of the need to work with other regional organisations and businesses outside of agriculture to increase the demand for regional or local produce and products and the importance of understanding consumer preferences.

These short regional supply chains can be applied to multiple regions throughout the north and with appropriate support built on to link into Asian markets. Using the rural development model as a framework and following the example of the RFN, the first step would be to audit the regions for existing businesses, facilities and resources to identify opportunities for development. The second step would be to encourage the involvement of local supply chain stakeholders, from farmers to consumers. Many people are reluctant to engage in new strategies or markets due to time and financial concerns, or are simply unaware of the supply chain and how to access it or have a lack of trust in the system (Marsden & Smith, 2005; Maxey, 2006). Barriers can be overcome, as demonstrated by the RFN, by effectively communicating information about the network's role, existing members and accreditation process to consumers and potential members of the network. Therefore, strong regional governance, including transparency in policy, clear communication to all stakeholders and demonstrating an understanding of stakeholder needs or barriers to engagement, is essential for successful development at a regional level (Michelini, 2013).

As is evident by a place-based approach, the types of systems put in place will inevitably vary from region to region. However, fundamental to success of a regional supply chain is a whole-of-system approach, whereby government and industry policies both encourage and facilitate farmer adoption of alternative supply chains and niche markets. Without this supportive framework, engaging farmers in alternative, local supply chains that build on established agri-industrial industries can be difficult.

## Conclusion

If we are to break out of the circular conundrum we need to learn from the past and take a new look at the ways that agriculture can contribute to regional development in Northern Australia. There are real opportunities to build on existing agri-industrial industries in Northern Australia, as these case studies have demonstrated. For too long, the main focus has simply been on new large-scale irrigated agricultural projects as the way to develop the north. History demonstrates, however, that starting small while developing the necessary human and physical assets and supply chains has been more successful (Andrews, 2014; Ash, 2014).

The place-based agriculture development framework provides a tool for policymakers, industries and communities to explore the different contributions that agriculture can make. Encouraging new narratives and visions for northern agriculture that are grounded not in old myths but in a deeper understanding of the physical, environmental and sociocultural assets of a region. When people are actively engaged and supported through place-based policies and institutional arrangements, they have the capacity to produce economic, environmental and social benefits that can uniquely leverage the assets and opportunities intrinsic to a place.

## Acknowledgements

The authors would like to acknowledge the Australian Government's Rural Industries Research and Development Corporation for funding the research that underpinned the development of the place-based agricultural development framework detailed in this chapter.

# References

Andrews, K. (2014). 'The Circular Conundrum': 150 years of cropping and complexity in north-west Australia (unpublished doctoral thesis). The Australian National University, Canberra, ACT.

Ash, A. J. (2014). *Factors driving the viability of major cropping investments in northern Australia—a historical analysis.* CSIRO.

Australian Government. (2014). *Green paper on developing Northern Australia.* Canberra, ACT: Department of the Prime Minister and Cabinet. Retrieved from www.regional.gov.au/regional/northernaustralia/

Australian Government. (2015). *Our north, our future: White paper on developing Northern Australia.* Retrieved from www.industry.gov.au/data-and-publications/our-north-our-future-white-paper-on-developing-northern-australia

Australian Labor Party. (2013). *Growing the north: A plan for Northern Australia.* Retrieved from d3n8a8pro7vhmx.cloudfront.net/australianlaborparty/pages/935/attachments/original/1376536954/Fact_Sheet_-_Growing_the_North.pdf?1376536954

Barca, F., McCann, P. & Rodríguez-Pose, A. (2012). The case for regional development intervention: Place-based versus place-neutral approaches, *Journal of Regional Science, 52*(1), 134–152. doi.org/10.1111/j.1467-9787.2011.00756.x

Bauer, F. H. (1985). A brief history of agriculture in north-west Australia. In R. Muchow (Ed.), *Agro-research for the semi-arid tropics: North-West Australia* (pp. 12–31). Brisbane, Qld: University of Queensland Press.

Bohnet, I. (2008). Assessing retrospective and prospective landscape change through the development of social profiles of landholders: A tool for improving land use planning and policy formulation. *Landscape and Urban Planning, 88*(1), 1–11. doi.org/10.1016/j.landurbplan.2008.07.002

Bohnet, I. & Smith, D. M. (2007). Planning future landscapes in the Wet Tropics of Australia: A social-ecological framework. *Landscape and Urban Planning, 80*(1), 137–152. doi.org/10.1016/j.landurbplan.2006.07.001

Brann, M. (2012, 20 September). Cattle giant to cash in carbon credits. *ABC Rural.* Retrieved from www.abc.net.au/news/2013-09-20/tipperary-carbon-credits/4970806

Bureau of Infrastructure, Transport and Regional Economics (BITRE). (2011). *Northern Australia statistical compendium 2011 update*. Canberra, ACT: BITRE. Retrieved from www.bitre.gov.au/sites/default/files/stats_014.pdf

Cocklin, C. & Alston, M. (Eds). (2002). *Community sustainability in rural Australia: A question of capital?* Wagga Wagga, NSW: Academy of the Social Sciences in Australia.

Cocklin, C., Dibden, J. & Mautner, N. (2006). From market to multifunctionality? Land stewardship in Australia. *Geographical Journal, 172*(3), 197–205. doi.org/10.1111/j.1475-4959.2006.00206.x

Commonwealth Scientific and Industrial Research Organisation (CSIRO). (2013). *Agricultural resource assessment for the Gilbert Catchment. An overview report to the Australian Government from the CSIRO Flinders and Gilbert agricultural resource assessment, part of the north Queensland irrigated agriculture strategy*. Brisbane, Qld: CSIRO.

Dale, A. P. (2014). *Beyond the north–south culture wars: Reconciling northern Australia's past with its future* (SpringerBriefs in Geography Series). The Netherlands: Springer.

Dale, A. P., McKee, J., Vella, K. & Potts, R. (2013). Carbon, biodiversity and regional natural resource planning: Towards high impact next generation plans. *Australian Planner, 50*(4), 328–339. doi.org/10.1080/07293682.2013.764908

Department of the Prime Minister and Cabinet. (2014). *Indigenous affairs budget 2014–15, Indigenous Advancement Strategy*. Canberra, ACT: Commonwealth of Australia.

The Economist Intelligence Unit. (2013). *A healthy future for all? Improving food quality for Asia*. Retrieved from perspectives.eiu.com/sites/default/files/A%20Healthy%20Future%20For%20All_main_Oct16_V3.pdf

Gammage, B. (2011). *The biggest estate on earth: How Aborigines made Australia*. Sydney, NSW: Allen & Unwin.

Hildreth, P. & Bailey, D. (2014). Place-based economic development strategy in England: Filling the missing space. *Local Economy, 29*(4–5), 363–377.

Hill, R., Pert, P. L., Davies, J., Robinson, C. J., Walsh, F. & Falco-Mammone, F. (2013). *Indigenous land management in Australia: Extent, scope, diversity, barriers and success factors*. Cairns, Qld: CSIRO Ecosystems Science.

Holmes, J. (2006). Impulses towards a multifunctional transition in rural Australia: Gaps in the research agenda. *Journal of Rural Studies, 22*(2), 142–160.

Holmes, J. (2012). Cape York Peninsula, Australia: A frontier region undergoing a multifunctional transition with Indigenous engagement. *Journal of Rural Studies*, *28*(3), 252–265.

Iyer, S., Kitson, M. & Toh, B. (2005). Social capital, economic growth and regional development. *Regional Studies*, *39*(8), 1015–1040.

Kneafsey, M. (2010). The region in food—important or irrelevant? *Cambridge Journal of Regions, Economy and Society*, *3*(2), 177–190.

Lawrence, G., Richards, C. & Lyons, K. (2013). Food security in Australia in an era of neoliberalism, productivism and climate change. *Journal of Rural Studies*, *29*, 30–39.

Liberal Party of Australia. (2013). *The Coalition's 2030 vision for developing Northern Australia*. Retrieved from parlinfo.aph.gov.au/parlInfo/search/display/display.w3p;query=Id%3A%22library%2Fpartypol%2F2550511%22;src1=sm1

Lockie, S. & Higgins, V. (2007). Roll-out neoliberalism and hybrid practices of regulation in Australian agri-environmental governance. *Journal of Rural Studies*, *23*(1), 1–11. doi.org/10.1016/j.jrurstud.2006.09.011

Marsden, T. (2003). *The condition of rural sustainability*. Assen, The Netherlands: Uitgeverij Van Gorcum.

Marsden, T. & Farioli, F. (2015). Natural powers: From the bio-economy to the eco-economy and sustainable place-making. *Sustainability Science*, *10*(2), 331–344.

Marsden, T. & Smith, E. (2005). Ecological entrepreneurship: sustainable development in local communities through quality food production and local branding. *Geoforum*, *36*(4), 440–451.

Marsden, T. & Sonnino, R. (2008). Rural development and the regional state: Denying multifunctional agriculture in the UK. *Journal of Rural Studies*, *24*, 422–431. doi.org/10.1016/j.jrurstud.2008.04.001

Maxey, L. (2006). Can we sustain sustainable agriculture? Learning from small-scale producer-suppliers in Canada and the UK. *Geographical Journal*, *172*(3), 230–244. doi.org/10.1111/j.1475-4959.2006.00211.x

Michelini, J. J. (2013). Small farmers and social capital in development projects: Lessons from failures in Argentina's rural periphery. *Journal of Rural Studies*, *30*, 99–109. doi.org/10.1016/j.jrurstud.2013.01.001

North Australian Indigenous Land and Sea Management Alliance (NAILSMA). (2014). *An Indigenous prospectus for northern development: Effective engagement, resilient communities, secure futures*. Submission to Parliament of Australia: Joint Committee on Northern Australia, Canberra.

Northern Australia Land and Water Taskforce. (2009, December). *Sustainable development in Northern Australia, A report to Government from the Northern Australia Land and Water Taskforce*. Canberra, ACT: Department of Infrastructure, Transport, Regional Development and Local Government.

Onyx, J. & Bullen, P. (2000). Measuring social capital in five communities. *The Journal of Applied Behavioral Science, 36*(1), 23–42. doi.org/10.1177/0021886300361002

Organisation for Economic Co-operation and Development (OECD). (2006). *The new rural paradigm: Policies and governance*. Paris, France: OECD.

Powell, J. M. (1977). *Mirrors of the New World - Images and Image-makers in the Settlement Process*. Folkestone, England: Dawson and Archon Books.

Productivity Commission. (2005). *Trends in Australian agriculture* (Research paper). Canberra, ACT: Productivity Commission.

Renting, H., Rossing, W. A. H., Groot, J. C. J., Van der Ploeg, J. D., Laurent, C., Perraud, D., … Van Ittersum, M. K. (2009). Exploring multifunctional agriculture. A review of conceptual approaches and prospects for an integrative transitional framework. *Journal of Environmental Management, 90*, S112–S123

Sharp, J. S. & Smith, M. B. (2003). Social capital and farming at the rural–urban interface: The importance of nonfarmer and farmer relations. *Agricultural Systems, 76*(3), 913–927.

Tomaney, J. (2010, November). *Place-based approaches to regional development: Global trends and Australian implications*. Sydney, NSW: Australian Business Foundation.

Turnour, J. (2014). Northern Australia agriculture policy: Opportunities and risks. In The Regional Australia Institute, *Green paper on developing Northern Australia: A joint submission to the Northern Australia taskforce* (pp. 63–70). Canberra, ACT: The Regional Australia Institute.

Turnour, J., Dale, A., McShane, C., Thompson, M., Prideaux, B. & Atkinson, M. (2015). *A place-based agriculture development framework* (Project report). Canberra, ACT: Rural Industries Research and Development Corporation.

Van Oosterzee, P., Preece, N. & Dale, A. (2010). Catching the baby: Accounting for biodiversity and the ecosystem sector in emissions trading. *Conservation Letters*, 3(2), 1–8. doi.org/10.1111/j.1755-263X.2009.00090.x

Van Oosterzee, P., Preece, N. & Dale, A. (2012). An Australian landscape-based approach: AFOLU mitigation for smallholders. In E. Wollenberg, M.-L. Tapio-Bistrom, M. Grieg-Gran & A. Nihart (Eds), *Climate change mitigation and agriculture* (pp. 193–202). Abingdon, England: Routledge.

Webster, T., Morison, J., Abel, N., Clark, N., Rippin, L., Herr, A., … Wilson, P. (2009). *Irrigated agriculture: Development opportunities and implications for Northern Australia*. Canberra, ACT: CSIRO.

Woodhouse, A. (2006). Social capital and economic development in regional Australia: A case study. *Journal of Rural Studies*, 22(1), 83–94. doi.org/10.1016/j.jrurstud.2005.07.003

# 3

# Investing in the Future: Human and Social Service Development in Northern Australia

Hurriyet Babacan and Narayan Gopalkrishnan

## Introduction

Development in Northern Australia has a long history of government and policy interest with renewed political and media attention in recent years. In particular, the need for economic diversification and economic growth has become a central focus (Australian Government, 2015). There is universal agreement that strong, resilient and healthy individuals, families and community play a vital role in building ongoing prosperity, wellbeing and economic development. It has been demonstrated that long-term economic growth in regions occurs through investment in human capital development (Babacan & Babacan, 2007; OECD, 2016; United Nations Economic and Social Commission for Asia Pacific, 2013). Lack of appropriate investment in the health and social services impedes Northern Australia's competitiveness and reinforces the persistence of human capital weaknesses, as well as increasing regional costs for the provision of social services (RAI, 2015; OECD, 2016).

Northern Australia is characterised by diverse populations living in communities that are regional, rural, remote or very remote. Northern Australia is challenged by critical factors that exacerbate aspects of spatial disadvantage. Northern Australia faces a significant range of social issues concerning the provision of, and access to, human and social services.

These have major impacts on human development and social capital. This chapter explores the nature of disadvantage in Northern Australia and key challenges in the provision of human and social services, and argues that a 'one-size-fits-all' approach will not work given the diversity, governance, social, environmental and economic issues unique to Northern Australia communities. The chapter examines the nature of social issues and current health and human services investment in Northern Australia. It also examines service delivery models and governance frameworks and argues that there is a need to develop models that provide preventative, sustainable outcomes for communities into the future.

## Brief Glance at Northern Australia

Northern Australia comprises over 1.2 million people; approximately 6 per cent of the national population (RAI, 2013). The area described as Northern Australia is located across three jurisdictions—Queensland, Western Australia (WA) and the Northern Territory (NT). It covers 74 local government areas (LGAs)—eight in WA, 16 in the NT and 50 in Queensland. There is a significant level of variability within and between regions in Northern Australia.

Aboriginal and Torres Strait Islander peoples have a strong presence and interest in Northern Australia. A quarter of the people who usually reside in Northern Australia are Indigenous (Stoeckl, 2010, p. 106). For example, 67,000 Aboriginal people represent 32 per cent of the total NT population (Manderson, 2008). The Indigenous population is expected to continue to grow at a faster rate than the non-Indigenous population (1.97 per cent per annum compared to 1.78 per cent) (Carson et al., 2009). Stoeckl (2010, p. 106) concludes that 'Indigenous people are not only an important and numerically significant part of this region's current population, but they will become even more important in the years ahead'.

Northern Australia can be considered regional, rural or remote. While there is much debate about what these terms mean, the rural, remote and metropolitan areas (RRMA) classification developed by the Australian Government specifies them as follows:

- 'regional' refers to non-urban centres with a population over 25,000 and with relatively good access to services
- 'rural' refers to non-urban localities of under 25,000 with reduced accessibility

- 'remote' communities are those of fewer than 5,000 people with very restricted accessibility
- 'metropolitan' has a population equal to or greater than 100,000 (Roufeil & Battye, 2008, p. 3).

Most of Northern Australia fits in the definition of regional, rural and remote, with only five towns having a population larger than 70,000, 13 comprising between 15,000 and 70,000 people, and 55 with populations of less than 15,000 in 2011 (RAI, 2013, p. 31). A range of social issues concerning the provision of, and access to, social services can be linked back to spatial location, as will be explored in the next section.

While there is a renewed focus on Northern Australia, disparities and inequities exist in a number of ways between Northern Australia and the rest of Australia, between Northern Australia locations and across population groups. The key priorities of the Regional Development Australia (RDA) Committees reflect the issues facing Northern Australia. The top issue identified by RDA was infrastructure, including basic infrastructure such as power, water and waste management. Diversification of the economic base, information and communication technologies and access to affordable housing, basic health services and education are other important areas of focus.

The Regional Australia Institute (RAI) (2013, p. 11), the think tank for regional development established by the Australian Government, states that 'regional development in northern Australia requires a range of approaches that address both the variability and the disparity; between the north and the rest of Australia, between and within regions, and between population groups'.

## Spatial Dimensions of Disadvantage in Northern Australia

Northern Australia comprises 2,773,000 km$^2$, comprising 36 per cent of the land mass of Australia. The connection between disadvantage, demography and geography are well established (AIHW, 2014a, 2014b; Cheers & Taylor, 2001; Chenoweth & Stehlik, 2001). The factors that exacerbate aspects of rural disadvantage have been identified as financial strain, family and community relationships, out-migration from rural areas, changing gender roles, lack of support services and social isolation

(AIHW, 2014a, 2014b; Hall & Scheltens, 2005). The AIHW (2017a, 2017b) has identified that life expectancy, income and education levels are lower for people in regional, remote and rural areas.

Cheers and Taylor (2001, p. 207) argue that people in rural areas are disadvantaged in comparison to urban people on most of the social and economic indicators including 'life chances, income levels, poverty, unemployment, living costs, housing quality, health status, education, and a range of social problems, and in gaining access to health, welfare, community, personal support, and essential services'. The AIHW (2014a, p. 4) points out that a lack of access to services in areas with geographically dispersed populations may affect the overall health and wellbeing of the populations living in those areas, especially in remote and very remote areas.

The persistence of locational inequality in rural/regional Australia is attributed to multiple factors including structural changes to the Australian economy, which 'through processes of circular cumulative causation' embed spatial disadvantage (Saunders & Wong, 2014, p. 132). In a national study of exclusion and deprivation, Saunders and Wong (2014) demonstrated that differences within and between where people live make a difference to wellbeing. They demonstrated that people living in rural and country towns (small and large) face deprivation in relation to economic status, wellbeing, material deprivation, social exclusion, disengagement and service availability. They posit that disadvantage can become entrenched and reinforce itself and be transmitted across generations.

There is a long list of social issues affecting people across Northern Australia, including mental health (Fragar et al., 2007) and acquired brain injury (Stephens et al., 2014), domestic violence (Wendt & Hornosty, 2010), aged care (Winterton & Warburton, 2011), disabilities (Massey et al., 2013) and poorer health, including lower life expectancy (AIHW, 2014a). Financial strain, high unemployment, low educational attainment, out-migration from rural areas, changing gender roles, domestic and family violence, suicide, social isolation, discrimination, marginalisation and deprivation are terms used to characterise the link between rural disadvantage and wellbeing (Hall & Scheltens, 2005). Significant to severe disadvantage persists in Indigenous and Torres Strait Islander communities across the north in key social areas such as life expectancy, education, income, labour market participation and health (Babacan, 2014).

Spatial disadvantage in Northern Australia is evident from the following data. The Australian Bureau of Statistics (ABS) calculates the Socio-Economic Indexes for Area (SEIFA). The index is derived from attributes that reflect disadvantage such as low income, low educational attainment, high unemployment and jobs in relatively unskilled occupations—the lower the SEIFA score, the higher the disadvantage. Based on 2016 Census data (ABS, 2016), the SEIFA index in Northern Australia demonstrates disadvantage in a significant number of LGAs (see Table 3.1). It should be noted that the average Australian SEIFA score is 1,000. The overall SEIFA score of Northern Australia is 970, based on 2011 Census data (Public Health Information Development Unit, 2014).

Table 3.1: Selected Socio-Economic Indexes for Areas (SEIFA) scores for Northern Australia.

| State | LGA | SEIFA score | State | LGA | SEIFA score |
|---|---|---|---|---|---|
| Qld | Aurukun | 641 | WA | Broome | 979 |
| | Burke | 915 | | Derby-West Kimberly | 796 |
| | Cairns | 971 | | Halls Creek | 718 |
| | Carpentaria | 874 | | Wyndham-East Kimberly | 941 |
| | Charters Towers | 914 | | | |
| | Cloncurry | 946 | NT | Alice Springs | 1015 |
| | Etheridge | 929 | | Central Desert | 697 |
| | Hopevale | 699 | | Darwin | 1057 |
| | Kowanyama | 676 | | East Arnhem | 562 |
| | Mackay | 966 | | Katherine | 990 |
| | Mareeba | 936 | | Palmerston | 1033 |
| | Mt Isa | 972 | | Roper Gulf | 709 |
| | Townsville | 976 | | Victoria Daly | 753 |
| | Tablelands | 932 | | West Arnhem | 735 |
| | Torres Strait Islands | 759 | | | |
| | Winton | 941 | | | |
| | Yarrabah | 651 | | | |

Note: LGA = local government area, Qld = Queensland, WA = Western Australia, NT = Northern Territory.
Source: ABS (2016) SEIFA Indexes Data.

Table 3.1 clearly demonstrates socioeconomic disadvantage across much of Northern Australia. The disadvantage is also evident in large regional cities such as Cairns and in more remote areas. Areas with high Indigenous populations have the lowest SEIFA scores in the nation.

The key indicators of the disadvantage is outlined by Catholic Social Services Australia (CSSA) (2014). They argue that there is greater government and welfare dependence in Northern Australia with indications such as lower median weekly income (i.e. 75 per cent of the Statistical Local Areas in Australia with a lower median individual weekly income), increased drug and alcohol issues, limited housing stock and poor infrastructure. The high cost of living is a critical issue in Northern Australia, particularly in food, housing and transport, which compounds the disadvantage of the people on low incomes (CSSA, 2014, pp. 6–7). The RAI identifies that Northern Australia is well below the national average for six of the nine indicators of the competitiveness index. They point out that while Northern Australia has a very high national average competitiveness in the economic fundamentals, it is hampered by significantly below average competitiveness in human capital and infrastructure and essential services (RAI, 2013, p. 21). The areas of human capital they identified include early childhood performance, school performance (primary and secondary) and English language proficiency. The RAI (2013, p. 26) also identifies barriers to accessing health services as a significant issue. The national *Patient Experience Survey 2017–2018* (ABS, 2017) verifies this. The survey identified that 21 per cent of people in outer regional/remote/very remote areas waited longer than they felt was acceptable to get an appointment with a general practitioner (GP) (compared to 18 per cent in major cities), and 33 per cent of people reported they could not see their preferred GP on one or more occasions (compared to 25 per cent in major cities). There are flow-on impacts of lack of access to services. For example, in Northern Queensland there is a high incidence of presenting to emergency departments of hospitals due to lack of access to primary health care providers; approximately 46 per cent of the population presented to emergency departments in 2015, compared to 25 per cent nationally (Northern Queensland Primary Health Network, 2017). The GP rate is calculated as number of GPs per 100,000 people. In Northern Queensland, the average GP rate is 86, compared to the national average of 110.6 and 105.5 in Queensland (Northern Queensland Primary Health Network, 2017, p. 30). Preventable hospitalisations for Northern Australia were higher than for North Queensland, with 2,981 people per 100,000. For the NT, this was 4,891 people, compared to the national figure of 2,430 (National Health Priority Areas, 2014). The number of people who could not access professional services for emotional health and wellbeing was approximately 19 per cent in remote areas, compared to 6.2 per cent in major cities (AIHW, 2017b).

Indigenous disadvantage continues in Northern Australia in key social areas such as life expectancy, education, income, labour market participation and health. For example, the gap in life expectancy between Indigenous and non-Indigenous people was 10.6 years for males and 9.5 years for females (Australian Government, 2014). Literacy levels are also poor. Between 2008 and 2013, the proportion of Indigenous students at or above the National Minimum Standards (NMS) in reading and numeracy has shown improvement in only two out of eight indicators. Only 31 per cent of Indigenous students in remote areas reached NMS in Year 9 in 2013. Only 38.5 per cent of Indigenous people aged 20–24 years in remote areas had completed Year 12 in 2012. The proportion of Indigenous people aged 15–64 who were employed in 2012 was 47.5 per cent, compared to 75.6 per cent for non-Indigenous people (Australian Government, 2014).

A number of government responses have been initiated over the last decade. Some of these have been highly contentious, particularly relating to the NT Intervention. A number of initiatives were delivered to address key issues and disadvantage including Closing the Gap and the National Partnership Agreement on Remote Service Delivery. The evaluation of Closing the Gap and the National Agreement noted some improvements in addressing Indigenous disadvantage and access to services, but concluded:

> there had been no improvement in Indigenous school attendance over five years. The record of progress against other targets has also been disappointing. There has been no progress on the employment target and while Indigenous life expectancy has improved, the pace of change is far too slow to close the gap by 2031 (Australian Government, 2014, pp. 3–4).

A review of Closing the Gap, a decade after its implementation, concluded that the progress on this major initiative 'has to date only been partially and incoherently implemented' and that 'mortality and life expectancy gaps are actually widening' in those localities due to improved life expectancy of non-Indigenous populations (Holland, 2018, p. 4). The government has called for a refreshed approach to Closing the Gap, as 'governments have not been able to make real in-roads into closing the gap in health equality and life expectancy for Australia's First Peoples' (Holland, 2018, p. 8).

This section has demonstrated the nature of social disadvantage and marginalisation in Northern Australia. The issues are complex and multidimensional. While Northern Australia is seen as having economic potential, there are significant challenges in relation to developing social and human capital.

## Investment in Human and Community Services Sector

Human service delivery agencies fall into three categories: community-based (also referred to as not-for-profit or third-sector) agencies, government agencies and for-profit agencies (mainly private sector). Health and human service delivery in rural and remote areas tends to be provided by a range of providers including the three tiers of government or community service organisations (which are often publicly funded) and the private sector. For example, in the area of residential aged care, for-profit providers constitute 40 per cent of services across Australia. However, only 4.1 per cent of services are located outside of major cities and inner regional locations. Conversely, 91 per cent of all services in rural or remote areas are operated by state or federal government agencies or community-based providers (Baldwin et al., 2013, p. 8). There is a gap in the evidence about the nature of this sector in Northern Australia. It is known that there are large charitable agencies such as CSSA across Northern Australia, as well as Indigenous health agencies, government agencies and a network of smaller community organisations.

In 2015–16, total government welfare expenditure in Australia was estimated at A\$157 billion (AIHW, 2017c)—cash payments for specific populations (not including unemployment benefits) accounted for 66.8 per cent, welfare services 26.9 per cent and unemployment benefits 6.3 per cent. In this same period, the total recurrent expenditure on health was A\$160.2 billion. It is worth noting that more than half (55.5 per cent) was spent in New South Wales and Victoria. Growth rates in health expenditures from 2010–11 to 2015–16 were 3.1 per cent in NSW, 3.0 per cent in Victoria, 4.1 per cent in Queensland, 4.3 per cent in Western Australia, 2.1 per cent in South Australia, 2.3 per cent in Tasmania and 1.8 per cent in the NT (AIHW, 2017b). In comparison with other developed nations, Australia ranks lower in welfare expenditure rankings. Australia's total social expenditure was estimated at 19.1 per cent of gross domestic product (GDP) in 2016 (OECD, 2018). Spending on welfare services in 2015–16 was A$42.3 billion for family and child welfare services, aged services, disability services and other services (AIHW, 2017a). The average amount spent by governments on welfare services per Australian resident in 2015–16 was A$1,763, up from A$1,512 in 2006–07 and A$1,667 in 2014–15 (AIHW, 2017a).

Examination of past data from 1999–2007 reveals chronic underinvestment in welfare in the states and territories that comprise Northern Australia. For example, the AIHW concludes that funding of recurrent expenditure on welfare services by all state and territory governments averaged A$421 per person in 2005–06. States with the lowest average government funding per capita were Queensland (A$358) and Western Australia (A$361) (AIHW, 2007). This means that the states that constitute Northern Australia are playing catch-up. Rural and regional service providers are disproportionately impacted by curtailment in public expenditure and cutbacks in location-specific public services (e.g. centralisation of services to a regional area) (Steiner & Teasdale, 2017; Babacan, 2013).

The data for Northern Australia is difficult to ascertain due to cross-jurisdictional data collection. Additionally, the AIHW (2013, p. 399) notes that 'there is currently no dedicated routine monitoring of total welfare expenditure, comprising government and non-government spending, in Australia'. While aggregated data exists for government expenditure, there is little disaggregated data based on locality, region and issues addressed. Thus, an accurate assessment of investment in social and community services is currently not possible in Northern Australia.

The real costs of meeting the needs in rural, remote and very remote settings continue to be inadequately factored into current funding allocations (First Peoples Disability Network, 2013; Massey et al., 2013). A number of factors influence welfare spending including population growth, the cost of providing services and rates of service use, and capacity to pay privately. The capacity to pay privately in Northern Australia is limited (CSSA, 2014) and reflected by the small private sector human service delivery. The reason why publicly funded welfare services are provided is given by government as improving 'the lives of Australians by creating opportunities for economic and social participation by individuals, families and communities' (Department of Families, Housing, Community Services and Indigenous Affairs, 2011, p. 13) and 'increasing national prosperity through improvements to productivity, participation and social inclusion' (DEEWR, 2011). There is a recognition by the Australian Government that investing in welfare yields socioeconomic returns to society (NEF Consulting, 2010). The social return on investment evidence undertaken in international and community development fields confirms this. For example, in the United Kingdom it was found that £1 invested in local area community development yielded a return valued at £15, a social return investment ratio of 2.16:1 (NEF Consulting, 2010, p. 4). On a macro scale, there is evidence around the connection between increased public spending on human capital and improved prosperity. For example, Lamartina and Zaghini (2008), in an analysis of 23 high-income countries from 1970–2006, confirmed a positive correlation between public spending and per capita rise in GDP. It is also well established that when support systems fail the result is severe personal and systemic disempowerment (First Peoples Disability Network, 2013).

In recognising the development and preventative role of social and human services sector in Northern Australia, the RAI argues that both sectors play a vital role in the early detection and treatment of preventable health conditions. They argue that lack of appropriate investment in the sector impedes Northern Australia's competitiveness, reinforces the persistence of human capital weaknesses over time and increases regional costs for the provision of social services (RAI, 2013). Similarly, the Mineral Council of Australia, in its submission to a Parliamentary Inquiry, pointed out the need for investment in community and community infrastructure in Northern Australia:

> Research suggests that communities that do not have sufficient infrastructure, social amenity and economic diversity will not attract new residents and this will in turn constrain the industry's recruitment capacity (House of Representatives Standing Committee on Regional Affairs, 2013, n.p.).

The complexity of government investment in Northern Australia is well demonstrated by the lack of progress in Closing the Gap. Holland (2018, p. 8) highlights the issues accurately:

> over the decade since 2008, Aboriginal and Torres Strait Islander affairs have experienced discontinuity and uncertainty. Regular changes to the administration and quantum of funding, shifting policy approaches and arrangements within, between and from government, cuts to services, and a revolving door of Prime Ministers, Indigenous Affairs Minister and senior bureaucrats have all but halted the steady progress hoped for by First Peoples.

Additionally, 'the introduction of new competitive tendering process for services to apply for funding grants was introduced, leading upheaval and led to uncertainty, lost continuity, and eroded engagement between Aboriginal and Torres Strait Islander organisations and government' (Holland, 2018, p. 8). Moreover, the level of funding was not commensurate with the complex needs and issues.

Recent studies have focused on social capital and community resilience. 'Resilience is the capacity for complex systems to survive, adapt, evolve and grow in the face of turbulent change' (van Opstal, 2007, p. 11). There is a positive and strong correlation between growth of human services and progressive change in communities. Winterton and Warburton (2011) demonstrated the connection between resilience and disadvantage for older adults living in rural areas. Chenoweth and Stehlik (2001) demonstrated in Queensland rural communities that human services were contributing to new forms of community resiliency. The authors cited examples from age and disability sectors, suicide prevention and mental health and financial counselling for drought-stricken communities. They argued that the potential for resiliency rests in partnerships and proactive planning at the local level. Other recent examples of building community resilience come from local government. For example, Dollery, Wallis and Akimov (2010) argue that local government service delivery scope and outreach was much broader in remote NT shires than for the city/town councils and other remote councils, covering many areas of community support. There is a strong imperative for strong communities given the challenges that face Northern Australia such as climate change, boom–bust economic cycles and significant disadvantage. Concepts of community and resilience have been associated with communities 'bouncing back', transforming' and being 'adaptive' (Kirmayer et al., 2009; Gow & Paton, 2008).

# Sustainable Rural and Remote Human Service Delivery

The delivery of human services in rural, remote and regional areas differs for a range of reasons. Distance impacts on service costs, and the productive time of community or social workers may be limited due to lack of allied supports and staff exhaustion due to travel commitments (Roufeil & Battye, 2008). CSSA (2014) argues that it costs much more to provide a service in Northern Australia than in other parts of Australia, a fact not often recognised in funding models. Other factors identified as a source of impost include community pressure on the few human service professionals or service delivery agencies to be 'all things to all people' in the absence of an adequate range of health and welfare services; the long time required to foster community acceptance; challenge of managing confidentiality in small communities; limited access to other support professionals, especially specialists; difficulty in recruiting and retaining staff; limited ability of communities to pay for services; and a general reluctance to seek help when needed (Roufeil & Battye, 2008; Judd et al., 2006).

These issues have been echoed in meetings held by one of the authors of this chapter across Northern Australia from 2010–13. An extensive consultation was undertaken in 2011, involving service providers in Far North Queensland comprising government and non-government agencies addressing issues relating to health, migrant and refugee community issues, domestic violence, mental health, substance abuse, child protection, women, Indigenous community issues, disability, ageing, housing and homelessness, poverty and community development. A number of key issues were identified including:

- Lack of resources and lack of appropriate service delivery. It was identified that, relative to need, funding did not take into account 'real service delivery costs' in rural and remote areas in Far North Queensland.
- Ad hoc planning and lack of coordination and integration, particularly across different tiers of government and service agencies. There were major gaps or duplication in services in specific locations. Non-profit service agencies competed with the processes of tendering for funding in a competitive environment, which acted as a major barrier for collaboration across service agencies. Many participants in the consultations felt this resulted in loss of effectiveness as a sector to speak and act in a unified manner. Others voiced concern about the inability to be proactive around community needs and limitations on responsiveness due to a culture of short-term competitive funding processes in the face of chronic social problems. They also emphasised the need for preventative and outcomes-based approaches to human service planning and delivery, rather than the current reactive and crisis-based approaches.

- Models of service delivery focused on addressing crisis intervention, rather than developing community capital and resiliency. This led to difficulties at times of crisis and major economic challenges such as climatic challenges and economic shocks.
- Difficulty of influencing policy and decision-makers who were long way away in Canberra or Brisbane. Many decision-makers had not visited Far North Queensland and did not have appropriate awareness of the issues in Far North Queensland. Community voices were inadequately represented due to a range of factors including distance, access to decision-makers and capability to translate Far North Queensland human service issues in relevant ways to policymakers. Many professional staff were identified as not having enough time to do the higher-order thinking and planning to be proactive as they were stretched responding to current demands.
- Workforce issues including difficulties of recruiting and retaining appropriately qualified workforce, loss of experienced personnel due to lack of funding and job security, and lack of career and personal development opportunities. Major concern was expressed relating to maintaining long-term service delivery viability with the 'churn over' of services and staff being commonplace. As a result, the human services sector was seen as variable in strength and coverage, often varying with funding opportunities, rather than addressing needs in any systematic manner (Babacan, 2011, 2014).

An analysis of the human services sector in Northern Australia requires an analysis of human service delivery models. As can be seen from the above list, major challenges exist across Northern Australia to achieve sustainable and functional service delivery models. Eversole (2017, p. 307) states that in the context of policy and political approaches, Australian regions are 'regularly defined through a deficit lens, and one which systematically overlooks the distinctive attributes of individual regions'. The author argues that resource management conflicts and social equity issues are regularly experienced 'in place' in regions, yet they are governed from afar by decision-makers with limited knowledge of the on-the-ground dynamics of particular regions (Eversole, 2017, p. 314).

Battye (2007, p. 5) defines a dysfunctional service model as one that does not support or enable professionals to provide care to individuals and communities on a sustainable basis. Identifying and implementing functional models of service in regional, rural and remote areas is not easy. Lessons learnt from Europe and OECD countries identify the need for broader approaches to human development (OECD, 2016). Policymaking is evolving and increasingly recognising social disadvantage, equity and environmental issues along with economic and imperatives for growth. There is emerging engagement with questions of sustainable regional development, recognising the interconnectivity between the economic with equity, community development, human and social capital, ecosystems, resilient institutions and strong cultures (Eversole, 2017; Babacan, 2017). The new policy lexicon demonstrates a change in focus to policy focusing on smart (linked with knowledge and innovation), sustainable (green, environmentally sound and climate change mitigation) and inclusive (equity, employment and cohesive) (Naldi et al., 2015).

Current practice in Northern Australia is mixed in service quality and sustainability, although there are no comprehensive studies available. In the absence of data, it is useful to apply a typology provided by Wakerman et al. (2008) from their study on rural and remote public health service delivery (see Figure 3.1).

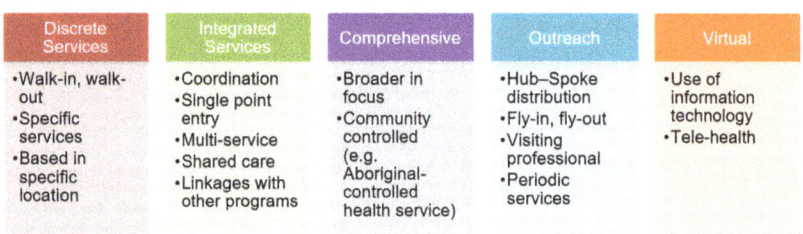

**Figure 3.1: Typology for service delivery in rural and remote regions.**
Source: Wakerman et al. (2008).

Each of these models has different features and advantages and disadvantages of which the scope of this chapter does not permit discussion. The authors identify essential elements of sustainable services and outline a number of enablers crucial in the provision of sustainable and accessible services. There are a number of environmental enablers, which include supportive policy that ensures sustained service funding, coordination of policy and funding, and an appropriate level of community readiness for involvement in planning and implementation of the service activity. At the service level, a number of requirements are necessary including the right number and mix of staff; adequate funding; strong governance, management and leadership; coordination and continuity of service with other agencies;

appropriate infrastructure; and, importantly, adequate information and communication technology. It is important to note that these factors are all inter-related.

The pressure on the health and human services sector continues to build as neoliberal approaches set a trend in which the state continues incrementally to withdraw support for traditional social service areas, accompanied by market-based models of funding such as outsourcing and contracting (Gopalkrishnan, 2007). New models of financial sustainability of social services are emerging such as social entrepreneurship—enterprises for a social purpose, of which the primary objectives are social and the profit or surplus generated by business activities is reinvested into these objectives (Steiner & Teasdale, 2017, p. 2). Research on social entrepreneurship in Northern Australia is scant and their contribution to rural development is not recognised. Unlike other parts of the world, social entrepreneurship is not recognised in policy frameworks and business development and capacity-building support is not provided by government trade and business departments. Experiences from overseas suggests that social entrepreneurship may be one of a diversity of options for Northern Australia, enabling multi-stakeholder, cross-industry and multi-level governance collaboration for sustainable outcomes (Steiner & Teasdale, 2017; Defourny & Nyssens, 2013) and for mobilising ideas, resources and support from external sources to benefit rural regions (Richter, 2017).

Sustainability issues need urgent attention as regional, remote and rural services are under enormous pressure and unable to meet the demands of the communities they serve (Baldwin et al., 2013; Alston & Kent, 2004). Services in Northern Australia face problems of accessibility, availability, relevance and acceptability, especially in the more remote areas (Limerick et al., 2012; Moran et al., 2009). Regional service centres attempt to cater for more remote surrounding areas without appropriate resources. CSSA (2014, p. 5), one of the major non-profit social service agencies in Northern Australia, argues that 'a "one size fits all" approach will not work for Northern Australia given the diversity, governance, social, environmental and economic issues'.

Identifying effective and sustainable models in Northern Australia is severely constrained by a lack of evidence about 'what works best'. While there is now a growing body of evidence about the needs of communities in Northern Australia, we have a scant research base about appropriate models of services and how to respond effectively to diverse community needs.

## Workforce Issues

The health and human services industry is one of the fastest growing industries, with trend forecasting by the Department of Jobs and Small Business (2018) identifying it as the largest employment increase in Australia (14.9 per cent) over the next five years. Currently, it comprises approximately 9 per cent of GDP and provides over 10 per cent of total employment in Australia. In Far North Queensland, in 2019–20, this sector provided 19,195 jobs—14.1 per cent of the total workforce—followed by retail; accommodation and food services (9.7%); construction (9.4%) and agriculture, fishing and forestry (7.1%) (Economy Id, 2021). In NT in 2021, largest industries by employment share are public administration and safety (17.4%), health and social services (17.3%), education and training (10%) and retail (8.9%) (Department of Industry, Tourism and Trade, 2021). The not-for-profit sector makes up just over 8.5 per cent of GDP, provides employment to about 10 per cent of the workforce and has nearly 3 million volunteers contributing an additional A$14.6 billion in unpaid work. It is the second-largest employing industry after health care and social assistance, and has more people than the construction (9.2%), professional, scientific and technical services (8.6%) and manufacturing (7.2%) industries (Social Ventures Australia and the Centre for Social Impact, 2020, p. 3). This sector is largely dependent on public funding, although private sector models are increasingly emerging. The sector has grown immensely in the context of significant increase in needs due to an ageing population, rise in chronic disease, increased longevity, increased mental health prevalence and a range of social issues (e.g. domestic violence, homelessness and unemployment). There are major service gaps and increased unmet needs with limitations of public expenditure resulting in targeted service delivery.

The community services workforce comprises people in paid employment who provide community services such as personal and social support, child care and corrective services (AIHW, 2013). This is complemented by volunteers, family members and informal carers. In 2011, there were more than 755,000 workers in community services occupations in Australia—an increase of 24 per cent since 2006 (AIHW, 2013, p. 25). Workers in community services occupations were more likely to be female (87 per cent), employed part-time (57 per cent), older and generally earning less than the average Australian worker (AIHW, 2013, p. 25). The relative ratios of community services staff per population in geographical areas vary greatly for different occupations. Table 3.2 provides a brief analysis of the people employed by community services occupations by remoteness in 2013.

**Table 3.2: People employed by community services occupations by remoteness (workers per 100,000 population) in 2013.**

| Occupation | Major cities | Inner regional | Outer regional | Remote/ Very remote | Australia |
|---|---|---|---|---|---|
| Registered nurses | 925.9 | 978.0 | 876.1 | 676.2 | 926.9 |
| Counsellors | 75.2 | 68.5 | 68.9 | 68.4 | 73.2 |
| Psychologists | 96.2 | 61.5 | 46.2 | 25.8 | 104.2 |
| Child care workers | 503.8 | 436.4 | 448.6 | 387.7 | 483.5 |
| Age and disabled care workers | 444.8 | 610.5 | 556.7 | 326.1 | 484.7 |
| Nursing support and personal care workers | 315.6 | 325.6 | 321.8 | 204.3 | 315.8 |

Source: AIHW (2013, p. 369).

The shortage of human and community services and health professionals in rural areas is well documented (Davies et al., 2009; Lonne & Cheers, 2004; Roufeil & Battye, 2008), although the Community Services and Health Industry Skills Council (2014) argues that there is a need for relevant and high-quality training and workforce data. They argue that appropriate planning in the sector is challenging without appropriate evidence, particularly in the context of a fast-changing policy and funding domain. The environmental scan conducted by the Community Services and Health Industry Skills Council (2014) identified shortages in aged care, child care, child protection, mental health, counselling, social workers, nurses and disability workers. The quantum of managers and senior staff in leadership roles in community services and the health sector was also identified as limited (AIHW, 2013). As can be seen from Table 3.2, the shortage of an appropriate community services workforce across different occupations increases with greater remoteness (AIHW, 2013). For example, early childhood teachers numbered 852 per 10,000 population in major cities, compared to 680 and 738 for outer regional and remote areas; nurses numbered 926 for major cities, compared to 876 and 676 for outer regional and remote areas; counsellors numbered 752 in major cities, compared to 689 and 684 in outer regional and remote areas; social workers numbered 806 in major cities, compared to 625 and 490 in outer regional and remote areas; and so on across the different occupational categories (AIHW, 2013, p. 17).

Babacan (2011) identified challenges in recruiting and retaining an appropriate community services workforce across Northern Australia, including systemic issues such as the difficulty of attracting appropriately qualified staff, problems with retaining staff in the face of short-term funding cycles and job insecurity, difficulty of career progression, burnout and stress and lack of opportunity for professional development. These findings are echoed by others. For example, Roufeil and Battye (2008, p. 8) suggest three key areas contributing to workforce shortages: professional issues (e.g. job dissatisfaction, overload/burnout, professional isolation, lack of support and training, burden of rural travel, inadequate orientation to rural/Indigenous practice, lack of adequate remuneration and inflexible award conditions), personal factors (e.g. housing, partner employment issues and access to quality child care/education) and community factors (e.g. establishment of social networks and local facilities). Similarly, Davies et al. (2009, p. xv) found that barriers to attracting staff included negative perceptions of rural employment and lifestyle opportunities; limited health, education facilities and services; lower wages and cost of living considerations; and cost, availability and quality of housing.

The difficulty of staff development in Northern Australia has been a long-term issue. For example, Trinidad (2001) highlighted the need to invest more in the ongoing professional development of staff, building on their knowledge, skills and qualities. He stated that 'the temptation for cash-strapped agencies like ours is to put that responsibility solely on the shoulders of the individual staff member' (Trinidad, 2001, p. 12). Suggested strategies for retaining staff were competitive employment packages, improving opportunities for structured career advancement pathways, generating activities and networks to overcome issues of social isolation, providing improved access to health and education facilities, and addressing limited housing options. Collaborative regional approaches were recommended to address workforce shortages as many small employers are unable to remediate key problems such as housing.

## Governance Challenges

Governance is a complex term that encompasses the way decisions are made to achieve a public good. Dale (2013, p. 5) reminds us to a take a wide view of governance and defines it as 'how the overall system of decision-making works to deliver social, economic and environmental outcomes for our society'. Governance arrangements in Northern Australia are critical as the urgency of social, economic and environmental challenges have been characterised as being on the 'knife's edge' (Dale, 2013, p. 10). The RAI (2013, p. 76) identifies the central role that government (local, state and federal) plays in the economy and society of Northern Australia and posits that the effectiveness of government policies across a range of economic and social issues are central to facilitating change in Northern Australia. Regions in Northern Australia are experiencing ongoing economic and social transformation and face multifaceted change processes in a complex environment in which global and local forces intertwine. Public policies developed by the three tiers of government have formed incrementally over decades and are fragmented, confused and lacking in coherence at times (Altman & Russell, 2012; Walker et al., 2012).

The efficacy and legitimacy of governance in Northern Australia has been the subject of discussion (Dale, 2013; Altman & Russell, 2012). Walker et al. (2012, pp. 39–53) outline six dysfunctions of governance in remote areas, drawing on three case studies in Northern Australia:

1. Government withdrawal, across the three tiers of government, from direct service delivery and outsourcing to third parties with the expectation that the market will deliver social policy outcomes. The increase in executive power of public servants has resulted in greater focus on accountability and audit. Additionally, the power to define social problems and priorities is centralised in public authorities; however, the resolution is pushed back to local communities and individuals.
2. Organisational arrangements that are not 'fit for purpose' and, hence, the inability to meet the needs of the communities. The variable success of organisations to engage with government is a source of frustration and deficiency of the client groups. Many of the participatory and representational processes of communities, particularly Indigenous communities, are challenged by structural change such as the abolition of bodies such as Aboriginal and Torres Strait Islander Commission.
3. A disconnect between policy and practice, with an overreaching of policy into wider domains of life and underreaching of the administrative aspects of delivery, with less resources and administrative capacity. The reason for the overreach is due to policymakers not being attuned to local realities, representational barriers, diversity, communication and the inability to apply local knowledge due to reliance on outside

staff. The result is a greater reliance by leaders in rhetoric and grand claims of strategy to address particular issues, and in so doing gain legitimacy.

4. Inability to balance general interests of society with specific or parochial needs where there are major differences across specific issues/needs due to differences in communities, welfare patterns, ethnicity and race markers. Applying a global standard over such diversity repudiates the various efforts by different actors.

5. Policy turbulence and instability, particularly in regard to how responsibilities are assigned up and down and across the system of government and between government, the community and the private sector. Programs come and go and various strategic plans are announced and imposed in the process by local, regional, state and federal governments. The result is the loss of accountability between government and citizens and loss of trust and build-up of animosity.

6. The mismatch between responsibilities and resources (such as funding available) is less than the cost of delivery of services, and gaps in infrastructure and the nature of funding programs undermines local solutions and abilities of local authorities.

The authors draw a number of very strong conclusions. Governance arrangements are a threshold cause of policy failure, and policy for remote Australia needs to be separately conceived, framed and 'custom-built' to meet its specific circumstances and needs. The challenge in designing new approaches to governing and administering remote Australia cannot be accommodated in the current governance framework and requires a paradigm shift in policy, one that addresses and changes structurally embedded habits, practices and approaches (Walker et al., 2012, p. 12).

The effectiveness of governance in Northern Australia is identified by other researchers. Governance arrangements are centralised in the state/territory capitals and Canberra (Babacan et al., 2012; Dale, 2013). For example, Dale (2013) identifies that people in the Kimberley may have a lot more in common with Weipa, but have to go through Perth or Brisbane without any connectivity. He concludes:

> by and large, the three jurisdictions tend to manage common issues in isolation. Canberra's relationships with them are also compartmentalised, with high levels of communication fragmentation in and across major Commonwealth ministries and programs (Dale, 2013, p. 10).

Dale (2013, p. 11) further argues that this leads to a 'high level of frustration both among northern Australian communities and even among the North's elected members'. This is supported by evidence from service providers and communities. For example, an Australian Government evaluation of remote Indigenous service providers found that the pace and volume of recent policy changes caused confusion and frustration largely due to a lack of clear and consistent information from departments. Service providers also noted that current funding arrangements are worse than those of five years ago, with increased red tape, reduced funding and impaired coordination between government departments (Australian Government, 2009, p. 5).

The need for cross–Northern Australia governance arrangements at different levels of government, business and community is being recognised with initiatives such as the establishment of the Northern Australian Ministerial Forum and RDA Boards. These are beginning to strengthen cross-jurisdictional policy debates and involve diverse stakeholders in the policy, planning and implementation processes. While these initiatives are to be applauded, they focus their attention on a limited number of areas, particularly those relating to economic and infrastructure development. As argued by Dale (2013), the vast majority of government-based policymaking, program design and budget development remains in the south. In Queensland and Western Australia, the locus of political decision-making sits in Brisbane and Perth respectively. The representation and participation of the stakeholders in northern Western Australia and Queensland to influence decision-makers is limited. Moreover, the level of interest in Northern Australia by departmental agencies is not strong (Dale, 2013, p. 14). While the NT's capital is located in Northern Australia, it does not have the status of a state and is largely dependent on the federal government located in Canberra, and has to compete for prioritisation with other national agendas.

Ways of addressing governance fragmentation in Northern Australia are beginning to be discussed (Dale, 2013; Babacan et al., 2012; Roux et al., 2014). For example, a pan–Northern Australia policy architecture is needed, which links into Council of Australian Governments (as a standing item) and WA, the NT, Queensland and Australian cabinet processes and budget cycles (Roux et al., 2014). Roux et al., in the context of economic development, argue that Australian, state and territory governments should seek bilateral agreement about how to best support connectivity in the north by:

> better defining the role of key regional and local players in strategic planning for (and the implementation of) regional economic development. There should be a focus on RDAs, Development Commissions, REDOs, local government and Indigenous organisations and positive approaches to improving the system. (Roux et al., 2014, p. xvi)

While regional bodies such as RDAs have been tasked with regional planning, and numerous consultative bodies exist to mediate complex governmental and regional socioeconomic systems, they lack authority, decision-making power and resources (Pugalis & Keegan, 2017; Pape et al., 2016). Walker et al. (2012, p. 65) argue for the need for place-based responses and regional innovations and call for the introduction of an authority with comprehensive oversight at regional levels, whereby any jurisdictional overlaps are negotiated.

There is very little collaboration across the human services sectors, although regional bodies exist. For example, the Cairns Social Services Alliance, a network of services in Far North Queensland, has called for policy and human services reform (Babacan, 2011). Diverse Indigenous governance systems characterise Northern Australia, organised around traditional owner groups, land trusts and not-for-profit service agencies. Indigenous leaders in Northern Australia have also been calling for governance reform such as rights-based reforms in the governance for land, community development and welfare work (North Australian Indigenous Land and Sea Management, 2012), and Noel Pearson (2013) has called for welfare reform.

Pointing to disconnect, disengagement and discontent, consultations undertaken by Desert Knowledge Australia revealed what people want: a say in decisions that affect them, equitable and sustainable financial flows, better services and a locally responsive public service, local control and accountability where possible, and inclusion in a greater Australian narrative (Walker et al., 2012, p. 9). This is supported by other researchers who argue that short-term, fragmented, inflexible and annualised government program delivery models simply do not work in Northern Australia (Dale, 2013). Walker et al. (2012, p. 10) provide an important caution not to view governance issues, particularly in remote locations, as 'Aboriginal issues'. They argue that this is a mistake, as many non-Aboriginal people face similar issues. It has been argued that centralisation of power and people, and the strict regulatory and policy measures adopted for funding for welfare services by federal and state governments, have resulted in highly standardised services that have problems with responding to diversity of needs and populations (Walker et al., 2012; Cheers, 1992). Walker et al. (2012, p. 18) concluded that 'funding criteria and rules relating to delivery and acquittal are centrally determined and provide little opportunity for local variation and for cross-program coordination and integration'. In an evaluation by the Office of Evaluation and Audit (Indigenous Programs) of service delivery to remote Indigenous communities, over 58 per cent of respondents thought the Australian Government was underperforming in relation to long-term funding agreements, and over 50 per cent rated as poor or below average the user-friendliness of grant application and reporting arrangements (Australian Government, 2009, p. 41). Conversely, in regard to the factors that mattered the most in having a good relationship with the Australian Government, having reliable and responsive staff was the most important and a good understanding of remote communities by the staff was the second-most important (Australian Government, 2009, p. 42). A quotation from one of the service providers summarises the key issues quite concisely:

> The ICC [Indigenous Coordination Centres] should be more hands on and less bureaucratic. It is not possible to make assessments and judgements about community needs based on a visit once or twice a year and for only a couple of hours. They also could be much more proactive in working with communities to identify needs and to follow up with various departments where funding or support could be obtained to meet these needs. (Australian Government, 2009, p. 45)

The importance of integrated and coordinated approaches cannot be overstated. For example, the OECD (2012, p. 10), in a study of 23 regional case studies across Europe, identified that success was based on improvements in horizontal coordination of policies, regional institutional capacities, infrastructure provision and human capital development. Quality of institutions, labour market fragmentation and connectivity were essential elements of prosperous regional development. Successful regional approaches require addressing a range of challenges at the same time, but, as many authors point out, not in a nuanced manner (Cheers, 1992; OECD, 2016).

Addressing governance issues in Northern Australia will require a shift to an approach that focuses on engagement of stakeholders who are most affected. However, who is engaged and the capacity of citizens to participate in the choices that affect them is integral to any conception of governance (Dale, 2013; Walker et al., 2012). Building civic capacity for participation is crucial. For example, in an Australian Government evaluation of Indigenous remote service delivery, it was identified that many of the service providers have a limited understanding of the structure and responsibilities of Australian Government departments. There was also confusion about the split of responsibilities between the Australian Government and state/territory governments (Australian Government, 2009, p. 4). It is argued that local institutions in Northern Australia are being overwhelmed by the changes taking place; many are unsuited to the tasks they confront and, as a consequence, they are unable to create durable and equitable arrangements to manage conflict, deliver services or sponsor entrepreneurial activity (Walker et al., 2012, p. 31). Developing strong communities and institutions is a key to the future of Northern Australia (Babacan, 2013).

Achieving integration and planning in human services will not happen by itself and will require intentional effort and resources. As Keast et al. (2012, p. 5) argue, integration and planning:

> is not easy to achieve nor is it an inexpensive undertaking, it requires dedicated consideration, planning, resourcing and adequate funding. In particular, interpersonal relationships are resource and labour intensive with associated (albeit often transparent) transaction costs and must be legitimised as a 'core' element of work and adequately funded. Coordination or linking points are critical in holding the elements of the system together and, when necessary, mobilise them to action.

Integration and coordination requires a shift of mindsets and practice of how policies and programs are designed and implemented. The RAI (2013, p. 76) posits that the challenge for policy is to create an approach that devolves genuine responsibility to people, incentivises their leadership in building a different future and provides the time needed for this seismic shift in approach to occur. The Productivity Commission (2017) states that regional development can take place with locally owned strategic approaches, capitalising on a region's strengths and endowments, investing in people's capabilities and regional connectivity. Northern Australia's diversity implies that generalised policies and programs will not be effective and the 'one-size-fits-all' approach to meeting community needs will not work. For this reason, many advocate place-based approaches (Walker et al., 2012; CSSA, 2014; Dale, 2013) to ensure responsiveness to local imperatives and the ability to tailor to local issues.

## Conclusion and Future Directions

Northern Australia is diverse, vast and sparsely populated. Most of Northern Australia spans the categories of regional, rural and remote. There is a significant link between geography, demography and social problems. There is considerable evidence that spatial location impacts negatively on wellbeing and increases disadvantage.

This chapter has demonstrated significant disadvantage in Northern Australia in general and severe and persistent Indigenous disadvantage in all major indicators of health and wellbeing in particular. Approaches to social problems is generally patchy and fragmented. A 'one-size-fits-all' approach is known not to work for Northern Australia, given the diversity, governance, social, environmental and economic issues unique to both Northern Australia and rural/remote and very remote communities (CSSA, 2014).

Services are disconnected and wide-ranging systemic failures pose a constant set of barriers to providing adequate support. One step towards improvement may be to fill major data gaps informing planning in governance arrangements, and the coordination and service delivery. There is insufficient evidence about what service models work best, in what locations, for type of services and for which social issue. What has been established is that the people living in regions across Northern Australia want a clear voice in the decisions that affect them, equitable and sustainable funding flows, improved locally based providers and public service, and local control and accountability (Babacan, 2014).

Northern Australia will continue to gain significance for a range of economic, political, social and cultural reasons. However, a renewed focus in Northern Australia is unlikely to succeed if human capital and social issues are not addressed. A number of areas require priority attention.

## Responsiveness to Community Need and Adoption of Place-Based Approaches

The social disadvantage in Northern Australia requires culturally and locally relevant approaches to produce socially just outcomes. Different policy and service sectors work across purposes within regions in a conflicting, disjointed or duplicating manner (Brown & Bellamy, 2010). The lack of capacity for identifying and planning for significant regional/

rural priorities has been demonstrated. The underlying causes included lack of capacity and expertise, inadequate data and evidence base, lack of collaboration, lack of coordination, lack of authority and lack of resources (Productivity Commission, 2017; Eversole, 2017; Pape et al., 2016). The lack of focus on strategic rural/regional planning has flow-on impacts for attracting investments for the region, policymaking and service delivery and design. The capacity of individuals and organisations to effectively participate in civic processes is fundamental to responsive outcomes. Appropriate representation and participation in human service planning, community development and policy processes by those who are affected can result in regional innovation and shift the effort from redistributive and welfare approaches to empowerment and place-based opportunities.

## Building an Evidence Base

There is a clear lack of evidence to guide decision-making in Northern Australia, particularly in human services. There is an urgent need to have appropriate data about the nature of social issues. Disaggregated data needs to be available to inform decision-making processes, particularly about topics such as welfare expenditure, service use and availability and workforce. Additionally, research is needed on a range of issues affecting the human services sector such as effectiveness of service delivery models, workforce issues, and the nature of need in specific locations and impacts of policy. There is a need to build capacity in Northern Australia to undertake social impact assessment, needs analysis and social research to better support human services sector in Northern Australia by the universities.

## Integrated Planning, Service Coordination and Relevant Policy Development

It is clear that centralised funding and policy models have produced variable results across Northern Australia. Walker et al. (2012) have argued that there is dysfunction in governance arrangements. The distance and the lack of presence of state and federal governments in Northern Australia has been noted, bringing with it criticism of lack of knowledge about the realities of Northern Australia in policymaking and the inability to influence key strategies and policies. Regional mechanisms that are devolved can produce integrated and coordinated approaches to service planning in Northern Australia. This means progressing mechanisms for formal, informal and cross-sectoral planning and delivery, driven by local stakeholders and local leadership. Moreover, it is critical that such devolved approaches are embedded in policy frameworks so that decision-making is not driven from Canberra, Brisbane, Darwin or Perth for Northern Australia. Effort is required to develop appropriate governance mechanisms at the third-sector level, clearly articulating connectivity, a vision for the sector and strategies to address capacity and social infrastructure constraints. There is a need for a Northern Australia community services umbrella agency or council, rather than the state/territory-based ones trying to undertake outreach, to be an advocate to address sectoral issues. Taking a cross–Northern Australia approach to address issues has been advocated in the recent past by Dale (2013, p. 21), who argued for 'communities across the north working more effectively as a block towards more joined-up and negotiated governance'. Governance and organisational mechanisms will need to be established to enable the ability to work across different levels of governments that are likely to have different policy agendas and delivery mechanisms. Dale (2013) identifies examples of such cross alliances emerging in Northern Australia in different sectors such as conservation, environmental sustainability and in higher education (particularly research).

## Ongoing and Secure Funding Models

There has been a chronic underinvestment in Northern Australia per capita for health and human service delivery. While the fragmentation in the sector is well known, the service gaps, capacity and resource constraints and priority areas are not well documented at the subregional level. There is a need to develop ongoing funding models that provide preventative, sustainable and outcome-based service delivery, rather than the current ad hoc, competitive and fragmented approaches. Programmatic approaches to funding over a number of years is critical, rather than one-off competitive models. The 'churning' of services and workforce due to poor funding models results in greater long-term inefficiencies and wastage of precious public resources. Best and Myers (2017, p. 7) conclude that there are benefits to funding relationships, which involve:

> multi-stakeholder, multi-agency active alliances, where it is possible to identify new and different routes to providing rural health and social care and to engage in networking and outreach activities that moved the focus of provision beyond traditional institutional boundaries into rural communities.

While government will continue to be the main funder of health and human services, there is a need to diversify the funding base with strategies to enable support from the private sector and philanthropic organisations, which requires incentives to trial different partnership models across sectors.

## Sector Capacity-Building and Workforce Development

It is important to document the nature of workforce and skills issues for the human sector across Northern Australia as there is a critical gap in our knowledge base. There is a need to address workforce loss of skills due to short-term funding in the non-government sector. Regional, coordinated and cohesive efforts are needed to attract and retain employees in Northern Australia, addressing professional, personal and community issues. It is important to develop improved future career progression strategies in the social and community services industry by education, training and professional development initiatives.

While Northern Australia continues to experience strong growth in the planning capacity of its economic and natural resource sectors, the social and human services sectors have not been supported at a strategic level. Building an environment conducive to this requires multidimensional approaches, and neglecting the human services sector will have serious long-term consequences economically, socially and in other ways. Failing to invest in the human services sector will have detrimental impacts on sustainable communities, the development of vibrant economies, opportunities for socioeconomic participation and inclusive cultural and social cohesion. It is critical that local service providers are enabled to find localised solutions. Providing adequate support, enabling cross-sector alliance, supporting capacity-building, enabling mobilisation of external assets/triggers and multi-level governance are key to innovation in, and revitalisation of, Northern Australia.

# References

Alston, M. & Kent, J. (2004). Coping with a crisis: Human services in times of drought. *Rural Society, 14*, 214–227.

Altman, J. & Russell, S. (2012). Too much 'Dreaming': Evaluations of the Northern Territory National Emergency Response Intervention 2007–2012. *Evidence Base*, *3*. doi.org/10.21307/eb-2012-003

Australian Bureau of Statistics (ABS). (2016). *Socio-economic indexes for areas* (No. 2033.0.55.001). Canberra, ACT: ABS. Retrieved www.abs.gov.au/websitedbs/censushome.nsf/home/seifa

Australian Bureau of Statistics (ABS). (2017). *Patient experience survey, 2017–2018* (No. 4839.0). Canberra, ACT: ABS. Retrieved from www.abs.gov.au/AUSSTATS/abs@.nsf/Lookup/4839.0Main+Features12017-18

Australian Government. (2009). *Evaluation of service delivery in remote Indigenous communities*. Canberra, ACT: Office of Evaluation and Audit (Indigenous Programs), Commonwealth of Australia.

Australian Government. (2014). *Closing the gap. Prime Minister's report 2014*. Canberra, ACT: Commonwealth of Australia.

Australian Government. (2015). *Our north, our future: White paper on developing Northern Australia*. Retrieved from www.industry.gov.au/data-and-publications/our-north-our-future-white-paper-on-developing-northern-australia

Australian Institute of Health and Welfare (AIHW). (2007). *Welfare expenditure Australia 2005–06*. Canberra, ACT: AIHW.

Australian Institute of Health and Welfare (AIHW). (2011). *Australia's welfare 2011* (Cat. No. AUS 142). Canberra, ACT: AIHW.

Australian Institute of Health and Welfare (AIHW). (2013). *Australia's welfare 2013* (Cat. No. AUS 174). Canberra, ACT: AIHW.

Australian Institute of Health and Welfare (AIHW). (2014a). *Australia's health 2014* (Australia's Health Series No. 14, Cat. No. AUS 178). Canberra, ACT: AIHW.

Australian Institute of Health and Welfare (AIHW). (2014b). *Health expenditure Australia 2011–12: Analysis by sector* (Health and Welfare Expenditure Series No. 51, Cat. No. HWE 60). Canberra, ACT: AIHW.

Australian Institute of Health and Welfare (AIHW). (2017a). *Australia's welfare 2017* (Cat No. AUS 214). Canberra, ACT: AIHW.

Australian Institute of Health and Welfare (AIHW). (2017b). *Health expenditure Australia 2015–16* (Health and Welfare Expenditure Series No. 58, Cat. No. HWE 68). Canberra, ACT: AIHW.

Australian Institute of Health and Welfare (AIHW). (2017c). *Survey of health care: Selected findings for rural and remote Australians* (Cat No. PHE220). Canberra, ACT: AIHW.

Babacan, H. (2011). Social and community services in Far North Queensland: Issues facing the sector (unpublished consultation report). Cairns, Qld: James Cook University.

Babacan, H. (2013). Social and community services in Northern Australia (unpublished consultation brief, in partnership with Regional Development Australia Far North Queensland).

Babacan, H. (2014). Human services sector development in Northern Australia. In The Regional Australia Institute (Ed.), *Green paper on developing Northern Australia: A joint submission to the Northern Australia Taskforce*. Canberra, ACT: RAI.

Babacan, H. (2017). *Investing in 'the Social' in Northern Australia*. Paper presented at the Developing Northern Australia Conference, 19–20 June, Cairns, Qld.

Babacan, H. & Babacan, A. (2007). Sustaining human security. *The International Journal of Environmental, Cultural, Economic and Social Sustainability*, *3*(1), 115–122.

Babacan, H., Dale, A., Andrews, P., Beazley, L., Horstman, M., Campbell, A., … Miley, A. (2012). *Science engagement and tropical Australia: Building a prosperous and sustainable future for the North* (Report). Department of Industry, Innovation, Science, Research and Tertiary Education. Retrieved from researchonline.jcu.edu.au/23871/

Baldwin, R., Stephens, M., Sharp, D. & Kelly, J. (2013). *Issues facing age care services in rural and remote Australia*. Canberra, ACT: Aged & Community Services Australia.

Battye, K. (2007). *Workforce shortages or dysfunctional service models?* Paper presented to the 9th Rural Health Conference, Albury, NSW. Retrieved from ruralhealth.org.au/9thNRHC/9thnrhc.ruralhealth.org.au/keynotes/docs/presentation/Kristine_Battye.pdf

Best, S. & Myers, J. (2017). Prudence or speed: Health and social care innovation in rural Wales. *Journal of Rural Studies*, 1–9. doi.org/10.1016/j.jrurstud.2017.12.004

Brown, A. J. & Bellamy, J. A. (2010). In the shadow of Federalism: Dilemmas of institutional design in Australian rural and remote regional governance. *Australasian Journal of Regional Studies*, *16*(2), 151–180.

Carson, D., Taylor, A. & Campbell, S. (2009). *Demographic trends and likely futures for Australia's tropical rivers.* Darwin, NT: Charles Darwin University.

Catholic Social Services Australia (CSSA). (2014). *Submission to the Joint Select Committee on Northern Australia.* Curtin, Canberra, ACT: CSSA. Retrieved from cssa.org.au/policies-and-submissions/

Cheers, B. (1992). Rural social work and social welfare in the Australian context. *Australian Social Work, 45*(2), 11–21.

Cheers, B. & Taylor, J. (2001). Social work in rural and remote Australia. In M. Alston & J. McKinnon (Eds), *Social work: Fields of practice* (pp. 206–209). Sydney, NSW: Oxford University Press.

Chenoweth, L. & Stehlik, D. (2001). Building resilient communities: Social work practice and rural Queensland. *Australian Social Work, 54*(2), 47–54.

Community Services and Health Industry Skills Council. (2014). *Environmental scan 2014: Agenda for change.* Retrieved from hdl.voced.edu.au/10707/299598

Dale, A. (2013). *Governance challenges for Northern Australia.* Cairns, Qld: The Cairns Institute, James Cook University.

Davies, A., Tonts, M., Troy, L. & Pelusey, H. (2009). *Australia's rural workforce: An analysis of labour shortages in rural Australia* (RIRDC Publication 09/008). Canberra, ACT: Rural Industries Development Corporation.

Defourny, J. & Nyssens, M. (2013). Social innovation, social economy and social enterprise: What can the European debate tell us? In F. Moulaert, D. MacCallum, M. Abid & H. Abdelilah (Eds), *The international handbook on social innovation* (pp. 40–52). Cheltenham, UK; Northampton, MA: Edward Elgar.

Department of Education, Employment and Workplace Relations (DEEWR). (2011). *DEEWR annual report 2010–2011.* Canberra, ACT: DEEWR.

Department of Families, Housing, Community Services and Indigenous Affairs. (2011). *FaHCSIA annual report 2010–11.* Canberra, ACT: FaHCSIA.

Department of Industry, Tourism and Trade (2021). *NT Key Business Statistics: Labour Market.* Retrieved from industry.nt.gov.au/economic-data-and-statistics/business/nt-key-business-statistics/labour-market

Department of Jobs and Small Business. (2018). *Industry employment projections 2018 report.* Retrieved from cica.org.au/wp-content/uploads/2018-Industry-Employment-Projections-Report.pdf

Department of Trade, Business and Innovation. (2017). *Northern Territory labour market, 2017*. Darwin, NT: Department of Trade, Business and Innovation.

Dollery, B. E., Wallis, J. & Akimov, A. (2010). One size does not fit all: The special case of remote small local councils in outback Queensland. *Local Government Studies*, *36*(1), 21–42.

Economy Id. (2021). *Employment by Industry*. Retrieved from economy.id.com.au/fnqroc/employment-by-industry

Eversole, R. (2017). Economies with people in them: Regional futures through the lens of contemporary regional development theory, Australasian. *Journal of Regional Studies*, *23*(3), 305–320.

First Peoples Disability Network. (2013). *Making the National Disability Insurance Scheme accessible and responsive to Aboriginal and Torres Strait Islanders: Strategic issues*. Sydney, NSW: First Peoples Disability Network (FPDN) Publications.

Fragar, L., Henderson, A., Morton, C. & Pollock, K. (2007). *The mental health of people on Australian farms: The facts*. Barton, ACT: Rural Industries Research & Development Corporation and Australian Centre for Agricultural Health and Safety.

Gopalkrishnan, N. (2007). Neo-Liberalism and infeatainment: What does a state do? In H. Babacan & N. Gopalkrishnan (Eds), *Racisms in the New World Order: Realities of culture, colour and identity* (pp. 22–23). Newcastle, England: Cambridge Scholars Publishing.

Gow, K. & Paton, D. (Eds). (2008). *The phoenix of natural disasters: Community resilience*. New York, NY: Nova Science Publishers.

Hall, G. & Scheltens, M. (2005). Beyond the drought: Towards a broader understanding of rural disadvantage. *Rural Society*, *15*(2), 347–358.

Holland, C. (2018). *A ten-year review: The Closing the Gap strategy and recommendations for reset*. The Close the Gap Campaign Steering Committee. Retrieved from humanrights.gov.au/sites/default/files/document/publication/CTG%202018_FINAL-WEB.pdf

House of Representatives Standing Committee on Regional Affairs. (2013). *Inquiry into the use of 'Fly-in, Fly-Out' (FIFO) workforce practices in regional Australia*. Retrieved from www.aph.gov.au/parliamentary_business/committees/house_of_representatives_committees?url=ra/fifodido/report.htm

Judd, F., Jackson, H., Komiti, A., Murray, G., Fraser, C., Grieve, A. & Gomez, R. (2006). Help-seeking by rural residents for mental health problems: The importance of agrarian values. *Australian and New Zealand Journal of Psychiatry, 40*, 769–776.

Keast, R., Waterhouse, J., Murphy, G. & Brown, K. (2012). *Pulling it all together: Design considerations for an integrated homelessness service system—Place-based network analysis*. Brisbane, Qld: Department of Families, Housing, Community Services and Indigenous Affairs.

Kirmayer, L. J., Sehdev, M., Whitley, R., Dandeneau, F. S. & Isaac, C. (2009). Community resilience: Models, metaphors and measures. *Journal of Aboriginal Health, 5*(1), 62–117.

Lamartina, S. & Zaghini, A. (2008). *Increasing public expenditures: Wagner's law in OECD countries* (Center for Financial Studies Report No. 2008/13). Retrieved from www.ifk-cfs.de/fileadmin/downloads/publications/wp/08_13.pdf

Limerick, M., Morris, R. & Sutton, M. (2012). *Local government service delivery to remote Indigenous communities. Review of service delivery models and approaches in various jurisdictions*. Sydney, NSW: Australian Centre of Excellence for Local Government.

Lonne, B. & Cheers, B. (2004). Retaining rural social workers: An Australian study. *Rural Society, 14*(2), 163–177.

Manderson, D. (2008). Not yet: Aboriginal people and the deferral of the rule of law. *ARENorthern Australia, 29*(30), 219–272.

Massey, L., Jane, A., Lindop, N. & Christian, E. (2013). *Disability audit— NE Arnhem Land/NT Gulf—A snapshot of Indigenous Australian disability in the very remote communities of the Groote Eylandt Archipelago (Angurugu, Umbakumba, Milyakburra), Elcho Island (Galiwin'ku), and Ngukurr (including Urapunga)*. Alyangula, NT: MJD Foundation Limited.

McGregor-Lowndes, M. (2014). *The not for profit sector in Australia: Fact sheet* (ACPNS Current Issues Information Sheet 2014/4). Brisbane, Qld: Queensland University of Technology. Retrieved from eprints.qut.edu.au/75397/

Moran, M., Anda, M., Elvin, R., Kennedy, A., Long, S., McFallan, S., … Young, M. (2009). *Desert services that work: Year one research report* (Working Paper No. 30). Alice Springs, NT: Desert Knowledge Cooperative Research Centre.

Naldi, L., Nilsson, P., Westlund, H. & Wixe, S. (2015). What is smart rural development? *Journal of Rural Studies, 40*, 90–101.

National Health Priority Areas. (2014). *Healthy communities: Potentially preventable hospitalisations in 2013–14*. Sydney, NSW: Commonwealth Government.

NEF Consulting. (2010). *Catalysts for community action and investment: A social return on investment analysis of community development work based on a common outcomes framework*. London, England: Community Development Foundation.

North Australian Indigenous Land and Sea Management Alliance. (2012). *Towards resilient communities through reliable prosperity. North Australian Indigenous Experts Forum on Sustainable Economic Development* (NKS 013/2012). Retrieved from web.archive.org/web/20150330172117/http://nailsma.org.au/sites/default/files/publications/Towards-resilient-communities-KS013-web.pdf

Northern Queensland Primary Health Network. (2017). *Health needs assessment update 2017-2018*. Cairns, Qld: NQPHN.

Organisation for Economic Co-operation and Development (OECD). (2012). *Promoting growth in all regions*. Retrieved from www.oecd.org/site/govrdpc/50138839.pdf

Organisation for Economic Co-operation and Development (OECD). (2016). *OECD regional outlook 2016: Productive regions for inclusive societies*. Retrieved from doi.org/10.1787/9789264260245-en

Organisation for Economic Co-operation and Development (OECD). (2018). *Social expenditure data*. Retrieved from stats.oecd.org/Index.aspx?DataSetCode=SOCX_AGG

Pape, M., Fairbrother, P. & Snell, D. (2016). Beyond the state: Shaping governance and development policy in an Australian region. *Regional Studies, 50*(5), 909–921.

Pearson, N. (2013, 15–16 June). Failures can't be pinned on Aborigines. *The Weekend Australian*, p. 19.

Productivity Commission. (2017). *Transitioning regional economies, study report*. Canberra, ACT: Commonwealth of Australia.

Public Health Information Development Unit. (2014). *Atlas of Northern Australia*. Adelaide, SA: PHIDU. Retrieved from www.atlasesaustralia.com.au/pmc/atlas.html

Pugalis, L. & Keegan, D. (2017). The regional economic development paradox: Attempting policy order in the face of societal complexity. *Australasian Journal of Regional Studies, 23*(1), 68–94.

Regional Australia Institute (RAI). (2013). *Rethinking the future of Northern Australia's regions*. Canberra, ACT: RAI.

Regional Australia Institute (RAI). (2015). *The future of regional Australia: Change on our terms*. Canberra, ACT: RAI.

Richter, D. R. (2017). Rural social enterprises as embedded intermediaries: The innovative power of connecting rural communities with supra-regional networks. *Journal of Rural Studies*, 1–9. doi.org/10.1016/j.jrurstud.2017.12.005

Roufeil, L. & Battye, K. (2008). *Effective regional, rural and remote family and relationships service delivery* (AFRC Briefing No. 10). Australian Institute of Family Studies. Retrieved from aifs.gov.au/cfca/publications/effective-regional-rural-and-remote-family-and-relationship

Roux, A., Faubel, M. & McCauchie, D. (2014). *Northern development: Creating the future Australia. Report of the ADC Forum, Northern Development Summit*. Melbourne, Vic.: ADC Forum.

Saunders, P. & Wong, M. (2014). Locational differences in material deprivation and social exclusion in Australia. *The Australasian Journal of Regional Studies*, *20*(1), 131–158.

Social Ventures Australia and the Centre for Social Impact. (2020). *Taken for granted? Charities' role in our economic recovery*. Social Ventures Australia. Retrieved from mk0socialventura85.kinstacdn.com/assets/200804_Taken for-granted-Charities-role-economic-recovery_CSI-SVA-lg.pdf

Steiner, A. & Teasdale, S. (2017). Unlocking the potential of rural social enterprise. *Journal of Rural Studies*, 1–11. doi.org/10.1016/j.jrurstud.2017.12.021

Stephens, A., Cullen, J., Massey, L. & Bohanna, I. (2014). Will the National Disability Insurance Scheme improve the lives of those most in need? Effective service delivery for people with acquired brain injury and other disabilities in remote Aboriginal and Torres Strait Islander communities. *Australian Journal of Public Administration*, *73*(2), 260–270.

Stoeckl, N. (2010). Bridging the asymmetric divide: Background to, and strategies for bridging the divide between Indigenous and Non-Indigenous economies in Northern Australia. In R. Gerritsen (Ed.), *North Australian political economy: Issues and agendas* (pp. 106–129). Darwin, NT: CDU Press.

Trinidad, M. (2001). Centacare in the Northern Territory. *Australian Social Work*, *54*(1), 10–13.

United Nations Economic and Social Commission for Asia Pacific. (2013). *Asia-Pacific trade and investment report 2013: Turning the tide: Towards inclusive trade and development.* Retrieved from www.unescap.org/publications/asia-pacific-trade-and-investment-report-2013-turning-tide-towards-inclusive-trade-and

van Opstal, D. (2007). *The resilient economy: Integrating competitiveness and security.* Washington, DC: Council on Competitiveness. Retrieved from www.compete.org/storage/images/uploads/File/PDF%20Files/Transform_The_Resilient_Economy_FINorthern AustraliaL_pdf.pdf

Wakerman, J., Humphreys, J. S., Wells, R., Kuipers, P., Entwistle, P. & Jones, J. (2008). *Primary health care delivery models in rural and remote Australia: A systematic review.* Alice Springs, NT: Centre for Remote Health.

Walker, B., Porter, D. & Marsh, I. (2012). *Fixing the hole in Australia's heartland: How government needs to work in remote Australia.* Alice Springs, NT: Desert Knowledge Australia.

Wendt, S. & Hornosty, J. (2010). Understanding contexts of family violence in rural, farming communities: Implications for rural women's health. *Rural Society, 20*(1), 51–63.

Winterton, R. & Warburton, J. (2011). Does place matter? Reviewing the experience of disadvantage of older people in rural Australia. *Rural Society, 20*(2), 187–197.

# 4

# Underpinning Development: Health and Health Workforce in Northern Australia

Scott R. Davis, Felicity Croker and Alexandra Edelman

The renewed focus on the economic potential of Northern Australia recognises its unique proximity to Asia and the Indo-Pacific region and its strategic position within the fastest growing global zone, the tropics (Commonwealth of Australia, 2012; State of the Tropics, 2014, 2017). Northern Australia is recognised as vital to Australia's future economic development over the next 30 years of the Asia-Pacific century (Australian Government, 2015; Commonwealth of Australia, 2012; Hill, 2013; State of the Tropics, 2014). With sustained policy and political commitment, Northern Australia has the capacity to be an international leader in providing health professional education, tropical health research and development, and innovative health service models that will enable development of a knowledge-based economic platform for the region (Australian Government, 2015; Edelman et al., 2018; Hill, 2013; Joint Select Committee on Northern Australia, 2014).

Achieving this vision requires recognising that the success of Northern Australia must be underpinned by a healthy and productive population. This population needs to be supported by a health system that can respond to significant demographic and epidemiological changes and transitions including population ageing, emerging tropical epidemics and the growing global prevalence of non-communicable diseases (WHO, 2016). Future-proofing Northern Australia's capacity within the tropics worldwide and throughout the Asia-Pacific century needs to be founded on a sustainable, adaptable, flexible health system with a workforce capable of responding to the dynamic opportunities and challenges ahead (ABS, 2018a; Commonwealth of Australia, 2012; Davis & Vernon, 2014; Department of Jobs and Small Business, 2018; Hill, 2013; Liberal Party of Australia, 2013; State of the Tropics, 2014, 2017).

Developing appropriate long-term strategies to enable Northern Australia to achieve its potential requires a strengths-based approach that recognises the geographic, environmental and sociocultural challenges as foundational to a knowledge-based economy. Northern Australia has the potential to be a leader in health systems innovation and health workforce training in the tropics worldwide, leading to significant health, social, cultural and economic benefits to both Australia and its near neighbours (Davis & Vernon, 2014; Edelman et al., 2018; Liberal Party of Australia, 2013). With appropriate policy and political support, this region can build on existing capacity and expertise in health, education and research sectors (ABS, 2018a; Australian Government, 2015; Commonwealth of Australia, 2012; Department of Jobs and Small Business, 2018; Hill, 2013; Mason, 2013; State of the Tropics, 2014).

This chapter outlines the critical health challenges facing Northern Australia, provides an overview of the raft of health and health workforce reforms that are leading to improved health outcomes, and makes recommendations for future actions based on key opportunities in the region.

## Northern Australia: The Context

Health in Northern Australia[1] reflects a combination of unique geographic and demographic factors. While the tropical cities of Cairns, Townsville and Darwin are uniquely positioned as thriving hubs servicing the region, the remainder of Northern Australia is classified as rural or remote,[2]

---

1  Northern Australia is defined as being above the Tropic of Capricorn by the Greater Northern Australia Regional Training Network (GNARTN) Council. This is consistent with the definition provided by the Joint Select Committee on Northern Australia (2014) and that used by the Australian Government (2015).

2  Based on the ABS Australian Standard Geographical Classification Remoteness Area classification, the term 'rural and remote' encompasses inner regional, outer regional, remote or very remote geographical areas. Increasingly, the Modified Monash Model (MMM) classifications are applied to categorise regionality and remoteness, with MMM 1–2 being metropolitan, MMM 3 being a large regional town and MMM 7 being a very remote community.

representing approximately one-third of Australia's outer regional and remote population (Joint Select Committee on Northern Australia, 2014). Northern Australia's population of 1.3 million people is distributed unevenly across a vast geographic area, and only four out of the 74 Local Government Areas have populations of over 100,000 people. Northern Australia also encompasses around 29 per cent of the nation's Aboriginal and Torres Strait Islander population (ABS, 2017, 2018a, 2018b; Mason, 2013). Currently, 5.5 per cent of Australia's workers are spread across the north occupying around 646,000 jobs, predominantly in the health and social services and construction sectors (Australian Government, 2015; Department of Jobs and Small Business, 2018; WHO, 2016). There is the potential to diversify employment through developing a workforce with internationally recognised expertise in health professional education, medical research and health systems innovation and reform (HWA, 2013; NHWPRC, 2010).

People living in rural and remote parts of Australia are at risk of poorer health status, shorter lives, higher rates of accident and injury, greater levels of illness, and lower rates of certain medical treatments. Mortality and hospitalisation rates and prevalence of health risk factors generally increase, and access to health services becomes more limited, with increasing remoteness (ABS, 2017; AIHW, 2013, 2018; Australian Medical Workforce Advisory Committee, 1998; Davis & Vernon, 2014; HWA, 2013; NHWPRC, 2010; Wakerman, 2004).

This is compounded for Indigenous Australians within the northern region. Indigenous Australians' health outcomes are significantly worse compared to either non-Indigenous Australians within the same region or other Indigenous Australians living in urban areas (AIHW, 2018; State of the Tropics, 2014). Health in Northern Australia also encompasses tropical, exotic and infectious disease, necessitating consideration of biosecurity, relationships with neighbouring countries and people movements across the northern border (Australian Government, 2015).

Multiple political, social, cultural and economic factors contribute to the health disadvantage experienced by people living in rural and remote communities, including population transience, high capital costs of infrastructure and a maldistributed workforce with recruitment and retention difficulties (NHWPRC, 2010; Australian Medical Workforce Advisory Committee, 1998; AIHW, 2013; Humphreys et al., 2006; Productivity Commission, 2005; Godwin et al., 2014; Insight Economics,

2012; HWA, 2012). These factors are compounded by significant geographical challenges in delivering accessible, affordable and appropriate health care services to low population densities, in small settlements and across large distances. Not all the trends are negative—Australians living in rural areas generally have higher levels of social cohesiveness, including higher rates of participation in volunteer work and feelings of safety in their community (AIHW, 2018).

Health care in Northern Australia has evolved unique characteristics and strengths, including a transdisciplinary practice environment requiring generalist (rather than specialist) skills and training. Health practitioners working in remote areas work in a cross-cultural context; serve small, dispersed and often highly mobile populations; operate in a physical environment of climatic extremes; and contend with geographical, professional and often social isolation (HWA, 2012, 2013; Insight Economics, 2012; NHWPRC; 2010). Many of these characteristics present unique challenges for health service providers and policymakers, with the following being highlighted in the Productivity Commission's (2005) report on Australia's health workforce:

- limited access to supporting health professionals, facilities and locum services
- less availability of continuing professional development
- lower housing standards
- more restricted education and employment opportunities for other family members.

One of the most pressing and persistent health challenges in Northern Australia is the geographic maldistribution of health professionals, meaning shortages in rural and remote areas. The *Review of Australian Government Health Workforce Programs* ('Mason Review') (Mason, 2013) identified maldistribution as the most significant health workforce issue, finding 'inadequate or non-existent service provision' in rural, remote and Indigenous communities (p. 6), populations of extreme disadvantage and some outer metropolitan communities coexisting with oversupply in other areas for some health professions (Davis & Vernon, 2014). The undesirable outcomes of workforce shortages and maldistribution—including poor access, unmet needs, poorer health outcomes for patients, overworked health professionals and expensive strategies to address immediate workforce shortages by government—have long been recognised (HWA, 2012; Mason, 2013; Universities Australia, 2014).

To remedy health workforce shortages, rural and remote areas have in the past relied heavily on migration of international health professionals. While skilled migration is under review as an oversupply of Australian medicine and health professional graduates is predicted (Godwin et al., 2014; HWA, 2012; Universities Australia, 2014), maldistribution remains a key policy challenge (Mason, 2013). A trend towards specialisation and sub-specialisation within the health professions has also resulted in a shortage of 'generalists' capable of practice in areas of workforce need (Murray et al., 2012; Scott & Joyce, 2014; United Nations, 2013).

There is now broad acknowledgement that a 'business as usual' approach to health workforce development in Australia is unsustainable (Mason, 2013; NHWPRC, 2010). Approaches going forward need to build on a history of significant health system and health workforce innovation targeted to the ongoing health disparities and health workforce challenges across Northern Australia.

# Innovation and Reform of Health Care and Health Workforce in Northern Australia

Successive administrations at the federal, state and territory levels have sought to address the complexity of providing health care to those rural and remote populations most in need, but many have been unsuccessful. Although significant challenges remain, the lessons learned from past initiatives and current policy successes position Northern Australia as a leader in innovative health and health workforce policy to meet the needs of a diverse and dispersed population.

Service models and models of care to provide high-quality patient care in rural and remote areas are different from those in larger communities, and while rural and remote heterogeneity means that no single model of service can be applied, exemplars provide a basis for future development of service models (Mason, 2013; NHWPRC, 2010; Productivity Commission, 2005; Universities Australia, 2014).

Recognising the benefits of local innovation and governance to meet local health needs, the National Health Reform Agreement of 2011 provided for the establishment of Local Hospital Networks (LHNs) with the aim of delivering better access to services, improved local accountability and transparency and greater responsiveness to local communities. Ten are located within Northern Australia (wholly or in part).[3] Decentralised hospital and health service management within the LHNs is provided for by local governance arrangements so that the health services located in Northern Australia will be more responsive to local needs and challenges.

To meet health workforce challenges, HWA was established by the Council of Australian Governments through the 2008 National Partnership Agreement on Hospital and Health Workforce Reform. HWA's mandate was to deliver a national coordinated approach to create a health workforce able to meet the current and future health care needs of all communities. HWA developed a significant array of programs to address some of the challenges in health workforce development across Australia, including innovative rural and remote workforce reform strategies (Mason, 2013; NHWPRC, 2010; Universities Australia, 2014). HWA as a statutory authority has been abolished, but many of its functions and programs are continuing through consolidation within the Commonwealth Department of Health.

One of HWA's key programs, the Clinical Training Funding (CTF) program, provided significant and welcome investment that successfully increased clinical placement capacity across the health professions, including expanding opportunities across a range of non-traditional placement settings. However, an unforeseen consequence of the payment of fees to placement providers for the clinical training of health professional students was the creation of an expectation of continuing payment from universities for placements across the health disciplines at the HWA rate. While the CTF has been discontinued, the expectation of payment for clinical placements continues.

Currently, there is significant variation in the rate charged by clinical placement providers across health services, jurisdictions and discipline areas. This is a significant challenge facing the health and higher education sectors across Australia, and particularly for providers in rural and remote

---

3   These have evolved into various entities with Hospital and Health Services in Queensland, Health Districts in the Northern Territory and Health Networks in Western Australia.

areas where there is a less established tradition of education, training and research; less investment and less infrastructure to support these activities; and high costs associated with providing clinical placements and student accommodation.

There is wide recognition of the vital role that Northern Australian universities working in partnership with health service providers play throughout Asia and the Indo-Pacific region as clinical education and training institutions (Universities Australia, 2014; United Nations, 2013). Further, the potential for collaborative initiatives between northern health services, universities and international partners is also emerging, such as Academic Health Centres (referred to as integrated health research centres in the 2013 McKeon Review) (Commonwealth of Australia, 2013) and institutions like the GNARTN and Cooperative Research Centre for Northern Australia (Australian Government, 2015). Future policy directions must address these trends and capitalise on the available opportunities to build tropical expertise and grow the knowledgeable, adaptable and appropriately skilled fit-for-purpose health workforce that the region needs.

The GNARTN was established in 2012[4] and has worked to build and enhance clinical placement and health workforce capacity across Northern Australia. GNARTN is a partnership between the director generals of Western Australia, Queensland and the Northern Territory Health Departments and has demonstrated the benefits, including efficiency gains, of east–west collaboration between all parties involved in health professional training (governments, non-government organisations and higher education providers). Since 2013, GNARTN, through a shared investment and governance model, delivered a range of initiatives at a price point that allowed a higher return on the investment made by the individual jurisdiction.

The challenges presented by the determinants of health in Northern Australia have created the opportunity for it to become a national leader in development and delivery of significant health service and health workforce innovations that meet population health needs, including:

---

4   For information on GNARTN governance and scope see www.gnartn.org.au (site discontinued).

- Building rural pipelines, or the continuum of training in rural or remote areas, in medicine (from recruitment to graduation, to junior doctor training, to employment as a junior doctor and on to vocational training in a medical speciality including general practice). Key recommendations of the Mason Review centre on the imperative to create coherent pathways for rural and regional education and training, particularly generalist medical training, with more appropriate resource allocation to nursing, midwifery, allied health and dentistry (Australian Government, 2015; Mason, 2013). The data on medical training at an undergraduate level, junior doctor level and vocational training level indicate that supporting rural and remote service providers and health professional trainees with accommodation, travel, supervision capacity and peer support while on rural and remote clinical placement leads to many health professionals returning to rural and remote areas following graduation (Sen Gupta et al., 2015). Supporting the articulation of rural training pipelines across the health professions is an important health workforce initiative and remains a critical area for further investment.

- Expanding scopes of practice for health practitioners. Rural and remote clinical practice in Australia already has established traditions of multidisciplinary team-based approaches to health care, including skill sharing and expanded scope of practice roles for nurse practitioners, midwives, practice nurses, enrolled nurses, remote area nurses, allied health professionals, rural pharmacists, Aboriginal and Torres Strait Islander health workers, rural paramedics and lay health care assistants. There is significant scope for expanded scopes of practice of other registered health professionals to address workforce shortages and help ensure that the evolving abilities of all members of the health care team can be fully applied.

- Smart use of technology, supported by the integrated telehealth system, point of care testing and 'tele-supervision' of students and trainees. The availability of broadband technology supported by effective models of care that utilise the existing rural and remote health workforce has the capacity to reduce cost of service while providing high-quality care to rural and remote patients. Western Australia and Queensland have already made significant advances in telehealth models of care. For example, Queensland has been piloting a telehealth supported model to deliver treatment and ongoing care to rural clients without them having to travel into the major urban centres. In Western Australia, the Western Australia Country Health Service has been effectively using videoconferencing to support nurses dealing with medical emergencies in small rural communities, thus providing immediate access to specialists who can support the rural practitioner in complex cases.

- Promoting rural and remote generalist specialists across all health professional groups, based on the model offered by rural generalist medicine, which is defined as the provision of a broad scope of medical care by a doctor in the rural context. Rural generalist medicine encompasses comprehensive primary, hospital and emergency care with a population health approach and within a multidisciplinary team, in contrast to medicine and medical training in major Australian cities, which has become increasingly sub-specialised and often shaped by income-earning opportunities, rather than by community needs. Rural generalism is well established in Queensland, with more recent adoption in the Northern Territory and other jurisdictions. A major initiative seeking to respond to the demand for generalist skills in other disciplines has been the development of the Allied Health Rural Generalist Pathway being undertaken in Queensland and rolled out across other states.

These areas of health and health workforce innovation and reform, within a cross-jurisdictional Northern Australian model, are outlined in Table 4.1.

As highlighted by the Mason Review, the current health reform era represents a shift away from acute care towards more coherent delivery of connected primary health care, with a focus on prevention and better management of chronic diseases and encouraging greater flexibility and productivity (Mason, 2013). This approach offers many benefits to health care in Northern Australia, and underscores the need for continuing investment in, and policy support for, key innovations and reforms that meet health care needs in rural and remote areas that are cognisant of demographic and epidemiological transitions.

**Table 4.1: Directions of health system and workforce innovation and reform in Northern Australia.**

| Cross-jurisdictional Collaborative Model for Improved Health Outcomes | | | |
|---|---|---|---|
| **Improve access to health services** | **Health professional workforce development** | **Telehealth** | **Reformed resourcing and governance model** |
| Fair, equitable and universal access to health services | Address maldistribution of the health workforce across Northern Australia | Enable greater access and equity to health services | Northern Australia governance mechanism to support the adoption of evidence-based models across jurisdictions |
| Smart use of technology, including telehealth, point of care testing and 'tele-supervision' of students and trainees | Appropriately educate and train workforce for rural/remote practice | Reduce costs and inconvenience associated with accessing specialist health services | Legislative and policy alignment (e.g. harmonised drugs and poisons regulations and clinical guidelines) |
| Regional partnerships between government and non-government organisations to support continuum of care | Share and mobilise workforce across jurisdictions | Improve access to quality, locally available clinical services | Co-investment model to reduce cost burden and risk, achieving greater access through greater equity in resourcing |
| Shared specialist health workforce in Northern Australia | Share recruitment models | Enable access to continuing education and professional development for health professionals | Integrated research, education and health care via an Academic Health Centre combining research, higher education and health sectors |
| Expand roles of practice for health professionals (generalist) | Increase access to specialist workforce across jurisdictions | Enable networking and collaboration to support workforce retention | Cost-effective service models based on collaborative service planning |
| Share collaborative health service/ population health planning models | Strengthen links between the health system and the higher education sector | Develop and deliver telehealth services across jurisdictions and geographical boundaries | Models recognising the cost of provision of services in rural and remote environments |

| Cross-jurisdictional Collaborative Model for Improved Health Outcomes | | | |
|---|---|---|---|
| Improve access to health services | Health professional workforce development | Telehealth | Reformed resourcing and governance model |
| Strengthen public health as a preventive mechanism | Enhance Aboriginal and Torres Strait Islander workforce development opportunities including health practitioner workforce | Achieve service delivery that reduces current inequity in access and associated poor health outcomes | Innovative service and workforce models |
| Strengthen Indigenous and rural and remote primary health care infrastructure | Technology-enabled solutions to address the significant maldistribution of the health workforce across rural and remote Northern Australia | | |

Source: Adapted from Davis and Vernon (2014).

# A Healthy Population Leading Australia in the Asia-Pacific Century

Northern Australia continues to establish itself as a leader in innovative health and health workforce policy to meet the needs of a diverse and dispersed population. Domestically, a healthy population means a healthy and productive workforce available to industry and business to underpin economic development. Looking further afield, Northern Australia is well placed to develop these areas of expertise as an export commodity. Northern Australia has established significant expertise in responding to disasters, managing tropical diseases and developing strategies to prevent and managing chronic diseases (Murray et al., 2012; United Nations, 2013). Combined with significant experience in rural and remote health workforce development and health system innovations—evidenced by the international demand for Australian-trained remote area nurses by international aid agencies for their skill, knowledge diversity and ability to work in resource-poor environments—Northern Australia also has a lot to offer other nations striving to achieve the goal of universal health coverage (United Nations, 2013).

Engagement with Asia and the Indo-Pacific region in education and health care has enormous strategic significance. Efficient and effective health systems with equitable foundations underpin sustainable development, security and economic growth, thus benefiting regional stability (Australian Government, 2015; Commonwealth of Australia, 2012; Hill, 2013; Murray et al., 2012; State of the Topics, 2014, 2017; United Nations, 2013). Additionally, Australia's reputation as a quality provider of health care and health professional education within a region with a growing middle class offers significant market opportunities in international education, health care and medical tourism.

The contribution of the higher education sector to the health and economic positioning of the region is significant. Universities in Northern Australia not only train the future health professionals of the region to meet health workforce needs, but strengthen the economy and build vital diplomatic links internationally. Currently, international education is Australia's largest export earner after resources and Australia's fourth largest export industry, earning around A$15 billion annual (Australian Government, 2015; Joint Select Committee on Northern Australia, 2014). Universities and research institutes are also driving research into emerging and re-emerging tropical infectious diseases and new models of care and service delivery for chronic disease, offering the potential for huge economic, social and health benefits to the local region, nation and neighbouring countries.

Ongoing investment in health services strengthening, health workforce development, and health and medical research will ensure that Northern Australia is recognised as a global leader in rural, remote and tropical health care and workforce innovation.

There are significant health and economic benefits to developing Northern Australia. To maximise these benefits, there is a need for sustained bipartisan political commitment to establish a robust Northern Australia east–west dialogue. This dialogue should be supported by a governance mechanism that enables collaboration between the Commonwealth and Western Australian, Northern Territory and Queensland governments.

4. UNDERPINNING DEVELOPMENT

# Key Summary Points

- A healthy population means a healthy and productive workforce available to industry and business to underpin economic development.
- Establishing an overarching east–west governance arrangement, supported by a series of alliances and focused on the critical issues identified in Table 4.1, will enhance the region's capacity to grow and develop, with significant benefits for Australia and its near neighbours.
- Health in Northern Australia reflects a combination of unique geographic and demographic factors, including poorer health status (with Northern Australia representing approximately one-third of Australia's outer regional and remote population), and geographic maldistribution of health professionals, meaning shortages in rural and remote areas.
- In health workforce development, ensuring availability and affordability of clinical training remains a significant challenge, particularly for providers in rural and remote areas where there is a less established tradition of education, training and research, less investment and less infrastructure to support these activities as well as higher costs associated providing clinical placements.
- Universities play an essential role in training future health professionals of the region to meet health workforce needs, strengthening the economy and building vital diplomatic links internationally.
- Northern Australia is leading the country in developing and delivering a number of health service and health workforce innovations to meet health needs in the region, including building rural pipelines in medicine, expanding scopes of practice for health practitioners, smart use of technology including telehealth, and promoting rural and remote generalist specialists across all health professional groups.
- Northern Australia is well placed to develop its health service and health workforce innovation expertise as an export, particularly to Asia and the Indo-Pacific region.

On the basis of the research evidence and the opportunities discussed in this chapter, the following recommendations are made for future policy and practices. Implementation of these recommendations enables strategic investment in the opportunities to build the capacity of the region to develop a healthy and productive population in Northern Australia.

**Recommendation 1:** Establish and strengthen inter-sectoral and cross-jurisdictional partnerships to provide accessible, effective and efficient health services across Northern Australia through:

- east–west governance arrangements that strengthen service delivery and collaboration between the not-for-profit sectors, private enterprise and state governments
- regional partnerships between government and non-government organisations that:
  - facilitate collaborative health services planning and modelling
  - provide an integrated and cooperative continuum of care across services and the region that supports the patient journey
  - effectively address inequities in access to services
  - collaboratively and inclusively address critical challenges to the health of the populations.

**Recommendation 2:** Employ strategies that develop an appropriate health workforce for Northern Australia and the region by:

- creating and further developing education and clinical training hubs that:
  - work cooperatively and collaboratively with health service providers across Northern Australia to grow an appropriate regional, rural and remote health workforce
  - provide affordable, quality clinical experiences for students
  - enable the export of health professional education and clinical training to the Asia-Pacific region
  - maximise opportunities to implement and evaluate innovative workforce models such as Indigenous health practitioners, nurse practitioners and tropical/rural training pathways
  - provide the expertise to develop rural generalist practitioners with the expanded scope of practice required in this context
  - provide continuing education and professional development for health professionals
  - leverage existing Northern Australia capability around disaster preparedness and management.

- east–west arrangements that transcend jurisdictional barriers and enable;
  - implementation of strategies to address the maldistribution of the health workforce
  - shared specialist health workforce in Northern Australia
  - shared recruitment and retention strategies
  - telehealth service delivery that provide access to networks, support and training without geographical barriers.

**Recommendation 3:** Reform resourcing and governance models across jurisdictions and sectors in Northern Australia to:

- align legislation and harmonise policies (e.g. around credentialing, scope of practice, drugs and poisons, and clinical guidelines)
- enable co-investment into training, resources and technology-assisted solutions that enable equitable access with a reduced cost burden
- developing and evaluating innovative service models and providing cost-effective service delivery
- integrate research, education and health care through formal Northern Australia governance structures to build capability and export regional expertise
- support and share evidence-based workforce models
- strengthen Indigenous and rural and remote primary health care infrastructure.

Prioritisation of, and ongoing investment in, health services strengthening, health workforce development, and health and medical research in Northern Australia will ensure the region is recognised as a global leader in rural, remote and tropical health care and workforce innovation. This needs to be underpinned by an overarching governance arrangement focused on the critical health and health workforce issues in the region. With sustained political commitment to Northern Australia, this tropical region has the potential and capacity to be the leading provider of innovative health service models, public health research and health professional education.

## Postscript

This chapter was originally written in late 2016. With proposed publication in 2021, there is a unique opportunity to reflect on progress towards addressing the challenges and leveraging the opportunities highlighted in this chapter.

Every year since 2016, the Annual Statement on Developing Northern Australia has been delivered by the current minister responsible for Northern Australia, and it would appear in the period between 2016 and 2021 that significant progress has been achieved in laying the foundations to support investment and leveraging of opportunities in Northern Australia.

The question remains in the minds of the authors as to whether the northern development agenda has delivered better outcomes for the communities of Northern Australia and, in particular, whether the recommendations identified in this chapter have been realised.

The establishment of the Cooperative Research Centre for Developing Northern Australia, a key recommendation from the 2015 White Paper, has served to support and invest in research, commercialisation and addressing supply chain issues with respect to Northern Australia health service delivery (including identifying new models and approaches, early detection, health-seeking behaviour and mental health). There appears to have been very little action in relation to the recommendations drafted in 2016, and in 2020 the CRCNA published a Northern Australia health service delivery situational analysis (Edelman et al., 2020). In this 2020 report the challenges identified and the recommendation to develop a systemic approach to enable collaboration and information-sharing are consistent with recommendations from 2016—namely, the lack of structural mechanisms to bring together key stakeholders to drive a strategic agenda remains an impediment to success. Pre-existing governance structures such as the GNARTN (which was funded by the Commonwealth Department of Health) were disestablished in June 2017, and the lack of systematic coordination, collaboration and co-investment in innovation and information-sharing between primary care networks, local health networks and LHNs and those universities and institutions with expertise in this area further exacerbate the fragmentation of effort and limits investment.

The Ministers Forum on Northern Australia, in combination with the Senior Officers forums supported by the Office of Northern Australia, does continue to provide a mechanism to enable strategic dialogue; however, evidence of the impact of this high-level collaboration is limited. While high-level dialogue is important, the ability to drive innovation, reduce duplication and improve outcomes through effective operational collaboration between states on shared issues remains limited without appropriate and strategic governance arrangements providing a foundation from which to invest.

Ongoing and regular changes in the funding and policy environment to increase health workforce clinical training capacity has had mixed outcomes. The ongoing investment in University Department of Rural Health (UDRH) and establishment of a UDRH in northern Western Australia is a positive outcome that will increase clinical training capacity in Northern Australia. All parties committed to supporting a regional homegrown medical, nursing, allied health and Indigenous health practitioner workforce to service local communities find their efforts confounded by the lack of a consistent and harmonised approach across Northern Australia. The diversity of positions taken by peak health professional bodies limits access and supervision in the provision of clinical placements. There is also legislative and regulatory discord between the three northern jurisdictions. The ongoing prioritisation to fund medical training over other health profession groups is also leading to a medically focused model, as opposed to a multidisciplinary team-based approach, which is more cost-effective and has better health outcomes, especially within Indigenous communities. Significant changes in policy have resulted in the loss of clinical training capacity, which had enabled universities to fund clinical placement opportunities in regional, rural and remote communities. There is evidence that providing well-supported clinical placement opportunities in regional, rural and remote areas increases the likelihood of students returning to a rural area and transitioning successfully into rural practice following graduation.

In 2021, workforce maldistribution in Northern Australia remains a key challenge, and a key recommendation of this chapter in 2016 was to develop a training system that leverages the existing training infrastructure of the Northern Territory, Queensland and Western Australia and, via collaborative partnerships, develop integrated training pathways that leverage this infrastructure and clinical training capacity so that students could systematically access this capacity across the north to enable an east–west training pipeline.

A significant gamechanger identified in Recommendation 3 of this chapter (in 2016) was a recommendation to work with the northern jurisdictions to harmonise legislation and policies to facilitate the health professional workforce to be more mobile between the three jurisdictions. Currently, there are a number of limitations and variances between the scope of practice of various health professionals in the north. The more these barriers to practice can be reduced, the more mobile health professional can be. Increasing mobility by minimising variances between the northern regions will contribute to addressing health workforce maldistribution, an area of work that has the potential to resolve a number of significant barriers to workforce mobility in Northern Australia, and could be within the remit of the CRCNA.

While the Northern Australia development agenda has created opportunities for Northern Australian communities, to date in 2021 outcomes in addressing workforce maldistribution in Northern Australia remain limited. The loss of any effective mechanism to drive collaboration and co-investment in innovative and systemic solutions across all three jurisdictions will continue independently of each other and not achieve the collective benefit from collaboration that the Northern Australia development foreshadowed.

The arrival of COVID-19 in 2020 reinforced Australia's position as being a centre of excellence in health service delivery and models of care, tropical public health and innovations in health professional training. However, our capacity to get this to market remains limited and marginal in the context of international market dynamics. Through effective and strategic collaboration between health system managers, universities and legislators, Northern Australia could address these issues and generate significant opportunities as a centre for expertise and education for the international market.

## References

Australian Bureau of Statistics (ABS). (2017). *Regional population growth, Australia, 2016.* (No. 3218.0). Canberra, ACT: ABS.

Australian Bureau of Statistics (ABS). (2018a). *Education and work Australia, May 2018* (No. 6227.0). Canberra, ACT: ABS.

Australian Bureau of Statistics (ABS). (2018b). *Estimates of Aboriginal and Torres Strait Islander Australians, June 2016.* (No. 3238.0.55.001. Canberra, ACT: ABS.

Australian Government. (2015). *Our north, our future: White paper on developing Northern Australia.* Retrieved from www.industry.gov.au/data-and-publications/our-north-our-future-white-paper-on-developing-northern-australia

Australian Institute of Health and Welfare (AIHW). (2013). *Nursing and midwifery workforce 2012* (National Health Workforce Series No. 6, Cat. No. HWL 52). Canberra, ACT: AIHW.

Australian Institute of Health and Welfare (AIHW). (2018). *Australia's health 2018* (Australia's health series no. 16, Cat. No. AUS 221). Canberra, ACT: AIHW.

Australian Medical Workforce Advisory Committee. (1998). *Medical workforce supply and demand in Australia: A discussion paper* (AIHW Cat. No. HWL 12). Sydney, NSW: AMWAC.

Commonwealth of Australia. (2012). *Australia in the Asian century.* Canberra, ACT: Commonwealth of Australia.

Commonwealth of Australia. (2013). *Strategic review of health and medical research.* Canberra, ACT: Department of Health and Ageing.

Davis, S. & Vernon, M. (2014). *Greater Northern Australia Regional Training Network submission to the Joint Select Committee on Northern Australia.* GNARTN.

Department of Jobs and Small Business. (2018). *ABS labour force regions—AA4 data.* Retrieved from lmip.gov.au/maps.aspx#layer=LabourForceRegions

Edelman, A., Grundy, J., Moodley, N., Larkins, S., Topp, S.M., Atkinson, D., Patel, B., Strivens, E. & Whittaker M. (2020). *Northern Australia health service delivery situational analysis.* CRCNA. Retrieved from crcna.com.au/resources/publications/northern-australia-health-service-delivery-situational-analysis

Edelman, A., Taylor, J., Ovseiko, P. V. & Topp, S. M. (2018). '"Academic" is a dirty word': Intended impact pathways of an emerging academic health centre in tropical regional Australia. *International Journal of Health Planning and Management, 34*(1), e661–e678. doi.org/10.1002/hpm.2681

Godwin, D. M., Hoang, H., Crocombe, L. A. & Bell, E. (2014). Dental practitioner rural work movements: A systematic review. *Rural and Remote Health, 14*(3). Retrieved from www.rrh.org.au/publishedarticles/article_print_2825.pdf

Health Workforce Australia (HWA). (2012). *Health workforce Australia, 2012. A summary of health workforce 2025—volumes 1 to 3.* Adelaide, SA: HWA.

Health Workforce Australia (HWA). (2013). *National rural and remote workforce innovation and reform strategy.* Adelaide, SA: HWA.

Hill, C. (2013). Australia in the 'Indo-Pacific' century: Rewards, risks, relationships. In D. Heriot (Ed.), *Parliamentary library briefing book—44th Parliament* (pp. 144–146). Canberra, ACT: Australian Government.

Humphreys, J., Wakerman, J., Wells, R., Kuipers, P., Jones, J. & Entwistle, P. A. (2006). *Systematic review of primary health care delivery models in rural and remote Australia 1993–2006.* Canberra, ACT: Australian Primary Health Care Research Institute.

Insight Economics. (2012). *Review of dental workforce supply to 2020.* Melbourne, Vic.: Australian Dental Association. Retrieved from hdl.voced.edu.au/10707/346119

Joint Select Committee on Northern Australia. (2014). *Inquiry into the development of Northern Australia — interim report.* Canberra, ACT: Parliament of the Commonwealth of Australia.

Liberal Party of Australia. (2013). *The Coalition's 2030 vision for developing Northern Australia.* Retrieved from parlinfo.aph.gov.au/parlInfo/search/display/display.w3p;query=Id%3A%22library%2Fpartypol%2F2550511%22;src1=sm1

Mason, J. (2013). *Review of Australian Government health workforce programs.* Canberra, ACT: Department of Health.

Minister for Resources and Northern Australia. (2018). *Northern Australia statement.* Retrieved from www.minister.industry.gov.au/ministers/canavan/speeches/2018-annual-statement-developing-northern-australia

Murray, K. A., Skerratt, L. F., Speare, R., Ritchie, S., Smout, F., Hedlefs, R. & Lee, J. (2012). Cooling off health security hot spots: Getting on top of it down under. *Environment International, 48,* 56–64.

National Health Workforce Planning and Research Collaboration (NHWPRC). (2010). *Refining the national workforce planning model. Final report.* Adelaide, SA: HWA.

Productivity Commission. (2005). *Australia's health workforce*. Canberra, ACT: Productivity Commission.

Scott, A. & Joyce, C. M. (2014). The future of medical careers. *Medical Journal of Australia*, *201*(2), 82–83.

Sen Gupta, T., Woolley, T., Murray, R., Hays, R. & McCloskey, T. (2015). Positive impacts on rural and regional workforce from the first seven cohorts of James Cook University medical graduates. *Rural and Remote Health*, *14*(1), 1–13. Retrieved from www.rrh.org.au/articles/showarticlenew.asp?ArticleID=2657

State of the Tropics. (2014). *State of the tropics report*. Cairns, Qld: James Cook University. Retrieved from www.jcu.edu.au/state-of-the-tropics/publications/2014-state-of-the-tropics-report

State of the Tropics. (2017). *2017 State of the Tropics Report: Sustainable infrastructure in the tropics*. Townsville, Qld: James Cook University. Retrieved from www.jcu.edu.au/state-of-the-tropics/publications/2017-state-of-the-tropics-report

United Nations. (2013). *Universal health coverage at the center of sustainable development: Contributions of sciences, technology and innovations to health systems strengthening*. Retrieved from www.un.org/en/ecosoc/julyhls/pdf13/concept_paper-uhc_during_ecosoc_amr.pdf

Universities Australia. (2014). *Universities Australia pre-budget submission 2014–15*. Universities Australia.

Wakerman, J. (2004). Defining remote health. *Australian Journal of Rural Health*, *12*(5), 210–214. doi.org/10.1111/j.1440-1854.2004.00607.x

World Health Organization (WHO). (2016). 'Travel and Health'. Retrieved from www.who.int/trade/en/

# Section 2

# Economic and Business Development in the North

Rolf Gerritsen

## Context

Economic and business development, particularly through large infrastructure projects, seems to be the current focus of the agenda for northern development. The chapters in this section provide a set of preliminary approaches that nuance this agenda. Each has a particular subject matter, but the five together in no way encompass the complexities of the economic development of the north—instead, they add further elements to a northern development debate that will occur over the coming years. In sum, they warn against over-centralised approaches and stress on-the-ground analyses.

## The Five Chapters

The five chapters in this section propose a theory of northern economic development, a perspective on an important northern industry (tourism), an interpretation of one of the persistent problems of northern development (equity) and a new 'ground-up' approach to Aboriginal economic development (the mixed-market).

### Gerritsen: Pulse and Pause in Northern Development

Gerritsen provides a synoptic view of northern development, which he sees as occurring in 'pulses' and 'pauses'—sudden booms being followed by long periods of stasis. He traces the history of these pulses from the mid-nineteenth century through to the recent resources boom. As in

Belich's (2009) 'Wests', these booms are exogenously derived and dependent upon capital inflows but reflect a changing economic geography both coincident with and consequent upon that process. Gerritsen stresses that the most recent resource pulse has created a suite of world-class Australian resource logistics and construction companies and also signalled the rise of Perth as the antipodean epicentre of this development. He points—as does Stoeckl (Chapter 7)—to the likelihood of persistent Indigenous disadvantage within this developmental framework.

## Prideaux et al.: The Future of Northern Tourism

This sombre chapter focuses on what the authors call the 'market failure' of the northern tourism industry. They demonstrate that this industry has stagnated and even declined since 2000. The authors are forthright about the industry's failures, both to recognise that its product needs rejuvenation and that simplistic appeals for more governmental expenditure on marketing is no answer to the industry's woes. They propose that the two areas of supposed northern competitive advantage—nature and the Indigenous experience—are not working on the demand (push) side of the tourism market. Similar to Stoeckl et al. (2014), they are critical of the centralisation of decision-making (not just with governments but also the private sector, viz the airlines, unreliability with routes and scheduling).

## Stoeckl: Equity and Major Development

Stoeckl explicitly rejects the 'trickle-down' theory of northern development and argues for a more nuanced approach. This recognises the prevailing inequities and that they have racial and gender elements. This builds on her earlier work about the distributional impacts of government program grants (Stoeckl et al., 2014). Equity is important because inequity vitiates economic development. Stoeckl identifies a syndrome that Wolf (1979) would describe as non-market failure. She proposes policy processes that would ameliorate this by ensuring that large-scale projects would be better connected to the communities within which they operate.

## Lovell and Zoellner and Zoellner and Lovell

These two, interlinked chapters seek to explore the interstices between what is happening on a range of Aboriginal communities in central Australia and what official statistics indicate is happening. They develop upon on a highly original model (Lovell et al., 2015) of what is described as mixed-market activity that is different from both Altman's 'hybrid economy' (Altman, 2001) and Gerritsen's (Chapter 5) nascent formulation of a multiplex economy. Using Wolf's (1979) formulation, Lovell and Zoellner propose that their form of mixed-market modelling reinterprets local capacity and 'advantage' and how these interact with contemporary markets. They have an essentially optimistic view—for them, mixed-markets can assist to overcome non-market failure (Wolf, 1979). The methodology these authors develop is unique, interesting and useful.

In the first chapter, Lovell and Zoellner argue that non-market interventions are not achieving their intentions in Aboriginal communities but that a locally based non-market sector persists, largely unrecognised by government. They point to neoliberal agendas that seek to individuate Aboriginal people and call for recognition of local socioeconomic systems.

The second chapter, Zoellner and Lovell, demonstrates in forensic detail how national data systems—such as household surveys (HILDA), youth labour markets (LSAY) and disadvantage measures (SEIFA)—do not represent remote Aboriginal community realities. This is especially the case with non-market activities. They propose a reorganisation of data systems, which they claim can aid the development of fit-for-purpose public policy. This would particularly target the pathology that the dominant non-market sector directs its economic gains away from the Aboriginal systems within which they occur and, thus, reduces the financial resources available to local economies. This conclusion augments Stoeckl's paper.

## Conclusion

This section is a collection of subjects that are of interest to us or we are fortuitously researching. It is not a strategic sample leading us ineluctably to 'solutions' for the problems of Northern Australia's skewed development and ongoing problems of disadvantage entrenched in particular localities.

For example, one of the economic problems of northern development is that, arguably, there is no Northern Australian economy. There is a series of regional economies, usually with their supply lines and bureaucratic/political command chains to different metropoles. In a sense, Northern Australia mirrors Australia before World War I when each colony/state economy was based on its metropole, each of which had its strongest direct economic relations with Britain and not other Australian capital cities. A 'national' economy did not begin to emerge until after World War I. Northern Australia operates like a pump—money comes in, mostly in the form of investment and governmental transfer payments of various kinds. Capital accumulation from the profit of the economic activities this 'investment' generates is repatriated via bank deposits, superannuation and housing investment, so the north disinvests (this happens also with the large resource corporations). This is the larger scale of the Zoellner and Lovell analysis in this section. We need to systematically investigate how to keep more money in the north and how to tie its regions together for economic development that is designed and implemented in place.

# References

Altman, J. (2001). *Sustainable development options on Aboriginal land: The hybrid economy in the twenty-first century* (Centre for Aboriginal Economic Policy Research, Discussion Paper No. 226). Canberra, ACT: ANU.

Belich, J. (2009). *Replenishing the Earth. The settler revolution and the rise of the Anglo world, 1783-1939.* Oxford, England: Oxford University Press.

Lovell, J., Guenther, J. & Zoellner, D. (2015). *Northern Australian aspirations.* Retrieved from www.cdu.edu.au/sites/default/files/research-brief-2015-07_0.pdf

Stoeckl, N., Esparon, M., Farr, A., Delisle, A. & Stanley, O. (2014). The great asymmetric divide: An empirical investigation of the line between Indigenous and non-Indigenous economic systems in Northern Australia. *Papers in Regional Science, 93*(4), 783–801. doi.org/10.1111/pirs.12028

Wolf, C. (1979). A theory of non-market failure: Framework for implementation analysis. *Journal of Law and Economics, 22*(1), 107–139. doi.org/10.1086/466935

# 5

# Pulse and Pause: Researching the Economic Future of Northern and Remote Australia

Rolf Gerritsen

## Introduction

With the current federal government interest in northern development (Australian Government, 2014), the opportunity supposedly exists both to position remote and Northern Australia for a prosperous and sustainable future and to make it a full participant in future Australian economic development. That outcome requires understanding of past developments to inform future assumptions and what they portend for Northern Australia. The nature of the past development of Northern Australia does not instil confidence that something will change that well-established pattern.

In the past, sudden rushes of optimism and investment were followed by decades of disappointment. Pearling rose and fell. Pastoralism rose and fell before establishing some equilibrium. Mining was characterised by brief 'booms'—mostly during the two World Wars—followed by slow 'busts', a pattern that recurred across remote Australia.

The future portends the likely erratic economic development of the region and the separate but continuing marginalisation and impoverishment of its Aboriginal population—features that provide particular challenges that set Northern Australia apart from the rest of the country.

In Darwin in 1900, the South Australian public servants that administered its northern territory wore clothes imported from Singapore. They ate some Asian food and Darwin had far more Chinese residents than European/Australian ones. Live cattle were exported to Asia from northern ports, particularly from the Kimberleys. The combination of the post-Federation policy of White Australia and governmental neglect (the north Queensland coastal area aside) reduced that Asian connection. In Darwin in 2000, or for that matter in Townsville or Broome, residents still wore clothes imported from Asia but they were wholesaled via Melbourne. After a post–World War I hiatus, live cattle exports to Asia resumed in the 1980s. In the period between, abattoirs across Northern Australia produced meat primarily for the domestic market. Asians were now in a minority of migrants (from overseas and from interstate Australia). But Asia was still the main market for most of Northern Australia's exports. But Asian imports bypassed the north, heading instead to the metropolitan ports of Southern and Eastern Australia. The economics of large-scale, long-range sea transport sidelined Northern Australia except for outward-bound cargoes of minerals.

Northern Australia has been enmeshed in a relationship with Asia almost since it was 'settled' and its resident Aborigines conquered. But the nature of that relationship has changed in ways that reflect the broader changes that have occurred in Australia over the last century. The economic relationship—agriculture, particularly sugar, the live cattle trade and some tourism aside—is now mediated through metropoles. As seen in the example of Northern Australians wearing clothes made in Asia but 'imported' via Melbourne.

This chapter begins an ongoing analysis of the economic development of Northern Australia that I will expand on in the future.

# Economic Development's History in the North

Economic development in Northern Australia historically parallels the 'pulse and pause' model ecologists use to describe the natural biological systems of the region. Development occurs rapidly (the boom) and then pauses into stasis, often for many years. The second half of the nineteenth century saw a dramatic 'pulse' as industries such as mining, pastoralism and pearling irrupted into Northern Australia (as did agriculture, particularly sugar, on the Queensland coast). In the 1950s, pearling disappeared, destroyed by the plastic button. That industry was later resurrected in a more sustainable form as represented by the cultured pearl industry, a high-tech industry aiming at the luxury consumer goods market and not the mass markets of the past.

Miners, now so important, were also significant in the expanding frontier of the north in the nineteenth century. Gold rushes in the Palmer River area and at Halls Creek in the 1870s and 1880s introduced large (for the north) populations briefly into the area. Many other areas featured mining booms and busts. The World Wars stimulated mining, particularly for the tin, copper and wolfram that was integral to the war effort each time (Jones, 1987, Appendix 1). From the 1960s, the development of Mount Isa and, later, the northern bauxite industry at Weipa and Gove and the Pilbara iron ore province and Bowen Basin coal in Queensland meant that mining replaced pastoralism and sugar and became the dominant 'productivist' private sector industry in the north. In the 1970s, the Pilbara natural gas province emerged as part of this first post-war mining boom. Gold and other base metals also joined this boom in Western Australia (WA) and Queensland. The post-2002 boom actually (notwithstanding the popular hype about the 'two-speed' economy in the past decade) had less structural impact on the Australian economy than the 1960s–70s resource boom (Connolly & Orsmond, 2011; Edwards, 2014). If anything, it consolidated the metropolitan heartlands. For example, Perth developed as the dominant centre for mining logistics and the provision of labour (via the fly-in/fly-out [FIFO] mechanism). For extractive industries, the Pilbara and the Northern Territory can now be considered as Perth's economic hinterland (Gerritsen, 2010).

After the rapid expansion of pastoralism from the 1880s to World War I, this industry has mostly paused. There have been brief revivals, as in the 1960s–70s with the Commonwealth beef road program and mechanisation and contractualisation to replace Aboriginal labour. This latter element was sped up by the equal wage case of 1967 but was underway before then. Essentially, pastoralists abandoned the labour-intensive model of production because it was uneconomic and seen as a state-sponsored exploitative appropriation of 'cheap' Aboriginal labour. More recently, the industry has sustained itself (as before World War I) by live exports, although it appears some companies are interested in developing a more sophisticated model based on vertically integrated supply chains. So, after a break of 30 years, abattoirs may return to the north (AACo constructed and briefly operated one near Darwin). Governments have also enhanced the potential for pastoral lands to contribute to future economic diversification by increasingly allowing use-purpose variations of pastoral leases. This process has developmental advantages. It shifts development risk onto the private capital that will benefit from any successful diversification of production; it is small-scale and potentially sustainable and avoids expensive, publicly funded, 'white elephant' projects, such as the Ord River scheme and other recent wild proposals to make the north the 'food bowl of Asia'. With Asian food demand predicted to continue to grow strongly until 2040, the market situation is promising, particularly for tropical fruits, grains and oilseeds. Investment will increasingly come from an Asia concerned more about food security than profits. Nevertheless, with improved herd and water management, experts propose that beef exports could increase by 80 per cent within three decades (Deane, 2014).

Apart from along the maritime littoral of Queensland, agriculture has not driven economic development in the north. The east coast of Queensland has managed intensive development, initially around sugar, and features a density of large towns and cities that portend self-sustaining development. This region exhibits economic dynamics (coal mining aside) that make it distinct from the rest of Northern Australia. It has large service centres (e.g. Townsville, or Mackay for mining), industrial cities (Gladstone) and mixed services/tourism centres (e.g. Cairns). This region of Queensland now has about two-thirds of the population of Northern Australia. It is here and in Darwin that most Northern Australian population increases will occur. The rest of the region can expect stasis or slow population rises below the national average.

In the rest of Australia's north, large-scale agriculture has not been successful. In the 1950s and 1960s, large schemes, such as Humpty Doo rice, failed and the Ord River project has never repaid its capital cost. Agricultural development is often the political driver of northern development, but rarely has it been an economic driver. It seems that this is currently the case. There is a case for more intensive agriculture in the north but designed sustainably around small locally efficient production and not dependent on federal investment in dams for irrigated broad acre cropping. Horticulture and specialist tropical crops appear to have the most environmentally and economically sustainable prospects. They can target high-value niche markets (the burgeoning Asian middle class) and so overcome expensive transport costs.

## Recent Economic Development: The So-Called 'Two-Speed' Economy?

The idea of Australia's two-speed economy that is driven from Northern Australia was fuelled by a recent gigantic investment boom in the construction of new mines and natural gas projects. This was accompanied until 2011 by a massive price rise for iron ore and coal, prices that recently have plummeted to nearer the long-term average and threaten much of the investment made during the boom. The novelty of the two-speed hypothesis, predicated on producing primary products to capitalise on rapid industrialisation in China, is overstated in two senses. Northern Australia's burgeoning resource extraction industries have been linked with Asian industrialisation since the 1960s, starting with Japan and then South Korea. The 1960s and '70s saw economic pulses in the north based on these industries. Because they saw the construction of new towns (mostly in the Pilbara), this initial phase had more impact on long-term northern development than the most recent boom/pulse of the first decade of this century. Second, the gross domestic product (GDP) share of mining during the 2002–11 boom did not expand faster than the general economy—so mining as a share of real GDP was the same in 2011 as in 2002 (Rayner & Bishop, 2013).

The core features of Australia's so-called two-speed economy are the concentration of a growth industry's central management in a growth metropole (i.e. Perth), with much of the value added in the mining industry being created there and the demand for labour at the resource-producing periphery. Although WA only employs 36 per cent of mining, including oil and gas, industry workers (Queensland employs 27 per cent and New South Wales 21 per cent), mostly in coal mining, it garners over 48 per cent of the mining industry's value added. Perth has become the epicentre of a wide range of resource extraction services companies engaged in support logistics, mining construction and design services, IT, finance, explosives and so on. Some of these, such as Leighton Holdings, Orica, Worley Parsons and Incitec, are now very large companies servicing resource extraction enterprises worldwide. These types of companies increased their share of nominal GDP from 3 per cent to 6.5 per cent during the recent minerals and energy investment boom (Rayner & Bishop, 2013). Some (probably most) of them will survive the current 'pause' because of their international diversification. This is arguably the most significant development in the Australian economy since the economic restructuring of the 1980s restored Australian competitiveness and coincided with a shift to service industries and a long downturn in manufacturing.

In effect, Northern and remote Australia has become part of Perth's economic hinterland. Queensland is a little more complex because coal mining is serviced from a number of larger north-east coastal regional cities, like Mackay. Brisbane is not establishing itself as an economic services metropole in the same way as Perth.

The problem for Northern Australia is the poor multipliers into the region of this resource extraction industry. Remote Central and Northern Australia are probably going to be weakly coupled to this engine of Australian growth over the foreseeable future.

All this will be significant—socially, politically, and economically—if the 'super-cycle' of resource demand principally created by the industrialisation of China (and probably India) continues. At present, it looks that the familiar pulse and pause (or in mining industry parlance, boom and bust) pattern is in a pause (bust) phase. Mines are closing because they were constructed during the boom and so were expensive and the low current primary commodities prices cannot justify their relatively high cost of production. None of this is surprising if you are a Western Australian. The eastern goldfields of WA are littered with the remnants of (usually expensively constructed) public buildings that are all that remain of once-thriving gold mining towns—think Sandstone, Menzies, Cue, Yalgoo, etc. These towns were not resurrected during the recent gold mining boom, which used FIFO labour.

This pattern of economic development has features that impact on Northern Australian governments. WA's overambitious scheme to make Port Hedland and Karratha cities of 50,000 people is explicable by the demands of the WA Nationals 'Royalties for Regions'—a result of the 2002 state election. It is temporary. The reality is that there was relatively little public infrastructure provision during the last resource pulse; existing infrastructure was more intensively used (Bureau of Infrastructure, Transport and Regional Economics, 2014). The last pulse saw labour sourced from places other than the operation point of the resource extraction project. The resource extraction labour force is largely supplied by FIFO workers commuting from large towns and cities, not in remote or Northern Australia (Queensland has a variation of this in drive-in/drive-out workers commuting from coastal cities to the coal mines of the Bowen and Galilee basins). Such arrangements are a consequence of how mining companies have developed new 'greenfields' projects (i.e. no longer providing a town to house workers because of the front-end costs and the associated exchange rate and interest rate risks) (Gerritsen, 2010, pp. 30–32). The provision of housing, education, health and other services for the workforce is left to the relevant state, territory or local governments. The extra costs of running a mine with FIFO labour comes off the Commonwealth's company tax receipts. So, FIFO makes eminent sense for mining companies; its only downside (for mining companies) is in exacerbating labour turnover. Governments have to worry about services, maintaining viable towns and relevant infrastructure, so they bear most of the social and fiscal costs of resource extraction.

The high cost of labour in the northern resource extraction industries means that mining companies will increasingly automate their operations. Driverless trucks and trains have already been introduced. Soon we will have mines run almost entirely by machines. Over the next two or three or so decades, mining output growth will not be matched by employment growth and FIFO will wane. The resource extraction industries will drive northern growth (in export-value terms) but not northern development. Here changes broadening the economy will be based in the metropoles, particularly Perth. The services industries (and possibly the military) will supply most future northern labour market and population growth and economic development.

So, future research must turn to the services sector to define growth possibilities. That does not mean that services will remain separate from resource extraction or agriculture. These industries can provide services opportunities, as indicated by the development of logistics and engineering services that accompanied the most recent resource pulse (boom) indicates. To grow current agricultural productivity requires a range of agronomic and soil science services (and finance, workforce training, etc. services). So, the services sector is where future labour and consumer markets will grow. The issue for Northern Australia (apart from the Queensland coastal cities and Darwin) is attracting labour to maintain services and economic viability. Overseas migration can be one means

(Taylor et al., 2014). Principally, this remains an issue of amenity—ready access to goods and services and at reasonable prices (Department of Regional Development, 2013), which is difficult to supply to remote and small towns. Labour constraints will continue to be a problem for Northern Australia.

## Indigenous Aspects

The economic development described above will have minimal beneficial elements for the Aborigines of remote and Northern Australia. Their well-known relative poverty, poor education and disconnect with the development of the larger Australian economy will—assuming current policy settings—probably get worse. Directly that is because Aborigines in remote and Northern Australia generally lack the skills or aptitudes that allow them to participate in the current economy. Even measures designed to benefit Aborigines mostly provide money to non-Aboriginal parties (Stoeckl et al., 2014). And it has been argued (Gerritsen & Straton, 2007) that the assumptions on which government services are delivered misread how Aboriginal settlements operate.

That situation is partly a legacy of history. Aboriginal people were forcibly accommodated into the colonial system after the British conquest of Northern Australia during the second half of the nineteenth century. Mostly, Aborigines resided on missions and cattle stations and, more recently, on supposedly self-governing communities. The autarchic economy of these places collapsed in the 1970s. In the latter part of the twentieth century, governments attempted to start Aboriginal enterprises but, for various reasons, these were mostly failures (Gerritsen, 2006). They were replaced by various training/workfare schemes, which persist to the present. The problem of Aboriginal engagement with the northern economy is partly that they reside on remote, poorly equipped communities far from real 'markets'. This residential pattern was initially the direct result of missions and governments historically seeking to keep Aboriginal people from the corrupting and debasing influences of white settlements. Later, it came from legal changes creating various forms of rights in land and the consequent return of many Aboriginal people to their traditional lands. Arguably, their culture also inhibits Aboriginal involvement in capitalist market activities (Austin-Broos, 2006; McRae-

Williams & Gerritsen, 2010). In conventional human capital terms, Aborigines have not 'invested' in their human capital to become job-ready (e.g. Gregory, 2005).

Indigenous disadvantage will persist, partly because there are paradoxes between Aboriginal society and the demands of Australian polities. That which is sought is internally contradictory—the state is inchoate. For example, some advocates and some policies value and privilege Aboriginal connection to and ownership of land. This currently has generally negative implications for access to mainstream economic opportunities because of institutional barriers to Aborigines selling or leasing their land (plus Aboriginal unwillingness to do so).

Other public policies require Aboriginal involvement in the mainstream economy ('real jobs' and 'Closing the Gap'). This paradox is replicated in Aboriginal society, where there is widespread recognition of poverty and that only 'real' jobs can reduce that problem. At the same time, patterns of relatedness and demand sharing are valued by Aborigines, notwithstanding that they prevent the achievement of the individual advancement that is at the core of capitalist economic progress (Austin-Broos, 2005; McRae-Williams & Gerritsen, 2010).

If Aboriginal labour remains immobile (i.e. they continue residing in remote communities), then the economic costs of distance will be great and economically conventional Aboriginal economic engagement will struggle. A solution here proposed is to reconceptualise Northern Australian economies into sectors—the capitalist, the state, a communal sector and a philanthropic sector. These would interact in a multiplex economy. My multiplex economy model is a development from Altman's (2001) 'hybrid economy' model and is presented in Appendix 1.

As originally proposed (Gerritsen, 2006), a multiplex economy would see the continuation of primarily government-sponsored Aboriginal enterprise creation and the entry of some Aboriginal persons into formal employment (mostly in government services). For example, the Northern Territory government (supported by Commonwealth funding) has, or recently has had, enterprise initiatives in areas such as aquaculture, forestry and agribusiness, mining services, pastoralism and tourism. These enterprises may create several hundreds of jobs in the foreseeable future. Relations between Aborigines and the mining industry have long been problematic (Scambery, 2013). It appears that Aborigines have secured better personal outcomes from mines operating under native title and better community development outcomes from mines within the land rights jurisdiction of the Northern Territory (Stanley, 2010). However, current economic approaches are an incomplete answer to the endemic unemployment on northern remote Aboriginal settlements. The best way to create the thousands of jobs required to reduce Aboriginal unemployment to levels comparable to those of the rest of Australia is in the communal sector element of the multiplex economy. For example, traditional Aboriginal skills in land and fire management could be augmented by roles in biosecurity and biodiversity protection to create a natural resource management (NRM) economy that would be an integral part of the multiplex economy of remote Australia. At present, public investment (via Caring for Country programs) is low. In 2012, the Australian Government funded only 680 Indigenous ranger positions across 90 ranger groups nationally. So, currently there are only a few hundred 'jobs' here where there should be thousands. Some successful Aboriginal industries, notably the Indigenous arts industry, already builds successful economics on top of Indigenous cultural resources (Morphy, 2005), although that industry has problems with intellectual property (Altman et al., 2002) and related oversupply and quality issues (Rothwell, 2015). The philanthropic sector, an integral part of my evolving multiplex economy, can provide capital, expertise and a spur to governments to persist with investment.

What my current iteration of the multiplex economy model adds to the equation is the introduction of the philanthropic sector. This was suggested by previous work on rangeland conservation (Salmon & Gerritsen, 2013). The condition of the Aborigines of Northern Australia attracts philanthropic attention. Increasingly, philanthropic foundations provide money for Aboriginal causes, like education and employment. The attempts by industry leaders to create 50,000 Aboriginal jobs in the mining industry, which has failed to date mostly because of the recent investment downturn, is a case in point. This philanthropy sectoral involvement (to my knowledge) has not been adequately documented but it is a potential core of any Aboriginal economic development in Northern Australia. It has two potentials, by its attention to spur/shame the efforts of governments and also as a positive bridge between the communal and capitalist/governmental sectors. Mapping out this interaction is an obvious subject for further research.

## What do we need to know to make a multiplex economy work?

Some of the research required for the multiplex economy has begun. Anthropologists and geographers have given us an understanding of Aboriginal land management (e.g. Baker et al., 2001). Traditional burning practices are now relatively well understood (Dyer et al., 2001; Russell-Smith et al., 2009) and the basic parameters of sustainable Aboriginal use of native flora and fauna have been sketched out (Altman & Whitehead, 2003). But there are large gaps in the research effort. Particular lacunae I will address here are in the demographic, economic and institutional realms. To some extent these raise inter-related questions.

If, to reduce unemployment, a communal land-based (or NRM) economy is to be encouraged, then it will be centred on dispersed outstation/ homelands settlements. Demographic research is required to determine the possibilities for future migration and settlement patterns. We know that Aborigines are highly mobile, within particular ranges (Memmott et al., 2006). But we do not know if the conventional economic development assumption (encouraged by some official policy) that urban drift is inevitable, probable, possible or even unlikely. We also do not know whether such migration is likely to be pervasive or even uniform, or whether that migration will occur in particular stages of the life cycle to be followed by reverse migration in later life. This knowledge requires more than just population movement surveys; we need to have a realistic view of underlying Aboriginal incentives and motivations.

Research (if not policy experience) has shown that the tension between 'work' and the web of kinship, ceremony and family incentives affects (conventional) economic behaviour (Austin-Broos, 2006; McRae-Williams & Gerritsen, 2010). In addition, basic economic research is required to determine the markets and production and marketing processes for the potential products of an Aboriginal NRM economy. The existing economic research relating to the value of land management and exotic flora and fauna control and other biosecurity issues is at present rudimentary. To it should be added research into enhanced possibilities for ecotourism and cultural tourism. The probable eventual emergence of carbon trading regimes will also have to be factored into the parameters for an Aboriginal NRM industry to emerge out of the welfare economy. In addition, the institutional/administrative rules and frameworks that will bound these communal activities, if they are to be assigned or achieve economic value, will have to be analysed. The implications of overelaborate accountability procedures and increasing interventions via mainstream non-government organisations are cases in point.

It appears that Aboriginal people are currently at the same sort of crossroads that marked the imposition of colonial control. If an alternative multiplex economy based on communal production and focused on natural resource–based activities is to emerge, it is important that the research that would allow this to happen is facilitated.

## Conclusions

What can we expect of northern development in the next few decades? Intensified urbanisation is likely. The major Queensland coastal cities will continue to grow, driven by a services economy, and their hinterland towns will languish relatively. Like Darwin, they have become 'soak' cities. Thus, the post–World War II growth pattern (Bureau of Infrastructure, Transport and Regional Economics, 2014) will continue, except that Gladstone will do better than Bundaberg and Rockhampton (Mackay, essentially a mining construction supply city, has suffered a post-construction bust). Darwin, the only other major northern centre, will continue to grow but the long-term driver will not be resource extraction but new Commonwealth governmental expenditure, possibly on national security and biosecurity. In WA, neither Karratha nor Port Hedland, notwithstanding former premier Barnett's stated intentions to make them cities of 50,000 persons each, is likely to match the growth of Darwin (or Townsville, Gladstone, etc.). The economics of agglomeration is against them. The continued growth of Darwin will exacerbate the problem of urban bias in the Northern Territory's public policy that leads to under-funded and under-performing services to Aboriginal communities (Gerritsen, 2010).

Indigenous disadvantage, particularly in economic terms, will persist. That is, unless research to develop new forms of economy—perhaps something like Altman's (2001) hybrid economy or my multiplex economy—in which Aboriginals can and will participate. Aboriginal advancement (even its definition) remains Northern Australia's most wicked problem.

There are core problems in Northern Australia that merit serious research, including:

- the environment—how to manage it to achieve not just conservation but sustainable economic growth and broadened economic opportunities. This requires new notions of the 'economic' and the application of more science to agricultural/horticultural development
- the population—how to retain residents and immigrants and educate them to produce a forward-looking labour market that can respond to new opportunities, especially in services industries and, crucially, how to produce an economy for the Aboriginal population
- infrastructure—how to create the infrastructure that makes Northern Australia both a worthwhile place to live (education, health and cultural and recreational infrastructure) and economically efficient (physical infrastructure).

These are the issues that researchers and policymakers interested in the economic development of Northern Australia must consider.

# Appendix 5.1: Conceptualising the Multiplex Economy of Northern Australia

| Production factors | State | Communal | Capitalist | Philanthropic |
| --- | --- | --- | --- | --- |
| Ecosystem | Regulation | Natural balance | Sustainability | Support |
| Technology | Promote | Traditional | Market (C-B) | Support/Provide |
| Knowledge | Research | Traditional | Applied/Adaptive | Support/Provide |
| Property rights | Regulation | Communal | Individual markets/profits | Support |
| Fiscal flows | Taxes/grants | Dependence | Tax expenditure | Donations |
| Capital | Infrastructure | Communal land | Market investment | Provide |
| Labour | Regulation/employer | Family | Individual | Support |
| **Values system** | | | | |
| | Promote | Family/traditional | Applied/Adaptive | Altruism |
| | Sustainability | | Growth | |

# References

Altman, J. (2001). *Sustainable development options on Aboriginal land: The hybrid economy in the twenty-first century* (Centre for Aboriginal Economic Policy Research, Discussion Paper No. 226). Canberra, ACT: ANU.

Altman, J., Hunter, B. & Wright, F. (2002). *Indigenous visual arts industry. Competition and consumer issues for Indigenous Australians.* Canberra, ACT: Australian Competition and Consumer Commission.

Altman, J. & Whitehead, P. (2003). *Caring for country and sustainable Indigenous economic development opportunities. Constraints and innovation* (Centre for Aboriginal Economic Policy Research, Working Paper 20/2003). Canberra, ACT: ANU.

Austin-Broos, D. (2005). Introduction. In D. Austin-Broos & G. MacDonald (Eds), *Culture, economy and governance in Indigenous Australia* (pp. 1–5). Sydney, NSW: Sydney University Press.

Austin-Broos, D. (2006). 'Working for' and 'working' among Western Arrente in central Australia. *Oceania, 76*(1), 1–15.

Australian Government. (2014). *Green paper on developing Northern Australia.* Canberra, ACT: Department of the Prime Minister and Cabinet. Retrieved from www.industry.gov.au/sites/default/files/2019-09/green-paper-on-developing-northern-australia.pdf

Baker, R., Davies, J. & Young, E. (2001). *Contemporary Indigenous management of Australia's lands and coastal regions.* Melbourne, Vic.: Oxford University Press.

Bureau of Infrastructure, Transport and Regional Economics. (2014). *The evolution of Australian towns* (Report 136). Canberra, ACT: Department of Infrastructure and Regional Development.

Connolly, E. & Orsmond, D. (2011). The mining industry: From bust to boom. In *The Australian economy in the 2000s.* Sydney, NSW: Reserve Bank of Australia.

Deane, P. (2014). *Molehill to mountain: Agriculture in Northern Australia.* Melbourne, Vic.: ANZ Bank Co.

Department of Regional Development. (2013). *Regional price index 2013.* Perth, WA: Department of Regional Development, Government of Western Australia.

Dyer, R., Jacklyn, P., Partridge, I., Russell-Smith, J. & Williams, D. (2001). *Savanna burning: Understanding and using fire in Northern Australia*. Darwin, NT: Tropical Savannas CRC.

Edwards, J. (2014). *Beyond the boom. A Lowy Institute paper*. Melbourne, Vic.: Penguin Books.

Gerritsen, R. (2006). A resilient future for Northern Australian? People, economics and policy issues. In N. Stacey, G. Boggs, B. Campbell & W. Steffan (Eds), *Prepare for impact! When people and the environment collide in the tropics* (pp. 4–10). Darwin, NT: Charles Darwin University Press.

Gerritsen, R. (2010). A post-colonial model for north Australian political economy: The case of the Northern Territory. In R. Gerritsen (Ed.), *North Australian political economy: Issues and agendas* (pp. 18–40). Darwin, NT: Charles Darwin University Press.

Gerritsen, R. & Straton, A. (2007). Coping with a tragedy of the Australian Aboriginal common. In A. Smajgl & S. Larson (Eds), *Sustainable resource use: Institutional dynamics and economics* (pp. 162–176). London, England: Earthscan.

Gregory, R. (2005). Between a rock and a hard place: Economic policy and the employment outlook for Indigenous Australians. In D. Austin-Broos & G. MacDonald (Eds), *Culture, economy and governance in Indigenous Australia* (pp. 135–150). Sydney, NSW: Sydney University Press.

Jones, T. (1987). *Pegging the Northern Territory: A history of mining in the Northern Territory, 1870–1946*. Darwin, NT: Northern Territory Government Printer.

McRae-Williams, E. & Gerritsen, R. (2010). Mutual incomprehension: The cross cultural domain of work in a remote Australian Aboriginal community. *International Indigenous Policy Journal, 1*(2). doi.org/10.18584/iipj.2010.1.2.2

Memmott, P., Long, S. & Thomson, L. (2006). *Indigenous mobility in rural and remote Australia* (Final Report No. 90). Melbourne, Vic.: Australian Housing and Urban Research Institute. Retrieved from www.ahuri.edu.au/research/final-reports/90

Morphy, H. (2005). Indigenous art as economy. In D. Austin-Broos & G. MacDonald (Eds), *Culture, economy and governance in Indigenous Australia* (pp. 19–28). Sydney, NSW: Sydney University Press.

Rayner, J. & Bishop, R. (2013). *Industry dimensions of the resource boom: An input-output analysis*. Sydney, NSW: Reserve Bank of Australia.

Rothwell, N. (2015, 2–3 May). Wilful blindness. *The Weekend Australian*.

Russell-Smith, J., Whitehead, P. & Cooke, P. (2009). *Culture, ecology and economy of fire management in north Australian savannas: Rekindling the Wurrk tradition*. Collingwood, Vic.: CSIRO Publishing.

Salmon, M. & Gerritsen, R. (2013). A more effective means of delivering conservation management: A 'new integrated conservation' model for Australian rangelands. *The Rangeland Journal*, *35*(2), 225–230. doi.org/10.1071/RJ12080

Scambery, B. (2013). *My country, mine country: Indigenous people, mining and development contestation in remote Australia*. Centre for Aboriginal Economic Policy Research Series No. 33. Canberra, ACT: ANU E Press. doi.org/10.22459/CAEPR33.05.2013

Stanley, O. (2010). Mining and Aboriginal economic development: Expectations unfulfilled. In R. Gerritsen (Ed.), *North Australian political economy: Issues and agendas* (pp. 130–141). Darwin, NT: Charles Darwin University Press.

Stoeckl, N., Esparon, M., Farr, M., Delisle, A. & Stanley, O. (2014). The great asymmetric divide: An empirical investigation of the link between Indigenous and non-Indigenous economic systems in Northern Australia. *Papers in Regional Science*, *93*(4), 783–801. doi.org/10.1111/pirs.12028

Taylor, A., Bell, L. & Gerritsen, R. (2014). Benefits of skilled migration programs for regional Australia: Perspectives from the Northern Territory. *Journal of Economic and Social Policy*, *16*(1), Article 3.

# 6

# Issues in the Future Directions of Tourism in Northern Australia

Bruce Prideaux, Benxiang Zeng and Sharon Harwood

## Introduction

The aim of this chapter is to raise a number of questions about the future direction of tourism in Northern Australia. As the following discussion highlights, little attention has been given to diagnosing the causes of market failure over the last decade or identifying new directions that the industry could take into the future apart from ongoing calls for additional marketing support or various forms of boosterism expenditure by the public sector. The chapter briefly considers the evidence to support the contention of market failure, examines the impact of externalities and the need for greater attention to competitiveness, examines the role of change, briefly reviews research (Prideaux, 2013a) that supports these views and suggests strategies that could be employed to address this issue. The discussion is supported by a case study that examines how many of these factors have affected the delivery of Indigenous tourism experiences in Alice Springs.

An analysis of general visitor tends in Northern Australia over the last two decades paints a picture of a tourism sector that has achieved limited growth or stagnated in some areas and is in a state of decline in others. More recently, the decline in the Australian dollar from 2014 and several new hotel developments in Cairns indicate grounds for some optimism that a new phase of growth may be possible. For most of the region, however, this is not the case. As a region, the situation looks even worse when compared to the growth of global tourism over the corresponding period. It also appears that the future role of tourism as an economic sector in the study region needs to be re-evaluated. Decision-making in these circumstances requires an understanding of the destination's comparative and competitive advantages, level of competitiveness, realistic assessment of tourist push factors (supply-side characteristics) in existing and potential markets, realistic assessment of the drawing power of the region's pull factors (demand-side perspectives), issues related to long-term economic and environmental sustainability, the involvement of the local community and an in-depth understanding of the structure of current and possible future markets. The following discussion will highlight a range of issues that the authors feel are central to identifying the causes of this situation and suggest questions that should be addressed when the future of the tourism sector is considered from a policy perspective.

## The Study Region

For the purposes of this research, the study region comprises three subregions based on state and territory political boundaries: Broome in Western Australia (WA), the entire Northern Territory (NT) and Tropical North Queensland centred on Cairns and including the Cassowary Coast Regional Council in the south, the Torres Strait Islands and Cape York and west to Burke Shire Council. State administrative control of both Broome and Tropical North Queensland is exercised by governments located in capital cities well outside the study area and all three regions are affected by decisions made in Canberra and domestic and international market forces. From a domestic tourism perspective, these subregions are generally seen, and marketed, as three distinct destinations. They also occupy a peripheral location in relation to domestic and international tourism markets.

One outcome of this policy environment is that many of the decisions that affect the study region are made within a state/territory or federal policy context where there is often limited understanding of the specific issues at a regional level and limited intergovernmental cooperation between local governments at state/territory level, between states and the territory, and between states/territory and the federal government. This situation has been described by Chaperon and Bramwell (2013) as being one of dependency where the periphery depends on the core (usually metropolitan cities) for economic leadership. The centralisation of decision-making in capital cities that is characteristic of the public sector is usually replicated by the private sector. Centralisation of this nature limits the ability of the region as a whole to engage with and influence political and economic decision-makers.

Within the study region the main tourism destinations are Darwin and Alice Springs in the NT, Broome in WA and Cairns in Tropical North Queensland; however, significant tourism activity also occurs in areas outside of these cities. Access to the study region is generally by air for long-haul domestic and international visitors, although significant numbers of domestic visitors travel by road and in more limited numbers by coach and rail. Short-haul or intra-regional travel is generally by road.

## Tourism Trends

The two-decade period from 2000 to 2020 was a turbulent period for tourism in northern Australia, a result of the loss of some international markets, the 9/11 terrorist attack on the USA, the Global Financial Crisis (2007–08), the rise and then decline in the value of the Australian dollar associated with the resources boom and, more recently, the COVID-19 pandemic. In Darwin, combined domestic and international arrivals fell from 574,000 in 2000 to 409,000 in 2016/17 before rebounding later in the decade. In the same two-decade period, global international arrivals more than doubled from 697 million in 2000 to 1.5 billion in 2019 (United Nations World Tourism Organization, 2020). In the same period international arrivals in Australia also doubled, increasing from 4.9 million in 2000 to 9.5 million in 2019 (Tourism Australia, 2020). These figures indicate that in the international market the region has rapidly lost market share over the two decades.

Although Cairns has avoided long-term decline to date, widespread coral bleaching in 2016, 2017 and 2020 highlighted the dependence of the city on the ongoing health of the Great Barrier Reef as a key destination pull factor. A report (Prideaux et al., 2018) on the impact of the 2016 and 2017 coral bleaching events found that Cairns and other coral reef–dependent destinations may experience a significant and sustained decline in international arrivals if further coral bleaching events occur in the near future.

# Competitiveness, Externalities and Change

Analysis of the trends outlined above raises a number of issues that need to be addressed by the tourism sector, the public sector and the host communities who rely on tourism for employment. In economic terms, the basic issues revolve around an imbalance in demand and supply, and on a broader scale relate to the long-term ecological, and in some cases cultural, sustainability of tourism in the study area, the desire of communities to continue to promote tourism as an economic sector, government policy directions and changing consumer demand for tourism experiences.

How individual subregions respond to change is important. For example, analysis of visitor trends over the last decade indicates that previously popular experiences have experienced a decline in demand or have not been refreshed in a manner that continues to attract substantial visitor interest. In the former case, where demand has declined, the most effective response may be to develop new tourism experiences to replace the inventory of unpopular experiences. In the latter case, the most appropriate response is to rejuvenate experiences to bring them into line with contemporary market expectations.

Not all changes in demand can be attributed to changes in the way visitors wish to engage in tourism activities. From a tourism perspective, changes in air services have had a major impact in both the NT and Cairns. For example, over the last decade, Qantas and Jetstar have reduced, deleted and later reinstated many services between Cairns and Japan. Alice Springs has faced similar problems with air connectivity. The rapid growth of new domestic markets and international destinations has also had an impact as has the rapid growth in low-cost carriers in the period since 2000. A large range of externalities must also be considered, including changes in exchange rates, political uncertainties, new and sometimes disruptive technologies and a series of global crisis events. The nature of tourism markets is also changing, driven by innovation, economic growth in many developing countries and evolving consumer tastes for lifestyle experiences such as gastronomy and wellness. Collectively, these factors have impacted on the competitiveness of the tourism industry.

Movements in the value of the Australian dollar in the 2007–17 period illustrate the impact that externalities can have on tourism. The rapid rise in value of the Australian dollar from January 2007 (A$1 = US$0.74) reduced the competitiveness of the tourism sector both domestically and internationally. The decline in the value of the Australian dollar between January 2013 (A$1 = US$1.03) and January 2018 (A$1 = US$0.74) had the reverse effect and increased the region's competitiveness. If the region is able to take advantage of the decline in the dollar, opportunities to attract domestic tourists and capture a greater share of the international market should emerge.

A number of researchers have focused on the concept of destination competitiveness (Dwyer et al., 2000) as a way of understanding how destinations evolve. Competitiveness may be assessed in a number of ways using metrics including visitor numbers, yield, growth in bed nights, profitability and investment, or in terms of comparative and completive advantages. Hassan (2000, p. 239) defined competitiveness as 'the destination's ability to create and integrate value-added products that sustain its resources while maintaining market position relative to competitors'. However, despite the growing interest in the notion of competitiveness a definitive model has yet to emerge, occasioning Dwyer and Kim (2003, p. 373) to comment: 'It is a complex concept because a whole range of factors account for it'. From another perspective, and one that has major implications for the study region, Ritchie and Crouch (2000, p. 5) commented that 'competitiveness is illusory without sustainability', indicating the need to closely monitor environmental carrying capacity at sensitive sites.

At a destination level, competitiveness can be described as the ability of a destination to identify its key selling propositions, identify markets that are likely to purchase these propositions, create a market space where these products are able to be purchased, identify change and future threats and have the ability to maintain this process over a long period of time in a manner that is both environmentally and economically sustainable (Prideaux et al., 2014). As consumption patterns change and consumers respond to innovation, comply with new regulatory requirements, adjust to personal and national financial conditions and adapt to ever-changing patterns of national culture and society, markets are forced to evolve or wither. In future, the need to adapt to changes in ecosystems and the visual environment driven by climate change is likely to have profound impacts not only on how the region is marketed but how it is protected and able to be used as a tourism resource (Williams et al., 2003).

Meeting the challenges of changing patterns of demand for tourism experiences and the impact of externalities that may affect the tourism sector requires an ongoing process of regular re-evaluation of key attractions and experiences, partnerships (domestic and international), competitors, potential new markets and planning to deal with the unexpected. Failure to adopt a strategy that incorporates these elements and recognise the needs for regional, inter-regional, state and national cooperation of this type can lead to reduced competitiveness, loss of opportunities and, possibly, long-term decline. Figure 6.1 attempts to outline why it is important to take a long-term view that is informed by past and emerging trends that are apparent in the present. Seen from the perspective of the present, the future has a number of alternatives that will be based on the decisions taken in the present timespace. The direction to be taken will in part be informed by a range of constraints as illustrated in Figure 6.1. Failure to make informed decisions about a desirable future has the potential to lead to an undesirable future.

While the most widely accepted strategies for the tourism sector both domestically and internationally focus on long-term growth in visitor numbers, growth may not always be the best alternative. In setting long-term targets there is a need to also consider community views, environmental capacity and the desirability of aiming for enhanced yields and/or longer visits rather than greater visitor numbers. Given that the study region is located in the national periphery and major decisions relating to infrastructure, planning and policy are made in the core, it is often difficult for subregions to either develop in a way they consider appropriate to their specific needs or to have their voice heard in the debates that ultimately determine policy directions. Overcoming problems of this nature are not easy and require skilful negotiation.

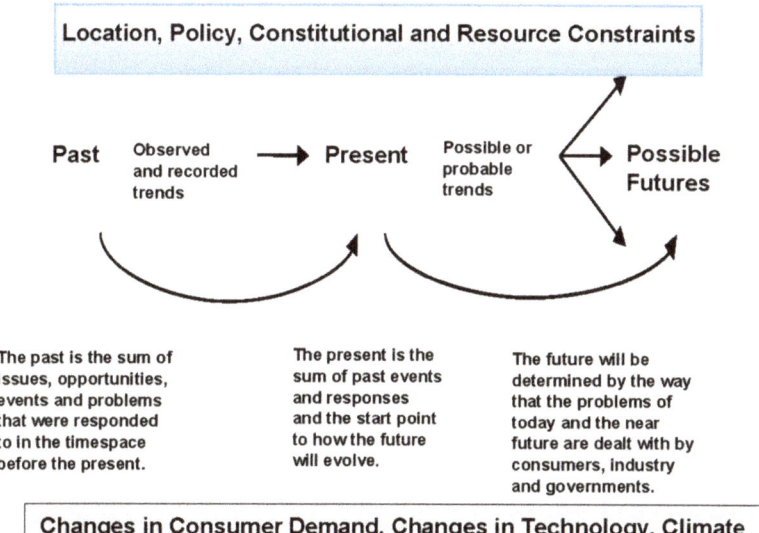

**Figure 6.1: The relationship between the past, present and future in linear time.**
Source: Adapted from Prideaux (2013a).

One model that may assist in understanding how a destination's past performance has the potential to influence the future is the push–pull model. Push factors originate in the demand side and are defined as factors that encourage people to travel for reasons such as the need for rest, relaxation, adventure, prestige and social interaction (Dann, 1977). Pull factors (Dann 1977; Crompton, 1979) originate in the supply side and include features and attributes of a destination including nature, cost, heritage and landscapes (Klenosky, 2002). A number of authors (Klenosky 2002; Cha et al., 1995) have commented that while push and pull factors may be viewed as two separate groups of consumer decisions, they are actually interdependent as consumers may simultaneously be pushed by their own internal desires and pulled by the attributes of the destination. Changing consumer demand is reflected in the push side of the model while the response to changes of this type can be observed in the pull side. Failure to respond to changes in consumer push factors may result in stagnation or decline.

Understanding the complexity of the relationships that exist between consumer demand and the willingness of destinations to refresh existing products and infrastructure and create new products is an essential start point for applying the model to the study region in the near future. Given the options that exist for future directions of both public and private sector investment, some understanding of the options available for the future is essential.

## Tourism Sector Stakeholder Views

A 2013 report (Prideaux, 2013a) examined the views of industry, government and academic respondents about the long-term environmental and economic issues facing the study region. Interviews were conducted in Darwin, Broome, Brisbane, Alice Springs, Brisbane, Gold Coast, Perth and Canberra. Results indicated that, with few exceptions, innovation has largely stalled and that overall there was a limited vision of the future mainly because of the reactive nature of the tourism industry's responses to market stagnation over the last decade. This is in stark contrast to the two decades commencing in 1980 when significant private and public investment underpinned the rapid growth of nature-based tourism across the study region. Since the publication of the report, the value of the Australian dollar has declined, enhancing the competitiveness of the region. However, the threat of future coral bleaching events and possible loss of the Chinese inbound market post COVID-19 may inhibit further growth unless new tourism experiences are developed.

Overall, however, the current situation is best summed up by the following statement:

> There appears to be a reluctance to accept that past plans and policies had failed to ignite growth or that the region's traditional product mix largely based on nature based tourism has consistently failed to stimulate a new phase of growth. The need for new activities and experiences to augment the study region's current suite of environmental experiences has not been widely recognised. (Prideaux, 2013a, p. 37)

Until the imbalance between the region's main pull factors and consumers' push factors is addressed, stagnation or decline will define the sector into the future.

Other points highlighted in the report (p. 38) include:

- the region's natural environment is currently being used in a sustainable manner
- there are concerns that insufficient resources have been allocated to the ongoing maintenance of the region's protected areas including combatting the Crown of Thorns Starfish, which can dramatically reduce coral cover, and control of invasive species such as crazy ants, which may adversely affect rainforest ecosystems
- as ecosystem resilience levels decline with increasing global warming, adjustments will need to be made to protected area boundaries to accommodate in and out migration of affected flora and fauna
- the potential for tourism may be affected as the carrying capacity of ecosystems decline
- there is a mismatch between consumer demand and what some subregions supply
- continued reliance on the region's ecosystems to attract tourists may lead to continuing decline, particularly if climate change begins to reduce the resilience of the region's ecosystems
- the long-term health of the region's tourism economy in part depends on the health of the region's ecosystem.

Previous research (McNamara & Prideaux, 2011) has highlighted the centrality of nature to the tourism experiences marketed by the tourism sector in Northern Australia. This being the case, the region faces either a situation where its natural experiences have become less appealing than in the past or the manner in which nature is presented is dated and needs to be refreshed. In Northern Australia, both trends appear to be occurring. In the NT, the decline in interest in nature-based experiences is demonstrated in Kakadu National Park where visitation has been steadily declining since the financial crisis of 2008. The following case study highlights the dilemma facing the region's tourism industry and also illustrates the type of solutions that may be required to reboot the tourism sector.

## Case Study: Alice Springs

This case study focuses on the area that includes Alice Springs Town, Central Desert Shire, McDonnell Range Shire and Yulara Management Area. Alice Springs has suffered a significant fall in international tourist arrivals in the past two decades with bed nights falling from 850,000 in 2010/11 to 445,00 in 2019/20 (Regional Development Australia, n.d.) Over the same period there was a very small increase in domestic bed nights from 925,000 to 1,060,000. Carson et al. (2012) attributed the decline in the city's tourism industry to its peripheral position, poorly defined marketing that has failed to recognise shifts in demand from mass tourism experiences to more niche experiences, a failure of the destination's large investors to rejuvenate their facilities and increasing social problems that have received international media coverage. Early in the first decade of this century, Alice Springs and the Petermann region ranked in the top 10 cultural tourism destinations for international visitors in Australia (Hossain et al., 2005).

Surprisingly, later research (Zeng et al., 2010) found that Indigenous culture was not included in the top attractions of the area. Although absent from the top of tourists' to-do lists, international visitors generally place a higher value on Indigenous culture and heritage than domestic visitors (Zeng et al., 2010). This in part supports the argument that developing Indigenous cultural tourism products is crucial for the international market. However, as international visitors comprise nearly a third of total visitors, there remains a need to balance cultural and nature-based tourism to both increase the area's attractiveness to international visitors and its appeal to domestic visitors.

Although many tourists have high expectations of experiencing Indigenous art and culture, a lack of engaging cultural experiences can lead to lower visitor satisfaction. Lack of access and information available on Indigenous cultural products and services might be one reason (Nielson Research, 2007). The dilemma here is that once tourists come to the region to seek Indigenous cultural experiences, they find themselves surrounded by Indigenous people but find it difficult to access Indigenous culture and daily life. This also suggests that the destination has not fully marketed its cultural dimensions and there has been an absence of culture-related tourism products. It might also point to a situation where many visitors do not fully realise the embodied cultural dimension of natural assets (e.g. the substantial association between Uluru and Indigenous culture). There also appears to be some difficulties in connecting Indigenous culture with natural assets. As a consequence, Indigenous culture is underproduced and opportunities for cultural experiences by visitors (especially for cultural visitors) are compromised. Indigenous culture is a part of real life in the region. One solution is to develop tourism experiences that broaden opportunities for engagement with Indigenous people. This could close the information asymmetry between tourism enterprises and tourists leading to a disconnection between supply and demands appears to be a problem.

In summary, market failure is evident through products failing to meet the expectations of some market segments; the disconnection and poor communication between products, services and tourists; and tourism marketing that seems not to engage local communities. There is also a clear disconnection between tourism markets and destination marketing.

While nature-based tourism is likely to continue to dominate, culture-based tourism can be developed as a complementary experience. The strategic development of both would provide an enhanced pull factor for the region and satisfy unmet demand suggesting scope for new products to supplement existing nature-based tourism.

The development of Indigenous cultural tourism products will require a shift from an emphasis on Indigenous artefacts to Indigenous cultural tours and interactive activities that integrate their cultural perspectives into specific landscapes or locations. A change of this nature will provide value-added products and generate benefits to Indigenous communities. Moreover, Indigenous tourism activity should not be seen as just activities that provide Indigenous experiences. Participation should be much broader and encompass the entire range of activities that constitute the tourism product.

In relation to Indigenous tourism, a participatory mechanism for local communities to engage in and benefit from tourism is critical. Enhancing opportunities for local Indigenous culture to contribute to tourism will not only encourage local Indigenous communities to participate in the tourism sector but will also appeal to cultural tourists and make a positive contribution to visitor numbers and expenditure.

To move forward on these issues will require identifying and acting on the causes of market failure (Carson et al., 2012). As part of this process, out-of-region research is required to identify how the region can use its comparative and competitive advantages to develop attractive pull factors that will appeal to contemporary visitors. This should be underpinned by consensus within the local community and Traditional Owners about the future 'look' of the regions' tourism industry. The next step will be to attract new investment and then promote the destination in appropriate market places.

# The Relationship between Change and the Future

Given that most of the study region's current stock of tourism experiences are nature centred, strategies for future development will need to consider long-term environmental sustainability as a key policy objective. Figure 6.1 highlighted the need to recognise the role of change. In the study region, three parallel though connected groups of change are occurring. The most obvious is the shift in consumer demand or push factors that have led to the current decline in demand for visiting some parts of the region. The second change that is beginning to occur is climate change, with evidence already emerging that elements of the future ecosystem will be different from those of the present. These changes, such as widespread coral bleaching on the Great Barrier Reef in 2016, 2017 and 2020, will necessitate a re-evaluation of the capacity of the future ecosystem to be used as a tourism experience. The third change is less obvious and concerns the conditions that have shaped human society in the past and will reshape society in the future (Prideaux, 2013b). Factors that will reshape the future include the transition to a net zero carbon economy, climate change, rapid urbanisation, ageing society, disruptive technologies such as autonomous electric vehicles and peaks such as peak land and peak water (see Figure 6.1).

The first group of changes focused on consumer push factors and is the most immediate and perhaps the easiest to deal with. Changing demand patterns for the consumption of natural experiences is one factor that has yet to be given serious attention. Most visitors to the region are from cities where nature takes a very different form to that experienced in the study region. Urban nature is manicured, ordered, constructed and non-threatening. Nature in the study region is the complete opposite—chaotic, untamed and, in some areas, threatening. Reconciling the two realities of nature, the tamed nature of the city and the untamed nature of the bush, creates a central dilemma for the region's tourism industry but must be addressed to deal effectively with the expectations of nature and how it is enjoyed by city dwellers. This will require the development of new products to enable urbanites to experience tropical nature within their personal comfort zones. From the push perspective of the region's visitors, there is an expectation that the region will provide at least similar levels of the lifestyle amenities that define everyday life in the city in areas such as dining experiences, coffee, shopping, entertainment, access to Wi-Fi and so on. Failure to offer lifestyle amenities at least at a level equivalent to the city not only reduces competitiveness vis-a-vis competing destinations but may also give an impression of backwardness. In this sense, the solution to identifying and rectifying some of the region's current problems lies in understanding the customer, where they come from and their expectations. Responding to these will require a re-engineering of the product offerings and experiences of the tourism sector in the study region. This might not be overly difficult and could, for example, start with relatively easy-to-implement initiatives such as service training for staff; re-engineering menus; rethinking product offerings in shops; and enhanced public amenities, opening hours and length of tours. It is already apparent that many businesses in the region have recognised this need, hence the growing number of personal services businesses such as wellness experiences.

Change is often a disruptive force that affects long-term demand and supply relationships and causes rapid shifts in the equilibrium position of the tourism sector. As demand and supply relationships change, new windows of opportunities emerge, some of which will replace previous markets. The shape of the future will arguably be ongoing interplay between change and at least four groups of drivers (Prideaux, 2013a):

1. The structure of contemporary society including governmental structures, institutions, society, legal systems, national culture and economy. The interplay of these factors provides the framework around which problems are identified, responded to and evaluated.
2. The version of the future that contemporary society and industry has adopted as its preferred course of progress. Without a vision of a preferred future, response to change is likely to be ad hoc and may

not deliver the desired results. Agreement on a specific version of the future creates a set of targets that can guide how the issues of today are addressed.

3. The manner in which change affects societies. The process of identifying change and recognising ongoing implications is important but often ignored until it is too late to channel change in a positive manner.

4. How society responds to change. Responses will include policy adjustments, investment by both the private and public sectors, innovation and adjustment of lifestyles.

To these need to be added a fifth external driver linked to climate change, which will eventually affect all human systems and force rapid adjustments to economic and social systems and urban settlement patterns. The change likely to occur in global economic production systems is a transition to a net zero carbon economy such as the circular economy based on renewable energy sources and extensive recycling.

## Discussion and Conclusion

It is apparent that stakeholders in the region need to consider how to respond to the problems that currently exist, and the responses to them will create, or extinguish, options for a different future. As part of this response a range of questions (Prideaux, 2013a) need to be considered by the public and private sectors and the region's community in relation to how the study region may respond to current visitor trends and to the changes that are currently taking place:

1. Why has anticipated growth largely failed to occur?
2. Is further growth achievable?
3. Is growth necessarily the best course for the future?
4. In the future, what externalities will have the greatest impact on tourism markets?
5. If growth is the best option, how can the study region's competitive position be strengthened?

These questions need to be addressed prior to further strategy development and will not be a simple task because the tourism sector has yet to accept the need for rejuvenation and the public sector has failed to recognise that the appeal of nature needs to be re-evaluated and presented in a form that appeals to contemporary consumers. Fundamental to any strategies and initiatives by either the public or private sectors is the need to understand the contemporary visitor and provide them with experiences they desire. This is not an easy task, particularly as visitor tastes are constantly changing. As of 2020, it appears that some parts of the region continue to experience difficulties in responding to changing customer expectations. Rectifying this situation will require action at both a strategic level and tactical level. At the strategic level, actions should include determining the long-term role of tourism in the regional economy and building appropriate infrastructure. At the tactical level, actions may include refurbishing existing infrastructure and marketing. Enablers required to achieve strategic and tactical objectives include funding to investigate new markets, building a visitor monitoring system that enables early detection of changes in demand and encouragement of the supply side to respond to changes in tourism demand by changing their product offering.

Irrespective of the direction that is determined to be the most appropriate for the region, a number of actions are required to guide the strategies that are adopted:

- develop a vision for the tourism industry that recognises its unique culture, landscapes, ecosystems and the quality of supporting infrastructure including attractions, accommodation and food and beverage infrastructure
- develop an intergovernmental and multi-sector mechanism for strategy coordination at regional, state and national levels
- establish a research capability able to support the region's tourism industry including the identification of new visitor markets and experiences such as Indigenous culture
- establish an ongoing monitoring mechanism to provide feedback on current trends.

Failure to incorporate these actions into future planning runs the risk of the future mirroring the past with destination pull factors failing to align with consumer push factors and below optimum levels of competitiveness.

The aim of this chapter was to raise a series of questions about the future direction of tourism in Northern Australia. As the discussion has indicated, part of the problem for the region as a whole is a collective failure to adequately respond to changing visitor demands. Responding to change will require the region as a whole to rethink the way it structures and delivers its experiences and visitor services. However, as the chapter argues, change is an ongoing process and for the region to both meet the challenge of change and to thrive in a future world that is constantly undergoing new threats and new challenges the region must first determine the future shape of its tourism sector and then establish and manage a pathway to the future that is forward thinking, rather than reactive.

## References

Carson, D., Carson, D., Cartan, G. & Vilkinas, T. (2012). *Research brief 201205: Saving Alice Springs tourism: Why it will never 'bounce back'—but might leap forward*. Retrieved from www.cdu.edu.au/sites/default/files/The%20Northern%20Institute/publications/Brief201205-Saving%20Alice%20Springs_leap%20forward%20not%20bounce%20backFinal.pdf

Cha, S., McCleary, K. & Uysal, M. (1995). Travel motivations of Japanese overseas travellers: A factor-cluster segmentation approach. *Journal of Travel Research*, *34*(2), 33–39.

Chaperon, S. & Bramwell, B. (2013). Dependency and agency in peripheral tourism development. *Annals of Tourism Research*, *40*, 132–154.

Crompton, J. (1979). Motivations for pleasure vacation. *Annals of Tourism Research*, *6*(4), 408–424.

Dann, G. (1977). Anomie, ego-enhancement and tourism. *Annals of Tourism Research*, *4*(4), 184–194.

Dwyer, L., Forsyth, P. & Rao, P. (2000). The price competitiveness of travel and tourism: A comparison of 19 destinations. *Tourism Management*, *21*(1), 9–22. doi.org/10.1016/S0261-5177(99)00081-3

Dwyer, L. & Kim, C. (2003). Destination competitiveness: Determinants and indicators. *Current Issues in Tourism*, *6*(5), 369–414. doi.org/10.1080/13683500308667962

Hassan, S. (2000). Determinants of market competitiveness in an environmentally sustainable tourism industry. *Journal of Travel Research*, *38*(3), 239–245. doi.org/10.1177/004728750003800305

Hossain, A., Heaney, L. & Carter, P. (2005). *Cultural tourism in regions of Australia*. Canberra, ACT: Tourism Research Australia.

Klenosky, D. (2002). The 'pull' of tourism destinations: A means-end investigation. *Journal of Travel Research, 40*, 385–395.

McNamara, K. & Prideaux, B. (2011). Planning nature based hiking trails—in a tropical rainforest setting. *Asia Pacific Journal of Tourism Research, 16*, 289–305.

Nielson Research. (2007). *Destination visitor survey—Indigenous cultural experiences: Summary of results.* Darwin, NT: Tourism NT.

Northern Territory Government. (2017). *Tourism NT annual report 2016.* Darwin, NT: Tourism NT.

Prideaux, B. (2013a). *An investigation into factors that may affect the long term environmental and economic sustainability of tourism in Northern Australia.* Cairns, Qld: James Cook University.

Prideaux, B. (2013b). Climate change and peak oil—two large-scale disruptions likely to adversely affect long-term tourism growth in the Asia Pacific. *Journal of Destination Marketing and Management, 2*(3), 132–136.

Prideaux, B., Berbigier, D. & Thompson, M. (2014). Wellness tourism and destination competitiveness. In C. Voigt & C. Pforr (Eds), *Wellness tourism: A destination perspective* (pp. 45–60). Oxon, England: Routledge.

Prideaux, B., Cassidy, J. & Pabel, A. (2018). *Impacts of the 2016 and 2017 mass coral bleaching events on the Great Barrier Reef tourism industry and tourism-dependent coastal communities of Queensland.* Retrieved from www.rrrc.org.au/wp-content/uploads/2018/11/RRRC-Impacts-2016-17-Coral-Bleaching-on-GBR-Digital.pdf

Regional Development Australia. (n.d.). *Alice Springs Town Council LGA: Tourism visitor summary.* Retrieved from economy.id.com.au/rda-northern-territory/tourism-visitor-summary?WebID=100

Ritchie, J. R. B. & Crouch, G. I. (2000). The competitive destination: A sustainability perspective. *Tourism Management, 21*(1), 1–7. doi.org/10.1016/S0261-5177(99)00093-X

Tourism Australia. (2020). *International market performance statistics.* Retrieved from www.tourism.australia.com/en/markets-and-stats/tourism-statistics/international-market-performance.html

Tourism NT. (2012). *Custom report: Central Australia Indigenous tourism visitors.*

Tourism NT. (2014a). *NT snapshot: Quick stats year end June 2014.*

Tourism NT. (2014b). *Tourism NT regional report Alice Springs and surrounds, April 2014.*

Tourism Research Australia (TRA). (2012). *Central Australia visitor profile and satisfaction report: Summary and discussion of results.* Canberra, ACT: Tourism Research Australia.

Tourism Research Australia (TRA). (2014). *Northern Territory visitor touch points: Executive summary.*

Tourism WA. (2018). *Australia's north west: 2017 factsheet.*

United Nations World Tourism Organization. (2020, 20 January). *International tourism growth continues to outpace the global economy.* Retrieved from www.unwto.org/international-tourism-growth-continues-to-outpace-the-economy

Williams, S., Bolitho, E. & Fox, S. (2003). Climate change in Australian tropical rainforests: An impending environmental catastrophe. *Proceedings of the Royal Society of London Series B, Biological Sciences, 270*(1527), 1887–1892. doi.org/10.1098/rspb.2003.2464

Zeng, B., Gerritsen, R. & Stoeckl, N. (2010). Contribution of Indigenous culture to tourism development. *International Journal of Cultural & Tourism Research, 3*(1), 165–185.

# 7

# Economic Equity and Major Development

Natalie Stoeckl

## Introduction

It does not matter whether one looks at labour income, non-labour income or different measures of income/wealth concentration, inequality has been increasing within and across many countries throughout the last few decades (Jaumotte et al., 2013). Australia is no exception. On some measures, Australia is more unequal than the majority of other OECD countries (specifically, the gap between the poorest and the richest 10 per cent of households) and regional inequality has also risen sharply in recent times (Rodriguez-Pose, 2012). Most notable has been the rise in the share of total income that has gone to the richest 1 per cent of Australians; in 1980, the richest 1 per cent received just 5 per cent of all income, but by 2008 the richest 1 per cent were receiving almost 12 per cent of income—the fourth highest of all OECD countries (Hoeller et al., 2012). Thus, despite Australia's progressive tax system and targeted cash transfers, which seek to redistribute incomes, its above-average wage dispersion and large share of part-time/casual workers (Watson, 2013) mean that household disposable incomes are unevenly distributed and are becoming even more unequal over time (Hoeller et al., 2012).

This recent increase in inequality is likely to have surprised earlier generations of economists, primarily because Kuznets (1955) observed that, in the United States, England and Germany, increases in inequality occurred during the early periods of urbanisation and industrialisation, but inequality fell once each country reached a certain level of prosperity. Yet, despite the fact that early empirical tests were largely supportive of the Kuznets hypothesis in a variety of different contexts (Ahluwalia, 1976; Papanek & Kyn, 1986; Campano & Salvatore, 1988), more recent studies have not found evidence of diminishing inequality beyond a given income level (e.g. Anand & Kanbur, 1993; Deininger & Squire, 1998). Recent research indicates that, contrary to the Kuznets hypothesis (which presumes that inequality is determined by economic growth), inequality and growth are jointly determined and dependent on preferences and choices of economic agents (Cheng, 2006; Yang & Zhang, 2003). The policy implication is that one cannot simply aim for economic growth hoping that inequality will (eventually) look after itself. If one cares about inequality (for any reason), one may need to take a more nuanced look at growth and development.

After discussing some of the costs of inequality (thus, establishing the need to consider it), this chapter briefly reviews literature that seeks to understand its causes, noting that inequality is often exacerbated by growth of high-tech industries, which increase the demand for (and wages of) skilled workers. It discusses that problem in the context of the Northern Australia development agenda, which has, among other foci, the goal of promoting growth by facilitating the development of large-scale (often high-tech) projects within the agribusiness, mining and energy sectors and, thus, may unintentionally serve to widen the gap between rich and poor in this region. It then proposes processes that would ameliorate the rising inequality likely to accompany such developments, suggesting ways in which those projects could become more financially connected to the communities within which they operate.

## The Cost of Inequality

Arguably, there appears to be more public concern with economic growth than with equality; compare the number of times, for example, that the media reports on (growth of) GDP versus the number of times the media reports on the gap between rich and poor. This is despite the fact that a wide body of research, going back as far as Pigou in the 1920s, has suggested that it is not just the amount of money one earns that is important, but the amount one earns when compared to other people. Feelings about the importance of fairness are commonplace (Fehr &

Schmidt, 1999; Dawes et al., 2007)—not just among humans but among monkeys (Brosnan & de Waal, 2003) and other animals. As such, failure to address inequity may generate social unrest (Wilkinson, 1996). Even those who do not feel that fairness is an important goal by and of itself may have good cause to worry about excessive concentration of wealth, since inequality has been linked to numerous social ills, including but not limited to crime, violence, drug abuse and large prison populations (Wilkinson, 1996; Wilkinson & Pickett, 2010). Inequality has also been linked to school bullying (Elgar et al., 2013) and, in developing countries, to poor health outcomes (Leigh et al., 2009). Prisons, lawyers, police officers and security guards and health services are not free, so inequality imposes costs on society (Detotto & Otranto, 2010; Cohen, 2012), often indirectly by placing pressure on government budgets.

Moreover, marginalised groups lack resilience and/or adaptive capacity and often live in regions (e.g. floodplains) that are particularly vulnerable to external shocks such as floods (Brouwer et al., 2009). These groups may require more government assistance to facilitate recuperation to unexpected shocks than less marginalised groups (Jaumotte et al., 2013), placing further strain on government budgets. Further, inequality of outcome is often associated with inequality of opportunity, which has long-term ramifications. It has been argued, for example, that low-income families are not be able to afford the same quality of education for their children as high-income families (Bailey & Dynarski, 2011; Duncan & Murnane, 2014). As such, today's unequal outcomes will contribute to tomorrow's unequal opportunities. This limits the growth potential of entire economies since not all members are able to fully contribute to or exploit emerging opportunities (Jaumotte et al., 2013).

Inequality is particularly profound in Northern Australia (Taylor et al., 2011). On one hand, it is the location of numerous mines with income-advantaged workers (Baum, 2006). But on the other, it is also home to some of the country's most disadvantaged people (as shown in the Australian Bureau of Statistics SEIFA indices) and many of the country's children most at risk of social exclusion (Tanton et al., 2009). Indeed, at least one-quarter of Australia's northern population belongs to the country's most socioeconomically disadvantaged and vulnerable group of people—Aboriginal and Torres Strait Islanders (Carson et al., 2009). Many of these Indigenous people live in abject poverty (Hunter, 1999), despite concerted policy attempts to 'close the gap'—a policy goal that many feel is largely unachievable within the near future (see, for example, Taylor &

Hunter, 1998; Hunter & Gray, 1999; Altman et al., 2008; Altman, 2009; Pholi et al., 2009). And the costs of that poverty are evident. There are, for example, significant differences in the life expectancy of Indigenous and non-Indigenous people (AIHW, 2010). There are also significant opportunity costs associated with this inequality; Taylor and Stanley (2005) estimate that the opportunity cost of poverty in just one remote Aboriginal settlement in Northern Territory likely exceeds A$40 million per annum (measured as the value of foregone production).

In short, inequality imposes costs on society. If policymakers are able to choose between two different development proposals, it is clear that (all else equal) they should choose that which does most to redress inequality. This requires a more nuanced understanding of the link between economic growth and equality, a topic to which the next section turns.

## Causal Links between Economic Growth and Inequality

Decades of work by researchers using various simple and numerous highly sophisticated techniques to analyse firm-level and country-level data has shed much light on and raised many questions about the causes of inequality, of which there are many. There is evidence to suggest, for example, that decentralisation may increase regional disparities (Ezcurra & Rodriguez-Pose, 2013). Trade is thought to increase regional inequalities in low-middle-income countries that are strongly integrated with the rest of the world, but trade has, in other circumstances, been associated with reduced inequality (Rodriguez-Pose, 2012; Jaumotte et al., 2013). Globalisation is also believed to have an important role to play—off-shoring workers is a practice that tends to marginalise workers who perform routine tasks, multinational firms tend to employ more high-income earners than national firms and trade-induced innovation impacts relative wages (Harrison et al., 2010).

Considering all factors, the balance of research has suggested that recent worldwide increases in inequality are most significantly attributable to advances in technology (Jaumotte et al., 2013; Rodriguez-Pose, 2012). Evidently, it is growth of high-tech industries that is most likely to be associated with rising inequality. Formally, technology is believed to affect inequality because technological developments increase the demand for (and thus the incomes of) skilled workers much more than the demand for (and incomes of) unskilled workers. More recently, researchers have considered three groups of workers (low, middle and highly skilled) in more sophisticated models (Acemoglu & Autor, 2010), but agree that technological progress favours the highly skilled (Jaumotte et al., 2013; Rodriguez-Pose, 2012). Thus, growth that is led by technology is frequently accompanied by rising labour market inequalities.

In remote areas across Northern Australia, skilled workers are often imported from other areas. For example, most local government areas within the Northern Territory import more workers than they export (Blackwell et al., 2015) and Brokensha et al. (2013) reported that 4.5 per cent of the Northern Territory's (NT) workforce and 23 per cent of the NT's mining workforce (a high-tech industry in this part of the world) were 'fly-in fly-out', 'drive-in drive-out' or 'bus-in bus-out' employees. Crucially, highly skilled imported workers do not always add to total employment. In their case study of the health industry in Tennant Creek, Carson and Carson (2014, p. 347) reported that 'the highly mobile medical professional part of the workforce did not just supplement a resident workforce, it completely replaced it'.

Other researchers have reported net income leakages from across the remote north, particularly from regions in which mining companies operate (Blackwell et al., 2015). Inequalities are also evident within mining regions. Reeson et al. (2012), for example, compared mining activity with measures of income inequality for both males and females in 728 Australian regions. They found evidence to support the Kuznets hypothesis for males (i.e. low inequality with no mining, moderate inequality with some mining and low inequality with high levels of mining), but for females, increases in mining activity were everywhere associated with increases in inequality. Reeson et al. (2012) argued that these marked differences were linked to the labour market—males are more likely to be employed in mining or associated industries than females and, thus, are in a better position to be able to capture either direct or indirect benefits from industrial expansion.

Having no way of earning money locally (be it through the sale of labour, hire of land and equipment or the sale of other goods and services) is also what seems to drive the marked inequities that exist between Indigenous and non-Indigenous people in Northern Australia (Stoeckl, Esparon et al., 2013). Far fewer Indigenous people are employed within the private sector or are the owner/operator of private businesses than would be expected on a per-capita basis (Stoeckl et al., 2007; Biddle et al., 2008). So, when regional developments occur, far fewer Indigenous people are able to benefit (directly or indirectly) from those developments than non-Indigenous people.

Other individuals who are not financially connected to the rest of the economy may also reap few benefits from regional development. Simply put, if segments of society are precluded from working or owning businesses,[1] they will not be able to sell labour, goods or services to new developments or projects (either directly, or indirectly by participating further down the supply chain). Thus, they have no means of benefiting, financially, from the projects. So, unless development projects provide other (public) goods or services that benefit society as a whole (e.g. roads, ports, schools and hospitals) they will not benefit the marginalised.

Moreover, financially marginalised groups (those who reap few benefits from development) may also have external costs imposed on them, perhaps manifested as higher housing prices (Rolfe et al., 2007) or reduced environmental services (Stoeckl, Jackson et al., 2013). As such, it is possible that some within the community will incur net financial benefit from new developments while others will unambiguously lose. This issue likely explains at least some of the community backlash and discontent associated with new development proposals in regional Queensland. Rolfe et al. (2010) found that the indirect (flow-on) benefits associated with the mining-industry[2] were higher in Brisbane (where mining does not occur) than in the regional areas (where the impacts of mining are felt).

The key point to be made here is that unless one can find ways of forging strong financial connections between broad sectors of the community, large-scale development projects (particularly those involving new or advanced technology) may exacerbate regional inequalities, imposing hidden costs on the wider community. Methods for doing so are discussed in the next section.

---

1   This seems to be the case for Aboriginal people in particular (Biddle et al., 2008), be it because of discrimination or otherwise. Options for redressing such issues are discussed in the next section.
2   Formally, the multipliers.

## Key Policy Directions

There has been much attention focused on strategies for promoting economic growth in Australia's north (Liberal Party of Australia, 2013), not just for the benefit of the region but the country as a whole. Some of these strategies seek to determine how to encourage and facilitate the establishment of large-scale agribusiness, mining and resource projects (Australian Government, 2015) such as the gas pipeline between Tennant Creek and Mount Isa (ABC News, 2015) and the Adani coal mine in Queensland.

If these large-scale projects are assessed and implemented as isolated enclaves (Faal, 2007), the growth that they generate may be uneconomic (Daly & Farley, 2004) in that the costs of achieving such growth (including those associated with increased inequality) may exceed the benefits. To ensure that growth is genuinely economic (rather than uneconomic), projects should not just be selected on individual merit and should not just be subjected to the usual factors included in environmental or social impact assessments. They should also be assessed on their ability to reduce inequalities (or, at the very least, not to exacerbate them) by forging strong financial links with existing residents and businesses of Northern Australia.

This suggests a primary need to use metrics that enable one to assess the extent to which large-scale projects connect, financially, to the local economy (see Stoeckl, 2007, for one example). Such metrics should be used in conjunction with other information when assessing the desirability, or otherwise, of project proposals. They could also be used in long-term monitoring programs, perhaps setting targets for increased financial connectivity over time.

Supporting policies that could be put in place to help meet those targets include, but are not limited to:

- Implementing institutional reforms, particularly those relating to the ownership of core assets such as land and water. This is extremely important for Indigenous people, since ownership facilitates income (e.g. by charging other people rent to use the asset or by using it to produce money earning goods and services). The importance of reform is recognised as an important priority in documents related to northern development (Australian Government, 2015).

- Devising community consultation processes (prior to projects being approved) that are specifically designed to identify opportunities for local residents and businesses to forge financial connections with project proponents.[3] There will clearly be some goods (e.g. high technology pieces of capital equipment) that will need to be sourced from outside the region, but there are numerous other ways in which members of the community might connect to large-scale businesses. For example, one could consider options for supplying the food or running the dining hall for businesses that house workers on site in remote locations (which would be a relatively large business in a remote area; before ceasing operations, Century Zinc employed more than 750 people and the proposed Adani coal mine in Queensland could increase the local workforce by approximately 1,400[4]).

- Related to the above, one could devise programs that support the development of small businesses that supply goods and services to large-scale projects. A large percentage of first-time businesses that are operating in less economically challenging environments than Northern Australia (e.g. in urban areas) fail during their first year of operation (up to 70 per cent, see Shane, 2009). Moreover, research indicates that education levels, and access to finance are highly correlated with business outcomes (Doms et al., 2010). So, simply encouraging people to start small businesses, particularly people who are at socioeconomic disadvantage, without providing long-term training and support may be all but dooming them to fail. Instead, one needs to develop long-term programs that might initially involve training, education and work experience, but that would evolve over time, culminating in the situation where participants took over management and then ownership of businesses that supply the goods and/or services to the large-scale developments. For example, if seeking to help develop locally owned and managed businesses that supply food for miners, one could, in the first instance, provide training programs focused on local food production (e.g. establishment of market gardens). The programs could evolve to focus on issues related to quality control, packaging and transport, and then evolve once more to include business/financial training. This would, in essence, build the foundations for a local (food-related) business. Once operating confidently, further support

---

3   Current processes relating to Environmental Impact Assessments require community consultation, but do not require proponents to consider these issues.
4   Exact numbers are difficult to ascertain. See Campbell (2015).

could be given to those associated with that business, helping them, for example, to source food (which cannot be grown locally) from elsewhere in Australia and, ultimately, taking over the food supply part of the mining operation.

- Enacting positive discrimination policies for large-scale projects specifically designed to favour local or marginalised employees or suppliers. One could, for example, require that project proponents ensure that a certain percentage of employees come from (locally) marginalised groups. Or one could require that a given per cent of project expenditure is undertaken with local businesses. Care must be taken to ensure that such measures do not create long-term incentives for economically inefficient behaviours (see Fryer & Loury, 2005, for a good overview), but if enacted appropriately could prove to be an effective means of ensuring that even marginalised groups reap benefits from northern development.

## Concluding Comments

The historical philosophy derived from the Kuznets hypothesis—that there is no need to worry about inequality since economic growth will, in the end, redress inequality—has been subsumed by a growing realisation that economic growth often exacerbates inequality. Likewise, the historical focus on literature assuming a trade-off between growth and equality (such as that considering the inefficiencies of taxation[5]) has been subsumed by body of evidence that growth and equality are not mutually exclusive (Koske et al., 2012). We now know that economic growth does not guarantee equality and that it will, instead, often exacerbate inequality. We also know that inequality imposes costs on society, the policy implication being that failure to consider inequality when assessing the desirability or otherwise of development proposals may mean that Northern Australian growth is uneconomic.

The exciting corollary to this realisation is that economic developments that help reduce inequality may generate substantial benefits beyond those normally considered (e.g. less government taxes being spent on unemployment benefits, health or on crime and protection). Thus, the current focus on Northern Australia provides policy and other decision-

---

5   See Ahmad & Stern (1991), Auerbach & Hines (2002).

makers with a heady opportunity to identify development proposals that both increase incomes and reduce inequality by providing marginalised groups (Indigenous and otherwise) with opportunities to engage, financially, with large-scale projects. Not only will this serve a fairer pie to communities in the north, but it will serve a larger one.

# References

ABC News. (2015, 17 November). Asian conglomerate Jemena wins tender to build NEGI gas pipeline from Northern Territory to Queensland. Retrieved from www.abc.net.au/news/2015-11-17/jemena-wins-negi-gas-pipeline-preferred-bidder-in-nt/6947746

Acemoglu, D. & Autor, D. H. (2010). *Skills, tasks and technologies: Implications for employment and earnings* (NBER Working Papers No. 16082). National Bureau of Economic Research.

Ahluwalia, M. S. (1976). Inequality, poverty and development. *Journal of Development Economics*, *3*(4), 307–342.

Ahmad, E. & Stern, N. (1991). *The theory and practice of tax reform in developing countries*. Cambridge, England: Cambridge University Press.

Altman, J. (2009). *Beyond closing the gap: Valuing diversity in Indigenous Australia*. (Centre for Aboriginal Economic Policy Research Working Paper No. 54). Canberra, ACT: ANU.

Altman, J., Biddle, N. & Hunter, B. (2008). *How realistic are the prospects for 'closing the gaps' in socioeconomic outcomes for Indigenous Australians?* (Centre for Aboriginal Economic Policy Research Discussion Paper No. 287). Canberra, ACT: ANU.

Anand, S. & Kanbur, S. M. R. (1993). Inequality and development: A critique. *Journal of Development Economics*, *41*(1), 19–43.

Athanasopoulos, G. & Vahid, F. (2003). Statistical inference and changes in income inequality in Australia. *Economic Record*, *79*(247), 412–424.

Auerbach, A. J. & Hines, J. R. (2002). Taxation and economic efficiency. In A. J. Auerbach & M. Feldstein (Eds), *Handbook of public economics* (pp. 1347–1421). Elsevier.

Australian Government. (2015). *Our north, our future: White paper on developing Northern Australia*. Retrieved from www.industry.gov.au/data-and-publications/our-north-our-future-white-paper-on-developing-northern-australia

Australian Institute of Health and Welfare (AIHW). (2010). *Australia's health 2010* (Australia's Health Series No. 12., Cat. No. AUS 122). Canberra, ACT: AIHW.

Bailey, M. J. & Dynarski, S. M. (2011). Inequality in post-secondary education. In G. J. Duncan & R. J. Murnane (Eds), *Whither opportunity?: Rising inequality, schools, and children's life chances* (pp. 117–132). Russell Sage Foundation.

Baum, S. (2006). A typology of socio-economic advantage and disadvantage in Australia's large non-metropolitan cities, towns and regions. *Australian Geographer*, *37*, 233–258.

Biddle, N., Taylor, J. & Yap, M. (2008). *Indigenous participation in regional labour markets, 2001-06* (Centre for Aboriginal Economic Policy Research Discussion Paper No. 288). Canberra, ACT: ANU.

Blackwell, B., Fischer, A., McFarlane, J. & Dollery, B. (2015). Mining and other industry contributions to employment leakage in Australia's Northern Territory. *The Journal of Developing Areas*, *49*(6), 263–278.

Brokensha, H., Taylor, A. & Carson, D. (2013). *The Northern Territory's non-resident workforce: One census on* (Northern Institute Research Brief Series, Issue No. 201304). Retrieved from www.cdu.edu.au/sites/default/files/research-brief-2013-4.pdf

Brosnan, S. & de Waal, F. B. M. (2003). Monkeys reject unequal pay. *Nature*, *425*(6955), 297–299.

Brouwer, R., Akter, S., Brander, L. & Haque, E. (2009). Economic valuation of flood risk exposure and reduction in a severely flood prone developing country. *Environment and Development Economics*, *14*(03), 397–417.

Campano, F. & Salvatore, D. (1988). Economic development, income inequality, and Kuznets' U-shaped hypothesis. *Journal of Policy Modeling*, *10*(2), 265–280.

Campbell, R. (2015, 31 August). Fact check: Will Adani's coal mine really boost employment by 10,000 jobs? *The Australian*. Retrieved from www.businessspectator.com.au/article/2015/8/31/policy-politics/fact-check-will-adanis-coal-mine-really-boost-employment-10000.

Carson, D., Taylor, A. & Campbell, S. (2009). *Demographic trends and likely futures for Australia's tropical rivers*. Darwin, NT: Charles Darwin University.

Carson, D. B. & Carson, D. A. (2014). Local economies of mobility in sparsely populated areas: Cases from Australia's spine. *Journal of Rural Studies*, *36*, 340–349.

Cheng, W. (2006). A new perspective on economic development and income inequality. *Economic Papers, 25*, 125–130.

Cohen, M. A. (2012). *The costs of crime and justice*. Routledge.

Daly, H. E. & Farley, J. (2004). *Ecological economics: Principles and applications*. Washington, DC: Island Press.

Dawes, C. T., Fowler, J. H., Hohnson, T., McElreath, R. & Smirnov, O. (2007). Egalitarian motives in humans. *Nature, 446*, 794–796.

Deininger, K. & Squire, L. (1998). New ways of looking at old issues: Inequality and growth. *Journal of Development Economics, 57*(2), 259–287.

Detotto, C. & Otranto, E. (2010). Does crime affect economic growth? *Kyklos, 63*(3), 330–345.

Doms, M. A., Lewis, E. & Robb, A. (2010). Local labor force education, new business characteristics, and firm performance. *Journal of Urban Economics, 67*, 61–77.

Duncan, G. J. & Murnane, R. J. (2014). Growing income inequality threatens American education. *Phi Delta Kappan, 95*(6), 8–14.

Elgar, F. J., Pickett, K. E., Pickett, W., Craig, W., Molcho, M., Hurrelmann, K. & Lenzi, M. (2013). School bullying, homicide and income inequality: A cross-national pooled time series analysis. *International Journal of Public Health, 58*, 237–245. doi.org/10.1007/s00038-012-0380-y

Ezcurra, R. & Rodriguez-Pose, A. (2013). Does economic globalization affect regional inequality? A cross-country analysis. *World Development, 52*, 92–103. doi.org/10.1016/j.worlddev.2013.07.002

Faal, E. (2007). Growth, investment and productivity in Papua New Guinea. *Pacific Economic Bulletin, 22*(1), 16–38.

Fehr, E. & Schmidt, K. M. (1999). A theory of fairness, competition, and cooperation. *The Quarterly Journal of Economics, 114*(3), 817–868.

Fryer, R. G. & Loury, G. C. (2005). Affirmative action and its mythology. *The Journal of Economic Perspectives, 19*(3), 147–162.

Harrison, A., McLaren, J. & McMillan, M. S. (2010). *Recent findings on trade and inequality* (NBER Working Papers, No. 16425). National Bureau of Economic Research.

Hoeller, P., Joumard, I., Pisu, M. & Bloch, D. (2012). *Less income inequality and more growth—are they compatible?: Part 1. Mapping income inequality across the OECD* (OECD Economics Department Working Paper No. 924). OECD Publishing. doi.org/10.1787/5k9h297wxbnr-en

Hunter, B. (1999). *Three nations, not one: Indigenous and other Australian poverty.* Canberra, ACT: Centre for Aboriginal Economic Policy Research.

Hunter, B. & Gray, M. (1999). *Income fluctuations over the lifecycle: A cohort analysis of Indigenous and non-Indigenous Australians, 1986–96.* Canberra, ACT: Centre for Aboriginal Economic Policy Research.

Jaumotte, F., Lall, S. & Papageorgiou, C. (2013). Rising income inequality: Technology, or trade and financial globalization? *IMF Economic Review, 61*, 271–309. doi.org/10.1057/imfer.2013.7

Koske, I., Fournier, J. & Wanner, I. (2012). *Less income inequality and more growth—are they compatible?: Part 2. The distribution of labour income* (OECD Economics Department Working Paper No. 925). OECD Publishing. doi.org/10.1787/5k9h2975rhhf-en

Kuznets, S. (1955). Economic growth and income inequality. *The American Economic Review, 45*(1), 1–30.

Leigh, A., Jencks, C. & Smeeding, T. M. (2009). Health and economic inequality. In W. Salverda, B. Nolan & T. Smeeding (Eds), *The Oxford handbook of economic inequality.* Oxford, England: Oxford University Press.

Liberal Party of Australia. (2013). *The Coalition's 2030 vision for developing Northern Australia.* Retrieved from parlinfo.aph.gov.au/parlInfo/search/display/display.w3p;query=Id%3A%22library%2Fpartypol%2F2550511%22;src1=sm1

Papanek, G. & Kyn, O. (1986). The effect on income distribution of development, the growth rate and economic strategy. *Journal of Development Economics, 23*(1), 55–65.

Pholi, K., Black, D. & Richards, C. (2009). Is 'close the gap' a useful approach to improving the health and wellbeing of Indigenous Australians? *Australian Review of Public Affairs, 9*(2), 1–13.

Reeson, A. F., Measham, T. G. & Hosking, K. (2012). Mining activity, income inequality and gender in regional Australia. *Australian Journal of Agricultural and Resource Economics, 56*, 302–313.

Rodriguez-Pose, A. (2012). Trade and regional inequality. *Economic Geography, 88*(2), 109–136.

Rolfe, J., Lawrence, R., Gregg, D., Morrish, F. & Ivanova, G. (2010). Impacts of the mining boom in the Bowen Basin 2004–2006. *Australasian Journal of Regional Minerals and Energy Studies, 13*, 134–153.

Rolfe, J., Miles, B., Lockie, S. & Ivanova, G. (2007). *Lessons from the social and economic resources sector in Queensland economic impact study*. Brisbane, Qld: The Eidos Institute.

Shane, S. (2009). Why encouraging more people to become entrepreneurs is bad public policy. *Small Business Economics, 33*, 141–149.

Stoeckl, N. (2007). Using surveys of business expenditure to draw inferences about the size of regional multipliers: A case-study of tourism in Northern Australia. *Regional Studies, 41*(7), 917–931.

Stoeckl, N., Esparon, M., Stanley, O., Farr, M., Delisle, A. & Altai, Z. (2013). The great asymmetric divide: An empirical investigation of the link between Indigenous and non-Indigenous economic systems in Northern Australia. *Papers in Regional Science 93*(4), 783–801. doi.org/10.1111/pirs.12028

Stoeckl, N., Jackson, S., Pantus, F., Finn, M., Kennard, M. & Pusey, B. (2013). An integrated assessment of some of the financial, hydrological, ecological and social impacts of 'development' on Indigenous and non-Indigenous people in Northern Australia. *Biological Conservation, 159*, 214–221.

Stoeckl, N., Stanley, O., Brown, V. & Stoeckl, W. (2007, October). *Regional economic multipliers in Australia's tropical savannas* (TS CRC Project Report). Townsville, Qld: James Cook University. Retrieved from www.nintione.com.au/resources/rao/regional-economic-multipliers-in-australias-tropical-savannas/

Tanton, R., Harding, A., Daly, A., McNamara, J. & Yap, M. (2009). Australian children at risk of social exclusion: A spatial index for gauging relative disadvantage. *Population, Space and Place, 16*(2), 135–150.

Taylor, J. & Hunter, B. (1998). *The job still ahead: Economic costs of continuing Indigenous employment disparity*. Canberra, ACT: Centre for Aboriginal Economic Policy Research.

Taylor, J. & Stanley, O. (2005). *The opportunity costs of the status quo in the Thamarrur Region* (Centre for Aboriginal Economic Policy Research Working Paper No. 18). Canberra, ACT: ANU.

Taylor, A., Larson, S., Stoeckl, N. & Carson, D. (2011). The *haves* and *have nots* in Australia's Tropical North—new perspectives on a persisting problem. *Geographical Research, 49*(1), 13–22.

Watson, I. (2013). Bridges or traps? Casualisation and labour market transitions in Australia. *Journal of Industrial Relations*, 55(1), 6–37.

Wilkinson, R. (1996). *Unhealthy societies: The afflictions of inequality*. London, England: Routledge.

Wilkinson, R. & Pickett, K. (2010). *The spirit level: Why equality is better for everyone*. Penguin Books Ltd.

Yang, X. & Zhang, D. (2003). Economic development, international trade and income distribution: The perspective of the new growth theories. *Journal of Economics*, *78*, 163–190.

# 8

# Other Views of Northern Australian Aspirations: Pre-Notions, Ideologies and Remoteness

Judith Lovell and Don Zoellner

## Introduction

This chapter explores ideology and remoteness through the configuration of markets and non-markets that operate in a sparsely settled region in Northern Australia. As non-Indigenous researchers analysing data from Aboriginal settlements, we acknowledge the primary and overarching configuration in these settlements is Aboriginal sovereignty and the standpoints of local residents and custodians (Ardill, 2013; Morrison, 2015; Nakata, 2007). A previous study of 15 remote Aboriginal settlements in the region (see Figure 8.1) revealed that certain mixed-market activities (aboriginal art centres, Indigenous ranger programs and Aboriginal community researchers) have remained active and produced socioeconomic benefits to residents over time. This is despite ideological shifts that are evident in public policy and national data analysis.

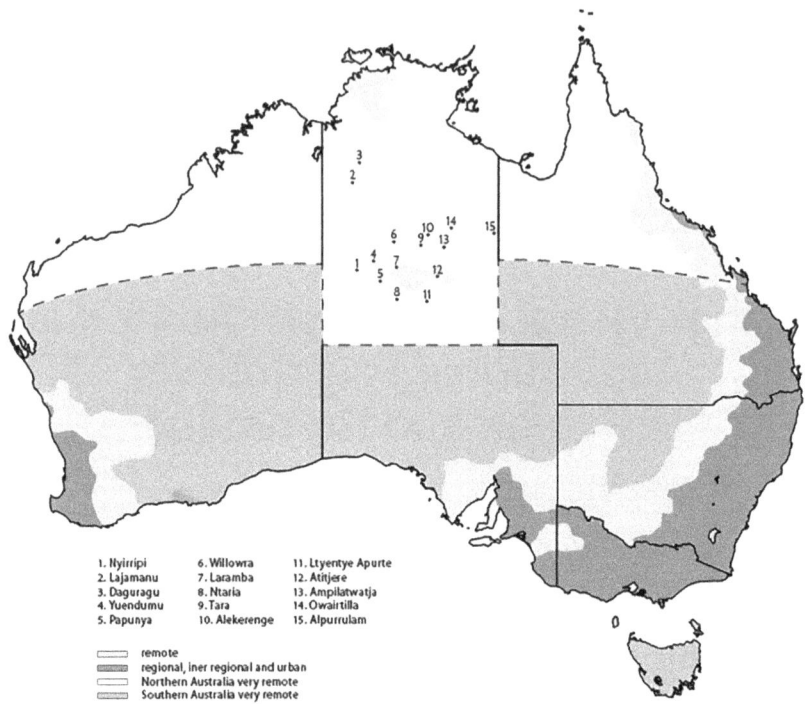

**Figure 8.1: Map of Australia with remote, very remote and Northern Australia boundaries and including the 15 settlements studied for mixed-market activity.**
Source: Ninti One Ltd (cartographer) and J. Lovell.

Non-markets are a category that includes governments, charities, not-for-profits and philanthropies. Non-markets exist when inputs are un-costed (Wolf, 1993). These institutions seek the equitable distribution of social and economic benefits in sectors where markets have failed or are not active (Wolf, 1993, p. 6). Markets are places where goods and services are openly traded and are priced. This chapter uses these terms in preference to the dualistic public versus private categorisation, which have severe conceptual limitations when describing the socioeconomics of these settlements (see Chapter 9). Mixed-markets are conceived as the mesh in which market and non-market traits interact along with customary forms of socioeconomic activity. In terms of the public data available to inform policy about remote economic participation, the sources of national data lack the definition required to accurately describe or interpret the impacts of mixed-markets at settlement level (Lovell et al., 2015b, p. 10).

Mixed-market activity shares features of socioeconomic benefit with social enterprises in other countries (Lovell et al., 2016). In two advanced market democracies, Canada and Australia, the constraints of national quantitative data and the lack of typological qualitative definition (McMurtry & Brouard, 2015; Sengupta et al., 2015) have prevented useful distinctions between social enterprises as market, mixed-market or non-market models. These constraints ignore evidence of historic context and other points of difference, such as culture and gender (Sengupta et al., 2015, p. 110), which distinguish settlement-level economic activity otherwise absent in the national data. The effect within the broad categories of market, non-market and Canadian Indigenous social enterprise (Sengupta et al., 2015) is that little information is available to contribute to understanding the agency required by local entrepreneurs (Pearson & Daff, 2014) or the usefulness of models of enterprise available under current legislation (Sengupta et al., 2015). Due to the constraints in remote population data and methodology, residents of sparsely populated regions experience unintended consequences of policy interventions in ways seldom experienced by larger populations of urban residents.

Analysis of the national and industry data available (see Chapter 9) suggested non-market interventions may have worked against the intended outcomes of policy in some of the remote settlements in the study area in Australia. There is evidence that non-markets failed to produce the intended equitable distribution of financial or social capital among employed residents in the study region. There were lower rates of Indigenous employment and lower average incomes for Indigenous residents in 2011 than in 2006 (ABS, 2012). The following points consider the configurations of ideology and remoteness that underpin conceptualisation of remote socioeconomic activity. Different and sometimes competing configurations are present, which, if unacknowledged, reduce opportunities for everyday market and mixed-market activity.

# Tipping Points

This chapter furthers the proposition that mixed-markets can provide a successful interface between non-markets, markets and residents as entrepreneurs acting collectively or individually. It seems there is a paradox between the priorities of the non-market and the aspirations of Aboriginal and Torres Strait Islanders that are neither classified through the geographic construct of 'remoteness' (ABS, 2013), nor represented by the national consensus of Australian values (Lovell et al., 2014). The agenda of developing Northern Australia is a tipping point at which entrepreneurial and mixed-market activity should be high on local, regional and national agendas (Morrison, 2015). Realistically, the management of unemployed adult residents into work programs remains the most dominant non-market response to remote economic participation at a settlement level in remote Australia (Moran & Porter, 2014). Current Australian welfare to work programs align with the 'liberal welfare' policies of a number of other developed nations (Whiteford, 2015, para. 7).

Since 2008, the impact of the global financial crisis on local, regional and national markets contributed to changes in mixed-market activity in the clusters of settlements in this chapter. There was a downturn in the value of products from remote Australian Aboriginal art centres entering the market after 2007 and an increase in the number of products entering the market at lower price points (Acker & Woodhead, 2015, p. 17). Also formalised in 2008, was the increasingly centralised approach of all tiers of government to the policy of *Closing the gap on Indigenous disadvantage* (Council of Australian Governments, 2008; Department of Families, Housing, Community Services and Indigenous Affairs, 2008). This program rerouted non-market expenditure into national priorities that continue to be a standard measure of non-market success or failure (Australian Government, 2015a). Additionally, in 2008, the Northern Territory Government undertook the 'largest scale, forced local government amalgamation in Australia' (Tiley & Dollery, 2010, p. 3) by restructuring local Aboriginal government authorities into large regional shires that operate from centralised service centres in a hub-and-spoke model (Local Government Association of the Northern Territory, 2014).

The Australian Government's Department of Industry green and white papers for the development of Northern Australia (Australian Government, 2014a, 2015c) do not mention the aspirations and capacity of the residents of remote settlements. This results in policy confusion at the local level because sustainable and prosperous businesses are priorities in the national policies contained in the Indigenous Advancement Strategy (IAS) that was developed by the Department of Prime Minister and Cabinet (Australian Government, 2014b). Earlier analysis of mixed markets confirms that remote Aboriginal and Torres Strait Islanders do not appear as consumers, producers or suppliers of markets or industries in census data (Lovell et al., 2015a) or in the policy papers mentioned.

There has been little attention paid in the public policy planning phases to bring distinctly different ideological positions and responses into public discussion of sustainable development (Morrison, 2015).

This omission leaves policy intentions and potential outcomes poorly understood from both the standpoint of Aboriginal and Torres Strait Islander custodians in Northern Australia and the dominant neoliberalism represented in national and territory governments' policy regarding sustainable Northern Australian development. The alternative to market-based employment or entrepreneurial activity in remote settlements is active social policy, currently called the Community Development Programme (Australian Government, 2015b). This is a 'work for the dole' employment activity. Correspondingly, the evidence of mixed markets in the clusters of 15 settlements suggests art centres, ranger programs and community researchers' activities have continued despite the unintended consequences of national policy decisions (Carson & Carson, 2014).

## Multidirectional Remoteness

Government and other non-market service providers have made use of geographic, spatial and demographic measures to classify settlements as remote or very remote as a measure of distance from the nearest regional or urban service centre. This classification is known as the Australian Statistical Geography Standard (ASGS) (ABS, 2012) through which approximately 86 per cent of the landmass and 2.8 per cent of the Australian population are classified as remote and very remote regions and residents. The use of this system of classification for policy and program development has funding and cost implications that affect the potential development of markets, non-market service delivery, taxation, governance and the prevalence or lack of infrastructure. Remoteness is frequently listed as a major contributor to market failure (Productivity Commission, 2014, p. 97).

In the ASGS framework, remoteness is a measure of disadvantage that is calculated against the sustainability of settlements (Morris et al., 2010), resource extraction opportunities (Foran et al., 2015), procurement practices (Dockery, 2014a), the resilience and vulnerability of marginalised regions and residents (Maru et al., 2014) and, most recently, the Northern Australian development agendas (Australian Government, 2015c; Carson et al., 2014; Mayes et al., 2014; Northern Territory Cattlemen's Association, 2014). The ASGS informs national polity and ideological positions, which are in turn subject to the forces of global, neoliberal developed economies (McMurtry & Brouard, 2015). Whether the tension is seen as top down or bottom up, in the neoliberal context the modification of non-market services, resources and opportunities is aimed at changing individual behaviours to align more closely with dominant ideological aspirations (Nethercote, 2015). The expectations, market-drivers and historical contexts generally reflect urban derivations and are inadequate as ways of configuring for remoteness.

The themes of remoteness and ideology cited in previous mixed-market analysis resonate with wider research synthesis and integration. In remote Australia, as elsewhere, research synthesis—as the bringing together of themes and findings across disciplines, stakeholders and programs—are part of 'a dynamic world, where everything is changing all the time' (Bammer, 2015, p. 289). This chapter is part of a synthesis and integration of the research programs of contiguous Cooperative Research Centres (CRCs) that are 'concerned with delivering solutions to the economic challenges of remote Australia' (Ninti One Ltd, 2010). The concept of 'remoteness' has emerged as contradictory when it is as much perceptual, social and temporal as it is proximal and spatial (Jacobsen & Tiyce, 2014). The lived experience of many residents in regional, remote and very remote Australia is that urban centres and populations are distant from those out bush in more ways than geographic (Woinarski et al., 2014). Remoteness conceived as multidirectional reveals complexity is at the heart of *The modern outback* (Woinarski et al., 2014). Geographers (Walker et al., 2012) argue that to reignite insight of remote human and natural landscapes is essential to the public interest. The future of regions and access to remote resources on which the national economy relies (Australian Government, 2014b, 2015c) depends on an articulation of complex multidirectional remoteness.

While recognising that the major limitations of national data are ideological and methodological, it is also evident that the dominance of non-market activity requires rethinking in relation the sustainable development of Northern Australia. Entrepreneurship is defined by the OECD (2015, p. 11) as 'the enterprising human action in pursuit of the generation of value' and entrepreneurial activities are 'not always related to the creation of financial wealth; for example, they may be related to increasing employment, tackling inequalities or environmental issues'. While there is an international literature exploring the value of entrepreneurship in relation to socioeconomic and wellbeing benefits (International Comparative Social Enterprise Models, 2013), this is not reflected in current Australian Indigenous policy and seems to lack the rhetorical fit with more recent and dominant ideology regarding employment and economic benefit for remote residents (Forrest, 2014; Wunan Foundation, 2015).

It is unsurprising that the recent mixed-market analysis reflects the near saturation of publicly funded employment initiatives when:

> the entrepreneurial culture in a country affects the attitude that individuals have towards entrepreneurship, the likelihood of choosing entrepreneurship as a career, the ambitions to succeed and start again after a failure or the support provided by family and relatives planning to set up a business. (OECD, 2015, p. 109)

Since colonisation, Australians have had a strong historical preference to first turn to government for funding and support of markets described as a form of 'colonial socialism' making entrepreneurship a secondary consideration in many cases (Barnard et al., 1982, pp. 320–321). Mixed markets are one glimmer of an entrepreneurial tendency that is sustained by the forms of capital central to the residents of remote Aboriginal settlements and which prevails despite the non-market reframing of remoteness and Indigeneity as forms of disadvantage (Guenther, 2015).

Adding yet another layer of complexity to policy development in remote and very remote Australia, human, cosmological and ecological structures in the modern outback (see Figure 8.2) reflect an extensive temporal continuity that existed pre-colonisation (Lovell, 2015; Maru et al., 2014). This continues to contribute to a presence in which 'Aboriginal people, lands, culture and socio-economic concerns are writ far larger than in a national context' (Woinarski et al., 2014, p. 33). Where land and waterways were once managed through kinship estates among language groups, various leaseholds also now cover and overlap the continent. Lease distributions in the arid and very arid regions of Australia that Woinarski et al. (2014, p. 121) defined as the modern outback are approximated as:

- 50 per cent pastoral leases
- 20 per cent conservation reserves
- 20 per cent Aboriginal-owned land
- 19 per cent unallocated crown lands
- >4 per cent intensive horticulture or forestry
- >1 per cent military use.

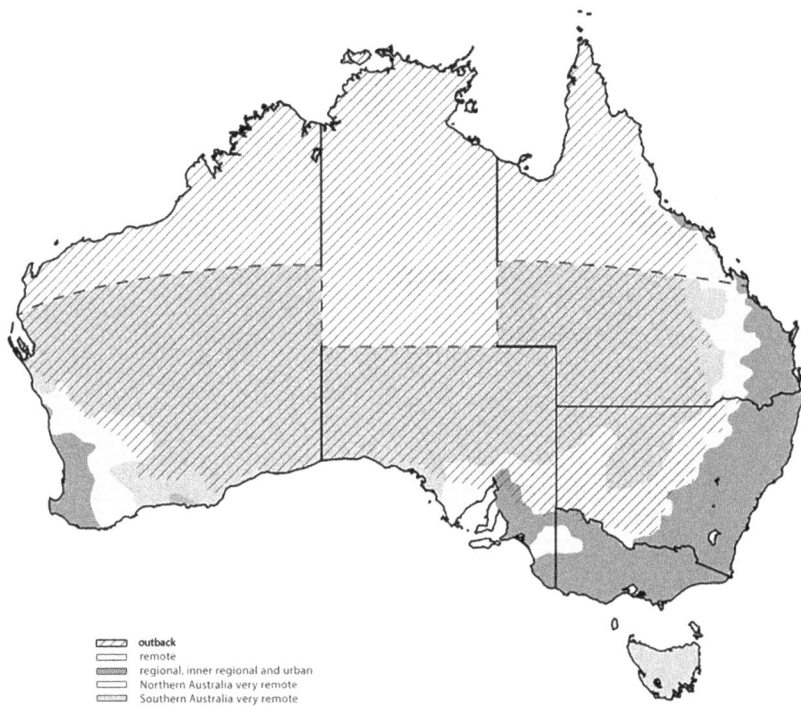

**Figure 8.2: 'Outback' region of the Australian continent, including remote, very remote and Northern Australia regions.**
Source: Woinarski et al. (2014).

Contemporary systems of leasehold and overlapping jurisdictions are cited by governments and industry as one of the most serious constraints for sustainable development throughout remote Australian regions (Forrest, 2014). The land tenure associated with such leases does not always reflect land use while mining and exploration leases overlay other tenure types (Australian Government, 2015c; Chaney & Walker, 2013; Morrison, 2015; Woinarski et al., 2014). Data regarding the flow-on socioeconomic benefits to remote residents through leaseholds on Aboriginal Land is not publicly available.

## The Invisibility of Non-Market Saturation

Three tiers of government administer remote and very remote Australia and, despite the prevalence of Aboriginal residents, businesses and custodian in these regions, there is no tier equivalent to an Aboriginal level of government (Sengupta et al., 2015). Instead, not-for-profit land councils have been established as statutory authorities of the national government, meeting the multiple roles of representation of custodians, managers of public funds received as lease monies and negotiators of reparatory payments to traditional owners and land rights (Central Land Council, 2015a). Land rights are the prevalent legislated mechanism for recognition of the communal structures of Aboriginal 'ownership' of country and they recognise the connection of people to land as sovereign rights that pre-exist European law. Walker et al. (2012) have suggested that the long-term change needed in remote Australia would involve new governance principals, ones that 'create locally appropriate institutions which have sufficient authority, legitimacy and effectiveness to fulfil their functions' (p. 64). However, Walker et al.'s vision of that authority is one of 'dual compact' reliant on 'the general public and the parochial interest' being adequately reflected in a 'common set of goals'. This orchestrates new forms of non-market institutions that carry out the task of 'mandating, mediating and settling contests' (p. 64). There is little in that proposition that recognises pre-existing sovereignty and standpoints within which social and economic systems of collaborative ownership, reciprocal responsibility and kinship ties already determine the socioeconomic multipliers and exchanges that benefit remote residents. Yet again, the solutions to the perceived problems of the outback are framed in ways that demand more non-market intervention and the eternal quest for better coordination between institutions.

While Woinarski et al. (2014) argued for modernisation of the outback and Walker et al. (2012) for its preservation, both recognised that systems of Aboriginal sovereignty have been in use to manage and define the human ecology of the continent over thousands of years. Both argued for increased non-market mediation for modernisation and preservation, yet non-market policy continues to consistently backfire against priority equity targets for employment and economic participation. Mixed markets represent an alternative entrepreneurial behaviour that can be responsive over time to changes in non-market polity (Acker & Woodhead, 2015; Central Land Council, 2015b; Woodhead & Acker, 2015).

Rather than redesigning the activity of an already immense group of non-market stakeholders in remote Australia as Walker et al. (2012) suggested, Lovell et al. (2015b) identified instances of successful mixed-markets. These are interfaces that challenge the misplaced assumption that national measures of disadvantage account for the advantages of local culture and capacity (Central Land Council, 2015b; Desart, 2014; Ninti One Ltd, 2014).

## Ideology and Intervention

It is the role of public policy to change the behaviour of the individual (Australian Public Service Commission, 2007), but the directives for change are based on population-level findings, combined with political aspirations and a governable populous. Currently, political aspirations occur in the context of critical discourse and neoliberal pragmatics (Hamilton, 2014; Nethercote, 2015; Whiteford, 2015) that are refined further by the situation in which Australia is one of the most urbanised and wealthiest developed nations (Hugo et al., 2013; Levine et al., 2015). The analysis of mixed-market activity described in earlier work (Lovell et al., 2015a) has revealed a resilience—among markets and producers—that continues despite changes in the direction that welfare and employment policies have taken in remote settlements.

In combining 150 program areas down to five priorities, the national IAS argued a framework within which children attend school and adults go to work in safe communities will ensure the wellbeing and health of residents (Australian Government, 2014b). This does not readily account for the ways that markets may intersect with and value remote Aboriginal custom, capacity or advantage (Larkin, 2009; Lovell, 2015; Zander et al., 2014), nor value Aboriginal and Torres Strait Islander longitudinal temporal and sovereign corporate knowledge (Ardill, 2013; Babie, 2013; Morrison, 2015). The IAS is aligned with Australia's liberal welfare policy, which is one of the major mechanisms through which the nation redistributes wealth in ways that provide for the marginalised and disadvantaged (Whiteford, 2015). Hamilton (2014, p. 453) argued that moving welfare policy via programming and implementation towards 'the individualisation of risk' aligned with neoliberalism has shifted emphasis from shared responsibility (individuals and the state) to responsible citizenry, in which the individual is expected to behave as an 'entrepreneurial self' bound to welfare through contractual arrangements.

Previous analysis identified that residents derive socioeconomic benefits from mixed markets (Lovell et al., 2015a; Lovell et al., 2016) through their capacity to use local assets—such as natural, cultural, social and knowledge capitals—to produce products or services with a market value. These assets are 'valued' quite differently by custodians, non-markets and markets (Lovell et al., 2015a, p. 3) and it is in an interface of activity, opportunity and transaction that residents derive socioeconomic benefits. Much of this asset base is collectively owned and managed and must be negotiated in addition to structures of the market place (Pearson & Daff, 2014). Sengupta et al. (2015) described a model of Indigenous social enterprise in which a quadruple bottom (social, cultural, environmental and financial benefits) line drives the aspirations and goals of any such organisation, but this remains contested among Indigenous scholars (Wuttunee, 2010).

In Australian policy, there is a difference in the remote welfare to work contract from programs applied to urbanites on the grounds of remoteness (see Australian Government, 2015a). This is a nuance that assumes Aboriginal residents in remote settlements are homogeneously disadvantaged and marginalised differently than city folk and need to work additional hours to receive their welfare payment (Altman, 2015). The close association of people of the land to trade, exchange, reciprocity and demand sharing is part of the inter-generational inheritance from those who managed the human ecology of homelands across the nation for thousands of years prior to European settlement and ensuing urbanisation (Woinarski et al., 2014). Indigenous sovereignty remains a fact of life. While not arguing for a return to pre-award wage economics, this chapter does question the standpoint in which the non-market intervention is one in which remoteness and Indigeneity are classified as disadvantages (Guenther, 2015). Currently, public services designed to counter remote disadvantage procure financial multipliers, often through private non-market actors, who are increasingly non-local and non-Indigenous and whose social and economic benefits are mostly redirected away from remote settlements, and in many cases, remote regions (see Chapter 9 for analysis of income data by Indigenous or non-Indigenous status).

# Convergence in Mixed-Markets in Remote Contexts

Analysis of the socioeconomic benefits derived from mixed markets is a theme from industry sector research in the CRC for Remote Economic Participation (CRC-REP) and wider academic and industry information. The flow of local enterprise back into settlements or membership cohorts and the concept of an interface of customary, market and state interests is not entirely new and has some features common with social enterprise (International Comparative Social Enterprise Models, 2013). Assessing from the settlement level, mixed markets appear to mesh market-type behaviours of customers who are prepared to pay for products and services with the local producers who have the assets required to provide them (Lovell, 2015).

Non-Indigenous and Indigenous researchers (Altman, 2015; Pearson, 2014; Sanders, 2015) analyse the socioeconomics of remote Indigenous settlements to inform public policy and public interventions. Altman (2007, p. 3) described 'customary economies' as interacting contributing factors along with market and state (government) in remote economies. He framed these as 'hybrid economies' and the concept has remained in use by some and contested by others for more than a decade (Langton & Mazel, 2008; Russell, 2011). Mixed markets are conceptualised from the standpoint of non-Indigenous researchers who have used national data sets to seek evidence of the remote industry activities of which they also have practical experience. Customary economies are embedded deep in the Aboriginal mediation of changing socioeconomic, cultural and natural human ecology (Lovell, 2015; Wallace & Lovell, 2009) and include forms of human capital aligned with Aboriginal standpoints and sovereignty (Ardill, 2013). The focus of mixed-market analysis to date has been how the interface where residents access market opportunity is counted (or not) through the systems of national data collection that inform policy. Entrepreneurial residents in remote settlements are increasingly influenced by the social welfare contracts and employment opportunities that are regulated by non-markets, yet residents continue to derive mixed-market socioeconomic benefits through products and services that rely on their local assets and sovereignty to supply markets.

The wider literature confirms that at settlement level a fit between local residents' aspirations, non-market and market is essential if socioeconomic activities are to succeed (Taylor et al., 2015). Mixed markets have produced socioeconomic benefits and remained active over time despite:

- proscribed non-market priorities including changes in behaviour to reflect the requirements of active social policy
- the impact of global markets on remote local markets
- the obscurity of mixed-market activities to policymakers and consumers of services and products (Lovell et al., 2015a, p. 16).

In contrast, the marketisation of government human service provision has created a type of 'market' behaviour among non-market providers—both commercial and not-for-profit—who are predominantly non-local and whose profits are removed from the local community without providing local multiplier benefits. The cash flow from this non-market market derives from the delivery of public services such as health, education and employment programs into remote settlements (Markham & Doran, 2015). In the original study region, public service delivery accounted for an increase in the number of non-local staff employed at higher income levels (ABS, 2014a) between collection points in 2006 and 2011. Significant policy driven intervention into public service provision and an increasingly contractual basis for obligational welfare (Nethercote, 2015) has driven the use of non-local and non-remote agencies to provide remote public services (Australian Government, 2014b). There is evidence that provision of remote housing, transport and communications for staff working in remote settlements has not improved local market or mixed-market activity or stimulated financial input into local economies through multiplier industries (see Chapter 9). Correspondingly, there is little infrastructure that supports visitor flow between settlements. Public transport is limited and delivered at high cost per capita (Spandonide, 2014), visitor facilities and local protocols for visitors are lacking and mobile communication is limited (Rennie et al., 2013).

In keeping with Wolf's (1993) theory, market and non-market are understood to derive success or failure through the distribution of a service or product, where success represents equitable and efficient costs and benefits. This theory opens to the convergence of complexity and critical success factors, among which correction of distributional inequities occurs through the one or more form:

- regulated industry
- production of public goods
- redress of market imperfection or failure.

Any of these redistributions 'place authority in the hands of some to be exercised over others' (Wolf, 1993, p. 83). The 'entrepreneurial self' is bound to a contract-type arrangement of active social policy—through taxation, welfare and superannuation (Whiteford, 2015) within an advanced market democracy. In the remote Aboriginal settlement context, the entrepreneurial self is additionally accountable to collectivised socioeconomic structures of sovereignty. The Indigenous entrepreneur manages the expectations of market-based supply and demand and obligations derived through kinship structures (Pearson & Daff, 2014).

Whiteford (2015, para. 10) suggested that 'another way of classifying and evaluating alternative welfare state arrangements is on the basis of the forms of redistribution they emphasise'. Policies that promote more market-driven behaviours to remote residents are based on significant 'private' employment. This so-called 'private' category of employment actually masks many people who are working for non-market entities, such as employment agencies, philanthropies and charities. Thus, this misrepresentation reported in the census data is likely to contribute to unintended programmatic outcomes. Forrest's (2014) policy for labour market activity is based on assimilation *from* customary and custodial economies to those of open and competitive markets. This policy drives behaviour-changing contracts through active social welfare on the assumption that economically rational behaviour will increase human capital capacity and cause behaviours conducive to neoliberal *homo economicus* aspirations. However, the socioeconomics of remote settlements suggest determinants of capital that stem from customary and cultural standpoints dominate and are not altogether those of neoliberal idealism (Altman & Kerins, 2012).

## A Changed Pre-Notion

Developing tourism as sustainable enterprise is a pillar in the policy for Northern Australian development (Australian Government, 2015c, p. 2). Currently, tourism reflected in the policy focuses on generating business between non-local tourists, iconic visitor locations and specialist tourism products and experiences. Tourism is a means of economic redistribution in rural, remote and regional settlements. It is a form of allocation through which local products or services have a transactional value in the market (Zeng, et al., 2015). The Northern Territory Government initiative to link Aboriginal tourism products to the opportunities of northern development reflects priorities aligned to Indigenous tourism with socioeconomic benefits to include remote Indigenous employment outcomes (Northern Territory Government, 2015).

As a theoretic case study, Indigenous tourism is used here to consider the impact of mobility of visitors on the redistribution of socioeconomic benefits at a settlement level, which requires a shift in thinking. Taylor et al. (2015, p. 10) posed the question *why not* prioritise amenities for local Aboriginal residents who move between settlements, and reconceptualise their contribution through mobility, as local tourists. Mobility that results in local tourism produces a financial flow through increased local spending (fuel, shopping, power, etc.), while the same movement away from settlement of origin has the reverse effect (Dockery, 2014b; Spandonide, 2014). The opportunistic and ad hoc behaviours that contribute to local mobility are not envisaged as market opportunities through policy and program design (Carson et al., 2014) but are managed as problematic in most service delivery scenarios.

Reconceptualising locally mobile residents as 'tourists' engaged in market behaviours as proposed by Taylor et al. (2015) is not without difficulty. Most often, those who are mobile between settlements are described as 'visitors', both in census data collection (ABS, 2014b) and in conversation among residents (Amunda Gorey, personal communication, 2011). In research consultations for ABS (2014b) about Indigenous perspectives on homelessness, the complexity of the expectations between Indigenous visitors and hosts is clear but not uniform across families, settlements, age groups and genders. The consulting group felt there was an opportunity to take the discussion further in relation to public housing as an instrument for organising and managing the flow of visitors at a settlement level, but this was not part of the research work. However, the opportunity for settlement-based responses to visitor/tourist facilities, via the instruments of existing public housing, is not without attributes common to the other mixed-markets of art centres, ranger programs and community researchers.

Non-markets respond to mobility of the same demographic group—remote Indigenous residents—differently across services. The impacts of mobility on educational service design and programming (Prout & Yap, 2012) are perceived as problematic and detrimental to the students' progress in learning, yet through the lens of certain social and cultural determinants, mobility is the correct response and contributes to the social and cultural capital of the individual (See Alice, school attendance, in Lovell et al., 2014). Access to country and cultural activity is shown to be beneficial in self-assessed wellbeing indices, including where this involves mobility, and reported benefits include social and cultural capital, and transfer of these into activities with socioeconomic benefits (Biddle, 2012).

## Conclusion and Further Comments

Using Wolf's (1993) criteria of market and non-market, it is clear that employment data from previous studies have produced findings that suggest an almost exclusively non-market economy exists in at least some regions of remote Australia. This is further determined through the data in which almost all employees report working for businesses they do not own. There appears to be close to zero 'market' activity, prompting the observation that the outsourcing of public services from government to other providers has not created market activity and the census data does not disclose the nature of 'private sector' as essentially non-market. Yet the ideological configurations in which these findings occur highlight a significant non-alignment exists in the perception of what works and what is work between urban and remote constituents. Applying a multidirectional understanding of remote Australia as a saturated non-market allows a transition to a more fit-for-purpose mixed-market. This brings with it the opportunity for local financial multipliers, economic and sociocultural benefits that can be generated and retained in remote settlements.

## References

Acker, T. & Woodhead, A. (2015). *The economy of place, a place in the economy: A value chain study of the Aboriginal and Torres Strait Islander art sector. Summary report*. Retrieved from nintione.com.au/resource/EconomyOfPlace/files/assets/basic-html/page-1.html

Altman, J. (2007). *Alleviating poverty in remote Indigenous Australia: The role of the hybrid economy.* Retrieved from pdfs.semanticscholar.org/373f/94ba0f8 ccd6a8d0b4c5218c98fd3bce97d5b.pdf

Altman, J. (2015, February–March). Indigenous policy 'reform'. *ARENA Magazine*, pp. 10–12.

Altman, J. & Kerins, S. (Eds). (2012). *People on country, vital landscapes, Indigenous futures.* Annandale, NSW: Federation Press.

Ardill, A. (2013). Australian sovereignty, Indigenous standpoint theory and feminist standpoint theory: First Peoples' sovereignties matter. *Griffith Law Review, 22*(2), 315–343.

Australian Bureau of Statistics (ABS). (2012). *Australian statistical geography standard (ASGS): Volume 5—remoteness structure, July 2011* (Cat. No. 1270.0.55.005). Retrieved from www.abs.gov.au/AUSSTATS/abs@.nsf/DetailsPage/1270.0.55. 005July%202011

Australian Bureau of Statistics (ABS). (2013, 29 October). *Glossary of statistical geography terminology, 2013* (Cat. No. 1217.0.55.001). Retrieved from www. abs.gov.au/ausstats/abs@.nsf/mf/1217.0.55.001

Australian Bureau of Statistics (ABS). (2014a, 18 December). *Australian demographic statistics* (Cat. No. 3101.0). Retrieved from www.abs.gov.au/AUSSTATS/abs@. nsf/Lookup/3101.0Main+Features1Dec+2014

Australian Bureau of Statistics (ABS). (2014b). *Information paper: Aboriginal and Torres Strait Islander peoples perspectives on homelessness* (Cat. No. 4736.0). Retrieved from abs.gov.au/ausstats/abs@.nsf/mf/4736.0

Australian Government. (2014a). *Green paper on developing Northern Australia.* Canberra, ACT: Department of the Prime Minister and Cabinet. Retrieved from www.industry.gov.au/sites/default/files/2019-09/green-paper-on-developing-northern-australia.pdf.

Australian Government. (2014b, 9 April). *Indigenous Advancement Strategy.* Indigenous Affairs. Retrieved from www.indigenous.gov.au/indigenous-advancement-strategy

Australian Government. (2015a). *Closing the gap. Prime Minister's report 2015.* Canberra, ACT: Australian Government. Retrieved from pmc.gov.au/sites/ default/files/publications/Closing_the_Gap_2015_Report.pdf

Australian Government. (2015b). *The community development programme.* Retrieved from www.desc.gov.au/community-development-program-cdp

Australian Government. (2015c). *Our north, our future: White paper on developing Northern Australia*. Retrieved from www.industry.gov.au/data-and-publications/our-north-our-future-white-paper-on-developing-northern-australia

Australian Public Service Commission. (2007). *Changing behaviour: A public policy perspective*. Canberra, ACT: Australian Government. Retrieved from legacy.apsc.gov.au/changing-behaviour-public-policy-perspective

Babie, P. (2013). Sovereignty as governance: An organising theme for 'Australian' property law. *University of New South Wales Law Journal*, *36*(3), 1075–1108.

Bammer, G. (2015). An approach to understanding change. In G. Bammer (Ed.), *Change! Combining analytic approaches with street wisdom*. Canberra, ACT: ANU Press. doi.org/10.22459/CCAASW.07.2015.01

Barnard, A., Butlin, N. & Pincus, J. (1982). *Government and capitalism: Public and private choice in twentieth century Australia*. Sydney, NSW; Boston, MA: Allen & Unwin.

Biddle, N. (2012). Measures of Indigenous social capital and their relationship with well-being. *Australian Journal of Rural Health*, *20*(6), 298–304.

Carson, D. & Carson, D. (2014). Local economies of mobility in sparsely populated areas: Cases from Australia's spine. *Journal of Rural Studies*, *36*, 340–349.

Carson, D., Carson, D. & Lundmark, L. (2014). Tourism and mobilities in sparsely populated areas: Towards a framework and research agenda. *Scandinavian Journal of Hospitality and Tourism*, *14*(4), 353–366.

Central Land Council. (2015a). *CLC homepage facts*. Retrieved from www.clc.org.au/

Central Land Council. (2015b). *Ranger program development strategy*. Retrieved from www.clc.org.au/publications/content/ranger-program-development-report

Chaney, F. & Walker, B. (2013). *Governance at the heart of reform in remote Australia*. Paper presented at the 12th National Rural Health Conference: Strong Commitment Bright Future, Adelaide, South Australia. Retrieved from www.ruralhealth.org.au/12nrhc/wp-content/uploads/2013/06/Chaney-Fred_Walker-Bruce_ppr.pdf

Council of Australian Governments. (2008). *Closing the gap on Indigenous disadvantage. The Challenge for Australia*. Retrieved from www.dss.gov.au/sites/default/files/documents/05_2012/closing_the_gap.pdf

Department of Families, Housing, Community Services and Indigenous Affairs. (2008). *Increasing Indigenous employment opportunity: Proposed reforms to the CDEP and Indigenous employment programs.*

Desart. (2014). *Desart. Culture first.* Retrieved from desart.com.au

Dockery, A. (2014a). The mining boom and Indigenous labour market outcomes. In M. Brueckner, A. Durey, R. Mayes & C. Pforr (Eds), *Resource curse or cure? On the sustainability of Western Australia* (pp. 75–89). London, England: Springer.

Dockery, A. (2014b). *Reconceptualising mobility for Aboriginal and Torres Strait Islander Australians.* Retrieved from www.crc-rep.com.au/resource/CW015_ReconceptualisingMobility.pdf

Foran, T., Williams, R., Spandonide, B., Fleming, D., Race, D. & Dowd, A. (2015). *A conversation about energy futures for remote Australian communities— theory and detailed workshop findings.* Retrieved from www.crc-rep.com.au/resource/CW022_ConversationEnergyFuturesRemoteCommunities_Theory.pdf

Forrest, A. (2014). *Creating parity – The Forrest review.* Canberra: Commonwealth of Australia. Retrieved from www.niaa.gov.au/resource-centre/indigenous-affairs/forrest-review

Guenther, J. (2015). *The advantaged and disadvantaged of remote schools.* Retrieved from www.crc-rep.com.au/resource/Guenther_AdvantagedAndDisadvantagedOfRemoteSchools.pdf

Hamilton, M. (2014). The 'new social contract' and the individualisation of risk in policy. *Journal of Risk Research, 17*(4), 453–467.

Hugo, G., Feist, H. & Tan, G. (2013). *Australian Population & Migration Research Centre policy brief.* Retrieved from arts.adelaide.edu.au/hugo-centre/#

International Comparative Social Enterprise Models. (2013, 28 September). *Introduction. International Comparative Social Enterprise Models.* Retrieved from www.iap-socent.be/icsem-project

Jacobsen, D. & Tiyce, M. (2014). *Aboriginal and Torres Strait Islander tourism enterprise approaches to creating value for visitors in remote Australia* (Report CR003). Retrieved from www.crc-rep.com.au/resource/CR003_AboriginalTorresStraitIslanderTourismEnterprisesCreatingValue.pdf

Langton, M. & Mazel, O. (2008). Poverty in the midst of plenty: Aboriginal people, the resource curse and Australia's mining boom. *Journal of Energy and Natural Resources Law, 26*(1), 31–65.

Larkin, S. (2009). Race blindness in neo-liberal and managerial approaches to Indigenous administration. *International Journal of Critical Indigenous Studies*, *2*(1), 36–42.

Levine, J., Chan, K. M. & Satterfield, T. (2015). From rational actor to efficient complexity manager: Exorcising the ghost of *Homo economicus* with a unified synthesis of cognition research. *Ecological Economics*, *114*, 22–32.

Local Government Association of the Northern Territory. (2014). *Local Government Association of the Northern Territory fact sheets*. Retrieved from www.lgant.asn.au/wp-content/uploads/2017/06/2017-06-01-Fact-Sheet-1-LGANT.pdf

Lovell, J. (2015). Customary assets and contemporary artistry: Multimodal learning and remote economic participation. *The Australian Journal of Indigenous Education*, *42*(2), 184–193. doi.org/10.1017/jie.2015.24.

Lovell, J., Blake, S., Alice, T. & Wallace, K. (2014). Red dirt service economies: A picture of trade-offs and choices. *Journal of Australian Indigenous Issues*, *17*(4), 131–151.

Lovell, J., Guenther, J. & Zoellner, D. (2015a, 20–22 July). *Developing Northern Australia: Recognising remote mixed-market economies*. Paper presented at the Developing Northern Australia: Economically, Socially, Sustainably conference, Townsville, Queensland.

Lovell, J., Guenther, J. & Zoellner, D. (2015b). *Northern Australian aspirations*. Retrieved from www.cdu.edu.au/sites/default/files/research-brief-2015-07_0.pdf

Lovell, J., Zoellner, D., Guenther, J., Brouard, F. & McMurtry, J. (2016). Contemporary Aboriginal settlements: Understanding mixed-market approaches. In A. Taylor, D. B. Carson, P. C. Ensign, L. Huskey, G. Saxinger & R. Rasmussen (Eds), *Settlements at the edge: Remote human settlements in developed nations* (pp. 246–269). Gloucester, England: Edward Elgar.

Markham, F. & Doran, B. (2015). Equity, discrimination and remote policy: Investigating the centralization of remote service delivery in the Northern Territory. *Applied Geography*, *58*, 105–115.

Maru, Y., Smith, M., Sparrow, A., Pinho, P. & Dube, O. (2014). A linked vulnerability and resilience framework for adaptation pathways in remote disadvantaged communities. *Global Environmental Change-Human and Policy Dimensions*, *28*, 337–350.

Mayes, R., McDonald, P. & Pini, B. (2014). 'Our' community: Corporate social responsibility, neoliberalisation, and mining industry community engagement in rural Australia. *Environment and Planning A*, *46*(2), 398–413.

McMurtry, J. & Brouard, F. (2015). Social enterprises in Canada: An introduction. *ANSERJ: Canadian Journal of Nonprofit and Social Economy Research/Revue canadienne de recherche sur les OSBL et l'économie sociale*, *6*(1), 6–17.

Moran, M. & Porter, D. (2014). Reinventing the governance of public finances in remote Indigenous Australia. *Australian Journal of Public Administration*, *73*(1), 115–127.

Morris, R., Callaghan, R. & Walker, B. (2010). *Rural-remote and Indigenous Local Government: Western Australian scoping study*. Retrieved from www.researchgate.net/publication/258839482_Rural-remote_and_Indigenous_Local_Government_Western_Australian_Scoping_Study_Report

Morrison, J. (2015). *Northern development: Embracing the Indigenous difference* [Press release]. Retrieved from www.nlc.org.au/uploads/images/Joe-Morrison-2015-NLC_JM_NPC_Address.pdf

Nakata, M. (2007). The cultural interface. *The Australian Journal of Indigenous Education*, *36*(5), 2–14.

Nethercote, M. (2015). Neoliberal welfare, minorities and tenancy support. *Social Policy and Society*, *16*(1), 15–32.

Ninti One Ltd. (2010, 1 April). *About CRC-REP. Cooperative Research Centre for Remote Economic Participation*. Retrieved from crc-rep.com/

Ninti One Ltd. (2014). *The key to the community intelligence of remote Australia*. Retrieved from www.nintione.com.au/resource/NintiOne_ACRProspectus_TheKeyToTheCommunityIntelligenceOfRemoteAustralia.pdf

Northern Territory Cattlemen's Association. (2014). *Northern Territory Cattlemen's Association*. Retrieved from www.ntca.org.au/

Northern Territory Government. (2015). *Indigenous Tourism Advisory Council to identify new job and business opportunities* [Press release]. Retrieved from newsroom.nt.gov.au/mediaRelease/13471

Organisation for Economic Co-operation and Development (OECD). (2015). *Entrepreneurship at a glance 2015*. Paris, France: OECD Publishing. doi.org/10.1787/entrepreneur_aag-2015-en

Pearson, C. & Daff, S. (2014). Female Indigenous entrepreneurship in remote communities in Northern Australia. *Information Management and Business Review*, *6*(6), 329–344.

Pearson, N. (2014). *Quarterly essay 55. A rightful place: Race, recognition and a more complete commonwealth*. Black Inc.

Productivity Commission. (2014). *Graphic labour mobility*. Retrieved from www.pc.gov.au/inquiries/completed/labour-mobility/report

Prout, S. & Yap, M. (2012). 'No-one's really aware of where they are': A case study of Indigenous student mobilities in Australia's northwest. *International Journal of Educational Research*, *54*, 9–20.

Rennie, E., Crouch, A., Wright, A. & Thomas, J. (2013). At home on the outstation: Barriers to home Internet in remote Indigenous communities. *Telecommunications Policy*, *37*(6–7), 583–593.

Russell, S. (2011). *The hybrid economy topic guide*. Canberra, ACT: ANU. Retrieved from caepr.cass.anu.edu.au/highlights/hybrid-economy-topic-guide

Sanders, W. (2015). *Experimental governance in Australian Indigenous affairs: From Coombs to Pearson via Rowse and the competing principles* (Centre for Aboriginal Economic Policy Research Discussion Paper No. 291). Canberra, ACT: ANU.

Sengupta, U., Vieta, M. & McMurtry, J. (2015). Indigenous communities and social enterprises in Canada. *ANSERJ: Canadian Journal of Nonprofit and Social Economy Research/Revue canadienne de recherche sur les OSBL et l'économie sociale*, *6*(1), 103–123.

Spandonide, B. (2014). *Transport systems in remote Australia: Transport costs in remote communities* (Working Paper CW017). Cooperative Research Centre for Remote Economic Participation. Retrieved from www.crc-rep.com.au/resource/CW017_TransportCostsInRemoteCommunities.pdf

Taylor, A., Carson, D., Carson, D. & Brokensha, H. (2015). 'Walkabout' tourism: The Indigenous tourism market for outback Australia. *Journal of Hospitality and Tourism Management*, *24*, 9–17.

Tiley, I. & Dollery, B. (2010). *Historical evolution of local government amalgamation in Queensland, the Northern Territory and Western Australia*. Retrieved from www.une.edu.au/__data/assets/pdf_file/0018/25416/02-2010x.pdf

Walker, B., Porter, D. & Marsh, I. (2012). *Fixing the hole in Australia's heartland: How government needs to work in remote Australia*. Retrieved from eprints.utas.edu.au/15065/

Wallace, K. & Lovell, J. (2009). *Listen deeply: Let these stories in*. Alice Springs, NT: IAD Press.

Whiteford, P. (2015, September). *Tales of Robin Hood (part 1): Welfare myths and realities in the United Kingdom and Australia*. Australian Review of Public Affairs Digest. Retrieved from www.australianreview.net/digest/2015/09/whiteford.html

Woinarski, J., Traill, B. & Booth, C. (2014). *The modern outback. Nature, people and the future of remote Australia*. Retrieved from www.pewtrusts.org/en/research-and-analysis/reports/2014/10/the-modern-outback

Wolf, C. (1993). *Markets or governments: Choosing between imperfect alternatives* (2nd ed.). Cambridge, MA; London, England: MIT Press.

Woodhead, A. & Acker, T. (2015). *Productivity, income and gender: Aboriginal and Torres Strait Islander artists* (Report CRO12). Retrieved from www.crc-rep.com.au/resource/CR012_ProductivityIncomeGenderAboriginalTorresStraitIslanderArtists.pdf

Wunan Foundation. (2015). *Empowered Communities: Empowered Peoples – Design Report*. Retrieved from apo.org.au/node/245871

Wuttunee, W. (2010). *Aboriginal perspectives on the social economy, co-operatives, and community economic development*. Toronto, ON: Edmond Montgomery Press.

Zander, K., Dunnett, D., Brown, C., Campion, O., Daniels, C., Daniels, G., … Carson, D. (2014). Indigenous cultural and natural resources management and mobility in Arnhem Land, Northern Australia. *Human Ecology*, *42*(3), 443–453.

Zeng, B., Ryan, C., Cui, X. & Chen, H. (2015). Tourism-generated income distribution in a poor rural community: A case study from Shaanxi, China. *Journal of China Tourism Research*, *11*(1), 85–104.

# 9

# National Data: Reflecting Northern Australian Aspirations?

Don Zoellner and Judith Lovell

## Introduction

This chapter reports on the continued exploration of the capacity of existing data sources to describe the economies of three groups of remote Aboriginal settlements in the Northern Territory (NT). The purpose is to contribute research that supports better place-based policy fit with remote settlements to augment opportunities for social and economic benefit. Understanding how the non-market (governments, philanthropic foundations and/or charities) might better amplify local, open and competitive market capacities requires rethinking fundamental constraints applied to the interpretation of national data. This includes an acceptance that remoteness has many facets and remains difficult to describe using existing economic and population data sets.

Building on an earlier analysis of the ways socioeconomic aspirations are manifested, each of the 15 settlements described below continued their assignment to one of three clusters. This was based on three types of economic activity, each of which was derived from combining various levels of mixed-market activity (Lovell et al., 2015a). Mixed-markets incorporate competitive market activity with non-market interventions taking into account customary socioeconomic practices. The original interrogation of the 2011 national census data, when combined with industry knowledge, confirmed that mixed-market economies are operating in remote and very remote Aboriginal settlements, but their activity is likely to be underestimated.

The analysis reported in this chapter examines and then dismisses longitudinal national data sources and returns to Australian Bureau of Statistics (ABS) categories of employment and income data to determine if a more comprehensive view of the mixed markets can be obtained and used to develop fit-for-purpose public policy responses. The field of this research is at the complex intersection of employment, occupation, labour force, taxation, social welfare and socioeconomic activity in remote communities, which are sparsely populated and whose residents are highly mobile—between settlements and beyond.

The work reported here extends the original analysis of three clusters of remote Aboriginal settlements in the NT, their economic capacity/advantage and the existence of mixed-market economies. The locations of these communities are shown in Figure 9.1. The previous research used a snapshot of national ABS census data from 2011 and available industry information to hypothesise that mixed-market economic activity is under-reported in these communities (Lovell et al., 2015a). In addition, these Australian clusters were compared to remote Canadian Indigenous communities, finding that similar issues are apparent in both countries regarding the limits to data adequacy, resulting in constraints on the understanding of economic activity and the development of public policy (Lovell et al., 2016).

There are vulnerabilities in analysis of sparsely populated settlements in remote regions and constraints in the data that present a methodological challenge to formal and social demographers (Carson et al., 2015). While the statistical limitations inherent in small sample sizes extracted from large data collections are well known, the ABS census data appears to be the best option available. The whole of population data has proven to be only marginally useful when attempting to understand, and exert policy influence on, the behaviour of individuals in the two advanced market democracies of Australia and Canada (Lovell et al., 2016; Pearson & Daff, 2014; Sengupta et al., 2015).

9. NATIONAL DATA

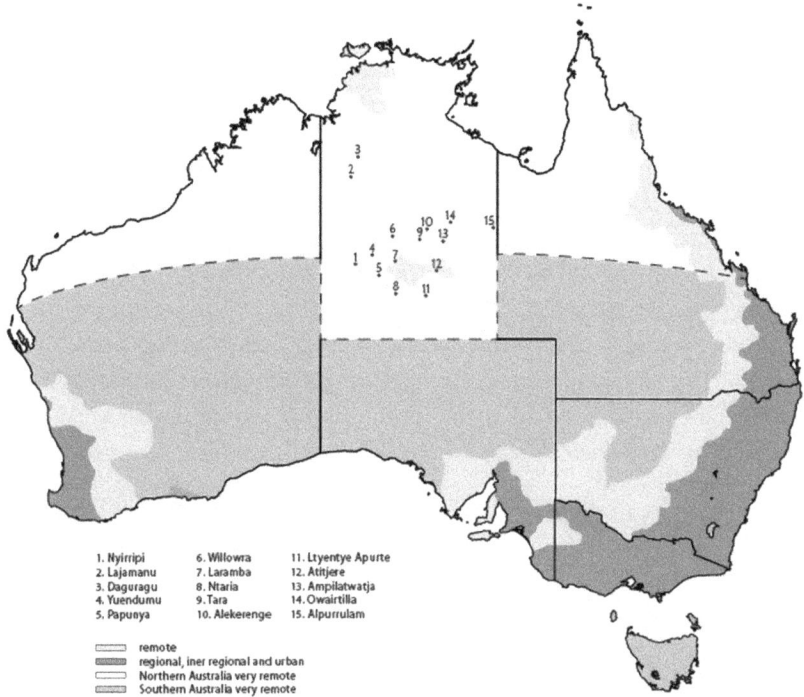

**Figure 9.1: Map of remote and very remote Australia indicating the locations of settlements included in Clusters One, Two and Three.**
Source: Ninti One Ltd (cartographer) and J. Lovell.

## Contextual Considerations

As non-Indigenous researchers writing about Aboriginal settlements, we acknowledge a configuration in which Aboriginal sovereignty and standpoints are part of the lived experience that Aboriginal residents of remote settlements bring to an interface with other ideological structures and standpoints (Morrison, 2015; Nakata, 2007). We do not claim to represent Aboriginal or Torres Strait Islander standpoints. It is the national construction of remoteness that provides the context for the arguments presented below on the basis of decades of working at the contemporary intercultural interface. It is the shortcomings of national data being used to develop policies that are the focus of this chapter and we acknowledge that the residents in these communities will have alternative perspectives.

## The Construct of the Clusters

The three clusters of Central Australian settlements under examination are not geographically contiguous, as opposed to the standard categories for the national census data collections. The 15 communities have been grouped on the basis of employment in three, one/two or none of the activities that can be reliably described by industry knowledge over time. These include ranger groups, art centres and Aboriginal community researchers (Lovell et al., 2015b, p. 4). Given the constraints of the data used to construct these novel assemblages and to seek further support for the hypothesised under-reporting of mixed-market activity and its economic contribution in these communities, the search for additional sources of information was undertaken. What follows are the results of that exploration.

### HILDA

The Household, Income and Labour Dynamics in Australia (HILDA) survey is conducted annually using a nationally representative sample to inform a longitudinal study that began with the first wave in 2001 (Wilkins, 2015, p. 4). Results are used to report national trends on a range of matters including those potentially relevant to the analysis of the mixed markets of very remote Australian communities. Specific items include income, expenditure, employment, education and attitudes and values on an array of subjects. Wave One contained 7,862 households occupied by 19,914 residents, of which only those aged 15 years and over were interviewed (Wilkins, 2015, p. 93).

The original design of the representative sample for HILDA's Wave One excluded five groups from consideration, including those who were in the defence forces, overseas residents, those institutionalised (e.g. in prison or hospitals) or 'people living in remote and sparsely populated areas' (Watson & Wooden, 2002, p. 3). This decision was made on the basis that:

> the focus of the HILDA [is] on producing nation-wide population estimates, [it is] our view that any benefits from a differential probability approach to sampling are outweighed by the negative impacts on overall statistical efficiency. (Watson & Wooden, 2002, p. 6)

As a result, the vast majority of the NT landmass was excluded from the national population reference sample, although the two larger towns nearest the clusters, Alice Springs and Tennant Creek, were included. This initial design decision to exclude very remote communities remains a feature of the newest waves studied through HILDA because the residents are not considered to be 'in-scope' (Wilkins, 2015, p. 93).

## LSAY

A second long-running longitudinal survey of young people has its roots in the 1970s and is currently known as the Longitudinal Surveys of Australian Youth (LSAY). It also relies on a nationally representative sample of Year 9 students chosen every third year since 1995 and each cohort has been 'topped up' to retain statistically relevant numbers (Jones, 2002, p. 1). In more recent times, the construction of the sample selection has also been aligned with the results of international testing schemes of reading, writing and mathematics conducted in Australian schools. Since 2003, about 14,000 students are recruited into the new cohort drawn from 350 schools in all states and territories (National Centre for Vocational Education Research, 2014, p. 18). The survey also collects information that would be relevant to the study of remote mixed markets, such as levels of education and training, work and social development; however, the word remote is not used in favour of a binary distinction—metropolitan or non-metropolitan (National Centre for Vocational Education Research, 2014, p. 18).

It is reported that one of the earlier studies in this series, the 1989 Australian Youth Survey, drew its sample 'from a list of ABS collection districts from non-remote areas' (Australian Council for Educational Research, 1997, p. 6). This survey gathered information on education and training pathways leading to engagement with the labour market from 5,350 16–19-year-olds and, again, new 16-year-olds were added in each year to maintain statistical validity (Australian Council for Educational Research, 1997, p. 2). By the mid-1990s, LSAY had incorporated the ABS measure of remoteness in preparing the selected sample of some 13,000 Year 9 students that would be tracked to post-school study and employment (Jones, 2002, p. 1). Because there were only 365 remote Indigenous students in the sample, Jones (2002, p. vii) proposed that 'in light of these sample distribution problems, the use of LSAY data for national reporting of outcomes by geographical location is not recommended'.

## SEIFA

The Socio-Economic Indexes for Areas (SEIFA) ranks areas in Australia according to 'relative socio-economic advantage and disadvantage' (ABS, 2013b, p. 1). The tool was initially produced with five indexes, of which one contained a rural measure, but none that are remote or very remote. In 2006, this was conflated into four indexes, again without remote or very remote scalable indices. These focus on various aspects of socioeconomic advantage and disadvantage in the form of a summary of subsets of census variables that assist in defining how access to material and social resources is related to the ability to participate in society. According to the ABS, 'the common uses of SEIFA include:

- determining areas that require funding and services
- identifying new business opportunities
- assisting research into the relationship between socio-economic disadvantage
- and various social outcomes' (p. 1).

With each census SEIFA updates its measures and in 2011 ceased using Indigenous/non-Indigenous status as a variable on the basis that there was an increase of 21 per cent of the population who indicated Indigenous status in 2011, which was recorded mainly in urban areas. In the past, Indigenous status has been used as a proxy for disadvantage in SEIFA, but this is no longer the case. The index is not designed for longitudinal or time series analysis—it is a snapshot of place and time. SEIFA reflects the collective characteristics of an area, settlement or neighbourhood and not the individual variances between residents.

The Index of Relative Socio-Economic Disadvantage (IRSD) ranks residents into levels of disadvantage, aggregated at settlement (or neighbourhood) level. There is less ranking of advantage in the IRSD than in the Index of Relative Socio-Economic Advantage and Disadvantage (IRSAD). IRSAD aggregates both advantage and disadvantage and the difference from one to the other is offset by the impact on the area from having advantaged residents. The Index of Economic Resources (IER) is based on area-level income data and assumes that 'areas with higher scores have relatively greater access to economic resources than areas with lower scores' (ABS, 2013b, p. 8). In 2011, the index discounted any income below A$1 per week. The Index of Education and Occupation (IEO) focuses on the skills and qualifications required to perform different occupations and aggregates the numbers of people with or without qualifications, with or without jobs and in high- or low-skilled jobs.

SEIFA has a process of exclusion for geographical areas in which census data cannot provide information for enough variables in some or all of the indices. This is where the index parts ways with national perspectives of remote and very remote settlement-level data as the data cubes available are already constrained to comparatives within a state or territory. On the basis of the 2011 exclusion rules, 2,231 Statistical Area 1 level blocks (SA1) were excluded and from a total of 54,805 areas (ABS, 2013b, p. 28). In the NT, the socioeconomic indexes for SA1 areas in 2011 returned summary data for 14 of the 15 settlements analysed. Unsurprisingly, the IRSAD, IRSD and IER scores across the clusters are all in the decile 1—that is, in the lowest 10 per cent of SA1 areas when compared within all NT SA1s.

The glaring exception to our clusters dominating the lowest deciles is in the IEO, which indicates a number of residents in the middle ranges in some settlements. Due to the fact that SEIFA no longer distinguishes Indigenous status, it is likely that these higher deciles reflect non-Indigenous/not-stated workers in schools, health clinics, business manager positions or other government positions. The deciles for IEO range from 1 (lowest 10 per cent) up to 4 (lowest 40 per cent) in the different communities.

## Constraints

With the total exclusion of remote residents in HILDA and the dubious nature of the sample base in LSAY, neither of these potentially useful longitudinal surveys can contribute to our basic understanding of remote mixed-market economies. The long-term nature of these surveys not only provides stable information from the same (or similar) persons but allows for trends to be observed and causal relationships to be surmised. For example, HILDA suggests that credible causal relationships can be inferred about 'the effects of various factors on life outcomes such as earnings, unemployment, income and life satisfaction' (Wilkins, 2015, p. 4). Similarly, LSAY proposes that the data it gathers allows for 'quasi-experimental' research designs (National Centre for Vocational Education Research, 2014, p. 10). This is because before-and-after information for interventions, such as gaining a qualification, can be analysed for effect (e.g. employment), providing some indications of causality, although readers are warned 'causality is never really established in the social sciences' (National Centre for Vocational Education Research, 2014, p. 10).

The integrity of these longitudinal studies relies on consistency and it seems unlikely that important features in the economic and social lives of the population who live in remote communities will be added to the samples, thus making it impossible to extract the same type of information that is readily available for urban and regional areas. This is problematic in public policy making because 'longitudinal data are very important to governments in the development of policy as they provide robust evidence to inform policy and debate' (National Centre for Vocational Education Research, 2014, p. 10). Those who contribute to policy debates on responses to remote Indigenous disadvantage, such as 'closing the gap' (Austin-Broos, 2011; Australian Government, 2015a) and the Indigenous Advancement Strategy (Department of the Prime Minister and Cabinet, 2014), do not have access to the same level of credible information and inferred causality as is used in making decisions for the vast majority of the population that have been included in the national longitudinal samples.

It is important to reiterate that differences shown in the derived data in the tables that follow must be understood as being snapshots of two points in time, unlike the longitudinal trend characteristics that can be described from HILDA and LSAY surveys. Comparisons are highly speculative and suggestions of causality cannot be supported from these point-in-time data. Nevertheless, this is the best statistical base available. There was an overall decline of 2 per cent in the Indigenous population of remote and very remote areas of Northern Australia (see Figure 9.1) between the census collection points of 2006 and 2011, with migration into regional and urban centres (Taylor et al., 2015). The combined Aboriginal population of the southern region of the NT is approximately 17,500 people including those normally resident in the three clusters of communities (Central Land Council, 2015a). Approximately 5,500 Aboriginal people were usually resident in the 15 settlements in these clusters, according to the 2011 census (ABS, 2014).

## Method

In this analysis, a census snapshot from 2006 is compared with the 2011 data and relevant industry information where it is available. With the addition of 2006 data, the presence or absence of mixed-market activity can be seen to have changed between the two census collection points. There is a slight change to the settlements with the inclusion of Tara in Cluster Three and Atitjere in Cluster Two in 2011, which is not evident in our search using TableBuilder Pro Census 2006 data (ABS, 2014). Otherwise, the groupings of communities, on the basis of known economic activity and industry knowledge, remains the same as in the previous research that used 2011 data (Lovell et al., 2015b, p. 4).

Using selected characteristics of labour force and population, employers and employees, and income and employment, this analysis provides the two snapshot points from ABS (2014) census data against which the magnitude of market and non-market activity can be considered, based on the presence or absence of the three mixed-market activities: art centres, ranger groups and Aboriginal community researchers. The clusters used here consist of the following communities:

- Cluster One includes Ntaria and Tjuwanpa, Lajamanu, Ltyentye Apurte (Santa Teresa), Yuendumu and outstations and Papunya and its outstations:
    - three settlements had an active art centre in 2006, and five in 2011
    - three settlements had an active ranger program in 2006, and five in 2011.
- Cluster Two includes Atitjere, Darguragu-Kalkarintji, Owairtilla (Canteen Creek), Ampilatwatja and Alekerenge (Ali Curung):
    - zero art centres in 2006 and two in 2011
    - one ranger group starting up in 2006 and three in 2011.
- Cluster Three includes Wirliyatjarrayi (Willowra), Alpurrurulam, Nyirripi, Laramba and Tara (which became a gazetted area in 2011 and, therefore, did not contribute to the 2006 data):
    - zero active art centres at either point
    - no formal ranger program at either point although one community has rangers locally based but employed through another community's program.

## Interpreting the Data

The 2006 and 2011 ABS census points are compared by using the following standard classifications (ABS, 2013a):

- Population, Occupation (OCCP)
- Labour Force (LFSP) statistics for Indigenous (INDG) and Non-Indigenous or Not-Stated (NI-NS) status
- Place of Usual Residence (POUR)
- Income (INCP)
- Employment (EMTP)
- Government/Non-Government Employment Indicator (GNGP).

The settlement data used throughout for comparison into Clusters One, Two and Three have been aggregated using the ABS TableBuilder Pro software (ABS, 2014) unless otherwise stated.

For the purpose of the Australian Census, participants in the labour force must be aged 15 years or older and employed at least one hour per week. The income data is calculated on the previous week and may not translate to annual amounts. The unemployed must be actively seeking work, be 15 years or older and not working more than one hour per week. The labour force in each settlement is a combination of those who are employed along with those who are officially unemployed.

Occupational data were found to be an inaccurate reflection of the mixed-market activities occurring in the industries selected. Some operate informally and without the correlation of financial income to product or service provided and residents often have more than one form of occupation, whereas the census question allows for a single response only (Lovell et al., 2015a). Economic participation is understood to be sporadic in remote and sparsely populated settlements, where variables include seasonal conditions, cultural obligations, shifts in policy and programs and movement of local residents in and out of communities (Carson & Carson, 2014; Dockery, 2014a, 2014b). In addition, migratory professional workforces account for high levels of mobility among non-local staff such as school and health staff, service managers and government business officers (Carson & Carson, 2014; Haslam McKenzie, 2011).

In 2006, the ABS added a series of questions relating to employment type, which 'classifies all employed people to either employees, owner-managers of incorporated enterprises, owner-managers of unincorporated enterprises or contributing family workers, on the basis of their main job' (ABS, 2012a). In the 2011 census, the Public/Private Employer Indicator classifies people 'as to whether their employment was in the government (public) or non-government (private) sector. The public sector is further broken down into National, State and Territory or Local Government' (ABS, 2012b). Both of these classifications discount persons who are under 15 years, unemployed, outside the labour force or whose status is not stated as within the labour force.

Using the two census collection points and the characteristics of employees and employers in the three clusters, two snapshots of the magnitude of market and non-market activity can be speculated on. As theorised by Wolf (1993, pp. 37–38), markets are characterised by free choice and strong price signals in which participants are protected by the minimum amount of regulation required to promote fair trading conditions resulting in efficiency and some measure of distributional equity of resources. The non-market alternatives generally include government-delivered programs, charitable efforts or philanthropic endeavours. Among the clusters in this study, non-market alternatives are more prevalent, but, as the data confirms, they do not necessarily produce equitable outcomes. Non-market failure often contributes to unintended consequences, disjunctions and tipping points that affect remote residents and settlements in ways contrary to the original intentions (Carson & Carson, 2014). Non-market failures are also reflected in the vision and management of remote environments (Woinsarski et al., 2014).

## Employers and Employees

Before examining the data for types of employment, several limitations concerning what is represented need to be stated. First, it is unlikely that philanthropic organisations will self-identify as a member of the non-market group, although Wolf (1993) theorised their activities as other than being active in the marketplace. In some cases, not-for-profit companies also contributed to the opportunity structures of the mixed-market sample described in the previous research brief (Lovell et al., 2015b). Second, it is equally unlikely that an employee of the Central Land Council will self-identify as working for the Australian Government, although the NT land councils are statutory authorities of the national government (Central Land Council, 2015a).

The choices of answers for the census question for government or private sector employment include one of the three levels of government or private sector (GNGP). Further choice for answering the question includes 'not stated' or 'not applicable'. When read in addition to the results for employment type, almost all respondents describe themselves in a government or private sector employment and as 'employees not owning a business' (EMPT). These classifications are aggregated in the figures below, for each cluster by using the GNGP and EMPT.

Using Wolf's (1993) criteria of market and non-market it is clear that employment data in these clusters suggests an almost exclusively non-market economy, despite the GNGP classifications as 'government' or 'private sector'. This is further supported through the EMPT data in which almost all employees report working for businesses they do not own. There appears to be close to zero open and competitive 'market' activity prompting the observation that the outsourcing of public services from government to other providers has not created market activity in the clusters. Crucially, this census data does not disclose that the nature of so-called 'private sector' employment is essentially non-market because industry knowledge indicates the ultimate source of revenue comes from taxes or other non-priced sources in most cases. For example, tracing back the source of funding for the ranger programs, a major form of 'private' employment, takes one to Australian Government 'Caring for Country' allocations to the Central Land Council (Central Land Council, 2015b). Likewise, this analysis does not describe fluctuations or changes in customary socioeconomic activities that are not captured by contemporary financial measures. However, it is recognised that such activities play an essential role in the wellbeing of residents throughout these settlements.

# Data

## Labour Force and Population

Figure 9.2 provides a comparison between clusters and collection points in labour force and population. The Cluster One census reported an Aboriginal and Torres Strait Islander population of 2,891 and NI-NS population of 260 in 2006. In 2011, those figures were 2,668 and 349 respectively, which indicates a decline in Aboriginal population (–23) and an increase in non-Indigenous population (+89) between collection points. The Indigenous labour force in 2006 was 606 and the NI-NS labour force was 180. In 2011, Indigenous labour force rose (+6) to 612 despite the decreased population, while the NI-NS labour force also increased (+37) to 249 in line with the reported population increase.

The Cluster Two census recorded an Indigenous population of 1,292 and NI-NS population of 74 in 2006. In 2011, those figures were 1,889 and 205 respectively, which indicates an increase in Aboriginal populations (+597) and an increase in NI-NS populations (+131) between collection points. The increase in the Indigenous population is partly explained through the addition of one settlement to the cluster data in 2011 (+164 Indigenous residents). The Indigenous labour force in 2006 was 340 and the NI-NS labour force was 48. In 2011, the Indigenous labour force increased (+6) to 346 and the NI-NS labour force increased (+131) to 205. The very slight increase in the Indigenous labour force (+6) cannot be adequately explained in light of the +164 Indigenous residents at Atitjere being added to the cluster in 2011 data. The increase in NI-NS population attributed to the additional settlement was +21, which contributes to the overall increase in NI-NS labour force in this cluster and also aligned to population increase.

The Cluster Three census showed an Indigenous population of 1,071 and NI-NS population of 172 in 2006. In 2011, those figures were 1,090 and 94 respectively, which indicates an increase in Aboriginal population (+19) and a decrease in NI-NS populations (–78) between collection points. The data for Cluster Three in 2011 also includes an added settlement with an Indigenous population of +53 and NI-NS population of +4. The Indigenous labour force in 2006 was 180 and the NI-NS labour force was 119. In 2011, the Indigenous labour force was 212 (+32) and NI-NS was 76 (–42). Some of the increases across the cluster are attributed to the inclusions of the newly gazetted settlement between censuses.

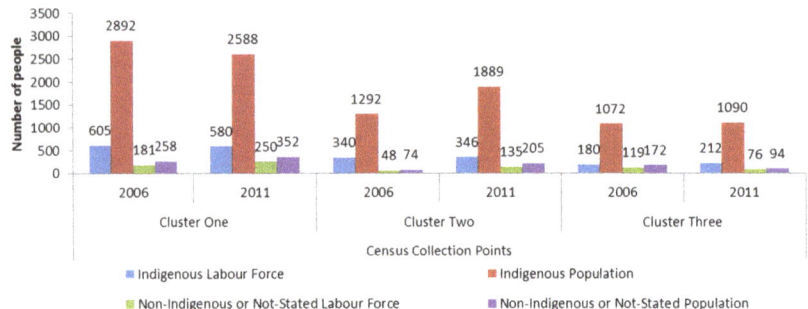

**Figure 9.2: Indigenous and NI-NS labour force and population by clusters and census points.**
Source: Authors' research.

Evidence of population mobility between census points is well documented (Carson et al., 2015; Dockery, 2014a; Taylor et al., 2015) and the population data above further supports findings of mobility. However, intra-settlement mobility does not fully explain the labour force changes across these settlements, which must be understood in relation to a national ideological shift in policy, which saw strong targeting of remote Indigenous employment across governments' policy agendas (Forrest, 2014; Limerick et al., 2014; Steering Committee for the Review of Government Service Provision, 2014). Cluster One labour force decreased 4.4 per cent and the population decreased 11.5 per cent. Cluster Two labour force increased 1.8 per cent whereas the population increased 32 per cent. Cluster Three labour force increased 16 per cent between collection points, whereas the population increased 1.7 per cent.

When comparing the absolute numbers of Indigenous people in the labour force, there are noticeable differences between the clusters. A stronger mixed market, larger population and higher levels of both Indigenous and non-Indigenous employment are present in Cluster One and are lowest in Cluster Three, which has been previously demonstrated to have minimal mixed-market activity. Of course, these observations cannot be interpreted as trends in each cluster nor can causality be determined. Nevertheless, it is not unexpected that larger population centres have more extensive social and physical infrastructure and may be more attractive places in which to invest in more complex mixed-market activities compared to smaller settlements. Clearly, this data also suggests that Indigenous population are not nearly as engaged in labour force activity as the non-Indigenous residents in each of the clusters. One reason for this is the migratory nature of non-Indigenous residents who travel and reside in a remote settlement on the basis of an employment contract, or as family members of those who relocate for employment.

## Government/Non-Government Employment Indices

The next set of ABS data that might be used to distinguish between market and non-market activity in the clusters comes from employment responses at the two census points (see Figure 9.3). The following is stratified from within labour force and population demographics presented above, according to the three classifications of not-stated, private sector and the combined governments sector (e.g. local, territory and federal). Additionally, the figure for persons employed, but not owning a business is marked on each bar with 'X'.

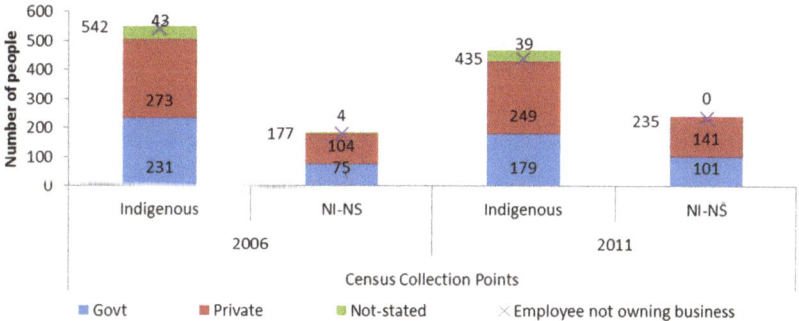

**Figure 9.3: Cluster One showing combined government and private sector employment indices and employment type for 2006 and 2011, using the categories of Indigenous and NI-NS.**
Source: Authors' research.

There are 547 Indigenous employees in Cluster One in 2006, of which 542 recorded they were employed in a business they did not own, while five nominated as owner-managers of unincorporated enterprises. In 2011, of a possible 467 Indigenous employees, 435 worked in a business they did not own and 32 worked as owner-managers of unincorporated enterprises. What the nature of those unincorporated enterprises was is not possible to define. These residents could be entrepreneurs producing goods or services for arts markets, undertaking fee-for-service for non-market agencies such as Land Councils or providing skills to not-for-profit or commercial employers in roles such as researchers and interpreters.

The correlating findings for NI-NS status people shows 183 employees in 2006, of which six selected owner-manager of unincorporated enterprise and the remaining 177 were employed in a business they did not own. In 2011, of a possible 242 NI-NS employees, 235 worked in a business they did not own and seven worked as owner-managers of unincorporated enterprises. The increase in NI-NS employees occurred predominantly in territory government (+32) and in those who indicated they held private sector employment (+37).

In Figure 9.4, Cluster Two data includes 230 Indigenous employees in 2006 who were employed in a business they did not own and no owner-managers of unincorporated enterprises. In 2011, of a possible 262 Indigenous employees, 258 worked in a business they did not own with four working as owner-managers of unincorporated enterprises. As in Cluster One, it is not possible to define these enterprises—they could be entrepreneurs producing goods and services or providing fee-for-service outputs to both market or non-market agents.

The correlating findings for NI-NS status people shows 66 employees in 2006, of which nine selected owner-manager of incorporated or unincorporated enterprise and the remaining 57 were employed in a business they did not own. In 2011, of a possible 184 NI-NS employees, 163 worked in a business they did not own and 21 worked as owner-managers of incorporated or unincorporated enterprises. The increase in NI-NS employees occurred predominantly in territory government (+38) and reported private sector employment (+71).

**Figure 9.4: Cluster Two shows combined government and private sector employment indices and employment type for 2006 and 2011, using the categories of Indigenous and NI-NS.**
Source: Authors' research.

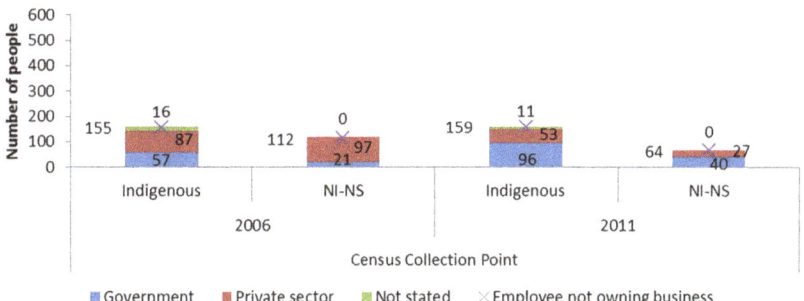

**Figure 9.5: Cluster Three shows combined government and private sector employment indices and employment type for 2006 and 2011, using the categories of Indigenous and NI-NS.**
Source: Authors' research.

In Figure 9.5, Cluster Three data suggests that, of 160 Indigenous employees in 2006, 155 were employed in a business they did not own, but figures for owner-managers of incorporated or unincorporated enterprises are so small it is not possible to know if they are valid. In 2011, of a possible 160 Indigenous employees, 159 worked in a business they did not own and again the figures for owner-managers of incorporated or unincorporated enterprises are too low to be valid. As with Clusters One and Two, it is not possible to define the nature of those unincorporated enterprises.

The correlating findings for NI-NS status people shows 118 employees in 2006, of which six selected owner-manager of incorporated or unincorporated enterprise and the remaining 112 were employed in a business they did not own. In 2011, of a possible 68 NI-NS employees, 64 worked in a business they did not own and four worked as owner-managers of unincorporated enterprises. The decrease in NI-NS employees occurred predominantly in private sector employment (–70).

In all three clusters, non-Indigenous employment and the size of the labour force correlate. In Clusters One and Two, the non-Indigenous labour force and employment both increased while they both decreased in Cluster Three. It is argued that employment drives the size of the non-Indigenous labour force in these remote communities because virtually all non-Indigenous persons must have a job to receive accommodation or be accepted into the settlement. This employment-driven explanation is further supported by the income data shown below that indicates virtually zero unemployment among the non-Indigenous residents of the three clusters.

For Indigenous residents, the linkage between the size of the labour force and the actual employment outcomes is not so clearly identifiable and might be more directly related to population size. In Cluster One, the Indigenous population dropped significantly, the labour force only contracted slightly, but employment went down considerably. In Cluster Two, Indigenous population went up by almost one-third, the labour market size was almost identical and Indigenous employment increased by a small amount. For Cluster Three, the population was nearly steady, the Indigenous labour force increased and the numbers of residents employed was almost the same at both time points. The data does not give a strong indication as to the drivers of Indigenous employment or unemployment, with the exception of a possible influence exerted by population size.

The information on employer type (i.e. government or private) seems unlikely to adequately describe the type and extent of mixed-market activity present in these clusters, at least in Wolf's (1993) definition of the non-market. Because the revenue for non-market activities is principally derived from taxes, donations or other non-priced sources (Wolf, 1993, p. 38), the classification of private sector employers who have tendered for and won contracts to deliver services for governments would be considered a non-market activity. However, it is unlikely that those who are working on the settlements are going to indicate they are working for government, if only because respondents to the census question may or may not know the ultimate source of the funds used to pay their wages.

Additionally, many of the employers who are operating in a more commercial environment, such as the art centres, frequently receive public grants or royalty funds to maintain their viability (Australian Government, 2015b). Again, it is unlikely that the art centre employees would indicate that they were anything other than in private employment. The large numbers of private employees in the ABS data superficially suggests the existence of a potentially significant amount of consumer-driven behaviour where the principal source of revenue comes from selling an output in an open market (Wolf, 1993, p. 39). For these remote settlements, the binary employer data is not nuanced enough to accurately understand the complexities of remote economies or their mixed markets. It is not possible to determine from the owner-manager data if any of these persons are operating in a fully commercial or entrepreneurial capacity. This distinction would assist in further distinguishing the relative contribution of markets and non-markets to determine the scale of the total mixed market. It would also inform better policy development.

Policies supporting more market-driven behaviours by remote residents on the basis of significant 'private' employment reported in the census data are unlikely to have their intended outcomes.

## Income and Employment

The next set of figures compares income and labour force data for Indigenous and NI-NS categories across clusters at the two census points. The income and labour force data in each cluster is aggregated into Indigenous, non-Indigenous or not-stated status. Income earners are classified as those actively seeking work or working at least one hour per week (ABS, 2014). Figures 9.6, 9.8 and 9.10 then aggregate income (INCP) and labour force (LFSP) data for each cluster into Non-labour force, Unemployed, Nil income or the total number of income earners (A$1+) during the week prior to census collection. Figures 9.7, 9.9 and 9.11 show brackets for income earned in the week prior to the collection point. Despite significant increases in public expenditure driven by Australian Government 'Closing the Gap' priorities (Australian Government, 2015a), the income difference between Indigenous and other employees in these remote settlements dramatically widens for income brackets above A$1,000 per week in all three clusters. It is recognised that in 2011 the value of the dollar is less than in 2006; however, the ABS does not adjust for inflation.

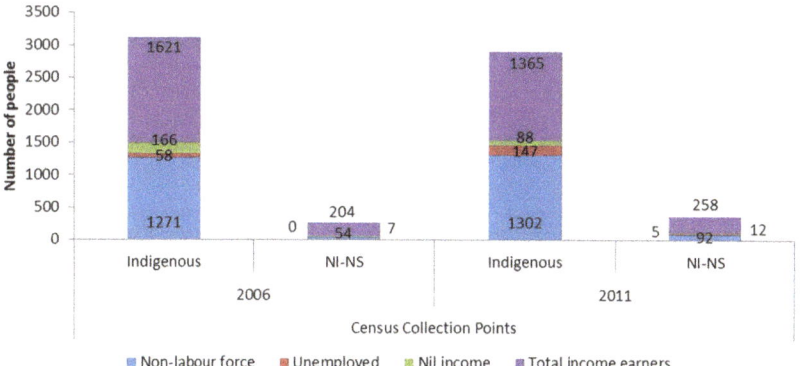

**Figure 9.6: Cluster One population aggregated as non-labour force, unemployed and nil income during the week leading up to census collection, and number of income earners at any level over A$1.**

Source: Authors' research.

Figure 9.6 shows the loss of Indigenous income earners accounted for the observed decline in population between the two collection points in Cluster One. The non-Indigenous population growth was more evenly distributed and shows very few unemployed or nil-income-earning persons, suggesting dependent partners and children contributed the NI-NS non-income increase.

Not unexpectedly, the number of income earners in Cluster One reflects the changes in population for each group. Figure 9.7 clearly demonstrates the disparity of income levels between Indigenous residents dominating the lower brackets and non-Indigenous residents occupying the bulk of the highest paid jobs in this group of settlements.

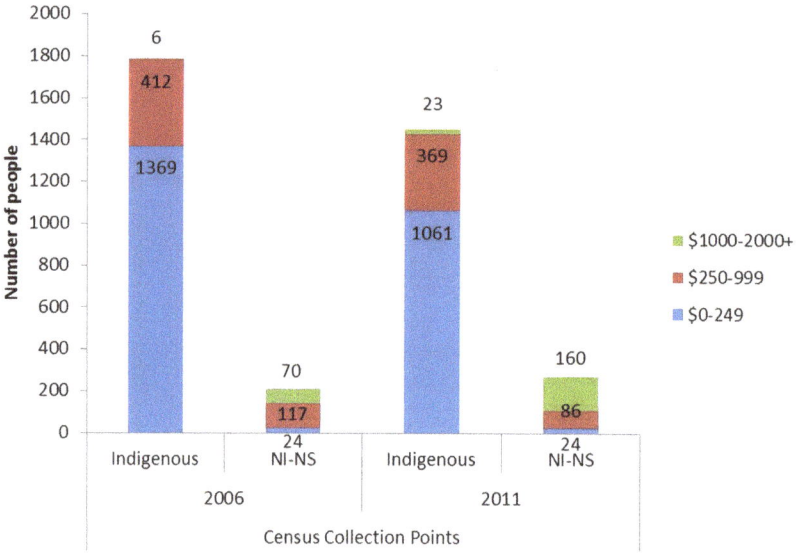

**Figure 9.7: Cluster One population aggregated as non-labour force, unemployed and nil income during the week leading up to census collection, and number of income earners between A$1 and A$2,000+ per week.**
Source: Authors' research.

In Cluster Two, Figure 9.8 suggests that population increase in both Indigenous and non-Indigenous residents accounts for increases in the total number income earners and the total number of non-labour force residents. The Indigenous unemployment reduced (−94), and nil income increased (+30) between collection points. The only change in those categories for NI-NS residents was slight increase (+3) in nil income.

9. NATIONAL DATA

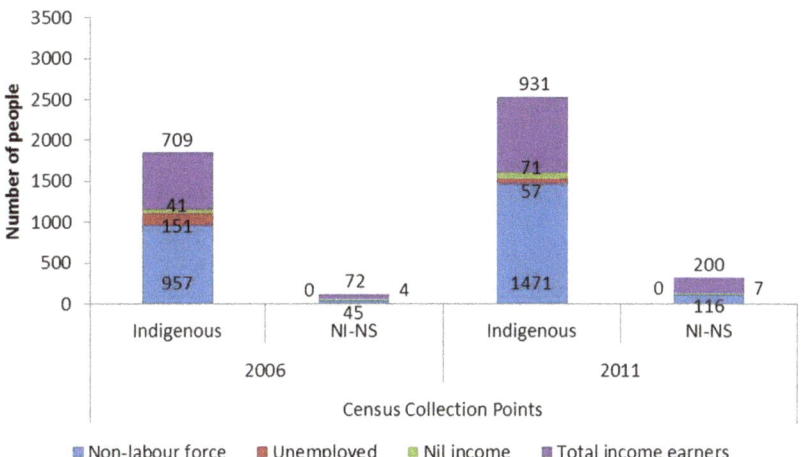

**Figure 9.8: Cluster Two population aggregated as non-labour force, unemployed and nil income during the week leading up to census collection, and number of income earners at any level over A$1.**
Source: Authors' research.

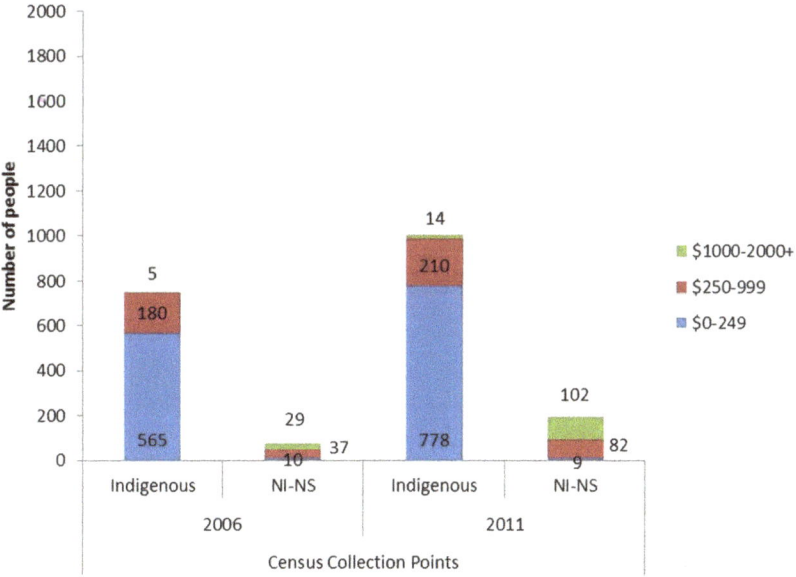

**Figure 9.9: Cluster Two population aggregated as non-labour force, unemployed and nil income during the week leading up to census collection, and income earners between A$1 and A$2,000+ per week.**
Source: Authors' research.

203

Figure 9.9 also demonstrates that while the growth in Indigenous income earners in Cluster Two was in the lower two income bands, the higher-paid employees in these communities were from the non-Indigenous population of income earners.

In Figure 9.10, the Indigenous non-labour force and income earners remain fairly static, with a slight increase in unemployment (+28) and reduction in nil income (–43). The non-Indigenous or not-stated category reflects a decrease in income earners (–46) and increases in all other categories (+59) combined.

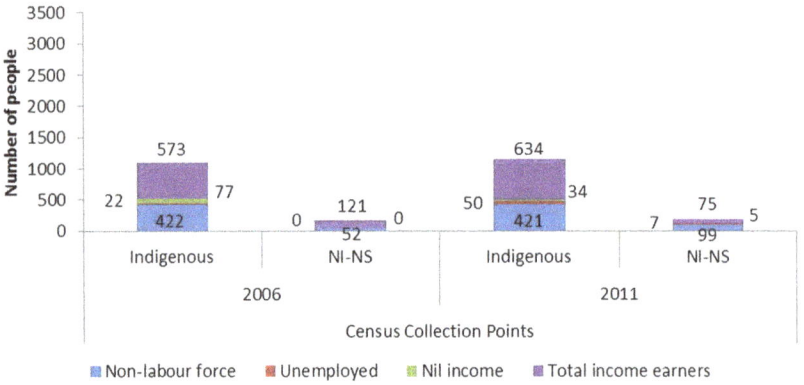

**Figure 9.10: Cluster Three population aggregated as non-labour force, unemployed and nil income during the week leading up to census collection, and number of income earners at any level over A$1.**
Source: Authors' research.

For Cluster Three, Figures 9.10 and 9.11 indicate relative stability in the Indigenous population at the two points in time, although none of the high-income earners from 2006 were still receiving that level of income in 2011 and the numbers of lower-income earners increased. While, yet again, non-Indigenous persons dominated the higher-income bracket in both years, the population loss was almost exclusively from the highest paid jobs in these settlements.

Industry experience shows that NI-NS higher-income earners seldom remain in any settlement for long periods of time and generally have accommodation and a motor vehicle supplied as a condition of employment. With a few minor exceptions, they spend very little of their incomes in the clusters and this disrupts any potential benefit of market-

9. NATIONAL DATA

related circulation of money through the local economy. Policy made on the basis of total community income levels would be seriously under-informed as to the level of potential economic activity that could take place without taking into account the disaggregation demonstrated in Figures 9.6–9.11.

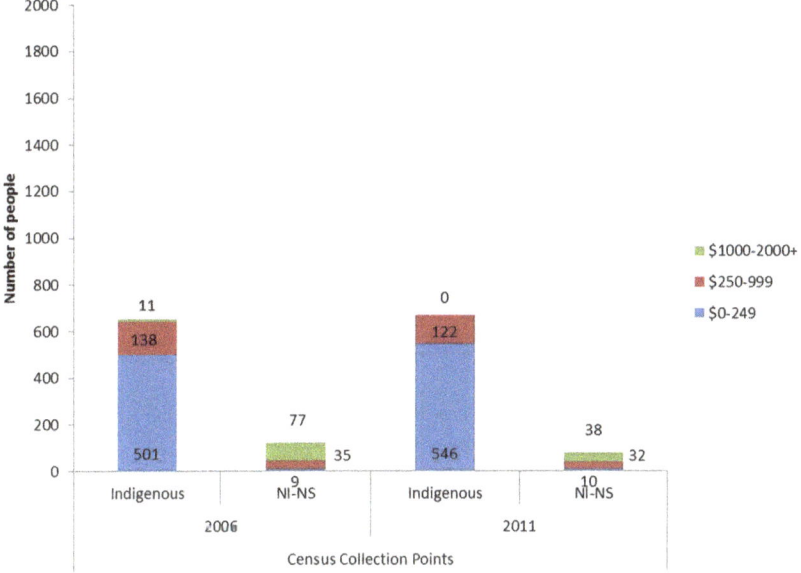

**Figure 9.11: Cluster Three population aggregated as non-labour force, unemployed and nil income during the week leading up to census collection, and income earners between A$1 and A$2,000+ per week.**
Source: Authors' research.

Additionally, the employer type data suggests that virtually none of these non-Indigenous high-income recipients is employed in a true market sector. The inclusion of non-Indigenous high-income earners in the SEIFA indexes skews the estimated levels of advantage upwards, as it overestimates the total of financial resources that are available in the mixed markets of these remote settlements. A variation in percentiles between settlements for the index of education and skilled employment reflects migratory staff with higher educational levels also attained higher levels of income. However, an unintended local consequence of this advantage is that the multiplier benefits of those higher incomes fall far from the remote region in which the income is derived.

Wolf (1993) argued that non-market failure occurs where there is lack of distributional equity and it would seem that despite increased expenditure on Aboriginal policy, gains in income and employment are clearly attributed to non-local migratory residents, while local Indigenous residents of the study area have experienced an overall decline in income. The evidence suggests that the economies of these settlements are almost exclusively non-market, and income that reaches and circulates among Indigenous residents has reduced between collection points. Additionally, there was no evidence of an overall increase in Indigenous employment. These findings confirm the earlier hypothesis that, despite additional public policy and expenditure, there is no evidence of increased economic benefit to local or migratory employees or business owners derived through true market activity between the two collection points in 2006 and 2011. In addition, most recent national Indigenous employment targets for closing the gap report further decline in employment (Australian Government, 2015a, p. 5).

## Mixed Market and Occupation in the Clusters

Aboriginal residents often undertake customary activity *despite* market or non-market ability to value or transact it (Lovell, 2015). Natural and cultural resource management, into which Indigenous ranger programs fit, is undertaken through both the mixed-market and customary structures. Aboriginal art is produced and sold opportunistically, both through and outside of Aboriginal art centres (Acker & Woodhead, 2015). There are a number of successful research and evaluation companies who undertake casual employment of Aboriginal researchers (Limerick et al., 2014). Aboriginal community research models tend towards fee-for-service or consultancy work, delivering an output that is classified here as a market activity.

Figure 9.12 shows Indigenous occupation at their POUR for selected occupations representing arts activity, natural and cultural resource management and education at each cluster, for both census points. Education-related occupations are placed here as a non-market correlate because Aboriginal community research activity cannot be calculated due to the lack of formal figures for 2006 and the 2011 data only reflected reports from a single employer. The arts and natural and cultural resource management occupational categories represent local jobs in art centres and ranger groups but may include other places of work.

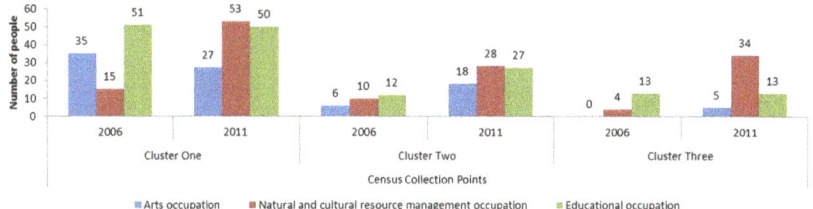

**Figure 9.12: Primary occupations of Indigenous persons at place of usual residence in 2006 and 2011 census points for each settlement cluster.**
Source: Authors' research.

Clusters One and Three are somewhat static in education-related occupations; however, there is a spike in Cluster Two. This suggests that there has been an increased level of employment relating to public education between 2006 and 2011 in that cluster, most likely related to the increased Indigenous population who are outside the labour force (children and parents of dependent children). The allocation of human resources to schools is directly related to student enrolment numbers and this is a likely contributor to both increases in the non-Indigenous labour force, employment and higher-level wages observed previously in this analysis. Because these settlement populations are small, natural fluctuations may contribute to the change as well. However, a spike like this might also reflect additional non-market program delivery in the cluster based on employment type data. Like other avenues of economic participation, educational initiatives come and go in remote communities and are highly dependent on (often short-term) funding cycles (Lovell et al., 2015a).

Additional federal funding (Australian Government, 2015c; Central Land Council, 2015b) for Indigenous ranger groups is reflected across all clusters by the increase in natural and cultural resource management occupations. In relation to occupational data, arts activities appear to have contracted in Cluster One, with the highest number of Aboriginal art centres and to have increased in the other clusters in spite of the total absence of formal art centres in Cluster Three. The industry navigated significant short-term program and market changes between census points as a result of welfare and employment policy shifts such as changes to Community Development Employment Programme (CDEP) and the contraction of the high-end and cosmopolitan Aboriginal arts market due to the global financial crisis in 2008 (Woodhead & Acker, 2014).

It can be conjectured that because the opportunistic nature of art production and sale supports a significant revenue source that derives from a market, the occupational record understates the informal economic activity. Fewer people classify art as a primary occupation since the CDEP ceased in 2008 and the arts centre–related activity changed significantly under new employment program policies (Acker & Woodhead, 2015).

Figure 9.13 compares 2006 and 2011 census snapshots of labour force at POUR with the annual aggregate taken from financial year measures at 30 June for 2006 and 2011. The results are displayed for each cluster. All five Cluster One settlements had an active art centre in 2011 and three had active art centres in 2006. In Cluster Two, there were two active art centres in 2011 and none in 2006 while Cluster Three had no active art centres at either point. In 2011, Cluster One data from the art centres (Tim Acker, personal communication, August 2015) shows that more people still sold at least one work of art through a local art centre than were registered as part of the labour force in that cluster.

In summary, Figures 9.12 and 9.13 confirm that where mixed-market data is available it reflects the availability of local opportunity structures. Non-market contribution and a market that values residents' agency can contribute sustainable economic and social participation, as proposed by Wolf (1993, pp. 89–90) that modern economies require a balance of the two.

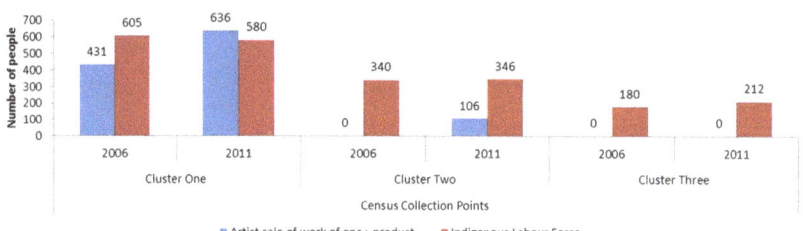

**Figure 9.13: Comparison of Indigenous artists recorded as selling one or more artworks and number of Indigenous people in the labour force at place of usual residence for 2006 and 2011 census points.**
Source: Authors' research.

## Conclusion

This chapter extrapolates from an earlier investigation of mixed-market activity in a sample of remote and sparsely populated Aboriginal settlements in Central Australia (Lovell et al., 2015a). That investigation found that describing some facets of mixed-market activity using national census and available industry data has provided a novel means of describing the potential for sustainable local economic participation. These findings further support the hypothesis that the concept of mixed market is a suitable lens for understanding the impact of public policy on the sustainable economic and social wellbeing of residents in remote and marginalised settlements.

In spite of their important contribution to national social and economic policy development, the two most relevant longitudinal surveys (HILDA and LSAY) are not fit for purpose when considering these mixed markets in the selected clusters of remote communities. Compared to the potential capacity of longitudinal surveys to suggest causality, the ABS census data cannot give a similar level of predictive possibility because it only captures points in time. Because SEIFA indices are constructed from ABS data, they suffer the same limitations and, unsurprisingly, correspond with the census employment and income data. The removal of Indigenous identification further reduces SEIFA's capacity to capture the mixed markets of remote NT communities.

The labour force data describes high levels of employment for non-Indigenous persons in each of the clusters and the exact opposite is true for Indigenous residents. Both groups are highly mobile, but it seems likely that while employment opportunities mobilise the non-Indigenous workforce, there are more complex factors, including population size, contributing to movements undertaken by 'locals'. The disparity in income between non-Indigenous and Indigenous residents further complicates the use of the data to determine the economy in the clusters. Averaging incomes across the entire workforce suggests higher levels of resources in the community than actually exist due to much of the non-Indigenous income never making it into the community in the first place.

The employment data, if not tempered by the application of local industry knowledge, is potentially very misleading when using the binary distinction of government or private. The large reported numbers of 'private' employees is more suggestive of suburban Canberra than remote communities and suggest the potential for more market-driven policymaking. This is where Wolf's (1993) more nuanced distinction between markets and non-markets, based on revenue source, becomes most illuminating. Except for a mere handful of owner-managers (most would be managers), the employees of organisations that operate in the clusters are almost exclusively in the non-market sector. On the other hand, it has been shown that both the sellers of art and artefacts and Aboriginal community researchers are operating in a market environment where their revenue is determined by a price linked to what the market will bear.

It is argued that the analysis presented here further supports the importance of mixed-market ideation to contribute to better socioeconomic policy if benefits are to be derived by local residents in remote settlements. In particular, there is evidence that in the mixed markets operating in these remote communities the market segment is dominated exclusively by individuals behaving as economically rational decision-makers. Conversely, the non-market sector is made up of organisations and their employees. Currently, these organisations and virtually all of their non-Indigenous labour force direct their economic gains away from the remote clusters in which they are derived and, therefore, reduce the financial resources available to circulate through the local economy and encourage greater market behaviour. Policy solutions that do not recognise the coexistence of individual Indigenous marketeers with those of non-market organisations seem destined to produce unintended outcomes at best and further impoverish these settlements at worst.

# References

Acker, T. & Woodhead, A. (2015). *The economy of place, a place in the economy: A value chain study of the Aboriginal and Torres Strait Islander art sector. Summary report*. Retrieved from www.crc-rep.com.au/resource/EconomyOf Place_WEB.pdf

Austin-Broos, D. (2011). *A different inequality*. Crows Nest, NSW: Allen & Unwin.

Australian Bureau of Statistics (ABS). (2012a, 24 October). *Employment type*. Retrieved from www.abs.gov.au/websitedbs/censushome.nsf/home/statements personemtp?opendocument&navpos=430

Australian Bureau of Statistics (ABS). (2012b, 24 September). Public/private employer indicator. *Australian census*. Retrieved from www.abs.gov.au/websitedbs/censushome.nsf/home/statementspersongngp?opendocument&navpos=430

Australian Bureau of Statistics (ABS). (2013a, 29 October). *Glossary of statistical geography terminology, 2013* (Cat. No. 1217.0.55.001). Retrieved from www.abs.gov.au/ausstats/abs@.nsf/mf/1217.0.55.001

Australian Bureau of Statistics (ABS). (2013b). *Census of population and housing: Socio-economic indexes for areas (SEIFA), Australia, 2011* (Cat. No. 2033.0.55.001). Retrieved from www.abs.gov.au/websitedbs/censushome.nsf/home/seifa

Australian Bureau of Statistics (ABS). (2014, 18 December). *Australian demographic statistics* (Cat. No. 3101.0). Retrieved from www.abs.gov.au/ausstats/abs@.nsf/mf/3101.0

Australian Council for Educational Research. (1997). *Longitudinal surveys of Australian youth: The Australian youth survey description*. Technical paper no. 7. Melbourne: Australian Council for Educational Research.

Australian Government. (2015a). *Closing the gap. Prime Minister's report*. Canberra, ACT: Australian Government. Retrieved from www.pmc.gov.au/sites/default/files/publications/Closing_the_Gap_2015_Report.pdf

Australian Government. (2015b). *Indigenous Languages and arts program*. Retrieved from arts.gov.au/topics/indigenous-arts-languages-and-culture/indigenous-languages-and-arts

Australian Government. (2015c, 6 February). *Indigenous Ranger Programs*. Retrieved from www.niaa.gov.au/indigenous-affairs/environment/indigenous-ranger-program

Carson, D. & Carson, D. (2014). Local economies of mobility in sparsely populated areas: Cases from Australia's spine. *Journal of Rural Studies*, *36*, 340–349.

Carson, D., Ensign, P. C., Rasmussen, R. & Taylor, A. (2015). Perspectives on 'Demography at the Edge'. In D. Carson, R. Rasmussen, L. Huskey, P. C. Ensign & A. Taylor (Eds), *Demography at the edge. Human populations in developed nations* (pp. 3–20). Farnham, England: Ashgate.

Central Land Council. (2015a). *CLC homepage facts*. Retrieved from www.clc.org.au/

Central Land Council. (2015b). *Ranger program development strategy*. Retrieved from www.clc.org.au/publications/content/ranger-program-development-report

Department of the Prime Minister and Cabinet. (2014). *Indigenous advancement strategy guidelines*. Canberra: Australian Government.

Dockery, A. (2014a). *Reconceptualising mobility for Aboriginal and Torres Strait Islander Australians.* Retrieved from www.crc-rep.com.au/resource/CW015_ReconceptualisingMobility.pdf

Dockery, A. (2014b). A wellbeing approach to mobility and its application to Aboriginal and Torres Strait Islander Australians. *Social Indicators Research, 125*(1), 243–255.

Forrest, A. (2014). *Creating party – The Forrest review.* Canberra: Commonwealth of Australia. Retrieved from www.niaa.gov.au/resource-centre/indigenous-affairs/forrest-review

Haslam McKenzie, F. (2011). Attracting and retaining skilled and professional staff in remote locations of Australia. *The Rangeland Journal, 33*(4), 353–363.

Jones, R. (2002). *Longitudinal surveys of Australian youth: Education participation and outcomes by geographic location* (Research Report No. 26). Retrieved from www.lsay.edu.au/publications/1865.html

Limerick, M. C., Department of the Prime Minister and Cabinet, Brunton, C., O'Brien Rich Research Group & Putt, J. C. (2014). *National partnership agreement on remote Service delivery evaluation 2013.* Canberra, ACT: Australian Government. Retrieved from www.niaa.gov.au/sites/default/files/publications/npa-remote-service-delivery-evaluation-2013.PDF

Lovell, J. (2015). Customary assets and contemporary artistry: Multimodal learning and remote economic participation. *The Australian Journal of Indigenous Education, 44*(2), pp. 184–193. doi.org/10.1017/jie.2015.24

Lovell, J., Guenther, J. & Zoellner, D. (2015a, 20–22 July). *Developing Northern Australia: Recognising remote mixed-market economies.* Paper presented at the Developing Northern Australia: Economically, Socially, Sustainably conference, Townsville, Queensland.

Lovell, J., Guenther, J. & Zoellner, D. (2015b). *Northern Australian aspirations.* Retrieved from www.cdu.edu.au/sites/default/files/research-brief-2015-07_0.pdf

Lovell, J., Zoellner, D., Guenther, J., Brouard, F. & McMurtry, J. (2016). Contemporary Aboriginal settlements: Understanding mixed-market approaches. In A. Taylor, D. Carson, P. Ensign, L. Huskey & R. Rasmussen (Eds), *Settlements at the edge: Remote human settlements in developed nations* (pp. 246–269). Oxon, England: Ashgate.

Morrison, J. (2015). *Northern Development: Embracing the Indigenous difference* [Press release]. Darwin: Northern Land Council.

Nakata, M. (2007). The cultural interface. *The Australian Journal of Indigenous Education, 36*(5), 2–14.

National Centre for Vocational Education Research. (2014). *Longitudinal surveys of Australian youth: Annual report 2013* Retrieved from www.lsay.edu.au/publications/2761.html

Pearson, C. & Daff, S. (2014). Female Indigenous entrepreneurship in remote communities in Northern Australia. *Information Management and Business Review, 6*(6), 329–344.

Sengupta, U., Vieta, M. & McMurtry, J. (2015). Indigenous communities and social enterprises in Canada. *ANSERJ: Canadian Journal of Nonprofit and Social Economy Research/Revue canadienne de recherche sur les OSBL et l'économie sociale, 6*(1), 103–123.

Steering Committee for the Review of Government Service Provision. (2014). *Overcoming Indigenous disadvantage: Key indicators 2014*. Retrieved from www.pc.gov.au/research/recurring/overcoming-indigenous-disadvantage/key-indicators-2014/key-indicators-2014-report.pdf

Taylor, A., Payer, H. & Brokensha, H. (2015). *The demography of developing Northern Australia*. Retrieved from www.cdu.edu.au/sites/default/files/research-brief-2015-06.pdf

Watson, N. & Wooden, M. (2002). *The Household, Income and Labour Dynamics in Australia (HILDA) survey: Wave 1 survey methodology* (HILDA Project Technical Paper Series No. 1/02 [Revised October 2002]). Retrieved from melbourneinstitute.unimelb.edu.au/assets/documents/hilda-bibliography/hilda-technical-papers/htec102.pdf

Wilkins, Roger. (2015). *The Household, Income and Labour Dynamics in Australia survey: Selected findings from waves 1 to 12*. Melbourne: Melbourne Institute of Applied Economic and Social Research, University of Melbourne.

Woinsarski, J., Traill, B. & Booth, C. (2014). *The modern outback. Nature, people and the future of remote Australia*. Retrieved from www.pewtrusts.org/en/research-and-analysis/reports/2014/10/the-modern-outback

Wolf, C. (1993). *Markets or governments: Choosing between imperfect alternatives* (2nd ed.). Cambridge, MA: MIT Press. Retrieved from www.rand.org/pubs/notes/N2505.html

Woodhead, A. & Acker, T. (2014). *The art economies value chain reports: Synthesis*. Retrieved from www.crc-rep.com.au/resource/CR004_AEVC_Synthesis.pdf

# Section 3

# Demographic Trends and Migration: Key Issues Facing Further Development in Northern Australia

Bruce Prideaux

This short section of two chapters outlines a number of key demographic and migration challenges that need to be addressed if the ambitious population targets contained in the Australian Government's *Our north, our future: White paper on developing Northern Australia* (2015) are to be achieved. Taylor and Yuhun note in their chapter that population is a key factor in determining development pathways for regions, complementing the observation of Rosenman et al. in their chapter that the small resident population of Northern Australia is one of the principle limitations hampering future economic and social development of the region. The population issues outlined by both chapters provide a useful insight into the issues raised by Brewer in his introduction to the six chapters dealing with water, land and energy (Section 4). Brewer notes that the long-running debate on developing the north has been marred by 'confusion and conflict generated by ambiguous and conflicting ideologies of laissez-faire economics'. The confusion noted by Brewer is reflected in comments made by Taylor and Yuhun in relation to the 2015 white paper's target of growing several of the region's cities to more than 1 million residents by 2060. As Taylor and Yuhun note, no research has been undertaken into the compatibility of the white paper's population targets with the white paper's policy ambitions.

In their discussion of the limitations on growth caused by labour shortages, Rosenman et al. note that little attention has been paid to the need for immigration to build a sustainable workforce and economically viable communities in Northern Australia. Part of the solution lies in attracting migrants. However, to ensure migrants feel welcome, communities and organisational cultures and structures must be developed to support both domestic and international 'newcomers'. This may require additional investment in community and health services as well as a more efficient system for skill recognition for overseas migrants. Taylor and Yuhun also highlight the need to attract migrants, particularly from overseas, but point out that there are numerous issues that must be addressed, given the long-established trend of migrants preferencing southern cities to the sparsely populated north. Another barrier identified by Taylor and Yuhun relates to gender balance, with the north having a greater number of males than females, an outcome of the difficulties in attracting women to and retaining them in the region.

Both chapters highlight the role that migration must play in strategies for developing Northern Australia and both identify a range of difficulties that currently inhibit migration. As Taylor and Yuhun note, it is unrealistic to expect that policies directed at growing the region's population will succeed in achieving the desired economic growth outcomes unless there is a deeper understanding of the various drivers that underlie both inward and outward migration from sparsely populated regions.

The observations made by both Taylor and Yuhun and Rosenman et al. about the need for a more detailed understanding of the role of migration and the composition of the region's current population highlight one of the key policy failures of past strategies to develop Northern Australia. Until there is a more detailed understanding of why people move into and out of the region and what is required to retain people who do move into the region, it is unlikely that the population strategies outlined in the 2015 white paper will be achieved. A more detailed understanding of the relevant population is also required if the economic growth targets outlined in the 2015 white paper are to have any chance of succeeding.

# 10

# The Demography of Developing Northern Australia

Andrew Taylor and Pawinee Yuhun

## Introduction

The size of populations and their changing compositions are at the forefront of determining economic development pathways for nations, states, regions and communities. In northern parts of developed nations, populations are relatively small, sparsely distributed (although becoming increasingly urbanised) and subject to rapid and significant changes (Carson et al., 2011). In addition, northern communities, more so than others on a per-capita basis, receive and send out transient non-resident populations including non-resident workers (Brokensha et al., 2013), tourists and mobile indigenous peoples (Carson & Carson, 2014). A growing body of literature has outlined the complexities of population systems in northern developed contexts and the importance of significant diversity in their characteristics, as well as their differences to southern areas (Hornstrom et al., 2015).

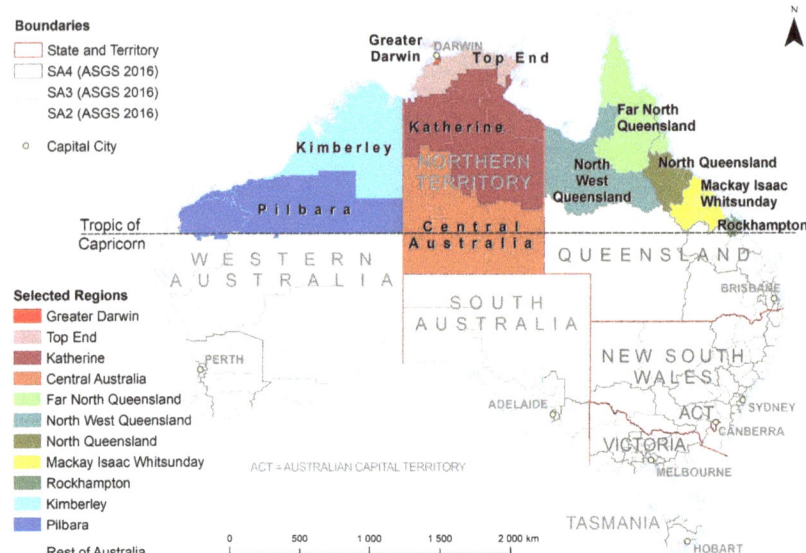

**Figure 10.1: Map of Northern Australia as defined in the 2015 white paper.**
Source: Constructed by the authors using open-source GIS software and Australian Bureau of Statistics digital boundaries.

In 2015, the Australian Government released its white paper on developing Northern Australia, *Our north, our future: White paper on developing Northern Australia*. The white paper set out policies and initiatives aspiring to deliver further and substantial economic development in and from northern parts of the nation. The policy hinges around five industries that the government feels have the most potential for growth: food and agribusiness; resources and energy; tourism and hospitality; international education; and health care, medical research and aged care (Australian Government, 2015, p. 3). 'Northern Australia' was defined in the policy as all areas north of the Tropic of Capricorn with the addition of the Central Australia (desert) area of the jurisdiction of the Northern Territory (NT), incorporating the service centre town of Alice Springs and its surrounding region (see Figure 10.1).

Both the 2015 white paper and its precursors, the *Green paper on developing Northern Australia* (Australian Government, 2014) and *Pivot North: Inquiry into the development of Northern Australia* (Joint Select Committee on Northern Australia, 2014), discussed the significance of population size and changes to population characteristics for determining economic development in the region. In all three documents, Northern Australia's small population size was identified as a critical barrier and this was reflected in the population-related targets and ambitions inherent in both the green and white papers. Indeed, the *Pivot North* report branded the north's small population as the 'key impediment to be overcome' (Joint Select Committee on Northern Australia, 2014, p. 109). This focus on increasing the size of the population in Northern Australia is shared with past iterations of Northern Australian development policies, which similarly connected economic growth potential with large increases in population size (Coombs, 1947; Harris, 1992; Carson, 2011).

The specific population-related targets and ambitions in the green paper were:

1. A focus on substantially growing 'urban zones': 'the White Paper will consider options for building on existing key urban zones—such as Darwin, Cairns, Townsville and Karratha—with the aim of substantially increasing their population' (Australian Government, 2014, p. 54).
2. Improve net internal migration flows: 'Greater migration from elsewhere in Australia would help boost population … The White Paper will explore practical options to remove some of the impediments to internal migration to northern Australia—recognising governments have limited ability to directly affect people's decisions as to where they live and work' (p. 54).
3. Increase international migration: 'the Australian Government is consulting across governments, industry, business and communities on ways migration policy can help increase the availability of skilled and unskilled labour, including in the north' (p. 56).

Population-related ambitions and policies were not so well defined in the white paper, with the focus instead on two main targets. The first was to grow several cities to more than 1 million residents to 'underwrite substantial exports of planning, design, architecture and construction services to the Tropics' (Australian Government, 2015, p. 3). In 2014, the largest city in Northern Australia was Townsville with a population of 192,000. The second target in the white paper was to achieve large absolute growth in the size of the region:

> Development will require many more people living in the north. Transformation won't happen if its population inches up by a few hundred thousand over the next 20 years. It would remain a high cost, small scale economy; more of a pilot project than a powerhouse. We need to lay the foundations for rapid population growth and put the north on a trajectory to reach a population of four to five million by 2060. (Australian Government, 2015, p. 4)

In 2014, the population of the region was estimated at 1.3 million residents (authors' calculations based on ABS, 2015).

The gaps between the white paper's targets and present-day populations are large. While population targets and ambitions are laid out and identified as vital to northern development in both the green and white papers, no research has previously been undertaken to assess the compatibility of the baseline demographic conditions in Northern Australia with the policy's ambitions. For example, there is no research-based review available on the critical issue of who comes, who leaves and who stays in the region. Such knowledge is vital in the context of the opportunities and barriers for growing the population and achieving the population goals embedded in the green and white papers.

This chapter reports on data extracted from the output files from the 2011 and 2016 Australian Censuses and analyses these against the specific population targets and aspirations outlined above. The aims are to identify whether and why current population characteristics might be compatible with the goals of the green and white papers and to assess how they might change, or be induced to change, to meet these. This provides the basis for subsequent commentary on the voracity of the population-related components of the present-day Developing Northern Australia agenda and discussion on what might need to change to help achieve the government's goals.

## Northern Australia Population Aspirations

The demographic context in Northern Australia is fundamentally different to southern parts of Australia, with the most obvious difference being the northern population is relatively small and is distributed over sparsely populated areas (although a significant share live in cities in the north). The need to dramatically increase the size of the population in Northern Australia mirrors sentiments in past northern development policies and initiatives (e.g. Coombs, 1947; Harris, 1992). However, in addition to absolute size, the composition of populations is crucial to determining economic development capacity (Carson et al., 2011). In northern areas of developed nations, there are a range of commonalities in relation to population compositions that determine that demographic change does not follow the same trajectories as might be expected elsewhere. One example is the high proportion of indigenous peoples in northern areas, which in the Australian context at least increases the youthfulness of the overall population's age structure. With a dearth of seniors, this makes for an imbalance of population across age groups (Zeng et al., 2015).

Demographic differences, both within northern regions and compared to elsewhere, mean that normal relationships between population and economy may not apply. For example, during 2015, the NT economy was indicated as booming (with low unemployment and high levels of private investment) at the same time as record numbers of residents were leaving for interstate; some 26,000 in 18 months, or the equivalent to its second-largest city of Alice Springs (see Payer & Taylor, 2015). These examples highlight that associations between population size and economic growth are not linear in northern economies, as they tend to be in the larger urban-focused southern economies (see Carson et al., 2011; Carson, 2011).

Theories on what matters up north for the causes and consequences of population change have begun to emerge from international cross-comparative studies. One theory (Carson et al., 2011) has proposed that the systems of human interaction (demography, economics, social systems, health systems, etc.) are different in sparsely populated areas such as Northern Australia compared to urban or rural zones. These differences can be conveniently described using eight words that start with 'D': detailed, diverse, discontinuous, dynamic, dependent, delicate, distant and disconnected. The tenet is that northern peripheral populations do not 'behave' like others, and demographic change can and does occur along non-standard pathways compared to other geographical areas.

Indeed, the green paper (Australian Government, 2014) identified some of the important differences in the population structure of Northern Australia including:

- high concentrations of population in urban areas (particularly Darwin, Cairns and Townsville)
- great diversity and polarity in the demographic and socioeconomic characteristics of settlements and their residents (especially comparing Indigenous to other residents)
- disparate population growth rates between urban and other areas
- the prevalence of a large number of small and very remote settlements away from coastal zones.

While these characteristics were recognised in the green paper, in the white paper (Australian Government, 2015) they have received no specific attention aside from the target to enact large size increases in the cities of the north and, consequently, for the region as a whole. The white paper population targets raise many questions about why and how such goals might be imperative. Not least is the issue of environmental carrying capacity and the potential for damage to fragile northern ecosystems from the fourfold increase in population outlined as desirable in the white paper. Further, and similar to previous northern development initiatives, there is scarce consideration of the population characteristics that may both differ from pre-existing resident characteristics and be considered as advantageous (in terms of age, gender, skills, education and so on) and for the purpose of facilitating economic growth aspirations. In light of the large differences in the characteristics of populations in the north, the reduction in granularity around population aspirations evident in the white paper (compared to the green paper) is interesting. While it may be reflective of limited understanding in policy circles about how populations in the north can contribute to harnessing opportunities for economic development, the rollout of white paper initiatives must be informed by knowledge of baseline demographic conditions and understanding about how these might change under future development scenarios.

# Sources and Data and their Application to the Research

The analyses in this chapter are primarily based on tables designed and extracted by the authors from the 2011 and 2016 Australian Censuses, as well as from ABS and Department of Immigration and Border Protection (2014) materials. 'Northern Australia' is defined as in the green and white papers (see Figure 10.1 above) as the area to the north of the Tropic of Capricorn but also including the Alice Springs region of the NT, in recognition of its importance for servicing surrounding communities and industry (Australian Government, 2014). In the present study, we replicated the definition in the green paper by developing a custom geographic area based on Statistical Areas Level 2 units to specify and extract customised Census tables using the ABS software Table Builder. The boundary of Northern Australia extends across parts of the states of

Queensland and Western Australia and encompasses the whole of the NT. Areas straddling both Northern and Southern Australia were allocated based on where the majority of their resident population was located.

The green paper identifies the cities of Townsville, Cairns, Darwin, Mackay, Rockhampton, Gladstone and Karratha as the key urban areas (or 'zones' as they are labelled) in Northern Australia. Interestingly, while the geographic scope of the policy includes Alice Springs (which is larger than Karratha), this city is not mentioned in the context of growth in the urban zones of the north. Our analysis of urban versus other populations and socioeconomic change in Northern Australia incorporates those cities defined as 'Significant Urban Areas' by the ABS in its publication *Regional population growth* (various editions): Townsville, Cairns, Darwin, Rockhampton, Mackay, Alice Springs, Mount Isa, Port Hedland, Yeppoon, Broome, Karratha and Emerald.

# Findings

The first part of the results section presents the baseline demographic and socioeconomic indicators for the region. The section then analyses and comments on the population targets in the white paper before analysis of the three key population aspirations identified in the green paper (substantially increasing the population of urban zones in Northern Australia, improving internal migration flows, and increasing international migration and retention of international migrants).

## Baseline Demographic and Socioeconomic Indicators for Northern Australia

Northern Australia comprised approximately 41 per cent of Australia's national land area, but only 5 per cent (1.1 million residents) of the total Australian population in 2016. This proportion was consistent with five years prior (see Table 10.1). Overall, Northern Australia population growth from 2011–16 was 4.1 per cent (compared to 8.5 per cent elsewhere). For the purpose of this study, the Estimated Resident Population figures (ERPs) were used to account for the net population undercount (see ABS, 2016). The overseas-born population living in the north grew by 12.9 per cent, such that their representation in the population increased from 16 per cent to 17 per cent (compared to 29 per cent in the rest of Australia by

2016). The Indigenous population in Northern Australia grew by 7.3 per cent, but the proportion of Indigenous people living in the north fell by 3 per cent. The ratio of men per 100 women (known as the gender ratio) decreased from 107 to 105, but remained the same in the rest of Australia (at 97 men per 100 women).

Table 10.1: Baseline demographic indicators for Northern Australia.

| Indicator | 2011 | 2016 | Change |
|---|---|---|---|
| Population of Northern Australia (ERPs) | 1,101,504 | 1,146,909 | 4.1% increase |
| Population elsewhere (ERPs) | 21,238,520 | 23,043,998 | 8.5% increase |
| Residents of Northern Australia born overseas (%) | 16% | 17% | 12.9% increase |
| Australians living in Northern Australia (%) | 5% | 5% | 2.9% increase |
| Indigenous people living in Northern Australia (%) | 28% | 25% | 7.3% increase |
| Males per 100 females in Northern Australia (rest of Australia) | 107 (97) | 105 (97) | −2 men per 100 women (no change) |

Note: ERPs = Estimated Resident Population figures.
Source: Authors' calculations extrapolated from ABS Table Builder software.

The resident population's age structure in Northern Australia differs from the rest of Australia, with a much younger population evident in the former. Some 21 per cent of the population were aged less than 15 years in 2016 compared to 19 per cent in the rest of Australia, while for the Indigenous population in Northern Australia this was 33 per cent compared to 19 per cent for other residents. Indigenous residents constituted 14 per cent of the population (around 160,000 residents) in 2016 (see Figure 10.2). Conversely, seniors were under-represented in Northern Australia, with 11 per cent of the population aged 65 years and over compared to 16 per cent in the rest of Australia in 2016. A 'bubble' in the age structure for Northern Australia is evident at 25–34 years, with a higher proportion evident in subsequent working ages up to 55 years.

The top 10 industries for employment in Northern Australia are shown in Figure 10.3. These accounted for 77 per cent of employment compared to 70 per cent for the top 10 industries in the rest of Australia (signifying a greater reliance on fewer industries). Mining and public administration and Safety (including defence) were more prominent in the north.

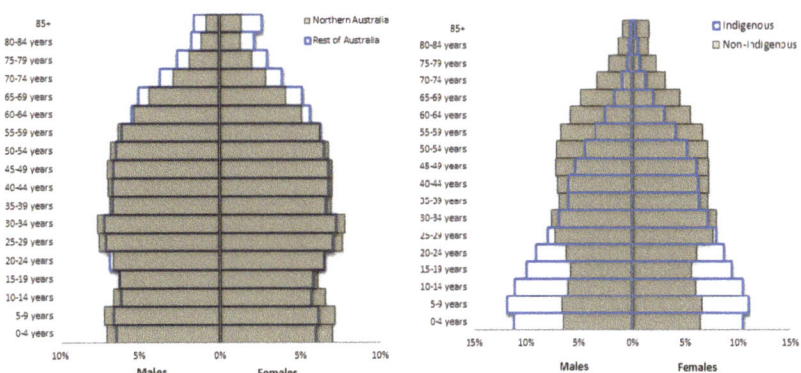

**Figure 10.2: Age–sex structures in 2016 for Northern Australia and the rest of Australia (left) and for Northern Australian Indigenous and non-Indigenous residents (right).**

Source: Authors' calculations extrapolated from ABS Table Builder software.

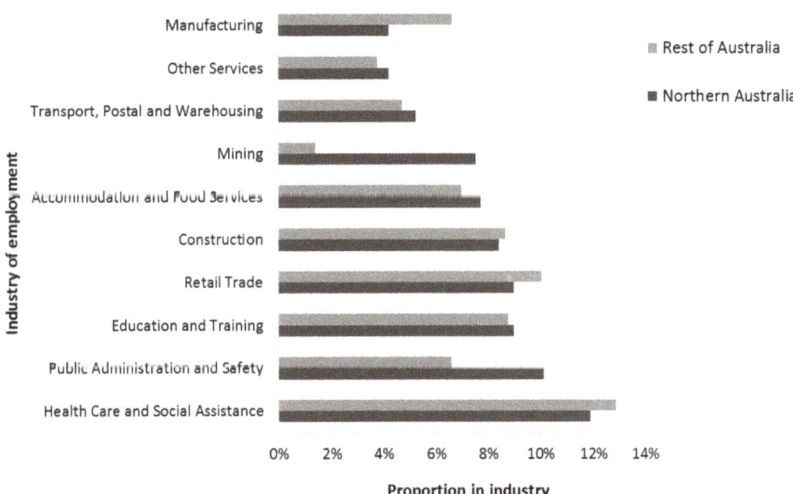

**Figure 10.3: Industry of employment in 2016 for Northern Australia and the rest of Australia.**

Source: Authors' calculations extrapolated from ABS Table Builder software.

Incomes in Northern Australia were higher on average than those in the rest of Australia in 2016, with the exception of Indigenous residents. Despite their relatively low incomes, 16 per cent of Indigenous residents earned $1,000 a week or more, while 37 per cent of Northern Australia residents overall earned $1,000 a week or more compared to 33 per cent for the rest of Australia (see Figure 10.4). While mining is a prominent northern industry, it was only the seventh-largest employer in the north in 2016. Substantial discussion and debate on the practice of fly-in/fly-out (non-resident) workers across the north has transpired, in particular for large resource-based projects. Nevertheless, non-resident workers were prominent in other industries in the north in 2016, including in the public administration and safety and health care and social assistance industries. The number of non-resident workers in Northern Australia grew by around 40 per cent from 2006–11. Around two-thirds of these were males. The trend of rapid growth in non-resident workers continued during the 2011–16 period. For example, in the NT, non-resident worker numbers increased by 65 per cent (compared to a 35 per cent increase in the rest of Australia) during the 2006–11 period.

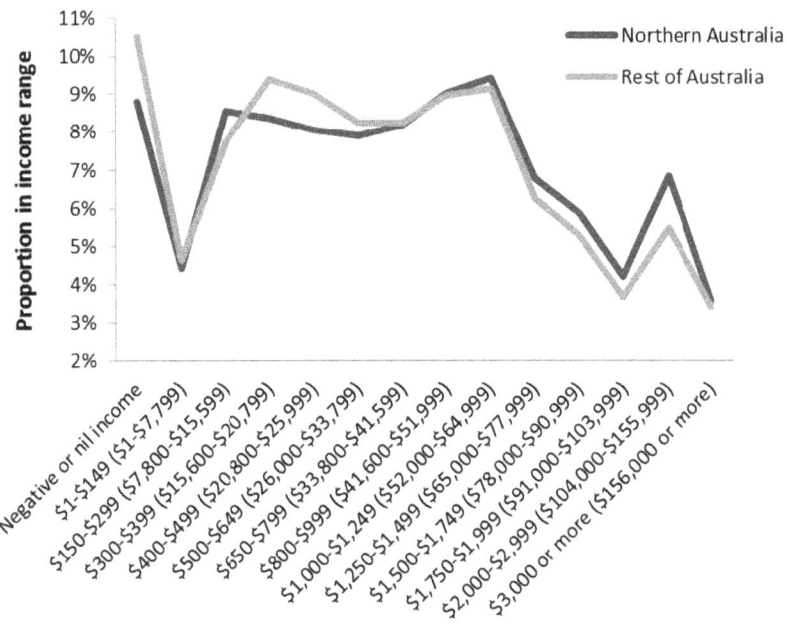

**Figure 10.4: Income distributions in 2016 for Northern Australia and the rest of Australia.**
Source: Authors' calculations extrapolated from ABS Table Builder software.

Over half of Indigenous residents in the north were not in the labour force in 2016 compared to 28 per cent for non-Indigenous people (see Table 10.2). The Indigenous unemployment rate was three times higher than that of non-Indigenous people. Educational data on individuals' highest post-school level of qualifications are an indicator of the overall level of skills in the community. For those with a post-school qualification, a smaller proportion of Indigenous people held a bachelor level or higher qualification in both Northern Australia and the rest of Australia (12 per cent and 19 per cent respectively) compared to non-Indigenous people in 2016. A far higher proportion of Indigenous people in Northern and Southern Australia hold certificate-level qualifications (see Figure 10.5).

**Table 10.2: Labour status in 2016 for Northern Australia and the rest of Australia.**

|  | Northern Australia | | Rest of Australia | |
| --- | --- | --- | --- | --- |
|  | Indigenous | Non-Indigenous | Indigenous | Non-Indigenous |
| Employed | 36% | 68% | 47% | 60% |
| Unemployed | 12% | 4% | 9% | 4% |
| Not in the labour force | 52% | 28% | 44% | 35% |

Source: Authors' calculations extrapolated from ABS Table Builder software.

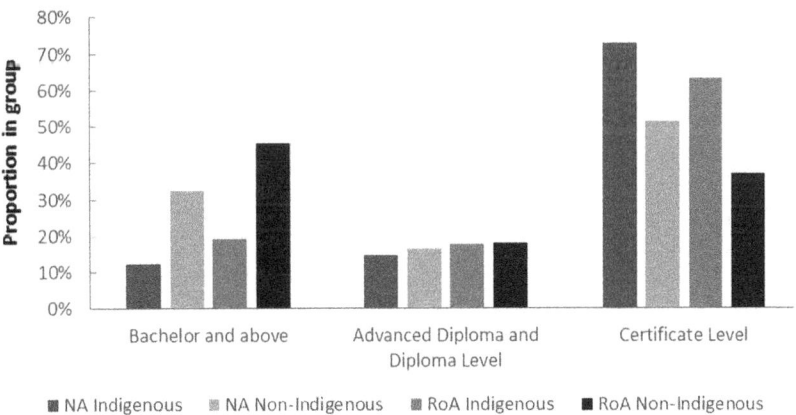

**Figure 10.5: Highest level of post-school qualifications in 2016 by Indigenous status for Northern Australia (NA) and the rest of Australia (RoA).**
Source: Authors' calculations extrapolated from ABS Table Builder software.

As a measure of Northern Australia's capacity to develop the industrial and services sectors, improving internet uptake rates is an important precursor and, indeed, a number of green paper submissions identified a lack of information and communications technology infrastructure as a barrier. In 2011, 21 per cent of households in Northern Australia did not have any form of internet connection, compared to 14 per cent in the rest of Australia. Of those households in the north who had a connection in 2011, less had broadband connections compared to the rest of Australia (71 per cent compared to 80 per cent respectively).

## Analysis of the White Paper's Population Targets

The white paper (Australian Government, 2015) articulates the duel targets for Northern Australia of having several cities of more than 1 million residents and a total population of between 4 and 5 million residents by 2060. Table 10.3 shows the estimated 2019 population for the larger northern cities and towns, with the right-most column showing the additional annual population growth required between 2020 and 2060 for each to reach a population of 1 million. Although the additional growth rates required for some cities (notably Cairns, Townsville and Greater Darwin) may appear to be low and achievable, in reality, accomplishing these year on year is highly unlikely. This is because the average annual growth rates during the decade leading up to 2014 were well above long-term averages, in part due to residual effects from the national mining boom. Growth rates are anticipated to be well below these peaks in the near future. For example, the 10-year average growth rate for Greater Darwin (from 2004–14) was 2.8 per cent, slightly above the average from 1991–2014 (2.7 per cent). To achieve 1 million residents by 2060, the city would need to grow twice as fast (by 4.6 per cent per annum). The second factor to consider in assessing the likelihood of achieving the population targets is that just one year of below-target growth will require growth rates in subsequent years to be higher still to effect a growth catch up.

For Northern Australia as a whole to reach 4.5 million residents (halfway between 4 and 5 million), additional population growth of 3.2 per cent per annum will be required. While this rate may not appear particularly high, achieving this would require a large transformation in the growth dynamics of the region. Not least, almost all of the growth in the region has been in the major centres, with the rest of the region in stagnation or decline. Consequently, cities would require growth rates over and above those shown in Table 10.3 to compensate for low growth elsewhere. The following sections discuss some of the reasons for these findings by way of examining the population targets and aspirations documented in the green paper.

10. THE DEMOGRAPHY OF DEVELOPING NORTHERN AUSTRALIA

Table 10.3: Population estimates and growth rates required to achieve the 2015 white paper's population targets.

| City | 2019 Population estimate | Target population | Difference | Additional p.a. growth needed based on 10-year average growth (2009–19) | Additional p.a. growth needed based on two-year average growth (2017–19) | Annual growth p.a. needed (2020–60) |
|---|---|---|---|---|---|---|
| Alice Springs | 26,390 | 1,000,000 | 973,610 | 9.6% | 9.3% | 9.0% |
| Broome | 14,371 | 1,000,000 | 985,629 | 9.4% | 11.1% | 10.6% |
| Cairns | 163,350 | 1,000,000 | 836,650 | 2.9% | 3.4% | 4.4% |
| Darwin | 147,255 | 1,000,000 | 852,745 | 2.9% | 5.2% | 4.7% |
| Karratha | 17,102 | 1,000,000 | 982,898 | 9.3% | 8.2% | 10.2% |
| Mackay | 116,763 | 1,000,000 | 883,237 | 4.8% | 5.2% | 5.2% |
| Port Hedland | 4,472 | 1,000,000 | 995,528 | 13.3% | 13.9% | 13.7% |
| Rockhampton | 119,590 | 1,000,000 | 880,410 | 4.3% | 4.7% | 5.2% |
| Townsville | 195,084 | 1,000,000 | 804,916 | 2.7% | 3.4% | 4.0% |
| Northern Australia | 1,204,043 | 4,500,000 | 3,295,957 | 2.4% | 2.9% | 3.2% |

Source: Authors' calculations extrapolated from ABS Table Builder software and ABS.Stat (Beta). Population targets drawn from Australian Government (2015).

# Analysis of the Green Paper's Population Targets and Ambitions

This section analyses the demographic and socioeconomic characteristics of Northern Australia pertinent to assessing the challenges and opportunities associated with the three broad population-related ambitions outlined in the green paper (Australian Government, 2014).

## Significantly Growing Northern Australia's Urban Zones

In 2016, the urban zones of Northern Australia (as defined above) accounted for 62 per cent of the population. The urban-based population grew by 6.6 per cent from 2011–16, compared to just 1.8 per cent for the rest of the region. Indigenous residents also increasingly gravitated towards urban zones, increasing by 11.6 per cent in those places over the five-year period (see Table 10.4).

Table 10.4: Demographic indicators for urban zones in Northern Australia and rest of the region in 2011 and 2016.

| Indicators | 2011 | | 2016 | |
| --- | --- | --- | --- | --- |
| | Urban zones | Rest of the region | Urban zones | Rest of the region |
| Population share of the region | 61.3% | 38.7% | 62.4% | 37.6% |
| Indigenous share of the region | 36.4% | 63.6% | 37.9% | 62.1% |
| Indigenous proportion in population | 9.0% | 24.6% | 9.4% | 26.1% |
| Proportion born overseas | 18.0% | 11.8% | 19.9% | 12.3% |
| Men per 100 women | 102.9 | 113.1 | 101.3 | 111.2 |
| Under 15 | 21.6% | 22.1% | 20.9% | 22.3% |
| Over 65 | 8.9% | 10.2% | 10.8% | 12.7% |
| Dependency ratio | 30.5% | 32.3% | 31.7% | 35.0% |

Source: Authors' calculations extrapolated from ABS Table Builder software.

There were 101 men for every 100 women in Northern Australian urban zones in 2016 compared to 111 per 100 in the rest of the region. This male bias in the population increased for both areas from 2011–16, especially for the rest of the region. Meanwhile, urban zones featured a larger and increasing share of overseas-born migrants in the population, at 20 per cent in 2016 compared to 12 pe cent in the rest of the region. The proportion of the population under 15 years of age was around 21–22 per cent across the north and remained consistent from 2011–16. However, the proportion aged 65 years and over grew in both the urban zones and remainder of Northern Australia from 2011–16.

## Improve Net Internal Migration Flows between the North and the Rest of Australia

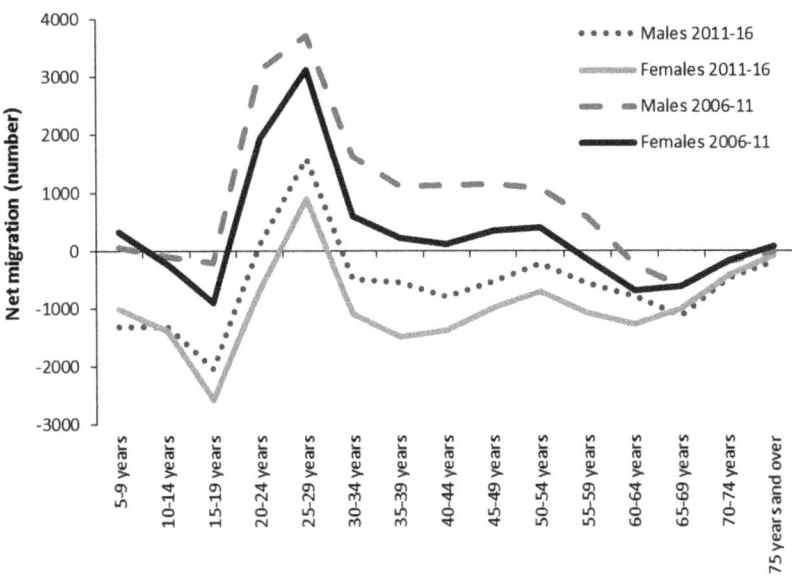

**Figure 10.6: Net migration for Northern Australia and the rest of Australia by age and gender from 2006–2011 and 2011–2016.**
Source: Authors' calculations extrapolated from ABS Table Builder software.

Critical to improving net interstate flows for Northern Australia is knowledge about who comes and who leaves through interstate migration. Overall, net interstate migration to Northern Australia from 2006–11 was 16,500 persons, with three-quarters attributable to the non-urban areas of the north. Growth in urban areas was driven by international migration, natural increase and internal migration within the region (to urban zones from other areas within Northern Australia). However, from 2011–16, Northern Australia suffered a net loss of 23,000 residents, of which 62 per cent (14,200) were females. Losses were particularly notable for those aged less than 20 years, including babies and toddlers, those in their final years of high school and those commencing university. The north failed to retain mid-career women and men, and although early career net migration was positive (for those in their 20s) for both genders, the extent of the net contribution was relatively small, especially for females. Figure 10.6 shows the difference in net migration between Northern Australia and the rest of Australia in 2006–11 and 2011–16.

A much greater number of males and females aged in their 20s migrated to Northern Australia in 2006–11 compared to 2011–16. The broad shapes of the in- and out-migration profiles are similar for men and women.

The gender differences in net interstate migration also validate the progression of the region towards a greater male bias, with nine extra men per 100 women moving into the region but fewer men per 100 women moving out.

Examining the reasons for people migrating out of Northern Australia assists to identify strategies for improving overall internal migration flows between the north and south of Australia. Census data provide some indications on factors associated with leaving. Those employed in the public administration and safety and education and training sectors were more likely to have left, as were those who were unemployed. Those not participating in the labour force were more likely to have stayed. Although no region-wide research on the motivations and triggers for leaving Northern Australia for interstate are available, research specifically for the NT provides some clues. A 2006 survey of people who had left the NT identified financial incentives, improvements to health services, career opportunities and housing subsidies as the main incentives that might attract them back as residents (Cunningham & Beneforti, 2008). Likewise, a large survey of NT seniors reported that those considering leaving the NT identified the cost of living (and particularly housing) as a motivator for leaving, as well as the desire to be closer to family (Zeng et al., 2015). However, none of these data incorporate full accounts of movements in and out of the region as they preclude non-resident workers who grew markedly in size from 2006–11 (e.g. by 35 per cent in the NT).

## Increased International Migrant Numbers in the North

Earlier analysis in this chapter shows that international migration is increasingly important for population growth in Northern Australia. Census data suggest there are significant structural and compositional differences between international migrants to the north and those in the rest of Australia, as well as between those who arrived to the north between 2011 and 2016 (the new arrivers) and longer-term overseas-born residents of the north (who arrived prior to 2011). Not least, the proportion of overseas-born residents in the population of Northern Australia remains significantly below the rest of Australia, at 17 per cent compared to 29 per cent respectively. This suggests a potential to increase numbers in the north. However, realising increased shares of international migrants will depend on policies targeted towards a complex range of issues, aside from those associated with visas and the use of skilled workers from overseas. These include redressing existing internal distributions of international migrants within Australia, which have long been heavily skewed towards the capital cities and their surrounding urban areas. In Queensland, for example, around 70 per cent of international arrivers settle in Brisbane or on the Gold Coast. In Western Australia, around 90 per cent settle in Perth. In the NT, 75 per cent of recent migrants settle in Darwin or Palmerston (Taylor, 2018). Northern jurisdictions have attracted a low per cent of recent migrants to the individual states or territory. Outside of the large population centres in the north this is lower still.

This analysis highlights some of the challenges inherent in encouraging new overseas migrants to settle and remain in sparsely populated northern regions. While state- and territory-specific migration programs encourage international migration to regional and remote areas (e.g. the Regional Skilled Migration Program), only a small portion of migrants choose to do so.

A further barrier to more substantial international migration flows to the north is attracting and retaining women. The gender ratio for overseas-born in the north in 2016 was 106 men per 100 women (much higher than for Australia-born residents at 95 men per 100 females), and migration flows to and from the region show females contributing at three times the rate on a net basis. The scale of the female deficit in the north is revealed in Figure 10.7, showing the 'missing' females in the north compared to the rest of Australia, broken down by overseas-born females and others. There are large deficits of overseas-born females aged 5–9 years and 60 years onwards. For non-migrants, deficits increase at a constant over the ages and peak from the age of 60 years onwards. A dearth of (non-Indigenous) women hampers the attraction and retention of more women who may be discouraged to move north or encouraged to move south by either a lack of females or more males than females in the populations of the most remote areas.

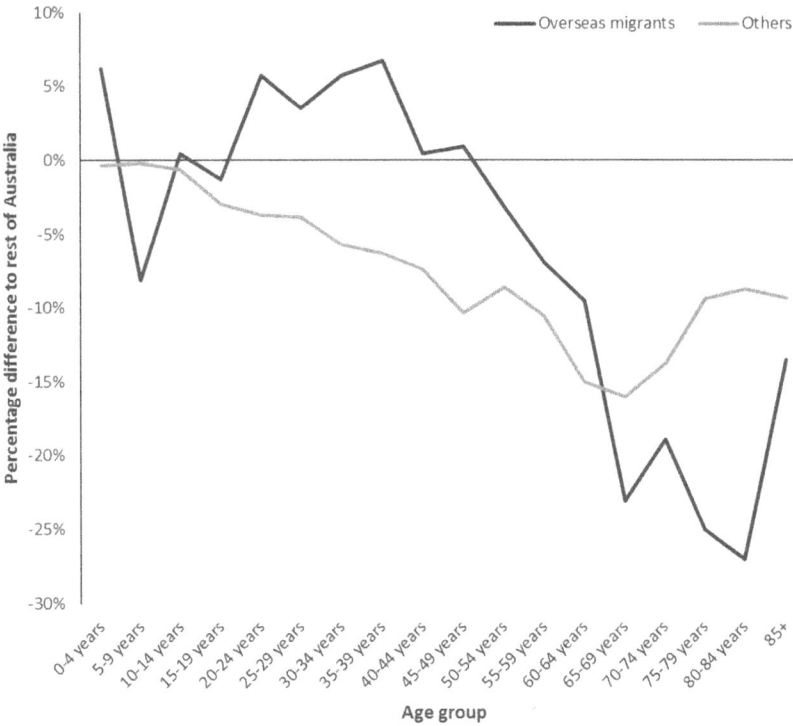

**Figure 10.7: The 'missing' women of Northern Australia by age group in 2016.**

Note: These calculations show the per cent difference in the number of women per 100 men between Northern Australia and the rest of Australia.

Source: Authors' calculations extrapolated from ABS Table Builder software.

## Discussion and Conclusions

Much of the analysis presented in this chapter involves comparisons and contrasts at a range of geographic and demographic levels: Northern Australia compared to the rest of Australia, urban areas in the north compared to others, overseas-born compared to others, and so on. These are just some of the breakdowns for which significant differences in the demographic and economic make-up across the region and between the region and elsewhere can be observed. There are also, of course, substantive intra-regional and cross-border differences warranting further research. For example, some areas like the Pilbara are in the midst of a significant downturn as the price of iron ore has plummeted, while the economy of the NT is purportedly booming from large resource projects but at the same time has lost record numbers of residents through net negative interstate migration from 2013–14 (Payer & Taylor, 2015).

These sorts of intra-regional differences in population systems and in the inter-relationships between population and economy are acknowledged to some extent in the green and white papers; however, there is little credence given to the importance of such differences for economic and population growth. Population systems in the north are relatively discrete, having been built and maintained around specific economic, strategic and other functions, which may well be temporary and certainly reinforce the sorts of population imbalances common across northern jurisdictions. Discrete areas of economic activity and population settlements themselves are largely poorly integrated when it comes to internal transport and flows of labour and capital (Carson, 2011).

What is common across the region is an increasing dependence on externally sourced capital and labour. Such conditions make the challenge of developing from within difficult and engender circumstances under which divergences in population and socioeconomic conditions between sub-groups, for example, between urban and non-urban residents or educated and less educated residents, can be expected to maintain and grow (Taylor et al., 2011). These sorts of challenges are longstanding for northern peripheral areas:

> Taking the structure and functioning of the Arctic regional economies and the degree of economic dependence as a point of departure … The fundamental problem is still the dependency Arctic regions have on their mother economies in the south. (Winther, 2010, p. 1)

The loss of university entrants to southern regions also emphasises the brain drain and loss of future innovation capacity from established migration patterns.

Several indications are apparent of a growing divide in the north between employed, educated and affluent residents (and non-residents), whose migratory patterns align with continuing such lifestyles, and a relatively non-migratory, under-educated and low-income cohort. The latter includes, but certainly is not limited to, many Indigenous residents in the north. Current approaches and articulations for northern development may identify these issues, but they provide very little in the way of direct suggestions on avoiding or rectifying the potential for a stuck underclass to continue to emerge and grow. Conversely, population aspirations articulated in the green paper may actually enhance the worrying trend towards a further male bias, a highly mobile high-income class and discrete geographical areas where boom-and-bust cycles attract and then repel increasing numbers of affluent men (Taylor & Carson, 2014). The Pilbara in Western Australia and Nhulunbuy in the NT (both areas suffered significant out-migration when resource-based industries were curtailed) are prime examples where the critical question is 'who is left?' after those who have the means to leave have done so.

The focus on urban growth, interstate migration and growing overseas migrant numbers in the green paper says little about how the north might grow from within. Urban zones are already far outstripping 'the rest', the number of international migrants is growing significantly (especially the skilled intake) and interstate migration flows are supporting the types of economic activities that might lead to further growth. This leaves the impression of both unrealistic targets in the white paper (as the short section in this chapter on the likelihood of reaching these shows) and an extemporaneous incorporation of the population ambitions embedded in the green paper. While the latter certainly incorporates some relatively sophisticated thinking on issues of population change and growth, the approach is timid in terms of broaching the difficulties of encouraging growth from within. The current iteration of developing the north, therefore, continues the focus on securing growth from externally sourced labour and capital and on sending goods and services overseas—notably to Chinese markets, which are portrayed in both documents as ready and waiting to consume our goods and services in large volumes.

One solution to generating long-term growth from within may be readily apparent from the analysis in this chapter, but also exceedingly difficult: attract and retain more women. The difficulties in achieving this were laconically laid out by Carson and Schmallegger in their 2009 article titled 'Why don't women like Darwin?'. In summary, northern peripheries are subject to a degree of demographic lock-in from legacy industries that are highly male preferred (e.g. fishing, agriculture and mining). Such industries 'trap' men into patterns of employment that, although changing in line with technological and workforce practices, contribute to a social atmosphere that is not favoured by women. Conversely, large cities 'down south' offer better education and career prospects, more favourable community amenities and are closer and more connected to locations of family members for support with children and finances.

The exploration of the baseline data here might also lead us to question whether and why a much bigger population in the north is inherently desirable, particularly if it is at the expense of a more appropriate population composition or the pristine and unique cultural and landscape environments. The tenet of present and past enquiries and reports on the potential of the region is that bigger is best, and this philosophy negates the importance and influence of the complexity and diversity of population systems in the north. A great array of settlement types, sizes, growth rates, ethnic compositions and workforce profiles (to name a few population characteristics) are found in Northern Australia. It is unrealistic to anticipate that growing the overall population size (in the white paper a fourfold increase was targeted) will deliver the required demographic and economic outcomes for up-scaled economic development. A more nuanced approach to understanding populations is preferable, with economic policies and investments informed by comprehensive scenario modelling using population projections to ascertain likely population outcomes.

Two further and poignant demographic issues are apparent for Northern Australia's development. First, and in line with global trends in developed nations, its population will age in the near future, although the onset of significant ageing is taking place a generation later than in the rest of Australia (Zeng et al., 2015). Population ageing in the north will be profoundly different due to the influence of rapid ageing in the Indigenous population. In the NT, for example, above 5 per cent growth per annum (although from a small base) is projected for Indigenous residents aged 65 years or more in the next 25 years (Zeng et al., 2015). Residents in very remote areas will require specific health and other services to facilitate ageing in place, likely to be the preferred choice for most seniors.

Second, the spatial distribution of Aboriginal and Torres Strait Islander people in Australia has undergone accelerated and dramatic changes in recent decades, with increasing proportions living in major Australian cities and a lower proportion living in the north (Taylor & Bell, 2013). Since World War II, for example, the Indigenous share in states and territories located wholly outside of Northern Australia (i.e. New South Wales, Victoria, South Australia, Tasmania and the Australian Capital Territory) more than doubled from 21 per cent to 48 per cent (ABS,

2014). More recently, the Indigenous share in Northern Australia declined from 28 per cent to 25 per cent from 2011–16. Despite absolute growth, the share living in the north has declined. From 1981–2006, for example, the Indigenous population of the NT grew by 85 per cent, but its share of the national Indigenous population (which grew by 185 per cent) fell from 18 per cent to 12 per cent, then to 10 per cent in 2011 (Taylor & Bell, 2013). This has affected finances for Northern Australia by changing the distribution of GST revenues to the states and territories and, consequently, the capacity for individual governments to address Indigenous outcomes in northern jurisdictions.

On the whole, the demography of Northern Australia features a range of population and settlement characteristics that are highly related to past pathways for economic development and the role of the region in national and strategic agendas (e.g. as strategically important militarily). These present a range of challenges and opportunities. An increasing focus on international migrants and non-resident workers creates opportunities around education and tourism-related services. The number of intergenerational families is growing, helping to balance out the heavy losses of residents in pre- and early retirement ages and providing social and financial capital to communities despite population ageing. However, the increasing male bias in the Northern Australian population signifies ongoing demographic and social imbalance in communities. To achieve the targets in the white paper will require a very big Australia. Past policies promoting a large population have received significant public backlash and it is interesting that the government has chosen to incorporate such targets, which are perhaps at best aspirational. Most importantly, the rollout of initiatives under the Developing Northern Australia agenda should incorporate sound demographic research, using projections and other forms of modelling, to plot the interplay between population change and economic development.

# References

Australian Bureau of Statistics (ABS). (2015). *Australian demographic statistics, December 2014* (No. 3101.0). Retrieved from www.abs.gov.au/ausstats/abs@.nsf/mf/3101.0

Australian Government. (2014). *Green paper on developing Northern Australia*. Canberra, ACT: Department of the Prime Minister and Cabinet. Retrieved from www.regional.gov.au/regional/northernaustralia/files/green-paper-on-developing-northern-australia.pdf

Brokensha, H., Taylor, A. & Carson, D. (2013). *The Northern Territory's non-resident workforce—one Census on*. Retrieved from www.cdu.edu.au/sites/default/files/research-brief-2013-4.pdf

Carson D. (2011). Political economy, demography and development in Australia's Northern Territory. *Canadian Geographer, 55*(2), 226–242.

Carson, D. B. & Carson, D. A. (2014). Local economies of mobility in sparsely populated areas: Cases from Australia's spine. *Journal of Rural Studies, 36*, 340–349.

Carson, D. & Schmallegger. (2009). Population Studies Research Brief. Why don't women like Darwin? Retrieved from www.cdu.edu.au/sites/default/files/research-brief-2009-36.pdf

Carson, D., Ensign, P., Rasmussen, R. O. & Taylor, A. (2011). Perspectives on 'Demography at the Edge'. In D. Carson, R. Rasmussen, P. C. Ensign, A. Taylor & L. Huskey (Eds), *Demography at the edge: Remote human populations in developed nations* (pp. 3–20). Farnham, England: Ashgate Publishing.

Coombs, H. (1947). *Development of Northern Australia*. Report of the Northern Australian Development Committee, Canberra, ACT.

Cunningham, T. & Beneforti, M. (2008). *NT Mobility Project: Movers out of the Northern Territory*. Retrieved from www.cdu.edu.au/sites/default/files/research-brief-2008-14.pdf

Department of Immigration and Border Protection. (2014). *Migration to Australia's states and territories 2012–13*. Canberra, ACT: Australian Government.

Harris, P. (1992). *A strategy for promoting the economic growth of Northern Australia. Report to the Commonwealth Government*. Townsville, Qld: Centre for Applied Economic Research and Analysis, James Cook University.

Hörnström, L., Perjo, L., Johnsen, I. & Karlsdóttir, A. (2015). *Adapting to, or mitigating demographic change? National policies addressing demographic challenges in the Nordic countries* (Nordregio Working Paper 2015:1). Retrieved from nordregio.org/publications/adapting-to-or-mitigating-demographic-change/

Joint Select Committee on Northern Australia. (2014). *Pivot North: Inquiry into the development of Northern Australia—Final report*. Canberra, ACT: Australian Government.

Payer, H. & Taylor, A. (2015). *Northern Territory seats in the Australian Parliament: It's a long way up, but not far down*. Retrieved from www.cdu.edu.au/northern-institute/ni-research-briefs

Taylor, A. (2018). *Heading north, staying north? The increasing importance of international migrants to northern and remote Australia*. Sydney, NSW: Lowy Institute for International Policy.

Taylor, A. & Bell, L. (2013). *The Northern Territory's declining share of Australia's Indigenous population: A call for a research agenda*. Retrieved from www.cdu.edu.au/sites/default/files/research-brief-2013-2.pdf

Taylor, A. & Carson, D. B. (2014). It's raining men in Darwin: Gendered effects from the construction of major oil and gas projects. *Journal of Rural and Community Development, 9*(1), 24–40.

Taylor, A., Larson, S., Stoeckl, N. & Carson, D. (2011). The haves and have nots in Australia's Tropical North - new perspectives on a persisting problem. *Geographic Research, 49*(1), 13–22.

Winther, G. (Ed.). (2010). *The political economy of northern regional development: Vol. I*. Copenhagen, Denmark: Nordic Council of Ministers.

Zeng, B., Brokensha, H. & Taylor, A. (2015). *Now you see us! A report on the policy and economic impacts from rapid growth in the number of senior Territorians*. Darwin, NT: Northern Institute, Charles Darwin University.

# 11

# Attracting and Retaining International Migrants: A Key Issue in Developing Northern Australia

Linda Rosenman, Kate Golebiowska, Andrew Taylor, Petra T. Buergelt, Hannah Payer, Huw Brokensha, Jan Salmon, Alicia Boyle, Kerstin K. Zander and Pawinee Yuhun

## Introduction

Reviews and enquiries into the development of Northern Australia have identified the small resident population as a key issue limiting future economic and social development: 'The small size of the population of Northern Australia, and its wide dispersal outside the handful of major centres … is perhaps the key impediment to be overcome [in development planning]' (Joint Select Committee on Northern Australia, 2014, p. 109).

Ambitious plans for economic expansion are limited by labour shortages due to difficulties in recruiting skilled workers and high staff turnover. These factors not only increase recruitment, relocation and training costs, but also negatively impact business performance, productivity, profitability and growth. Companies may be unable to pursue market opportunities or have to cancel or delay strategic investments because of labour constraints. In key service areas such as health and education, high staff turnover has negative impacts on service delivery and client outcomes. Small populations and high turnover restrict the development of thriving communities and services that attract and retain workers and families.

Despite the fact that Australia is an immigrant nation, with almost 30 per cent of the population born overseas, relatively little attention has been given to immigration as a key strategy for building a sustainable workforce and economically viable communities for Northern Australia. On a national scale, most of the research on immigration to regions has focused on southern parts of Australia (e.g. Taylor & Stanovic, 2005; Flanagan, 2007; Piper & Associates, 2007, 2008, 2009; Hugo, 2008; McDonald et al., 2008; Boese, 2015). This chapter complements this research. It also aims to better embed studies of immigration to Northern Australia conducted by researchers based in the north into the national body of knowledge. This chapter focuses on attracting and retaining immigrants and the ways they contribute to the development of economic and social capital.

We start with an analysis of the census data on recent (2011–16) and longer-term immigrants (those who arrived prior to 2011) to Northern Australia to develop a profile of immigrants to the north. This is a novel and ambitious approach that required more work 'behind the scenes' compared to the usual approach of analysing the census data for an entire state or territory, which is unsuitable for this study due to the definition of Northern Australia. We then review research on immigration and immigrants to regional areas, particularly in Northern Australia, that addresses key factors identified in attracting and retaining immigrants:

- employment and business opportunities
- family, psychosocial social and cultural connectedness
- place characteristics of Northern Australia.

Based on research on specific occupational groups that rely heavily on immigrants in Northern Australia, we conclude with identifying some of the strategies that may assist in attracting and retaining immigrants as workers and community members. This research was predominantly carried out in the Northern Territory (NT).

# A Demographic and Socioeconomic Profile of International Migrants Living in 'the North'

To provide a profile of the demographic and socioeconomic characteristics of overseas-born residents living in Northern Australia, we extrapolated custom tables from the 2016 Census. We compared and contrasted the profiles of overseas-born residents living in Northern Australia to those living in the rest of Australia. We also compared recent arrivals (those who arrived from 2011–16) to longer-term overseas-born residents (those who arrived prior to 2011) to identify changes and differences in migration patterns and characteristics.

## Size, Distribution and Sources

In 2016, overseas-born residents comprised 17 per cent of the population of Northern Australia, lower than for the rest of Australia (29 per cent). Twenty-five per cent of overseas-born residents were new arrivals, higher than the average for the rest of Australia (22 per cent). The distribution of overseas-born residents is very city centric. High proportions, around 40 per cent, of the population are found in the suburbs and centres of the two largest cities of Northern Australia (Darwin and Cairns), including Wagaman (NT), Brinkin–Nakara (NT), Cairns City (Queensland), Coconut Grove (NT) and Darwin City (NT).

Table 11.1 shows the top five source countries and regions for overseas-born residents of Northern Australia. Northern Australia differs from the rest of Australia in that its immigrant share from New Zealand (17 per cent compared to 8 per cent) and Maritime Southeast Asia (13 per cent compared to 8 per cent) is higher, but its immigrant share from Southern Asia is lower (9 per cent compared to 12 per cent).

However, countries and regions of origin for overseas-born residents in Northern Australia appear to be changing markedly with large differences between those who arrived before 2011 (long-term residents) compared to those arriving after 2011 (recent arrivals). While the share of migrants from New Zealand and United Kingdom has declined, more Asian-born immigrants are now choosing to live in Northern Australia.

**Table 11.1: Main sources for overseas-born residents including long-term residents versus new arrivals (per cent).**

| Source country/region | All of Australia | | Northern Australia | |
|---|---|---|---|---|
| | Northern Australia | Rest of Australia | Arrived before 2011 | Arrived after 2011 |
| United Kingdom | 19.5 | 17.6 | 22.8 | 10.3 |
| New Zealand | 16.6 | 8.2 | 17.8 | 12.8 |
| Maritime Southeast Asia | 12.6 | 8.2 | 11.1 | 17.3 |
| Southern Asia | 8.7 | 12.0 | 6.6 | 15.6 |
| Southern and East Africa | 6.3 | 4.6 | 6.6 | 6.0 |

Note: Maritime Southeast Asia includes Brunei Darussalam, Indonesia, Malaysia, Philippines, Singapore and Timor-Leste. Southern Asia comprises Bangladesh, Bhutan, India, the Maldives, Nepal, Pakistan and Sri Lanka.

Source: Census data extracted from Australian Bureau of Statistics (ABS, 2016) using ABS Table Builder software.

## Personal and Family Characteristics

The age profile for overseas-born residents of Northern Australia is strikingly different to residents born in Australia (see Figure 11.1), with the overseas-born population being generally older and the majority being over 25 years old. This is primarily the result of skilled migration programs encouraging settlement of people of working age and with appropriate qualifications and experience.

In terms of marital status, a greater proportion of overseas-born residents in Northern Australia were in a de facto relationship (13 per cent) compared to those in the rest of Australia (8 per cent). Fewer overseas-born residents in Northern Australia (53 per cent) were married compared to married, overseas-born residents in the rest of Australia (57 per cent).

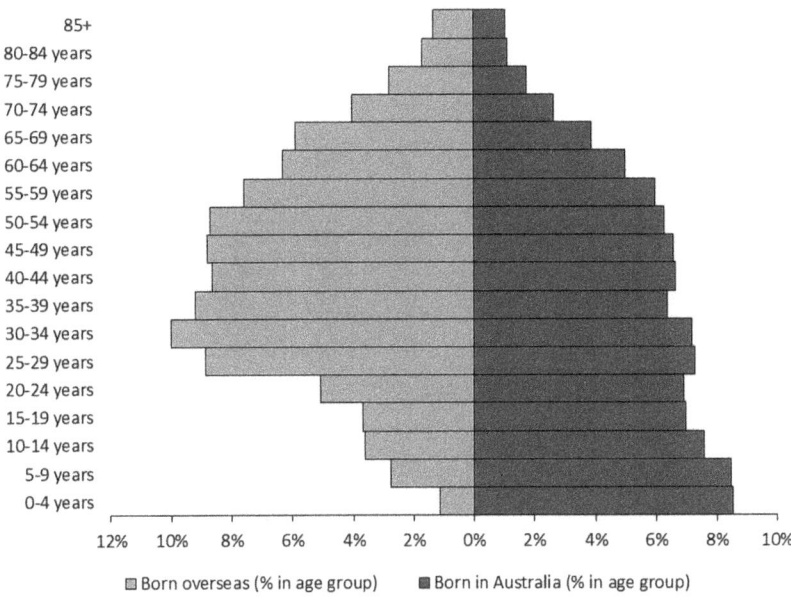

**Figure 11.1: Age profile for Northern Australia residents born overseas and in Australia (2016).**
Source: Census data extracted from ABS (2016) using ABS Table Builder software.

## Qualifications and Workforce Indicators

A lower proportion of Northern Australian overseas-born residents with post-school qualifications (45 per cent) held a bachelor degree or higher qualification compared to overseas-born residents elsewhere in Australia (56 per cent). However, certificate-level qualifications were more prominent in the north. With the increase in migration under the skilled migration streams, a much larger proportion of recent arrivals (59 per cent) to Northern Australia held a bachelor or higher-level qualification than long-term overseas-born residents (41 per cent).

Compared to long-term overseas-born residents, a lower proportion of recently arrived immigrants worked in professional, managerial or clerical occupations in 2016, while higher proportions worked as labourers and community and personal service workers (see Figure 11.2).

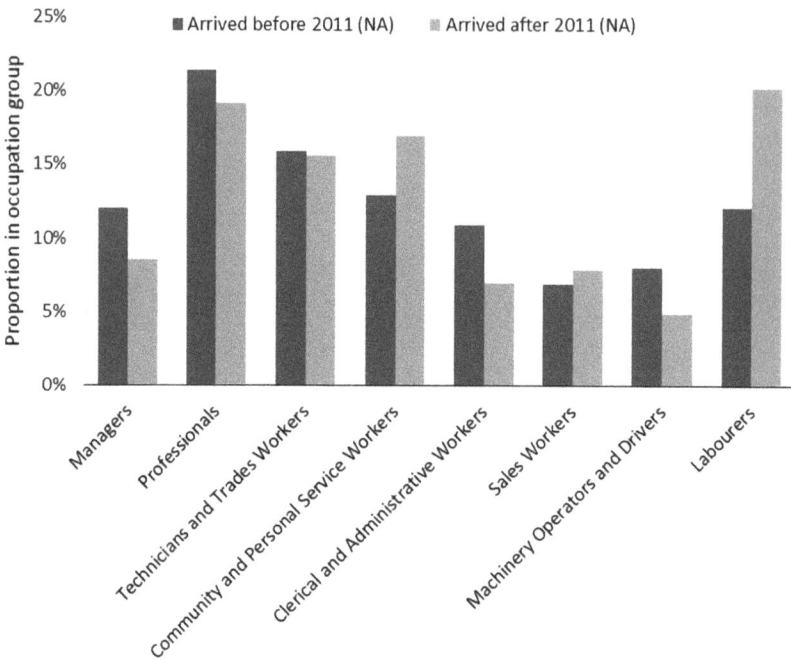

**Figure 11.2: Occupations of employed long-term overseas-born residents and recent arrivals in Northern Australia (2016).**
Note: NA = Northern Australia.
Source: Census data extracted from ABS (2016) using ABS Table Builder software.

The main industries of employment in 2016 for overseas-born residents in Australia were health care and social assistance followed by accommodation and food services (see Table 11.2). For recent arrivals, both industries are prominent employers, while a higher proportion of long-term overseas-born residents are employed in public administration and safety and education and training. Mining is a comparatively more important employer in Northern Australia, while manufacturing is more prominent in the rest of Australia.

Incomes of overseas-born residents in Northern Australia were markedly higher than those in the rest of Australia in 2016. For example, 39 per cent of overseas-born residents in Northern Australia stated they earned A$1,000 per week or more compared to 32 per cent in the rest of Australia (see Figure 11.3). A large proportion of recent arrivals (18 per cent) stated they usually earned no income at all.

## 11. ATTRACTING AND RETAINING INTERNATIONAL MIGRANTS

**Table 11.2: Industry of employment for overseas-born residents in 2016 (per cent).**

| Industry of employment | Northern Australia | Rest of Australia | Northern Australia long-term overseas-born residents | Northern Australia recent arrivals |
|---|---|---|---|---|
| Health care and social assistance | 16.5 | 15.3 | 16.7 | 16.0 |
| Accommodation and food services | 12.9 | 8.6 | 10.3 | 21.3 |
| Public administration and safety | 8.1 | 5.2 | 9.1 | 4.8 |
| Retail trade | 7.8 | 8.8 | 7.7 | 8.1 |
| Education and training | 7.8 | 7.4 | 8.6 | 5.2 |
| Construction | 7.3 | 7.2 | 7.6 | 6.4 |
| Mining | 6.6 | 1.2 | 7.2 | 4.8 |
| Transport, postal and warehousing | 5.4 | 5.5 | 5.8 | 3.9 |
| Administrative and support services | 4.6 | 4.5 | 4.3 | 5.6 |
| Professional, scientific and technical services | 4.5 | 9.3 | 4.6 | 4.3 |
| Manufacturing | 4.1 | 8.0 | 4.1 | 4.3 |
| Other services | 3.5 | 3.7 | 3.5 | 3.6 |
| Agriculture, forestry and fishing | 3.3 | 1.3 | 2.7 | 5.1 |
| Wholesale trade | 1.8 | 3.4 | 1.8 | 1.7 |
| Rental, hiring and real estate services | 1.5 | 1.7 | 1.6 | 1.5 |
| Arts and recreation services | 1.4 | 1.3 | 1.4 | 1.6 |
| Electricity, gas, water and waste services | 1.1 | 0.9 | 1.2 | 0.7 |
| Financial and insurance services | 1.0 | 4.7 | 1.0 | 0.7 |
| Information media and telecommunications | 0.7 | 2.0 | 0.8 | 0.5 |

Source: Census data extracted from ABS (2016) using ABS Table Builder software.

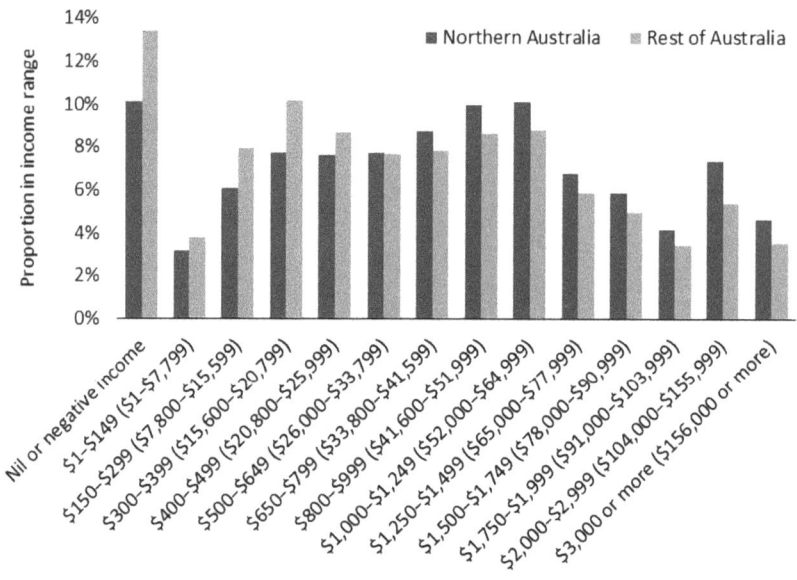

**Figure 11.3: Weekly income profiles for employed overseas-born residents in Australia (2016).**
Source: Census data extracted from ABS (2016) using ABS Table Builder software.

## Turnover and Retention

It is possible to approximate interstate migration turnover rates and net interstate migration numbers for overseas-born residents by examining movements into and out of Northern Australia between 2011 and 2016. For Northern Australia, gross interstate turnover for overseas-born residents was more than double the turnover for Australian-born residents (4.8 per cent and 1.4 per cent respectively), indicating overseas-born residents of Northern Australia are more mobile. Unfortunately, it is not possible to differentiate whether the overseas-born residents of Northern Australia who leave move within Australia, leave Australia to step-migrate to another country or return to residing overseas.

Net interstate migration suggests that there has been a net outflow of overseas-born residents from Northern Australia, which from 2011–16 was equivalent to approximately –2.5 per cent of the 2016 overseas-born population of Northern Australia. Net migration was negative for both males and females (around –1,000 males and –3,500 females).

## 11. ATTRACTING AND RETAINING INTERNATIONAL MIGRANTS

The age profiles for net interstate migration of overseas-born residents (see Figure 11.4) reveal a predominantly net negative pattern for both males and females with the exception of males of working age (25–39 and 50–54 years old) and females aged between 25–29 years old. A net loss of children and especially of teenagers incorporates movements to attend secondary and tertiary educational institutions (often with parents), while the net loss of older migrants parallels that of the general population who tend to leave Northern Australia once they retire. Collectively, these data suggest that employment is the key driver of movements into the region. The range of reasons for leaving the region is more diverse.

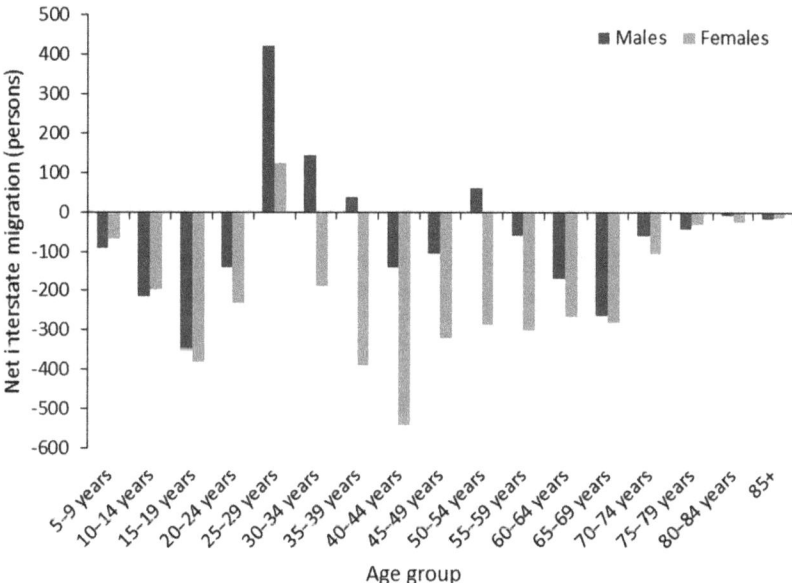

**Figure 11.4: Overseas-born net interstate migration into Northern Australia by age and gender (2011–16).**

Note: These data show the net result of subtracting overseas-born residents of Australia who lived in Northern Australia and then moved to the rest of Australia (negative figures) from those who lived in the rest of Australia and moved to Northern Australia during the period 2011–16 (positive figures).

Source: Census data extracted from ABS (2016) using ABS Table Builder software.

## Employment and Business Opportunities

The availability of a long-term job, better job or more suitable job for immigrants or their family members and business opportunities fundamentally influence the decisions to settle and remain in a particular area (Griffiths et al., 2010).

Currently, the majority of immigrants to Australia enter on skilled migration visas. Regional and state-sponsored programs in particular aim to attract and retain skilled immigrants to regional areas outside the southern capitals. Skilled migrants made up 58.3 per cent of total immigrants to the NT in 2011–12 and almost 40 per cent in Queensland (DIBP, 2013a). The most recent state and territory statistics reveal that these grew to 71 per cent in the NT and 63.2 per cent in Queensland in 2013–14 (DIBP, 2014). In recent years, regional and state-sponsored programs have driven the growth of skilled migration to the NT (Golebiowska, 2015).

The social and ethnic makeup of immigrant groups is changing. This is the case in regional Australia with growing numbers of immigrants from Asia, particularly the Indian subcontinent and the Philippines (Taylor et al., 2014). These immigrants are highly skilled and contribute significantly to the workforce, particularly in areas such as health and community services where it is difficult to attract and retain workers. Retaining these skilled immigrants and their families within regional areas and within their occupations reduces the costs of employee turnover and provides greater population stability.

## General Observations from Recent Studies

Taylor et al. (2014) surveyed 400 recent skilled immigrants in the NT, who arrived under regional migration programs, to assess rates of retention in sponsored occupations. They found that regional skilled migration schemes are delivering positive labour market outcomes and relatively high residential retention rates among this immigrant cohort to the NT. The primary applicants as well as their (employed) partners were helping to address skills and labour shortages, particularly in health care and social services and accommodation and food services. Most participants intended to permanently settle in the NT, with 89 per cent of respondents still resident after initial settlement and 80 per cent of respondents stating an intention to remain. Job opportunities were the prime reason for intending to stay.

These results are consistent with Griffiths et al. (2010) who interviewed 110 immigrants, 26 employers and 15 government officials in regional Australia. Their study focused on four regional areas, three of which were in Northern Australia (Darwin, Mt Isa and Karratha) as were over 90 per cent of the respondents. They identified that:

> Employment factors clearly played a central role in the settlement decision for many skilled migrants … Availability of employment and business opportunities are fundamental factors in influencing decisions to settle and remain in a particular regional area. A high proportion of skilled migrants who … reported settlement difficulty attribute[d] their difficulty to trouble in finding a job. Long-term employment opportunities for skilled migrants are crucial to the future of migration to regional areas. (Griffiths et al., 2010, pp. 5–6, 8)

State and regional skilled migration programs seem effective in attracting migrants and are a major opportunity to address skills shortages in Northern Australia. However, there is evidence that the potential contribution of immigrants may be under-utilised. While they have a higher employment rate in the NT (75 per cent) than Australian-born residents (67 per cent), many seem to be underemployed. For example, 47.3 per cent of permanent visa holders who arrived in 1997–2007 held overseas qualifications suitable for professional-level jobs, but only 28.3 per cent of those performed such jobs at the time of the 2006 Census and 42 per cent were employed in lower and unskilled occupations (Golebiowska, 2009, pp. 4, 6). This supports the previously discussed qualifications and workforce indicators findings and suggests that under-utilisation of qualifications and skills is an established pattern.

Buergelt (2011) found that recognition of overseas qualifications and experience and under-utilisation of skills can be major hurdles to attracting and retaining immigrants. She identified that under-utilisation of immigrants' skills is due to several factors including the processes professional bodies put in place for gaining recognition of qualifications and/or experience (e.g. under-valuing of overseas qualifications or prior experience, requirements to re-sit exams despite years of work experience, high costs and long processing times) and negative perceptions by employers (e.g. uncertainty regarding skill levels, lack of Australian-specific knowledge in area of work, language issues including professional terminology, managing cross-cultural issues, and possibly fear of being outperformed due to having lower qualifications and less experience). This research suggests that it is crucial to identify the specific individual and contextual factors that influence under-employment among immigrants in Northern Australia to design effective strategies that ensure that the skills immigrants bring when they migrate are fully utilised.

## Observations from Recent Workforce-specific Studies

Several of the challenges identified are evident in research on employment and mobility of nursing professionals in the NT (Garnett et al., 2008).[1] Garnett et al. (2008) interviewed overseas-qualified professionals because they would have had to have deal with issues of foreign qualifications recognition and the transfer of their knowledge and skills in the Australian health context. The study revealed that in the 2001–06 intercensal period, the NT recorded a proportional decrease of nursing professionals born in the United Kingdom and New Zealand and a simultaneous increase in the share of nursing professionals born elsewhere, in particular in the Philippines and India. For health services in the NT, this requires dealing with greater variances in the levels of education in the future.

Garnett et al.'s (2008) survey results revealed that the skills of some overseas-qualified nursing professionals are under-utilised, although this needs to be seen in the context of their transferability to the Australian context. Higher proportions of overseas-qualified immigrants are qualified to work in critical care/emergency (4.6 per cent difference), mixed medical/surgical (15.8 per cent difference), medical (16.5 per cent difference) and surgical (15.5 per cent difference) areas than are actually working in them. Managers expressed reservations about the ability of some overseas-qualified nurses to work at full capacity and independently soon after arrival due to lack of familiarity with Australian medical terminology and variances in clinical skills. However, they agreed that

---

1   In this study, a survey questionnaire was distributed to Australian and overseas-qualified professionals. Responses were received from 1,006 individuals of whom 127 were overseas qualified. Semi-structured interviews were conducted with some individuals from the latter group. Managers of overseas-qualified professionals in public hospitals were also interviewed.

although considerable initial support was required, the benefits were that overseas-qualified nurses tended to have a lower turnover rate than their Australian-qualified counterparts.

Data from the Department of Immigration and Citizenship (DIAC)[2] revealed that between 1996 and 2007, employer-linked permanent visas granted to registered nurses in the NT were the most common immigration avenue (surpassing skilled independent migration and family-linked skilled migration) (Garnett et al., 2008). DIAC data also revealed that the number of registered nurses granted employer-nominated temporary skilled visas (formerly 457 visas) in 2006–07 was nearly double the number of employer-nominated permanent skilled visas granted in this period to registered nurses destined for the NT (80 versus 46 respectively). The high volume of 457 visas granted is consistent with the information obtained from interviews with nurse managers who added that nurses would typically convert to permanent skilled visas once they were eligible (Garnett et al., 2008). Despite annual fluctuations in numbers from 130 to 40, between 2009–10 and 2012–13 registered nurses were the top occupation nominated for 457 visas in the NT (primary applicants only) (DIAC, 2011; DIBP, 2013b). Similar occupation-level data are not immediately available for permanent migration to the NT.

Garnett et al.'s (2008) analysis of immigrant age distribution and period of arrival data (from the 2006 Census) showed that the NT nursing workforce had a higher percentage of recently arrived overseas-born professionals aged 20–39 years old than Australia as a whole. These immigrants were probably less experienced than the rest of the immigrant workforce, but their longer working lifespan meant that if they gained the necessary experience and decided to remain in the NT, they could form the core of a future nursing workforce. This, in turn, could provide some continuity of service, which is a challenge due to a high turnover of the Australian-born nursing workforce in the NT.

Nurses come to the NT for a number of social and economic reasons. The three most common reasons for Australian- and overseas-qualified nurses are opportunities for new experiences, expectations of an opportunity to use a wider range of skills and expectations of job availability. For overseas-qualified nurses, the main reasons for staying

---

2   The DIAC was renamed the DIBP in September 2013, and this department was absorbed into the Department of Home Affairs in late December 2017.

in the NT were a sense of professional independence and responsibility, income and the NT lifestyle. The main reasons for leaving the NT were further travel, career opportunities elsewhere, completion of employment contract, stressful work (burnout) and dissatisfaction with management. Australian-qualified nurses cited family and social networks (elsewhere) and burnout as their main reasons for leaving the NT.

Another workforce-specific study investigated the characteristics of overseas-born residents in the early childhood education and care (ECEC) workforce in the NT (Golebiowska & Boyle, 2014).[3] In the 2011 Census (ABS, 2011), overseas-born residents represented 27.5 per cent of the ECEC workforce in the NT, compared to 24 per cent in the 2006 Census. Asian-born residents represented the single largest share in the NT ECEC workforce after Australian-born residents, with their share having increased from 10.5 per cent to 15.7 per cent between the 2006 and 2011 censuses and remaining higher in the NT than in Australia as a whole (Golebiowska & Boyle, 2014; ABS, 2011, 2016). This provides another illustration of the ongoing shift in countries of origin.

In contrast to overseas-qualified nurses who were skilled migrants, the majority of interviewed overseas-born ECEC workers (63 per cent) were family category migrants. All skilled interviewees (15 per cent) were dependent on their husbands' skilled visas. Workers with refugee backgrounds accounted for 11 per cent of interviewees, and the majority of the remaining 11 per cent were in non-visa categories (e.g. overseas-born children of Australian citizens). Regardless of immigration category, migration served to reunite or keep a family together.

People who move to Australia under the family migration category are often skilled and, per Golebiowska and Boyle's (2014) study, making an equally valuable economic contribution. All interviewees had post-school qualifications, and in some cases these were a level higher (e.g. a bachelor or diploma) than the minimum required to work in the ECEC sector in Australia (usually a Certificate III in Children's Services).

Due to a lack of formal work experience in the ECEC sector overseas (78 per cent of interviewees) and the majority having formal qualifications in areas other than ECEC, most interviewees were working in the ECEC

---

3   This study analysed unpublished 2006 and 2011 census statistics, immigration statistics from the DIAC and involved 27 face-to-face interviews with overseas-born residents employed at selected long day childcare centres in Darwin and Palmerston.

for the first time. The lack of formal ECEC work experience overseas is likely because formalised childcare arrangements are not as well developed overseas as in Australia and looking after children is part of the assumed family duties of females. The key motivations for joining the ECEC workforce included a passion for working with children; prior experience of looking after children in family settings; finding the studies required to join the workforce interesting and enjoyable; suggestions from family, friends and Centrelink; and the awareness that as educators they can influence the development of young children (Golebiowska & Boyle, 2014).

At the time of interviews in mid-2012, the ECEC workforce Australia wide was in the process of upskilling to meet the new regulations for minimum formal qualifications (a Certificate III in Children's Services). Over two-thirds (68 per cent) of interviewees had already met or exceeded the qualification requirement and 70 per cent were either interested in furthering their studies or already studying. A significant proportion of interviewees identified that although their English-language speaking and listening skills were high, they believed that their reading and writing skills were not sufficient to enable them to continue their studies at a higher level (Golebiowska & Boyle, 2014).

Family ties and the NT lifestyle/climate were cited by interviewees as the two principal reasons for migration to and staying in the NT. A friendly and multicultural community and a small city ranked third in the reasons for migrating and second in the reasons for staying (ex aequo with overall work satisfaction). The third reason for staying was support from management ex aequo with good relationships with other staff. Importantly, 85 per cent of interviewees intended to live in the NT permanently or longer term, primarily for family reasons. As 81 per cent of interviewees anticipated working in the NT ECEC sector in the next 5–10 years, it can be surmised that nearly all stayers would remain employed in the ECEC industry for this period of time (Golebiowska & Boyle, 2014).

Interviewees suggested that higher wages (85 per cent), more time to upgrade formal qualifications (48 per cent), better financial recognition of higher-level qualifications (22 per cent) and more flexible modes of formal training (22 per cent) would improve their employment experience. Importantly, 7 per cent of interviewees representing Asian and African countries noted that their prior learning should be better recognised by the Australian ECEC sector. Unsurprisingly, given their own roles as educators, all but one of these improvements relates exclusively to education. This suggests their genuine desire to pursue further education if it is accessible, appropriately recognised and suitably remunerated.

Suggestions as to how overseas-qualified professionals could be helped to remain in the NT long term were related to work and their settlement in the local community. Garnett et al. (2008) identified that providing an information package about Darwin and helping with securing affordable accommodation would facilitate settling in. Buergelt (2011) suggested that the challenges immigrants and employing organisation experience initially could be addressed by providing intensive training in English, Australian-specific professional terminology and Australian- or organisation-specific work culture.

Notwithstanding the shortages of skilled workers in Northern Australia, many take a long time to find a job that matches their professional qualifications and aspirations. High living expenses and absence of income push many immigrants to take any employment. Regardless of their job status in their home country, many migrants are compelled to engage in whatever work they find from cleaning to sales jobs to childcare to hospitality. Working in jobs that do not match their skills and are lower paid and of lower status than they had in their home location causes dissatisfaction that may result in migrants re-evaluating their initial migration decision and deciding to leave for a place where they can secure more appropriate employment (Buergelt, 2011). This is a longstanding issue for immigrants settled in the Darwin area (Haines, 2001) and is not unique to the NT (Tani, 2018).

## Observations from a Historical Study

Vietnamese farmers are now an integral part of the horticulture industry in Darwin's hinterland. The story of the Vietnamese farming community is part of the local mythology caught up with images of 'boat people'. It is commonly believed that these refugees came from farming backgrounds, but this is incorrect. In 1980, the Federal Government and new NT Government entered into an agreement to take relatively large numbers of Vietnamese refugees from camps in Southeast Asia to create a Vietnamese 'community' in Darwin and increase the population. The criteria included good education, skills and urban background, 'young families' and precluded single unattached uneducated males (Haines, 2001, p. 11).

Haines estimated that more than 1,000 Vietnamese arrived in Darwin in the early 1980s. However, by 1986, more than half had migrated interstate to find better employment opportunities than were available in Darwin (Haines, 2001, p. 60). The ones who stayed were more likely to have found employment and to have family support (Haines, 2001, p. 105).

Haines (2001) reported that there were 21 Vietnamese farmers in the Darwin region in 1995. These individuals often had little knowledge or experience of farming, but gravitated towards farming because speaking English was not a requirement and it provided a pragmatic solution to providing for their families (Haines, 2001, pp. 83–85). According to the 2011 Census (ABS, 2011), 883 people in the NT indicated that they had Vietnamese ancestry. Of these, 33.6 per cent were born in Australia. Most of those with Vietnamese ancestry lived in the Darwin region (85.2 per cent), the majority in the urban areas. Of these that were employed, 36.2 per cent worked in agriculture, forestry and fishing.

## International Students

Skill shortages in the north could also be reduced by attracting and retaining other classes of immigrants, in particular, international students who can apply for permanent residence and add to the skill pool. The contribution of international students to the labour force is significant, especially in industries such as hospitality and retail trade that offer casual and part-time employment at times congruent with study demands. Education is now one of Australia's largest export industries. Hawthorne (2010, pp. 6, 10, 29, 30) observed that the majority of onshore immigrants are former international students:

> This phenomenon of 'two-step' student migration is one proliferating world-wide … The next challenge will be to keep them, in an increasingly competitive global environment where students have been prioritized for selection by multiple OECD countries … Within this context, international students will become highly discerning education and migration consumers—researching global options to select the optimal study, migration and lifestyle 'package'. Multiple factors will inform their decisions, including the speed and certainty of selection, access to work rights and citizenship (for family as well as primary applicants), and the quality of employment outcomes.

However, institutions in Northern Australia attract only a small percentage of international students coming to Australia. Overall, only 3 per cent of international students studying in Australia go to regional areas. In 2018, 10 per cent of the 26,789 international students studying in Australia were located in the NT (almost all in the Darwin area), while 7 per cent were in Townsville and 9 per cent in Cairns. Between 2017 and 2018, there have been small increases in the percentage studying in Darwin, but corresponding decreases in those studying in North Queensland (Department of Education and Training, 2019). Increasing the number of international student enrolments has been identified in a number of reports as a significant potential contributor to the economy, predominantly through student's fees, living costs and demand for services. To illustrate, in the NT in 2007–08, the presence of international students[4] contributed 196 full-time jobs (54 in the education industry and 142 in other industries) (Access Economics, 2009, p. 8). This indicates that international education has a spillover effect on other sectors in the economy. International education (spending by onshore students) contributed A$38 million to the NT economy in 2010–2011 and A$55 million in 2014–15 (Australian Education International, 2012, 2015). International students also participate in the labour market and their contributions to local economies need to be better understood and appreciated by authorities. The focus of governments and educational institutions has largely been on attracting full-fee-paying international students, rather than their potential contributions to addressing skills shortages and how to retain them as permanent residents on completion of their studies. This requires a concerted and cooperative approach by the relevant state and territory governments that often do not focus on such regional issues.

## Family, Psychosocial, Social and Cultural Connectedness

Migration decisions need to be seen in the context of individual life courses and lifespan processes. Strong family and community ties contribute to an immigrant's sense of stability and likelihood of staying in Australia.

---

4   International students at the tertiary study level, in ELICOS (now English Australia) and other non-award courses and schools.

Analysis of the census data (see above) indicates that the majority of immigrants are in marital-type relationships, although lower proportions of those in Northern Australia are actually married.

It is recognised that migration places numerous stresses on families:

> These factors may take many years to resolve and include: changed economic status—either loss of status or better economic conditions that alter relationships; conflict and stress relating to having to re-establish themselves … adapting to a different environment, language and culture … loss of human and social capital … lack of a sense of recognition, belonging and inclusion … strict migration laws can erode traditional family structures, reduce family support structures and limit the connection between generations. (Queensland Government, 2011)

Further, migration has disproportionately negative impacts on women, particularly in terms of family incomes, loss of family and social support, and discrimination (Queensland Government, 2011).

However, if partners and children are settled and feel welcome, migrants are more likely to intend to stay in a regional location (Griffiths et al. 2010). Khoo et al. (2013) had similar findings, but warned that:

> While most family migrants already contribute to their families' welfare and many also contribute to the economy and the community, some of them have had difficulty in finding employment or have expressed low satisfaction with their jobs and financial situation. There is scope for improving employment outcomes of family migrants to increase their economic contributions and improve their families' economic welfare and their own level of life satisfaction. (p. 92)

Migration entails substantial mental, emotional and financial investment, and is highly risky and uncertain. Not mastering the mental, emotional and physical preparation and integration processes can lead to psychological and physical health issues, isolation, alienation and homesickness; relationship issues with partners children and extended family; work performance issues; financial hardship; and, ultimately, antagonism towards locals and their culture. All of these can lead to migrants leaving. However, these negative outcomes can be prevented and reduced, and positive outcomes facilitated by assisting migrants to successfully adapt to their new environment. Buergelt (2011, 2012) showed that success in moving between cultures is determined by the mindset and capabilities of people migrating and by a set of contextual factors in the locations of origin and destination. High turnover rates are partly due to migrants and their families experiencing problems adapting to their new work and living environments, but also due to employers and government poorly selecting, preparing and supporting migrants.

## Place Characteristics

A wide variety of natural, cultural and social place characteristics play a critical role in attracting and retaining migrants. While immigration policies are focused on attracting immigrants to regional Australia, retention appears to be a problem with a significant percentage of immigrants moving to capital cities once they have met the visa conditions. Several characteristics have been identified as deterring migrants from choosing to move to and stay in Northern Australia. Anwar and Prideaux (2005) hypothesised that climate extremes and remoteness from (southern) population centres cause high rates of population turnover among immigrants once their minimum duration of stay under their migration program is completed. However, Taylor et al. (2014) provided a more positive view with lifestyle and amenity noted as significant pull factors.

Other research points to factors that may have a mitigating effect on a decision to leave once contractual visa obligations have been met. Griffiths et al. (2010) found that 70 per cent of survey respondents were positive about their chosen regional area, citing the quality of life in regional environments and smaller communities, with many preferring it to larger cities. Immigrants from South and Southeast Asia appreciated the hot and humid climatic conditions which are comparable to their home country and the relative proximity of Northern Australian cities to their country of origin. However, 30 per cent of respondents were dissatisfied with the living conditions. They expressed concerns about climate, high costs of living (especially the cost of housing) and the low standard of public and community facilities including schools, housing and transport—all were disincentives to them staying in Northern Australia.

Taylor et al. (2014) reported very high retention rates for regional skilled migrants in the NT (90 per cent) and even higher rates for migrants on specific visas like the Regional Sponsored Migration Scheme (RSMS) visa (93 per cent), with more than half of RSMS respondents stating that they intended never to leave the NT. 'This indicates that, at worst, skilled migrants are no less likely to leave the NT … than other residents and at best that the majority might remain there for the longer term' (Taylor et al., 2014, p. 15).

Research undertaken for Multicultural Affairs Queensland and Welcoming Australia suggested a number of essential strategies for retaining immigrants in regional communities (van Kooy et al., 2019), in particular, the importance of locally driven coordination, consultation and planning at the local/regional council level; consultation with migrant organisations and local Indigenous communities; accessible, affordable housing, transport and culturally appropriate services; and creating a culture of welcome in receiving communities.

## Summary and Conclusions

Small resident populations and skill shortages limit the economic development of Northern Australia. Since white settlement, Australian states have relied on immigration to build their economies and labour forces. Nevertheless, Northern Australia attracts only a very small percentage of the total immigrant intake to Australia. The research presented in this chapter provides evidence that permanent and temporary immigrants to Northern Australia contribute to the economy and labour force, particularly in the services areas. These immigrants are also more likely than migrants elsewhere in Australia to settle permanently in the north with their families and so build the population. In light of the higher turnover of overseas-born workers compared to Australian-born workers, continued research into attraction and retention factors for the former is needed, including in sectors of the economy other than health services and ECEC. Immigration, especially from the regions close to Northern Australia (Southeast Asia, the Philippines, India and China), could be a significant contributor to growing both the working population and stable and vibrant communities in Northern Australia. Successfully attracting and retaining immigrants requires understanding and addressing the challenges that they and their families face in obtaining employment that is appropriate to their skills and qualifications, housing, education, transport and community connections.

Notwithstanding the benefits they bring to the community and economy, immigrants face many challenges in migration to and settlement in Northern Australia. These include lack of skills recognition, adaptation to the local labour force including assistance with job search, and orientation to local organisational cultures. The research reported in this chapter has identified a number of strategies to facilitate successful employment. These include a more streamlined qualifications translation process, recognition of experience, profession specific English language programs and employment-orientation programs that assist immigrants in understanding local organisational and social cultures. On the other side, managers need training and support in selection, orientation and integration of immigrants from very diverse social, educational and linguistic backgrounds into work and organisational cultures.

Migrating to and settling into a community is often a family decision. Accordingly, creating community and organisational culture and structures to support immigrants and their families before, during and after they move to Northern Australia is vital in ensuring that families feel welcome and choose to settle and stay in Northern Australia. Employment opportunities for partners are important, as is recognition of the educational and language needs of children from different linguistic and social backgrounds. Culturally appropriate health and community services including those directed towards families are particularly important and require additional investment that may be hard to justify for very small populations. While these challenges exist throughout Australia, they are particular important in the small and geographically isolated communities in Northern Australia.

Orientation to the destination culture, society and economy is important for all immigrants. Northern Australia is home to large numbers of Indigenous Australians, many of whom live in their traditional communities. Gaining an understanding and appreciation of their culture and the impact that immigration and development plans have on their societies is particularly important for all migrants living and working in the north.

# References

Access Economics. (2009, April). *The Australian education sector and the economic contribution of international students.* Retrieved from globalhighered.files.wordpress.com/2009/04/theaustralianeducationsectorandtheeconomiccontributionofinternationalstudents-2461.pdf

Anwar, S. & Prideaux, B. (2005). Regional economic growth: An evaluation of the NT. *Economic Papers, 24*(3), 194–214.

Australian Bureau of Statistics (ABS). (2011). *2011 Census of population and housing*. Available from www.abs.gov.au

Australian Bureau of Statistics (ABS). (2016). *2016 Census of population and housing*. Available from www.abs.gov.au

Australian Education International. (2012, April). *International education snapshot*. Retrieved from internationaleducation.gov.au/International-network/ Australia/InternationalStrategy/IEAC2/Consultation(IEAC)/Documents/ DataSnapshot.pdf

Australian Education International. (2015, November). *Export income to Australia from international education activity in 2014–2015*. Retrieved from international education.gov.au/research/Research-Snapshots/Documents/Export%20Income %20FY2014-5.pdf

Boese, M. (2015). The roles of employers in the regional settlement of recently arrived migrants and refugees. *Journal of Sociology, 51*(2), 401–416. doi.org/ 10.1177/1440783314544994

Buergelt, P. T. (2011). Contemporary migration between developed countries: Transformation processes towards actualising authentic selves and lives (unpublished doctoral thesis). Massey University, New Zealand.

Buergelt, P. T. (2012, March) *Migration motives and challenges: Implications for countries of origin and settlement*. Keynote address at the Intergovernmental Consultations on Migration, Asylum and Refugees (IGC) Chair's Theme Workshop on Motives for Migration, IGC, Geneva, Switzerland.

Department of Education and Training. (2019, February). *International students studying in regional areas*. Retrieved from internationaleducation.gov.au/ research/Research-Snapshots/Documents/Location%20of%20International %20Students%20in%202018.pdf

Department of Immigration and Border Protection (DIBP). (2013a). *Migration to Australia's states and territories, 2012–13*. Retrieved from www.homeaffairs.gov. au/research-and-stats/files/migration-australia-state-territories-2012-13.pdf

Department of Immigration and Border Protection (DIBP). (2013b). *Subclass 457 State/Territory summary report, 2012–13 to 30 June 2013*. Retrieved from www.homeaffairs.gov.au/research-and-stats/files/state-territory-summary-2012-13-to-30-june-2013.pdf

Department of Immigration and Border Protection (DIBP). (2014). *State and territory migration summary, 30 June 2014*. Retrieved from www.home affairs.gov.au/research-and-stats/files/state-territory-migration-summary-june-2014.pdf

Department of Immigration and Citizenship (DIAC). (2011). *Subclass 457 State/ Territory summary report, 2010–11 to 30 June 2011*. Retrieved from www.home affairs.gov.au/research-and-stats/files/457-stats-state-territory-jun11.pdf

Flanagan, J. (2007). *Dropped from the moon—the settlement experiences of refugee communities in Tasmania*. Retrieved from www.anglicare-tas.org.au/research/dropped_from_the_moon/

Garnett, S., Coe, K., Golebiowska, K., Walsh, H., Zander, K., Guthridge, S., Li, S. Q. & Malyon, R. (2008). *Attracting and keeping nursing professionals in an environment of chronic labour shortage*. Darwin, NT: Charles Darwin University Press.

Golebiowska, K. (2009). *Country of origin and labour market participation of the overseas-born in the NT* (Research Brief Issue 2009039). Population Studies Group, School for Social and Policy Research, Charles Darwin University. Retrieved from www.cdu.edu.au/sites/default/files/research-brief-2009-39.pdf

Golebiowska, K. (2015). Are peripheral regions benefiting from national policies aimed at attracting skilled migrants? Case study of the Northern Territory of Australia. *Journal of International Migration and Integration 17*, 947–971. doi.org/10.1007/s12134-015-0431-3

Golebiowska, K. & Boyle, A. (2014). Professional integration and belonging of the immigrant-born early childhood education and care (ECEC) workers in Darwin, Northern Territory, Australia. *International Journal of Organisational Diversity, 13*(2), 1–17.

Griffiths, J., Laffan, W. & Jones, A. (2010, June). *Factors that influence skilled migrants locating in regional areas. Final report*. Retrieved from www.dss.gov.au/sites/default/files/documents/01_2014/factors-influence-skilled-migrants-locating-regional-areas.pdf

Haines, T. K. (2001). 'Replacing Vietnam'. A longitudinal study of a refugee population in isolation: The Vietnamese of Darwin (unpublished doctoral thesis). University of Queensland, Brisbane, Qld.

Hawthorne, L. (2010). How valuable is 'two-step migration'? Labour market outcomes for international student migrants to Australia. *Asian and Pacific Migration Journal, 19*(1), 5–36. doi.org/10.1177/011719681001900102

Hugo, G. (2008). Australia's state-specific and regional migration scheme: An assessment of its impacts in South Australia. *Journal of International Migration and Integration, 9*(2), 125–145. doi.org/10.1007/s12134-008-0055-y

Joint Select Committee on Northern Australia. (2014). *Pivot North: Inquiry into the development of Northern Australia—Final report*. Canberra, ACT: Australian Government. Retrieved from www.aph.gov.au/Parliamentary_Business/ Committees/Joint/Former_Committees/Northern_Australia/Inquiry_into _the_Development_of_Northern_Australia/Tabled_Reports

Khoo, S.-E., McDonald, P. & Edgar, B. (2013, April). *Contribution of family migration to Australia*. Report to the Department of Immigration and Citizenship.

McDonald, B., Gifford, S., Webster, K., Wiseman, J. & Casey, S. (2008). *Refugee resettlement in regional and rural Victoria: Impacts and policy issues*. Retrieved from library.bsl.org.au/jspui/bitstream/1/977/1/RefugeeResettlement_Report_ Mar08.pdf

Piper, M. & Associates. (2007, March). *Shepparton regional humanitarian settlement pilot*. Summary report of an evaluation undertaken by Margaret Piper and Associates for the Department of Immigration and Citizenship.

Piper, M. & Associates. (2008, November). *Regional humanitarian settlement pilot Mount Gambier*. Report of an evaluation undertaken by Margaret Piper and Associates for the Department of Immigration and Citizenship.

Piper, M. & Associates. (2009, January). *Regional humanitarian settlement pilot Ballarat*. Report of an evaluation undertaken by Margaret Piper and Associates for the Department of Immigration and Citizenship.

Queensland Government. (2011). *Supporting information: Understanding the effects of migration and settlement*. Retrieved from www.qld.gov.au/web/ community-engagement/guides-factsheets/cald-communities/introduction/ understanding-migration-effects.html

Tani, M. (2018, 8 February). Australia's jobs and migration policies are not making the best use of qualified migrants. *The Conversation*. Retrieved from theconversation.com/australias-jobs-and-migration-policies-are-not-making-the-best-use-of-qualified-migrants-90944

Taylor, A. J., Bell, L. & Gerritsen, R. (2014). Benefits of skilled migration programs for regional Australia: Perspectives from the Northern Territory. *Journal of Economic and Social Policy*, *16*(1), article 3.

Taylor, J. & Stanovic, D. (2005). *Refugees and regional settlement: Balancing priorities*. Retrieved from library.bsl.org.au/jspui/bitstream/1/6212/1/regional_ refugee_summary.pdf

van Kooy, J., Wickes, R. & Ali, A. (2019). *Welcoming regions*. Retrieved from welcomingcities.org.au/wp-content/uploads/2019/03/WelcomingRegions_ Summary.pdf

# Section 4

# Water, Land and Energy in the North

Tom D. Brewer

## Introduction

Water, land and energy lie at the core of the contemporary policy narratives and discourse of Northern Australia. This section of five chapters offers a rich set of ideas that together portray northern development in a different light. The chapters range from the critical reflections on and possible solutions to the northern development dilemma to governance of natural resource management. Connecting themes include the fluid and intertwined nature of northern people, places and policy; the emergence of the north as a place with a past and present able to speak for its future; and the north as a place of undervalued uniqueness and potential for innovation.

Brewer et al. begins the section by exploring local landscape values and development preferences in and around Darwin Harbour as juxtaposed to northern development rhetoric. Their work is grounded in a comparison between the current iteration of the land use plan for the Darwin region and empirical data collected from a sample of households from the Darwin region. The identified values do not conform to hard planning boundaries but are diffuse and diverse, mirroring the people of the region. They identify the need to revisit development ideologies in a more sophisticated, open and shared way. These ideas are further developed by Carter in the last chapter in this section. Brewer et al. also offers pragmatic means of incorporating local interpretations of development and values into governance architecture and development language and policy.

Dale et al. bring us to land tenure as central to northern policy discourse. Land tenure underpins a broad range of government policymaking and program delivery and function including land administration, taxation, administrative boundaries and land use management. Therefore, a functioning, transparent and efficient land tenure governance arrangement, both in structural and functional terms, is vital to planning for economic growth, social stability, reducing investment risk and land management and sustainability. Dale et al. synthesise the history of land tenure in Northern Australia as an anchor for highlighting the importance of resolving land tenure complexities, including the multitude of tenure arrangements layered across northern landscapes, to move the northern development agenda forward. They outline both the impediments and opportunities for reform and, in doing so, present a synthetic mud map for moving northern development forward. Many of the most significant gains in terms of improving investor certainty and development outcomes for northern enterprises and communities will come from engaging with tenure complexity in constructive and more informed ways that recognise the unique mix of land uses, resources, rights and interests in northern lands.

The theme of land continues in the third chapter, where Dale et al. discuss governance of community-based natural resource management. They deliver a clear and succinct history of northern natural resource management governance and explore differences between natural resource management policy and program delivery at the national-level and in Northern Australia. They highlight key differences including strength of Indigenous land management, climatic constraints and the need to focus on maintaining ecosystem function rather than rehabilitation as occurs in the south. They end by offering some insights into the progression of the model to date in the north and suggest some key continuous improvements needed for better landscape outcomes. Both chapters led by Dale provide well-considered and pragmatic land use policy recommendations for future northern development informed by significant experience across key domains of land use policy.

In the fourth chapter, we return to water and maintain the conversation with our Southeast Asian neighbours. Here, Steenbergen et al. explore the impact of national and regional legislation on small-scale fisheries, as a readily overlooked yet important marine resource use system, at Warruwi in the Northern Territory and at Ohoiren in Eastern Indonesia. Using the trepang fishery as a case study, they show how local actors become entangled in legislation, which, while aiming to create fair and sustainable access to fisheries, creates a system of rights that can undermine the ability of local actors to engage in commercial activities. Local actors must navigate not only these legally complex environments but local prescriptions governing access and use. They conclude that, despite the vastly different country settings similar tensions can be observed at local, regional and national scales in the challenge of balancing economic demands and sustainable resource management needs. This chapter reinforces the importance of placing Commonwealth-level development visions in the context of lived realities and forces us to think more deeply on the consequences of sweeping policy.

We end with an evocative interpretation of the elephant in the room of developing frontiers debates: confusion generated by ambiguous and conflicting ideologies of laissez-faire economics that consumes frontier resources and of protectors of the wild and pristine that was here before the frontier was conceived, demarcated and conquered. In essence, Carter highlights the mixed metaphor of nature and nurture of development and calls for resolution of confusion around the language of economic utopianism that dominates current development policy debates. Inspired by watery northern landscapes, Carter responds to this confusion by proposing a shift in thinking, defining and doing development, from the current dry, static and techno-centric approach to a more fluid, wet and dynamic interpretation and practice of development devoid of hard boundaries and binary thinking. A development that builds connections among and celebrates the academic and poetic dimensions of language to enable us to both grapple with the myriad interpretations of development and plot a development course more amenable to frontier landscapes and communities. He shows the metaphorical value of water in a policy landscape that traditionally values water in economic and ecological production terms.

# 12

# A Case-Based Discussion on the Disjuncture between Local Values and Federal, State and Territory Development Policy in Northern Australia

Tom D. Brewer, Sharon Harwood, Ainsley Archer, David Williams and Allan P. Dale

## Introduction

Northern Australians have seen repeated waves of politically fashionable development-focused policy prescriptions devised in Perth, Adelaide, Darwin, Canberra or Brisbane by the Commonwealth and the states over the preceding century. While some policies have had positive outcomes for the region, many have failed to deliver expected outcomes and have arguably in some cases had negative effects on human communities and their land and sea environments across the north (Adamson, 2013; Bell et al., 2014). A historical and growing literature points to a number of factors that contribute to the failure of northern development, including climatic, soil and remoteness constraints on primary and secondary industries including agriculture and mining (Ash, 2014; Davidson, 1965; Northern Australia Land and Water Taskforce, 2009); top-down engagement with Indigenous communities that occludes other ways of knowing and doing (Stephens et al., 2015); and pro-environmental agendas driven by southern lobbyists that, knowingly or ignorantly, disregard northern land- and sea-management rights and practises and livelihoods embedded in the north (Dale, 2014).

Democracies, in theory, function by the will of the people; political parties are elected, decisions are made and laws are passed based on majority rule. Within our Australian democracy, the federal government is answerable to the largest number of constituents. While different tiers of government are responsible for different elements of governing, public policy devised and enacted at the federal level, such as welfare reform, will generally affect a more socioculturally diverse body of constituents than local-level public policy. Equally, federal policy focused on a particular geography or demography will face the challenge of reconciling national agendas with individual-, local- and region-level idiosyncrasies and aspirations. This potential mismatch of scale between national- and local-level aspirations (Cash et al., 2006; Termeer et al., 2010), coupled with sociopolitical changes, including reduced nation-state autonomy, increased multiculturalism and the rise of the market as the preferred mode of policy delivery (Lockwood et al., 2009), makes formulation and implementation of public policy challenging.

While the national government consults the community on public policy using a broad range of tools (including letters to local members, submission platforms, opinion polling, meetings and white papers), we argue that effective modes of acquiring and integrating public views are lacking. There remains, in our view, a marginalised silent majority that lacks the means, or desire, to engage in public policy processes. Additionally, neoliberalism, the dominant paradigm in Australian politics, tends to view alternate values as disruptive to markets (Springer, 2010) and, consequently, precludes their influence, rather than drawing on the sociocultural diversity embedded within society (Stephens et al., 2015). Here, neoliberalism refers to the political belief that economic liberalism and privatisation and reduced government taxation, spending and regulation are good for society. It assumes that the market is capable of recognising individual and social values and preferences. A concern with this mode of policy delivery, in our view, particularly in places like Northern Australia, is that forcing conformity to maintain market function occludes diversity, leading to erosion of social resilience and reduced long-term prosperity (Grieves, 2015). This chapter urges the greater incorporation of the embedded diversity of sociocultural values of Northern Australia (Altman, 2009; Grieves, 2015) into planning processes and development policy as a means of achieving desirable development. In doing so, we are not discounting the role of markets in achieving positive social outcomes but are suggesting that the full engagement of multiple belief systems have a role in realising desirable development:

> Good governance does not simply default to the power of global capital. Good governance enables the input of, and negotiation with, small populations and remote, and at times divided, Indigenous communities. Good governance recognises the value of diversity and the value of the north's proud non-conformity. (Bell, 2013)

We argue that a mismatch between federal- and state/territory-level policy and local values and development preferences contribute to chronic past failure of federal visions of northern development (Carson et al., 2010). Overcoming this mismatch through embracing local values, aspirations and knowledge, rather than marginalising or normalising them (Stephens et al., 2015), will lead to an improvement in the development trajectory of the north. However, this will require an understanding of northern conceptions of development (Dale, 2013), rather than ones that hold market-driven development as the preeminent goal. Our development vision (synthesised from Stephens et al., 2015) is one of a governmentality that enables marginalised views to gain legitimacy and voice, rather than simply endorsing the current neoliberal paradigm. It is one of genuine self-determination and improved wellbeing of both mainstream and Indigenous communities of Northern Australia (Altman & Markham, 2014; Morrison, 2013), secure environmental assets and a flourishing and diverse economy that dampens boom–bust demographic and economic cycles (Carson, 2011). It is one of greater internal autonomy, drawing on the knowledges and networks of those residing in the north and their links to Southeast Asian neighbours.

The recent *White paper on developing Northern Australia* (Australian Government, 2015) is an example of larger-scale federal public policy initiative that highlights federal ambitions in Northern Australia. Leading up to the white paper, the federal government released the Liberal Party's 2030 vision for developing Northern Australia (Liberal Party of Australia, 2013) and the *Green paper on developing Northern Australia* (Australian Government, 2014). Discussion around land use; growth in mining, agriculture, industry and residential; and a streamlining of native title processes 'to drive growth in jobs and investment for the benefit of all Australians' (Australian Government, 2014, p. vi) are dominant across the pages of both documents. Both documents were designed to instigate debate on northern development, but, more significantly, they are statements of intent on utilising the north by reducing regulation and increasing privatisation for economic development. Publicising the federal vision prior to broad consultation in Northern Australia meant discussions on northern development would begin from the position presented by the government, potentially reducing opportunity for dissent and increasing apathy arising from inadequate engagement (Peel & Lloyd, 2007). The resulting white paper (Australian Government, 2015) was distinctly focused on economic growth and development, including simpler arrangements to support development; developing the north's water resources; our business, trade and investment gateway; infrastructure to support growth; a northern workforce for growth; and good governance for Northern Australia. The most significant tangible development resulting from the white paper was the announcement of A$5 billion in concessional loans to encourage private sector investment in economic infrastructure development.

Essentially, the geographically distant, short-term economic view of the utility of Northern Australia is limited to growth of human and financial capital, a source of immediate revenue for national prosperity. However, enduring development, including ongoing liveability of places, additionally requires genuine consideration of other forms of capital including natural, social and cultural (Beeton, 2006; Woolcock, 1998, 2001) to strengthen and maintain sustainable development of communities.

Darwin, as a capital city, significant seaport and gateway to Southeast Asia, has experienced rapid economic growth over recent years, representing a focal point of development through free market means. Darwin can, therefore, be seen as antagonistic to alternate values and ideas of development and not representative of broader Northern Australia including rural and remote communities. We posit, however, that comparing manifestations of the current paradigm with local values in a place where free market policies dominate enables some inference that if there is a mismatch between the current development policies and local values in Darwin then there is likely to be mismatch in other northern regions. Contemporary examples include conflict between Woodside Petroleum and local residents in Broome, Western Australia, and the AQUIS mega-resort proposed for Cairns, Queensland.

This broader federal agenda is reflected in the previous NT Government's Draft Regional Land Use Plan for the Darwin region (NT Planning Commission, 2014). The purpose of the Regional Land Use Plan is to 'define and respond to the essential characteristics and needs that will shape land use and development in the Darwin Region in the long term' (NT Planning Commission, 2014). Land use planning is controlled by a legislative hierarchy. Development for the entire NT is controlled through the NT Planning Scheme (NT Government, 2007) and is subordinate to the territory-wide planning legislation, the NT *Planning Act* (2008). Per Section 2A, the objects of the Act are 'to plan for, and provide a framework of controls for, the orderly use and development of land' and these objects are to be achieved by:

a. strategic planning of land use and development and for the sustainable use of resources;
b. strategic planning of transport corridors and other public infrastructure;
c. effective controls and guidelines for the appropriate use of land, having regard to its capabilities and limitations;
d. control of development to provide protection of the natural environment, including by sustainable use of land and water resources;
e. minimising adverse impacts of development on existing amenity and, wherever possible, ensuring that amenity is enhanced as a result of development;
f. ensuring, as far as possible, that planning reflects the wishes and needs of the community through appropriate public consultation and input in both the formulation and implementation of planning schemes; and
g. fair and open decision-making and appeals processes.

Unlike the Queensland equivalent, the objects of the NT *Planning Act* do not specifically mention the identification and protection of landscape amenity or the enhancement of community social wellbeing and, more importantly, the protection of Indigenous Australian culture and tradition. Rather, the focus is on the creation of a system of land use and development control for the purposes of economic development as opposed to balanced perspective of sustainable development (after Campbell, 1996). NT land use plans cannot incorporate aspects of planning not outlined within the Act, which limits the inclusion of local values and preferences. The land use plan can, however, be used to guide interpretation of the provisions outlined in the Planning Scheme. The draft plan places strong emphasis on efficient allocation of infrastructure—industrial, residential, roads and rail required for continued economic growth (see Figure 12.1)—reflecting the tenor of the federal white paper. Similar to the federal agenda in Northern Australia, the regional planning process, as required by the Act, is focused on built and financial capital as vehicles for economic growth, providing limited consideration for other forms of capital. As with the federal development agenda, the land use planning process is top down, limiting opportunity for consideration of alternative values and development preferences at more local scales. It has been suggested that Darwin in particular experiences periodic economic stagnation due to, among other factors, prioritisation of the short-term interests of external investors in land use planning and construction (Carson et al., 2010). Carson et al. (2010) suggested that addressing this periodic stagnation requires a change in the political approach to development at the Territory level that prioritises local interests that generates internal development, including more consultative planning with long-term residents and City of Darwin Council.

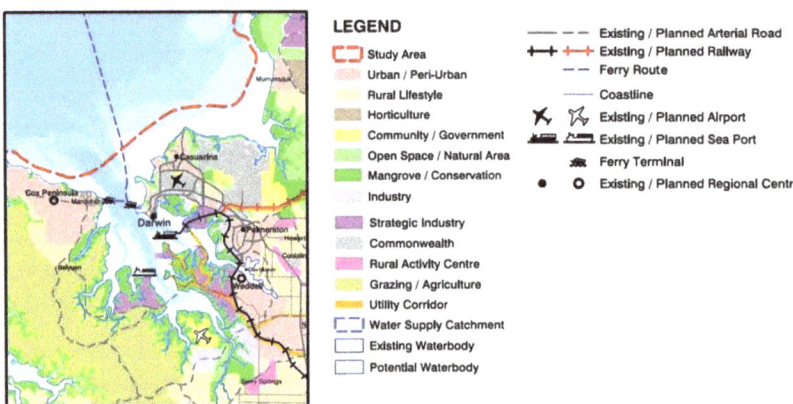

**Figure 12.1: Overview of the Darwin Harbour section of the Draft Darwin Regional Land Use Plan.**
Source: NT Planning Commission (2014).

Since the publication of the draft plan, the NT Planning Commission has conducted public consultation including information displays, briefings and submissions (Munday, 2014). Stakeholder values were elicited as part of the consultation process and included but were not limited to rural lifestyle, heritage/culture, Indigenous culture, tropical lifestyle, recreation, old Darwin culture and values and environment. Inadequate recognition for cultural and heritage values, natural environments and the conservation estate has been identified as a problem, suggesting the final plan might include some changes that reflect this new knowledge on local values and priorities; however, it cannot be expected to extend beyond its purpose as defined by the *Planning Act*. Importantly, the consultation highlights discrepancies between citizen priorities and the market values driving federal and territory agendas. This discrepancy is succinctly summarised in a statement in the community consultation report: 'It was clear during consultation that development can be an emotive topic, particularly when it threatens people's values, lifestyle and amenity' (Munday, 2014, p. 35).

We have highlighted the chronic failing of federal and state/territory capital visions of development in Northern Australia, as others have done, and suggested that part of the cause is the continued application of a singular ideology that prioritises short-term economic gain to the occlusion of non-market values and local preferences held by long-term residents that do not conform. To overcome these limitations, there is a need to ensure the marginalised, who add to the current landscape knowledge, diversity and resilience, do not remain marginalised or become normalised, but play a role in shaping northern development (Altman & Hinkson, 2007; Morrison, 2013). Specifically, we ask to what extent do local values, presented as spatial data on non-market values, reflect state and federal policy priorities, presented as key policy documents and a regional land use plan.

## Methods

To explore predicted disjuncture between local values and federal and state policy prescriptions, we elicited, using a survey instrument, spatially explicit landscape values and development preferences for Darwin Harbour and foreshore. We followed the method of Brown and others (Brown, 2005, 2006, 2012; Raymond & Brown, 2006; Brown & Raymond, 2007) to elicit the landscape values and development preferences. The 12 landscape values are a typology of both material/instrumental (e.g. economic and biodiversity) and non-use/symbolic values (e.g. cultural, intrinsic and aesthetic). Thus, they allow an exploration of what people value in landscapes, beyond the market values that are the focus of regional planning and federal priorities. Landscape values in the typology are 'aesthetic', 'biodiversity', 'economic', 'future', 'heritage', 'intrinsic', 'knowledge', 'life sustaining', 'recreation', 'spiritual', 'therapeutic' and 'wilderness'. Development preferences presented here include 'no development', 'residential development', 'tourism development' and 'industrial development'. Landscape values mapping enables the local community to be involved in the planning from the outset, rather than predefining the agenda as has occurred in the white paper process and the Darwin Regional Land Use Plan process. The landscape values loosely represent forms of non-market capital (e.g. cultural, social and natural) overlooked in the white paper process, and not made explicit in the regional plan. The spatial nature of the exercise enabled comparison with the Draft Darwin Regional Land Use Plan.

To elicit landscape values and development preferences, we administered a questionnaire to 2,000 households in the Darwin Harbour catchment. Probability (random) sampling was used to sample that part of the population that does not normally participate in the planning process (Brown, 2005)—the silent majority. A small prize incentive and a reminder postcard were used to increase response rate. It was also made clear to respondents that the information derived from the survey would be made available to the government to consider in future planning. Determining landscape values and development preferences involved respondents placing stickers on a map (scale 1:125,000). Six stickers were available for each of the landscape values and development preferences allowing respondents to identify multiple locations as having particular values and preferences. The landscape value sticker dots were worth different points (50, 20, 10, 10, 5 and 5) to indicate the relative importance of different locations on the provided map (Brown, 2005). The map, derived from a satellite image, included Darwin Harbour and foreshore to 500 metres inland from the estimated coastline (coastline source data). Data were aggregated across respondents. Here, we briefly present the spatially explicit landscape value and development preference data to inform a discussion comparing the results of the survey with the white paper process and Darwin Regional Land Use Plan process.

## Results

The results presented here are preliminary and not necessarily fully representative of the population, including only 130 households, of the approximately 60,000 residential addresses within the study area, that responded to the survey and completed the mapping exercise. The response rate from the initial 2,000 surveys administered was low. No Larrakia people, the traditional land owners, responded to the survey.

A total of 3,157 of a possible 9,360 (34 per cent) landscape value sticker dots were placed on the provided maps. The spatial extent was relatively well covered by the summed values of the 130 respondents (see Figure 12.2); however, there was significant clustering around the built landscapes including Darwin City (1) and the Cullen Bay Marina (2) and relatively natural landscapes including Charles Darwin Nation Park (3), Fast Point (4), Nightcliff foreshore (5) and Casuarina Coastal Reserve to Lee Point (6).

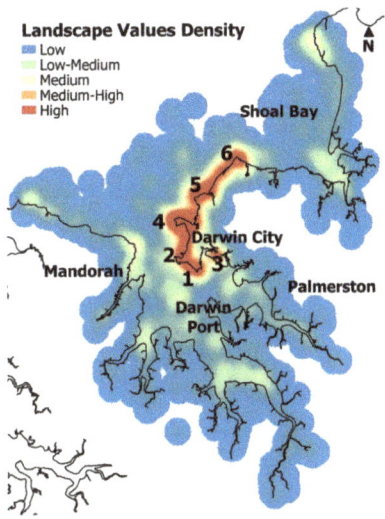

**Figure 12.2: Cumulative distribution of all landscape values across the spatial extent of the study represented as a heat (density) map based on 130 surveys (difference in assigned value is equal between each of the categories).**

Source: Authors' research.

Disaggregating the landscape values revealed differences in both the average total scores assigned to the different values and in their spatial distribution. Recreation and aesthetic values were, on average, assigned the highest total value by respondents (see Figure 12.3). These values are associated with open spaces and natural areas, which received only cursory recognition in the draft land use plan (NT Planning Commission, 2014, p. 27). Economic value, arguably the only value here that has been revealed to the market, was the eighth-highest scoring value. These differences, we assume, reflect a relative difference in perceived importance of the different values. However, economic value is, arguably, not well represented spatially and so comparing scores and spatial distribution between values should be done with caution. Individually, the landscape values differ in their degree of spatial clustering (see Figure 12.4), with some values having clear hot spots and others as a spatial mosaic across the harbour and foreshore. Notably, the only values that are clearly evident in the more urban areas of

Darwin are historic value and economic value. This finding highlights the perceived importance of natural landscapes, across a range of values, to the survey respondents. Generally, the differences in spatial distribution highlight both the relative uniqueness of each of these perceived values and the complexity of incorporating such values into regional land use planning if not mapped explicitly.

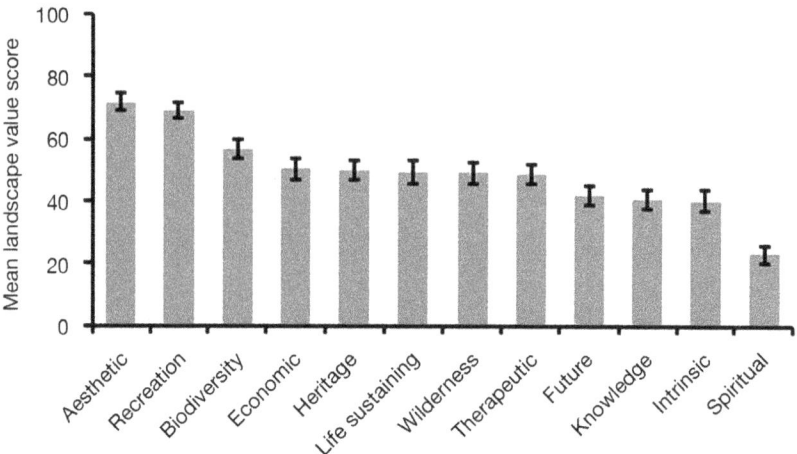

**Figure 12.3: Mean percentage of landscape value assigned by respondents of a possible 100 based on sum of all points for each value.**
Source: Authors' research.

Direct overlay of development preferences with the draft land use plan shows some clear differences between the two data sources (see Figure 12.5). For example, survey results show a strong preference for industrial development (see Figure 12.5A) to be focused around the east arm of the harbour; this is in contrast to the draft development plan, which proposes greater spatial spread of 'industry' and 'strategic industry' (purple shading). When aggregated, respondents had a clear preference for 'no development' (see Figure 12.5B) along much of the harbour foreshore, including the embayment to the north of East Point where there has been a proposal to engineer an island for residential housing, and towards the top of Shoal bay (top right of map) in close proximity to the Glyde Point Port proposal. It is possible that the high density of preference for no development is in response to the proposed Glyde Point Port, yet this is speculative because the spatial extent of the mapping exercise did not encompass the proposed port site. While there are clear differences in both method and results between the two data sources, it is not possible to conclude that either data source adequately represents the views of local residents. Further sampling and analysis is required to conduct a more robust comparison. Beyond further sampling, further analysis correlating proposed land use zones with the point data on landscape values and development preferences would give a quantitative measure on compatibility of the two data sources.

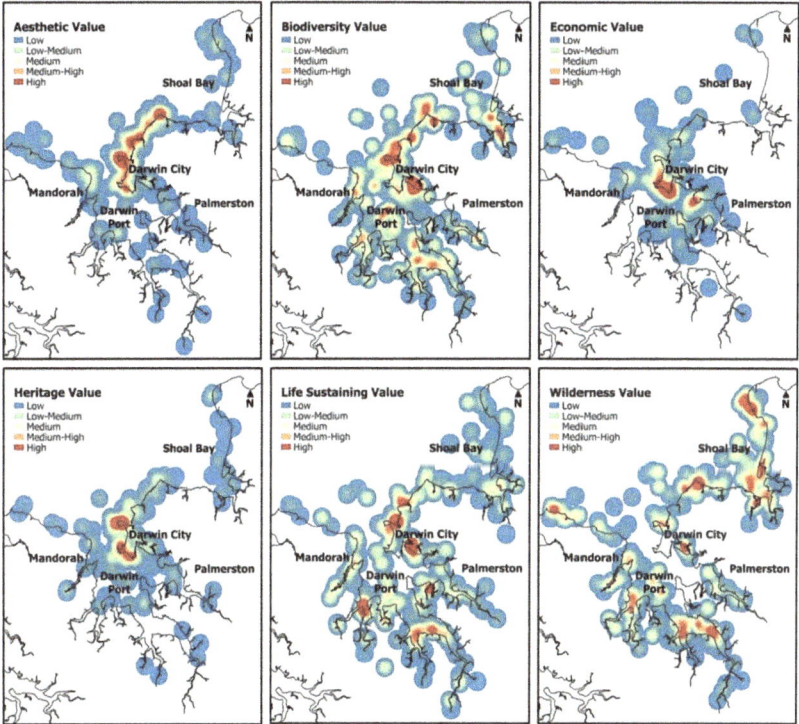

**Figure 12.4: Spatial distribution of a sample (6/12) of individual landscape values derived from 130 surveys of the catchment community represented as heat (density) maps.**

Note: Black line shows coastline of Darwin Harbour.

Source: Authors' research.

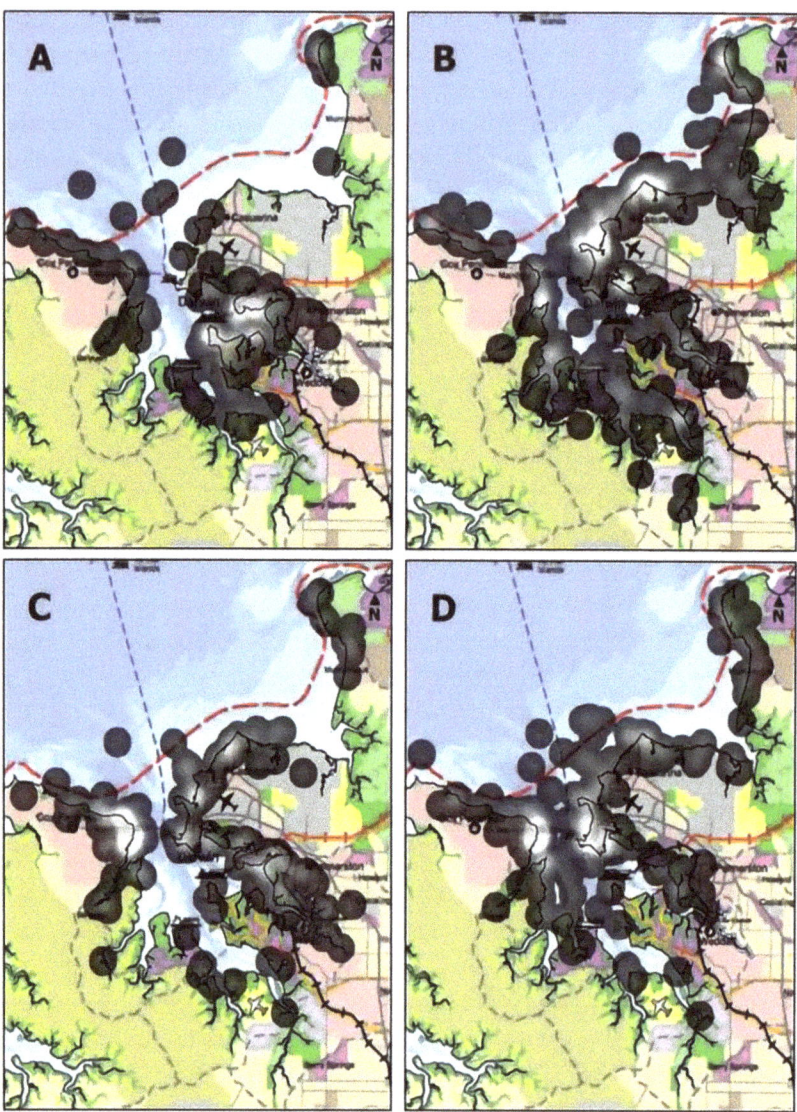

**Figure 12.5: Spatial distribution of development preferences displayed as 2 km radius heat map including preferences for 'industrial development' (A), 'no development' (B), 'residential development' (C) and 'tourism development' (D) overlaying Draft Darwin Regional Land Use Plan.**

Note: White areas of density map reflect higher density sticker placement by survey respondents. See Figure 12.1 for draft land use plan legend.

Source: Authors' research and NT Planning Commission (2014).

## Discussion

Federal policy that aims to make northern landscapes economically productive, to the exclusion of other understandings of utility, has a long history of conflict and failure. A swathe of biophysical factors including a harsh and variable climate, poor soils, variable water availability and pests and disease have prevented the success of the Anglo-centric development model. Further, excluding some communities' input of value placed on the landscape will potentially alienate them from long-term shared purpose. Here, we suggest the need for identifying an alternate development paradigm for Northern Australia; a less rigid paradigm that respects and, in doing so, reflects tropical social and cultural values that work with the biophysical realities and that are resilient to exogenous vagaries. To be clear, this paradigm of adaptive and resilient development is not about abandoning economy and markets as an important component of northern futures, but about ensuring the northern economy is compatible with the diversity of existing northern values that have emerged (and flourished) through enduring northern experience. As a contribution towards challenging the legitimacy of the dominant northern development paradigm, we have highlighted the depth and diversity of localised non-market values that are embedded in a region where market values are dominant in the policy and planning landscape. To illustrate our case, we have shown the landscape values and development preferences held by people residing in the Darwin Harbour catchment as a counterpoint to the white paper process and Draft Darwin Regional Land Use Plan. The breadth of landscape values that respondents identified with, and the higher relative weighting assigned to non-use/symbolic values reflects the feedback on the Draft Regional Land Use Plan (Munday, 2014) of a range of non-market values that are largely overlooked in the planning process, because they are not explicitly recognised in the Act.

Mapping of landscape values and development preferences occurred after the release of the Draft Darwin Regional Land Use Plan, so no opportunity to incorporate this new information into the plan occurred. It is hoped that, within the limits of the *Planning Act*, the derived data will be presented to the NT Planning Commission for consideration in future planning processes. However, despite the predicted importance of landscape values in land use planning (e.g. Brown, 2012; Klain & Chan, 2012; Zube, 1987), landscape values and development preference mapping exercises have, historically, failed to tangibly influence land use planning elsewhere (Brown, 2012). According to Brown (2012), the main reason for this is that planning processes tend to include superficial, obligatory and tokenistic public participation. In Brown's view, for public participation, using mapping exercises to have a meaningful impact on planning outcomes, planning agencies must meaningfully engage the public in the process irrespective of the mapping component. We would add to Brown's (2012) observations that to make spatially explicit values and development preferences meaningful in regional planning there needs to be a mechanism for translating spatially explicit values into an understanding of how this affects public and private spaces (Ives et al., 2015). Trade-offs are required between values in space and more abstract but equally valid issues such as how much space should be dedicated to, for example, aesthetic and spiritual values (which are spatially fluid compared to discrete landscape objects such as biodiversity, which can be measured using repeatable methods). To their credit, the NT Planning Commission has conducted extensive public consultation regarding controversial rezoning and urban infill proposals. The low response rate to the survey on landscape values and development preferences is telling of the difficulties associated with engaging the public in planning processes. Identifying why residents do not actively engage would aid more targeted future engagement. The data on landscape values of Darwin Harbour and foreshore will be further dissected to begin exploring these and other issues around improved regional land and sea decision-making in Northern Australia.

Assuming that future federal and state development policy that explicitly recognises, respects and negotiates with local values will deliver long-term development gains both in the north and Australia at large through generating greater internal development, how can we achieve better uptake of local values in current governance arrangements? We discuss four potential strategies below.

First, we believe there is need for transparent discussion on the varied interpretations of 'development'—what 'development' means to different people and through different political ideologies and who is likely to gain and lose from the different interpretations. Until development is explicitly defined, it is not possible to have productive conversations around policy expectations. Reframing the agenda as 'Developing (in) Northern Australia' might reposition the agenda as being development defined by Northern Australia rather than implicit economic development through external agency as currently occurs. A northern definition of development will require a shift in governance power towards greater northern autonomy so that the northern collective can articulate development that suits the north and see it realised. This will be made possible as large-scale institutions with vested power work in unison across the north (e.g. via new and emerging cross-jurisdictional governance mechanisms).

Second, there is a need to reveal the importance of landscape values to quality of life and understand the trade-offs between maintaining current landscapes and proceeding with major projects. Not all values are commensurable and, therefore, untradeable. Therefore, a sensible way forward would be to recognise a greater breadth of values within policy. Similarly, there is a need to better account for the beneficial and detrimental aspects of major projects associated with clientelism (Carson et al., 2010) in Darwin and across the north. To illustrate, the Darwin Harbour region has been declared, within the NT *Water Act* (1992), as having a suite of beneficial uses and recreational, cultural and aesthetic values. Yet the NT Government has been actively supporting the approval and development of large industrial sites on the foreshores of Darwin Harbour. When, in 2003, the first liquefied natural gas (LNG) project was initiated, effort was invested in public forums to inform the community on the expected benefits from the project and how the project would affect the aesthetics of the harbour. Much of what was shown was that the LNG plant would be hidden from view behind a small hill and the fringing mangroves. However, on completion, the facility is clearly visible from many locations around the harbour. When the second LNG project was initiated, public information sessions focused on economic benefits and assurance of significant environmental regulation. Although the investors conducted useful studies and produced extensive reports, none of the data has been made publicly available. Neither was an effort to show the visual impacts of the final development and the second LNG development is readily seen from many locations around the harbour. With the construction phase complete and on-site employment reduced, future financial benefits to the community will be limited (David Williams, personal communication, 3 June 2015). The short-term economic gains from these major projects must be weighed against adverse effects on the environment, including landscape values and the local community including traditional owners.

Third, spatially explicit tools that aid the nuanced incorporation of local values and preferences need to be employed in planning and development decision-making (Archer et al., 2009). Components of these tools can be agent based—agents respond autonomously to changes in their environment, driven by rules that can be qualitative, quantitative or both. Agents can reflect different communities and viewpoints within communities within a defined landscape. Using a participatory action research approach, iteratively, would enable calibration of the tool and increase community buy-in through participant observation of the potential consequences of development-related choices. This process would enable community-driven development of alternative development scenarios based on local ideology and values, which could inform a more nuanced land use planning process.

Fourth, the purpose of the NT *Planning Act* is primarily about the process of planning and provides no substantive matter to guide the creation of a regional plan. Explicit inclusion of matters related to enhancing the liveability of the NT and Darwin in particular, for its residents, is critical. The *Northern Territory Planning Act (1999)* does not require plans to consider matters such as landscape values, climate change, urban congestion, human health, diversification of housing and the economy and infrastructure efficiency. Nor does the Act provide for the creation of regional plans (unlike Queensland and Western Australia) and, as such, both the substance and procedure associated with this regional planning process is neither transparent nor accountable.. Regional plans should be more than strategic investment documents for government to achieve economic efficiency of municipal and transport infrastructure. Regional plans should be about deciding how to enhance the liveability of a region through strategic investment in public and private infrastructure. Finally, there is a lack of coordination between major projects and land use planning in the NT. Darwin and the entirety of the NT should not be regarded as remote frontiers or even new frontiers that should be grateful for any development. Rather, Darwin and the balance of lands and waters within the NT are home or a place treasured by its residents and, as such, these values should be protected and enhanced through planning activities that explicitly acknowledge the presence and validity of these values.

## Conclusions

Despite century-old rhetoric on the economic potential of Northern Australia, outcomes, as measured against expectations, have been limited. We have argued, as others have done, that the narrow laissez-faire ideology which occludes and suppresses alternative practises, ideologies and values scattered throughout Northern Australia partly explain this failure.

Explicitly, we have shown disparity between local values and federal, state and territory priorities using land use planning as our exemplar and conclude that reduced clientelism and stronger engagement with local diversity, values and place-based knowledge will enable development to be better suited to the context. Our recommendations for incorporating local views and values are not meant as an exhaustive list of instructions but as a sample of pragmatic means of moving the development conversation in a more north-centric direction.

## Acknowledgements

This work was funded by the Department of Industry, Innovation, Science, Research and Tertiary Education via the Northern Futures Collaborative Research Network. We thank three anonymous reviewers for their thoughtful reading of the manuscript and suggestions.

## References

Adamson, D. (2013, 28 June). Romancing the north: The food bowl furphy. *The Conversation*. Retrieved from theconversation.com/romancing-the-north-the-food-bowl-furphy-15469

Altman, J. C. (2009). *Beyond closing the gap: Valuing diversity in Indigenous Australia* (Centre for Aboriginal Economic Policy Research working paper no. 54). Canberra, ACT: ANU.

Altman, J. C. & Hinkson, M. (2007). *Coercive reconciliation: Stabilise, normalise, exit Aboriginal Australia*. Arena Publications.

Altman, J. C. & Markham, F. (2014). *Inquiry into the development of Northern Australia: A submission by Jon Altman and Francis Markham*. Canberra, ACT: ANU.

Archer, A. A., Higgins, A. J. & Thorburn, P. J. (2009). A method for comprehending and adapting complex supply chains in agriculture. *Journal on Chain and Network Science*, 9(1), 9–15.

Ash, A. J. (2014). *Factors driving the viability of major cropping investments in northern Australia—a historical analysis*. Retrieved from industry.gov.au/ONA/Reports-and-publications/Documents/NA-food-fibre-supply-chain-appendix-3-1.pdf (site discontinued)

Australian Government. (2014). *Green paper on developing Northern Australia*. Canberra, ACT: Department of the Prime Minister and Cabinet. Retrieved from www.industry.gov.au/sites/default/files/2019-09/green-paper-on-developing-northern-australia.pdf

Australian Government. (2015). *Our north, our future: White paper on developing Northern Australia*. Retrieved from www.industry.gov.au/data-and-publications/our-north-our-future-white-paper-on-developing-northern-australia

Beeton, R. (2006). *Society's forms of capital: A framework for renewing our thinkings*. Prepared for the 2006 Australian State of the Environment Committee. University of Queensland, Gatton Campus.

Bell, S. (2013, 10 September). The shipping news: The north's new frontier is a complex place. *The Conversation*. Retrieved from theconversation.com/the-shipping-news-the-norths-new-frontier-is-a-complex-place-17997

Bell, S., Campbell, A. & Larkin, S. (2014, 5 March). Northern Australia, the sequel: Remaking an old policy classic. *The Conversation*. Retrieved from theconversation.com/northern-australia-the-sequel-remaking-an-old-policy-classic-23833

Brown, G. (2005). Mapping spatial attributes in survey research for natural resource management: Methods and applications. *Society and Natural Resources, 18*(1), 17–39.

Brown, G. (2006). Mapping landscape values and development preferences: A method for tourism and residential development planning. *International Journal of Tourism Research, 8*(2), 101–113.

Brown, G. (2012). Public Participation GIS (PPGIS) for regional and environmental planning: Reflections on a decade of empirical research. *URISA Journal, 24*(2), 7–18.

Brown, G. & Raymond, C. (2007). The relationship between place attachment and landscape values: Toward mapping place attachment. *Applied Geography, 27*(2), 89–111.

Campbell, S. (1996). Green cities, growing cities, just cities?: Urban planning and the contradictions of sustainable development. *Journal of the American Planning Association, 62*(3), 296–312.

Carson, D. (2011). Political economy, demography and development in Australia's Northern Territory. *The Canadian Geographer/Le Géographe canadien, 55*(2), 226–242.

Carson, D., Schmallegger, D. & Harwood, S. (2010). A city for the temporary? Political economy and urban planning in Darwin, Australia. *Urban Policy and Research*, *28*(3), 293–310. doi.org/10.1080/08111146.2010.509886

Cash, D. W., Adger, W. N., Berkes, F., Garden, P., Lebel, L., Olsson, P., … Young, O. (2006). Scale and cross-scale dynamics: Governance and information in a multilevel world. *Ecology and Society*, *11*(2). Retrieved from www.ecologyandsociety.org/vol11/iss2/art8/

Dale, A. (2013, 6 August). Northern Australia should have a say in its own future. *The Conversation*. Retrieved from theconversation.com/northern-australia-should-have-a-say-in-its-own-future-16469

Dale, A. (2014). *Beyond the north-south culture wars: Reconciling Northern Australia's recent past with its future*. Springer.

Davidson, B. R. (1965). *The northern myth: A study of the physical and economic limits to agricultural and pastoral development in tropical Australia*. Cambridge University Press.

Grieves, V. (2015, 17 March). Aboriginal lifestyles could fix the hole in the heart of Australia. *The Conversation*. Retrieved from theconversation.com/aboriginal-lifestyles-could-fix-the-hole-in-the-heart-of-australia-38701

Ives, C. D., Biggs, D., Hardy, M. J., Lechner, A. M., Wolnicki, M. & Raymond, C. M. (2015). Using social data in strategic environmental assessment to conserve biodiversity. *Land Use Policy*, *47*, 332–341.

Klain, S. C. & Chan, K. M. A. (2012). Navigating coastal values: Participatory mapping of ecosystem services for spatial planning. *Ecological Economics*, *82*, 104–113. doi.org/10.1016/j.ecolecon.2012.07.008

Liberal Party of Australia. (2013). *The Coalition's 2030 vision for developing Northern Australia*. Retrieved from parlinfo.aph.gov.au/parlInfo/search/display/display.w3p;query=Id%3A%22library%2Fpartypol%2F2550511%22;src1=sm1

Lockwood, M., Davidson, J., Curtis, A., Stratford, E. & Griffith, R. (2009). Multi-level environmental governance: Lessons from Australian natural resource management. *Australian Geographer*, *40*(2), 169–186. doi.org/10.1080/00049180902964926

Morrison, J. (2013, 3 September). Indigenous participation in the developing north: A national emergency. *The Conversation*. Retrieved from theconversation.com/indigenous-participation-in-the-developing-north-a-national-emergency-17733

Munday, M. W. (2014). *Community consultation report: Draft Darwin regional land use plan 2014*. Retrieved from www.planningcommission.nt.gov.au/__data/assets/pdf_file/0020/43409/DRLUP-Consultation-Report.pdf (site discontinued)

Northern Australia Land and Water Taskforce. (2009). *Northern Australia land and water science review 2009. Chapter summaries*. Retrieved from www.econnect.com.au/wp-content/uploads/2011/08/NA_Taskforce_chapter_summaries_2009.pdf

Northern Territory Government. (2007). *Northern Territory Planning Scheme*. Retrieved from nt.gov.au/property/building-and-development/northern-territory-planning-scheme/introduction

Northern Territory Planning Commission. (2014). *Draft Darwin regional land use plan 2014*. Retrieved from www.planningcommission.nt.gov.au/__data/assets/pdf_file/0017/41642/Draft-Darwin-Regional-Land-Use-Plan-2014-full.pdf (site discontinued)

Peel, D. & Lloyd, M. G. (2007). Neo-traditional planning. Towards a new ethos for land use planning? *Land Use Policy, 24*(2), 396–403. doi.org/10.1016/j.landusepol.2006.05.003

Raymond, C. & Brown, G. (2006). A method for assessing protected area allocations using a typology of landscape values. *Journal of Environmental Planning and Management, 49*(6), 797–812. doi.org/10.1080/09640560600945331

Springer, S. (2010). Neoliberalism and geography: Expansions, variegations, formations. *Geography Compass, 4*(8), 1025–1038. doi.org/10.1111/j.1749-8198.2010.00358.x

Stephens, A., Oppermann, E., Turnour, J., Brewer, T., O'Brien, C., Rayner, T., … Dale, A. P. (2015). Identifying tensions in the development of Northern Australia: Implications for governance. *Journal of Economic and Social Policy, 17*(1), 96–118.

Termeer, C., Dewulf, A. & Van Lieshout, M. (2010). Disentangling scale approaches in governance research: Comparing monocentric, multilevel and adaptive governance. *Ecology and Society, 15*(4), 29.

Woolcock, M. (1998). Social capital and economic development: Toward a theoretical synthesis and policy framework. *Theory and Society, 27*(2), 151–208.

Woolcock, M. (2001). The place of social capital in understanding social and economic outcomes. *Canadian Journal of Policy Research, 2*(1), 11–17.

Zube, E. H. (1987). Perceived land use patterns and landscape values. *Landscape Ecology, 1*(1), 37–45. doi.org/10.1007/BF02275264

# 13

# Land Tenure and Development in Northern Australia

Allan P. Dale, Bruce Taylor and Marcus B. Lane

## Introduction

While principles of land ownership (predominantly freehold) under 'common law' have been relatively stable in large parts of Southern Australia, in the north there is limited freehold title and it is often clustered around major centres. Across the wider Northern Australian landscape, concepts of ownership on lands previously held by the Crown (and consequently land titles) have also changed significantly in the last 30 years, with pre-existing Indigenous rights (e.g. native title) now recognised in law and new statutory forms of land rights established. Further, in recent decades Commonwealth, state and territory regulation has placed restrictions on many of the tenure rights that would otherwise have accrued with land and natural resource ownership (e.g. the Commonwealth's *Environment Protection and Biodiversity Conservation Act 1999* or Queensland's *Vegetation Management Act 1999*).

Given this difference, land tenure is often touted by governments and industry alike as being one of the most significant barriers hindering development and investment in Northern Australia (Australian Government, 2014; Joint Select Committee on Northern Australia, 2014). Debates about land tenure in the north have been increasingly driven by economic development and, in particular, control of important resources such as minerals, prime agricultural land and conservation assets. These debates are not confined to Commonwealth, state and territory policy circles; there has been a significant and long-standing academic interest in tenure as a policy tool and social institution (e.g. Holmes, 2011). This work has included interest in the reform of land tenure and administration systems, with calls for greater investment in and coherence of national spatial data infrastructures underpinning land administration, particularly in federated countries like Australia where land information is generally held across multiple agencies and levels of government (Bennett et al., 2012). For example, information systems that underpin land administration are argued to be critical public good infrastructure, rather than the property of particular land administration agencies (Bennett et al., 2013).

Internationally, there has also been a long focus on human rights dimensions of the rights, responsibilities and restrictions created by land tenure policies, institutions and systems of administration (Enemark et al., 2014). In the Australian context, for example, some authors have argued that key factors underpinning Indigenous disadvantage can be characterised as 'market failure relating to the disjunction between the Indigenous land base and the broader market economy' and low levels of public investment in infrastructure on the Indigenous estate (Altman & Dillon, 2005, p. 252). The focus has more recently turned to more specific issues of the relationship between secure tenures of home ownership and economic development on Indigenous-owned lands (Wensing & Taylor, 2012).

Finally, there are a number of themes in the literature that are important for understanding the evolution of tenure as a policy instrument (aimed at facilitating either development or conservation) in Northern Australia's northern rangelands in particular. Holmes' (2000, 2011, 2012, 2014) significant contribution, for example, highlights pastoral leasehold tenures and native title, emphasising that tenure instruments and the administrative architecture and policy goals that govern their use are not static. Instead, they have been responsive to changing political, economic and land management requirements over time. Indeed, Holmes' work highlights how understanding tenure instruments as an evolving set of socio-legal institutions that are responsive to an ever-widening suite of public policy goals, rights and interests is central to designing appropriate interventions in contemporary landscapes. This requirement for a responsive system of tenure becomes more important when we consider economic development opportunities in broader northern regional contexts. This is because regions in Australia's north are described as experiencing a multifunctional transition, where the mix and dominance of different values in a given landscape or region (e.g. amenity or consumptive values and conservation, Indigenous or pastoral values) are rapidly changing (Holmes, 2011, 2012). The Cape York region in particular provides stark evidence of such a rapid transition in recent decades where new regional and place identities are being formed as a result of changes to property rights, tenures and economic opportunities (Holmes, 2012).

Against this background, this chapter focuses on the relationship between tenure considerations and the broader policy concept of Northern Australian development.

# The Importance of Land Tenure to Northern Australian Futures

Land tenure refers to the legal regime under which land is owned. In all states and territories of Australia there are statutory definitions of what is meant by 'land'. While the general principles of land ownership under common law have long been established, the extent of ownership has changed significantly in interpretation over the last 100 years. In particular, the rights and benefits entailed in land ownership have been interpreted, codified and, in some cases, restricted by statutory law. This has been particularly important in Northern Australia where freehold title is limited and the contention between development and conservation interests is so important. This has given rise to a concern that the potential for tenure rights to be diminished by policy and legal change has reduced the confidence of investors in the north.

In the context of Northern Australia, the focus on land tenure has been increasingly driven by matters that relate to clarifying the rights of economic and cultural development and, in particular, control over important resources such as minerals, prime agricultural and traditional lands. Consequently, Australia's land tenure systems are fundamental to several important policy domains including the resolution of historical social injustice; development planning and economic growth strategy;

welfare, housing and employment; economic development and property markets; and natural resource, environmental and cultural management (JCU & CSIRO, 2013).

Land ownership systems also underpin much of government policymaking and program delivery and functions such as taxation, land administration, administrative boundaries, regulation and land use management. One critical difference about the north, however, is that settlement, occupancy and land use patterns vary markedly from those in southern and eastern Australia. The Northern Australian system of land tenure was designed to expedite land settlement, secure investment in traditional agricultural development and reserve land for Indigenous and later conservation purposes (Holmes, 2000). The landscape scale consequence of this approach is that the vast majority of land (75.4 per cent) is Crown owned, two-thirds of which is pastoral leasehold (JCU & CSIRO, 2013). Another 18.5 per cent is Indigenous land (most previously held by the Crown). Native title resolution processes continue across many parts of the crown land estate. Privately owned land accounts for only 6.1 per cent of the total area. Clearly, the proportions of Indigenous land and leasehold land are significantly higher than in Southern Australia. Native title claims and mining and gas exploration permits also cover significant parts of the landscape.

In a major reform to the purpose of the original Northern Australian system of land tenure, over 40 years ago major new tenures emerged with innovations under the *Aboriginal Land Rights (Northern Territory) Act 1976*, followed by the *Aboriginal Land Act and Torres Strait Land Acts 1991* in Queensland. These statutes sought to provide measures of national social and land justice for Indigenous Australian and Torres Strait Islander peoples who were physically and/or legally dispossessed at the time of colonial acquisition (Hibbard et al., 2008).

As a consequence of this complexity, in recent decades, a wide range of diverse parties have advocated for change and reform to northern tenure arrangements. The more significant of these include:

- the pursuit of pastoral enterprise diversification, in some instances, via the development of irrigation, tourism or conservation on leasehold (Gleeson et al., 2012; van Etten, 2013)
- persistent interest in the expansion of agriculture in Northern Australia, particularly the expansion of irrigated cropping (Chilcott, 2009; Northern Australia Land and Water Taskforce Science Review, 2009)

- the Council of Australian Governments (COAG) National Water Reform Agenda changed the character of water rights and access, separating water from land title, thus providing for the establishment of water markets
- major growth in the mining and gas sectors and a boom in exploration has meant that these activities are operating across a range of tenures and entitlements. This growth has also led to increased frequency of tensions related to access on rural and Indigenous lands
- native title has delivered the prospect of social reparation and tenure security for Indigenous people, while also posing legal and practical challenges as to how traditional owners can leverage investment on native title lands and other tenures
- Indigenous water interests are an emerging policy area, with new interests such as cultural flows and Strategic Indigenous Reserves being defined (NAILSMA, 2013)
- growing recognition of conservation values in northern landscapes, both within the formal conservation estate, on other tenures, and new private and not-for-profit sector investors.

There has also been a growing interest among governments, landholders and investors to seek benefits from emerging ecosystem service-based markets, in particular for carbon. Here, opportunities are being explored for banking or mitigation services and market-related knowledge services (e.g. buyers, brokers, partners and information providers) (CSIRO, 2012; Whitten et al., 2008). Researchers have reported that the negotiation of conservation or biodiversity outcomes at landscape scale on pastoral lands, for example, requires better communication with and involvement of 'new' land managers such as mining companies—now major holders of pastoral leases in Western Australia (van Etten, 2013).

As a consequence of this history, there are several features of land tenure and its administration in the north that make it both complex and unique:

- there are multiple and often overlapping tenure types for the same area of land (e.g. the existence of non-exclusive native title rights over leasehold land)
- administrative arrangements for land tenure and classifications of similar tenure types vary across state and territory jurisdictions

- in regions like Cape York, tenure change is happening rapidly (Holmes, 2012)
- for potential investors, multiple interactions are often required with government to gather the information needed to assess sovereign risk and to seek tenure changes
- there are numerous implications arising from the ongoing task of identifying untested native title rights
- there are emergent tenures or changes to rights related to assets such as water, carbon and biodiversity, with uncertain and evolving tenure regimes (JCU & CSIRO, 2013).

## Reform Foci from the Recent Past

There are efforts to improve tenure management arrangements within each of the north's four primary jurisdictions (see Table 13.1). For instance, each of the state and territory jurisdictions have over the last decade undertaken reviews of their own tenure arrangements, particularly with respect to pastoral leasehold lands. These recent and proposed changes aim to enable more diverse uses within tenures and to clarify access and use rights in circumstances where there are multiple entitlement holders. In addition to proposed pastoral land reforms, other recent work has focused on improving the secure allocation of water entitlements and clarifying Indigenous interests in land and water.

Reforms are also progressing in all jurisdictions in relation to land administration and land-related information management. In Western Australia, for example, progress is being made towards the creation of a Single Registration System for all Crown and freehold land (under the *Land Administration Act 1996*). There is also emerging national progress towards the establishment of a National Electronic Conveyancing system.

## 13. LAND TENURE AND DEVELOPMENT IN NORTHERN AUSTRALIA

Table 13.1: Point in time tenure reform process during 2015.

| | Mining | Pastoral and irrigated agriculture | Water | Conservation and ecosystem services | Indigenous land/native title |
|---|---|---|---|---|---|
| WA | *Reforming Environmental Regulation and Multiple Land Use Framework. Water in Mining Guide.* | *Rangelands Reform Program* proposes more flexible rangelands or perpetual leases and addresses 2015 lease renewal deadlines. | Water allocation plans in La Grange groundwater area, the Ord River area and the Pilbara groundwater allocation plan. Review of Broome Water Plan (2008). | Proposed permit of conservation uses and ecosystem service investment on rangelands leases. Progress on a major Kimberley Science and Conservation Strategy. | Investigating options for land tenure reform on the Aboriginal Lands Trust estate. Recent review of native title processes in major development. |
| NT | Exploration licences may be renewed indefinitely. Emerging consideration of codes for gas-sector land access arrangements. | Review of *Pastoral Land Act 1992* considering non-pastoral use permits. Removal of time-bound renewal periods of permits provides registration to title, third-party involvement and transferability. | Water planning in Tindall Limestone Aquifer (Katherine) Water Resource Plan (2009), Mataranka, Oolloo, Howard East and Berry Springs areas in progress. | Proposed amendments to the *Pastoral Land Act 1992* suggest approval required to carry out any activity likely to significantly modify landscape health. | Lease conversions underway and payment for leases. NT Government involved in Commonwealth review of *Aboriginal Land Rights Act 1983* and native title. |
| Qld | Land Access Code (2010) introduced for the coal seam gas industry. Reforms to regional land use planning, major project assessment, state planning policies and one-stop shop approvals (also relevant to agriculture). | Amendments to the *Land Act 1994*, (2008) linking improved tenure security to land use condition. Report on Parliamentary Inquiry into pastoral tenures (2013). March 2013) to allow clearing for high value agriculture, removing high value regrowth regulations from freehold and Indigenous land. | Water Resource Plans for Gulf catchments (2011), Mitchell (2009), Great Artesian Basin (2012) and Wet Tropics. Wet Tropics and Gulf plans consider cultural flows and Strategic Indigenous Reserves. | Consideration under the *Land Act 1994* to seek to improve for conservation-based investments. Amendment of state legislation to allow the transfer of carbon and forestry rights from the state to lessees (2011). | Pastoral Indigenous land Use Agreement (ILUA) template and guide established. Amendments to *ATSI Land Holding Act* to address sub-lease uncertainty. Discussion paper on tenure reform for home ownership. Queensland Government involved in Commonwealth native title reviews. |

299

|  | Mining | Pastoral and irrigated agriculture | Water | Conservation and ecosystem services | Indigenous land/native title |
|---|---|---|---|---|---|
| CTH | National Partnership on CSG and Large Coal Mining Development (2012). Current COAG process regarding delegation of assessment via *Environment & Biodiversity Conservation Act 1999*. | Investigation of mosaic agriculture development, including the North Queensland irrigated agricultural strategy and strategic development of beef industry. | *New Policy Guidelines for Water Planning and Management* 2011. Developing new policy guidance (NWC Northern Australian Position Statement). | *Carbon Credits (Carbon Farming Initiative) Act 2011* and *Carbon Credits (Carbon Farming Initiative) Regulations 2011* and *Clean Energy Act 2011* establishes basis for trading carbon equivalents. *Biodiversity Carbon Fund. National Wildlife Corridors Plan*. | Native Title Amendment Bill 2012 clarifies 'good faith', 'right to negotiate' and enables parties to disregard extinguishment in parks and reserves. Streamlines ILUAs. NIRA reforms. Reviews of Native Title Rep Bodies, Department of Families, Community Services and Indigenous Affairs (FACSIA) and Home Ownership (COAG). |

Source: Updated from JCU and CSIRO (2013).

## Opportunities for Tenure Reform and Barriers for Progression

The opportunity for reform in land tenure to drive diverse investment in the sustainable development of Northern Australia is significant. Such changes might serve to reduce conflict and encourage more optimal use and management of the north's natural resources, while also protecting the rights of interests of traditional owners. Potential new reforms could also enable land owners to manage and trade vital ecosystem services such as water, biodiversity and carbon while providing additional economic development opportunities. Based on wide discussion across key Northern Australian stakeholders, JCU and CSIRO's (2013) report to the Northern Australia Ministerial Forum (NAMF) proposed a number of broad areas of focus for realising these opportunities in the short, medium and long terms. Table 13.2 provides a summary of the individual opportunity that might be actioned and the feasibility and benefit likely to be derived over time.

Table 13.2: Key opportunities for improving land tenure arrangements in Northern Australia.

| Opportunity | Feasibility | Benefit | Timescale | | |
| --- | --- | --- | --- | --- | --- |
| | | | 1 yr | 2–5 yrs | >5 yrs |
| **Tenure improvements** | | | | | |
| Harmonise key tenure-related practices across jurisdictions | H | H | | ✓ | |
| Provide a single 'whole of government' point of contact for tenure resolution | M | M | | ✓ | |
| Adopt consistent principles to improve flexibility and diversify land use especially on pastoral and Indigenous lands | H | H | ✓ | | |
| Complete rollout of National Water Initiative principles and statutory water plans across the north | H | H | | | ✓ |
| Develop and implement a consistent approach to Indigenous water including rights to water for commercial purposes | H | H | | ✓ | |
| Ensuring consistency of tenure arrangements for carbon/biodiversity in the landscape | H | M | | ✓ | |

| Opportunity | Feasibility | Benefit | Timescale | | |
| --- | --- | --- | --- | --- | --- |
| | | | 1 yr | 2–5 yrs | >5 yrs |
| Continuous improvement in progressing native title/statutory claims | M | H | | | ✓ |
| Provide more flexible means of transition from leasehold to freehold on small land parcels for intensive uses | M | H | | ✓ | |
| **Information, planning and major project assessment** | | | | | |
| Develop a nationally-consistent and spatially explicit tenure (and registered interests) data system | H | M | ✓ | | |
| Reduce project delays by improving development assessment practice | M | H | | ✓ | |
| Initiate stable, regionally-scaled strategic land and resource use planning | M | M | | | ✓ |

Note: H = High and M = Medium.
Source: Updated from JCU and CSIRO (2013).

While different sectors and interests across Northern Australia face distinct investment issues, stakeholder engagement undertaken in the development of JCU and CSIRO's (2013) report to the NAMF identified common and significant tenure-related barriers to investment (see Table 13.3). These include the underlying complexity of tenures and entitlements on a given area of land, the capacity for investors to manage across multiple tenures and jurisdictions and resolve disputes efficiently, and the limits of some types of tenure to allow owners to leverage land assets for capital and development purposes such as on some Indigenous tenures. It is also important to understand that while tenure is an important consideration, it is only one of a number of factors that may impede investment. Infrastructure, distance to market, land values and terms of trade all have significant weight in investment decisions.

## 13. LAND TENURE AND DEVELOPMENT IN NORTHERN AUSTRALIA

**Table 13.3: Tenure-related impediments to investment as they relate to different sectors and interests.**

| Impediments | | Frequency | Impact |
|---|---|---|---|
| **Mining** | Delays converting and establishing extraction permits | H | M |
| | Negotiation of native title agreements and access | H | M |
| | Inconsistent water pricing regimes and securing water access | H | M |
| | Negotiating single projects across complex multiple tenures | M | M |
| | The non-tax-exempt status of native title payments | M | M |
| **Pastoral and agriculture** | Poor flexibility to diversify and realign boundaries | H | H |
| | Uncertainty with lease renewal processes/term security | H | H |
| | Lease rental policy not aligned to land productivity | M | H |
| | Native title 'Future Act' triggers are unclear/third-party respondent funding | H | H |
| | Multiple tenures and limitations on who can hold a lease | M | M |
| | Insecurity due to exploration and mining rights | M | M |
| | Limited system of vendor disclosure of government land interests | L | L |
| **Conservation and ecosystem services** | Some pastoral lease conditions inhibit conservation | H | M |
| | Costs, restrictions and uncertainties to change lease conditions | M | M |
| | Legislative inconsistency on carbon rights between jurisdictions | L | M |
| | Resumption of rights and issuing of third party rights on Nature Refuges | L | H |
| **Water** | Nascent status of National Water Initiative–compliant water plans | H | L |
| | Unresolved Indigenous rights with respect to water | M | L |
| | Cross-basin trading can be inconsistent with Indigenous values | L | L |
| | Inadequate water data and mapping | M | M |

303

| Impediments | | Frequency | Impact |
|---|---|---|---|
| **Traditional owners and Indigenous home ownership** | Unresolved native title and other land and sea claims | H | H |
| | Lack of finance leveraging capacity on tenures | H | H |
| | Lack of guarantee for mortgaging associated with inalienability | H | H |
| | Uncertain process for government-leasing of native title lands | M | H |
| | Insufficient or crude registration of Indigenous tenures | L | L |

Note: H = High, M = Medium and L = Low.
Source: JCU and CSIRO (2013).

## New Directions in Tenure Management

The case for improving tenure arrangements in Northern Australia is compelling, but the challenge in doing so is substantial, requiring significant cross-jurisdictional cooperation and national investment in research and development. It will not happen quickly. JCU and CSIRO's (2013) report to the NAMF proposed that efforts to reduce impediments to investment and development in Northern Australia might be pursued in three distinct ways. The first is attending to tenure complexity through administrative or legislative reform. This could involve supporting collaborative research and policy development partnerships on critical issues of investment and financing on Indigenous tenures, developing consistent principles to guide tenure reviews in the different jurisdictions and improving the quality and accessibility of tenure-related data for northern regions. The second main pathway involves improving the efficiency of development assessment and regulation, including clarifying major project assessment responsibilities between jurisdictions, better resourced negotiation and streamlined administration of assessment processes and resources to assist with tenure-resolution processes that arise following project approval. The third main pathway could focus on actions to improve the effectiveness of land and resource (including water) planning so that broader 'regional'- or 'landscape'-level signals exist about the preferred infrastructure and resource use futures for different northern regions. Such planning would provide the broader context in which local-level conflicts over tenure can be resolved.

Tenure reform in the north, however, must preserve the rights of and create opportunities for the north's traditional owners. Tenure is implicated in the ongoing social and economic disadvantage suffered by Indigenous people. Indigenous-led tenure reform on Indigenous tenures, therefore, has a role to play in ameliorating this situation. Finding the means by which traditional owners can leverage their land assets to raise capital for social and economic development offers great national and local benefit. However, this needs to be able to accommodate informed consent and the inalienability of title. In considering these issues (see also NAILSMA, 2013), support is required to progress policy options which will have general applicability to traditional owners across Northern Australia. Such work could focus on:

- progressively resolving ongoing native title/land claim issues and water rights
- supporting and resourcing the capacity of traditional owners to develop country-based/land use planning across their estate, township-based land use planning and wealth generation strategies
- exploring further the most appropriate tenure and financial mechanisms for facilitating investment leverage (within Indigenous land estates)
- supporting traditional owners to explore new and innovative governance models for managing aspirational/country-based planning and 'wealth funds' emerging from economic development
- exploring some form of Northern Australian 'guarantee or trust fund' to support traditional owners with sound business investment projects to secure commercial finance, funded either from amendment to existing or new government funds, private sector investment or innovative investment of local traditional owner-based sovereign wealth funds at the local scale
- pan-northern partnering with lending institutions to build investment confidence.

Given the complexity and diversity that exists within land tenure arrangements in Northern Australia described above, it would be understandable to presume the goals of efficiency and consistency are paramount in the quest for improving opportunities for investment. However, many of the most significant gains in terms of improving investor certainty and improving development outcomes for northern enterprises and communities will come from engaging with this complexity in constructive and more informed ways that recognise the unique mix of land uses, resources, rights and interests in northern lands.

## Acknowledgements

Much of this work was originally supported by the Australian Government within the context of the North Australia Ministerial Forum. It was also supported by the Department of Industry, Innovation, Science, Research and Tertiary Education via the Northern Futures Collaborative Research Network, the Australian Government's Stream 2 Climate Adaptation Program and the Australian Research Council. We would also like to thank Andrew Johnson for his leading contributions to the original JCU and CSIRO (2013) report and the wide range of contributors, practitioners and experts from across Northern Australia consulted during that process.

## References

Altman, J. & Dillon, M. (2005). Commercial development and natural resource management on the Indigenous estate: A profit related investment proposal. *Economic Papers*, *24*(3), 249–262. doi.org/10.1111/j.1759-3441.2005.tb00377.x

Australian Government. (2014). *Green paper on developing northern Australia*. Canberra, ACT: Department of the Prime Minister and Cabinet. Retrieved from www.industry.gov.au/sites/default/files/2019-09/green-paper-on-developing-northern-australia.pdf

Bennett, R., Rajabifard, A., Williamson, I. & Wallace, J. (2012). On the need for national land administration infrastructures. *Land Use Policy*, *29*, 208–219. doi.org/10.1016/j.landusepol.2011.06.008

Bennett, R., Tambuwala, N., Rajabifard, A., Wallace, J. & Williamson, I. (2013). On recognizing land administration as critical, public good infrastructure. *Land Use Policy*, *30*, 84–93. doi.org/10.1016/j.landusepol.2012.02.004

Chilcott, C. (2009). Growing the north - Opportunities and threats to developing agriculture in the north of Western Australia. *Farm Policy Journal*, *6*(2), 11–17.

Commonwealth Scientific and Industrial Research Organisation (CSIRO). (2012). *The emerging carbon economy for Northern Australia: Challenges and opportunities*. Canberra, ACT.

Enemark, S., Hvingel, L. & Galland, D. (2014). Land administration, planning and human rights. *Planning Theory*, *13*(4), 331–348. doi.org/10.1177/1473095213517882

Gleeson, T., Martin, P. & Mifsud, C. (2012). *Northern Australian beef industry: Assessment of risks and opportunities. ABARES report to client prepared for the Northern Australia Ministerial Forum* (ABARES project 43220). Canberra, ACT: ABARES.

Hibbard, M., Lane, M. B. & Rasmussen, K. (2008). The split personality of planning: Indigenous people and planning for land and resource management. *Journal of Planning Literature*, *23*(2), 136–152. doi.org/10.1177/0885412208322922

Holmes, J. (2000, 21–22 February). *Land tenure and administration in Northern Australia: Needed future directions.* Paper presented at the Tropical Savannas CRC Forum: Land Administration and Management in the Tropical Savannas: A Better Way, Darwin, Australia.

Holmes, J. (2011). Land tenures and policy instruments: Transitions on Cape York Peninsula. *Geographical Research*, *49*(2), 217–233. doi.org/10.1111/j.1745-5871.2011.00692.x

Holmes, J. (2012). Cape York Peninsula, Australia: A frontier region undergoing a multifunctional transition with Indigenous engagement. *Journal of Rural Studies*, *28*, 252–265. doi.org/10.1016/j.jrurstud.2012.01.004

Holmes, J. (2014). Explorations in Australian legal geography: The evolution of lease tenures as policy instruments. *Geographical Research*, *52*(4), 411–429. doi.org/10.1111/1745-5871.12083

James Cook University (JCU) & Commonwealth Scientific and Industrial Research Organisation (CSIRO). (2013). *Land tenure in Northern Australia: Opportunities and challenges for investment.* Brisbane, QLD: CSIRO.

Joint Select Committee on Northern Australia. (2014). *Pivot North: Inquiry into the development of Northern Australia—Final report.* Canberra, ACT: Australian Government. Retrieved from www.aph.gov.au/Parliamentary_Business/Committees/Joint/Former_Committees/Northern_Australia/Inquiry_into_the_Development_of_Northern_Australia/Tabled_Reports

North Australian Indigenous Land and Sea Management Alliance (NAILSMA). (2013). *Indigenous futures and sustainable development in north Australia: Towards a framework for full Indigenous participation in economic development* (Discussion paper 018/2013). Darwin, NT: NAILSMA.

Northern Australia Land and Water Taskforce Science Review. (2009). *Northern Australia land and water science review 2009: Full report.* Darwin, NT: Australian Government.

van Etten, E. J. B. (2013). Changes to land tenure and pastoral lease ownership in Western Australia's central rangelands: Implications for co-operative, landscape-scale management. *The Rangeland Journal*, *35*(1), 37–46. doi.org/10.1071/RJ11088

Wensing, E. & Taylor, J. (2012). *Secure tenure for home ownership and economic development on land subject to native title* (Australian Institute of Aboriginal and Torres Strait Islander Studies research discussion paper no. 31). Canberra, ACT: AIATSIS.

Whitten, S., Abel, N. & Cowell, S. (2008). *A scoping study of the market-based opportunities available to eco-entrepreneurs in the rangelands. Report prepared for Bush Heritage Australia*. Canberra, ACT: CSIRO Sustainable Ecosystems.

# 14

# Governing the Community-Based Natural Resource Management System in Northern Australia: Challenges and Opportunities

Allan P. Dale, Gabriel Crowley, Tom D. Brewer, Kate Andrews, Brian Warren, Karen Vella and Ruth Potts

## Introduction: Australia's Community-Based Natural Resource Management System

Australia's community-based NRM (CBNRM) system is underpinned by cohesive policy, program and delivery arrangements. It uses suasive, non-regulatory approaches to achieve outcomes at the landscape scale. Dale et al. (2017) and Curtis et al. (2014) reviewed the origins and health of the nation's CBNRM system. They find that while these systems originated via state government efforts in soil conservation and catchment management, Commonwealth efforts began with the National Soil Conservation Program (1983–92), evolving into the National Landcare Program (NLP, 1993–present), the Natural Heritage Trust (NHT1, 1997–2001 and NHT2, 2001–08), the National Action Plan for Salinity and Water Quality (NAP, 2001–08) and the Caring for our Country (CfoC) Program and associated funds (2008–13). CfoC later transformed into the NLP (Dale et al., 2017).

The establishment of a national framework for regional NRM under NHT2 in the early 2000s was a major step change for Australian CBNRM and saw the establishment of 56 regional NRM bodies—a move informed by the National NRM Policy Statement Steering Committee's (1999) report. A significant consequent improvement in the national CBNRM system was the tying together of agricultural and environment goals through this framework. The mechanisms have changed through time but a constant approach has been the contribution of funds from both Commonwealth agriculture and environment portfolios and the involvement of both ministers and the states/territories. This rare and difficult cooperation across governments and government agencies and policy silos has been pivotal to achieving landscape-scale management.

While the CBNRM system originally emerged from both statutory and Landcare models in the southern states, it was later, in part, appropriated by Commonwealth agencies. With increasing Commonwealth influence, a bilaterally agreed policy framework for CBNRM was negotiated with state and territory governments which, except for the Northern Territory (NT), all have capitals south of the Tropic of Capricorn. Consequently, the basic form and function of governance and design of the CBNRM system and its evolution paid little attention to the challenges facing communities and landscapes in Australia's remote north.

From 2001, regional NRM bodies were established to develop and maintain regional NRM plans to guide management action (Paton et al., 2004)—planning that aimed to secure regional consensus on aspirational and (nationally-guided) resource condition targets. NRM bodies also developed investment and engagement strategies to motivate land managers to improve management practices. Programs and projects given auspice under these arrangements were delivered by partner organisations such as Landcare groups, Traditional Owners, industry bodies, environment groups, councils or consultants (Dale et al., 2017). Despite the centralisation and move away from government bilateral agreements from 2007 onwards, the governance system retained some of these core features. Hence, a difference in the north has been that, while some southern jurisdictions (e.g. Victoria and New South Wales) delivered bilateral NRM via pre-existing statutory-based catchment management institutions (Ryan et al., 2010), the three governments across Northern Australia established non-government delivery organisations. With the decline of bilateralism between the Commonwealth and the states/territories, this has limited the institutional capacity of NRM bodies through limited government commitment and resourcing for long-term planning and implementation within the regional NRM framework.

Additionally, NRM planning in Northern Australia has also been impeded by a lack of environmental inventories, maps, monitoring systems, asset identification or knowledge of ecosystem function, so it was disproportionately affected by the disbanding of the National Land and Water Resources Audit in 2008 and Land and Water Australia in 2009. NRM planning in northern and remote areas had generally used tailored approaches (such as expert elicitation) to progress action in the face of data deficiencies while also prioritising investment in improving the research and knowledge base (Dale, Pressey et al., 2014). However, as northern assets remained under-represented in national databases, northern NRM was once again disadvantaged when CfoC shifted investment prioritisation from regional NRM plans to identified national assets and reduced support to research and knowledge building activities at the cross-regional and regional scales.

While the national emergence and refinement of the regional NRM framework was a governance innovation from the early 2000s, regional NRM governance capacity was uneven geographically and between sectors (Hill et al., 2013; Ryan et al., 2010). This was an issue in the north, where reduced institutional capacities slowed the engagement of Indigenous, industry and conservation interests. Similarly, blunt bilateral negotiations saw some parts of the national landscape under-resourced for implementation efforts (e.g. Central Australia). On the whole, however, all landholders in most regions across Australia, for the first time, were able to elect to become part of a predictable NRM process via extension, training and incentive-based activities (Dale et al., 2017). Collaborative projects were encouraged and stable resourcing had become available to implement priority actions.

# Systemic Governance Challenges in the North

With this policy and program-focused history in mind, this chapter first considers those contextual differences in Northern Australia that pose challenges for the successful design and delivery of nationally oriented and state/territory-based CBNRM policies and programs.

## Northern Australia is an Indigenous Domain

Dale (2013) considered Northern Australia culturally very different to the south of Australia and one of the world's most expansive Indigenous domains. He suggested that as Aboriginal and Torres Strait Islander people have control of, and/or interests in, the vast majority of the landscape, from a human rights perspective, Australia will continue to face pressure to engage seriously in Indigenous aspects of natural resource use to close the socioeconomic gap between Indigenous and non-Indigenous Australians. Statutory land and native title rights must also continue to be resolved across the wider landscape, while native title remains an evolving area of case law (JCU & CSIRO, 2013). The challenge this creates is that NRM policies/programs designed in Southern Australia, generally, are not well placed to meet the aspirational and practical needs of Traditional Owners (Dale, 2014).

## Climatic Differences and Limited Operational Windows

Climatically, the windows available for implementing CBNRM activities in Northern Australia are seasonally constrained in a major way. Accessibility is severely hampered during the wet season when the north's limited road networks are frequently impassable. Deep dry seasons bring altogether different challenges associated with fire management and water stress. Cyclones and severe flooding are a real possibility each wet season (Bureau of Meteorology, 2015). Consequently, project/budgetary cycles designed for more benign southern climates do not match northern conditions in practical ways. These constraints must be taken into account when reviewing NRM program progress against expectations.

## Institutional and Human Resource Capacities

Anyone trying to run an institution in Northern Australia understands the implications of limited human resource capability. This is relevant for the strategic development, implementation and monitoring of programs and projects. Workers in not-for-profit institutions face a higher cost of living in the north and, by and large, are paid less than their southern counterparts. High-paying industrial and public service sectors compete for available skills, leading to booms and busts in skilled workforces. Both local and migration-based workforces can also be both younger and more transient, a consequence of lower levels of liveability and isolation (Dale, 2013). Remoteness can lead to transience and higher cost in doing business (Martell et al., 2013), with implications for the capacity of both strategic and delivery-oriented NRM institutions.

## A Focus on Landscape Protection versus Restoration

National NRM programs continue to focus on tree planting and other rehabilitative activities to restore ecological function in largely agricultural landscapes. As the north retains most of its tree cover (an artefact of the vast expanses of economically marginal country), it is perceived to be in better condition than southern landscapes. Serious environmental degradation, however, has progressed under the tree canopy higher grazing pressures, disruption of fire management, and weeds and feral animals contributing to the most serious species losses to occur in the last half-century (Doody et al., 2009; Franklin, 1999; Russell-Smith et al., 2003; Woinarski et al., 2007; Woinarski et al., 2015; Woinarski et al., 2007). CBNRM initiatives, therefore, should focus on the identifying causes of ecosystem dysfunction and measures to address them. Durable and stable on-country programs are essential to restore the nexus between people and the environment and to maintain knowledge of ecosystem function via fire, weed and feral animal management (Woinarski et al., 2014).

There are many examples where this is working well, notably the Western Arnhem Land Fire Abatement (WALFA) project (Whitehead et al., 2009) and emerging community-based pollution reduction programs in the Great Barrier Reef (Brodie & Waterhouse, 2012). Like much of the rest of the nation, however, such projects can only be effective if there is a more widespread change from the current project-based and short-term funding model. They need to be underpinned by community support, on-ground (often traditional) knowledge and robust science, including extensive use of satellite imagery and modelling. They also need governance frameworks designed to ensure gradual incorporation of ecosystem service delivery into a marketable commodity. WALFA, for example, has transitioned from an on-country fire management project to a major savanna-burning program supporting some 33 carbon abatement projects over 140,000 km$^2$. This foundation promises to support land management at levels never before seen in the north. Similar approaches of scaling up from local to cross-regional activities that can be converted to marketable commodities would ensure the delivery of enduring landscape outcomes. Such initiatives, however, are hampered through policy and price uncertainty in Australia's carbon market and a general lack of ecosystem service policy (Dale et al., 2014).

## Conflicts Between Resource Exploitation and Preservation

One of the more difficult challenges facing NRM governance in the north is balancing economic development through resource exploitation with landscape preservation (Stephens et al., 2015). The historical introduction of improved pasture plants later classified as weeds and environmental and industry competition over water allocation are two examples. Often the poor management of conflict between these competing agendas leads to failed development *and* failed environment policy and investment (Stephens et al., 2015). These problems are exacerbated by a dearth of adaptive approaches to land use planning across Northern Australian landscapes. However, the emergence of new ecosystem service markets, including carbon farming, solar radiation capture, Indigenous land and sea knowledge and innovative nature tourism opportunities, could reduce conflict. They can provide additional income streams to complement more traditional forms of development (Dale, 2014). Their growth, however, requires NRM governance arrangements to build private and public partnerships that improve access to funding and shares costs across multiple sectors.

# The Northern Progression of Community-Based Natural Resource Management

Having built the above understanding of major challenges facing the progression of CBNRM in Northern Australia, the following explores specific aspects of historical development of the concept across the three key jurisdictions (Queensland, NT and Western Australia [WA]). This allows us to draw out key conclusions for the growth and development of appropriate CBNRM governance systems in the north.

## Progression of the System in Northern Queensland

The early 2000s saw a progressive maturation of regional CBNRM programs in Queensland. This provided an enhanced institutional capacity for NRM in the north. The Queensland Government opted for a community-based form of regionalism and continuous improvement through cooperative bilateralism, the accreditation of evidence-based and engaged regional NRM plans and the designation of regional NRM body capacity. Between 2001 and 2007, this policy phase ushered in a growth in more integrated NRM (INRM) efforts in the north, including the establishment of 12 designated regional NRM bodies. These emerging institutions were, however, weakened with the more centralised program delivery approach ushered in under CfoC in 2007. CfoC's introduction heralded great financial uncertainty for regional bodies and delivery partners, a problem only partially resolved by the Australian Government eventually committing some 60 per cent of stable pre-2007 investment as guaranteed funding via regional NRM bodies and their delivery partners (Dale et al., 2017).

By 2013, the swing in Commonwealth support away from integrated regionalism had reduced institutional stability in northern regions and increased policy/financial uncertainty as well (Dale et al., 2017). In the Wet Tropics, for example, while the region's NRM body fared well under the CfoC program (e.g. via Reef Rescue funding), from 2007, there was a parallel short-term collapse in the capacity of the regional body to support biodiversity, pest management and Indigenous land and sea management. Importantly though, the Wet Tropics region's capacity to secure Reef Rescue and Indigenous Protected Area (IPA) funds was, in part, a legacy from the stable institutional arrangements operating pre-CfoC.

The Australian Government's shift away from bilateralism also left North Queensland regions more vulnerable to shifting policy environments within the state government. Also, using the Wet Tropics as an example, the introduction of CfoC stalled progressive improvements in the development of cohesive delivery systems in local government, the conservation sector and in the Landcare and catchment management sectors. Conversely, by exception, time-bound programmatic funding (with a specific investment horizon) via CfoC's Reef Rescue Program, for example, improved capability in the agricultural sector while IPAs funded capacity advances in the Indigenous sector (Dale et al., 2017).

## Progression of the System in the Northern Territory

Formalised INRM in the NT began in 2003 with the signing of the bilateral agreement for NHT delivery between the NT Government and the Commonwealth (Commonwealth of Australia & Northern Territory, 2003). The Landcare Council of the NT (LCNT) was recognised as the regional delivery body (LCNT, 2005). LCNT had been established in 1990 as the peak community and industry body advising the NT Government on NRM matters. All 14 council members were NT Government appointees and included diverse participants. The NT was alone with the Australian Capital Territory in having one body covering the whole jurisdiction. LCNT was tasked with developing the first NT INRM Plan (LCNT, 2005). On completion of this plan, LCNT was replaced by the NRM Board of the NT (NRMBNT), later called Territory NRM. Changes to the governance of Territory NRM since 2012 have included updating the constitution to replace responsibility for board appointments from the NT Government to a community member–based panel. The INRM Plan was revised in 2010 (Territory NRM, 2010) and is currently undergoing a second revision.

From 2005, NRMBNT operated as a priority-setting and funding body. It administered competitive funding for projects delivering on INRM Plan priorities. It supported NRM activities of community, industry and government aligned to the plan. With the transition to CfoC in 2007, Commonwealth funding that would previously have supported this process was delivered through open funding rounds to meet the newly devised Commonwealth priorities, rather than regional plans. This restricted the capacity of NRMBNT to implement the plan and the role of NRMBNT in supporting NRM activities. Following the demise of

NRM-based bilateral agreements, Commonwealth grants to the regional body fell from over A$8 million in 2007/08 to about A$6.4 million in 2009/10 and A$5.2 million in 2013/14, with no cash contributions to from NT Government (Department of Natural Resources, Environment, The Arts and Sport, 2011; Territory NRM 2014). Despite the reduced funding, improved program security was maintained through five-year base-level funding for regional bodies through CfoC from 2011 and in the NLP.

Commonwealth budget allocations to the NT have always been disproportionately small. The NT constitutes some 17.5 per cent of Australia's land area and 17.5 per cent of its marine area, but typically receives less than 5 per cent of Commonwealth environmental management funds. Indeed, NHT funding from 1996–2000 fell to 3.1 per cent of the national total (Williams et al., 2001). Inadequate funding was exacerbated in the national open-call process, as NRM organisations in the NT were uncompetitive under the CfoC priorities of: 1) rehabilitation of degraded landscapes, 2) the management of a priority asset lists, or 3) increased participation rates. Substantial Commonwealth support for the operation of the Northern Australian Indigenous Land Management Alliance (NAILSMA) projects were a notable exception.

The destabilising result of decoupling Commonwealth funding from the NT INRM plan was illustrated by the outcome of the CfoC 2009–10 Business Plan, in which one of two projects funded in the NT were for control of rats on Truant Island. While the control of rats on islands was a Commonwealth priority (Department of the Environment, Water, Heritage and the Arts, 2009) and eradication from Truant Island was specifically mentioned in the CfoC Business Plan (Australian Government Land and Coasts, 2008), neither Traditional Owners nor conservation ecologists contributing to the 2010 NT NRM Plan identified either as a priority. The project eventually foundered because of lack of support from the Traditional Owners and funding was withdrawn.

The NT, thus, presents a unique case. Its regional body covers the entire Territory and its plan reflects priorities of the community, industry and government. Increasing integrated regionalism to underpin of delivery of Commonwealth funding through the regional body should, therefore, deliver on Territory priorities, but would also ensure that the science behind the funding allocation is well suited to the region and that high levels of community ownership of projects would deliver high success rates.

## Progression of the System in Northern Western Australia

The northern area of WA is large with a low population density. The 2011 Census shows the Kimberley has a total population of about 34,794 with over half of these people in the major towns. The remaining 16,500 are in smaller centres and/or engaged in pastoralism across an area of about 42.1 million hectares. About 40 per cent of the population are Indigenous. Establishment and development of regional NRM programs in WA has similar characteristics to the Queensland model. This is true even to the extent that the 2007 Commonwealth pullback from NRM support made the WA regional NRM groups and communities vulnerable to the changed state government policy environment, even though direct state government funding to NRM in WA had been low since the demise of NHT-NAP in 2007. The Commonwealth–WA Government bilateral agreement during NHT supplied matching funding that was almost always delivered through in-kind by the state. This was important for providing skills and technical resources to northern NRM activities and these are now much reduced.

As in Queensland and the NT, the NHT-NAP period was progressive for regionally based NRM. In northern WA, there was a unique situation where very disparate communities, spread across large areas, needed to be engaged to deliver a broad suite of NRM programs, often for the first time. This difficulty was recognised at the time of establishment of the NHT programs in the early 2000s and the regional NRM group (Rangelands NRM WA) undertook a planning process to engage communities and to develop a genuine community basis for the NHT-NAP programs. Rangelands NRM WA consulted with communities and individuals across the north to identify the natural resources in their areas and to secure regional consensus on aspirational and resource condition targets and possible management options. This process was undertaken over a period of more than 12 months and led to a Rangelands NRM Investment Plan (Rangelands NRM Coordinating Group, 2005) to guide investment and engagement through NHT and NAP. This was the first time such an intense and detailed community consultation process had been carried out across the WA rangelands and communities, and individuals had good ownership of the investment plan and were supportive of the NHT-NAP programs (via the plans and community committees were established). Such support across communities in WA's north is unique and eventually paved the way for over 100 projects addressing many of the NRM issues identified in the consultation process. Several special interest environmental groups were also established to deliver programs and some continue to operate in the region (B. Warren, personal communication, 3 April 2015). This background highlights the importance of and opportunities for engaging people and retaining their participation to achieve social, economic or environmental benefits.

The more recent development of CfoC post-2007 and the more prescriptive formulas endorsed reduced community ownership. Projects that met CfoC criteria did not always align or support community-identified NRM issues. As a result, many communities and groups became disillusioned and negative to the regional group and to the Commonwealth's programs, and several local groups have since failed due to capacity problems. The limited number of CfoC-identified natural assets in a region made it difficult to re-establish previous relationships and community ownership as achieved under NHT-NAP. The individual relationships with both Indigenous and non-Indigenous land managers across the north was also weakened, although the Sustainable Agriculture stream of CfoC provided an alternative, albeit relatively poorly funded, mechanism for engagement of pastoral land managers.

Most of the programs supported under CfoC did not take account of rangeland systems and frequently, in northern WA, support was only available to address issues of degradation and not protection of high-quality assets. Although work on feral animal and weed control was vital, it did not engage well with many land managers. Control work generally had to be undertaken by trained professionals and was not 'suasive and community-based'. The loss of commitment to CBNRM by the land managers of the north became a critical issue. There was no genuinely demonstrated understanding by government that the people living and managing the land must be involved and own the actions required for positive and sustainable NRM outcomes (B. Warren, personal communication, 3 April 2015).

As previously stated, the prescriptive system developed for the agricultural areas of Southern Australia does not fit the needs of the north and will fail unless a new, community-focused approach that recognises the knowledge and commitment to country of the northern land managers is adopted. To deliver good NRM management outcomes across the remote north, it is absolutely essential that all land managers are engaged and committed to sustainable NRM. The vast areas that need management cannot be maintained without the land managers in place providing the services needed to sustain asset quality and slow degradation. It is clear that one size does not fit all in the NRM space and that a move to a different paradigm, where recognition of the importance of local communities is again understood, is essential to protect our Northern Australia assets.

# Some Common Learnings for Northern Australia

## Cohesive Scale-Based Planning and Effort Mobilisation

Northern Australian regional NRM bodies and communities generally experienced the CfoC era as a shift from an outcome-focused policy agenda, which aimed to mobilise bilateral and regional NRM effort, to a centralised and narrowly focused national grants program. These centralised changes responded to the 2008 Australian National Audit Office (2008) report on the regional delivery model that criticised a lack of reporting on investment outcomes. This put further pressure on constrained institutional and human resources. In respect to the Wet Tropics, Dale et al. (2017) reported:

- less alignment between state and Commonwealth policy efforts and diminished alignment of local government, industry and community investment against agreed targets
- declining collaborative effort among many major regional institutions (including state and local governments, regional NRM bodies, statutory authorities and research institutions)
- with some sectoral exceptions (e.g. parties funded under IPA, Working on Country [WoC, now Indigenous Ranger Programs] and Reef Rescue), increased competition with consequent transaction costs facing all parties
- declining planning and delivery capability among NRM stakeholders, but increased capacity in the Indigenous domain and investment in the national reserve system (see Hill et al., 2013).

A retreat from target-driven bilateralism and coordinated regionalism, while intended to reduce transaction costs for the Australian Government, to a large extent simply increased the overall transaction costs in northern regions. Stakeholders now had to spend significant resources developing project proposals that were not necessarily compatible with regional priorities and achieved low success rates.

## Collaborative Frameworks for Research and Knowledge Management

Without collaborative regional research frameworks, including knowledge exchange, investment in northern NRM research and development is driven by researchers or funding agencies. This limits the regional relevance and impact of research and its benefit to strategic long-term decision-making. Since 2010, the Australian Government has tended to centralise control and management of significant regional NRM research programs (Expert Working Group on Science Engagement into and for Australia's Tropical Region, 2012). This has increased transaction costs for regional communities in the north, and regional NRM bodies became less able to influence the development and monitoring of their internal programs with well-engaged science management arrangements. This additionally reduced the capacity of their regional communities to influence policy and investment decisions affecting regional NRM (Dale et al., 2017). Over the last decade, new consultation arrangements have been revitalised through the establishment of cluster-based research partnerships through Clean Energy Fund (CEF) funds from 2013 (e.g. see Hilbert et al., 2014), the new evolving National Environmental Sciences Program (NESP) hubs and the new Collaborative Research Centre for Northern Australia (CRCNA). These new approaches could help rebuild previous arrangements such as the older Tropical Savanna, Reef and Rainforest Collaborative Research Centre, Tropical Rivers and Coastal Knowledge (TRaCK) approaches. The new Collaborative Research Centre for Northern Australia (CRCNA) is also now strongly playing in the space, integrating efforts across the NESP hubs and southern research and development corporations (RDCs).

## Environmental Accounts, Reporting and Adaptive Management

Regional stakeholders require evidence about the condition and trend of natural resources to devise solutions and to know whether current practices, policies and investments are working and to help engage and mobilise the region's key land managers. Since 2007, however, there has been a shift away from building a nationally integrated resource condition monitoring framework that could provide national-scale baseline data on natural resource conditions. National monitoring frameworks for key assets have been progressing (e.g. water and vegetation) but this has tended to occur via centralised and fragmented effort based on key asset classes, weakening the capacity of northern regions to influence state and national policy and investment agenda. Additionally, a less focused national framework has diverted coordinative effort in the states and the NT with regard to holistic resource condition and trend monitoring. Some years ago, in recognition of these issues, collaborative, pilot-based work on monitoring and reporting regional natural resource condition and trend within a national accounting context was progressing in partnership between northern regional NRM bodies and the Wentworth Group (2008). This could inform positive new thinking and development in this area.

## Devolved Regionalism: Shared Common Success Factors

While the broader CfoC framework eschewed devolved, multiscale approaches as a core tenet, some CfoC subprograms did use less centralised methods. The IPA subprogram, for example, provided devolved funds to Traditional Owner groups to plan the declaration and management of new IPAs. This funding was followed up with long-term delivery contracts through the WoC subprogram. These subprograms were also managed by a dedicated team of centrally based Indigenous NRM specialists and given operational flexibility. Consequently, Indigenous groups across Northern Australia made real gains in capacity and delivery. Similarly, the Reef Rescue subprogram, arguably CfoC's most high-profile success, was also negotiated by regional NRM, industry and conservation bodies ahead of the main CfoC framework (Dale et al., 2020). Governance innovations established under the NAP-NHT, however, had helped drive the evolution of these subprograms.

## Landscape Based Carbon: An Emerging Opportunity

Northern Australia has significantly influenced national thinking about using ecosystem service markets to deliver CBNRM outcomes. The initiation and operation of WALFA was supported with direct Commonwealth funding and the NRMBNT at times provided stop-gap funding for on-ground fire management, methodology development and the guiding of land managers through the Carbon Farming Initiative (CFI) accreditation process. While these developments emerged from a strong Indigenous agency, particularly through the NAILSMA, such groups were able to cast their work into policy frameworks that were also substantially influenced by other regional NRM bodies, particularly in Queensland (Dale, 2014). Hence, Australian Government reforms (from 2013 and earlier) under the CEF framework established the foundations for new ecosystem service markets/products of international standing in the north.

Attracting and guiding these emerging markets was a key goal underpinning the updating of regional NRM plans in the Monsoon, Arid Lands, Wet Tropics and South Eastern Queensland Clusters (Dale, Vella et al., 2014). By supporting the agricultural and land use sectors to trade in greenhouse gas abatement and other complementary ecosystem services (like biodiversity), these markets could transform NRM in Northern Australia. Enabling mitigation and abatement activities to become ecosystem service commodities would also allow northern regions to gain relative economic advantage from climate change rather than letting vulnerable regions be overwhelmed by it (Van Oosterzee et al., 2013). The Australian Government's new Emission Reduction Fund retains most of the key opportunities established under the CEF, ensuring real prospects for solid landscape outcome across the north.

## Conclusions

While reforming the wider CBNRM governance system is nationally important in its own right, the system has specific weaknesses when considered in the Northern Australian context. Program short-termism and poor links between science and decision-making are key problems. More problematic, however, is the gap between a centralised policy agenda and the way it fails to address the needs of Traditional Owners and the pastoral and farming sectors in managing extensive estates across the north. Many of these needs relate to building long-term capacity of pastoralists and Indigenous land and sea institutions for NRM. This chapter argues that any reform of the national NRM governance system must pay attention to the needs of Northern Australia. The new and emerging discussions associated with implementation of the Commonwealth's Northern Australia white paper, ongoing refinement of the nation's CBNRM system and the emerging new NESP hubs and the new CRCNA present some opportunities to commence a pan-northern dialogue on these issues.

## Acknowledgements

This work was funded by the Department of Industry, Innovation, Science, Research and Tertiary Education via the Northern Futures Collaborative Research Network, the Australian Government's Stream 2 Climate Adaptation Program, and the Australian Research Council. We would also like to thank the wide range of practitioners and experts involved in the Northern Australian CBNRM system for contributing their knowledge and experience to the chapter.

## References

Australian Government Land and Coasts. (2008). *Caring for our country business plan 2009–2010*. Canberra, ACT: Department of Sustainability, Environment, Water, Population and Communities and Department of Agriculture, Fisheries and Forestry.

Australian National Audit Office. (2008). *Regional delivery model for the National Heritage Trust and the National Action Plan for Salinity and Water Quality* (Report No. 21). Canberra, ACT: Australian National Audit Office.

Brodie, J. & Waterhouse, J. (2012). A critical review of environmental management of the 'not so Great' Barrier Reef. *Estuarine, Coastal and Shelf Science, 104–105*, 1–22. doi.org/10.1016/j.ecss.2012.03.012

Bureau of Meteorology. (2015). *Australian weather and season: A variety of climates*. Retrieved from www.australia.gov.au/about-australia/australian-story/austn-weather-and-the-seasons (site discontinued)

Commonwealth of Australia & Northern Territory. (2003). *Bilateral agreement between the Commonwealth of Australia and the Northern Territory of Australia to deliver the Natural Heritage Trust*. Canberra, ACT: Australian Government.

Curtis, A., Ross, H., Marshall, G. R., Baldwin, C., Cavaye, J., Freeman, C., … Syme, G. J. (2014). The great experiment with devolved NRM governance: Lessons from community engagement in Australia and New Zealand since the 1980s. *Australasian Journal of Environmental Management*, *21*(2), 175–199. doi.org/10.1080/14486563.2014.935747

Dale, A. P. (2013). *Governance challenges for Northern Australia* (The future of Northern Australia Discussion Paper Series). Cairns, Qld: The Cairns Institute. Retrieved from researchonline.jcu.edu.au/29868/2/29868_Dale_2013.pdf

Dale, A. P. (2014). *Beyond the north-south culture wars: Reconciling northern Australia's past with its future*. London: Springer.

Dale, A. P., Pressey, R., Adams, V. M., Álvarez- Romero, J. G., Digby, M., Dobbs, R., … Gobius, N. (2014). Catchment-scale governance in northern Australia: A preliminary evaluation. *Journal of Economic and Social Policy*, *16*(1), Article 2.

Dale, A., Ryan, S. & Broderick, K. (2017). Natural resources management as a form of multi-level governance: The impact of reform in Queensland and Tasmania. In K. A. Daniell & A. Kay (Eds), *Multi-level governance: Theory and case studies* (pp. 327–359). Canberra: ANU Press. doi.org/10.22459/MG.11.2017

Dale, A. P., Vella, K. & McKee, J. (2014). Analysing governance of Australia's system of landscape-based greenhouse gas abatement. *Australasian Journal of Environmental Management*, *21*(4), 378–395. doi.org/10.1080/14486563.2014.954644

Dale, A. P., Vella, K., Ryan, S., Broderick, K., Hill, R., Potts, R., … Brewer, T. (2020). Governing community-based natural resource management in Australia: International implications. *Land*, *9*(7), 234. doi.org/10.3390/land9070234

Department of the Environment, Water, Heritage and the Arts. (2009). *Threat abatement plan to reduce the impacts of exotic rodents on biodiversity on Australian offshore islands of less than 100 000 hectares*. Canberra, ACT: DEWHA.

Department of Natural Resources, Environment, The Arts and Sport. (2011). *Annual report 2010–11*. Darwin, NT: Department of Natural Resources, Environment, The Arts and Sport.

Doody, J. S., Green, B., Rhind, D., Castellano, C. M., Sims, R. & Robinson, T. (2009). Population-level declines in Australian predators caused by an invasive species. *Animal Conservation, 12*(1), 46–53. doi.org/10.1111/j.1469-1795. 2008.00219.x

Expert Working Group on Science Engagement into and for Australia's Tropical Region. (2012). *Science engagement and tropical Australia: Building a prosperous and sustainable future for the north.* Kingston, ACT: Department of Industry, Innovation, Science, Research and Tertiary Education.

Franklin, D. C. (1999). Evidence of disarray amongst granivorous bird assemblages in the savannas of northern Australia, a region of sparse human settlement. *Biological Conservation, 90*, 53–68. doi.org/10.1016/S0006-3207 (99)00010-5

Hilbert, D. W., Hill, R., Moran, C., Turton, S. M., Bohnet, I., Marshall, N. A., ... Westcott, D. A. (2014). *Climate change issues and impacts in the Wet Tropics NRM Cluster Region.* Retrieved from publications.csiro.au/rpr/download? pid=csiro:EP14913&dsid=DS3

Hill, R., Maclean, K., Pert, P. L., Rist, P., Joyce, A., Schmider, J. & Tawake, L. (2013, December). *Project 12.1 Technical Report: Participatory evaluation of co-management in wet tropics country. Interim report—December 2013.* Cairns, Qld: Reef and Rainforest Research Centre Ltd. Retrieved from www.nerptropical.edu.au/publication/project-121-technical-report-participatory-evaluation-co-management-wet-tropics-country

James Cook University (JCU) & Commonwealth Scientific and Industrial Research Organisation (CSIRO). (2013). *Land tenure in northern Australia: Opportunities and challenges for investment.* Brisbane, Qld: CSIRO.

Landcare Council of the Northern Territory (LCNT). (2005). *Integrated natural resource management plan for the Northern Territory: Sustaining our resources—people, country and enterprises.* Darwin, NT: Department of Infrastructure, Planning and Environment.

Martell, C., Carson, D. & Taylor, A. (2013). Changing patterns of migration to Australia's Northern Territory: Evidence of new forms of escalator migration to frontier regions? *Migration Letters, 10*(1), 91–100.

National Natural Resource Management Policy Statement Steering Committee. (1999). *Managing natural resources in rural Australia for a sustainable future: A discussion paper for developing a national policy.* Canberra, ACT: Department of Agriculture, Fisheries and Forestry (Australia).

Paton, S., Curtis, A., McDonald, G. & Woods, M. (2004). Regional natural resource management: Is it sustainable. *Australasian Journal of Environmental Management*, *11*(4), 259–267. doi.org/10.1080/14486563.2004.10648622

Rangelands NRM Coordinating Group. (2005). *Rangelands NRM strategy & investment plan*. Perth, WA: Rangelands NRM Coordinating Group.

Russell-Smith, J., Yates, C., Edwards, A., Allan, G. E., Cook, G. D., Cooke, P., … Smith, R. (2003). Contemporary fire regimes of northern Australia, 1997–2001: Change since Aboriginal occupancy, challenges for sustainable management. *International Journal of Wildland Fire*, *12*(4), 283–297. doi.org/10.1071/WF03015

Ryan, S., Broderick, K., Sneddon, Y. & Andrews, K. (2010). *Australia's NRM governance system: Foundations and principles for meeting future challenges*. Canberra, ACT: Australian Regional NRM Chairs. Retrieved from nrmregionsaustralia.com.au/wp-content/uploads/2013/12/NRM-Governance-in-Australia.pdf

Stephens, A., Oppermann, E., Turnour, J., Brewer, T., O'Brien, C., Rayner, T., … Dale, A. P. (2015). Identifying tensions in the development of northern Australia: Implications for governance. *Journal of Economic and Social Policy*, *17*(1).

Territory NRM. (2010). *Northern Territory integrated natural resource management plan 2010–2015*. Darwin, NT: Territory Natural Resource Management.

Territory NRM. (2014). *Annual Report 2013–14*. Darwin, NT: Territory NRM.

Van Oosterzee, P., Dale, A. & Preece, N. D. (2013). Integrating agriculture and climate change mitigation at landscape scale: Implications from an Australian case study. *Global Environmental Change*, *29*, 306–317. doi.org/10.1016/j.gloenvcha.2013.10.003

Wentworth Group. (2008). *Accounting for nature. A model for building the national environmental accounts of Australia*. Sydney, NSW: Wentworth Group of Concerned Scientists. Retrieved from wentworthgroup.org/2008/05/accounting-for-nature-a-model-for-building-the-national-environmental-accounts-of-australia/2008/

Whitehead, P., Purdon, P., Cooke, P., Russell-Smith, J. & Sutton, S. (2009). The West Arnhem Land Fire Abatement (WALFA) project. In J. Russell-Smith, P. J. Whitehead & P. Cooke (Eds), *Culture, ecology, and economy of fire management in North Australian Savannas: Rekindling the Wurrk tradition* (pp. 287–312). Collingwood, Vic.: CSIRO.

Williams, J., Read, C., Norton, T., Dovers, S., Burgman, M., Proctor, W. & Anderson, H. (2001). Biodiversity theme report. In Australian State of the Environment Committee (Ed.), *Australia state of the environment report 2001* (pp. 69–82). Canberra, ACT: CSIRO Publishing on behalf of the Department of the Environment and Heritage. Retrieved from soe.environment.gov.au/sites/g/files/net806/f/soe2001.pdf?v=1487243878

Woinarski, J., Mackey, B., Nix, H. & Traill, B. (2007). *The nature of northern Australia: Its natural values, ecological processes and future prospects*. Canberra, ACT: ANU Press. doi.org/10.22459/NNA.07.2007.

Woinarski, J. C. Z., Burbidge, A. A. & Harrison, P. L. (2015). Ongoing unraveling of a continental fauna: Decline and extinction of Australian mammals since European settlement. *Proceedings of the National Academy of Sciences of the United States of America, 112*(15), 4531–4540. doi.org/10.1073/pnas.1417301112

Woinarski, J. C. Z., Pavey, C., Kerrigan, R., Cowie, I. & Ward, S. (Eds). (2007). *Lost from our landscape: Threatened species of the Northern Territory*. Palmerston, NT: Department of Natural Resources, Environment and the Arts.

Woinarski, J. C. Z., Traill, B. N. & Booth, C. (2014, 14 October). *The modern outback: Nature, people and the future of remote Australia*. The Pew Charitable Trusts. Retrieved from www.pewtrusts.org/en/research-and-analysis/reports/2014/10/the-modern-outback

# 15

# Comparing Roles and Rights of Indigenous Groups in Local Governance of Trepang Fisheries in Northern Australia and Eastern Indonesia

Dirk J. Steenbergen, Gemma Wickens and Jackie Gould

## Introduction

The trepang[1] trade has historically sustained livelihoods in the Arafura Timor Seas (ATS) region and continues today (Adhuri, 2013b; Fox, 2000). The early trade was centred on the port of Makassar and undertaken predominantly by Makassarese, Bugis, Butonese and Bajau fishers based in southern Sulawesi (Clark & May, 2013a). Now generally referred to as 'Macassans', these traders negotiated with the Indigenous landowners in Indonesia and Northern Australia for rights to access trepang stocks and sell the dried product to the Chinese market for hundreds of years (MacKnight, 1976). Such arrangements were typically organised around customary governance regimes on land and sea territory that recognised Indigenous ownership. Throughout the twentieth century, much of the region came under the jurisdiction of some form of central nation-state government, while international trade increasingly became subject

---

1  Trepang is the saleable product of sea cucumber, most commonly sandfish (*Holothuria scabra*), also referred to as *teripang* (in the Southeast Asia region) or *bêche-de-mer* (in the Pacific region).

to control under various national and international trade agreements. The role of local Indigenous groups remains subject to complex political structures despite centrally legislated processes to determine rights and roles of local proprietary systems.

This chapter explores the national and regional influences that give shape to fisheries legislation in the Northern Territory (NT), Australia and eastern Indonesia and how these respectively impact on local access to small-scale fisheries (SSF). Using two cases of trepang fishery, this chapter shows how local actors become entangled in legislation that, while aiming to create fair and sustainable access to fisheries, creates a system of rights that can undermine the ability of local actors to engage in commercial and livelihood-sustaining activities. First, we set out the wider context of relevant policy development in Northern Australia and eastern Indonesia. We discuss the most important influences on fisheries policy design in each region and how these materialised into legislation. Second, we compare the Indigenous community at Warruwi in West Arnhem Land, Australia and Ohoiren in the Kei Islands of Moluccas Province, eastern Indonesia (see Figure 15.1) to show how local practices operate in relation to national policy. We observe that despite the vastly different socioeconomic and political settings, similar tensions exist between local-level practice and policy design at various scales of government that reflect the challenges of balancing economic demands and need for sustainable environmental management.

This chapter draws from a review of SSF policy and the authors' ongoing engagement in qualitative research on local rights-based management over natural resources in Northern Australia (Gould, 2011, 2015) and eastern Indonesia (Steenbergen, 2013a, 2013b) through their respective research projects.[2] For this study, enquiries were made on different actors' understanding of fisheries legislation and perceived opportunities and associated challenges, responsiveness of local practices to this legislation and how policy design progressed along particular agendas.

---

2   Steenbergen, 'Integrating Local Resource-Dependent Groups into Marine Resource Management in the Arafura Timor Seas Region' (NAMRA Postdoctoral research) (2014–2017); Wickens, 'Commercial Aboriginal Fisheries in the Northern Territory' (PhD project); Gould, 'Warruwi Fisheries and Aquaculture Knowledge Partnership Project' (Postdoctoral research).

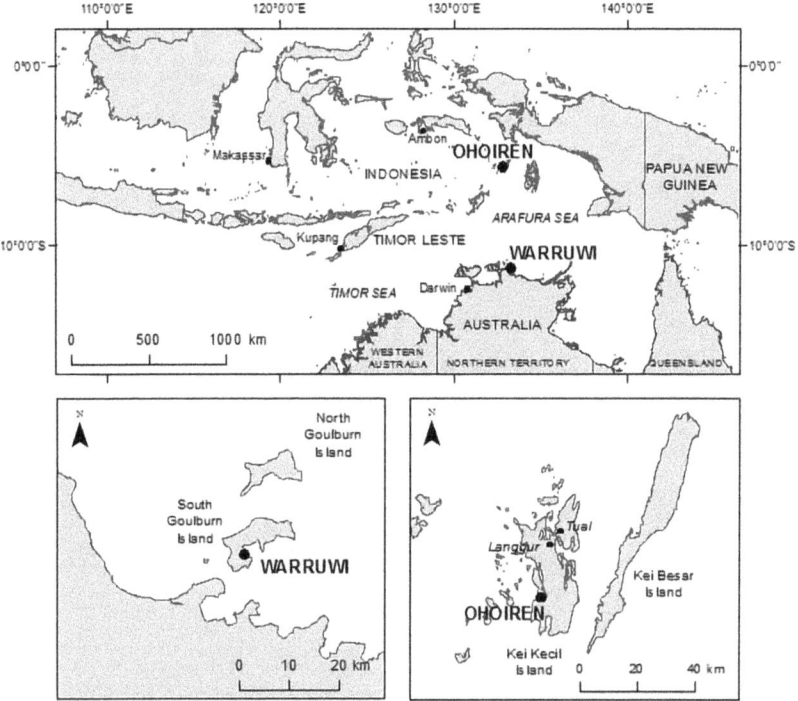

**Figure 15.1: Map of the Arafura Timor Seas Region showing the two cases studies of Warruwi (West Arnhem Land, Northern Australia) and Ohoiren (The Moluccas, eastern Indonesia).**
Source: Map created by the Research Institute for the Environment and Livelihoods, CDU, using Arc-GIS.

## The Wider Fisheries Policy Contexts

Due to its remoteness, the ATS region was not subject to particularly active nation-state control for much of the twentieth century. In Northern Australian waters, lower levels of European settlement, compared to other parts of the coast, allowed local Indigenous people greater ability to continue the custodial role of their sea country, including significant subsistence fishing. However, regulation has, more recently, reduced their role in the commercial trade from resource owner to casual labourer. In eastern Indonesia, the early absence of fishery authorities also allowed the continuation of traditional resource management practices around communal inshore waters. However, increased central government rule and encroaching market actors mean these coastal communities no longer operate along singular governance frameworks. The following section outlines in further detail the major ways in which contemporary fisheries governance has come about in the two different contexts.

## Northern Territory, Australia

Indigenous people have sophisticated rules governing the sea (Barber, 2010; Bradley & Yanyuwa, 2007; Dillon, 2002; Nursey-Bray, 2005; Palmer, 1998; Palmer & Brady, 1983; Peterson & Devitt, 1997; Smyth & Monaghan, 2004). Systems that designate land and sea country rights vary regionally, with those applying to the sea typically reflecting the complex tapestry of ancestral, ecological, sociocultural and economic values applicable to the land (Bagshaw, 1998; Barber, 2005; Morphy & Morphy, 2006). Rights to resources are asserted through reference to kinship structures and totemic and spiritual relations. Coastal Indigenous groups retain significant cultural connections to marine areas and rely heavily on them for subsistence (Gray & Altman, 2006; Henry & Lyle, 2003).

In the NT, the land rights movement of the 1970s led to the passage of the *Aboriginal Land Rights (Northern Territory) Act 1976* (ALRA) (see Figure 15.2). The ALRA allows Indigenous people a form of inalienable community freehold where land is held by designated Indigenous land trusts under regional land councils. Following the legal case of Blue Mud Bay,[3] Indigenous land trusts, with land awarded to the mean low water mark under the ALRA, have the right to exclude people from their inter-tidal zone. Although the NT Government retains the property right to trepang and other marine resources and can control capture, use and sale, Aboriginal people can limit access to trepang habitats in inter-tidal waters across 85 per cent of the NT coastline.[4] This is a significant portion of trepang habitat in the NT due to the large tides.

---

3   *Northern Territory of Australia v Arnhem Land Aboriginal Land Trust* [2008] HCA 29; 236 CLR 24; 82 ALJR 1099; 248 ALR 195 (30 July 2008).
4   The right to exclude parties from the inter-tidal zone has been a highly politicised issue in the Northern Territory, and in the main access to inter-tidal waters by commercial and recreational fishers has continued. Negotiations over how long-term access might be managed remain unresolved. For the latest iteration of access arrangements, see www.nlc.org.au/tidal-fishing.

*The Fisheries Act 1904 (SA):*
Commercial Fishery licences introduced—non-commercial Aboriginal fishing is exempt. Indonesian traders were not issued a licence.

*Aboriginal Land Rights (Northern Territory) Act 1976 (Cth) (ALRA):*
Land was granted to Aboriginal claimants in the Northern Territory. Many claims extended to the mean low water mark but the sea was not thought to be included until 2008. ALRA set up the administrative system of local land trusts and regional land councils.

*Fisheries Act 1988 (NT):*
Manages fisheries in Northern Territory. Section 53 allows for traditional Indigenous fishing. Section 17 allows for development permits.

*Fisheries Act Regulations 1993 (NT):*
Allows for Aboriginal coastal licences. Until July 2015, these were restricted to one per community, for non-commercial species and only allowed catch to be sold to end users within the licensed community.

*Native Title Act 1993 (Cth):*
Grants 'bundles' of rights to Aboriginal and Torres Strait Islander claimants who can establish that they have continued to use such rights in an area. Section 211 stipulates the right to traditional fishing, however, this is limited to non-exclusive and non-commercial use.

*Commonwealth v Yarmirr (2001) 208 CLR 1:*
The first native title claims granted over sea country. The public right to fish and navigate was found to be inconsistent with exclusive rights.

*Western Australia v Ward (2002) 213 CLR 1:*
Native title claim was accepted over sea country, but the public right to fish and navigate was found to extinguish any exclusive rights.

*Northern Territory v Arnhem Land Aboriginal Trust (2008) CLR 29 (Blue Mud Bay Case):*
The High court affirmed that Traditional Owners with land granted under the ALRA that extends to the low water mark have the right to exclude others from that part of sea as they would the land. Fishing regulation extinguished public right to fish. Fisheries legislation still applies. No extra rights to marine resources were implied.

*Fisheries Amendment Regulations (No. 2) 2015 (SL No. 18, 2015)* and *Fisheries Amendment (Coastal Line Fishery and Other Matters) Regulations 2015 (SL No. 19, 2015):*
Amendments to the Aboriginal coastal licence allow Aboriginal people to sell marine resources to third parties and allow for more commercial gear.

**Figure 15.2: Key legislation defining the rights of Aboriginal people to trepang in the Northern Territory.**
Source: Authors' research.

Beyond the mean low water mark, Indigenous Territorians have limited legal rights to their traditional waters. Section 211 of the *Native Title Act 1993* (Cth) stipulates the right to traditional fishing; however, this is limited to non-exclusive and non-commercial use.[5] Traditional fishing is also allowed under section 53 of the *Fisheries Act 1988* (NT). The NT *Fisheries Regulations 1993*[6] allow Indigenous people to apply for an Aboriginal coastal licence, which permits the limited sale and trade of aquatic resources. The regulations were amended in 2015 to remove many restrictions that had practically reduced rights to those already permitted

---

5    Exclusive rights to fish (property rights) were denied to native title claimants due to being inconsistent with the public right to fish (Commonwealth v Yarmir (2001) 208 CLR 1), extinguishing any exclusive right (Western Australia v Ward (2002) 213 CLR 1). A native title claim in the Torres Strait does include non-exclusive commercial rights (Akiba on behalf of the Torres Strait Regional Seas Claim Group v Commonwealth (2013) 300 ALR 1).
6    Part 11, Division 2.

under section 53. Now, Aboriginal coastal licensees are permitted to sell fish to third parties and can use limited commercial gear, although most commercially valuable species are excluded from the licences. This builds on earlier trials carried out under development licences.[7]

The Macassan trepang trade flourished across the north of Australia from at least the 1700s to 1907 (Clark & May, 2013b), when regulations were enforced to support an Australian takeover of the industry (Macknight, 1969, 1976). For the first half of the twentieth century, scant landing reports suggest the catch was many times higher than recent times; however, this slowed after 1945 to zero (Department of Primary Industries and Regional Development, 2004). Interest was renewed by an NT Government financial viability study in 1986 (Department of Industries and Development, 1988), which led to six new licences being issued to established commercial fishers in 1992. The licensed areas were large and conditions of the licence ensured only those who were able to 'demonstrate sufficient experience and skills to safely and effectively maintain commercial operations'[8] were considered, excluding many local Indigenous people. Further financial incentives were added by merging fishing areas and making licences transferable in 1993. Consequently, all six licences are now owned by a single fisher based in Southern Australia, to the exclusion of local actors.

The NT trepang fishery is managed by NT Fisheries, part of the Department of Primary Industry and Resources (previously the Department of Primary Industry and Fisheries [DPIF]) (DPIF, 2016). Under division 13 of the NT Fisheries Regulations 1993, the licensed area extends three nautical miles from the high water mark and only manual collection is permitted. Most activity occurs along the Arnhem Land coast. In 1999, catch peaked at 250 tonnes, with a value of A$2.4 million (DPIF, 1999). In 2012, this fell to 33 tonnes (DPIF, 2014), attributed to limitations in labour force rather than market failure (DPIF, 2013). In 1995, a four-year research project commenced to record Indigenous knowledge of sandfish (a trepang species) and evaluate the possibility of creating an Indigenous trepang industry. Without Indigenous-held licences in place, Indigenous groups could not capitalise on the research. Instead, despite

---

7   Section 17 of the *Fisheries Act 1988* (NT) and Part 8, Division 14 of the NT Fisheries Regulations 1993.
8   NT Fisheries Regulations 1993, Regulation 68.2(a)

confidentiality agreements, the information was used by the sole trepang licensee to expand into the mapped areas and achieve record harvest and profits gains (Carter & Hill, 2007).[9]

The extended period of Macassan contact had a significant impact on Indigenous economic and cultural dynamics (Berndt & Berndt, 1954; Blair & Hall, 2013). Some coastal communities express a strong desire to draw on this heritage to foster sustainable future livelihoods by engaging with the commercial trepang trade. While legislation recognising rights to sea country has progressed, it remains limited and has evolved separately to fisheries management regimes. The structure of the fisheries legislation is focused on balancing economic and environmental outcomes, with little consideration of social impacts, Indigenous cultural and historical connections or the ability of remote communities to engage in the industry. This acts to undermine access to potential benefits of resources by these groups.

## Eastern Indonesia

Of the people employed in Southeast Asian capture fisheries, over half come from Indonesia, and the majority of Indonesia's rural population lives within 10 km of the coast (Asian Development Bank, 2014). This makes Indonesia's maritime space an important source of national and local income and cultural distinction. Contemporary fisheries policy, to which local fishers are subject in Indonesia, has been shaped by influential political agendas since the country's independence in 1945 (Muawanah et al., 2018). Early national laws and decrees that governed Indonesia's maritime space were primarily geared towards promoting economic development and securing national sovereign rule (see Figure 15.3). Indonesia's bountiful seas (like the ATS) were regarded primarily as economic assets that saw limits only in fishers' capacity to extract (Moss & van der Wal, 1998; Novaczek et al., 2001). The first Fisheries Act (No. 9 of 1985) echoed this perspective, passing policies that ensured both subsistence and commercial access to marine resources.

---

9   This was prior to the Blue Mud Bay decision that could have prevented exploitation.

*National Law No. 4 of 1960 on defining Indonesia's territorial maritime boundaries as an archipelagic state [Djuanda Declaration]:*
Acknowledged the seas and all its resources as the property of the national government. National fisheries and coastal management consisted of rules and regulations administered across more than 20 ministries.

*Ministerial Decree No. 607 of 1976 on fishing zonation under the Ministry of Agriculture:*
Established initial zonation to partition (foreign) commercial and artisanal fishing access. Vessels >5GT were allowed to fish only beyond the 3NM coastal limit, while vessels >25 GT beyond the 4 NM limit and vessels >100GT beyond the 5 NM limit.

*Presidential Decree No. 39 of 1980 on trawling ban:*
Imposed a ban on trawling along the Malacca Straits and off the north coast of Java (regarded the two most important fishing grounds). The ban extended nation-wide in 1981, except across the Arafura Timor Seas.

*UN Convention of the Law of Sea (UNCLOS) of 1982:*
Recognised Indonesian maritime borders, which led to institution of international boundaries under National Law No. 5 of 1983 on the exclusive economic zone (EEZ).

*National Law No. 9 of 1985 on fisheries [Fisheries Act]:*
Prohibited use of destructive fishing gear (e.g., explosive and poison fishing); designated inshore fishing to artisanal fishing subject to regulation (i.e., mesh sizes >25 mm for reef fishing and >60mm for pelagic seine nets). Commercial access to fishing ground required license (i.e., foreign or domestic vessels >30GT from national authority, 10–30 GT from provincial authority and <10 GT from district authority).

*National Law No. 5 of 1990 on Conservation of Biological Natural Resources and Ecosystems [Biological Conservation Act]:*
Stipulated protection of habitats (i.e., priority habitats: mangroves, seagrass beds and coral reefs) and species (i.e., threatened species: 48 mammals [dugong, turtles, cetaceans, etc.], birds, crabs, shellfish and coral).

*National Law No. 23 of 1997 on environmental management [Environmental Protection Act]:*
Established framework for environmentally sustainable development and situating natural resource management under national government coordination.

*Ministerial Decree No. 51 of 1997 on fishing aggregation device (FAD) installation and use under the Ministry of Agriculture:*
Stipulated district responsibility over FADs within the 3 NM coastal zone, provincial responsibility between 3–12 NM and beyond that under national fisheries directorate.[3]

*National Law No. 22 of 1999 on local government [Local Autonomy Act]:*
Stipulated revisions to coastal zonation for governance under Articles 4 and 10 (i.e., <4 NM coastal zone under district regulation, <12 NM under provincial regulation and beyond that under national legislation).

*Presidential Decree No. 177 of 2000 on the organizational structure and task of ministries:*
Formed and defined duty and function of Ministry of Marine Affairs and Fisheries (MMAF): assisted the president to conduct governance of marine affairs and fisheries. This included primarily implementing new devolved governance structures at provincial and district level, revising fisheries licensing and authorization, and governing the beyond the 12 NM coastal limit. MMAF (at respective levels: national, provincial and district) became responsible for: (i) Exploration, exploitation, conservation and management of marine resources; (ii) Administrative function; (iii) Spatial planning; (iv) Law enforcement of local regulation and central legislation; (v) Support in Security issue; and (vi) Support in Defence.

*National Law No. 32 of 2004 regarding regional government [Revised Regional Government Act]:*
Replaced previous *Local Autonomy Act of 1999* and defined regional government to include provincial, district and city levels. Article 14 denoting full authority to regional government, except for functions/responsibilities attained by central government (the role of province decreased with most sectors devolving from national and provincial to district and city level).

*National Law No. 31 of 2004 concerning fisheries [Revised Fisheries Act, enacted on 6 October 2004]:*
Replaced former *Fisheries Act of 1985* with focus on economic and environmental concerns, with particular mention on coral reef zones and their ecosystems. Article 7 provided MMAF the right to implement management measures and control fisheries activities (i.e., specified method or gear, determining maximum sustainable yield [MSY] or total allowable catch [TAC] for domestic and foreign fishers, prevented pollution and destructive fishing, and rehabilitation of resources and habitats).

*Article 18 of National Law No. 32 of 2004:*
Emphasised management of natural resources and maintenance of environmental preservation (by regional government) pursuant of the law with similar maritime zonation division for governance.

*National Law No. 27 of 2007 on management of coastal zones and small islands [Coastal Zones and Small Islands Act]:*
Established coordination, integration and consistency in management and planning decisions. Facilitated further decentralised community-based coastal management schemes by allowing concession rights to be granted to individuals (Indonesian citizens), *adat* communities and the private sector for up to 20 years, and could be used for extraction, conservation and tourism.

*CTI-CFF leader's declaration signing of 2009:*
Initiated the CTI-CFF among six countries (Indonesia, Malaysia, Philippines, East Timor, Papua New Guinea and Solomon Islands). Driven by conservation lobby groups, with five main objectives: (i) Design and effectively manage priority seascapes; (ii) Apply ecosystem-based management of fisheries and other marine resources; (iii) Establish and effectively manage marine protected areas (MPAs); (iv) Achieve climate change adaptation measures; and (v) Improve threatened species status.

*National Law No. 32 of 2009 on environmental management [Revised Environmental Protection and Management Act]:*
Defined (marine) eco-regions, and stipulating improvement of legislation on the protection of marine ecosystems (previously not explicitly marine). Authorised central government to make and implement the policy on the protection of marine and coastal environment, coordinated by Ministry of Environment.

*National Law No. 1 of 2014 on the Management of Coastal Areas and Small Islands [Revised Coastal Zones and Small Islands Act]:*
Annulled coastal water concession provisions under *National Law No. 27 of 2007* (following constitutional court ruling (No. 3/PUU-VII/2010) in 2011). Article 20 noted that permissions to use local resources/areas may not interfere with traditional livelihood and use of coastal resources. Article 26A noted foreign investment in coastal resources must comprise public access, including fishing access.

Legend
- Fisheries-oriented — Policy Shifts in Governance Centrality
- Conservation-oriented — Policy Shifts Relevant to Marine NRM Governance

**Figure 15.3: National policy developments relevant to marine natural resource management in Indonesia.**

Source: Cribb and Ford (2009); Kusuma-Atmadja and Purwaka (1996); Novaczek et al. (2001); Satria and Matsuda (2004); Wever et al. (2012); De Alessi (2014); Rosen and Olsson (2013).

Following Indonesia's political reform ('*reformasi*') in 1999, responsibility for fisheries management was transferred to the newly established Ministry of Marine Affairs and Fisheries (MMAF). The change in Indonesia's political environment allowed for involvement of a wider set of stakeholders in processes of national policy design and regional collaboration. The already strong presence of conservation non-government organisations (NGOs) lobbying for environmental sustainability initiated a shift from an 'economic and exclusivity' driven fisheries agenda to one that included considerable attention for biological conservation.

The Biological Conservation Act (No. 5 of 1990) (see Figure 15.3) first incorporated formal policy that addressed the need to protect particular habitats and species (Novaczek et al., 2001) and saw the establishment of the first marine protected areas (MPAs). Their implementation lacked effective management and enforcement (Moss & van der Wal, 1998; Persoon et al., 1996). Nevertheless, the environmental lobby campaigns continually gained a political voice and, almost two decades later, new revisions were passed into laws that addressed marine-oriented environmental concerns (e.g. Environmental Protection and Management Act [No. 32 of 2009]). Capitalising on the momentum of the environmental NGO sector, Indonesia initiated the declaration of the Coral Triangle Initiative on Coral Reefs, Fisheries and Food Security (CTI-CFF)[10] in 2009, which proposed a regional framework for implementation of marine conservation measures (Fidelman et al., 2012).

Alongside the various agendas working on Indonesia's fisheries policy, wider devolution of management and decision-making occurred that significantly altered the way fisheries were managed. Prior to 1999, official governing responsibilities were defined and refined per maritime zone (see Figure 15.3), although supreme ownership of and governance over all marine areas remained strongly centralised. After the 1999 government decentralisation, greater recognition developed for existing forms of local governance, acknowledging local customary law and management systems that, to varying degrees, still dictate coastal communities' access and use of marine resources (Satria & Adhuri, 2010). Such customary management practices, typically applied to shallow inshore coastal zones, are based around tenure claims of particular social groups, are an integral part of local

---

10  The Coral Triangle covers an area marine scientists regard as the epicentre of global marine biodiversity, spanning the national territories of Indonesia, Malaysia, Philippines, East Timor, Papua New Guinea and the Solomon Islands.

belief systems and have formed around longstanding cultivation practices of economically important marine resources (e.g. trepang and trochus). Government legislation and resource co-management planning initiatives increasingly seek to incorporate such customary systems into modern governance frameworks (Cohen & Steenbergen, 2015; Steenbergen & Visser, 2016). For example, under the national Coastal Zones and Small Islands Act (No. 27 of 2007) (see Figure 15.3), traditional custodians of particular territories were recognised and could be granted a mandate to sanction practices that impeded on local law (De Alessi, 2014). Such initiatives, although positive in that local tenure was recognised, formalised customary arrangements and moulded these to function in official government structures, leading to considerable loss of flexibility and fluidity of customary law. The law was later revised under No. 1 of 2014, which cancelled particular articles that formalised customary law (see Figure 15.3). As a result, in regions like the Kei Islands, coastal communities such as Ohoiren village face contemporary challenges in their management of trepang stocks that mirror both local and higher-level political developments.

## Local Governance Practices Around Small-Scale Trepang Fisheries

### Case Study 1: Trepang Fishery at Warruwi, Northern Territory

Approximately 400 people live at Warruwi, on South Goulburn Island in Western Arnhem Land. Land and seas are held by patrilineal clans called *nguya*. Substantial management responsibilities and use rights are also conferred through maternal links. Additional less primary layers of rights and responsibilities flow from other sacred and secular relationships that underpin daily life (Gould, 2011). Livelihoods at Warruwi continue to have a seaward orientation. For many residents, their traditional estates are located within the coasts and seas on or around the island and nearby mainland. The marine environment remains an important source of food and plays an important role in social and cultural life, particularly in the passing on of ecological and cultural knowledge (Gould, 2011; Petheram et al., 2013). Resources are accessed, used and redistributed according to locally prescribed kinship and clan-based lines of responsibility.

The Methodist mission, established at Warruwi in 1916, participated in the commercial harvesting of trepang and other seafoods. From oral history accounts, the mission involvement in the trepang trade continued until the 1950s or 1960s (Gould, 2011). Attempts to initiate a modern community-based trepang enterprise at Warruwi commenced in the early 2000s, when trepang management was discussed at community planning workshops and informally among community leaders. A business plan was developed in 2005, focused on the development of a local hatchery and the sea-based cultivation of stock. This required an aquaculture licence and sea lease excised from the commercial wild harvest licence area. Attempts to attain the sea lease were unsuccessful due to a lack of scientific data that identified the area needed to establish a viable enterprise, thus stalling any immediate progress towards developing community-based enterprises at Warruwi.

At the time, little research into trepang breeding, growth dynamics, movement or preferred habitats had been conducted in Northern Australia. In recent years, however, interest in community-level enterprises from the commercial sector, NT Fisheries and an international aid agency has led to a suite of research projects being undertaken. This research has been complemented by projects at Warruwi focusing on building governance, infrastructural and technical capacity (Fleming, 2012), and on the commercialisation of other marine products like oysters, clams and fish (Fleming, 2015).

Although considerable technical data is now available, the licensing system used to manage the fishery assumes large-scale operations to the exclusion of Indigenous small-scale initiatives. As with other fishing sectors, substantial capital is required to purchase a licence, boats and the other equipment required to operate over a large licence area. Specialised technical skills are required to use and maintain this equipment, with costs and logistical issues inherent to remoteness presenting further challenges. To ensure financial viability, staff must work to a rigid framework with little room for considerations such as the need to care for young, elderly or sick family members, ceremonial obligations, and local prescriptions governing the allocation and use of resources collected from different areas. Warruwi's residents have exceptional knowledge of the local marine environment and aspirations commonly prioritise cultural and social resilience over commercial profit. Thus, a viable local industry would be one that allows this knowledge to be drawn on using low-technology inputs, with trepang collected by kinship-based groups from areas in which people have acknowledged traditional proprietary interests, and with products sold through a cooperative structure.[11]

Small-scale, wild-caught, commercial trepang fisheries would still require, under current legal structures, a licence to be attained on the free market from the sole licensee who may be unwilling to sell such a right and is likely to demand a prohibitively high price. Indigenous communities can harvest trepang under agreement with the licence holder, selling their product exclusively to the licensee. Two trial harvests using such a model were undertaken in 2015 and 2017. Although the trials were successful, this model does not allow any community participation in the industry beyond the harvesting stage of production. There remains the possibility of obtaining an aquaculture licence and sea lease for ranching trepang. As this would see the licence area excised from the wild harvest licence area, it requires political will to favour the social and cultural interests of Indigenous people over the corporate interests of commercial fishers. Finally, the recent changes to the Aboriginal coastal licence regime gives the Director of Fisheries discretionary powers regarding whether trepang collection is permitted. At the time of fieldwork, five licences had been issued, although none requested limited local collection and sale of trepang.[12] There are few opportunities to leverage sea rights beyond the inter-tidal zone to raise capital. Overall, the current legislative regime creates a range of pathways towards SSF development, but each incurs insurmountable barriers for Indigenous communities such as Warruwi.

## Case Study 2: Trepang Fishery at Ohoiren, Eastern Indonesia

Ohoiren is located along the western coast of Kei Kecil Island, with a small population of 567 people spread across about 120 households (Kecamatan Kei Kecil Barat, 2010). People sustain livelihoods through diverse engagement in small-scale agriculture, subsistence fishing and artisan activities (e.g. iron smithing, weaving and boat building). Collective income-generating activities are important and include trepang fisheries. These fund communal activities often linked to the village's Catholic church (e.g. restoration/maintenance of church grounds).

---

11  The Yagbani Aboriginal Corporation was established at Warruwi in 2011, in part for this purpose.
12  The inclusion of trepang in any Aboriginal coastal licence would have similar commercial implications to the creation of an aquaculture licence and, therefore, is likely to be similarly controversial.

Ohoiren's customary resource management and tenure regimes developed from a long history of trepang cultivation across Kei's coastal communities (Thorburn, 2000). Communal territory (*petuanan kampung*) is typically overseen by a local traditional 'lord of the land' (*tuan tanah*) (Adhuri, 2013a; Laksono, 2002). Customary marine resource management systems developed locally within the cadres of local ownership. These customary systems, although more recently altered through co-management initiatives seeking to build on both customary and science knowledge bases (see also Cohen & Steenbergen, 2015), still determine how resources are accessed locally. As a result, local fishers typically operate loosely within what is defined in national policy, particularly given the limited capacity for central enforcement.[13]

In 2004, residents of Ohoiren started collaborating with an Indonesian conservation NGO in response to local concerns regarding the continued withering of customary practices and increased infringements by outsiders extracting resources. The collaboration promoted sustainable marine resource management practices through strengthening traditional governance. Village regulations were formulated as an extension of existing traditional laws to control the cultivation, harvest and sales of trepang and were enforced locally by community groups. The NGO identified opportunity under the Coastal Zones and Small Islands Act to provide legal subdistrict recognition of these village regulations, which allowed Ohoiren to legally sanction infringements on their trepang access regulations. Moreover, as part of the collaboration with the NGO, particular small marine areas were allocated as permanent no-take zones to form trepang sanctuaries. Regular trepang monitoring activities were conducted within and outside these no-take zones to supposedly inform when and how much could be harvested at any one time. These local control and management structures influenced how local management was conducted. Entrepreneurial connections of the NGO enabled Ohoiren to obtain official legal recognition of local ownership and village resources use regulations.[14]

---

13   Throughout eastern Indonesia, documented cases exist of outside fishers subjected to custodian action by residents based on locally perceived rights as custodians of land and sea (Steenbergen, 2013a, 2013b).
14   Ohoiren was one of only two communities in the subdistrict to have gained such legal recognition of village regulations. Both obtained this through collaboration with the same NGO.

Simultaneously, but distinct from these local developments, a larger MPA was gazetted in the western Kei Islands as a direct result of increased conservation-oriented projects in the last decade. An international conservation NGO responsible for driving the implementation of this larger MPA initially had commenced a participatory planning strategy with local communities. However, these efforts failed to capture local interest or build on traditional governance. Several communities, including Ohoiren, eventually withdrew from collaboration with the international NGO. The NGO, however, persisted in its endeavour to establish an MPA and shifted strategy towards gaining district political leverage that eventually facilitated its implementation. So, although this MPA encompasses communal territories that had pre-existing management regimes in place, planning and implementation resulted from the international conservation NGO's negotiations with local government with very low community participation. Among community fishing groups, such as in Ohoiren, little was known of this gazetting or what implications it had for local practices. Ironically, the opportunities in legislation that officially recognised Ohoiren's traditional village regulations were now applied by other actors to recognise superseding laws under the MPA and inadvertently undermined the recently established local authority.

Considering the developments in and around Ohoiren, it is clear that Indigenous fishers operate in and between plural governing structures: 1) official government policy imposed through district authorities (e.g. the establishment of the large MPA), 2) traditional tenure regimes that are part of local customary law systems and, midway between these, 3) co-management frameworks that attempt to develop management systems that draw from both customary and science-based practices (e.g. Ohoiren's trepang management village regulations). At various instances in their local livelihood practices, Indigenous fishers contradict one or several of these governing frameworks. For example, the extraction of trepang for commercial sales as managed under the village co-management scheme breaches the resource protection regulations of the MPA regulations. Similarly, annual fishing gear handouts from the fisheries department to local fishers as a means to bolster local production and food security was perceived locally to contradict other restrictive fishing policies endorsed by the same government department.

The complexity and inadequate dissemination of higher-level policy meant Indigenous fishers tended to adhere to more familiar regulations, which often involved rules developed locally under co-management arrangements or that were part of customary law. In cases where fishers violated official district-level regulations, such as larger MPA regulations, they were often unaware they were acting illegally. Consequently, the governance frameworks formed in part by strategic interest groups from the conservation sector clearly steered what kinds of measures were implemented. However, without adequate information sharing and participation, mechanisms also significantly fell short in advancing desirable local practice.

## Discussion

In both locales, historic engagement around resource use, between Indigenous groups and outsiders, have been sidelined during centralisation of political and economic power following nation-state building agendas over the twentieth century. The contemporary settings in both Northern Australia and eastern Indonesia sees involvement of powerful national and international actor groups engaging with, or at least active in the same areas as, Indigenous groups who have little political leverage on their own. Recent trends towards recognising traditional proprietary systems in both countries create legislative contradictions regarding access to and use of marine areas and resources.

At Warruwi, the development of fisheries legislation has effectively come to favour larger non-local corporate interests and excludes remote Indigenous community small-scale participation in the trepang industry. Land rights legislation has emerged separately and has not impacted on the ways in which extractive rights to marine resources are allocated. The contemporary economic marginality of remote communities in the context of a regional economy based on large-scale projects leave remote communities with few commercial or political assets to leverage in their attempts to build sustainable futures (Howitt, 2010). Substantial investments have been made by the community, a partnering aid agency and within NT Fisheries to develop the technical and governance capacities required to establish a small-scale trepang enterprise,[15] but these efforts have, to date, failed to impact on the higher-level political structures that favour existing large commercial interests in the designation of land and sea rights and fisheries management regimes.

---

15   We note these sit alongside investments by the commercial licence holder into trepang ranching research and development.

In Ohoiren, the development of policy and legislation at various levels has brought forth both restrictive and supportive regulations and created a complex arena of legal pluralism. Thus, local governance arrangements based on customary laws exist in one form or another alongside central government policy and legislation. Centrally managed MPAs, for example, are being established over waters that include communal areas where local no-take zones have been independently designated by communities. Communities like Ohoiren, in their collaboration with the NGO, have been able to partially navigate these complexities and secure their claims over tenure and local ownership by having their customary law recognised in state law. In such cases, communities have benefited from collaborations with well-informed and well-connected NGOs—the community in Ohoiren, for example, was able to curb potential encroachments on its right to access and manage resources through passing of higher-level legislation. The large majority of coastal communities in the wider eastern Indonesian context do not have access to facilitating agents. In such cases, lack of political entrepreneurship leaves communities functioning somewhere in the middle between official central state and district law on one hand and local customary law on the other. So, although national policy presents opportunity for communities to play a more significant role, without trusted and well-informed politically facilitating agents in place, local actors appear unlikely to capitalise on such opportunities.

In both cases, divergent discursive trajectories appear to inform legislation, impacting the way local Indigenous communities go about using resources. In the NT, fisheries legislation aims to regulate the extraction of resources in a sustainable manner. Land and sea rights legislation has, in more recent times, emerged to partially recognise Indigenous entitlements to the access and use of country. Although this latter legislation has, to some degree, limited the rights of those holding commercial fisheries licences (allowing potential control over access to the inter-tidal zone), it has not allowed Indigenous communities to enter into spaces vacated by the commercial sector (by allowing access to the marine resources). Additionally, with no formal platform for the integration of Indigenous voices into the management of the NT's fisheries, Indigenous systems of resource allocation and use are not able to inform wider extractive and environmental management regimes. In eastern Indonesia, policy brought forward through the MMAF subjects resource users both to measures that bolster rural coastal economic development and measures that restrict capture fisheries. The suite of conflicting measures distort local understandings of what sustainable resource management means—namely, balancing interests of economic rural development and environmental protection.

Reflecting on these findings, it is important to consider what the implications are for wider narratives that dictate development in the two case studies. In the push to 'Develop the North', it is imperative that the Australian and NT governments look beyond the rhetoric that is giving direction to legislative change. Creating tensions between stakeholders, without real benefits accruing to either, does little to stimulate economic or environmental outcomes. The recognition of Indigenous rights to control access to inter-tidal zones has the potential to create economic benefits for remote communities in the form of royalty schemes. However, NT governments may wish to consider taking the additional step of developing policies that favour small-scale extractive (as opposed to mere access) rights to marine resources, if their stated agenda of promoting Indigenous community development is genuine. The recent changes to the Aboriginal coastal licensing regime represent a significant move in this direction. They create a policy space that allows local SSF business to be developed, although it is too soon to see whether the Director of Fisheries will use their discretionary powers under this regime to do so—for example, by allowing the collection of trepang at Warruwi.

In eastern Indonesia, SSF policy narratives are brought forward under the regional multilateral partnership of the CTI-CFF to focus on local food security and environmental sustainability. Such policy narratives need to translate locally to function in or with local customary governing systems, rather than simply acknowledging their existence while implementing parallel SSF management schemes (see also Courtney et al., 2017; van Nimwegen, 2017). Opportunity for recognition in government law already exists, as is evident in Ohoiren's case where local tenure rights were endorsed by subdistrict authority. However, to prevent this process of local ownership recognition becoming a reactionary measure to fears of higher-level (restrictive) policy developments, both governance contexts require effective information and knowledge exchange. Implementing enduring information-sharing platforms across policy levels may provide a catalyst for developing understanding across the multi-scaled fisheries frameworks that Ohoiren, Indonesia and ATS regions are all governed by.

A notable priority under the NT Government's development agenda is to foster development in remote communities. Rights-based management over natural resources offers the opportunity to enhance livelihoods and establish effective local governance capacity. Support for SSF in the NT is emerging but underdeveloped; however, in drawing from the above discussion on legal recognition of local tenure claims in the eastern Indonesia case, lessons can be learned in terms of the sort of complexity and potential challenges of plurality involved in establishing legislative recognition of local authority structures.

## Conclusion

In the context of wider regional development narratives aspiring to address local socioeconomic development challenges while also achieving environmental sustainability, local resource user groups clearly stand to play an important role. However, as the case studies have shown, there are particular voices that remain unheard or are inadequately responded to. For effective policy to emerge in remote Indigenous communities, rights-based policy design processes must secure socially and politically just outcomes. Particularly, the position of local Indigenous peoples in negotiations over resource access with powerful competing industry or public sector interest groups needs strengthening. Contemporary governance design processes proceed with too little genuine input from local customary owners of particular land or seascapes who claim value of a place for its cultural capital and as a primary source of livelihood and living environment. Instead, such processes appear more responsive to larger economic development plans (e.g. NT's 'Developing the North') and powerful conservation lobby movements (e.g. CTI-CFF).

The need for more inclusive processes refers to planning, design and implementation stages that extend beyond local spheres into multiple policy scales. Tools and mechanisms facilitating effective rights-based resource management on the ground, as seen in eastern Indonesia, must be made to fit within existing sociopolitical arenas. Such arenas have existing forms of local governance, strong social hierarchies, legacies of past development and strong competing interests from other stakeholders, which all affect how resources are accessed. Establishing channels of information sharing, integrating adequate checks and balances in management design and building platforms for suitable 'institutional bricolage' (Cleaver, 2012) to take place at interfaces between different stakeholder groups may provide the necessary exchange and dual-way understanding to address conflicting governance structures or co-option of resources by powerful groups over weaker groups.

Given a complex legislative environment with many stakeholders extant across varied spatial scales, the need for an effective balance between social, economic and environmental prerogatives is fundamental but challenging. Without unfairly compromising the legitimate interests of existing commercial sectors, Indigenous communities require access to the legislative spaces necessary for engaging with the national and global economies. In considering legislative reforms in the context of the Northern Development Agenda, thought must be given to the adverse unintended consequences of policy implementation, such as occurs with the interaction of fisheries management and land rights regimes. Enabling Indigenous economic development is a prerogative for governments and Indigenous communities alike. Progress is more likely to happen through the resolution of tensions created by contradictory legal regimes than through the retraction of land and sea rights.

# References

Adhuri, D. S. (2013a). *Selling the sea, fishing for power: A study of conflict over marine tenure in Kei Islands, Eastern Indonesia*. Canberra, ACT: ANU E Press. doi.org/10.22459/SSFP.02.2013

Adhuri, D. S. (2013b). Traditional and 'modern' trepang fisheries on the border of the Indonesian and Australian fishing zones. In M. A. Clark & S. K. May (Eds), *Macassan history and heritage journeys, encounters and influences* (pp. 183–203). Canberra, ACT: ANU E Press. doi.org/10.22459/MHH.06.2013

Asian Development Bank. (2014). *Economics of fisheries and aquaculture in the Coral Triangle*. Mandaluyong City, Philippines: Asian Development Bank. Retrieved from www.adb.org/sites/default/files/publication/42411/economics-fisheries-aquaculture-coral-triangle.pdf

Bagshaw, G. (1998). Gapu Dhulway, Gapu Maramba: Conceptualisation and ownership of saltwater among the Burarra and Yan-nhangu peoples of northeast Arnhem Land. In N. Peterson & B. Rigsby (Eds), *Customary marine tenure in Australia* (pp. 247–283). Sydney, NSW: University of Sydney Press.

Barber, M. (2005). Where the clouds stand: Australian Aboriginal relationships to water, place, and the marine environment in Blue Mud Bay, Northern Territory (unpublished doctoral thesis). ANU, Canberra, ACT.

Barber, M. (2010). Coastal conflicts and reciprocal relations: Encounters between Yolngu people and commercial fishermen in Blue Mud Bay, north-east Arnhem Land. *The Australian Journal of Anthropology*, *21*, 298–314. doi.org/10.1111/j.1757-6547.2010.00098.x

Berndt, R. & Berndt, C. (1954). *Arnhem Land: Its history and its people*. Melbourne, Vic.: Cheshire.

Blair, S. & Hall, N. (2013). Travelling the 'Malay Road': Recognising the heritage significance of the Macassan maritime trade route. In M. Clark & S. May (Eds), *Macassan history and heritage journeys, encounters and influences* (pp. 80–100). Canberra, ACT: ANU E Press. doi.org/10.22459/MHH.06.2013

Bradley, J. & Yanyuwa, F. (2007). *Barni-Wardimantha Awara Yanyuwa sea country plan*. Retrieved from Mabunji Aboriginal Resource Association.

Carter, J. & Hill, G. (2007). Indigenous community-based fisheries in Australia. *Journal of Environmental Management*, *85*(4), 866–875.

Clark, M. & May, S. (2013a). *Macassan history and heritage: Journeys, encounters and influences*. Canberra, ACT: ANU E Press. doi.org/10.22459/MHH.06.2013

Clark, M. & May, S. (2013b). Understanding the Macassans: A regional approach. In M. Clark & S. May (Eds), *Macassan history and heritage: Journeys, encounters and influences* (pp. 1–18). Canberra, ACT: ANU E Press. doi.org/10.22459/MHH.06.2013

Cleaver, F. (2012). *Development through Bricolage: Rethinking institutions for natural resource management*. New York, NY: Routledge.

Cohen, P. J. & Steenbergen, D. J. (2015). Social dimensions of local fisheries co-management in the Coral Triangle. *Environmental Conservation*, *42*(03), 278–288. doi.org/10.1017/S0376892914000423

Courtney, C. A., Pomeroy, R., De Alessi, M., Adhuri, D., Yuni, C. & Halim, A. (2017). *Marine tenure and small-scale fisheries: Learning from the Indonesia experience*. Retrieved from land-links.org/wp-content/uploads/2018/03/USAID_Land_Tenure_TGCC_Indonesia_Marine_Tenure_Report_Updated.pdf

Cribb, R. B. & Ford, M. (2009). *Indonesia beyond the water's edge: Managing an archipelagic state*. Singapore: Institute of Southeast Asian Studies.

De Alessi, M. (2014). Archipelago of gear: The political economy of fisheries management and private sustainable fisheries initiatives in Indonesia. *Asia & the Pacific Policy Studies*, *1*(3), 576–589. doi.org/10.1002/app5.40

Department of Industries and Development. (1988). *Beche-de-mer (trepang) harvesting preliminary economic feasibility study*. Northern Territory: DID, Division of Primary Production.

Department of Primary Industry and Fisheries (DPIF). (1999). *Fishery status reports 1999*. Retrieved from dpir.nt.gov.au/__data/assets/pdf_file/0012/233121/fr55.pdf

Department of Primary Industry and Fisheries (DPIF). (2013). *Annual report 2012–2013*. Retrieved from industry.nt.gov.au/__data/assets/pdf_file/0005/227840/dpif_ar1213.pdf

Department of Primary Industry and Fisheries (DPIF). (2014). *Fishery status reports 2012*. Retrieved from dpif.nt.gov.au/__data/assets/word_doc/0011/233678/fr113_compat.docx

Department of Primary Industry and Fisheries (DPIF). (2016). *Status of key Northern Territory fish stocks 2014*. Retrieved from dpif.nt.gov.au/__data/assets/pdf_file/0006/366117/FR115.pdf

Department of Primary Industries and Regional Development. (2004). *Fishery status reports—2003*. Retrieved from hdl.handle.net/10070/222882

Dillon, R. (2002). Seeing the sea change and Indigenous sea rights. *Maritime Studies*, *2002*(123), 12–16.

Fidelman, P., Evans, L., Fabinyi, M., Foale, S., Cinner, J. E. & Rosen, F. (2012). Governing large-scale marine commons: Contextual challenges in the Coral Triangle. *Marine Policy*, *36*(1), 42–53.

Fleming, A. (2012). *Sea ranching of sandfish in an Indigenous community within a well-regulated fishery (Northern Territory)*. Retrieved from coastfish.spc.int/doc/coastfish_docs/Meetings/PPT19_Fleming.pdf

Fleming, A. (2015). Improving business investment confidence in culture-aligned Indigenous economies in remote Australian communities—A business support framework to better inform government programs. *International Indigenous Policy Journal*, *6*(3). doi.org/10.18584/iipj.2015.6.3.5

Fox, J. J. (2000). Maritime communities in the Timor and Arafura Region: Some historical and anthropological perspectives. In S. O'Conner, P. Veth & A. A. Balkema (Eds), *East of Wallace's Line: Studies of past and present maritime cultures of the Indo-pacific region* (pp. 337–356). CRC Press.

Gould, J. L. (2011). Being in the black: The business of development in Northern Australia (unpublished honours thesis). Charles Darwin University, Darwin, NT.

Gould, J. L. (2015). Caught in the tides: The (re)development of a trepang industry at Warruwi, Northern Territory. *Reviews in Fish Biology and Fisheries*, *26*(4). doi.org/10.1007/s11160-015-9400-3

Gray, M. & Altman, J. (2006). The economic value of harvesting wild resources to the Indigenous community of the Wallis Lake Catchment, NSW. *Family Matters*, *75*, 24–33.

Henry, G. & Lyle, J. (Eds). (2003). *The national recreational and Indigenous fishing survey*. Retrieved from eprints.utas.edu.au/2526/1/Henry_Lyle_Nationalsurvey.pdf

Howitt, R. (2010). Sustainable Indigenous futures in remote Indigenous areas: Relationships, processes and failed state approaches. *GeoJournal*, *77*(6), 817–828.

Kecamatan Kei Kecil Barat. (2010). *Kei Kecil Barat Dalam Angka* [Western Kei Kecil in Numbers]. Retrieved from Central Board of Statistics Indonesia (Badan Pusat Statistik, BPS)—Maluku Tenggara District.

Kusuma-Atmadja, M. & Purwaka, T. H. (1996). Legal and institutional aspects of coastal zone management in Indonesia. *Marine Policy*, *20*(1), 63–86. doi.org/10.1016/0308-597x(95)00034-4

Laksono, P. M. (2002). *The common ground in the Kei Islands: Eggs from one fish and one bird*. Yogyakarta, Indonesia: Galang Press.

Macknight, C. C. (1969). The Macassans: A study of the early trepang industry along the Northern Territory coast (unpublished doctoral thesis). ANU, Canberra, ACT.

MacKnight, C. C. (1976). *The voyage to Marege': Macassan trepangers in northern Australia*. Melbourne, Vic.: Melbourne University Press.

Morphy, H. & Morphy, F. (2006). Tasting the waters: Discriminating identities in the waters of Blue Mud Bay. *Journal of Material Culture*, *11*(1–2), 67–85. doi.org/10.1177/1359183506063012

Moss, S. M. & van der Wal, M. (1998). Rape and run in Maluku: Exploitation of living marine resources in eastern Indonesia. *Cakalele*, *9*(2), 85–97.

Muawanah, U., Yusuf, G., Adrianto, L., Kalther, J., Pomeroy, R., Abdullah, H. & Ruchimat, T. (2018). Review of national laws and regulation in Indonesia in relation to an ecosystem approach to fisheries management. *Marine Policy, 91*, 150–160. doi.org/10.1016/j.marpol.2018.01.027

Novaczek, I., Sopacua, J. & Harkes, I. (2001). Fisheries management in Central Maluku, Indonesia: 1997–98. *Marine Policy, 25*(3), 239–249.

Nursey-Bray, M. (2005). *Having a yarn: Engaging with Indigenous communities in natural resource management.* Paper presented at the International Conference on Engaging Communities. Retrieved from citeseerx.ist.psu.edu/viewdoc/download?doi=10.1.1.574.7680&rep=rep1&type=pdf

Palmer, K. (1998). Customary marine tenure at Groote Eylandt. In N. Peterson & B. Rigsby (Eds), *Customary marine tenure in Australia* (pp. 227–245). Sydney, NSW: University of Sydney Press.

Palmer, K. & Brady, M. (1983). *A report prepared in support of an application to control entry onto seas adjoining Aboriginal land. Prepared on behalf of the Minjilang Aboriginal Community and other traditional owners.* Darwin, NT: Northern Land Council.

Persoon, G. A., de Iongh, H. & Wenno, B. (1996). Exploitation, management and conservation of marine resources: The context of the Aru Tenggara marine reserve (Moluccas, Indonesia). *Ocean and Coastal Management, 32*(2), 97–122.

Peterson, N. & Devitt, J. (1997). *A report in support of an application for recognition of the native title to areas of sea by the Mangalara, Mandilarri-Ildugij, Murran, Gadura, Mayarram, Minga and Ngaynjaharr of the Croker Island region.* Northern Land Council.

Petheram, L., Fleming, A., Stacey, N. E. & Perry, A. (2013). *Indigenous women's preferences for climate change adaptation and aquaculture development to build capacity in the Northern Territory.* National Climate Change Adaptation Research Facility.

Rosen, F. & Olsson, P. (2013). Institutional entrepreneurs, global networks, and the emergence of international institutions for ecosystem-based management: The Coral Triangle initiative. *Marine Policy, 38*, 195–204. doi.org/10.1016/j.marpol.2012.05.036

Satria, A. & Adhuri, D. S. (2010). Pre-existing fisheries management systems in Indonesia, focusing on Lombok and Maluku. In K. Ruddle & A. Satria (Eds), *Managing coastal and inland waters: Pre-existing aquatic management systems in Southeast Asia* (pp. 31–55). Dordrecht, Heidelberg, London and New York: Springer Science and Musiness Media.

Satria, A. & Matsuda, Y. (2004). Decentralization of fisheries management in Indonesia. *Marine Policy*, *28*(5), 437–450.

Smyth, D. & Monaghan, J. (2004). *Living on saltwater country: Review of literature about Aboriginal rights, use, management and interests in northern Australian marine environments*. Hobart, Tas.: National Oceans Office.

Steenbergen, D. J. (2013a). Negotiating the future of local 'backwaters': Participatory marine conservation on small islands in eastern Indonesia (unpublished doctoral thesis). Murdoch University, Perth, WA.

Steenbergen, D. J. (2013b). The role of tourism in addressing illegal fishing: The case of a dive operator in Indonesia. *Contemporary Southeast Asia*, *35*(2), 188–214.

Steenbergen, D. J. & Visser, L. E. (2016). Caught between mediation and local dependence: Understanding the role of non-government organisations in co-management of coastal resources in eastern Indonesia. *Anthropological Forum*, *26*(2), 115–137. doi.org/10.1080/00664677.2016.1148012

Thorburn, C. C. (2000). Changing customary marine resource management practice and institutions: The case of Sasi Lola in the Kei Islands, Indonesia. *World Development*, *28*(8), 1461–1479.

van Nimwegen, P. (2017). Shifting waters—Indonesia's dynamic marine protected area policy seascape (unpublished Master's thesis). Murdoch University, Perth, WA.

Wever, L., Glaser, M., Gorris, P. & Ferrol-Schulte, D. (2012). Decentralization and participation in integrated coastal management: Policy lessons from Brazil and Indonesia. *Ocean & Coastal Management*, *66*(2012), 63–72. doi.org/10.1016/j.ocecoaman.2012.05.001

# 16

# Dry Thinking, Wet Places: Conceptualising Fluid States

Paul Carter

Development and semiotic enclosure go together. In narratives of regional development, dreams and visions belong to an earlier historical phase. As the maps are filled in and the legal and administrative structures imposed, the room for imaginative manoeuvre is correspondingly contracted. The initial El Dorado romance progressively yields to narratives of heroic geographical conquest, imperial assimilation and subsequent Ersatz identifications of place. Ersatz because, despite the rhetoric of independence and autonomy, the measures of social, economic and environmental viability remain tied to the normative values of the nation-state and the global economy. In the myth of loosely flexible renegotiations of identity and habit, the frontier plays a symptomatically ambiguous role. On one hand, it suggests a hard-and-fast line, while on the other it implies a wave moving forward. Solid and fluid states coexist. Northern Australia is presented as a land of opportunity; in reality, it produces extreme bureaucratic arteriosclerosis. Depending on one's social proclivities, sustainable development requires a new model of complexification, integration and their planning, one that retains the generative myth of place making (memorably inscribed in Darwin's name).

Development refers to the unfolding of new meanings—to develop is etymologically to 'unwrap' and to unwrap a country is, presumably, to reveal its meanings. At the same time, the capitalistic and colonialist thrust towards the exploitation of the Earth's resources ensures that the meanings attributed to the newly occupied territories are those that translate into quantifiable benefits (economic, social and political). The generative core of the country unfuelled and unveiled through development is identified with entrepreneurial knack and technological ingenuity. The notion that the country might write back—that it possesses a cryptic script of its own, a system of sustaining inter-relations and exchanges that also produce wealth, is harder to assimilate. Because of this, the development of the new society occurs through the counter-envelopment of the environment. As the environment is progressively parcelled out, classified and demarcated for discrete acts of development, its natural capacity for development is smothered. In relation to the transformational potential of a region understood creatively, the theory and practice of Western development acts surprisingly like the surfeit of bureaucratic measures that, in other circumstances, business interests so loudly lament. The principle of laissez faire is not extended to river systems, for example, and certainly not to processes that measure change in terms of geological time.

What, then, is the endgame of development conceived as a matter of planned, strategic investment in the region's resources? While thinking about the language of development, it is impossible to ignore the mixed metaphor at work here—to develop is to unwrap, to invest is to clothe. On one hand, we strive to strip away nature's disguises (e.g. to extract mineral wealth), on the other we are driven to endow what is naked and needy with dignity, agency, grace and power. Obviously, these twinned goals of development enjoy an uneasy alliance and there is an extreme ambiguity about the way they are deployed. Investment in what is already well endowed (projects that harness the earth's mineral or energy) is not recuperative but is driven by the profit motive. In this case, investment disguises a certain lack of vision, concealing the possibility of handling where we live differently. Equally, the continuing viability of the developmental society depends on an environment that is not entirely divested of its value (through overexploitation). Whatever the societal El Dorado these practices envisage, it is clear that it will be dogged by confusion unless the language of their economic utopianism is sorted out. What—to introduce a variation on the development/investment dialectic—is the relationship between folding out (as in, folding out the map) and folding up (as in, the collapse of a business)? Is there another way of thinking about change, one in which folding out means something like spreading and folding up means an act of bending that brings formerly distant surfaces together?

Ocean Connections, a research conversation convened as part of the Cooperative Research Network (CRN), responded to this question of thinking about development differently by relocating development both conceptually and environmentally. Conceptually, the rhetoric of development in Northern Australia embodies what I have elsewhere called 'dry thinking', where the ground of thinking is idealised as a flat, dry and featureless *terra nullius* available for exclusive occupation, division and development (Carter, 2008b). Ocean Connections proposed a conversation between planning, the creative arts, the ecosciences and Indigenous knowledge systems and practices that was, in contrast, characterised by 'humid thinking' (p. 76). As already implied, this proposition had a strong geographical analogue—to think more fluidly about development is also to redefine the environment of development. Instead of thinking of development in terms of separable spatial units, whose functionality is directly linked to their consistency, dryness and passivity, humid thinking would bring into play environments usually regarded as too indefinite or shifting to be of strategic value. In illustration of this, we pointed to the land/water zones of Northern Australia, the coasts, estuaries, offshore currents and inland distributary systems—these may be essential to the vitality of natural systems and the resilience of human ones, but they are largely thought about (for development purposes) in dry terms.

A dry approach to environmental management is not only conceptually and environmentally impoverished but reflects the outdated disciplinary foundations of the technical knowledge underpinning governance of the public domain. Although they obviously overlap, different federal, state and territory departments are responsible respectively for health; the environment, tourism, recreation; and infrastructure. Periodically, attempts are made to find common ground (as documented elsewhere in this book) but the 'dry' mentality, which places operational self-consistency over any consideration of large societal value, means that these overtures tend to fail. This failure rests on the larger failure of our teaching and research institutions to shoulder the task of rethinking the disciplines. Ocean Connections was a pragmatic response to this intellectual desiccation—in placing artists at the heart of discussion about alternative environmental governance practices, it accepted the argument that:

> The topography of thinking is drying out. And the thinkers are implicated in this. They have dematerialized the medium of thought—language. They have tried to dry up the wellsprings of memory that inform speaking and writing, and reduce language to an instrument of rational communication. They have eliminated

> the poetic dimensions of language that allow it to flow—from one idea to another, from one mouth to another. They have taken the liquid syllables of living words and, in the presses of their arguments, dried them out like flowers between sheets of blotting paper. (Carter, 2008b, p. 77)

These general claims have a particular resonance in the context of Ocean Connections where, first, multidisciplinary approaches to fragile environment management and design already exist and where, second, the rationalisation of such approaches is often figurative or poetic. So well established, for example, is the combination of Indigenous and non-Indigenous environmental management methods and practices in eastern Arnhem that the Yolngu 'refer to the two way approach as *ganma*—like brackish water which combines saltwater and freshwater' (Ens., 2012, p. 47). The application of the concept of *ganma* to a bicultural environmental management strategy illustrates the point that intellectual fluidity brings into being different fields of action and interaction. Banduk Marika remarks, 'We do not make a distinction between land and sea in the same way as Ngapaki do when talking about country; it is all country' (Marika et al., 2012, p. 136). This country is neither dry nor wet but is the combination of these qualities. Likewise, this way of thinking about country, which habitually combines qualities rather than separating them out, is not only absorptive; it extends its sense of the world through a kind of capillary action until its realm of action and responsibility links up to universal coordinates of time and space. The *Yolnguwu Monuk Gapu Wänga Sea Country Plan*, subtitled *A Yolngu Vision and Plan for Sea Country Management in North-East Arnhem Land, Northern Territory* (Dhimurru, 2006), states:

> Ancestral Spirit beings of the Yirritja and Dhuwa moieties created us and the known world—the celestial bodies, land, sea, living plants and animals. The journeys of these ancestral creators crisscrossed the sea and the land creating the land and the seascape and breathing life into the living things that inhabit it ... From these ancestral journeys and the network of important sites created across land and sea, we gain our names, our identity, and our way of life. (Verran, 2007, p. 7)

The relational philosophies of north Australian peoples find parallels around the limits of the Ocean Connections zone of interest. Originally inspired by an invitation to consider sustainable design solutions for a severely compromised river system in Chennai, and migrating to conversations about the sea-land governance of estates in West Sulawesi, Ocean Connections has repeatedly encountered humid geographies whose capacity to crisscross elementally distinct land and seascapes is predicated on the human analogy. Instead of positing a sharp distinction between human and non-human cultures, the middle ground of environmental exploration, exchange and care is populated with symbolic forms that provide mythopoetic proof of an ultimate reciprocity between the world and human interests. These understandings of place perceive a complexly interwoven system of relations that underwrite the vitality of the environment and that should inform everyday social praxis. In the context of a reorientation from dry, functionalist management practices towards participatory, relational and self-actualising senses of place, relational philosophies suggest how multifactorial strategies for habitat maintenance and renewal can be put in place.

In 2007, the distinguished Australian architect Greg Burgess and I were invited to conceptualise and design a bridge for the Adyar Poonga recuperative ecology project in Chennai, Tamil Nadu. This project exemplified stresses and strains between Western-style administrative managerialism and community-based cultural understandings of place with which we are quite familiar in the Top End. In writing the reverse brief, I noted some other familiar biases and omissions from the proposed recuperation strategy. Given the downstream pre-estuarine Adyar was brackish and, in particular, composed of a fractal pattern of shallow flows, porous edges and tidal meanders, it was an oversight not to articulate the character of these edges. In the classic Tamil period, the Tamil land was divided into five kinds of country. One of these was the 'Neydal, the coastal or littoral tract'. This was not simply a physiographic tract but denoted a distinctive mode of behaviour ('Tinai'), social or moral. The notion of Tinai comprised 'the features of the plant life as well as of the human beings, their tribes, and clans and the gods and religious ideas … In fact, each of the regions was conceived as a total web of life in itself' (Pillay, 1975, p. 164).

This web of life ontology assumed a new significance and poignancy a few months later when the tsunami overwhelmed our project—and dumped a tent village of tsunami survivors on the beach immediately outside the heads. In this complex (multifactorial) situation of traumatic change, what was the function of the bridge? How might a bridge not span water, starting and finishing in dry land, but become something different? Yolngu people understand that the vitality of places resides in their humid potential to interconnect, in their possessing a track that embodies their vitality, so that places come alive through the spirit that moves across and through them. 'The two names for the open sea are the names of multiple ancestral spirits that flow along the coast to join with the waters of the open sea' (Magowan, 2005, p. 79). We are told that 'The perceptions of water are fluid and ambiguities depending on context and a person's ancestral affiliation reflecting the many faces of those looking at it' (p. 80). The Manybuynga and Rulyapa currents are forms of connectivity, not so much in-between places as stretches of vitality. They cannot be defined in terms of hard-and-fast boundaries—they cross salt and freshwater edges, walls with interiors like snakes. Moving inside themselves, the currents are the jointure of the sea, the darker colour suggesting muscular depth. Local knowledge of this kind cannot be used as a template for ecological rehabilitation elsewhere, but, in the context of Ocean Connections, it cannot help but raise important questions about the environmental assumptions underlying Western-style infrastructure renewal projects. How does a bridge become a web? How does a web flow?

Different topographies will inspire different personifications, narratives and strategies. Zerner (2003, p. 66) said this about the beliefs Mandar people of West Sulawesi hold about oceanic connections:

> While the edge of the sea is haunted by a restless, ceaselessly moving female *spirit, the shallow waters, reefs, coasts,* and promontories are inhabited by unpredictable, shape-shifting guardians. These regions are watched over and governed by potentially cruel spirits known as the 'guardians of the points' (B.M. *pukammi tanjung*).

The skills needed to navigate this unpredictable anthropomorphised archipelago are also those needed to locate shoals of fish and, more generally, to manage an environment of constant change and intermittent tumult. Any suggestion that non-Western environmental philosophies such as these are quietist or perennial can be rejected—articulated in terms of energetic flows and powerful resistances, they are adept at handling crisis, riding change and negotiating the unexpected.

Translated into infrastructure provision, the developmental imperative organises investment through the mechanism of the master plan. Master plans define the spaces of operations in terms of a jigsaw of ideally flat territories. These divisions correspond to the capitalistic need to quantify opportunity, risk and return. A comparable social economy is imagined: flows are contained and enclosures of reception designed; relationships are discounted as existing between projects—spatial connectivity, on the other hand, is synonymous with social progress. Evidently, a fluid understanding of place making and design means far more than a late recognition of different Indigenous epistemologies (and their perhaps illegitimate appropriation). It involves a reclassification of living spaces in terms of their relational infrastructure—their active flows, exchanges, and spatio-temporally active arrangements and rearrangements. More than this, an altered conception of development involves a reinvigorated discourse of development.

To reconceptualise places actively, in terms of spiritual, social and biological reciprocities, is, in linguistic terms, to foreground analogy and metaphor. More profoundly, it acknowledges that processes of place management may be indistinguishable from outcomes. Protocols for the maintenance of fragile environments may be scarcely different from the practice of their navigation. In temporal terms, the object is not to jettison the present and bring forward the future. It is to extend the envelope of the present to incorporate the rhythmic order of time. A Sea Breeze Dreaming in Marri Ammu language from the Kimberley runs, in English, 'Oh, brother Sea Breeze, he is eternally making himself active right here and now' (Marett, 2005, pp. 27–28). The words translated in this way mean 'he makes himself active', 'he has done it forever' and 'right here and now'. Here grammatically articulated is a fluid, 'self-manifesting and eternally active nature' that corresponds to Heraclitus' Logos. Becoming is merged into the temporal extension and differentiation of the present through the performance of the singer. Asked what the Marri Ammu term translated as 'he makes himself active' meant, a leading *wannga* dancer, Ambrose Piarlum, 'stood up and danced its meaning. By rotating a cloth held in his hand … he performed in that place and in that moment the self-manifesting nature of the Tjerri's wind activity' (Marett, 2005, p. 28).

A performance of this kind might be thought to be entirely local. It has the piquancy of an anecdote but cannot generate the kinds of general principle associated with planned development. In reality, it not only expresses a collective sensibility; when brought into dialogue with other cultures that identify environmental wellbeing with human self-actualisation, it makes concrete a philosophy of flow simultaneously social and environmental. To put it another way, the performative praxis is born of the place where it happens—it does without the metaphysicalist ground of Western instrumental logic (whose colonial counterpart is the exclusively held territory). The *Tjerri* or Sea Breeze Dreaming (*ngirrwat*) has a site and 'Both humans and non-human phenomena born of these sites are seen as incarnations of the *ngirrwat*' (Marett, 2005, p. 28). Because these places speak, they connect. They are ground, they do not need to be grounded. Where there are cliffs, there are caves (p. 31). The sense is of continuous production at and of that place through a concomitant act of self-actualisation. And this *relational* reality—in the double sense of being mediated through story and mediating passage between elements and places—produces, geographically speaking, a region of care, one defined in terms of tidal returns.

In her book *Reef Passions*, Allen (in press, p. 17) writes about 'Coral reef communities of land and sea' in the Mediterranean and in West Sulawesi. Noting that in early etymologies the word 'island' had nothing to do with 'isolation' but signified 'watery lands', she characterises them as formed of 'multitudinous crossings'. She goes further, imagining landfall entirely from the point of view of oceanic energy transfer. It is, as she indicates, a reversal of perspectives that dry thinkers are likely to find dizzying:

> The practice of thinking water from water while suspended in the rapid churning, entrapments, disruptions and stillness of the most voluminous through flow of water on the planet occasions a perturbation of the mindscapes that conjoin human and marine dimensions. Amazingly, the currents' circumnavigation of the more than 17,000 islands, along with the underwater trenches, basins, channels, ridges, shelves, and sills, which form Indonesia, consumes so much energy that it slows the spinning of the globe. (p. 132)

From a less marine, coastal perspective, Allen describes an archipelagic reconfiguration of geographical, cultural and social relations. Hence, according to Hamzić (2012, p. 158), 'the world's largest archipelagic state' (Indonesia) exhibits a distinct 'cultural and spiritual plurality':

> The turbulent tides of trading, migration and warfare have raged along their shores for centuries, moulding syncretic ethnoscapes, wherein an islandic self is dynamically negotiated between the allegiance to local narratives and the need to adjust to foreign winds, be they of Indic, Arab, colonial European or some other more or less distant origin.

It is interesting to compare this outlook with the continentalist definition of Australian identity prevalent in Australia's political rhetoric and media stereotypes. 'Archipelagic thinking', in Glissant's (1997, p. 31) formulation:

> flows along with the course of our worlds. It borrows from their ambiguity, fragility, and derivativeness. It accepts the practice of détour, which is neither escape nor renouncement … Is it to renounce self-government? No, it is to accord with that which, from the world, has diffused into the archipelagos precisely, the diversities in expanse, which nevertheless gather the shores and marry the horizons.

Fluid relations correspond to the humid constitution of the archipelagic environment. They stem from a classification of country that respects its amphibious nature, and that aligns its cultural, social and political practices with the creative turbulence of currents, tides, flows and their multitudinous crossings. As Langton (2006, p. 154) writes in another context, 'Along with other features of the natural world, the estuarine zone is not just a bio-physical feature, but a metaphorical reference to knowledge'. Sullivan (2014, p. 161), noting that in the Yawuru community of Broome 'Use of land is not distinct from use of the sea', emphasised the complementarity of environmental and social behaviour:

> Off the coast there are areas of shallows stretching for several kilometres out to sea which are mud flats at extreme low tides and permit wading to reefs and sandbars. It is an area, then, where water, salt and fresh, is a constant, and constantly changing features of the people's lives. (pp. 161–162)

Responsive to these circumstances, 'the adaptation favoured by the Yawuru is flexibility in the distribution of land and sea rights supported by an ideology of relatedness and common property among those of the same and related languages' (p. 162).

In the context of a developmentalist discourse, these countercultures and counter-environments represent a significant choice. The political geography of the archipelagic mindset can be ignored and each community land/seascape treated as an isolated challenge to dry-style development. Alternatively, a different understanding of the meaning of development can be fostered, a capacity to work with and alongside what is already changing, self-renewing and related. The fragile environments of the nation-building infrastructure program are products of that program. They are the supplement of water-related environments, communities and traditions that resist enclosure and the desiccation of abstract planning. They resist government from a distance in favour of a tidal arrangement of differences, one that habitually expresses itself in properly performed meetings. In terms of a new approach to planned place making, one that recognises the strength and fragility of humid regions, much can be learnt from the educative function of the Yolngu Garma festival. For the space of potential to be realised, for Garma to become an event place 'where ideas are shared and negotiated in order to facilitate agreement', there needs to be an intensification of interests and alignment. This notion is conceptualised in the Yolngu term *galtha*:

> [a] connecting spot … a spot where people make solid contact with the earth, when they have been brought together from different places, and now they are having a discussion together to agree on a plan of action. Anywhere there is ceremony, there will be *galtha*. Every ceremony must be different, because its art lies in creating that ceremony to specifically reflect the participants and the place and the time. (Marika-Munnungirritj & Christie, 1995, p. 59)

Per Christie (2007), '*Galtha* is at once a moment and a place, a process and a manifestation' (p. 74), 'While a ceremony has a *galtha*, so can individuals have their own *Galtha* when they become truly themselves in line with ancestral imperatives' (p. 75).

Here we can reasonably touch on the issue raised later in this volume, the challenge of developing appropriate planning frameworks for the development of Darwin Harbour. In this case, instead of anticipating the discussion about scaled-up local knowledge models and their application to the production and governance of regions of care, we might ask what role a distinctively coastal (or estuarine) sensibility might play in the *design* of a zone such as this, of obvious strategic value but archipelagic in its humid constitution. One approach might be educative—to design a consultative process where people with convergent interests are brought together from different places, not simply to confer on the future of this place but to relate their own experience. A practical example of this approach is the link the Ocean Connections project has made to the Mellon Foundation–supported Changing Humanities Centers and Institutes/Integrative Graduate Humanities Education and Research Training (CHCI-IGHERT) program *Indigeneity in an expanded field: Transnationality, migration and human/non-human belonging*.[1] Indigeneity, this initiative contends, is due for redefinition and the scope of its meaning

---

1   See Müller & Vuletić (2014) for a report on the September 2014 workshop held at the University of California, Santa Cru.

expanded. Supporting a 'problem-based approach to research, applicable to problems of profound human significance which cannot be definitively resolved by more knowledge or technical measures, but which demand ongoing debate, reinterpretation, reflection on values, and adaptation', this program promotes new alliances between transnational institutions and movements operating across borders and newly emergent transnational networks of Indigenous people themselves (CHCI-IGHERT Program Proposal and Pilot Project, 2014–16).

Another approach, also educative, embodies the ethics and aesthetics of fluid states in the design of a facility that acts as a filter, a meeting place of alternative strategies for the definition, representation, design and maintenance of fragile environments. In this context, Ocean Connections proposes to capture the wealth of material it has generated under the CRN arrangement in Pearl, a virtual exhibition space that also exists as the design concept for a physical building, originally commissioned for construction at the Darwin Waterfront by the Darwin Waterfront Authority.[2] By developing Pearl as a digital facility or online museum, a methodological relationship is established between the themes of the creative research projects exhibited in the virtual gallery and the way these themes are conceptualised, narrated and related. The resulting virtual walk-through of approximately concentric corridors models a knowledge that emerges incrementally in response to the visitor's route. Repeated walk-throughs can be said to perform the process of interfolding different understandings of place. Like the accumulating laminations that form Pearl, concomitant acts of exploration, reflection and renewal draw the visitor-researcher into the path of their own responsibilities.

A work like Pearl conceptualises the coast differently—agreeing with Langton's (2006, p. 154) remark that 'the estuarine zone is not just a biophysical feature, but a metaphorical reference to knowledge', it translates this insight into design terms. To go back to the invitation to design a bridge for the Adyar Poonga project, we argued there that any bridge should be conceptualised as a passage.

> The form of the Adyar estuary is the rationalisation of fluidity. The mingling fresh- and salt-water of estuary produces a complex system of water currents. This operates at different and overlapping temporal scales (daily, seasonal, intermittent), and produces

---

2  See www.materialthinking.com.au for a visual summary of the project.

> a comparably shifting land-water border. So-called 'Quibble Island' was in pre-colonial times not an 'island' but a network of creeks—inter-tidal channels. Relics of this distinctively estuarine environment survive in the low spits in the main river. (Material Thinking, 2007, p. 1)

Further, reimagined as an act of casting, the bridge could be fluid (see Carter, 2002, pp. 140–143, for the 'opening' and 'closing' of the river; see Carter, 2008a, pp. 173–202, for a developed discussion of humid edge design). Referring to the existing bridge built in the colonial period, we wrote:

> When the Elphinstone Bridge was thrown across the Adyar River, the outrage to the river gods can only be imagined: the bridge may have 'opened' a land passage but it 'closed' the passage of water and desecrated the sacred economy of continuous transformational flux associated with life-giving water. To reverse this imprisonment, we need to remake the bridge in the form of a net. (Material Thinking, 2007, p. 2)

Place as passage, self as other or spirit double, orientation as authority and responsibility—these are perceptions of place integral to life in the archipelago. And, in practical terms, they focus attention on the coast, its conceptualisation and inhabitation. An idea of place as a boundary ecology emerges, the wet/dry boundary as a filtration system in which flux is endowed with a network character, as if it could be imagined as a double figure integrating wall and way, fence and flow (see Forman, 1995, p. 82ff, for the concept of 'boundary ecologies' in ecological discourse). The architecture of passage is characterised by knots where different story lines do not simply meet but entangle, hybridise or otherwise activate a principle of mere coincidence to improvise a chiasmatic or riddling formation. To riddle is to speak enigmatically, to veil senses—it is also to sift coarse material. The act of sifting serves to preserve data that do not conform, which for this reason hold the potential to attract new associations or revive old, neglected ones. In design terms, data of this kind are forms that may look strangely familiar but that resist identification. Such forms serve as hinge works, mediating between different physical states, diverse story lines and cultures of settling. In the context of designating a boundary, ecology poles have this function—stylised islands, mooring posts, palisades, sticklike figures, gills and nets—they are twinned in this typology with hollows, bays, ears, shells and other sail-like receptacles materialising the history of passage.

It is evident that these signatures of passage localise, materialise and connect, but the sense of place they might incubate does not correspond to the 'place making' rhetoric of the master planned urban environment. The inhabitant of this networked place experiences the suspension of settlement, the creative and recreative potential of passage to produce out of chiasmatic events ambiguous settings. These offer creative templates not for the restoration of invariant cultural stereotypes but for things to take place. Staged here is the setting of exchange rates and the shadows cast by the processes of filtering, selecting, classifying and quarantining essential to the constitution of stable forms and identities. These are clearly choreographies with a global application, but they educate not by leading out from the neighbourhood but by marking and re-marking exploratory *sentiers* amid it. These *sentiers* are not paths yet. In fact, they may never evolve into signposted ways through the labyrinth. Passage here will have the same oscillatory nature as breathing; always timed and placed, always expressive, relational, dependent and poised between inspiration and expiration. Such emotionally engaging networks of *sentiers* as these suggest what Hokari refers to in Gurindji philosophy as the 'Right Way'—where a design is ethical not because it successfully cites traditions associated with the place but because it rightly orients people, teaching them 'how to look after this created world' (Hokari, 2005, pp. 216–217).

In encouraging dialogue between Indigenous place-based knowledge systems, and between these and the frontier rhetoric of development, Ocean Connections aspires to inaugurate a new orientation. In this, environments classified as fragile or, indeed, as lacking clear identity not only come into view as primary sites of cultural and biological biodiversity, they assume an ontological and epistemological value. They ground human relations differently, archipelagically. They correspond to forms of governance that are flexible, performative, localised but regional. The potential of this reconceptualisation to influence the political, administrative and legal cultures whose dry thinking currently dominates Northern Australia's development remains to be seen. The constructive critique will need to be pursued directly, through the demonstration of alternative approaches to the theory and practice of place making, and indirectly through the application of humid thinking to such inter-related areas as archipelagic geographies and performative, relational governance practices.

# References

Allen, J. (in press). *Reef passions: Postcolonial aesthetics between coral reefs*.

Carter, P. (2002). *Repressed spaces: The poetics of agoraphobia*. London, England: Reaktion Books.

Carter, P. (2008a). *Dark writing, geography, performance, design*. Honolulu, HI: University of Hawai'i Press.

Carter, P. (2008b, Winter). Trockenes Denken: vom Verlust des Wasserbewustseins und von der Poesie des Fluiden [Dry thinking: On praying for rain]. *Lettre International*, 76–81.

Christie, M. (2007). Yolngu language habitat: Ecology, identity and law in an Aboriginal society. In G. Leitner & I. G. Malcolm (Eds), *The habitat of Australia's Indigenous Languages: Past, present and future* (pp. 57–78). Berlin, Germany; New York, NY: Mouton De Gruyter.

Changing Humanities Centers and Institutes (CHCI)/Integrative Graduate Humanities Education and Research Training (IGHERT) Program Proposal and Pilot Project. (2014–16). *Indigeneity in an expanded field: Transnationality, migration, and human/non-human belonging*. University of California, Santa Cruz, 2014–2016.

Dhimurru. (2006). *Yolnuwu Monak Gapu Wana sea country plan: A Yolngu vision and plan for sea country management in North-East Arnhem Land, Northern Territory*. Dhimurru Land Management Aboriginal Corporation.

Ens, E. (2012). Conducting two-way ecological research. In J. Altman & S. Kerins (Eds), *People on Country: Vital landscapes, Indigenous futures* (pp. 26–64). Sydney, NSW: Federation Press.

Forman, R. T. T. (1995). *Land mosaics: The ecology of landscapes and regions*. Cambridge, England: Cambridge University Press.

Glissant, É. (1997). *Traité du tout-monde*. Paris: Gallimard.

Hamzić, V. (2012). Unlearning human rights and false grand dichotomies: Indonesian archipelagic selves beyond sexual/gender universality. *Jindal Global Law Review*, 4(1), 157–170.

Hokari, M. (2005). Gurindji mode of historical practice. In *AIATSIS Conference 2002: The power of knowledge and the resonance of tradition* (pp. 214–222). Canberra, ACT: AIATSIS Press.

Langton, M. (2006). Earth, wind, fire, water: The social and spiritual construction of water in Aboriginal societies. In B. David, B. Barker & I. J. McNiven (Eds), *The social archaeology of Australian Indigenous societies* (pp. 139–160). Canberra, ACT: Aboriginal Studies Press.

Magowan, F. (2005). A sea has many faces: Multiple and contested continuities in Yolngu coastal waters. In L. Taylor, G. K. Ward, G. Henderson, R. Davis & L. A. Wallis (Eds), *The power of knowledge: The resonance of tradition* (pp. 74–85). Canberra, ACT: Aboriginal Studies Press.

Marett, A. (2005). *Songs, dreamings & ghosts: The Wangga of North Australia*. Middletown, CT: Conn Wesleyan University Press.

Marika, B., Munyarryun, B., Munyarryun, B., Marawili, N. & Marika, W. (2012). Ranger djama? Manymak! In J. Altman & S. Kerins (Eds), *People on Country: Vital landscapes, Indigenous futures* (pp. 132–145). Sydney, NSW: Federation Press.

Marika-Munnungirritj, R. & Christie, M. J. (1995). Yolngu metaphors for learning. *International Journal of the Sociology of Language*, *113*(1), 59–62.

Material Thinking. (2007, 29 August). 'Adyar Poonga: Creative Inceptions 2', 1–3. Available from the author.

Müller, F.-M. & Vuletić, S. (2014). IGHERT Project Workshop at the Institute for Humanities Research. University of California, Santa Cruz, 19-20 September Retrieved from www.uni-giessen.de/faculties/gcsc/newsboard/ighert-project-workshop

Pillay, K. K. (1975). *A social history of the Tamils* (Vol. 1). Madras, India: University of Madras.

Sullivan, P. (2014). Salt water, fresh water and Yawuru social organization. In N. Peterson & B. Rigsby (Eds), *Customary marine tenure in Australia* (pp. 159–180). Sydney, NSW: Sydney University Press.

Verran, H. (2007, 29–31 August). *Contemporary Australian NRM as nature/culture dichotomy amnesia. How can we do politics of nature without politics or nature?* Paper presented at Performing Nature at World's Ends, Department of Social Anthropology, University of Oslo, Norway.

Zerner, C. (2003). Sounding the Makassar Strait: The poetics and politics of an Indonesian marine environment. In C. Zerner (Ed.), *Culture and the question of rights: Forests, coasts, and seas in Southeast Asia* (pp. 56–108). Durham, NC: Duke University Press.

# Section 5

# Thriving in Northern Climates

Linda Rosenman

Climatic conditions are widely viewed as having negative implications for the development of Northern Australia. Against a backdrop of predictions of major climate changes, the chapters in this section consider the climate of the region and its implications for human living and working conditions and the future economic development of Northern Australia. All authors identify adaptive strategies to reduce the impacts and mitigate the negative effects of climatic extremes to facilitate people living and working healthily in Northern Australia. Since Northern Australia encompasses almost half of the Australian landmass, the climatic variation is considerable; however, it is broadly characterised by extremes of temperature and (in coastal areas) of humidity and a marked hazardscape that includes cyclones, droughts, bushfires and flooding, which are likely to intensify with climate change. Ambitious plans for industrial and agricultural development and population growth will need to be cognisant of the adaptations needed due to climate and the environment to allow people to live and work happily and productively in Northern Australia.

Each of these papers takes a different perspective on northern climates. Chapter 17 (O'Brien et al.) focuses on the high degree of variability in rainfall in Northern Australia and shows that while advocates for development in Northern Australia claim that water is plentiful and rainfall reliable for intensive agricultural development, the rainfall record indicates otherwise. There is a high degree of variability in the timing of rainfall annually and over decadal and longer time periods. Reflecting rainfall patterns, stream and river flows are also extremely variable and heavily influenced by land use patterns, including diversion for agricultural production. The policy implications of climate variability for Northern Australia need to distinguish between climate variability, climate change and extreme weather events. They also suggest that large-scale changes to land and water use such as for intensive agriculture or to house growing populations is likely to have significant additional impacts on river flows and water quality.

Chapter 18 (Buergelt et al.) focuses on how to build viable and resilient communities in Northern Australia in the context of its extreme hazardscapes. They suggest that the unique social and environmental conditions in Northern Australia are ideal for utilising natural hazards to facilitate the sustained development of adaptive, competent and thriving communities. By focusing on developing community capacity to capitalise on social and environmental amenities, the emphasis is on community development, with risk management being explicitly included as part of social and environmental capital building. They suggest that social capital development activities organised around planning for disaster risk reduction, recovery and rebuilding based on community strength and integrating risk management, community and economic development and poverty alleviation can 'kill two birds with one stone'. Building community capital will not only create more disaster-resilient communities but build community connectedness that facilitates attracting and retaining residents in Northern Australia.

To understand Indigenous adaptation to climatic conditions and climate change, Chapter 19 (Zander et al.) reports research with four different Indigenous communities across Northern Australia regarding their observations about changing climate and living conditions, the impact that this might have on their lives and potential adjustments. They suggest that Indigenous communities who are living traditional lifestyles and those in towns are aware of the likely impacts of climate change on their food sources, livelihoods, health and wellbeing. They suggest that the cultural and social capital of Indigenous communities needs to be understood and valued in terms of their adaptability and adaptive strategies to climatic variation. One key to dealing with the climatic extremes and variations is to learn from the Indigenous inhabitants (and the inhabitants of other tropical zones to Australia's immediate north and worldwide) who have adapted to and thrived over millennia in climates comparable to those in Northern Australia.

The high heat and humidity and hazardscape characteristic of Northern Australia and the need to design and build more socially and ecologically sustainable communities create challenges for urban form and housing design. More environmentally appropriate designs must be considered if the expectations of population growth are realised in Northern Australia. Chapter 20 (Law et al.) identifies that urban design and housing standards that have been developed in more temperate climates need to be reimagined for Northern Australia to break the current pattern of reliance on high energy use in the form of car travel and use of air conditioning to create comfortable living environments. They conclude that 'current building rating systems assume that air conditioning is essential in tropical conditions and, thus, favour buildings designed to ensure that air conditioners work efficiently'. The authors suggest that buildings and precincts should rather be designed to minimise the use of air conditioning through 'maximising ventilation, shading and green space'.

Imposing national standards, measurements and cultural attitudes towards work practices, urban and housing design and community and social relationships that have evolved in and for temperate climates and for Western industrial societies can exacerbate the difficulties of building viable economies and societies across Northern Australia due to its different climatic, environmental and cultural contexts.

The chapters in this section present a starting point for providing regionally specific analyses of climate to support appropriate measures to enable populations to thrive in Northern Australia.

# 17

# Timing and Climate: Rainfall Variability in Northern Australia

Chris O'Brien, Sara Beavis, Andrew Campbell and Tom Griffiths

People have observed the skies over Northern Australia for millennia. First, Indigenous peoples garnered knowledge linking land, seas and sky. Then, the colonial invaders imported their own ways of seeing and knowing. The two have long existed side by side and the dominance of Western knowledge has, until recently, rendered Indigenous knowledge invisible beyond the Aboriginal population. Depending on your cosmology, we in the north have long experienced a common weather but different climates and seasons in the very same places.

Nevertheless, Western meteorology in Northern Australia has long been of remarkably high quality. The colonial Departments of Astronomy in the colonies of South Australia, Western Australia and Queensland saw to this before the establishment of the Commonwealth Bureau of Meteorology in 1908. The Bureau itself has seen to this since. The first systematic daily weather records for Darwin were taken in March 1869. Records for Katherine, Daly Waters and other NT locations soon followed. Several lines of telegraph wire tied each of these 'outposts' to each other and to the already well-developed meteorological networks in South Australia, Victoria and New South Wales (NSW), and through them to the broader networks throughout the British Empire. Now they bequeath a legacy of millions of pieces of 'local' weather data. Despite this, responding to the federal government's green paper on northern development, the Australian

Academy of Science argued that climate variability in Northern Australia is still so little understood that this deficiency is a barrier to the northern development agenda (Australian Academy of Science, 2014).

How can this be? Millions of data! In recent decades, the Bureau has produced maps of rainfall variability across Australia. As long ago as 1916, the distinguished Geographer Griffith Taylor did the same. During the 1980s, climatologists investigated the timing of both the Wet Season and the Monsoon in Northern Australia (Nicholls et al., 1982; Holland, 1985), albeit with a statistical rather than an analytical historical approach. One answer is that Indigenous knowledge was pushed aside. But there are other important answers in the way we do meteorology, which is one focus of this paper. We will outline historical variability in rainfall for Darwin, Pine Creek, Katherine, Daly Waters, Wyndham, Broome and Burketown. Here we demonstrate variability by showing that the timing of rainfall across the north, historically, has frequently and consistently varied from year to year over a 70-year period. We also look at variability in streamflows in the Elizabeth and Daly river systems. This history illustrates the importance of timing, and volumes, and that time matters on numerous scales. We finish with a discussion of policy implications, especially in light of expected climate change. Variability and cycles are not evidence against anthropogenic climate change; variability is exacerbated by and cycles interact with a warming global atmosphere.

## Ideas

Aboriginal meteorology is characterised by interconnections between events on the land, in rivers and seas and, of course, in the sky. Change of season is not related to the calendar. Clusters of natural events mark changes of season—when certain animal behaviours match particular appearances of plants, when these are accompanied by specific known winds, or kinds of rain or even patterns of rainfall. In Northern Australia, these vary from community to community. So, ideas of season and climate are place based and markedly local. Not being bound to the calendar, these concepts of season allow for variability from year to year, in stark contrast to Western scientific understandings of season. North Australia's Aboriginal and Torres Strait Islander peoples conceive of season and climate in holistic, ecological terms.[1]

---

1   For more see O'Brien (2016).

## 17. TIMING AND CLIMATE

Two compelling ideas infuse the scientific study of weather and climate. Both have somewhat sidelined variability in the meteorological literature. First is the notion of the 'clockwork climate' (O'Brien, 2014), the elegant idea that weather and seasons happen in a timely manner, year after year. The oldest surviving expression comes from the oldest farmer's almanac Hesiod's *Works and Days* dating to the eight century BCE. More examples abound in the corpus of Greek and Roman literature. More than 2,000 years ago, the idea of the four seasons inextricably linked to what we know as the rotation of Earth on its axis became established. The atmospheric clock has long appeared to have a mechanism. The concept has seemed to explain what people experienced. This idea made sense to people in modern times and as Europeans voyaged to other climates they formulated the notion of the wet/dry seasonal dyad for the tropics. Jan Huyghen van Linschotten and Edmund Halley were among early promulgators of this idea during the seventeenth century, though they defined the seasons by wind regimes or monsoons. William Dampier was the first to explicitly identify wet and dry seasons for the tropics. Versions of the clockwork climate for the tropics and temperate zones spread through nautical guides, almanacs and, later, popular press. Not merely an idea, this was something people lived. It organised trade, travel, farming, commerce, festivals for centuries. It shaped individual and communal life and was integral to how people made sense of the natural and cultural world. Empirical observation here and throughout Australia was organised by this powerful concept, not used to test its veracity. Unsurprisingly, Darwin's weather-watcher extraordinaire J. A. G. Little, in 1902, said of the Top End's weather that 'the different changes of these seasons are so uniform and regular that they may be predicted to almost a day' (Little, cited in Taylor, 1918, p. 70). Even now, local media in Darwin effectively do the same thing every 1 October when they declare a change of season irrespective of the weather. Weather has long been seen to have an almost precise regularity, more so than empirical evidence supports. Through this conceptual lens, variability is sometimes difficult to see as a significant aspect of climate.

The second idea is virtually a statistical version of the first. Before meteorology incorporated hydrodynamics and thermodynamics in the first quarter of the twentieth century, it was, practically, a statistical discipline. After the 'physical turn', averages for rainfall, temperature, humidity and any element that can be measured and enumerated remain at the core of weather and climate study. But means have long borne a compelling meaning. In the early 1800s, Belgian Astronomer Royal Adolphe Quetelet argued that in a distribution of measurements of multiple observations, individual readings contain error but the mean, provided sufficient measurements—this reflects reality (Hacking, 1990). Philosopher Ian Hacking showed in his work *Taming of Chance* that this concept became a template for understanding measurable phenomena throughout the nineteenth century and for much of the twentieth. It is certainly evident in Australian weather records through to the 1980s. The mean indicated true rainfall, temperature etcetera and a mean of means revealed climate. Variation was understood as deviation from an idealised norm. Reality/normality was indicated by a point, not ranges or distributions. Through these understandings, the statistical practices of meteorology occluded variability. In a dominant mechanistic metaphysics where weather and climate were seen as repeating on an annual basis according to Earth's rotation on its axis and, hence, tied to the calendar, climatic variability was often seen as variation—sets of singular aberrations not part of an elemental pattern.

## Realities

Experience, however, often challenges the conceptual. In the mid-nineteenth century, George Goyder grappled with rainfall variability in South Australia in drawing a line to demarcate places of reliable rainfall from those of unreliable rains. During the 1880s, Charles Todd and his counterparts in NSW, Victoria and India corresponded about weather teleconnections[2] between Australia and India after observing remarkable rainfall variability. Geographer Griffith Taylor calculated rainfall variability across Australia in the 1910s and, with perhaps the most comprehensive understanding of Australia's climates at the time, argued that this continent had a limited carrying capacity. Griffith Taylor and Goyder bore inconvenient truths that were sidelined by politics. The teleconnections studied by Todd and colleagues were the start of a long process that eventually led to the revelation of El Niño–Southern Oscillation (ENSO). But since there was then no explanatory mechanism for their observations, they were seen as deviations rather than as part of a variable climate that worked over cycles of 3–8 years.

---

2   Teleconnections are large-scale climatic anomalies in air pressure and atmospheric pressure usually manifesting in prolonged periods of drought or flood across a variety of large-scale regions.

Variability is more visible now. But it is studied in limited ways. Variability has been applied to volumes. The formula is 90th percentile to 10th percentile readings divided by the median. This is useful but conceals temporal variability. When do rains come? What are the consequences on the land? These are issues that play out on a variety of timescales, not just the calendar month or calendar year at the core of so much weather and climate research. To make sense of temporal variability, this chapter notes the 10th and 90th percentiles of the timing of a particular milestone. So, if the data set extends to a period of 70 years, the date by which the seven earliest and from which the seven latest instances occur is noted. With records spanning 50 years, the corresponding times for the five earliest and the five latest are highlighted. Where seasons are defined as lasting six months, we posit that a difference of one month is a reasonable mark of variability. The greatest consequences of variability are ecological—the critical points at which timing of rain would cause significant impact differ from plant to plant, animal to animal, crop to crop and season to season. Given this, it is more useful now to outline the variability rather than calculate any one-size-fits-all statistics. In any case, the need to look at timing of rains and variability is evident.

First, a word on the data.[3] To avoid confounding with rainfall variability, most data date to when anthropogenic climate change is understood to have had minimal influence. Climatologists have no standard definition of the onset of the wet (Nicholls et al., 1982). To examine rainfall variability then, across time, we look at four rainfall milestones. The first is simply the timing of first rains, which is important enough to feature in north Australia–based fiction of authors such as Xavier Herbert and Jeannie Gunn. Rainfall histories reveal a temporal variability at odds with the clockwork climate. Between 1871 and 1941, the earliest seven first rains in Darwin came before 15 July and the latest seven from mid-October, with a range from 1 July to 16 November. Three months separates the earliest 10 per cent from the latest 10 per cent.

Usually comprising numerous rain events, the date when 50 mm of cumulative rain from the start of the seasons is a more reliable measure. Variability is still evident; the earliest seven came on or before 7 October and the latest seven from 27 November, three of which were well into

---

3   Unless otherwise stated, all data is from the Bureau of Meteorology, Climate Data Online.

December. Seven weeks span the differences between the earliest and latest 10 per cent of instances. The range runs from 24 September to 13 December.

We still see marked variability for the timing of 100 mm cumulative rain; the earliest came on 6 October and the latest on 26 December, with the seven earliest by 25 October and the seven latest from 8 December. This is still a big difference in timing—six weeks between the earliest 10 per cent and the latest 10 per cent. Crucially, this is six weeks at a time of maximum insolation and evaporation, which gives such variability enormous ecological significance. Figure 17.1 illustrates the historical variability of this marker. Last rains are also variable in timing. The earliest seven (or 10 per cent) came mid-April or earlier and the latest seven (or 10 per cent) from mid-June, ranging from 9 April 9 to 30 June.

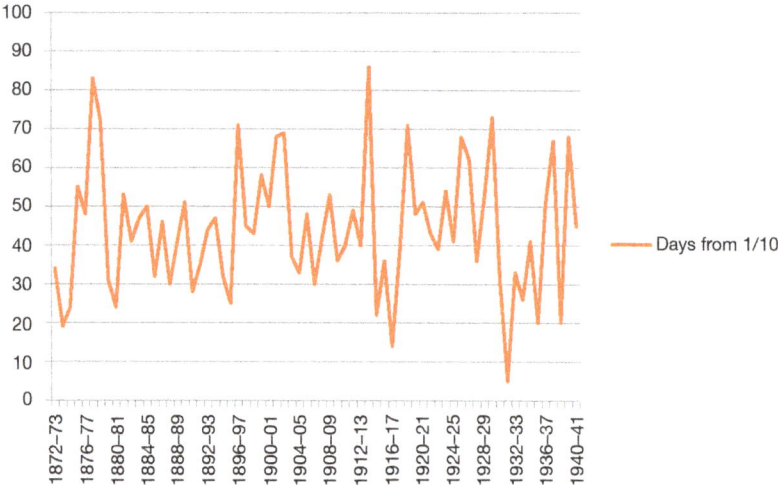

**Figure 17.1: Darwin Post Office, temporal variability 100 mm cumulative rains.**

Note: The x-axis indicates years, the y-axis the number of days from 1 October that the 100 mm cumulative volume was reached. Defining wet season onset as the date when 100 mm of rain has been recorded we see large variability in its timing and that it frequently happens long after 1 October.

Source: Chris O'Brien, original research.

Records across the north tell the same story.

The timing of rain has varied remarkably from one year to another at Pine Creek, 250 km inland from Darwin. Between 1890 and 1941, the first rains come as early as 1 July and as late as 6 November. The earliest five occasions happened on or before 9 July and the latest five on or after 29 October. The 50 mm cumulative mark was reached as early as 26 September and on five occasions had been reached by 12 October. Five times it came on or after 24 November, with the latest being 18 December. The range for the 100 mm cumulative mark is 8 October to 28 December, with the five earliest happening by 22 October and the five latest from 9 December onwards. Rain fell as late as 29 June, with the five latest occasions being on or after 17 June. Yet, there were five years when rains had stopped by 28 March, one of which saw last rains on 14 March. For all milestones, the differences between the earliest and latest 10 per cent of instances was at least six weeks and, more typically, more than two months.

Rainfall at Daly Waters, 600 km south of Darwin, showed similar year on year differences between 1880 and 1941. First rains came as early as 1 July and as late as 13 November. On the six earliest occasions, the six earliest rains (10 per cent) had fallen by 12 July and the six latest on or after 31 October. In six of these years, the 50 mm cumulative mark for rainfall had been reached by 7 October and during another six it was not reached until 8 December or after, with a range of 27 August to 8 January. The 100 mm cumulative mark came as early as 4 October and as late as 25 February. Six times this happened by 15 November and another six not until 29 December or after. Last rains have fallen as late as 30 June and rain has ceased as early as 25 February. Six times rains have stopped as early as 18 March and six times they have come on 21 June or later. On each measure, the earliest and latest 10 per cent of instances have happened at least two months apart from each other.

Temporal variability is clear from records taken at Burketown, in Queensland's Gulf Country, between 1888 and 1941. For first rain, the range is 2 July – 2 November with the earliest five, or 10 per cent, by 24 July and the latest five from 14 November onwards. For the 50 mm cumulative mark, five times was reached by 12 November and five times on or after 3 January, ranging from 8 October – 26 January. For five years during this period, 100 mm of accumulated rain had fallen by 27 November, once occurring as early as 13 November. In five years, this point was not reached until 27 January or later and once as late as 19 February. Last rain fell as early as 21 February and as late as 30 June. Five times it had fallen by 21 March, another five it came on 22 June or later. Again, the typical difference between the earliest and latest 10 per cent of instances was two months.

Between 1898 and 1941, rainfall at Wyndham, in the north-east Kimberley, shows something similar. First rains came as early as 1 July, on four occasions (10 per cent) coming by 16 July. First rains have fallen as late as 11 November, and 6 November or later in four years. In four years, 50 mm of rain had accumulated by 7 November. Four other years saw this not happen until 18 December or later, ranging from 9 October to 10 January. The 100 mm mark was reached as early as 14 November and as late as 7 February. Four times this happened by 28 November and four times on or after 10 January. In four years, last rains have come by 2 April, and another in four from 24 June, with a range from 15 March to 26 June. For all milestones, the difference between the earliest and latest 10 per cent of occurrences is six weeks or longer.

These indices tell a story largely untold in the meteorological literature of the time. The timing of rain is subject to enormous temporal variability across Northern Australia. Rainfall records contradict received ideas of the region's climates. It is wrong, however, to infer from these records that wet seasons are necessarily longer than people have thought, as implied by first rains in July and last rains in June. First and last rains are singular events. In a place of such intense insolation and potent evaporation it is overall patterns of rain—the shape of seasons—that matters ecologically. Regrettably, determining these shapes is beyond the scope of this chapter. The natural environment is dynamic and contingent. Organisms have slowly evolved to function within particular ranges and these relate to timing and duration. In a place where solar radiation bakes the environment with fierce intensity, follow-up rains matter as much as volumes. A season with recurrent periods of rain will create a remarkably different environment to one with only one brief burst or one with long enough gaps between rain to desiccate the land. Statistics yield vital information but they smooth away these contingencies. History is about contingency, the particular and the uncertain and so is ideally suited to investigating the shapes of seasons and the complexities of weather, climate and the broader environment.

Policies that ignore rainfall variability are likely to be mugged by reality. Regrettably, amnesia has long characterised discussions about northern development. Historian Libby Robin (2007) devoted an entire chapter to this in her book *How a Continent Created a Nation*. Past failures are forgotten so crucial lessons go begging—chiefly that development needs to be geared to the ecological limitations of particular locales. Rainfall variability is integral to this. In a region where insolation is so fierce that even a modest delay in the timing of rain can be lethal for stock and crops, weeks actually matter. Successful policies must be sensitive to the decisive effects of rainfall variability across time and space throughout Northern Australia. Successful policies must incorporate hard-won knowledge that has been forgotten or ignored. They must also heed new work that identifies the historical intricacies of the region's ecologies. Unless weather and climate are properly understood—on a variety of timescales—they are likely to continue to undermine all large-scale initiatives, just as they have done throughout the post-invasion history of Northern Australia.

## Longer Cycles

Climate variability also happens on much larger timescales. It occurs not only at seasonal but also interannual and decadal timescales as responses to the Indian Ocean Dipole and the ENSO. Less well known is a much larger oscillation in annual rainfall thought to occur over a 50–100-year cycle. Kraus (1955) first noted this pattern in coastal NSW, where the latter part of the nineteenth century was wetter than the first half of the twentieth century. Later studies have shown that an increasingly wetter phase occurred in the second half of the twentieth century and it now appears that eastern and south-eastern Australia are entering the next drying phase now. Over approximately 100 years, there are alternating drying and wetting periods demarcated by tipping points at which a change occurs over a very short period of time. For these regions, phase change at those tipping points has been associated with severe, prolonged drought (the Federation and Millennium droughts) and major flooding in the 1950s. Plotting data for Katherine and Daly Waters (from 1900–2013), with overlays for Broome and Darwin (from 1941–2013), demonstrates a similar long-term oscillation, despite a short perturbation in the 1980s (see Figure 17.2). The tipping points for Northern Australia occurred around 1910 and 1971–74, a lag of approximately 15–20 years with eastern Australia. The first tipping point around 1910 reflected a change to drying that lasted until the early 1970s, when the next shift occurred to an increasingly wetter regime. Conditions are still wetting up, but if the lag with the eastern states is an indication then the next tipping point could be expected in the next 10 years.

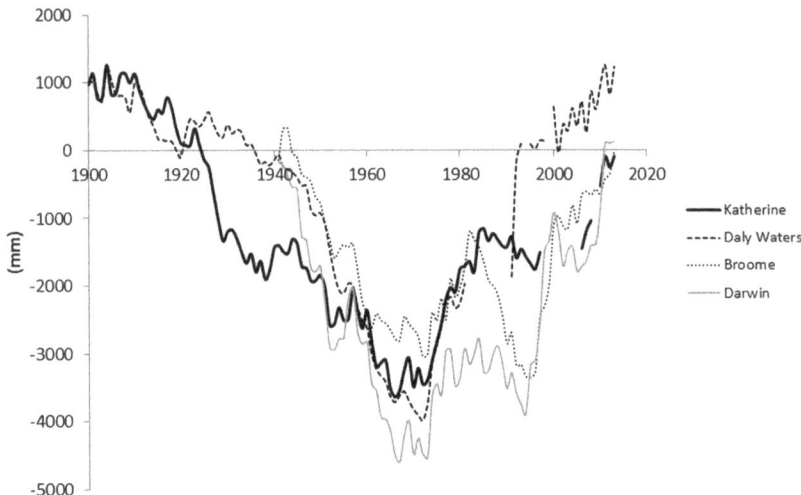

**Figure 17.2: Long-term trends in rainfall for Katherine and Daly Waters (1900–2013) and Darwin and Broome (1940–2013).**

Note: Figures along y-axis represent cumulative departure of annual rainfall from long-term annual mean. Increasingly wet conditions are depicted by a rising limb and increasingly dry conditions by a falling limb.

Source data: Bureau of Meteorology (2014); Sara Beavis, original research.

## Variable Rivers

For Northern Australia, the percentage of rainfall that is converted to streamflow varies from 60 per cent along the coast to less than 3 per cent inland. Unlike in the Murray-Darling, most runoff is generated in the lower catchment rather than in upland regions. Monsoonal troughs and depressions associated with cyclones account for this. Therefore, rainfall patterns, regardless of temporal scale, are reflected in streamflow variability; higher flows occur during wet periods and lower or no flows during dry periods.

Hydrological gauging networks are less extensive and more recent than meteorological networks in Northern Australia. Nevertheless, 40 to 50 years of records illuminate the salient characteristics of two contrasting river systems in the Northern Territory, the Daly and Elizabeth rivers.

The iconic Daly River is one of the largest perennial streams in Northern Australia. With a total catchment area of over 53,000 km$^2$, the Daly rises in the arid foothills of Arnhem Land and flows ~320 km into the Timor Sea.

Estuarine conditions occur in the final 65 km as the river opens out into a typical funnel-shaped tide-dominated estuary surrounded by abundant tidal flats and salt marshes. Dry season flow is maintained by groundwater discharging from extensive limestone aquifers (the Cambrian Tindal Limestone and Ordovician Oolloo Dolostone), which recharge during the wet season, when some 92 per cent of annual streamflow occurs. This means that the river is flood dependent in the 'Wet' and groundwater dependent in the 'Dry'. These different water sources have distinct physico-chemical properties that affect the nutrient load and primary production in the stream environment. The extreme seasonality also means that the upstream extent of tidal waters, and the associated salinity gradient from seawater to freshwater, varies over tens of kilometres depending on the volume of freshwater flowing down the system across the wet and dry seasons. High-value ecosystems have evolved that are dependent on these rhythmically changing environments, providing habitat to numerous reptile, fish and plant species, including the vulnerable pig-nosed turtle (*Vallismeria nana*) and the giant whip ray (*Himantura dalyensis*). Climate change will likely interfere with these sensitive rhythms.

Significant changes to these flow regimes in terms of the frequency and duration of wet season flood flows and dry season low flows will impact these ecosystems (Georges et al., 2002). With this in mind, the high interannual and interdecadal variability in flow that also mimics rainfall temporal patterns is also important for water-dependent biota at longer timescales.

The Elizabeth River flows into Darwin Harbour, draining a catchment of ~23,000 km². The catchment includes extensive inter-tidal flats and groundwater-fed wetlands in the estuary and low-lying floodplain areas, agriculture, horticulture, urban, peri-urban and industrial land uses. Streamflow is highly seasonal with 98 per cent of annual flow occurring during the Wet and only 2 per cent during the Dry. Conditions of no flow or very low flows characterise the dry season throughout the non-estuarine reaches of the river system. Most of the wet season streamflow is derived from rainfall, with some contributions from groundwater discharging from underlying shallow Cainozoic laterite and Cretaceous sandstone aquifers. In the Dry, flows cease in all but the main river due not only to a lack of rain and surface runoff but the disconnection between the river and the underlying aquifer as groundwater levels drop, so that groundwater flows into the river system cease.

Despite the differences in catchment area, geology, topography and mean annual rainfall, the Daly and Elizabeth river systems share some commonalities when long-term streamflow data are examined. Fifty-year records for the Daly River at Mt Nancar (gauging station #G8140040) and Elizabeth River at Stuart Highway (gauging station #G8150018)[4] show that streamflow mimics climate at a range of scales. For example, rainfall anomalies (that is, the departure of annual rainfall from the long-term mean) closely correlate with the Southern Oscillation Index in both systems (see Figure 17.2). At seasonal scales (again, using long-term data), the distribution of rainfall and runoff follow similar patterns. Although the Daly is perennial, maintaining flows throughout the year, and the Elizabeth is seasonally ephemeral, both systems not only reflect rainfall dominance throughout the wet season but have a one-month lag in stream response to the beginning of the dry season and a two-month lag at its end. This is due to the key role of surface–groundwater connectivity with groundwater continuing to discharge into the streams after the dry season commences, but with steady depletion of the aquifers and lowering of the water table. The very dry catchment conditions when the wet season breaks means that most rainfall infiltrates the soil or is partitioned into evaporation pathways. Until the catchment becomes saturated, streams continue to experience low flow conditions, and in the case of the Elizabeth River the stream and aquifer do not reconnect until sufficient recharge raises the water table to threshold levels.

Streamflow records are not yet long enough to determine whether these two river systems experience 50–100-year oscillatory patterns of rainfall. However, a very close correlation has been observed during the current phase of increasingly wetter conditions since 1992 to 1994.

Both of these systems are vulnerable to land use changes that divert rainfall that is naturally partitioned into streamflow and groundwater recharge. In recent decades, approximately 6 per cent of the total Daly River catchment has been cleared for agricultural land use, with an increase in the number of bore licences issued in areas undergoing development. Pressure to further develop agriculture will increase demand for groundwater extraction during the dry season. This risks reduced streamflows and consequent impacts on water quality, aquatic habitats and cultural values of the river system. In the Elizabeth River catchment, which is undergoing rural and peri-urban

---

4   From Bureau of Meteorology, Climate Data Online.

development, bore data provide clear evidence of water table lowering in response to land use change over the last few decades. Reduced flows will impact water quality and also extend the period over which the river is dry. The hydrogeology of both catchments has been mapped (Verma, 2003; Tickell, 2005) and the ecological risks have been identified (Hart, 2004; Chan et al., 2012). However, a sound understanding of the sustainable yields of the aquifers is yet to be developed.

Policy must anticipate not only the smoothed, typical, expected and normalised aspects of climate, rivers and environment, but also the contingent and the possible, however unlikely. Policy needs to understand how particular improbabilities coalesce to create challenging realities. Historical understanding helps in numerous ways—it uncovers forgotten particulars, gives a sense of the range of the possible and tells of problems already faced and how people have or have not dealt with them. Crucially, history can show comprehensively how environmental events relate to each other and the contingencies under which these relationships develop. With climate change, a location's future may well be discontinuous with its past but continuous with the past of another place. In this case, history will be vital in helping people adjust to their changing future and anticipating policy challenges.

## Policy: Problems

In discussing the policy implications of climate variability for Northern Australia, it is important to distinguish between three climatic phenomena:

- climate variability—the 'natural' variation in climatic parameters such as temperature and rainfall within and between years
- climate change—shifts in the long-term underlying conditions in parameters such as temperature and rainfall
- extreme weather events—including cyclones and severe storms, flooding rains, heat waves and droughts.

These phenomena are inter-related. The climate change we have been experiencing over the last century—accelerating in recent decades—creates a warmer atmosphere with a higher moisture content, which is inherently more volatile. This amplifies climate variability, disrupts traditional patterns of atmospheric and oceanic circulation, and increases the likelihood of extreme weather events. Extreme weather events are one artefact of climate variability. An analogy used in climate science is that of a dice that has been weighted such that warming conditions with associated weather patterns (e.g. droughts, storms, floods and heat waves) are much more likely than extremes of cold.

Projections from the CSIRO and Bureau of Meteorology's *Monsoonal north cluster report* (Moise et al., 2015) suggest that the following are probable in Northern Australia over coming decades:

- warmer temperatures on land and in the ocean, with a rise in days above 35°C in Darwin from 11 per year to 43 in a median year to over 74 per year in the warmest 10 per cent of years by 2030
- amplified variability—wetter Wets and drier Drys
- fewer but more severe cyclones, but with a 60 per cent increase in the intensity of severe storms by 2030, and a higher proportion of Category 4 and 5 events
- rising sea levels (currently 7 mm/year off Darwin, but with the potential for step changes this century if the accelerating melt of the Greenland Ice Sheet continues).

The potential impacts of such changes in climatic conditions are likely to include:

- increased risk of vector-borne diseases
- potential changes in the range of weeds and pests (as more tropical conditions extend further south)
- increasing challenges in managing bushfire extent and intensity
- more pressure on water supplies towards the end of longer dry seasons
- greater risk of damage to human settlements, food, water and energy supplies and infrastructure during extreme events
- increased heat stress and ticks on cattle (20 per cent impact on beef production by 2030)
- greater risks of flooding and storm surge impacts such as erosion and salt water intrusion in coastal areas.

From a public policy perspective, this is a classic nest of intertwined wicked problems (Brown et al., 2010) characterised by technical complexity and uncertainty; large scales in space and time; a mix of social, economic and biophysical drivers; and contested issues among diverse stakeholders. These challenges encompass issues as diverse as public health and safety, water security, food production, fire management, transport logistics, energy supplies and networks and intensified pressure on infrastructure, particularly near the coast where most people live. The diagram in Figure 17.3 illustrates that different types of developments operate over a range of planning and decision horizons, and that planning for more than 2°C of warming and metre(s) of sea level rise needs to be transformational, rather than incremental.

As we move along the 100-year timeframe in Figure 17.3, the boundaries between climate change, climate variability and extreme weather events, and even between climate change adaptation and mitigation, blur. The overarching policy challenge has been described as managing the unavoidable (adaptation) while avoiding the unmanageable (mitigation). Long term, mitigation (reducing net greenhouse gas emissions) becomes a key plank of adaptation.

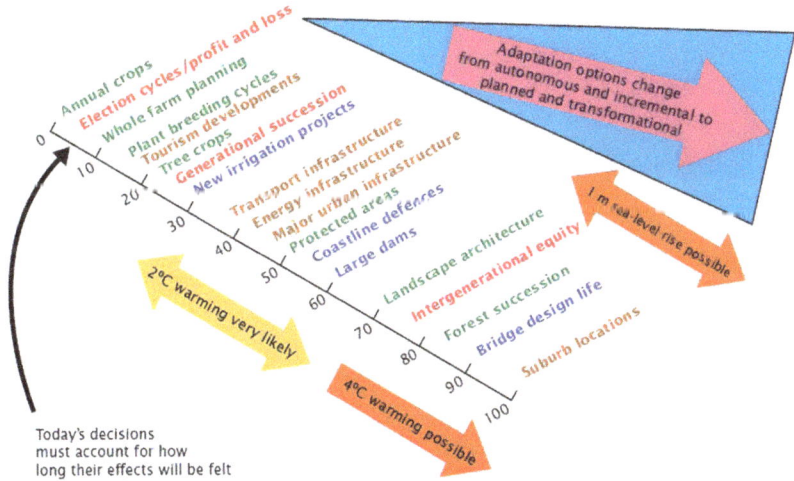

**Figure 17.3: Climate change, adaptation options and human planning horizons.**
Source: Cleugh et al. (2011).

## Solutions

Climate change and its likely consequences demand sophisticated approaches to planning and risk management. A climate-smart policy menu for Northern Australia would likely include approaches to planning and development approval processes that:

- are robust under a range of climate change and demographic scenarios
- build in resilience thinking (e.g. protect coastlines, improve habitat connectivity and buffering, protect refugia for threatened species)
- encourage carbon pollution mitigation in energy, transport and food systems
- encourage sustainable tropical design (carbon, water, energy, liveability, performance during and after extreme events) in the built environment at household, precinct and community levels
- safeguard productive soil and allow for increased food production and shorter supply chains
- manage demand for and facilitate recycling of water, nutrients and energy.

Policymakers must also adapt a place-based, rather than regional, approach. The historic variability of climate across the north means that rainfall and river flow vary not only from one place to another, but also from one year to another. Add climate change to this natural variability and regional-scale development such as the food bowl appears unviable. Agricultural development only has a chance if tied to the ecological particularities, limits and possibilities of individual places.

One question immediately presents itself: is this better done in a largely knowledge- and services-based economy, rather than in a resources-based economy?

The implications of a warming, more variable climate for Northern Australia are not all negative, nor are the policy implications all about defensive risk management. Developing low-carbon economies is one of the fastest-growing economic opportunities globally. Anticipating, planning for and responding to extreme events and associated mass movements of people is also a rapidly growing industry. The inherent geological instability of Southeast Asia, particularly Indonesia, has implications for human settlements and infrastructure comparable to extreme climatic events. The tropical zone is the fastest-growing region of the world economy. Solutions developed for urban and remote communities in Northern Australia are likely to be applicable elsewhere in the tropics, even though Australia's tropics are more climatically variable than other tropical regions, creating export opportunities for knowledge, technologies and services. With astute planning and strategic investment in capacity and regional partnerships, Darwin could position itself as a Southeast Asian centre of excellence for low-carbon economies and for disaster risk management and response, attracting international private and public investment and selling expertise and services throughout Asia and beyond.

If we distil governance to its essence—how society shares risks, benefits and costs through space and time—then it is clear that the climate challenge is fundamentally a test for our systems of governance. At a macro level, the climate policy challenge is equally about how society sets policy directions and makes decisions, and what decisions are made by whom. Ideally, climate policy demands approaches—or at least core objectives and principles—that are bipartisan, extend beyond government to civil society and industry, and endure over multiple electoral cycles. Unfortunately, contemporary Australian politics is moving further and further away from this, for now. But it is also worth considering that many of the policy objectives canvassed above are worthwhile whether or not climate change is a factor. In any case, future prosperity relies on a deep understanding of the north's environmental history.

# References

Australian Academy of Science. (2014, February). *Submission to the Joint Select Committee on North Australia*. Canberra, ACT. Retrieved from www.science.org.au/files/userfiles/support/submissions/2014/submission-joint-select-committee-northern-australia.pdf

Brown, V. A., Harris, J. A. & Russell, J. Y. (Eds). (2010). *Tackling wicked problems: Through the transdisciplinary imagination*. London, England: Earthscan.

Bureau of Meteorology. (2014). *Climate data online, daily and monthly rainfall data*. Retrieved from www.bom.gov.au/climate/data/

Chan, T., Hart, B., Kennard, M., Pusey, B., Shenton, M., Valentine, E. & Patel, S. (2012). Bayesian network models for environmental flow decision making in the Daly River, Northern Territory, Australia. *River Research and Applications*, *28*(3), 283–301.

Cleugh, H., Stafford Smith, M., Battaglia, M. & Graham, P. (Eds). (2011). *Climate change: Science and solutions for Australia*. Collingwood, Vic.: CSIRO Publishing.

Georges, A., Webster, I., Guarino, E., Jolly, P., Thoms, M. & Doody, S. (2002). *Modelling dry season flows and predicting the impact of water extraction on a flagship species – the pig nosed turtle (Carretochelys insculpta)*. Report prepared for the Northern Territory Department of Infrastructure Planning and Environment, Darwin.

Hacking, I. (1990). *Taming of chance*. Cambridge, England: Cambridge University Press.

Hart, B. (2004). Environmental risks associated with new irrigation in Northern Australia. *Ecological Management and Restoration, 5*, 106–11.

Holland, G. J. (1985). Interannual variability of the Australian summer monsoon at Darwin: 1952-82. *Monthly Weather Review, 114*, 594–604.

Kraus, E. B. (1955). Secular changes of east-coast rainfall regimes. *Quarterly Journal of the Royal Meteorological Society, 81*, 430–439.

Moise, A., Abbs, D., Bhend, J., Chiew, F., Church, J., Ekström, M., … Whetton, P. (2015). *Monsoonal north cluster report* (Climate change in Australia projections for Australia's natural resource management regions: Cluster reports). CSIRO and Bureau of Meteorology, Australia. Retrieved from plan.northerngulf.com.au/wp-content/uploads/2015/11/Monsoonal-North-regional-climate-change-projections-report.pdf

Nicholls, N., McBride, J. L. & Ormerod, R. J. (1982). On predicting the onset of the Australian wet season at Darwin. *Monthly Weather Review, 110*, 14–17.

O'Brien, C. (2014). Imported understandings: Calendar, weather and climate in tropical Australia, 1870s–1940s. In J. Beattie, E. O'Gorman & M. Henry (Eds), *Climate, science and colonization* (pp. 195–211). New York, NY: Palgrave Macmillan.

O'Brien, C. (2016). Rethinking seasons: Changing climate, changing time. In T. Bristow & T. Ford (Eds), *A cultural history of climate change* (pp. 38–54). New York, NY: Routledge.

Robin, L. (2007). *How a continent created a nation*. Sydney, NSW: UNSW Press.

Taylor, T. G. (1918). *The Australian environment (especially as controlled by rainfall)*. Melbourne, Vic.: Government printer.

Tickell, S. (2005, 1 April). *Groundwater resources of the Tindall Limestone*. Darwin, NT: Department of Natural Resources, the Environment and the Arts.

Verma, M. (2003). 1:250,000 hydrogeological map of Darwin Harbour, DIPE. In T. Haig & S. Townsend, An understanding of the groundwater and surface water hydrology of the Darwin Harbour Plan of Management Area. *Proceedings of the Darwin Harbour Public Presentations*. Darwin: Northern Territory Government.

# 18

## Killing Two Birds with One Stone: Developing Northern Australian Adaptive Capabilities to Sustainably Develop Competent and Thriving Communities Capable of Responding Effectively to Natural Hazards

Petra T. Buergelt, Douglas Paton, Andrew Campbell, Helen James and Alison Cottrell

## Introduction

Northern Australia has the potential to become a powerhouse within Australia (Australian Government, 2015). However, as the same report pointed out, the realisation of this potential is threatened by Northern Australia's exposure to substantial natural hazards. These hazards include bushfires, cyclones and flooding as well as extreme heat and humidity for six months of the year. At the same time, the resources and capabilities required to mitigate the complex natural hazard risk are declining. Infrastructure issues that can be traced to how extreme weather and climatic conditions make construction and maintenance difficult and expensive. Social factors such as low population densities, communities of varying degrees of remoteness, low population diversity and population turnover compound to introduce other significant challenges to the human component of mitigation planning. Additional challenges arise in remote Indigenous communities from differences between Indigenous and non-Indigenous stakeholder views about how to interpret, reduce and respond to risks. These conditions have conspired to create circumstances in which even relatively large remote communities in Northern Australia have almost no formal emergency management capacity, and little spare capacity to fall back on when a hazard event occurs.

In this chapter, the above challenges provide the backdrop to understanding and exploring how to reduce and respond to the continuing and increasing risk natural hazard events present to the development of Northern Australia. This backdrop is also used to frame disaster risk reduction (DRR) capabilities (UNISDR, 2015) that can be used to sustainably develop adaptive and thriving communities capable of responding effectively to natural hazards. Utilising the work of Paton et al. (2014) and the holistic emergency management and capacity development model advanced by Buergelt and Paton (2014), we propose that integrating community development and disaster risk management that includes and utilises all sectors and levels of community approach would be the most effective pathway.

We start by describing how the substantial natural hazard risk in Northern Australia is a serious threat to developing this region. Next, we propose pathways for creating innovative solutions that facilitate developing Northern Australia. We deliberate how DRR strategies must collectively consider and address the social, economic and cultural challenges faced by communities, particularly remote Indigenous communities, across the region. From this discussion, an integrated, holistic and community-based DRR framework emerges.

This framework shows how we could 'kill two birds with one stone'. The 'stone' is community development (Dalton et al., 2007). The first 'bird' derives from applying community development principles and practices to strengthen the *everyday* capacities and capabilities of communities. The second 'bird' emerges from recognition that the person, household and community capacities and capabilities developed by using community development strategies are fundamental to the development of sustained community-based DRR strategies (Paton et al., 2014; Paton & McClure, 2013). Integrating community development and DRR in the manner envisaged offers a mechanism for reconciling the development of Northern Australia with the management of the natural hazards that have been identified as constraints on that development. We conclude this chapter by discussing the unique participatory research opportunities Northern Australia affords and the research needed to facilitate developing and implementing an integrated, holistic and community-based DRR and development framework.

## Northern Australia's Unique Context and Substantial Hazard Risks: A Serious Threat to Developing the North

In Northern Australia, adaptive and thriving communities are a prerequisite to fulfilling the potential of the region to become a powerhouse within Australia (Australian Government, 2015) by ensuring societal, economic and environmental sustainability in the context of increasingly rapid change, uncertainty, insecurity and wicked problems (Cutter et al., 2015).[1] In Northern Australia, the key contextual challenges to fulfil the region's potential include closing the gap between Indigenous and other Australians; ensuring education, employment and welfare outcomes; attracting and retaining people in regional economies reliant on volatile commodity markets; and food, energy and water insecurity (Garnett et al., 2009). However, the major challenge to realising this potential derives from Northern Australia's unique hazardscape.

Northern Australia is dominated by substantial natural hazards. The natural hazards include bushfires, cyclones and flooding as well as extreme heat and humidity for six months of the year. Bushfires in the region burn, on average, 430,000 km$^2$ (an area larger than Germany) every year and contribute nearly 50 per cent of regional greenhouse emissions (Murphy et al., 2015). If bushfires are not properly interacted with, they can have disastrous consequences for communities and ecosystems.

Besides its threat to human life, the ecological, household, infrastructure and societal costs associated with bushfires are enormous. In Australia, these costs average US$1.58 billion per year (Mortimer et al., 2011). It is difficult to define specific costs in Northern Australia due to issues with record keeping (Allan & Tschirner, 2009), but specific costs per property

---

1   'Wicked problems' are problems that are difficult to clearly define, complex due to the interaction of a large number of inter-related factors, constantly changing and requiring a transformation of mindset of a large number of people to be solved.

have been estimated to reach A$420,000. Additional social and economic costs can arise from short- and long-term bushfire-related evacuation and migration, and from loss of land, homes, livestock and critical community and business infrastructure (Commonwealth of Australia, 2012).

In addition to bushfires, Northern Australia's hazardscape is also characterised by moderate to high frequency cyclones, which affect Indigenous and non-Indigenous communities, particularly within 50 km of the coast (Commonwealth of Australia, 2012). Further, the widespread flooding that accompanies the monsoonal wet season disrupts lives and livelihoods in many communities, often for up to 90 days per year. Climate change will increase the frequency and intensity of these hazards, amplifying their potential destructiveness and making them more difficult to interact with (Department of Environment, 2015).

Northern Australia also has to confront the consequences of sea surface temperature increases. Temperatures in the Timor Sea are rising faster than almost any part of the world's oceans. Warming oceans and warmer air increase risk from possibly fewer but more destructive cyclones, with a higher proportion of Category 4 and 5 cyclones (CSIRO & Bureau of Meteorology, 2014).

The impact of these cyclones is compounded by rising sea levels. Sea levels around Darwin have risen by 18 cm over the last 20 years, threatening coastal infrastructure and livelihoods of Indigenous communities dependent on formerly freshwater floodplain wetlands (CSIRO & Bureau of Meteorology, 2014).

Climate change also adds threats from heat stress and vector-borne diseases (Department of Environment, 2015). It is estimated that monsoonal wet seasons will get wetter, and dry seasons longer and drier with the number of 35°C+ days anticipated to rise from the current average of 11 to 60 days per year by 2030 (Bureau of Meteorology & CSIRO, 2015). These climatic conditions will increase physical and mental health issues related to heat stress and potentially deter people from moving to or staying in Northern Australia. In addition, vector-borne diseases affecting both humans (e.g. mosquitos) and animals (e.g. ticks in cattle) will also increase. Individually and collectively, this increasingly hazardous environment will create significant risks to life, human health and wellbeing, economic productivity, infrastructure and ecosystems in

Northern Australia. However, humans are also substantially contributing these natural processes becoming the kinds of events that represent the (hazardous) challenges introduced above.

While the process that ultimately underpins events societies label disasters are natural, the so-called 'natural disasters' are not 'natural' per se. Natural processes (e.g. fire and cyclones) become hazards only when they interact with people. These hazards, in turn, become disasters when the scale and consequences of hazard activity exceed the societal capacity to contain or respond to these natural processes.

Natural events only become disasters when two basic conditions are present. The first condition manifests when people decide to live in areas where natural hazards occur and to develop these areas by (e.g. building houses, infrastructure and businesses) in ways that are independent of their environment. That is, their decisions are based on exploiting the amenities and resources of an area, but do not consider the hazardous potential that arises from their societal development decisions. The need to consider this linkage introduces a social ecological dimension to understanding natural hazard risk and a need for more active considerations of the social contribution to this equation.

By choosing to live in an environment in which natural processes and resources offer people benefits and amenities, people also choose to live in an environment that can occasionally turn hazardous. To effectively coexist with this environmental dynamic, it is important that people and communities choose to accommodate both the beneficial and hazardous potential inherent within the environment. The latter can be facilitated by people and communities taking steps to reduce the likelihood of natural events turning into disasters by increasing their capacity to anticipate detrimental impacts and develop ways to adapt to and recover from periodic hazard consequences.

Developing adaptive capacities will become more important given that Northern Australia's hazardscape will become more challenging due to climate change processes. Thus, the second condition reflects the degree to which people and communities anticipate the consequences that could arise when extreme natural events occur and that these consequences could exceed their capacities to respond and act. Only if people and communities engage in this kind of environmental vigilance will they develop and implement the planning, mitigation and preparedness processes required to reduce their risk and to increase their capacity to cope, adapt and recover.

Consequently, to prevent or at least reduce losses to communities and ecosystems, it is crucial to improve environmental understanding and develop hazard mitigation and response strategies that focus on societal coexistence and the development of adaptive capabilities that increase the capacity of people and communities to proactively respond to social and environmental change and periodic natural hazard events. The cost effectiveness of these endeavours can be framed in terms of reducing costs (e.g. less disruption and quicker recovery) and increasing a multitude of co-benefits for residents and communities (e.g. creating novel approaches to ensuring that securing benefits from environmental engagement accommodates the mitigation of hazardous circumstances). However, given the complexity of social–environmental interactions, this will take some new ways of thinking and acting (see Pathways for Creating Innovative Solutions section below).

Reducing the risk of and responding to natural hazards is complicated by natural hazards being wicked problems that are characterised by a wealth of complex interconnected ecological relationships and interdependencies that are constantly evolving and changing (BNHCRC, 2013; Brown et al., 2010). Consequently, the development of new ways of thinking and acting must accommodate the ecological nature of development. The need for the latter was anticipated by Buergelt and Paton (2014) and Buergelt et al. (2017a) when they developed their ecological all-hazard interdisciplinary risk management and adaptation model (see Figures 18.1, 18.2 and 18.3). This work emphasises that it is paramount to identify, understand and interact holistically with the multitude of individual and contextual/environmental factors that affect ecological relationships for both development and DRR strategies. A need for this kind of holistic approach is acknowledged as being important for addressing the wicked challenges associated with anticipating, preparing for, responding to and recovering from natural hazard events (BNHCRC, 2013; Paton et al., 2015).

18. KILLING TWO BIRDS WITH ONE STONE

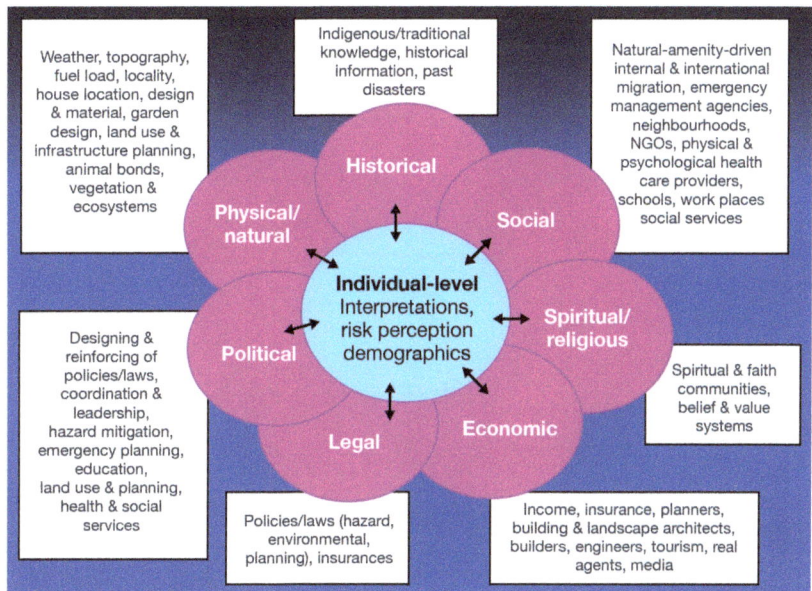

**Figure 18.1: Ecological risk management and capacity building model: overview of community-level dimensions.**
Source: Buergelt and Paton (2014).

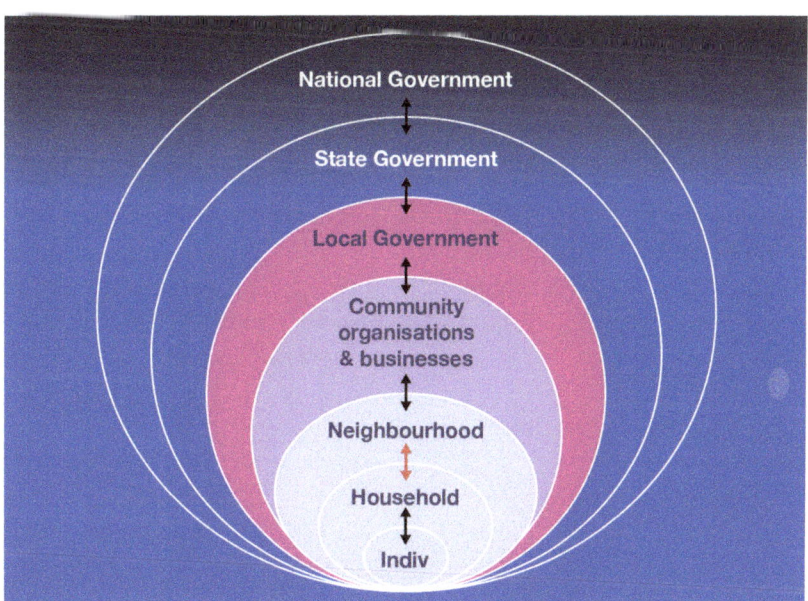

**Figure 18.2: Ecological risk management and capacity building model: overview of community levels.**
Source: Buergelt and Paton (2014).

397

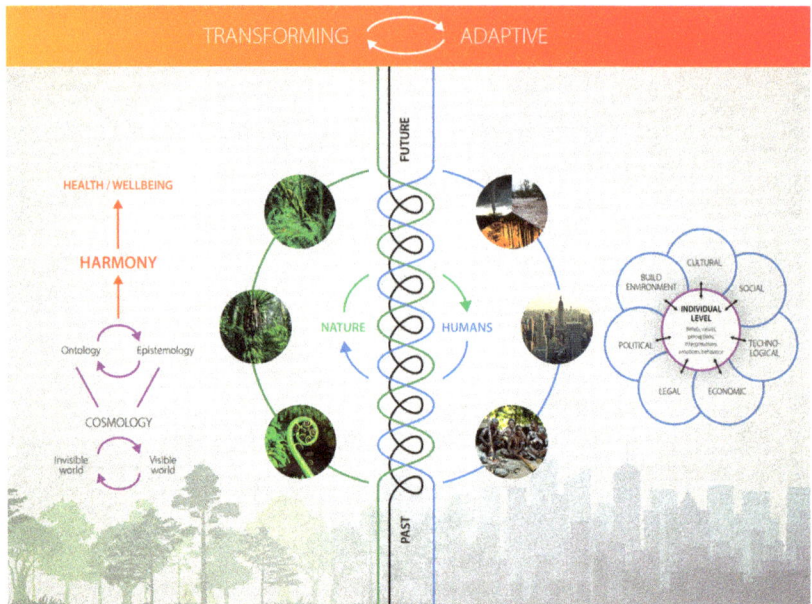

**Figure 18.3: Revised risk management and capacity building model.**
Source: Buergelt et al. (2017a).

At the same time, worldwide, it is becoming increasingly apparent that currently available resources and capabilities are increasingly inadequate for addressing the wicked challenges associated with anticipating, preparing for, responding to and recovering from natural hazard events (BNHCRC, 2013; Paton et al., 2015). In Australia, the predominant response to this issue has been framed in the national strategy for disaster resilience discussed in the *National disaster resilience framework* (Commonwealth of Australia, 2013). This report argued that developing community disaster resilience is crucial for effectively reducing the risk of natural hazards turning into disasters. The model outlined in Figures 18.1–18.3 provides a comprehensive overview of domains and how they interact over time that need to be considered when developing community disaster resilience. Consequently, realising the benefits of the national strategy will require strategies that consider and plan for accommodating and utilising, as far as possible, the domains described in Figure 18.1 at the different scales depicted in Figure 18.2. This is particularly important in the Northern Australian context.

As outlined earlier, the development of community resilience throughout Northern Australia is complicated by infrastructure development and maintenance challenges. A resilience strategy must also accommodate weather and climate extremes and how they interact with a social environment characterised by population diversity and turnover, cultural diversity and communities of varying degrees of remoteness (some 360,000 people live in communities ranging from 'outer regional' to 'very remote', with an increasing proportion of Indigenous people living remotely). Cultural diversity introduces a need to accommodate the wide variety of views of Indigenous and non-Indigenous stakeholders about how to interpret, reduce and respond to hazard risks. The challenges inherent in this scenario are magnified by the remote geographical location of Northern Australian communities and the implications of this for the time and costs associated with assistance coming from other states due to colonising practices having undermined and continuing to erode the substantial adaptive individual and collective capacities Indigenous peoples and communities developed over millennia (Ali et al., 2021; Buergelt et al., 2017a).

In sum, the substantial natural hazard risk in Northern Australia poses a serious threat to realising the potential of the region to become the powerhouse that Australia's government envisages (Australian Government, 2015). At the same time, the unique social and environmental conditions prevailing in Northern Australia introduce several challenges to the task of developing the community disaster resilience required to reduce the threat by reducing the risk of extreme natural events and responding effectively to them when they occur (Commonwealth of Australia, 2013). In addition to their acting to constrain the development of resilience in Northern Australia, these conditions combine to impede developing the north's strategically important national and international role as Australia's base for responding to major natural hazards (bushfires, cyclones, tsunamis, earthquakes, volcanic eruptions), pandemics and terrorist attacks that occur elsewhere in the world (Commonwealth of Australia, 2012).

However, the significance of the issues that constrain the development of Northern Australia is amplified by focusing predominantly on the hazardous environmental factors and not pay adequate attention to the human and social factors that influence the likelihood of natural events turning into disasters. Yet, focusing on the human and social factors makes it is possible to argue, as we do here, that it is precisely the substantial, continuous and increasing threat of natural disasters that could be used to act as a catalyst for the development of the north. In the next section, we discuss how hazard events could act as catalysts by enhancing the day-to-day capacities of people and communities. We outline pathways we believe would facilitate developing Northern Australia in ways that reconcile the substantial natural hazard threats with continued, sustained development of individual and collective adaptive capacities.

# Pathways for Creating Innovative Solutions that Facilitate Developing Northern Australia

We propose that the challenges posed by a complex and dynamic hazardscape to developing Northern Australia can be attributed, at least in part, to the fact that current DRR approaches, which focus predominantly on managing the natural environmental contributions to risk (e.g. mitigation and traditional risk communication), have not been particularly successful (Paton & McClure, 2013; UNISDR, 2015). Thus, more effective approaches require new ways of thinking and acting to reduce and respond to disaster risk that are capable of contributing to realising the significant strategic and economic potential Northern Australia holds. That conclusion echoes Einstein's[2] contention that 'a new type of thinking is essential if mankind is to survive and move toward higher levels'. That is, problems cannot be solved with the same kind of thinking that created them, pointing to the need to transform people's mindsets to create the collective transformations required to accomplish the desired outcomes. Individual and collective transformations must accommodate the complex and constantly changing ecological dialogical interactions pointed out by Buergelt and Paton (2014) and Buergelt et al. (2017a) in their ecological all-hazard interdisciplinary risk management and adaptation model (see Figures 18.1–19.3).

---

2   'The real problem is in the hearts of men' [Michael Amrine interview with Einstein] (1946, 23 June), *New York Times Magazine* as quoted in Icarusfalling (2009, 24 June), Einstein enigmatic quote [Blog post]. Retrieved from icarus-falling.blogspot.com.au/2009/06/einstein-enigma.html.

## Developing Transformed Ways of Thinking and Acting

The first shift in mindset involves facing and accepting the reality that hazard events are inevitable, can happen to us and are likely to become more frequent and severe in future. It also involves accepting the fact that while the activity of natural processes is inevitable, people can do much to reduce and respond to the nature and implications of the consequences hazard activity has for themselves and others. Accepting this reality would be facilitated by developing a mindset that focuses on coexisting with environmental benefits and the challenges and threats posed by natural environmental processes. A corollary of this is that any disaster that does occur can act as a catalyst for development. This potential is embodied in Sendai's call (UNISDR, 2015) to include the 'Build Back Better' concept in disaster recovery planning (Paton & James, 2016). To fulfil this potential, it is necessary to fundamentally shift what people and communities think and do in their everyday lives prior to hazard events occurring.

Berkes et al. (2003) specified the mindset required. They argued that communities can more readily cope with and adapt to complex, dynamic and rapid change and challenges if the majority of people in communities are able to learn fast, understand complexity, synthesise seemingly separate pockets of knowledge and apply this new knowledge to continuously create and implement innovative solutions. From a DRR perspective, this introduces a need to focus on community development and change processes in DRR planning (Paton et al., 2014). A consequence of this approach is that DRR becomes fundamentally a community development activity that is complemented by risk management, rather than one that focuses on managing hazard processes directly or indirectly via reliance on, for example, hazard-focused risk communication processes. It is this latter shift, and one that focuses on creating adaptive transformative communities, that offers the potential for the complex Northern Australian hazardscape to become a catalyst for social and economic development.

According to Berkes et al. (2003), developing the mindset required to plan for and realise this potential necessitates dissolving barriers to learning; building on the substantial and diverse existing local knowledges and experiences; learning from experience of what worked, did not work and might work; synthesising diverse knowledges; focusing on high-level analyses; engaging in critical thinking; and imagining different scenarios from business as usual. However, the key to success in twenty-first-century societies will not only require the knowledge of how to effectively navigate through rapid change but the knowledge of how to effectively lead people and groups through change and pass that knowledge on to others to facilitate the evolution of change (Berkes et al., 2003). Pivotal to successfully conceptualising and enacting such ideas requires more comprehensive interdisciplinary perspectives and thinking.

Buergelt and Paton's (2014) ecological all-hazard interdisciplinary risk management and adaptation model (see Figures 18.1–18.3) offers a framework for the development of an interdisciplinary perspective. In accordance with this model, Buergelt and Smith (2015) argued that to thrive in the face of uncertainty due to environmental risk from bushfires, cyclones, flooding and heat (threat) and to create safe, sustainable and thriving communities (possibility) it is necessary to facilitate residents developing matching diverse physical, mental, emotional, social, cultural and spiritual capabilities. The challenge is to identify *how* to best create and facilitate individual and societal transformations that create the required mindsets in practice. The sense of shared fate and common purpose that can be engendered by the threat of natural hazards and by the possibility of developing a thriving Northern Australia could provide an ideal context for creating the willingness and openness to engage in transformative education (Paton et al., 2014).

Traditional informative education programs have proven to be ineffective in facilitating the required capabilities (Lindell et al., 2009). In contrast, innovative transformative education technologies such as transformative education, experiential learning, collaborative learning, neurolinguistic programming and scenario planning are capable of dissolving old ways of being and thinking that proved unproductive and creating the required new ways of being and thinking (DePoerter, 1992; Andreas & Faulkner, 1996; Mezirow, 1996; DePoerter & Hernacki, 1998; Smith, 1998; DePoerter et al., 1999; O'Sullivan et al., 2002; Cranton, 2006; Beard & Wilson, 2006; O'Connor & Seymour, 2011; Rose, 2011; Zaffron & Logan, 2011). Transformative education facilitates people reconstructing the interpretations or meanings they assign to their experiences, resulting in ontological and epistemological transformations or shifts that motivate actions that are more adaptive (Mezirow, 1996; O'Sullivan et al., 2002).

The holistic approach advocated above (Figures 18.1–18.3) means that there is urgent need for holistic systemic transformations in all components. This view is echoed by Berkes et al. (2003). Given that contextual components are the result of groups of people acting together and interacting with other groups within communities (e.g. governments, NGOs and businesses), systemic transformation requires transformations at the organisational and community level. Integrating community development and disaster risk management could facilitate the required systemic transformation. The threat of natural hazards to developing Northern Australia could be utilised to create the impetus for systemic shifts.

Transformative education pedagogies facilitate people seeing reality more clearly and actively facing it (Mezirow, 1996; O'Sullivan et al., 2002). Hence, transformative education holds the potential of people and communities to be able to see, accept and be with the complexity and uncertainty inherent in natural processes. This shift would enable people and communities to anticipate what they might have to contend with. This knowledge would inspire people and communities to seek, develop and implement solutions capable of adapting to the challenges identified. The key to adaptation is effective and efficient everyday competencies and relationships within communities (Paton & McClure, 2013). Accordingly, it is crucial to give community development a more prominent place in DRR and management than has hitherto been the case.

## Integrating Community Development and Disaster Risk Management to Sustainably Develop Thriving Communities and Reduce Disaster Risk

One reason people and communities are generally failing to anticipate the significance of the natural hazard risk they face and/or their ability to take responsibility for reducing their risk has been the separation of risk management from other aspects of social policy and practice designed to develop communities (O'Keefe et al., 1976; Paton & McClure, 2013). This separation derives from a focus of formal risk management on the hazard and its physical characteristics. This focus has two basic consequences. The first consequence is that people commonly fail to differentiate the cause (over which they have no control) from the consequences of hazard activity that they can influence (Paton & McClure, 2013). Second, and following from the last point, a predominant focus of traditional risk management on advising people of physical hazard activity (and its magnitude, severity, etc.) and using this to frame the recommended actions required to prepare has resulted in neglecting the development of the interpretive social and psychological capacities required to, for example, realistically interpret risk and make decisions under uncertain conditions (Lindell et al., 2009; Paton & McClure, 2013).

As a result, traditional approaches fail to increase people's commitment to reducing risk and to developing their individual and collective capacities to reduce, adapt to and respond to extreme natural processes (Paton et al., 2014; Paton & McClure, 2013). The cost of not developing individual and collective adaptive capacities is evident in the growing recognition of the important role these capacities play in how people collectively interpret risk and develop the capacities that enhance their ability to adapt to complex and rapid change (Norris, et al., 2008; Paton & Johnston, 2006).

The national risk management approach discussed in the national disaster resilience framework suggests that developing community resilience also creates an access for reducing the risk of disasters (Commonwealth of Australia, 2013). The emphasis on community resilience provides a foundation for an approach that recognises that peoples' capacity to reduce and adapt to hazardous circumstances derives more from social capital developed from everyday personal and social experiences and interpretations, rather than from additional, specific risk management strategies. Hence, we go a step further and propose that the development of community resilience would be more successful and cost effective if we integrate community development and risk management strategies (Paton et al., 2014).

The focus of community development could change from seeking to encourage community support for reducing losses from hazard events to taking steps to safeguard and further enhance the everyday lifestyle, amenities and resources that attract people to the north by developing people's individual and collective capability to adapt (Norris et al., 2008; Paton et al., 2014). Buergelt and Paton's (2014) and Buergelt et al.'s (2017a) ecological all-hazard interdisciplinary risk management and adaptation model supports this approach, because it shows that all sectors of community are involved in and influence DRR (see Figures 18.1–18.3).

In Northern Australia, integrating community development and managing disaster risk could include, for example, identifying and developing strength-based strategies that build on the intrinsic aspects that make Northern Australia an attractive place to live, work and play, while enhancing community capacity to respond effectively when the environmental processes that create these amenities turn hazardous. Strength-based strategies could include learning from people who have lived in Northern Australia for generations. Learning is especially useful from Indigenous people who have built up in-depth and holistic knowledge and developed strategies for effectively coexisting with natural hazards for millennia (Buergelt et al., 2017a). The strategies could also include relevant Indigenous and non-Indigenous leaders and organisations from various sectors truly working together with urban and remote communities long term to co-create sustained, novel processes and contexts that further enhance their capacities to adapt (Ali et al., 2021; Buergelt et al, 2017).

## Utilising Threat of Natural Hazards and Potential of Northern Australia as Catalysts for Transformation

Reconciling how community development and DRR can be integrated requires people and society to do things differently. However, people dread change because it entails leaving the familiar and stepping into unfamiliar territory, can be challenging and offers the prospect of failing. Typically, only two conditions inspire change. First, crisis, or the threat of a crisis, propels people to change because crisis results in changes within the environment that render habitual ways of thinking and acting ineffective. An argument for pursuing this line of thinking derives from the Chinese symbol for crisis—it encompasses 'danger' and 'opportunity'. In Northern Australia, the key is combining both the threat and the possibilities to increase people's collective motivation to transform. This raises a question of how to create the kind of opportunity or desired outcome that can inspire people to change. One answer to this question may lie with facilitating transforming how people relate to their environment to focus on the need to safeguard against periodic hazardous circumstances if they are to sustainably avail themselves of the amenities and benefits afforded by the environment they live in.

Such ways of thinking are possible. Chinese (and other Asian) environmental philosophies argued for relationships between people and environment to be based on principles of harmonious coexistence (Tianchen, 2003). While it is unrealistic to assume that the wholesale adoption of an environmental philosophy can be imported from one culture into another, the existence of beliefs and actions that facilitate the kind of environmental coexistence envisaged here does at least suggest that it is a goal worth pursuing (Buergelt et al., 2017a). To trigger the required transformations, however, will require something that will catalyse shifts in thinking. We propose that the Northern Australian hazardscape could be utilised as such a catalyst to facilitate the transformation required for the sustained development of adaptive, competent and thriving communities capable of more effectively responding to natural hazards.

While this pathway has not been attempted, the mechanisms that could be used to develop and implement this kind of change do exist. For example, the hazardscape could be used to create the kind of superordinate goal that can catalyse collective action (Paton & Buergelt, 2012) using transformative pedagogies such as those highlighted above as a vehicle for transforming, reconciling and integrating stakeholder beliefs and practices. Because hazard effects are widespread, and involve and affect all sectors and levels of society, integrating community development and DRR offers the potential for whole-of-community efforts involving community, government, businesses, and researchers collaborating.

By encouraging all stakeholders (e.g. community members, communities and local and regional governments) to develop DRR approaches that focus on creating community capacity by utilising local individual and collective resources, disaster risk reduction and management become a subset of activities subsumed within environmental, cultural, social and economic community adaptive capacity building. This change in focus creates an opportunity to frame the Northern Australia hazardscape as a catalyst to inspire and lead holistic community development and social change. The shared challenges posed by natural hazards might propel people and communities to cooperate and collaborate. The threat also provides the urgency that focuses people to act. The threat could provide a useful context in which stakeholders can be identified, their respective views and interests elicited and transformed, and governance and planning processes that seek to accommodate diversity of views and interests developed to create high levels of cooperation and collaboration.

## Developing Unprecedented Levels of Cooperation and Collaboration

Because natural hazards do not respect human-made boundaries, unprecedented levels of cooperation and collaboration will be required among and between sectors across local, state, national and international levels to continually create and implement innovative responses as suggested by Buergelt and Paton's (2014) ecological risk management and capacity building model. This cooperation and collaboration will create cross-sectoral transformation, development and ownership of adaptive mindsets and actions and embed these adaptive capacities and responses into everyday community beliefs and practices.

At the coalface of community-based DRR, pre-existing networks can function as resources for the focus of community-based activities (e.g. professional, cultural, religious, sporting, environmental, artistic, women's and men's groups, schools and health services) (Buergelt & Paton, 2014). According to Norris et al. (2008), resilience resides in four sets of interlinked, networked resources. Leadership is essential in creating these competencies. Often, such leadership comes from existing social networks operating both within and external to the community, which enable both intra- and inter-community resources to be activated. By empowering and linking the resources and leaderships of these groups, the adaptive capacity and competence of communities can be enhanced manifold (James & Paton, 2016).

For this participatory civil society–based approach to be successful, the natural, human, man-made, cultural, social, spiritual, economic and political resources of local communities need to be able to operate at a high level of capability and competence (Buergelt & Paton, 2014; Norris et al., 2008). However, people growing up in and living in individualistic cultures commonly do not develop the mindset and skills required for cooperating and collaborating. Moreover, governance structures developed by individualistic cultures can impede cooperating and collaborating. Hence, to respond effectively to natural hazards, people and communities need to further develop the mindset and skills necessary for collaborating. Communities also need to create governance structures that facilitate collaboration such as sociocracy (Buck & Villines, 2007;

Endenburg, 1998, 2002) and that explicitly consider risk and shape community expectations around responses to extreme events (Buergelt & Smith, 2015; Paton et al., 2015).

One feature of the Northern Australian social context currently defined as a limiting factor regarding collaboration and cooperation could be turned into a driver of cooperative action. This limiting factor is low population numbers and density, which means that more cultural, social, economic and religious/spiritual roles, including leadership roles, required for societal and community functioning are available than there are people to fill them and that organisations are under resource constraints (James & Paton, 2016). More roles and resource constraints can have both facilitating and limiting implications.

On the upside, more roles than there are people to fill these roles means there are more opportunities for people to step up and take up roles and to fulfil a variety of roles (Barker & Gump, 1964; Bechtel & Churchman, 2002). Further, people are used to taking on and being responsible for fulfilling roles. Both scenarios build capacities—they facilitate people making and having a wide variety of experiences and learning many new ways of thinking and acting within a short timeframe. Additionally, having to manage with limited resources creates the necessity for people to work together across organisations and sectors. Accordingly, they are more likely to have developed the mindset and skills necessary for working effectively in diverse teams.

On the downside, the same people being involved across a variety of roles increases the risk of them burning out. There may also be less diversity of views, reducing the capacity of communities to develop new views to create novel solutions and to anticipate alternative futures (Bechtel & Churchman, 2002). This diminished capacity would make it more difficult to anticipate, plan for and respond to future events that may be more challenging than anything hitherto experienced, such as extreme natural hazards. Therefore, it is important to empower as many people as possible to become active participants in social civic life by taking up roles. People accepting the responsibilities of roles and effectively fulfilling roles can be facilitated using transformative education pedagogies.

Together, the outlined pathways create an integrated, holistic and community-based DRR framework that would enable people and communities to actively and continuously reduce, respond and adapt to extreme natural and potentially dangerous hazards. This capacity would facilitate developing Northern Australia. We now turn to a more detailed discussion of the benefits of this framework.

## Integrated, Holistic and Community-Based DRR Framework: Benefits

The holistic, integrated and community-based DRR framework that emerged is being promoted as an effective means to enhance the capacity of people, communities and societies in disaster-prone areas to adapt and respond to natural hazards. The Hyogo Framework for Action (HFA) argued that adaptive capacities are a function of the capability of social systems to organise themselves in ways that increase its capacity for learning from past disasters, offering better future protection (UNISDR, 2007). Accordingly, as Paton and Johnston (2006, pp. 7–8) emphasised, natural hazard threats and disasters can be a 'catalyst for development opportunities'. This perspective is also supported by Thomalla and Schmuk (2004) and the IFRCRCS (2009). The latter highlighted the role DRR programs play in contributing to creating employment, building social capital and to developing a culture of hazard preparedness embedded in everyday community life. By facilitating and (re)activating local civil society capabilities inherent in Indigenous and non-Indigenous communities in both rural and urban areas, and creating conditions that enable them to collaborate and learn two-way effectively, the participatory approach to disaster governance can achieve several outcomes.

First, the integrated, community-based DRR framework described above enhances the reviving and redeveloping of capacities of local communities and values local worldviews, knowledges and practices (James & Paton, 2016; Buergelt & Paton, 2014). By identifying, activating, drawing out and reviving the resources and capacities inherent in Indigenous and non-Indigenous communities in rural and urban regions, and enabling diverse community members to effectively collaborate and learn two-way, the participatory approach to disaster governance not only draws out, and on, the resources and capacities inherent in the local communities, but also creates sociocultural, financial, health and environmental outcomes that create communities that attract and retain people.

Second, local participatory governance is more likely to be effective in a long-term, sustainable way than top-down national-level approaches, which evaporate once the immediate crisis has passed. The role of the state or national governments is to provide an enabling policy framework for the implementation of participatory DRR governance. Third, this comparatively new approach to disaster governance can help to more effectively save lives and resources by embedding a culture of disaster preparedness in local communities (Mallick, 2014). Community-based DRR creates DRR as an ongoing process that is built into the community's everyday activities and improves quality of life in communities rather than being an additional task along with all the other tasks people and communities have to manage (see Paton et al., 2014, and James & Paton, 2016, for examples).

Fourth, in the proposed framework groups traditionally perceived as vulnerable—especially Indigenous Australians, women, immigrants/refugees and older people—are reframed as highly valuable resources due to having specific and sophisticated local, ecological, spiritual and cultural knowledge, experiences, perspectives and capabilities. As a result, these groups are included in community-based DRR and their input is highly valued, sought and harnessed.

Fifth, developing adaptive and thriving communities will also contribute to addressing the substantial attraction and retention issue Northern Australia is confronting by facilitating people becoming psychologically and socially attracted to the region and embedded into their communities (e.g. Norris et al., 2008; Paton et al., 2014; Paton & McClure, 2013). Being attached to a place increases people's interactions in physical settings (Kyle et al., 2005) and creates the conditions necessary for the development of a sense of community (Tuan, 1977). The more people interact and feel they belong, the more they believe that members matter to one another and to the group, and that members' needs will be met through their commitment to be together (McMillan & Chavis, 1986). The more people interact with each other, the more they care for each other. As a result, people are more interested in and motivated to take responsibility for improving their community and in getting actively involved in preparing for and responding to natural hazards because they want to protect the people they care for. Further, people are more committed to rebuilding their communities after natural hazards (e.g. Paton & McClure, 2013). These aspects are reinforcing each other, setting an upward spiral in motion.

However, currently high population turnover, particularly in the Northern Territory (Australian Government, 2015; Roseman et al., Chapter 11, this volume), may be diluting these important aspects of social capital. Place attachment develops from people's perception of the capacity of a location to meet their personal and lifestyle goals (the amenity value of place) in ways consistent with their beliefs, feelings, values, goals and behaviours (place identity) (Norris et al., 2008). Consequently, strategies that increase the amenity value need to be identified and implemented to facilitate people more strongly identifying with and becoming attached to Northern Australia. People being attracted to and staying in Northern Australia is essential for creating the social capital that will contribute to community development and community-embedded DRR (e.g. James & Paton, 2016). At the same time, because high turnover has long been an issue in the north and is likely to continue, it might be worthwhile to start considering designing social learning systems that assume a high turnover (albeit with a stable population of long-term residents in many communities), rather than focusing only on reducing the level of turnover.

Assigning key roles to developing sense of community and place attachment provides a foundation for motivating the development of shared responsibility between all sectors of society to support the social capital–building activities organised around strengths-based DRR strategies (see Paton et al., 2014, for an example). Strategies that integrate risk management, community and economic development and poverty alleviation will play integral roles in fostering adaptation and transformation of at-risk communities (Norris et al., 2008).

## Northern Australia: Unique Participatory Research Opportunities and Needs

Developing effective holistic, integrated, transformative and community-based DRR in Northern Australia necessitates community-based participatory action research and evaluation. Northern Australia's unique urban, rural, environmental, social and cultural diversity creates ideal contexts for participatory hazard and recovery research. While large enough to encompass, for example, major social and societal aspects of urban life, social organisation and governance issues, the urban areas are small enough to conduct whole-of-community case studies. In addition, the social and cultural diversity due to high numbers of Indigenous peoples, national and international immigrants, fly-in/fly-outs and rural–urban mix provides a context for conducting research on major aspects of diversity.

In cities such as Darwin, the relatively high proportion of Indigenous residents creates a context not only for learning and understanding Indigenous hazard knowledge but comparing individualistic versus collectivist cultures. Darwin's proximity to Asia makes it an ideal location for researching cross-cultural similarities and differences, and international collaboration. This unique combination of valuable conditions creates a context for valuable comparative Indigenous and cross-cultural DRR research. While the relatively high population turnover in Darwin can create issues regarding key aspects of community resilience (such as diluting sense of community, place attachment and hazard knowledge), this same turnover provides unrivalled opportunities to shed light on social change processes over time.

The increase in natural hazards in Asia coupled with the proximity of Northern Australia to Asia also means that disaster and/or humanitarian aid (e.g. managing the influx of large numbers of dislocated people from Asia due to natural hazards or pandemics) is likely and that related scenarios can be simulated. Natural hazards in Northern Australia typically have an impact across state boundaries (Northern Territory and Queensland or Western Australia), requiring these states to work together across jurisdictional boundaries. Both aspects allow for creating and testing multi-state, national and international disaster and humanitarian aid collaboration.

Darwin and its surrounds do have human and social resources at least comparable to other Australian cities of similar size. The uncertainty stemming from the specific path and size of future cyclones being unpredictable creates a relatively uniform risk in the Darwin urban area (i.e. no one can say beforehand that they will definitely not be affected). This uniform risk is important for researching individual and collective DRR beliefs and behaviours. Additionally, emerging risk from bushfires around Darwin creates opportunities to investigate an emergent hazard and to further develop understanding of changes in DRR beliefs and action that need to be understood to proactively develop social capability to deal with climate change issues.

Finally, but most importantly, Indigenous peoples and communities have historical, ecological, psychological, cultural, social and spiritual capacities that, if recognised, valued, listened to, revived and strengthened, would reduce the risk of extreme natural events occurring, and create adaptive and thriving Indigenous communities. Additionally, Indigenous worldviews, knowledges and practices also hold the key for creating adaptive and thriving communities in general (Ali et al., 2021; Buergelt et al., 2017a). Northern Australia provides unique and critical opportunities to build on existing relationships and knowledges of working with Indigenous communities to co-design, co-implement and co-evaluate Indigenist community-based participatory action research with Indigenous communities for the benefit of both Indigenous and Western peoples and societies (Ali et al., 2021; Buergelt et al., 2017b). These strong foundations could be used to create, together with Indigenous communities, effective community-based DRR approaches. This research would also contribute to finding and creating pathways towards addressing the 'gap' between Indigenous and non-Indigenous citizens (Commonwealth of Australia, 2012).

# Conclusion

Taken together, utilising both the natural hazard threat and the possibility of Northern Australia to be Australia's powerhouse to motivate and implement a holistic, integrated and community-based participatory community development approach, based on Buergelt and Paton's (2014) ecological disaster management and capacity-building model, would facilitate developing Northern Australia effectively by killing two birds with one stone. First, this approach would contribute to the (re) development of adaptive, competent and thriving communities capable of utilising the unique opportunities Northern Australia offers and of fulfilling the potential critical national and international roles the Australian Commonwealth identified for Northern Australia. Second, this approach would reduce the likelihood of extreme natural events to occur and minimise the potential of them to turn into disasters, facilitating the development of Northern Australia. The suggested approach also points to value of community-based participatory action research approaches, especially those that are co-designed, co-implemented and co-evaluated. Finally, this approach creates many opportunities that answer the call of Australia's BNHCRC (2013) to think in new ways and develop high-quality research, together with communities, that takes into account and addresses the needs of communities and the complex and interdependent nature of disaster dimensions and processes.

## References

Ali, T., Buergelt, P. T., Maypilama, E. L., Paton, P., Smith, J., Yuŋgirrŋa, D., Dhamarrandji, S., & Gundjarranbuy, R. (2021). Facilitating sustainable disaster risk reduction in Indigenous communities: Reviving Indigenous worldviews, knowledge and practices through two-way partnering. *International Journal of Environmental Research and Public Health, 18*(3), 855. doi.org/10.3390/ijerph18030855

Allan, G. E. & Tschirner, A. (2009). Pastoralists' perspectives on the costs of widespread fires in the pastoral lands of the southern Northern Territory region of central Australia, 2000–02. In G. P. Edwards & G. E. Allan (Eds), *Desert fire: Fire and regional land management in the arid landscapes of Australia* (pp. 187–208). Alice Springs, NT: Desert Knowledge Cooperative Research Centre.

Andreas, S. & Faulkner, C. (1996). *NLP: The new technology of achievement*. New York, NY: William Morrow.

Australian Government. (2015). *Our north, our future: White paper on developing Northern Australia*. Retrieved from www.industry.gov.au/data-and-publications/our-north-our-future-white-paper-on-developing-northern-australia

Barker, R. & Gump, P. (1964). *Big school, small school*. Stanford, CA: Stanford University Press.

Beard, C. & Wilson, J. P. (2006). *Experiential learning: A best practice handbook for educators and trainers*. London, England: Kogan Page.

Bechtel, R. B. & Churchman, A. (2002). *Ecological psychology*. New York, NY: Wiley.

Berkes, F., Colding, J. & Folke, C. (2003). *Navigating social-ecological systems: Building resilience for complexity and change*. Cambridge, England: Cambridge University Press.

Brown, V. A., Harris, J. A. & Russell, J. Y. (Eds). (2010). *Tackling wicked problems through the transdisciplinary imagination*. London, England: Earthscan.

Buck, J. & Villines, S. (2007). *We the people: Consenting to a deeper democracy: A guide to sociocratic principles and methods*. Washington, DC: Sociocracy Info.

Buergelt, P. T., Maypilama, L. E., McPhee, J., Dhurrkay, G., Nirrpuranydji, S., Manyturrpuy, S., Wunungmurra, M., Skinner. T., Lowell, A., & Moss, S. (2017b). Working together with remote Indigenous communities to facilitate adapting to using energy wisely: Barriers and enablers. *Energy Procedia, 121*, 262–269.

Buergelt, P. T. & Paton, D. (2014). An ecological risk management and capacity building model. *Human Ecology, 42*, 591–603.

Buergelt, P. T., Paton, D., Sithole, B., Sangha, K., Campion, O. B. & Campion, J. (2017a). Living in harmony with our environment: A paradigm shift. In D. Paton & D. Johnston (Eds.), *Disaster resilience: An integrated approach* (2nd ed) (pp. 289–307). Springfield, Ill: Charles C. Thomas.

Buergelt, P. T. & Smith, R. (2015). Wildfires: An Australian perspective. In D. Paton, P. T. Buergelt, S. McCaffrey & F. Tedim (Eds), *Wildfire hazards, risks and disasters* (pp. 101–122). Hazards and Disasters series. London, England: Elsevier.

Bureau of Meteorology & Commonwealth Scientific and Industrial Research Organisation (CSIRO). (2015). *About monsoonal north*. Retrieved from www.climatechangeinaustralia.gov.au/en/impacts-and-adaptation/monsoonal-north/ (site discontinued).

Bushfire and Natural Hazards Cooperative Research Centre (BNHCRC). (2013). *Call for papers*. Melbourne, Vic.: BNHCRC.

Commonwealth of Australia. (2012). *Australian emergency management hub: Bushfire*. Retrieved from knowledge.aidr.org.au/

Commonwealth of Australia. (2013). *National disaster resilience framework*. Retrieved from www.em.gov.au/Publications/Program%20publications/Pages/NationalDisasterResilienceFramework.aspx (site discontinued)

Cranton, P. (2006). *Understanding and promoting transformative learning* (2nd ed.). San Francisco, CA: Jossey Bass.

Commonwealth Scientific and Industrial Research Organisation (CSIRO) & Bureau of Meteorology. (2014). *State of the climate 2014*. Canberra, ACT: Commonwealth of Australia.

Cutter, S. L., Irasema Alcántara-Ayala, A., Altan, O., Baker, D. N., Briceño, S., Gupta, H., ... Wu, G. (2015). Global risks: Pool knowledge to stem losses from disasters. *Nature, 522*, 277–279. doi.org/10.1038/522277a

Dalton, J. H., Elias, M. J. & Wandersman, A. (2007). *Community psychology: Linking individuals and communities* (2nd ed.). Belmont, CA: Wadsworth.

Department of Environment. (2015). *Climate change impacts in the Northern Territory.*

DePoerter, B. (1992). *Quantum learning: Unleashing the genius in you.* New York, NY: Dell.

DePoerter, B. & Hernacki, M. (1998). *Quantum learning in business: How to be more confident, effective and successful at work.* London, England: Piatkus Books.

DePoerter, B., Reardon, M. & Singer-Nourie, S. (1999). *Quantum teaching: Orchestrating student success.* London, England: Allyn and Bacon.

Endenburg, G. (1998). *Sociocracy as social design.* Delft, The Netherlands: Eburon Academic Publishers.

Endenburg, G. (2002). *Sociocracy: The organisation of decision-making.* Delft, The Netherlands: Eburon Academic Publishers.

Garnett, S. T., Sithole, B., Whitehead, P. J., Burgess, C. P., Johnston, F. H. & Lea, T. (2009). Healthy country, healthy people: Policy implications of links between Indigenous human health and environmental condition in Tropical Australia. *Australian Journal of Public Administration, 68*(1), 53–66.

International Federation of Red Cross and Red Crescent Societies (IFRCRCS). (2009). *Early warning, early action.* Geneva, Switzerland: IFRCRCS.

James, H. & Paton, D. (2016). *The consequences of Asian disasters: Demographic, planning and policy implications.* Springfield, IL: Charles C. Thomas.

Kyle, G., Graefe, A. & Manning, R. (2005). Testing the dimensionality of place attachment in recreational settings. *Environment and Behavior, 37*, 153–177.

Lindell, M. K., Arlikatti, S. & Prater, C. S. (2009). Why people do what they do to protect against earthquake risk: Perceptions of hazard adjustment attributes. *Risk Analysis, 29*(8), 1072–1088.

Mallick, B. (2014). Cyclone shelters and their locational suitability: An empirical analysis from coastal Bangladesh. *Disasters, 38*(3), 654–671.

McMillan, D. W. & Chavis, D. M. (1986). Sense of community: A definition and theory. *Journal of Community Psychology, 14*(1), 6–23.

Mezirow, J. (1996). Contemporary paradigms of learning. *Adult Education Quarterly, 50*, 5–23.

Mortimer, E., Bergin, A. & Carter, R. (2011). *Sharing risk: Financing Australia's disaster resilience* (Australian Strategic Policy Institute, Special Report Issue 37).

Murphy, B., Edwards, A., Meyer, C. P. & Russell-Smith, J. (2015). *Carbon accounting and savanna fire management*. Melbourne, Vic.: CSIRO Publishing.

Norris, F., Stevens, S., Pfefferbaum, B., Wyche, K. & Pfefferbaum, R. (2008). Community resilience as a metaphor, theory, set of capacities, and strategy for disaster readiness. *American Journal of Community Psychology, 41*(1–2), 127-150.

O'Connor, J. & Seymour, J. (2011). *Introducing NLP: Psychological skills for understanding and influencing people* (Neuro-Linguistic Programming). San Francisco, CA: Conari Press.

O'Keefe, P., Westgate, K. & Wisner, B. (1976). Taking the naturalness out of natural disasters. *Nature, 260*, 566–567.

O'Sullivan, E., Morrell, A. & O'Connor, M. A. (Eds). (2002). *Expanding the boundaries of transformative learning: Essays on theory and practice*. New York, NY: Palgrave.

Paton, D. (2014). *Disaster management for community workers*. Taipei, Taiwan: Ministry of Health and Welfare.

Paton, D. & Buergelt, P. T. (2012). Community engagement and wildfire preparedness: The influence of community diversity. In D. Paton & F. Tedim (Eds), *Wildfire and community: Facilitating preparedness and resilience* (pp. 241–259). Springfield, IL: Charles C. Thomas.

Paton, D. & James, H. (2016). Identifying new directions in post-disaster livelihood, resilience and sustainability in Asia. In H. James & D. Paton (Eds), *The consequences of disasters: Demographic, planning and policy implications* (pp. 357–369). Springfield, IL, Charles C. Thomas.

Paton, D. & Johnston, D. (2006). *Disaster resilience: An integrated approach*. Springfield, IL: Charles C Thomas.

Paton, D. & McClure, J. (2013). *Preparing for disaster: Building household and community capacity*. Springfield, IL: Charles C. Thomas.

Paton, D., Buergelt, P. T., McCaffrey, S. & Tedim, F. (Eds). (2015). *Wildfire hazards, risks and disasters.* Hazards and Disasters series. Oxford, England: Elsevier.

Paton, D., Johnston, D., Mamula-Seadon, L. & Kenney, C. M. (2014). Recovery and development: Perspectives from New Zealand and Australia. In N. Kapucu & K. T. Liou (Eds), *Disaster & development: Examining global issues and cases* (pp. 255–272). New York, NY: Springer.

Rose, C. (2011). *Accelerated learning for the 21st century: The six-step plan to unlock your master-mind.* New York, NY: Random House.

Smith, A. (1998). *Accelerated learning in practice.* New York, NY: Continuum.

Tianchen, L. (2003). Confucian ethics and the environment. *Culture Mandala: The Bulletin of the Centre for East-West Cultural and Economic Studies, 6*(1).

Thomalla, F. & Schmuk, H. (2004). We all knew that a cyclone was coming: Disaster preparedness and the Cyclone of 1999 in Orissa, India. *Disasters, 28*(4), 373–387.

Tuan, Y. F. (1977). *Space and place: The perspective of experience.* Minneapolis, MN: University of Minnesota Press.

United Nations International Strategy for Disaster Reduction (UNISDR). (2007). *The Hyogo Framework for Action (HFA) 2005–2015: Building the resilience of nations and communities to disasters* (UN Document A/CONF.206/6).

United Nations International Strategy for Disaster Reduction (UNISDR). (2015). *Sendai framework for disaster risk reduction.* Geneva, Switzerland: UNISDR. Retrieved from www.undrr.org/implementing-sendai-framework/what-sendai-framework

Zaffron, S. & Logan, D. (2011). *The three laws of performance: Rewriting the future of your organisation and your life.* Hoboken, NJ: Jossey-Bass.

# 19

# Perceptions About Climate Change Impacts and Adaptation— Case Studies from Indigenous Communities in Northern and Central Australia

Kerstin K. Zander, Yiheyis T. Maru, Digby Race,
Supriya Mathew and John Rainbird

## Introduction

The impact of climate change is one of the most significant environmental challenges facing humans. Australia is likely to face temperature increases in the range 0.6–1.5°C by 2030 and 2.2–5°C by 2070 compared with the climate of 1980–99 (CSIRO & Bureau of Meteorology, 2014). Extreme events are likely to become more severe and frequent in many locations across Australia, thus demanding preparatory measures to mitigate the potential risks (Addison, 2013). These extreme events include cyclones, and associated storm surges, riverine and flash flooding, heatwaves, coastal erosion, bushfires and more frequent droughts.

Indigenous communities are likely to feel the consequences of climate change in terms of maintaining their health and wellbeing, and outdoor living and housing comfort (Green et al., 2010). Indigenous peoples' ability to pursue education and employment opportunities, and the viability of community businesses are also likely to be affected by increases in intensity and frequency of extreme events such as heatwaves and flash flooding, which can cut off transport and communication to remote communities. The strong dependence of many remote Indigenous Australians on their traditional country for food (Altman, 2004), health (Garnett et al., 2009) and culture (Altman et al., 2007) may further increase the vulnerability[1] of Indigenous communities to climate change (Adger et al., 2005; Green et al., 2010).

There is a growing body of literature on understanding how Indigenous communities perceive, and might adapt to, climate change, globally (Berkes & Jolly, 2001; Sakakibara, 2008; Byg & Salick, 2009; Turner & Clifton, 2009) and in Australia (Green et al., 2010; Petheram et al., 2010; Petheram et al., 2015; Bardsley & Wiseman, 2012; Bird et al., 2013; Zander et al., 2013; Maru et al., 2014; Race et al., 2014). Recent studies in this area increasingly refer to adaptive capacities derived as a combination of vulnerabilities (e.g. socioeconomic disadvantage, distant governance and services for remote communities) and resilience (e.g. experience living in uncertain and harsh climates) (Petheram et al., 2010; Maru et al., 2014). In Australia, remote Indigenous communities typically have strong social networks (McAllister et al., 2008), a unique relationship to their country and considerable family and kinship responsibilities (Salmon, 2000; Burgess et al., 2009). These can create opportunities to improve their resilience (e.g. high mobility could allow relocation) to climate-related risks and increasing vulnerabilities (e.g. overcrowding and health implications). Adaptation should be considered as a dynamic, long-term, transitory and transitional process that involves repeated decisions, better described as adaptation pathways (Maru & Stafford Smith, 2014).

To inform Indigenous peoples' pathways to adaptation, there is a need for understanding what impacts climate change and extreme events have on Indigenous communities, how climate change–related changes and impacts are perceived and what might be feasible adaptation responses. In this chapter, we aim to present a synthesis of research conducted in four case studies (see Figure 19.1) that address these issues. We focus on the jurisdictions with the highest proportion of Indigenous people in Australia—the Northern

---

1    We used Intergovernmental Panel on Climate Change definitions as follows: adaptation = 'adjustment in natural or human systems in response to actual or expected climatic stimuli or their effects, which moderates harm or exploits beneficial opportunities'; vulnerability = 'the degree to which a system is susceptible to, and unable to cope with, adverse effects of climate change, including climate variability and extremes'; resilience = 'ability of a social or ecological system to absorb disturbances while retaining the same basic structure and ways of functioning, the capacity for self-organisation, and the capacity to adapt to stress and change' (Intergovernmental Panel on Climate Change, 2007).

Territory (NT) with nearly 30 per cent and the Torres Strait Islands in northern Queensland with 79 per cent of their populations identifying as Indigenous or Torres Strait Islanders. The NT (both coastal and central desert areas) and north Queensland including low-lying islands of Torres Strait are prone to extreme weather events (Hennessy et al., 2007).

Three case studies are from the NT: 1) Lajamanu at the northern end of the Tanami Desert, 2) town camps of Alice Springs in Central Australia and 3) Yirrkala in East Arnhem Land. In all three case studies, in-depth interviews, focus group discussions and workshops were conducted with community members, using a range of participatory methods in collaboration with local Indigenous researchers. The fourth case study is from Queensland and presents a Human Development Index (HDI) and adaptation implication analysis for the people in the Torres Strait region. A more detailed description of the methodology for the research in Lajamanu and Alice Springs (see Race et al., 2014; Race et al., 2016), Yirrkala (Petheram et al., 2010; Zander et al., 2013) and the Torres Straits (Butler et al., 2014) is provided in the cited literature. The research for the case studies was conducted at different times with varying foci and data collection methods (see Table 19.1).

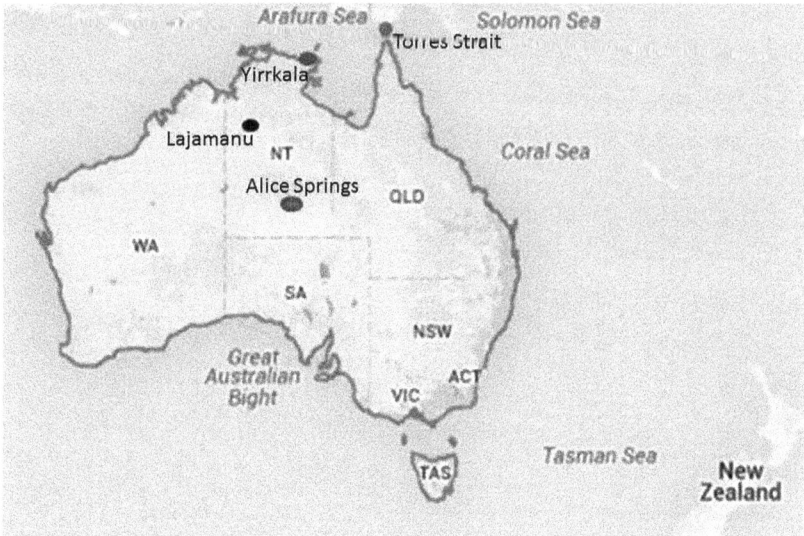

**Figure 19.1: Locations of the case study regions—communities in Lajamanu, Yirrkala and Torres Strait and town camps around Alice Springs.**
Source: Authors' research.

**Table 19.1: Details of the four case studies.**

| Case study | Objectives | Methods |
|---|---|---|
| Lajamanu community case study and Alice Springs town camps | To gather information about:<br>1. major weather changes (over seasons and over years) in study participants' lifetimes<br>2. major weather events that affect the participants<br>3. adaptive strategies used to cope with extreme weather. | • research was conducted by a team of experienced researchers from multiple organisations (Ninti One Ltd, Tangentyere Council, Charles Darwin University and CSIRO—partners in the Cooperative Research Centre for Remote Economic Participation) together with experienced Aboriginal researchers at both locations<br>• collection of information through a few cycles of interviews and focus group discussions<br>• stratified sample of the Indigenous population at the two sites (to include people across different ages, gender and language groups)<br>• total participants were 36 Indigenous people at Lajamanu and 43 Indigenous people in Alice Springs (see Race et al., 2014; Race et al., 2016). |
| Yirrkala | To understand Indigenous peoples' perception of climate change and associated coping strategies now and in the future to integrate those into mainstream in planning adaptation policy. | • in-depths interviews conducted by Indigenous co-researchers and workshops facilitated by Indigenous co-researchers<br>• initial selection of participants defined by the research situation (contacts and available participants) and later guided by emergent data and theory, in a process of 'theoretical sampling'<br>• total number of participants was 21<br>• four workshops—two with a total of nine male Indigenous land/sea rangers from the Dhimurru Aboriginal Corporation and two workshops with a total of 12 female participants from a women's organisation and local households<br>• use of visual techniques to support discussions<br>• data collected over two years (2008–10). |
| Torres Strait region | 1. assess regional resilience<br>2. explore potential future scenarios in the face of climate and other changes<br>3. identify adaptation options. | • two regional and three community-level workshops conducted between July 2012 and December 2014<br>• surveys on perceptions of the meaning, elements and status of resilience of communities, the region, climate change and other social and environmental changes<br>• analysis of a Human Development Index (HDI) for the Torres Strait region for global comparison<br>• HDI combined with 2006 Australian Bureau of Statistics census data for Torres Strait region. |

## Case Study: Yirrkala

Yirrkala is situated in North East Arnhem Land (see Figure 19.1) with a population of approximately of 800. This area, as part of tropical Northern Australia, is expected to become hotter, experience sea level rise and more extreme cyclonic events and associated storm surges. Sea levels rose 7–10 mm per year along Australia's northern coastline between 1993 and 2009, about three times the rate of sea level rise along the southern and eastern coastlines (CSIRO & Bureau of Meteorology, 2014). Many off-shore islands, wetland areas and coastlines are likely to be vulnerable to erosion and saltwater intrusion (Green, 2008) leading to significant negative impacts on the distribution of plant and animal species (Dunlop & Brown, 2008).

The Indigenous people in this case study area are referred to as Yolngu and consist of more than 50 Indigenous clans. Their language group, Yolngu Matha, comprises about 12 different dialects (Omniglot, 2009). The conducted research was in collaboration with local co-researchers and the Dhimurru Aboriginal Corporation (ranger group). We conducted in-depth interviews and a series of workshops (see Table 19.1). Using visual techniques such as drawing maps and diagrams, participatory sculpting and participant-generated photography (see Petheram et al., 2010; Petheram et al., 2011), respondents were asked to identify changes in their environment (which also included social/political changes) that they have noticed. Causes of these changes were then discussed, of which climate change was one.

Workshop participants always talked about climate change impacts in relation to non-climate (social) issues and observed landscape changes have almost always been attributed to a combination of climate change and mining (Yirrkala and surrounding communities are very close to a bauxite mine) and development (e.g. increasing tourism). When discussing possible ways to adapt, people in Yirrkala also invariably linked climate change to current wider problems such as lack of employment opportunities, housing and facilities for the youth and violence (see Petheram et al., 2010). However, many said that their current problems will worsen as exposure to extreme weather events increase. Rather than responding to a top-down approach, Indigenous people in Yirrkala stressed the importance of dealing with climate change adaptation in culturally acceptable ways by fostering self-sufficiency, independence and empowerment. Some also stressed the importance of observing and knowing the environment (their traditional country) in enabling people to adapt to climatic changes and, more broadly, any environmental change (e.g. changes in seasons, abundance of animals, fires and existence of plants used for food).

## Case Study: Lajamanu

Lajamanu is a small remote town in the NT with the majority of its 650 residents being Indigenous. The projected climate change indicates there will be an increase in temperatures, with more hot days and extended periods of warm temperatures and fewer frosts for the northern rangelands region, which includes both Lajamanu and Alice Springs. Rainfall projections are unclear for this region.[2] As in most remote Australian locations, occurrences of extreme events (e.g. floods and cyclones) can result in damage to infrastructure, road closures and spread of diseases.

During the survey and focus group discussions with the participants at Lajamanu, people indicated that most of them are deeply aware of the short-term weather and long-term trends of the climate where they live. The surrounding natural environment remains an important indicator of the local climate, even when the environment is in various stages of alteration (e.g. dams used to trap and store surface water, thereby affecting creeks and waterholes) and degradation (e.g. overgrazing by feral animals and prevalence of weeds). Not surprisingly, people who spend more time living and working outdoors (e.g. hunting and gathering wild food in the surrounding country or employed as rangers to manage the surrounding natural resources) reported more detailed experiences and insights about the climate and changes to their country.[3] The results of this research indicated that the rich and deeply embedded traditional ecological knowledge (TEK) held by remote Indigenous communities is affected by the frequency and nature of access to their country. Recent policy and organisational changes are formalising avenues for this TEK to be shared and documented (according to cultural protocols) and included in

---

2   See northern rangelands Coupled Model Intercomparison Project data, www.climatechange inaustralia.gov.au/en/.
3   'Country' is a term used by Aboriginal people to refer to the land to which they have a long cultural connection to and their place of Dreaming (see australianmuseum.net.au/glossary-indigenous-australia-terms#sthash.bnq5gbOw.dpuf).

decision-making in relation to natural resource management. Participants in the focus group discussions acknowledged that the Aboriginal Ranger Groups are one such avenue, where small teams of men and women from the local community are employed to manage the surrounding natural environment.

## Case Study: Alice Springs Town Camps

Alice Springs is an established town in Central Australia with a population of about 28,000, which fulfils an important role as a service hub providing education, employment, health, welfare and financial services to the wider population in the Central Australian region. About 19 per cent of the Alice Springs population is Indigenous. It has a semi-arid climate but is still prone to flash flooding, which can result in the outbreak of infectious diseases, bushfires following the increase in vegetation, damage to infrastructure and disruption to transport links (Beer et al., 2013). The projected increase in the number of hotter days is likely to result in health-related challenges, such as heat stress affecting vulnerable members of communities such as the elderly and those with poor health (see Webb et al., 2014). Climate change is also expected to affect the pastoral and tourism industries (Beer et al., 2013; Race, 2015).

Participants in the research conducted in the Alice Springs town camps (public housing for Aboriginal communities in Alice Springs) mentioned that they had observed many changes to the climate (e.g. hotter and longer summers and more variable rainfall) and natural surroundings (e.g. more weeds and less bush food). The respondents indicated that modern housing and associated services (e.g. reliable supply of fresh water) provided a comfortable adaptation to heat in comparison to what was available to them prior to the 1990s. Their adaptive strategies mainly focused on: 1) energy intensive measures (e.g. air conditioners) to moderate building temperatures at comfortable levels; 2) housing designs as a shelter against extreme weather; and 3) movement to communal buildings such as shopping or art centres to escape harsh weather. They also mentioned gathering under tree shade and hosing the ground as heat stress mitigation measures. The strong social networking interests of these communities have also been highlighted in their adaptation preferences (e.g. gathering under the shade of trees and visiting shopping or art centres). Participants noted an increased reliance on modern technology to adapt to the increasing heat in Alice Springs.

## Case Study: Torres Strait Region

The Torres Strait region is part of the northern border of Australia that stretches from the tip of Cape York to the south-western coast of Papua New Guinea. The region has 18 communities with 17 islands supporting permanent settlements (Foreign Affairs, Defence and Trade References Committee, 2010). The Torres Strait region is home to about 7,500 people of whom 84 per cent are of Torres Islander and Aboriginal origin (ABS, 2012). The Torres Strait Islander people have deep connections with and extensive local knowledge of their land and sea (Foreign Affairs, Defence and Trade References Committee, 2010; Butler et al., 2012).

Geographic location and island characteristics, cultural factors and socioeconomic conditions put the Torres Strait Islands at high risk of impacts from climate change and associated increases in frequency and intensity of extreme weather events (Green et al., 2010). Some communities on low-lying islands, especially in the central coral cay islands of Masig, Poruma, Iama and Warraber and northwest mud islands of Boigu and Saibai, are already experiencing inundation and erosion impacts of sea level rise and storm surges. Communities are very concerned by their current experiences and potential impacts of climate on the long-term liveability of their islands and their ability to undertake traditional livelihoods including hunting and fishing (Green et al., 2010; McNamara & Westoby, 2011). Potential community dislocation as result of climate change will likely have negative impacts on the physical and mental health of Torres Strait Islander people as it disrupts close attachments of communities to country and challenges their strong view of community health and wellbeing connections to the state of their land and sea country (Green & Minchin, 2014). Potential impacts of climate change (Butler et al., 2012) include:

- increasing coastal erosion and major damage to settlement infrastructure including houses, transport facilities, sewerage, water and power plants with risk of mortality, morbidity and disruption of livelihood and potential dislocations

- inundation of cemeteries and other culturally sacred sites with potential for a high level of physical and psychological health implications
- increase in insect-borne diseases due to change in favourable climate and breeding conditions
- changes in breeding patterns, abundance and location of important totemic (e.g. dugong and turtle) and other animals and plants with implication for nutrition, health and community wellbeing
- increased risk of heat-related impacts such as heat stress, water shortage and bushfire risk.

Communities have received urgent support from state and federal governments to build sea walls as an adaptation response to reduce exposure to sea level rise. In recent participatory adaptation and resilience planning work carried out by the Torres Strait Regional Authority (2016), community leaders recognised the importance of immediate hard adaptation responses (those involving physical infrastructure). However, they also noted the widespread health and socioeconomic disadvantage and high level of dependence on welfare as core causes of weakening culture, thus adding to the social vulnerability of these communities to climate change impacts.

Our calculations of HDI for the Torres Strait region puts the region's disadvantage into a global perspective. The HDI had a scale ranging from zero (lowest) to one (highest), based on a country's life expectancy, adult literacy and school enrolment in the particular year. UNDP (2009) ranked 187 nations in 2007 and used ABS (2006) data for Australia, which ranked second. Our estimate of the HDI score for the Torres Strait Islands resulted in 0.736, ranking 110th out of 187 and close in ranking to Fiji and other developing countries. The score for Indigenous Torres Strait Islanders indicated a gap of 0.274 in favour of the non-Indigenous population in the Torres Strait region, showing a significant disparity in the health and the socioeconomic conditions of Indigenous and non-Indigenous communities.

The Steering Committee for the Review of Government Service Provision (2014) report indicated that there has been slight improvement in life expectancy, average income and post-secondary education outcomes. However, Indigenous rate of disability and chronic diseases remains very high, mental health problems and adult imprisonment rates have worsened and no change has occurred in juvenile detention, family and community violence and literacy and numeracy results.

Climate change impacts already evident, particularly in the low-lying islands, may worsen the health and socioeconomic disadvantage of Torres Strait Islander people and the worsening conditions may, in turn, amplify the vulnerability of communities to climate change and associated increases in the severity of impacts of extreme weather events. This forms a trap that requires a transformative action (Maru et al., 2012). A transformative action involves addressing the root cause to achieve a substantial qualitative and systemic change in the system. Torres Strait Islander communities have adapted to changes in climate in the past and still retain many elements of resilience in their culture, local language and traditional knowledge. Efforts for transformation must build on these resilient elements. However, transformation will require addressing root causes of current health and other socioeconomic conditions and a substantial reduction in welfare dependence of Torres Strait Islander communities as in the other case studies.

## Concluding Remarks

The research conducted in the four case studies indicates the importance of building on the strengths of the local community (e.g. existing resources, social networks and traditional knowledge) to explore and develop feasible adaptation options, rather than introducing adaptation measures that may be effective elsewhere for different populations. The social capital cultural values and knowledge of the Indigenous communities that need to underpin efforts to build the adaptive capacity to climate change are often undervalued by outside researchers, policymakers and service providers. While modern buildings can provide immediate relief from extended periods of hot weather or storms (e.g. shopping centres), these can be expensive to operate and may not be affordable to operate as currently practised over the long term for the highly dispersed population across Central Australia. The example of the Aboriginal Ranger Groups (described above) are creating a new adaptation knowledge that blends TEK with contemporary science and equipment that simultaneously addresses vulnerability (e.g. using contemporary technology to record and analyse changes in the local environment and using modern equipment and vehicles to control pest animals and plants to enhance the health of the native biodiversity) and builds resilience (e.g. draws on knowledge and wisdom of Elders and builds the skills and knowledge of younger generations about how to care for their country) amid complex changes.

As such, learning how best to blend the existing strengths of remote Indigenous communities with that offered by outsiders (e.g. individuals, organisations and governments) is most likely to afford an effective way forward so that remote Indigenous communities can build their resilience to the changes they confront.

Despite the exposure to different impacts of climate change and associated extreme events, there is communality and similarity in the level of health and social wellbeing disadvantages and welfare dependency of communities across all four case studies, which is at the core their heightened sensitivity and low capacity to adapt. We argue that a stronger understanding of the cultural and social capital within remote Indigenous communities, particularly those still strongly framed by traditional culture, can enhance the development of bottom-up approaches for effective climate adaptation (e.g. approaches initiated, developed and supported by local residents). In three communities, Indigenous people pointed out the need for integrating climate change policies into other mainstream policies. However, Indigenous communities in all four case studies face multiple and immediate socioeconomic problems such as lack of education, jobs and housing, violence, and medical problems. Therefore, climate change policies and responses to climate risks should not be implemented in isolation from other policies that community members wish the government to pursue to alleviate the more urgent problems (Petheram et al., 2010; Mathew et al., 2012).

This means paying attention to multiple immediate issues while simultaneously addressing the root causes of vulnerability of Indigenous communities to climate change and associated extreme events. An attention only to immediate community issues poses the risk of resulting in maladaptive actions. The adaptation decision process in Indigenous communities should simultaneously address both short- and long-term issues and combine incremental and transformation actions as suggested by Maru et al. (2014). The balance of attention to incremental (e.g. short-term options such as use of electric air conditioners to adapt to heat stress and community education) and transformational adaptation actions (e.g. transforming to renewable energy) that need to be given in building adaptation pathways will depend on whether a community is in a maladaptive or an adaptive space (Wise et al., 2014). While incremental adaptation has a place, the significant health and socioeconomic disadvantage and the welfare dependence are such that transformation options that build on the resilient elements of the communities are required to effectively address the combination of changes (including climate change) affecting remote Indigenous communities in Northern Australia.

# References

Addison, J. (2013). *Impact of climate change on health and wellbeing in remote Australian communities a review of literature and scoping of adaptation options* (CRC-REP Working Paper CW014). Alice Springs, NT: Ninti One Ltd.

Adger, W. N., Hughes, T. P., Folke, C., Carpenter, S. R. & Rockström, J. (2005). Social-ecological resilience to coastal disasters. *Science*, *309*(5737), 1036–1039.

Altman, J. (2004). Economic development and Indigenous Australia: Contestations over property, institutions and ideology. *Australian Journal of Agricultural and Resource Economics*, *48*(3), 513–534.

Altman, J., Buchanan, G. J. & Larsen, L. (2007). *The environmental significance of the Indigenous estate: Natural resource management as economic development in remote Australia* (Discussion Paper No. 286). Canberra, ACT: ANU.

Australian Bureau of Statistics (ABS). (2006). *Population characteristics, Aboriginal and Torres Strait Islander Australians, 2006* (Cat. No. 4713.0). Canberra, ACT: ABS.

Australian Bureau of Statistics (ABS). (2012). *2011 census of population and housing. Aboriginal and Torres Strait Islander peoples (Indigenous)* (Cat. No. 2002.0). Canberra, ACT: ABS.

Bardsley, D. K. & Wiseman, N. D. (2012). Climate change vulnerability and social development for remote Indigenous communities of South Australia. *Global Environmental Change*, *22*(3), 713–723.

Beer, A., Tually, S., Kroehn, M., Martin, J., Gerritsen, R., Taylor, M., … Law, J. (2013). *Australia's country towns 2050: What will a climate adapted settlement pattern look like?* Gold Coast, Qld: National Climate Change Adaptation Research Facility.

Berkes, F. & Jolly, D. (2001). Adapting to climate change: Social-ecological resilience in a Canadian western arctic community. *Conservation Ecology*, *5*(2), Article 18.

Bird, D., Govan, J., Murphy, H., Harwood, S., Haynes, K., Carson, D., … Larkin, S. (2013). *Future change in ancient worlds: Indigenous adaptation in Northern Australia*. Gold Coast, Qld: National Climate Change Adaptation Research Facility.

Burgess, P.C., Johnston, F.H., Berry, H.L., McDonnell, J., Yibarbuk, D., Gunabarra, C., Mileran, A. & Bailie, R.S. (2009). Healthy country, healthy people: The relationship between Indigenous health status and caring for country. *Medical Journal of Australia, 190*(10), 567–572.

Butler, J. R., Tawake, A., Skewes, T., Tawake, L. & McGrath, V. (2012). Integrating traditional ecological knowledge and fisheries management in the Torres Strait, Australia: The catalytic role of turtles and dugong as cultural keystone species. *Ecology and Society, 17*(4), 1–19.

Butler, J. R., Skewes, T., Mitchell, D., Pontio, M. & Hills, T. (2014). Stakeholder perceptions of ecosystem service declines in Milne Bay, Papua New Guinea: Is human population a more critical driver than climate change? *Marine Policy, 46*, 1–13.

Byg, A. & Salick, J. (2009). Local perspectives on a global phenomenon—climate change in eastern Tibetan villages. *Global Environmental Change, 19*(2), 156–166.

Commonwealth Scientific and Industrial Research Organisation (CSIRO) & Bureau of Meteorology. (2014). *State of the climate 2014*. Retrieved from www.bom.gov.au/state-of-the-climate/documents/state-of-the-climate-2014_low-res.pdf?ref=button

Dunlop, M. & Brown, P. R. (2008, February). *Implications of climate change for Australia's National Reserve System: A preliminary assessment*. Canberra, ACT: Department of Climate Change.

Foreign Affairs, Defence and Trade References Committee. (2010, November). *The Torres Strait: Bridge and border*. Canberra, ACT: Commonwealth of Australia. Retrieved from www.aph.gov.au/~/media/wopapub/senate/committee/fadt_ctte/completed_inquiries/2010-13/torresstrait/report/report.ashx

Garnett, S. T., Sithole, B., Whitehead, P. J., Burgess, C. P., Johnston, F. H. & Lea, T. (2009). Healthy country, healthy people: Policy implications of links between Indigenous human health and environmental condition in tropical Australia. *The Australian Journal of Public Administration, 68*(1), 53–66.

Green, D. (2008). *Garnaut climate change review. Climate impacts on the health of remote northern Indigenous communities*. Sydney, NSW: University of New South Wales.

Green, D., Alexander, L., McInnes, K., Church, J., Nicholls, N. & White, N. (2010). An assessment of climate change impacts and adaptation for the Torres Strait Islands, Australia. *Climatic Change, 102*(3), 405–433.

Green, D. & Minchin, L. (2014). Living on climate-changed country: Indigenous health, well-being and climate change in remote Australian communities. *EcoHealth, 11*(2), 263–272.

Hennessy, K., Fitzharris, B., Bates, B. C., Harvey, N., Howden, M., Hughes, L., … Warrick, R. (2007). Australia and New Zealand climate change 2007: Impacts, adaptation and vulnerability. In M. L. Parry, O. F. Canziani, J. P. Palutikof, P. J. van der Linden & C. E. Hanson (Eds), *Contribution of working group II to the fourth assessment: Report of the intergovernmental panel on climate change*. Cambridge, England: Cambridge University Press.

Intergovernmental Panel on Climate Change. (2007). *Climate change 2007, glossary*. Retrieved from www.ipcc.ch/site/assets/uploads/2019/01/SYRAR5-Glossary_en.pdf

Maru, Y. T., Chewings, V. & Sparrow, A. (2012). *Climate change adaptation, energy futures and carbon economies in remote Australia: A review of the current literature, research and policy* (CRC-REP Working Paper CW005). Alice Springs, NT: Ninti One Ltd.

Maru, Y. T. & Stafford Smith, M. (2014). Reframing adaptation pathways. *Global Environmental Change, 28*, 322–324.

Maru, Y. T., Stafford Smith, M., Sparrow, A., Pinho, P. F. & Dube, O. P. (2014). A linked vulnerability and resilience framework for adaptation pathways in remote disadvantaged communities. *Global Environmental Change, 28*, 337–350.

Mathew, S., Trueck, S. & Henderson-Sellers, A. (2012). Kochi, India case study of climate adaptation to floods: Ranking local government investment options. *Global Environmental Change, 22*, 308–319.

McAllister, R. R. J., Cheers, B., Darbas, T., Davies, J., Richards, C., Robinson, C. J., Ashley, M., Fernando, D. & Maru, Y. T. (2008). Social networks in arid Australia: A review of concepts and evidence. *Rangeland Journal, 30*, 167–176.

McNamara, K. E. & Westoby, R. (2011). Local knowledge and climate change adaptation on Erub Island, Torres Strait. *Local Environment, 16*, 887–901.

Omniglot. (2009). *Yolngu (Yolŋu matha)*. Retrieved from www.omniglot.com/writing/yolngu.php

Petheram, L., High, C., Campbell, B. M. & Stacey, N. (2011). Lenses for learning: Visual techniques in natural resource management. *Journal of Environmental Management, 92*, 2734–2745.

Petheram, L., Stacey, N. & Fleming, A. (2015). Future sea changes: Indigenous women's preferences for adaptation to climate change on South Goulburn Island, Northern Territory (Australia). *Climate and Development, 7*, 339–352.

Petheram, L., Zander, K. K., Campbell, B., High, D. & Stacey, N. (2010). 'Strange changes': Indigenous perspectives of climate change and adaptation in NE Arnhem Land (Australia). *Global Environmental Change, 20*, 681–692.

Race, D. (2015). *The impacts of, and strategies to ameliorate, the intensity of climate change on enterprises in remote Australia* (CRC for Remote Economic Participation Working Paper CW020). Alice Springs, NT: Ninti One Ltd.

Race, D., Campbell, M., Hampton, K., Foster, D., Fejo, C. & Robertson, D. (2014). Observations of climate change by remote communities: Lessons from the bush in central Australia. *Journal of Australian Indigenous Issues, 17*, 23–39.

Race, D., Mathew, S., Campbell, M. & Hampton, K. (2016). Understanding climate adaptation investments for communities in remote Australia: Experiences from desert communities. *Climatic Change, 139*(3–4), 461–475.

Sakakibara, C. (2008). 'Our home is drowning': Iñupiat storytelling and climate change in Point Hope, Alaska. *Geographical Review, 98*, 456–475.

Salmon, E. (2000). Kincentric ecology: Indigenous perceptions of the human-nature relationship. *Ecologcal Applications, 10*(5), 1327–1332.

Steering Committee for the Review of Government Service Provision. (2014). *Overcoming Indigenous disadvantage: Key indicators 2014*. Canberra, ACT: Productivity Commission. Retrieved from www.pc.gov.au/research/recurring/overcoming-indigenous-disadvantage/key-indicators-2014

Torres Strait Regional Authority. (2016, June). Torres Strait Adaptation and Resilience Plan 2016–2021. Report prepared by the Environmental Management Program, Torres Strait Regional Authority.

Turner, N. J. & Clifton, H. (2009). 'It's so different today': Climate change and Indigenous lifeways in British Columbia, Canada. *Global Environmental Change, 19*, 180–190.

United Nations Development Programme (UNDP). (2009). *Human development report 2009*. New York, NY: Author.

Webb, L., Bambrick, H., Tait, P., Green, D. & Alexander, L. (2014). Effect of ambient temperature on Australian Northern Territory public hospital admissions for cardiovascular disease among Indigenous and non-Indigenous populations. *International Journal of Environmental Research and Public Health*, *11*(2), 1942–1959.

Wise, R. M., Fazey, I., Stafford Smith, M., Park, S. E., Eakin, H. C., Archer Van Garderen, E. R. M. & Campbell, B. (2014). Reconceptualising adaptation to climate change as part of pathways of change and response. *Global Environmental Change*, *28*, 325–336.

Zander, K. K., Petheram, L. & Garnett, S. T. (2013). Stay or leave? Potential climate change adaptation strategies among Aboriginal people in coastal communities in Northern Australia. *Natural Hazards*, *67*(2), 591–609.

# 20

# Design for Liveability in Tropical Australia

Lisa Law, Shokhida Safarova, Andrew Campbell and Edward Halawa

> The ABS [Australian Bureau of Statistics] predicts a high population figure of 62.2 million Australians by 2101. This represents an extra 39,402,415 people. To accommodate these extra millions, we would need over 17 million houses—some 14,276km$^2$ of new suburbia ... Despite the likelihood of such growth, Australia's current collection of major city planning frameworks only accounts for about an extra 5.5 million people. (Weller & Bolleter, 2013, p. vi)

In their agenda-setting book on the future of Australia cities, Weller and Bolleter (2013) contemplated Australia's rapid and continual growth and its implications for the future Australian landscape. Setting views about a Big Australia to one side, these trends present Australian cities with some immutable challenges. Will Australians have to adapt to a deteriorating quality of life as cities accommodate this growth? Will the extra accommodation be built in the precincts where jobs are concentrated? Can cities grow to quarter more and more people without losing their liveability?[1] Are there any special issues to consider in tropical Australia, a region that has experienced high population growth over the past decade and where the government has earmarked future development (Australian Government, 2014)?

---

1  The term 'liveability' is understood here as 'the quality of urban life that is determined predominantly by the physical nature of the built environment' (see State of the Environment 2011 Committee, 2011).

Australia is not alone in facing an expanding urban footprint. Growing rapidly from 746 million people in 1950 to 3.9 billion people in 2014, the world's urban population is now expected to surpass 6 billion by 2045 (United Nations, 2014). As Rob Adams (2011), Director of City Design in Melbourne, put it, 'We are going to have to build almost as much urbanism again in the next 40 or 50 years as we have since the start of civilization'. In a context of scarce resources and climate change, designing and managing sustainable, ecologically sensitive cities is a crucial global challenge for the next century. We need to adapt locally relevant good urban design to create better cities—to minimise energy use and net greenhouse gas emissions but also to improve physical and mental health and social outcomes for urban dwellers.

In Northern Australia—a region that encompasses the parts of Australia north of the Tropic of Capricorn, including parts of Western Australia, the Northern Territory and Queensland —new suburban development to accommodate growing populations only rarely follows principles of sustainable tropical design (cf. Bay & Ong, 2006; Emmanuel, 1995; Safarova et al., 2017; Safarova et al., 2018). New subdivisions tend to offer large concrete block dwellings with many internal walls and small window openings, with tiny backyard/green spaces that are often enclosed with a substantial fence (see, for example, Figure 20.1; Law, 2019). Small backyards prohibit landscaping for shading buildings and reducing ambient temperatures, fencing prohibits breezeways and the block homes themselves need air conditioning for a large portion of the year. Such subdivisions tend to have poor environmental and social outcomes, with residents retreating to the climate-controlled privacy of their home. Australian New Urbanism has made some headway in planning circles, creating more diverse and walkable communities with better access to green/public spaces. Urban consolidation projects have also tended to encourage smaller lot sizes to enable higher urban densities (Hall, 2010). Most new subdivisions in cities and towns across tropical Australia are consequently energy hungry and overly reliant on car use.

**Figure 20.1: Google Earth image of a tightly packed, air-conditioned neighbourhood in Cairns (16 August 2016).**
Source: Google Earth.

Therefore, urban growth and consolidation presents urban designers and architects in Northern Australia with unique challenges in terms of creating habitable/comfortable indoor and outdoor spaces. The main design challenge is to reconcile two opposing thermal comfort parameters in a hot and humid tropical climate characterised by a high ambient air temperature and high relative humidity. On one hand is the need for ventilation and air movement, a parameter promoted by proponents of passive troppo design. On the other is the need to reduce hot and very humid air, which even when moving across human skin can still be within what is normally considered to be the heat stress zone. In short, this is the difference between a porous building envelope that embraces prevailing breezes and a less permeable building that is more efficient at mechanical cooling. For the second half of the twentieth century, the response to the northern tropical climate has shifted from passive design to active cooling through air conditioning. This shift helped displace the traditional Queenslander, a high-set timber house with breezy undercroft spaces, casement windows to direct breezes and large verandas for shade and outdoor living. Air-conditioned residential suburbs are now dominant in Northern Australia and houses tend to look much like they do elsewhere, with high thermal mass, high embodied energy, limited shading and the active elimination of natural ventilation. These are not buildings designed with tropical liveability in mind.

Given the increasing attention directed towards Northern Australia due to its potential for growth, proximity to Asia and specialised expertise in tropical development, urban issues must be a pivotal part of any northern development strategy. Unfortunately, that has not been the case in the most recent green paper on northern development (Australian Government, 2014). This chapter puts urban growth in the context of a developing tropical Australia, where an increase in the number of residential detached buildings will contribute to mounting energy demands and greenhouse emissions unless more regionally responsive/climate sensitive subdivision designs are advocated for the region. Although the chapter sets out some of these challenges, it also provides case studies of innovation in the field, arguing that efforts to provide climatically adapted design will make new suburban development more liveable for growing populations in a growing Northern Australia.

# Challenges to Liveability in Tropical Australia

Our research focus is to work from design principles that seek to manage thermal comfort at the scale of individual buildings and precincts in ways that are also cognisant of wider sustainability and liveability concerns including energy, water, resource depletion, amenity and biodiversity. To do that, we need to understand the basic drivers of thermal comfort. Thermal conditions in urban areas are influenced by many factors, including building designs and materials, and the type and amount of urban vegetation (Emmanuel, 2005). These factors combine to create urban heat islands (UHI) where temperatures can be 4°C higher than in less built-up areas, sometimes leading to increases in heat stress–related morbidity and mortality (Wong & Yu, 2005; Loughnan et al., 2013; Bi et al., 2011). Architects and urban designers can apply different design techniques to mitigate these heat stress conditions, but environmentally responsive, tropical architecture has tended to recede in the face of modernising cities where international building styles are constructed from materials travelling long distances.

Many scholars and practitioners stress the importance of passive cooling techniques in tropical building design, including the layout of buildings but also the urban design techniques that affect human thermal conditions in tropical places more generally (Baker, 1987; Givoni, 1992; Aynsley, 2006; Cheng et al., 2007; Yilmaz, 2007; Kibert, 2012). The environment in and around any building can be enhanced through design elements such as good orientation for shading and capturing prevailing winds, creating enough distance between buildings to enable breezeways and vegetation for shade, using appropriate building forms that enable good ventilation (both from external breezes and also ceiling fans) and selecting building materials with appropriate thermal mass for the site. In addition to design techniques at the individual building scale, the layout, geometry, material and density of buildings within the wider urban fabric can contribute to increased air temperatures by storing heat and preventing natural ventilation, while parks and other green areas play a crucial role in reducing the impact of UHI at a local level (Ali-Toudert & Mayer, 2007; Bowler et al., 2010; Shashua-Bar et al., 2012). Urban designers can mitigate heat stress by addressing these issues, using appropriate building and surface materials and considering the cooling effects of green spaces on urban ambient temperatures.

Designing lots and subdivisions that minimise solar radiation and allow access to prevailing breezes is considered a major factor in improving the thermal performance of a residential housing. Lot layout in particular is crucial to the thermal performance and energy efficiency of a building envelope (Miller & Ambrose, 2005; CRCCI, 2006; Ambrose, 2008). Miller and Ambrose (2005) considered the influence of lot orientation on the energy efficiency of buildings' envelope in the subtropics, for example, and found that changing the orientation of the house can increase or decrease the energy load by 10–32 per cent. In 2006, the CRCCI carried out a related study of the role of natural ventilation in cooling South-east Queensland houses. The study found that the small lots (18–25 m deep) had very poor cross-flow ventilation and that energy efficiency was harder to achieve in houses built on these lots because of the ratios of lot area to building floor area.

These design techniques notwithstanding, there is no agreed way to measure the effectiveness of mitigation strategies. But measuring thermal comfort is important because of the very small margin between the upper limit of comfort and the 'onset of heat stress' in the tropics (Aynsley, 1997, p. 168). Two widely used thermal comfort prediction methods in the academic literature include the Predicted Mean Vote (PMV) (developed by Fanger, 1986) and the Adaptive Model (AM) (Auliciems & Szokolay, 1997; de Dear & Brager, 1998; Humphreys & Fergus Nicol, 2002). The PMV index is calculated by using variables such as the metabolic rate and clothing type of survey participants, the internal air temperature and the radiant temperature and relative humidity and velocity of the air. However, the PMV method has been criticised as inappropriate for predicting thermal comfort in naturally ventilated buildings. De Dear and Brager (1998) suggested that the AM better predicts thermal comfort because it considers outdoor temperature, behavioural adjustment, physiological acclimatisation and psychological habitation or expectation. Halawa and Van Hoof (2012) suggested the development of a new method that would incorporate the best of the PMV and AM.

In a policy context, Australia's National House Energy Rating System (NatHERS) has adopted the far simpler Effective Temperature (ET*) index for assessing indoor thermal comfort. NatHERS is a national framework regulating thermal performances of Australian homes and encourages energy-efficient building design and construction by providing a reliable way to estimate and rank the potential thermal performance of residential buildings. The ET* index adopted by NatHERS is a dry bulb temperature of a uniform enclosed space at 50 per cent relative humidity, 'which would produce the same net heat exchange by radiation, convection and evaporation as the environment in question' (Auliciems & Szokolay, 1997, p. 36). According to NatHERS, active cooling is required if indoor temperature is over the upper limit of neutral temperature range; in the tropical climate zones of Darwin and Cairns, this upper limit is 26.5°C (NatHERS, 2014).

Research on thermal comfort in a hot and humid tropical climate such as Darwin shows that passive design techniques alone cannot significantly reduce indoor temperature and humidity levels, but increased ventilation can help improve thermal comfort more generally (Kane et al., 2009). Kane et al. (2009) used TRNSYS energy simulation software to simulate 24-hour ventilation, night-only ventilation and insulation and shading in lightweight elevated and concrete houses. Their research suggested an upper limit of thermal comfort at 29.3°C with 90 per cent satisfaction during the January–March period—a temperature higher than that suggested by the NatHERS rating scheme. During the measurements for the study, the outdoor temperature reached a maximum of 35.5°C with a relative humidity of 91.5 per cent. In the completely closed concrete house the indoor temperature reached 32.4°C in the living room and 36.2°C in the bedroom, with 76.9 per cent and 82.4 per cent relative humidity respectively. Indoor maximum temperature and relative humidity in the open elevated house reached 36.5°C and 79.6 per cent in living room, and 34.5° C and 82.6 per cent in bedroom. In other words, Darwin's overnight temperature and humidity are too high during the warm months for design techniques such as shading and insulation to make sufficient impact.

Passive design for the hot and humid tropics focuses mainly on addressing heat, and seems to overlook the oppressive northern humidity, especially in the 'Build Up' and monsoon seasons. Ventilation and shading alone are insufficient to maintain thermal comfort for most people during the seasonal rains. Conversely, designing dwellings so that the air conditioning works efficiently in extreme heat and humidity has to date resulted in buildings that are relatively inefficient and unsustainable over the whole year.

Research on human thermal comfort in the hot and humid Australian tropics is sparse, with only a few studies of indoor comfort and no published research on outdoor conditions in the wider urban environment. There is also very little research about relative senses of thermal comfort, which might be especially relevant as the towns and cities of Northern Australia grow and bring new migrants from different climate zones (see Oppermann et al., 2017, for a critical review of tropical heat). For example, Kenawy and Elkadi's (2013) research in Melbourne showed some correlation between cultural and climatic background and experiences of heat stress, which has implications for human thermal comfort in both indoor and outdoor spaces (see also Hansen et al., 2013). These gaps in research, combined with the Northern Australia development agenda, inspired us to share two case studies of innovation in the field of tropical design. The first is a project that evolves criteria for assessing good design in the tropics, highlighting examples from the Far North Queensland region. The second is a residential precinct in suburban Darwin that implements passive design features at the neighbourhood and individual lot level. These case studies emphasise design principles that shape thermal comfort, while at the same time keeping in sight a broader sustainability/liveability agenda.

# Case Study 1: Tropical Design Case Studies Project

The first case study is a joint initiative of the Tropical Green Building Network (TGBN) and James Cook University (JCU) that aims to document and share the knowledge and best-practice tropical expertise in the built environment in tropical north Queensland (see JCU, 2018). The TGBN/JCU case studies record key features of selected sustainable/green/tropically adapted building projects in the region, from large projects to domestic homes, including work carried out in national parks, tourist accommodation, multi-units and in remote Aboriginal communities. Several of the projects already have green star ratings from various sources, but other projects are well adapted to the tropical environment but are difficult to rate using criteria typically based on temperate models (see Figure 20.2). The project's aim was to consolidate existing knowledge and expertise and develop a vocabulary of features that work well in a tropical environment.

**Figure 20.2: Sunbird House.**

Note: The Sunbird house uses passive design for shade and natural ventilation and renewable energy use, with sustainably sourced materials for durability and low maintenance in the tropical climate. Its porous building envelope is not encouraged by rating software, even though it enables the natural ventilation that enhances thermal comfort for most of the year.

Source: JCU (2018).

The case studies were developed through consultation with a working group of industry experts, mostly architects but also engineers, planners and others involved in the construction industry. The group acknowledged that rating tools had not been particularly effective in providing good outcomes for tropical sustainable design, so the project evolved specific criteria for defining what constitutes good tropical outcomes. The working group drew on the current Australian rating, accreditation and approval systems underpinned by codes and standards for sustainable construction and supplemented this with a working knowledge of building in tropical, regional Australia. Through the process the group created a standardised set of sustainability criteria that enabled comparison across different types—residential, commercial, industrial, civil, civic and retrofitted/renovated buildings. The group helped prepare a guiding document and data collection sheet that could be distributed to those in industry practising good tropical design.

The group identified common criteria and categories to define what was important in each from a regional, tropical perspective. In total, the criteria provided information on the content of six primary focus areas of sustainable tropical design that were deemed critical—planning and management, site, design, materials, energy and water. Through this process, the research revealed that tropical sustainable design expertise is about planning for tropical wet/dry seasonality; using passive design for good solar orientation and capturing breezes; developing and applying building materials and technologies for extreme heat, cyclones, humidity and heavy rainfall; and encouraging sustainable environmental practices through the efficient use of renewable natural resources and the protection of natural assets.

While the case studies focus on a wider range of building/development types beyond suburban development, many examples of good tropical residential design are documented that might not score well with current ratings software. Although ratings tools are fast evolving with feedback from different sectors, they often privilege fully sealed buildings with a high thermal mass, rather than the more desirable lightweight construction with a porous building envelope that enables good ventilation in tropical climates. In other words, they tend to further entrench the increasingly ubiquitous concrete block home with concrete slabs (colloquially known as 'eskies'). Block homes are favoured by the project home market, and while they may be more efficient at retaining air conditioning for a few months of the year, it is also possible they increase the number of days climate control is used in tropical Australian towns and cities. More research in the field is clearly needed, and the TGBN/JCU case studies project aims to inspire more research in the field of tropical design.

## Case Study 2: Breezes Muirhead as Sustainable Subdivision

Another case study worthy of discussion is a residential development in suburban Darwin, Breezes Muirhead. Located in in Darwin's northern suburbs, the developer Defence Housing Australia (DHA) in partnership with Investa has aimed to deliver an environmentally responsive master planned community. The development is designed to strategically optimise the cooling impact of year-round sea breezes, dry season south-easterly trade winds and wet season westerly, north-westerly winds. This was achieved by orienting the master plan to enable maximum cross ventilation of each home and to ensure the penetration of breezes throughout the development. This model challenges standard master planning practice in terms of solar access and lot orientation.

The low density master plan design includes extensive open green space, parklands and neighbourhood pocket parks, staggered blocks and a street layout that provides for the movement of prevailing cool breezes through the subdivision. The orientation and width of lots and a specifically designed breezeway (see Figure 20.3) are designed to provide access to breezes for all houses in the development. The Breezes Muirhead Design Guidelines for house builders outlines the requirements and recommendations that should be reflected in the proposed plans submitted to the Breezes Muirhead Design Review Panel for approval. Requirements include roof colours, size of rooms, cross ventilation for main living areas and deep eaves.

To ensure the penetration of breezes throughout the development, design guidelines control fencing and landscaping and dictate window locations and room span. To prevent the obstruction of cool breezes the guidelines also require a 4.5 m site setback (see Figure 20.4), minimum 50 $m^2$ of open space, pool type or slat fencing and the use of particular vegetation specified in the document.

20. DESIGN FOR LIVEABILITY IN TROPICAL AUSTRALIA

**Figure 20.3: Google Earth image of Breezes Muirhead (24 April 2015).**
Note: When compared to the subdivision in Figure 20.1, this neighbourhood has larger setbacks, more footpaths, lighter roof colours and more open space.
Source: Google Earth.

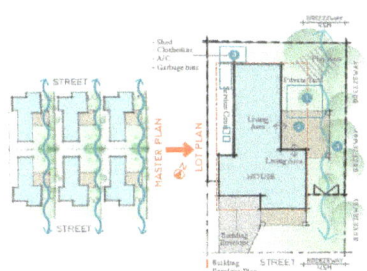

**Figure 20.4: Requirement for breezeway provision.**
Source: Defence Housing Australia (2016).

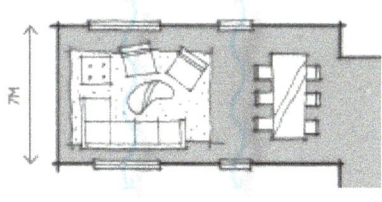

**Figure 20.5: Provision for cross ventilation.**
Source: Defence Housing Australia (2016).

To ensure building cross ventilation the guidelines require designing at least one room with windows situated parallel to each other and having 50 per cent of louvres on the front facade out of total window area (see Figure 20.5). The guidelines also regulate roof and wall colour to increase the effect of albedo and reduce the heat radiation from the building surface.

445

In this way, Breezes Muirhead is an experiment in tropical urban design, drawing on ideas of best practice. With the subdivision soon due for completion there is an opportunity to assess how this new master planned development mediates urban thermal comfort for its residents. The authors are collaborating on a project with Investa, DHA and Power and Water Corporation NT to do just that.

## Conclusion

Current building rating systems assume that air conditioning is essential in tropical conditions and, thus, favour buildings designed to ensure that air conditioners work efficiently. They do not favour buildings or precincts designed to minimise the use of air conditioning in number of days per year and number of hours per day through maximising ventilation, shading and green space. There are compelling arguments for a renewed focus on design for sustainability in tropical built environments in Northern Australia. Good design increases the liveability of urban areas but also minimises energy use and net greenhouse gas emissions, making maximum use of natural and recyclable materials, retaining water within urban landscapes and improving the quality of run-off. The hot and humid climate poses a serious design challenge to deliver thermal comfort and improve sustainability. Research is underway to critically assess the best design approach for this climate, and there are likely to be useful lessons in/for the countries to our north.

## References

Adams, R. (2011, 4 October). *Creating places for people: The Melbourne experience* [Video file]. Retrieved from www.youtube.com/watch?v=lfnynzD0yDI

Ali-Toudert, F. & Mayer, H. (2007). Thermal comfort in an east–west oriented street canyon in Freiburg (Germany) under hot summer conditions. *Theoretical and Applied Climatology, 87*(1–4), 223–237.

Ambrose, M. (2008). Energy-efficient housing and sub-division design. In P. Newton (Ed.), *Transitions: Pathways toward sustainable urban development in Australia* (pp. 425–435). Melbourne, Vic.: CSIRO.

Auliciems, A. & Szokolay, S. V. (1997). *Thermal comfort: Passive and low energy architecture*. Brisbane, Qld: Department of Architecture, University of Queensland.

Australian Government. (2014). *Green paper on developing Northern Australia.* Canberra, ACT: Department of the Prime Minister and Cabinet. Retrieved from www.industry.gov.au/sites/default/files/2019-09/green-paper-on-developing-northern-australia.pdf

Aynsley, R. M. (1997). Tropical architecture: The future. In *Proceedings of the ANZAScA conference* (pp. 167–175). The Australian and New Zealand Architectural Science Association.

Aynsley, R. (2006). Indoor wind speed coefficients for estimating summer comfort. *International Journal of Ventilation, 5*(1), 3–12.

Baker, N. V. (1987). *Passive and low energy building design for tropical island climates.* London, England: Commonwealth Secretariat.

Bay, J.-H. & Ong, B.-L. (2006). *Tropical sustainable architecture: Social and environmental dimensions.* Oxford, England: Architectural Press.

Bi, P., Williams, S., Loughnan, M., Lloyd, G., Hansen, A., Kjellstrom, T., … Saniotis, A. (2011). The effects of extreme heat on human mortality and morbidity in Australia: Implications for public health. *Asia-Pacific Journal of Public Health, 23*(2), 27S–36S.

Bowler, D. E., Buyung-Ali, L., Knight, T. M. & Pullin, A. S. (2010). Urban greening to cool towns and cities: A systematic review of the empirical evidence. *Landscape and Urban Planning, 97*(3), 147–155.

Cheng, V., Ng, E. & Givoni, B. (2005). Effect of envelope colour and thermal mass on indoor temperatures in hot humid climate. *Solar Energy, 78*(4), 528–534.

Cooperative Research Centre for Construction Innovation (CRCCI). (2006). *The role of natural ventilation in building sustainable subdivisions in south east Queensland.* Brisbane, Qld: CRCCI. Retrieved from eprints.qut.edu.au/27032

de Dear, R. & Brager, G. S. (1998). *Developing an adaptive model of thermal comfort and preference.* Center for the Built Environment, UC Berkeley. Retrieved from escholarship.org/uc/item/4qq2p9c6

Defence Housing Australia. (2016). *Breezes Muirhead: Design guidelines.* Retrieved from www.breezesmuirhead.com.au/assets/uploads/2018/05/Breezes_Design_Guidelinesweb.pdf

Emmanuel, M. R. (2005). *An urban approach to climate-sensitive design: Strategies for the tropics.* London, England; New York, NY: Spon Press.

Emmanuel, R. (1995). Energy efficient urban design guidelines for warm-humid cities: Strategies for Colombo, Sri Lanka. *Journal of Architectural and Planning Research*, *12*(1), 58–79.

Fanger, P. O. (1986). Thermal environment—human requirements. *Environmentalist*, *6*(4), 275–278.

Givoni, B. (1992). Climatic aspects of urban design in tropical regions. *Atmospheric Environment. Part B. Urban Atmosphere*, *26*(3), 397–406.

Halawa, E. & Van Hoof, J. (2012). The adaptive approach to thermal comfort: A critical overview. *Energy and Buildings*, *51*, 101–110.

Hall, A. C. (2010). *The life and death of the Australian backyard*. Collingwood, Vic.: CSIRO Publishing.

Hansen, A., Bi, L., Saniotis, A. & Nitschke, M. (2013). Vulnerability to extreme heat and climate change: Is ethnicity a factor? *Global Health Action*, *6*, 1–7.

Humphreys, M. A. & Fergus Nicol, J. (2002). The validity of ISO-PMV for predicting comfort votes in every-day thermal environments. *Energy and Buildings*, *34*(6), 667–684.

James Cook University. (2018). *Tropical sustainable design case studies*. Retrieved from www.jcu.edu.au/TUDLab/research-projects/tropical-sustainable-design-case-studies

Kane, A., Fuller, R. J., Luther, M. B. & Boldys, R. (2009). Improving comfort levels in Darwin houses through passive design. In *ANZSES 2009: Proceedings of Solar 2009, the 47th ANZSES annual conference* (pp. 1–10). Brisbane, Qld: Pictorial Press Australia in conjunction with Impress Media Brisbane.

Kenawy, I. & Elkadi, H. (2013). The impact of cultural and climatic background on thermal sensation votes. In *PLEA 2013: Proceedings of the 29th sustainable architecture for a renewable future conference* (pp. 1–6). Munich, Germany: Technische Universität München and PLEA Organization.

Kibert, C. J. (2012). *Sustainable construction: Green building design and delivery*. Hoboken, NJ: Wiley.

Law, L. (2019). The tropical backyard: Performing environmental difference. *Geographical Research*, *57*(3), 331–343.

Loughnan, M. E., Tapper, N. J., Phan, T., Lynch, K. & McInnes, J. A. (2013). *A spatial vulnerability analysis of urban populations during extreme heat events in Australian capital cities*. National Climate Change Adaptation Research Facility, Gold Coast. Retrieved from nccarf.edu.au/wp-content/uploads/2019/03/Loughnan_2013_Spatial_vulnerability_analysis.pdf

Miller, A. & Ambrose, M. (2005). *Sustainable subdivisions: Energy-efficient design report to industry*. CRC for Construction Innovation. Retrieved from eprints.qut.edu.au/27250/1/27250.pdf

National House Energy Rating System (NatHERS). (2014). *Occupancy settings*. Department of Industry.

Oppermann, E., Brearley, M., Law, L., Smith, J. A., Clough, A. & Zander, K. (2017). Heat, humidity and health in Australia's tropical monsoon zone: A critical review of heat stress in a changing climate. *WIREs Climate Change, 8*(4), 1–23.

Safarova, S., Garnett, S., Halawa, E., Law, L., van Hoof, J. & Trombley, J. (2018). Sustainable urban design and energy consumption of households in the hot and humid tropical climate of Darwin. In W. L. Filho, J. Rogers & U. Iyer-Raniga (Eds), *Sustainable development research in the Asia-Pacific region: Education, cities, infrastructure and buildings* (pp. 421–435). Switzerland: Springer.

Safarova, S., Halawa, E., Campbell, A., Law, L. & van Hoof, J. (2017). Pathways for optimal provision of thermal comfort and sustainability of residential housing in hot and humid tropics: A critical review. *Indoor and Built Environment*. doi.org/10.1177/1420326X17701805

Shashua-Bar, L., Tsiros, I. X. & Hoffman, M. (2012). Passive cooling design options to ameliorate thermal comfort in urban streets of a Mediterranean climate (Athens) under hot summer conditions. *Building and Environment, 57*, 110–119.

State of the Environment 2011 Committee. (2011). *Australia state of the environment 2011*. Canberra, ACT: Department of Sustainability, Environment, Water, Population and Communities.

United Nations. (2014). *World urbanization prospects: The 2014 revision, highlights* (UN Document ST/ESA/SER.A/352). Department of Economic and Social Affairs, Population Division.

Weller, R. & Bolleter, J. A. (2013). *Made in Australia: The future of Australian cities*. Perth, WA: UWA Publishing.

Wong, N. H. & Yu, C. (2005). Study of green areas and urban heat island in a tropical city. *Habitat International, 29*(3), 547–558.

Yilmaz, Z. (2007). Evaluation of energy efficient design strategies for different climatic zones: Comparison of thermal performance of buildings in temperate-humid and hot-dry climate. *Energy and Buildings, 39*(3), 306–316.

# Section 6

# Governance Systems in Northern Australia

Allan P. Dale

This book reminds us that charting a vibrant future for Northern Australia will rely on our communities envisioning and securing sound economic, environmental and social development outcomes. Some refer to this as genuine or triple bottom line development. Development where there is wealth creation defined by more inclusive forms of growth. Development where policy and decision-making about natural resources delivers economic outcomes, efficient resource use and protects and manages the wider cultural and environmental services needed by society. Achieving this, however, requires both a strong and underpinning societal culture and systems of societal governance that are purposeful, deeply engaging, evidence based and adaptive.

Consequently, the final section of this book picks up on the key feature of the quadruple bottom line—the social culture and emergent governance system(s) that underpin decision-making. Weak societal governance could see a dystopian future for the north emerge—deep and entrenched disadvantage and poverty in many communities, populations and regions; boom–bust economies; continuing demographic instability; and a progressive decline of the north's environmental assets. Stronger or healthier systems of governance could set the scene for a much brighter future.

The section starts with a discussion of potential new pathways for governance of the north by Dale et al. This chapter unfolds some of the past myths of unidimensional forms of development ranging from the grand economic schemes of past governments to extensive regulatory and distantly managed forms of landscape protection. The chapter introduces the importance of regionally and locally led forms of development that sit happily within a more nuanced national policy frame. This particularly reminds us of the importance of Indigenous-led development as an alternative to more top-down, nationally competitive forms of program management under the Closing the Gap policies. The authors' stress most importantly that development must be both engaged and evidence based.

The second chapter in this section further explores the notion of Indigenous governance systems needed at the centre of Indigenous-led notions of development. Ford et al. particularly reflect on the important role of researchers as partners in improved, but community-led governance in the contemporary environment. They provide hope that development might best spring from local aspirations, capacities and innovations, rather than from remotely anchored Commonwealth and state/NT-driven intervention or funding programs.

In the third chapter, at a perhaps wider scale, Carter absolutely reinforces the importance of place, and the perspectives of those that live there, in driving development narratives and outcomes. He takes the importance of local knowledge and aspirations—concepts frequently challenged by development plans and approaches derived from higher policy scales. He implores the importance of co-design, deeply infused by local knowledge, in reconciling different development narratives and producing results that are culturally rich and ultimately more meaningful to all.

The fourth chapter takes us more into a methodological space, exploring the further potential for the development and application of critical systems theory and, more specifically, the Governance Systems Analysis (GSA) method (in part developed and applied through the Northern Futures Collaborative Research Network [CRN]). Positioning societal governance as a more systemic concept worthy of equally systemic and collaborative analysis is a feature of this chapter. Stephens et al. collectively and critically evaluate the importance and potential for further application of the GSA tool as a mechanism that could better inform shared conversations about continuously and adaptively refining our governance systems. Such systemic approaches could help to reconcile the seemingly incommensurable tensions between the three arms of triple bottom line outcomes. They could see a more policy-centric form of governance emerge that enables people and place to re-emerge as important features of decision-making.

Finally, as one might expect from the focus of this book, Cram explores the critically important role of the academy and researchers in infusing our governance systems (from pan-northern to local scales) with new governance concepts and the theoretical thinking and empirical evidence required to inform good decision-making and monitor the impacts of those decisions. Consequently, he reviews the important governance-building contribution of the Commonwealth's recent investment in developing the CRN. The CRN has been instrumental in building the new thinking and contributions essential to this book.

Together, these chapters remind us that, for Northern Australia and Northern Australians to have a prosperous and meaningful future, we all need to get the governance foundations right. I have previously argued that bilateral and bipartisan establishment of a northern development policy framework, while extremely economically focused, presents the opportunity for discussion about what the future of Northern Australia might look like and how it is governed. I equally think that, for the first time, we have quite powerful pan-northern governance frameworks emerging. With clever thinking, Northern Australians have the opportunity to grab the initiative and help drive these arrangements to identify and drive innovative policy and investment decisions to imagine a more durable, engaged and evidence-based system of governance for the north.

# 21
# New Pathways for the Governance of Northern Development

Allan P. Dale, Andrew Campbell, Michael Douglas, Alistar Robertson, Ruth Wallace and Peter Davies

## Introduction

In the last decade, the future of Northern Australia has once again been the focus of national discussion, culminating in the development of the *White paper on the development of Northern Australia* (e.g. see Australian Government, 2014, 2015). Dale (2013, p. 2) described this wider national debate by saying:

> the north has again been cast as the nation's frontier saviour through bold new resource and agricultural developments, both real and imagined. Yet others have dreamt of the north's expansive landscapes being secured as an iconic wilderness. Big human rights-centred debates have raged about the success or otherwise of Commonwealth, State and Territory interventions in Indigenous communities.

Dale (2014) went further to consider that these divergent narratives represent conflict between very different sectoral interests within Australian society and have been based on vastly different visions about the future of the north. He suggested, however, that there are real opportunities for Northern Australians within these new national debates.

With a view to learning from the past to help secure a brighter future, this chapter explores some of the deep cultural drivers behind these quite divergent visions or narratives and, to some extent, longstanding but pervasive mythologies about the best way to govern the north. It explores how these vastly divergent narratives need to be better reconciled if the nation as a whole is to benefit from the Australian Government's currently proposed and potentially new phase of northern development. Our key take-home message is that this currently unfolding future can build upon those things that are already working very well, and that new approaches do not need to repeat major policy and development conflicts and investment failures that have punctuated the story of the north since European settlement.

We consider, in particular, that the key to genuine progress relies on new governance approaches to de-risking major government and private sector decisions about policy and investment in the north by:

1. taking a strategic approach to building the more detailed evidence base needed to overcome some of the north's most significant tyrannies (distance and access to markets, limited soils, failed business models, labour, climate, knowledge, capacity, seasonal water availability, etc.)
2. empowering northern communities (places, enterprises, industries and people), seriously engaging with regions and building effective and long-term partnerships.

This means finding new and more effective pathways for policy development and planning at the pan-northern and the regional and landscape scale, combined with substantive reform in the way decisions are made in the assessment and approval of major development projects. While addressing power imbalances and real equity issues, this also means governments, Indigenous people, conservation interests, industries, regions and those in the north focusing on what has worked, while discarding past approaches that have not worked. This will require all the parties sitting together to jointly decide the future directions that we need to take for the long term. Quality and defensible science and evidence needs to underpin decision-making processes, and together we need to monitor joint progress towards shared goals.

## Defining the North

Northern Australia could perhaps be best defined as one of Australia's most contested landscapes. There is often a sharp contest between different visions and realities about the future visions of the north and this means that defining Northern Australia can itself be a contentious business. For the north's traditional owners, for example, there is not so much a place called Northern Australia but a series of Indigenous nation-states that share a similar culture, a long history of interaction and regular international relationships with Indonesia, East Timor and Papua New Guinea. Territorians would often not necessarily see themselves as being part of a wider Northern Australian polity, and likewise for northern Queenslanders or northern West Australians. Many others within the broader Australian society make clear distinctions between remote and developed Northern Australia (e.g. Walker et al., 2012). Other federal administrative structures view the north as variously the Northern Territory (NT), the Monsoonal Rangelands or other self-defined geo-realities depending on their particular policy and administrative needs. This suggests there are many different communities and geographies in the north that require individual attention.

We generally take the view that the north can loosely be delineated by the Tropic of Capricorn (see Figure 21.1). However, while many may not think of Northern Australia as a 'place' in a geo-political sense, its residents experience similar cultural, historical, economic, climatic, environmental and social conditions. People in the Kimberley, for example, face day-to-day realities more akin with Weipa than Perth. As such, there are many areas to the near south of that line (such as the Gascoyne-Murchison or the Alice Springs districts) that relate both to the north *and* the south. Consequently, care needs to be taken in interpreting facts and figures for 'Northern Australia'. Distinctions of 'who's in' and 'who's out' of the north are perhaps not that useful in real terms.

**Figure 21.1: Australia north of the Tropic of Capricorn.**
Source: Dale et al. (2020).

No matter how we define it though, Dale (2013) outlines several characteristics of Northern Australia that distinguish it from the vastly different south of the country. These include 1) the extent and potential of Northern Australian lands and water; 2) its location, population and strategic importance; 3) the significant Indigenous population and extent of Indigenous rights (e.g. see Sullivan, 2011); 4) the nature of land ownership and tenure; 5) the boom-and-bust history of the north's economic cycles; 6) the economic opportunity possible through the north's competitive advantage in tropical knowledge; 7) Northern Australia's vulnerability to climate change, extreme weather events and biodiversity loss; and 9) the existence of energy dependency in a land of energy opportunities. Given these features, Dale (2013) goes on to explore the fragmented nature of the north's overarching system of governance. He considers that many of the current economic, social and environmental outcomes that are being secured should be celebrated and expanded. However, along with Walker et al. (2012), he also foreshadows the need for radical governance improvements to avoid a punctuated future arising from development.

## Northern Development: A Punctuated History

### The Three Big Northern Development Narratives

There have always been and continue to be grand national narratives regarding the future prospects for the north. In exploring more recent history over the past 50 years, however, Stephens et al. (2015) suggested three big narratives have tended to reappear predictably. One is based on the perception that Northern Australia is a place of endless economic bounty and limitless opportunity (see McGregor, 2015). The second derives from those who would like to see extensive conservation within the Northern Australian landscape (e.g. see Roberts, 2009). Both these narratives are based on important realities. There are significant resource development opportunities in the north, while at the same time, the region is a largely intact biocultural landscape of immense international and national value (Woinarski et al., 2007). Both narratives, however, discount major physical, climatic, economic and social barriers (see Ash, 2014; Dale, 2014).

The third narrative is more complex and relates to the way many non-Indigenous Australians have viewed Indigenous interests in the north. At one extreme, some have failed to see that the concept of *terra nullius* was indeed a colonial myth, leading to engagement approaches that have treated Indigenous interests as marginal or inconsequential. Alternatively, others involved in policy development may have not fully grasped the fact that traditional owners are indeed self-determining, with proposed Indigenous development approaches assuming Indigenous people will simply adopt many well-intentioned national, state and territory government policies. Together, both views perhaps reflect a broader myth that traditional owners across the north do not have significant ongoing sovereignty over much of the Northern Australian domain (see JCU & CSIRO, 2013). Together, these three northern narratives have often created the foundations for grand plans and even grander failures in the distant and recent history of northern development.

In the more distant period of colonial history prior to World War II (see Reynolds, 2003), development in the north was characterised by significant frontier conflict and sometimes tenuous colonial advances and retreats—consider the determined but failed attempts to establish colonial outposts at places like Port Essington and Somerset. Initially established in 1824, the outpost developed at Port Essington was abandoned in 1849 because of isolation, disease, cyclones and difficult climatic conditions that made it hard to attract a stable labour force. The demise of the settlement saw the end of British attempts to occupy the far Northern Australian coast. There would be one further unsuccessful attempt, by the South Australian colonial government in 1864, at Escape Cliffs (also known as Palmerston), before the first permanent settlement was established at Darwin (also initially known as Palmerston), in 1869 (Parks and Wildlife Commission of the NT, 2000).

By the start of the World War I, the main economic bulkheads were well established in places like Rockhampton (1858), Mackay (1862), Townsville (1866), Darwin (1869), Katherine (1871), Cairns (1876) and Broome (1883). Mainstream economic activity was represented by short-term resource industries (e.g. mining, forestry and crocodile hunting) or somewhat marginal harvesting regimes (pastoralism, fishing and beche-de-mer), often made viable only by the participation of underpaid Indigenous or indentured labour. Equally, government and church mission stations across the north also ran their own, often-failed approaches to assimilating Indigenous north Australians into the new settler culture and economy. The fear of Northern Australia being an 'empty' land on Asia's doorstep continued to drive much development effort, with the mantra of 'populate or perish' driving several government-backed schemes. The approach of World War II sparked greater fears about security in the north of the nation, and perception in both the north and the south of Australia that the government still was not doing enough to develop the region. Some, such as Ted Theodore, even called for the formation of a separate northern state (Fitzgerald, 1994).

Post-war Australian optimism saw the success of impressive nation-building projects in the south (such as the Snowy Mountains Scheme) and revived enthusiasm for nation-building public investment in the north. This happened even though the foundational barriers and issues limiting the prospects of northern development remained largely in place. These major proposals included bold schemes like the proposed Bradfield irrigation scheme, a massive irrigation scheme that envisaged turning several rivers in Queensland's Wet Tropics inland. Some of these schemes progressed to the development phase, but many fundamentally struggled to deliver a return on investment. The Ord River Irrigation

Scheme, for example, with its intended focus on cotton, initially failed to deliver a return on the significant public investment made during the late 1960s and 1970s (Greiner, 2000).

As early as 1965, Bruce Davidson summarised the core reasons why ambitious development plans for the north from the past had largely failed to deliver lasting results. His first published assessment of agricultural and pastoral development in tropical Australia concluded that most forms of agriculture north of the Tropic of Capricorn would be inefficient because prospective agricultural products could not be produced more cheaply than in the south (Davidson, 1972). In his view, several insurmountable cost impediments included transport, labour and pest management. In particular, he considered that the many arguments behind calls for major development reflected a non-economic political agenda, leaving them open to future commercial failure under changing policies or dependent on the expenditure of ongoing subsidies. He did, however, see ongoing potential for sugar and extensive cattle grazing as they could be produced in the tropics more cheaply than in temperate Australia. Not inconsistent with this, and in a deeper analysis of both privately and publicly funded agricultural development since the 1950s, Ash (2014) found that:

- the natural environment (climate, soils, pests and diseases) makes agriculture in Northern Australia challenging, but in the agricultural developments assessed, these inherent environmental factors were not, with a couple of exceptions (e.g. insect pests and cotton in the early phase of the Ord River Irrigation Area), the primary reason for lack of success
- management, planning and finances were assessed to be the most important factors in determining the ongoing viability of agricultural developments; in particular, unrealistic expectations of achieving a reasonable return on investment in the first few years. This included overly optimistic expectations of being able to scale up rapidly, and not coming to grips with the limitations in the real-world operating environment
- supply chains and markets were also important factors in determining the success of a number of the developments. For broadacre commodities that require processing facilities, these facilities need to be within a reasonable distance from production and at a scale to make them viable in the long term. In more remote regions, higher

value products such as fruit, vegetables and niche crops have to date proved to be more successful, though high supply chain costs to both domestic and export markets remain impediments to expansion.

Overall, Ash (2014) showed that for developments to be successful, all factors relating to climate, soils, agronomy, pests, farm operations, management, planning, supply chains and markets need to be thought through in a comprehensive system-scale design. He considered that particular attention needs to be paid to scaling up at a considered pace and being prepared for reasonable lags before positive returns on investment are achieved.

In a similar vein, several authors have investigated the very high level of failure of major (largely) government-funded developments inspired by federal or state Indigenous development policies. The philosophical intent behind these developments has shifted dramatically over the years. From the late 1800s, government- and church-run missions established projects aimed both to make mission communities self-sufficient, but also to provide meaningful work and skills development. Later policy phases included assimilationist, integrationist, self-determination and, later, normalisation agendas. In nearly all cases across these policy eras throughout Northern Australian history, Indigenous development projects have tended to fail for two reasons:

- the same types of technical reasons identified by Ash (2014) in his assessment of agricultural developments across Northern Australia
- a common and sharp divergence between the policy-based intent of projects and the far more localised aspirations of Indigenous project clients.

Dale (1993), for example, explored the failure behind several rural development projects in two Indigenous communities in northern Queensland. In all cases, these projects failed to achieve their stated policy and programmatic objectives because the technical constraints were too great, and/or because the projects simply did not mesh well with the aspirations of their Indigenous clients. Project success, on the other hand, emerges when Indigenous development aspirations match policy objectives and when the preconditions for successful and profitable enterprise development align.

Finally, while there have been many iconic visions, and indeed actions, to secure the wide-scale protection of Northern Australia for conservation purposes (e.g. Kakadu National Park), many of these visions have themselves sparked conflict between supportive and opposed stakeholders and communities, both within Northern Australia and beyond. Some telling examples in recent north Australian history include high levels of both support and conflict associated with the wild river declarations in northern Queensland and the listing of Cape York Peninsula for its World Heritage values. At present, several of these ambitious plans have failed to garner bipartisan political support (see Stephens et al., 2015).

While many of the above debates have raged in relation to the agricultural development and conservation protection of the north, it needs to be remembered that, since the 1960s, many of the constraints to development outlined above have become more tractable as a result of the changing locus of markets, emerging infrastructure and regulatory reform. As a consequence, agriculture and fishing have grown dramatically, while Indigenous communities also now lead and oversee significant economic activities within their land estates across a range of industries (Australian Government, 2014, 2015).

Additionally, significant mining, energy and tourism industries have now emerged across the Northern Australian landscape. In general (but with significant exceptions), these industries have worked hard to meet their environmental obligations. As an economic driver in particular, mining and energy dwarf all other industries in terms of gross product in the north, delivering significant social and economic benefit to the whole nation, but not necessarily delivering real and lasting benefit to local or regional communities (Stoeckl et al., 2013). The mining and energy industries have contributed to the overall health of the Australian economy, and the keys to the successes of mining and energy development in the north are different to agricultural development in that there is a clear competitive advantage in international terms (Port Jackson Partners, 2013). In the case of metals and ores, Northern Australia has commodities in abundance that are not available as cheaply elsewhere in the world. Hence, notwithstanding the boom–bust nature of many ventures, mining can succeed in certain contexts in the north, whereas agriculture (perhaps with the exceptions of sugar, horticulture and cattle in some regions) has less comparative value compared to other global supplies. Tourism growth has equally relied on its international competitiveness.

The vitality of the tourism, mining and energy industries, however, rises and falls with the strength of the resources sector, exchange rates and global economic confidence. Hence, while critically important, without greater diversity being built into the Northern Australian economy, these industries alone do have the tendency to subject northern regions to boom-and-bust cycles. Welters (2013), for example, showed the stabilising influence of defence spending in economies in places like Darwin and Townsville relative to the tourism-dependent economy of Cairns. The growing strength of Australia's export-focused mining and energy services sector has also been an increasingly stabilising influence.

More recently, particularly in the NT, new partnerships have formed that are working to develop a conservation economy, where several non-government and corporate organisations have been some of the strongest proponents, supporters and funders of innovative, Indigenous-led land management. Examples include the Indigenous savanna-burning programs funded by Conoco-Phillips and Caltex. The Kimberley to Cape process has also engendered a more inclusive Northern Australian dialogue on important aspects of environmental sustainability within northern landscapes. Such approaches establish a platform for new models of sustainable development across the north. These models are of great interest to multinational resources companies and leading pastoral houses (e.g. AACo and Consolidated Pastoral) who are interested in ways of supporting the active and constructive engagement of traditional owners on country in their areas of operation.

The above suggests that the key take-home message for northern development, if we are to deliver genuine economic opportunity, is that it will require real access to knowledge, collaborative capacity building and cross-governmental mobilisation of effort within Northern Australian regions, coupled with serious analysis of the global comparative advantage of the resource to be developed. The history of grand northern visions based on policy myths rather than well-informed and well-engaged reality has generally resulted in conflict, economic failure and a continuation of a boom–bust economy. The very clear result of all three narratives has been persistent underdevelopment. Indeed, Megarrity (2011) showed that political promises for northern development not based on economic and social reality have tended to be sacrificed on the altar of economic austerity once the political commitments made during election campaigns are assessed in the cold hard light of day.

Very importantly, however, as suggested by the Australian Government *White paper on the development of Northern Australia* (Australian Government, 2015), there are great opportunities and, at the same time, many complex issues to be identified, analysed and resolved. Significant trade-offs will need to be negotiated and real partnerships established between development, Indigenous interests and conservation. If we do this, the genuine opportunities in targeted agriculture, tourism, mining, fishing and forestry, carbon, conservation and ecosystem services and tropical knowledge services will grow. There is, however, a real need to ensure this effort is underpinned by stronger evidence, engagement and improved governance of the north.

## More Recent Approaches to Northern Development

In the last 15 years there have been at least three new Australian Government–led efforts to revitalise northern development. These have included:

- The Australian Coalition Government's formation of a Northern Development Taskforce in 2007 (the Heffernan Committee). The committee included Aboriginal leader Noel Pearson, media magnate Lachlan Murdoch, tourism leader David Baffsky and politicians Dave Tollner and Senator Ron Boswell.
- The Australian Labor Government's scrapping of the Heffernan Committee to replace it with a new stakeholder-based Northern Australia Land and Water Taskforce. Supporting and informing that Taskforce's efforts, CSIRO examined the potential for development of Northern Australian industry through the Northern Australia Land and Water Science Review (CSIRO, 2009).
- The Taskforce's efforts were complemented by the Australian Government's formation of the Office of Northern Australia, the formation of the North Australian Ministerial Forum and the commissioning of several key pieces of work informing the deliberations of the Forum through the Northern Australia Expert Advisory Panel, established to provide in-depth analyses of issues (e.g. see CSIRO, 2014; JCU & CSIRO, 2013).

The evidence emerging from these landmark processes and studies and subsequent Green and White Paper development work, all of which have drawn on an ever-growing knowledge base and wide engagement, have identified significant growth prospects for major industries and attendant impediments and enablers. In effect, while the prospects for both development and extensive conservation are good, the focus on building the evidence and engaging local communities remain critical. The new Australian Government's Green and White Paper processes and the aligned Northern Australian Joint Parliamentary Committee present an additional new opportunity (Joint Select Committee on Northern Australia, 2014). With the exception of deep engagement with the north's traditional owners, these processes are both heavily engaged (via the Parliamentary Committee) and evidence based (through the White Paper process) and early thoughts are emerging about the long-term governance arrangements required to institutionalise the changes needed to deliver on the policy intent.

## Opportunities and Possible Futures

The Australian Government's 2015 White Paper assessed the significant economic opportunities available to Northern Australia. This process, however, did not focus as much on the north's Indigenous development and environmental sustainability challenges. With all three of these key themes in mind, we explore the opportunities ahead given the megatrends facing our global future (Hajkowicz et al., 2012). We first need to speculate about how the future of the north might look if we do not resolve or reconcile some of the critical mythologies and cultural divides from the past. In a topical book regarding the future of Northern Australia, Dale (2014) posited that, depending on how successful the nation is in charting this next critical phase of northern development, two vastly different scenarios could emerge. He suggested that, if future governance and decision-making about the future of the north goes spectacularly wrong, then a failed state scenario is indeed possible. However, with engaged decision-making based on sound evidence, a much brighter future is a real possibility. While this unfolding opportunity represents many possible futures, this could look something like the emergence of a stable alliance of dynamic regional economies across Northern Australia.

## What Might a Failed State Scenario Look Like?

In envisaging such a scenario, one could imagine more fast-growth mining towns with limited infrastructure and services and no sense of community, and significant boom–bust features based on the strength of the resources sector, exchange rates and commodity prices (e.g. see Laurie, 2008). Second, one could imagine the further decline of social function in remote Indigenous communities, housing sometimes the third and fourth generations of people facing social dysfunction and abject poverty. Finally, under this scenario, one could imagine a wider (non-Indigenous) population retreat from Northern Australia. Climatic risks could see an insurance redline from Rockhampton to Port Hedland, above which the insurance industry would seek to reduce exposure. Rising fuel prices could push the cost of travel and domestic cooling beyond reach for many. We could, at the same time, see north Australia continue to lose market share from international and domestic tourism (Prideaux, 2013). Equally, under this scenario, regulatory complexity and increasing corporate takeovers may cause the demise of family-based pastoralism. Pockets of deep rural resentment could build in hinterland communities nearer the coast once people migrate there from the bush. Without capable, resourceful individuals out in the landscape, it would no longer be manageable, leaving it exposed to the consequences of rampant hot fires late in the dry season and weed and feral animal invasion.

## A Stable Federation of Dynamic Regional Economies

Consistent with Dale (2013, 2014), we see a better scenario being one of several stable and vibrant regional economies linked together by a common purpose and direction. Each region would have their own economic and service centres, ensuring we have both an urban and rural dynamic to maintain home-grown capacity locally and attract and retain human capital from elsewhere. The vibrant economic regions could at the very least include the Gascoyne, the Pilbara (based on Karratha/Port Headland), the Kimberley (maybe even the eastern region based on Kununurra and western based on Broome), the Darwin Top End, the Katherine-Daly-Roper region, Arnhem Land (based on Jabiru), the Centre (based around the Alice Springs region), the Torres Strait and Northern Peninsula Area, the Southern Gulf (based on Mt Isa), the northern Gulf (based on the vibrant towns of Mt Surprise, Georgetown, Normanton and

Karumba), the Wet Tropics (based on the Cairns, coastal and tablelands areas), Cape York Peninsula (based on Cooktown, Weipa and Coen), Longreach, Townsville, Mackay and Rockhampton and their western hinterlands. Under this scenario, there would need to be a greater spread of national investment across these regions, rather than simply a focus on Cairns, Townsville and Darwin. For the first time, government money aimed at securing the future of Indigenous communities would be devolved more effectively to regions and communities. A real effort would be put into preparing the Australian workforce to go bush and stay there. Land and tenure reform in Indigenous communities and the pastoral landscape would have also led to more equitable outcomes and a decentralised spread of wealth and power from bigger towns. Nevertheless, under this scenario, Darwin, but also Townsville and to a lesser extent Cairns, would enjoy considerable growth as major centres for service industries (health, education, welfare and public administration) and defence industries, and export ports and technology hubs for the resources sector.

A regionally aggregated and managed ecosystem services economy could also see a new layer of economic activity that is gradually emerging (e.g. see CSIRO, 2012). Under this economy, traditional owners and pastoralists across the north would gain a real and paid role for the management of landscapes to deliver environmental services such as habitat conservation, protection of water resources and abatement of greenhouse gas emissions. New agricultural development would retain a good mix of larger corporate and small to medium enterprises. The key resource extraction industries in each of these regions would start strategically reinvesting in the region's social and economic future. A better process for managing project assessment and approvals would have resulted in real and lasting community development initiatives being established alongside major project development (e.g. through sustaining employment for Indigenous ranger groups). However, such improvements would need to provide greater certainty to both mining companies and communities alike. More money would not just stay in the region; this investment would be more effectively used to help build infrastructure and a better region for the future.

These regions would also be more resilient to natural disasters. Strategic investment in transport and communications infrastructure and new technologies would mean they are not cut off from the rest of Australia for various periods of time in most years. Planning laws would ensure that communities are not located in harm's way (e.g. within storm surge zones) and all dwellings would have appropriate building standards, designs more suited to the tropics and greater cost efficiency. This capacity for dealing with risk would itself present a major opportunity for the region, with Northern Australia being well placed as a high-end knowledge provider and exporter in disaster risk reduction, management and response, climate change adaptation, and water, food and energy security.

While discussing the knowledge opportunity, it is worth stressing that the potential of the knowledge-based economy in the north, both with an Australian focus on lifting productivity and also an export-revenue focus, is extensive. Health, education and training, public administration, retail and tourism will likely remain the big employers in the north, and jobs in professional and technical services will likely exceed those in the resources and agriculture sectors over the longer term.

If we are to get things right, Australia needs to be picking up on the White Paper themes about the size and growth rate of the global tropical economy, the need for knowledge services as a key element of that growth and the need to make Australian research institutions globally competitive in this dynamic region. Of all OECD countries, Australia is arguably the most 'tropical', with the largest percentage of its land mass in the tropics. There are few globally competitive research institutions headquartered in the tropics, and for the time being Australia has a disproportionate share of them. With clever investment centred on Australia's tropical universities (e.g. JCU, Charles Darwin University [CDU] and Central Queensland University), we could develop a leadership position in this market, while delay may leave us far behind emerging institutions across the tropical world.

Additionally, these northern regions already have a clear cultural and climatic link to Southeast Asia and the Pacific, so they should be actively supported by government policy and the location of key agencies to be Australia's face to those cultures and economies. Given their shared histories and experiences, Indigenous cultures in these northern regions could also play a bigger role in building cultural relationships with our near northern neighbours. These regions would also play a bigger role as Australia's customs, biosecurity and defence frontlines. Regional communities in the north already have an important role in international trade, research, education and defence-related relationships.

These regions would also have greater energy security and affordability. Well planned and carefully designed water storage and harvesting schemes (more likely based on groundwater in carefully targeted districts rather than large dams on major rivers) would also have generated innovative local water supply projects and a diversification of the economy into some major new agricultural and industrial opportunities. Development that is mindful of minimising environmental impacts would ensure the continued strength of nature-based tourism. Flexible land tenure and regulatory arrangements would also help facilitate change. Investment in renewable energy, particularly in off-grid situations to reduce dependence on diesel, would reduce costs and increase resilience for remote communities, mines and pastoral enterprises. For the first time, there would be coordinated Australian, state, territory and local government investment in supporting each region to have a clear vision for the future and the durable regional institutions needed to mobilise the international, national, regional and local community effort and investment needed. Lifestyle and liveability would be a big and consistent theme in rural/urban planning, making each region's residents feel that they are making genuine progress while achieving the lifestyles they desire.

## What Will Deliver Genuine Northern Development?

To secure the future, it has been important to analyse the contemporary opportunities that could be used to secure key reforms and to escape past mythologies and southern dreams of Northern Australia. In anticipation and support of the Green and White Paper process, a Northern Australia research and development (R&D) dialogue emerged to inform critical debates about the future. It comprised R&D and education institutions with historic experience and a substantive footprint in Northern Australia: CDU, CSIRO, JCU and the University of Western Australia. In addition to specialist capabilities these and other institutions such as the new Collaborative Research Centre for Northern Australia (CRCNA) bring:

- an established history of successful collaboration on large-scale R&D projects across Northern Australia
- demonstrated capacity, such as through the Tropical Savanna Cooperative Research Network (CRN), Tropical Rivers and Coastal Knowledge consortium, National Environmental Research Program

Hubs and the Northern Research Futures CRN, to draw on robust national and international networks that can generate world-class research capability in the north
- commitment and experience in working collaboratively and in culturally respectful ways with Indigenous people and organisations.

As the White Paper has confirmed, with economic foundations in pastoralism, mining, agriculture, health, education, defence and tourism, the north is poised to play a larger role in Australia's economic future. With the nation's largest reserves of iron ore and with globally significant offshore and onshore gas and coal reserves, Northern Australia has the energy and raw materials to help fuel the rapidly expanding economies to the north. Seasonally abundant water supplies and significant interest from Australian and foreign investors have also led to a re-examination of the potential for the north to increase the supply of food to the wider region. These are economic opportunities of a scope and scale that could position the north to play a critical role in delivering energy, mineral, food and water security for Australia and beyond. Given the combined needs of government, conservation, Indigenous and industrial interests, however, we also have an unprecedented opportunity to develop the north in a new way—a better way. If we seize this opportunity, northern development could be inclusive and secure a prosperous future for all people of the region.

We consider, however, that the north is not as well understood as southern Australia. Consistent with the White Paper, we consider that there are six key uncertainties and challenges that must be understood and solved to provide the confidence to unlock future investment:

- resolving regional-scale land use and tenure-related conflict
- assessing the capacity of soil, water and other resources, their suitability and the environmental consequences of alternative uses
- improving production technologies, practices and sustainability
- enhancing/informing new and improved markets and labour access, including appropriate opportunities for participation of Indigenous organisations and communities
- increasing the efficiency and resilience of transport and supply chains
- enhancing policies, regional and project governance and the capacity for informed decision-making processes.

Northern development could secure certainty around both resources for industry and the future of the natural and cultural assets that define the region. Indeed, if done well, northern development could avoid the mistakes that have left many other Australian regions with social, economic and environmental legacies that are costly or impossible to repair. Getting it right in Northern Australia, however, will require cohesive and integrated cross-jurisdictional decisions about policy and investment that are engaged, transparent, defensible and based on sound evidence. Achieving this will mean addressing some significant challenges.

## Evaluating Opportunities

It is not just the climate that is different in Northern Australia. The high proportion of Indigenous people within the population requires solutions that fully empower and involve them in the pursuit of secure and sustainable development. Further, in comparison to other parts of Australia, Indigenous and government-controlled lands dominate tenure arrangements. With the exception of a few small cities, population density in the north is very low and is highly dispersed across a very wide region. Relatively poor infrastructure and vast distances inhibit service delivery, resulting in logistic challenges and poor connections to markets. This contributes to a challenging environment for industry development, a situation exacerbated by the challenges of attracting and retaining a skilled and stable workforce. Finally, a high level of government investment is common across the north as it supports all aspects of the economic and social fabric of the region.

Despite these challenges, opportunities abound for further sustainable development in primary industries, resources and tourism and in the development of a range of smart, specialised enterprises and industries. Many of these opportunities, however, are at different stages of development and some are just starting out along the innovation pathway. Further, there is generally a history of opportunities in Northern Australia being overstated, resulting in under-delivery or unexpected and adverse outcomes. The primary reason for poor outcomes has been limited evaluation of the opportunities and the risks that attend them.

There is great value and a public interest in employing integrated (across institutions), cross-cutting (employing several disciplines and cross-sectoral) analysis of opportunities to inform government policy, reduce the risk and lower the threshold for investment. Unlocking potentially significant new investment and development also requires investor confidence about the scale of the opportunities and the risk associated with their development. Hence, embedding an integrated R&D and education capacity as a key part of the future governance arrangements for Northern Australia can provide the engine needed for the smart evaluation of these opportunities.

## Securing Opportunities

Working with Northern Australians to progress development opportunities is not a new endeavour. Australia has more than 100 years of experience to draw on, some successes to build on and some key failures to learn from. From the R&D perspective, the notion of 'securing opportunities' conveys two meanings, both of which are important for Australia's overall development. On one hand, there is a need to build the momentum for development as local industries and communities have legitimate development aspirations that align with their local interests and values. The wider Australian nation also looks to Northern Australia to play a more vital role in our social and economic future—including as our interface to a rapidly changing Asia-Pacific region.

On the other hand, to be real and sustained, the development opportunities in the north have to be 'secure' in the following ways:

- only development that does not generate unexpected or unacceptable damage to the unique mix of natural assets of Northern Australia (land, water, ecosystems) will deliver long-term value
- development that fails to recognise and align with the diverse mix of cultural values and aspirations of Northern Australian people will generate divisions and will also be insecure and of lesser value
- investors and other stakeholders in development activity need security of resource access and this requires deep knowledge and analysis of short-term variability and long-term change in resource trajectories
- past and considerable legacy effects, which continue to be exacerbated by policies that treat the north as a social problem, need to be overcome
- communities need the assurance of long-term planning that identifies and works towards opportunities beyond extractive resource projects

- Northern Australia is uniquely placed to contribute to Australia's engagement in the wider tropical world and the Asia-Pacific region in particular, and this can add to national security, including helping to address particular challenges such as cross-border illegal activity
- Northern Australia is exposed to a host of natural hazards (cyclone, drought, fire, etc.) and development needs to be progressed in ways that are resilient to these hazards
- Northern Australia is also in the front line of the many national biosecurity challenges that can quickly turn into serious threats to industry viability, environmental integrity or human health—securing development opportunities in the north implies that we fully embrace a proactive biosecurity stance.

Progressing development opportunities without taking on board what is needed to secure these opportunities for local communities, for the wider national interest and for the long term will lead to disappointment and wasted resources and may cause irreversible damage to our largely intact natural asset base. The R&D community can partner with initiatives led by governments, the northern community and proponents to help avoid such disappointments. Similarly, the education community can also help contribute to the longer-term development of the skills and institutions needed to secure a positive future for Northern Australia.

## Doing Things Differently in Northern Australia

This particular moment in time presents a great chance to rethink the approaches needed to secure the best future for the north that arise from emerging opportunities. This rethink needs to include the role of R&D within that wider governance system, ensuring a strong foundation for evidence-based private sector investment, community-led strategy and government policy and program development. Overall, improved evaluation based on integrated knowledge can reduce risks and lower the thresholds for public and private investments. Some early steps in the right direction have recently emerged through cross-jurisdictional government processes with the three Northern Australian jurisdictions and the Australian Government working together on strategic issues, seeking advice and evidence from the wider science community in the north, and engaging major northern stakeholders (e.g. Indigenous people and the beef industry) in finding the right solutions.

Building on these emerging approaches and making them more effective can deliver on northern development needs and showcase best-practice approaches to evidence-based and inclusive governance across the tropics. This knowledge could become an exportable smart specialisation across the tropical world. To this end, a more enduring and more widely based Northern Australian R&D dialogue could form to:

- strengthen Northern Australia's R&D capacity through a collaborative network of key research and education institutions with a major footprint in Northern Australia
- broker a much wider range of R&D capabilities nationally and internationally to help secure emerging Northern Australian opportunities
- provide pathways for cohesive engagement with northern jurisdictions, stakeholders and the private sector to help inform major policy, program and investment opportunities
- more broadly, apply smarter technologies for solving problems (e.g. new generation remote sensing and an ability to analyse 'big data')
- coordinate northern efforts to lift human/institutional capability via teaching/training, knowledge building and increasing the critical mass of R&D capability within the north
- provide integrated science to solve complex problems beyond the capacity of any single R&D agency.

The additional benefit of a pan-northern R&D dialogue would be to drive demand-driven R&D, resulting in improved public and private sector decision-making. This engaged and evidence-driven approach could be the key to securing real opportunities for Northern Australia.

## Acknowledgements

This chapter represents an updated and now formally published version of a conference paper delivered to the ADC Northern Australian Development Forum in 2014 (Dale, A., Campbell, A., Douglas, M., Wallace, R., Robertson, A., & Davies, P. (2014). From myth to reality: New pathways for northern development. Paper presented at the Northern Australian Development Conference, Canberra).

# References

Ash, A. (2014). *Factors driving the viability of major cropping investments in northern Australia—an historical analysis*. Australia: CSIRO.

Australian Government. (2014). *Green paper on developing northern Australia*. Canberra, ACT: Department of the Prime Minister and Cabinet. Retrieved from www.industry.gov.au/sites/default/files/2019-09/green-paper-on-developing-northern-australia.pdf

Australian Government. (2015). *Our north, our future: White paper on developing Northern Australia*. Retrieved from www.industry.gov.au/data-and-publications/our-north-our-future-white-paper-on-developing-northern-australia

Commonwealth Scientific and Industrial Research Organisation (CSIRO). (2009). *Water in northern Australia: Summary of reports to the Australian Government from the CSIRO Northern Australia Sustainable Yields Project*. Retrieved from www.clw.csiro.au/publications/waterforahealthycountry/nasy/documents/nasy-summary-report.pdf

Commonwealth Scientific and Industrial Research Organisation (CSIRO). (2012). *The emerging carbon economy for northern Australia: Challenges and opportunities*. Retrieved from www.aph.gov.au/parliamentary_business/committees/house_of_representatives_committees?url=jscna/subs/sub052%20attachment%20a.pdf

Commonwealth Scientific and Industrial Research Organisation (CSIRO). (2014). *Flinders and Gilbert agricultural resource assessment*. Brisbane, Qld: CSIRO.

Dale, A. P. (1993). An assessment of planning for government-funded land-use development projects for Aboriginal communities in eastern Australia (unpublished doctoral thesis). Griffith University, Brisbane, Qld.

Dale, A. P. (2013). *Governance challenges for northern Australia*. Cairns, Qld: The Cairns Institute. Retrieved from researchonline.jcu.edu.au/29868/2/29868_Dale_2013.pdf

Dale, A. P. (2014). *Beyond the north-south culture wars: Reconciling northern Australia's past with its future*. London, England: Springer.

Dale, A. P., Keith, C., Matz, J. & MacLean, B. (2020). *Securing outcomes and measuring progress: A preliminary report into agricultural development and tropical health servicing in Northern Australia*. Townsville, Qld: CRCNA.

Davidson, B. (1972). *The northern myth: Limits to agricultural and pastoral development in tropical Australia* (3rd ed.). Melbourne, Vic.: Melbourne University Press.

Fitzgerald, R. (1994). *Red Ted: The life of E.G. Theodore*. Brisbane, Qld: University of Queensland Press.

Greiner, R. (2000, January). *The northern myth revisited: A resource economics research response to renewed interest in the agricultural development of the Kimberley region*. Paper presented at the 44th Annual Conference of the Australian Agricultural and Resource Economics Society, Sydney, NSW.

Hajkowicz, S., Cook, H. & Littleboy, A. (2012). *Our future world: Global megatrends that will change the way we live. The 2012 revision*. Brisbane, Qld: CSIRO.

James Cook University (JCU) & Commonwealth Scientific and Industrial Research Organisation (CSIRO). (2013). *Land tenure in northern Australia: Opportunities and challenges for investment*. Brisbane, Qld: CSIRO.

Joint Select Committee on Northern Australia. (2014). *Pivot North: Inquiry into the development of northern Australia—Final report*. Canberra, ACT: Australian Government. Retrieved from www.aph.gov.au/Parliamentary_Business/Committees/Joint/Former_Committees/Northern_Australia/Inquiry_into_the_Development_of_Northern_Australia/Tabled_Reports

Laurie, V. (2008, 13–14 September). Abandoned outback a 'failed state', *The Weekend Australian*, p. 5.

McGregor, R. (2015). *On the northern treadmill*. Australian Policy Online. Retrieved from apo.org.au/node/59055

Megarrity, L. (2011). 'Necessary and urgent'? The politics of Northern Australia, 1945-75. *Journal of the Royal Australian Historical Society*, 97(2), 136–160.

Parks and Wildlife Commission of the Northern Territory. (2000). *Cobourg Peninsular historic sites: Gurig National Park*. Darwin, NT: Parks and Wildlife Commission of the Northern Territory.

Port Jackson Partners. (2013). *Opportunity at risk: Regaining our competitive edge in mineral resources*. Retrieved from www.minerals.org.au/file_upload/files/presentations/mca_opportunity_at_risk_FINAL.pdf (site discontinued)

Prideaux, B. (2013). *An investigation into factors that may affect the long term environmental and economic sustainability of tourism in northern Australia*. Cairns, Qld: The Cairns Institute. Retrieved from researchonline.jcu.edu.au/30100/10/30100_Prideaux_2013.pdf

Reynolds, H. (2003). *North of the Capricorn: The untold story of the people of Australia's north*. Crows Nest, NSW: Allen & Unwin.

Roberts, G. (2009, 19 May). Cape splits over wild rivers, *The Australian*, p. 1.

Stephens, A., Oppermann, E., Turnour, J., Brewer, T., O'Brien, C., Rayner, T., … Dale, A. P. (2015). Identifying tensions in the development of northern Australia: Implications for governance. *Journal of Economic and Social Policy*, *17*(1). researchonline.jcu.edu.au/37994/1/Identifying_Tensions_in_the_Development_of_Northern_Australia.pdf

Stoeckl, N., Esparon, M., Farr, M., Delisle, A. & Stanley, O. (2013). The great asymmetric divide: An empirical investigation of the link between indigenous and non-indigenous economic systems in Northern Australia. *Papers in Regional Science*, *93*(4), 783–801. doi.org/10.1111/pirs.12028

Sullivan, P. (2011). *The policy goal of normalisation, the national Indigenous reform agreement and Indigenous national partnership agreements* (Working Paper 76). Retrieved from crc-rep.com/resource/NintiOneWorkingPaper_76_PolicyGoal ofNormalisation.pdf

Walker, B., Porter, D. & Marsh, I. (2012). *Fixing the hole in Australia's heartland: How government needs to work in remote Australia*. Alice Springs, NT: Desert Knowledge.

Welters, R. (2013). *The Australian defence organisation and tropical Australia: Its socio-economic impact in Cairns, Darwin and Townsville*. Cairns, Qld: The Cairns Institute. Retrieved from researchonline.jcu.edu.au/30101/7/30101_Welters_2013.pdf

Woinarski, J., Mackey, B., Nix, H. & Traill, B. (2007). *The nature of northern Australia: Its natural values, ecological processes and future prospects*. Canberra, ACT: ANU E Press. doi.org/10.22459/NNA.07.2007

# 22

# Collaborative Research into Contemporary Indigenous Governance

Linda Ford, Michael Christie, Catherine Bow, Tanyah Nasir, Michaela Spencer, Matt Campbell, Helen Verran and John Prior

## Introduction

This chapter aims to describe activities of researchers within the Contemporary Indigenous Knowledges and Governance group at the Northern Institute in the changing relations of state governance under conditions imposed by an advanced liberal economy in contemporary Northern Australia and how it intersects with Indigenous governance. This is done by detailing situations where the researchers have found themselves engaged in brokering between Indigenous and modern state (and university) governance practices as they emerge when contemporary Indigenous institutions and contemporary government organisations (GOs) and non-government organisations (NGOs) work together but struggle to conduct their different governance practices together. The chapter details the role of the institute, and of academic work, within this struggle while recognising differences.

While governance issues and practices are of concern to a wide range of research and public engagements in Northern Australia, it is perhaps the issues of governance practices relating to Indigenous communities and organisations that have garnered the most interest and substantial amounts of funding. The problematics of Indigenous governance practices arise with the acknowledgement that traditional forms of Indigenous governance are still alive and well in Northern Australia and different to modern practices of nation-state governance in several ways. This chapter describes projects where governments, Indigenous people and researchers are together designing ways of conducting Indigenous and modern governance practices together in productive and sustainable ways.

We begin by defining terms. First, we note that according to the Google program viewer, which tells us about the frequency of word usage in the 'lots' of published English-language books that Google has digitised, the term 'governance' was almost absent up until the 1960s. It seems the term 'government' was the term frequently employed when the relations between states and their peoples and citizens were discussed. However, in the late 1960s the usage of 'government' began to decrease and usage of 'governance' began to increase very rapidly. We take the slow retreat from 'government' and the increase in usage of 'governance' as a significant indicator that something is happening in the ways that states and their peoples relate politically, and in the technical arenas where states manage their populations (Verran & Christie, 2015). Here, 'government' refers to the mode of governance of and by the Australian state. Nowadays, states often operationalise policies as services provision by NGOs, so the intersecting self-driven governance of Indigenous people and the corporate governance practices of Indigenous NGOs are of interest to us, as are those of GOs.

Consequently, we are interested in governance taken as the overall interplay among multiple 'governances'—odd though that sounds. We are concerned with governance as the Australian state currently understands and practices it in GOs; wider Indigenous governance, inclusive of the corporate governance of a variety of NGOs; and governance as various Indigenous communities understand and practice it in their places. We understand governance as describing relations between 'rules' and 'what is ruled'. 'Rules' of government are laws made by parliaments and regulations devised by civic services, and what governments rule are peoples, citizens or populations and territories. As corporations, NGOs are obliged to make public their rules and what is ruled, and the personnel they employ or whom they retain as volunteers in a formal sense. In contrast, multiple Indigenous people-places (community members, clans and their places) have both unwritten and written rules that are variously formalised, and what is ruled are entities we might, in English, call 'people-places'; entities that are indissoluble complexes comprised of elements that are both human and non-human, and material and conceptual—places and their songs, stories and ceremonies.

This chapter presents several case studies. Linda Ford, working with her daughters Chloe and Emily, discusses working with two systems of ethical accountability in 'New Ways for Old Ceremonies'. Michael Christie and Cathy Bow consider some of the challenges of working with texts configured by disparate practices of ownership in 'The Living Archive of Aboriginal Languages'. Linda Ford details the careful work of community engagement in 'Arrakpi Aquaculture' on Goulburn Island. Tanyah Nasir and Michaela Spencer reflect on some of the potential effects of governance work in 'Tiwi Community Governance', and Matt Campbell considers questions around the production of evidence in Indigenous research in 'Tangentyere Research Hub'.

Five projects are briefly described through these case studies. Being careful to respect the profound differences between these projects, we nevertheless suggest that they might be thought of as falling into two groups. One group is concerned with what we might call 'objects of governance'—'New Ways for Old Ceremonies', concerned with archival records of ceremonies, songs, performances, rituals and stories, assembled largely in past anthropological research; 'The Living Archive of Aboriginal Languages', concerned with written texts and their digitised web-based doppelgangers; and 'Arrakpi Aquaculture', concerned with wild harvest of fisheries products. The second group is concerned with organisational processes—'Tiwi Community Governance' and 'Tangentyere Research Hub'. In describing these projects, this chapter shows how we, as researchers, are embedded in the 'action', the 'doing' to recognise who and what the other participants are, in being and recognising that their interests differ from ours, as researchers. Being explicit about the knowledge drawn on and the governance practices of our research is the way we as researchers participate in good faith.

# New Ways for Old Ceremonies: An Archival Research Project

Linda Ford

The New Ways for Old Ceremonies: An Archival Research Project aims to develop and implement suitable frameworks for the preservation, interpretation and dissemination of recordings of ceremonial performances of the Mak Mak Marranunggu people of the Northern Territory (NT). The focus is a body of recordings by early anthropologists and missionaries (from 1824–2009) of the final mortuary ceremonies performed. The ceremonial performance is a key process for integrating Indigenous knowledge from many different domains—a socially powerful site of exchange, transmission and transformation of relationship to country, kin and identity (Ford et al., 2014).

As a Mak Mak Marranunggu person, this research has involved me working with the ceremonial knowledge of my own people and places. We call ourselves Tyikim. During my PhD, I worked with my mother, Ngulilkang Nancy Daiyi, and other elders from my community to find ways to bring my Tyikim knowledge traditions into the university classroom (Ford, 2010). Now, I seek to work the other way and bring the knowledge and technologies of the university to help my daughters, Chloe and Emily, and extended family and related clan groups keep our traditional ceremonies alive.

This project is just beginning, and it will take a long time to organise and finalise all the complex negotiations required for this work. However, I have already encountered a dislocation between the forms of ethical accountability recognised by the university and the practices of ethical accountability observed and undertaken by my people. I am sometimes caught in the middle. As we look through old video footage, I need to set up systems that allow for negotiations around who may view the film, and how it may continued to be used and exhibited in the future. In doing this work, I am guided by my elders and act on their instruction. I am accountable to their directives and the way they guide me to observe proper protocols for managing cultural objects in the work we are doing together. To do this carefully and well, I depend on the good faith and goodwill of my elders who are supporting me in the project.

Aware of my accountability in these terms, I felt confident that I would be able to carry out this research with the support of my colleagues and family members. However, a letter from the university ethics committee asked me to account for my research and its impacts in a rather different way, challenging me on several issues that were very difficult for me to address. They wanted to know if the outcomes of the research might 'consolidate and strengthen' the status of my family compared to others and whether this 'might cause disharmony or offence' to other families. The ethics committee also wanted to know how my Elders would be involved, how their involvement might differ from a 'consultation and negotiation processes' and how I would make that clear in a 'plain language statement'.

It was immediately clear to me that the ethics committee did not really understand how I was being guided by protocols of ceremony, and so did not really understand how the project was going to be negotiated. Or, if they did understand, perhaps they were constrained by their own protocols, rules and regulations, which saw research as dealing with the standard research subjects of a university—anonymous subjects, who are not induced to participate or rewarded, and who are subjects of the research, not researchers.

When working with my own people, I do not need to account for my work in these ways. However, when also doing this work with and for the university, I do need to justify myself to the ethics committee and be completely honest with them. I had to discuss the questions with my elders and be quite upfront. Yes, the status of my family may be consolidated and strengthened through this project, but the 'family' that is represented in this ceremonial context is spread through a large geographical area including the Batchelor, Darwin, Belyuen, Wagait and Daly regions, and includes many people and multiple clans and language groups. It is fully expected that other ceremonial groups, such as the Wangga, Lirrga and Djanba, will be very interested in my work and inspired to undertake a search for archived materials that might help them with similar work. My family would be very happy to support them with this.

But what is important is continuing to listen to the elders to express their knowledge within our work together. It is for them to tell me how to do this research. The ethics committee may have been a little surprised by my answers, but they have accepted them and, so far, I have been able to work Tyikim governance and university governance together without any trouble.

# The Living Archive of Aboriginal Languages
Michael Christie and Catherine Bow

In the 'Living Archive of Aboriginal Languages project, we are involved in designing and developing an archive of rare texts in over 50 endangered Indigenous languages of the NT.[1] Between 1974 and 2000, thousands of books were produced in remote communities in an era of significant government support for vernacular education and the training of Indigenous teachers and language workers for bilingual education. We now find ourselves in an era when bilingual education is no longer supported by the Australian state, and the use of English in teaching and literacy is official policy, resulting in disuse and endangerment of these materials of cultural and linguistic importance.

Funding was obtained to work in collaboration with other tertiary institutions and government and non-government departments to 'rescue' the literature and to catalogue, digitise and configure it using web technologies. The creation of a website for the use of the language owners and authorities (Christie 1993; Christie & Perrett, 1996), and new generations, as well as for classroom teachers and students, academic teaching and research nationally and globally, required careful consideration of the needs of different users and different requirements of the technology (Bow et al., 2014).

We recognise that the items that constitute this archive are in a strong sense owned by the communities in which they were produced; that ownership lies with those whose languages and stories are mobilised in the texts. Yet at the same time, in being produced as written texts generated in the work of state-funded literature production centres, the items in the archive are equally in some ways owned by the governments of the Australian state. Thus, the items are subject to disparate traditions of governance, which, in constituting the archive, we as researchers must negotiate in good faith

---

1   See laal.cdu.edu.au/.

(Christie et al., 2014; Bow & Hepworth, 2019). We do not have the space here to detail how and where those disparate traditions of governance clash in some places and mesh in others when it comes to the day-to-day practices of constituting the archive.

The conventional academic view of the academic researcher is that they should be removed, impartial and somehow 'all seeing', so that the knowledge claims they might make about, say, the worth or otherwise of such an electronic archive, and how it might be subject to a transparent regime of good governance, might be epistemically valid. We doubt that such an idealised position was ever achievable, but irrespective, it is certainly not a position we aspire to. So, from what sort of a position might we generate valid and useful generalisations about such an archive and an appropriate governance regime? And how do the technical requirements fit into this?

This work involves careful ongoing balancing between the centralised top-down configurations for robust coding and sustainable and extensible development (as described in Bow et al., 2014), and the dispersed localised reappropriation and enrichment of documents on country under the authority and for the benefit of their owners. The negotiation of permission and copyright issues also requires careful consideration of both Indigenous and Western concepts of ownership and access to knowledge. This work finds us re-examining our role as experts and researchers in the changing worlds of government policies, education, technology and remote community sustainability. And it opens more fundamental metaphysical questions around the nature of language itself and its relation to country, people, identity and technology. Each new challenge needs to be carefully thought through, not least with respect to what good faith participation requires.

# Arrakpi Aquaculture

Linda Ford

While working on the New Ways for Old Ceremonies: An Archival Research Project, I was also invited to participate in a project developing an aquaculture industry in the Indigenous community at Warruwi on Goulburn Island, NT. It was part of a wider project called 'Identifying the key social and economic factors for successful engagement in aquaculture ventures by Indigenous communities'.

The original project came from the Fisheries Research and Development Corporation (FRDC), as part of an effort to build sustainable aquaculture in remote communities. Its focus was around identifying key factors for success in Indigenous businesses and the development of a fisheries-based community development program.

When I first became involved in this project in 2013, its 'community engagement' aspect had been running for a long time but had only minimal success. Work had been continuing for many years, but while it had, in the words of one of the scientists, 'ticked all the boxes', the project was still not progressing. Nobody seemed to be interested.

The FRDC milestone identified the senior Arrakpi women from the community to work together under the auspice of the Yagbani Aboriginal Corporation to make some decisions and support the project. The women were busy, they were from quite different families and clan groups who did not seem interested in the project and the project was not their idea in the first place. This might have been why engagement had minimal uptake and progress was slow. The Yagbani Aboriginal Corporation, registered in 2012, was up and operating, and the Arrakpi directors were familiarising themselves with their roles and responsibilities as board members.

I have a few distant kinship relationships at Warruwi, so I agreed to accompany them and seek authorisation from the Traditional Owners of the aquaculture area to join the research project team. They were happy to invite me to be a researcher on the aquaculture enterprise development project because I was connected to them through both my Indigenous and research backgrounds. My first priority was identifying and locating the right people to talk to, to see if they would be happy for me to join the research team. Gradually, I began to meet a few more women, many of whom I could trace some connection to. We had several meetings and discussions. The women were mostly interested in food for the community's children and elders, so it was through focusing on the traditions associated with seafood that we finally began to work together and develop a collective interest in how this aquaculture project, if it was going to work, should be negotiated and implemented.

It was through the stories that connected them to each other, the sea and the new generation that the women elders became engaged. One day, we had a breakthrough. I spotted leaning on the wall of the Warruwi school staff room an old chart that had been produced by senior women and men back in the days of bilingual education. The chart had names and a few pictures of dozens of sea (and a few land) animals good for eating at different times of the year. The names were arranged into a circle, as a seasonal calendar with the seasons, months and prevailing winds all in the local language, Maung. It promoted much discussion and brought the women together because it was a sign, of senior women who had gone before them and whose knowledge and connections were so valuable, and for the new generation of young children. We used some of our funding to make the old drawing into a new poster, and then into a digital version, which eventually ended up on the Warruwi Fisheries and Aquaculture Knowledge Partnership Project website.[2] It was through this new work, this object we were gradually creating together, that community engagement that was meaningful to both parties (and that was supported by an emerging new Indigenous enterprise) began to be conducted.

# 'Tiwi Community Governance'
Tanyah Nasir and Michaela Spencer

In this project, we (Nasir and Spencer) were involved in developing governance and leadership capacities in the community of Wurrumiyanga. Amid continually shifting responsibilities of local, regional and state governments, and as new forms of enterprise development were springing up in the Tiwi Islands, we worked collaboratively with people in the community, telling stories and learning together about governance. We talked about how governance work was being done and explored ways that young people might be supported to confidently participate in these processes in the future.

This work was funded as part of an NT Government project on governance and leadership in remote Indigenous communities. It was born out of a recognition that amid the proliferation of government and corporate governance training practices in remote Indigenous communities, there was very little work being conducted on the ground, taking account of how existing and new governance structures were being negotiated and engaged with by local people. Working under the guidance of elders, and led by two Indigenous facilitators, we ran a series of workshops focused

---

2    yagbaniac14.wix.com/aquacultureknowledgeproject#!warruwi-projects/c10d6. The Yagbani Aboriginal Corporation manages this site.

on 'problems of the moment' arising in the community, moving between Tiwi and English languages and working through Tiwi skin groups and family hierarchies, while being explicit about the forms of university administration and protocols that we were required to follow.

Many of the Tiwi people attending the workshops knew, or were in some way related to, the facilitators. They felt comfortable to raise and discuss issues that were important to them, but that might otherwise go unarticulated. We also worked closely with a local elder, Bonaventure Timaepatua, who guided us regarding who were the right people for us to invite and where our discussions should be focused. Identifying that there is often a disconnect between governance and leadership work being done in the community, and governance and leadership work being conducted in council offices and board meetings, we often used this as a place to work collaboratively with Tiwi people while supporting them to feel confident in engaging multiple sets of governance practices, while also continuing to work with and within the community.

However, in doing this work we were frequently reminded that our own practical assumptions were themselves artefacts of earlier activities—temporary working settlements that had enabled Tiwi governance and Western governance to mingle and coexist. Working in groups to tell stories about how 'Tiwi Way' was involved in the work of councils, boards, schools and tiers of government, we began by talking about the four Tiwi skin groups—Warnarringuwi, Miyartuwi, Takaringuwi and Mantimapila. But very soon, we found ourselves delving into the recent past of Tiwi governance relations. As it turned out, while there actually are 16 subgroups it had become common to work only with the main four. This simplification was an artefact of needing to organise meetings and arrange for equal representation of the four groups within council and other meetings. It was, in part, a shift and a solidification brought about through the requirements and opportunities of representational governance.

Recognising that our government-specified brief is to participate and intervene in shaping the ways in which community governance is done, we began to see ourselves as also working to craft partial and temporary settlements, working compromises and moments of collaboration that produce particular separations and connections.[3] Wary of these becoming solidified and the contingency of their creation lost, we hesitated before

---

3   For further explanation of the methods involved, see www.cdu.edu.au/centres/groundup/.

writing definitive accounts or reports of our work and the outcomes it has achieved. Instead, we were pushed back towards offering accounts of our practices that retained these difficulties and governance work in communities that supported capacities to produce new and different temporary settlements into the future.

## Tangentyere Research Hub

Matt Campbell

The Tangentyere Council is the governing body for 17 Aboriginal 'Town Camps' in the Alice Springs area. It runs the Tangentyere Research Hub as one of its key services, and I, as the coordinator of this research unit, work both with Indigenous researchers in the Alice Springs Town Camps and (at times) with Charles Darwin University. The Research Hub was established within the Tangentyere Council to give Town Camp residents a chance to provide feedback for the evaluation of the first Alice Springs liquor trials, introduced by the NT Government in 2002 as a strategy for addressing alcohol-related problems in Alice Springs. Since then, the Tangentyere Research Hub has grown and conducted a wide range of projects. In 2020, it continues to plan, undertake and report on research on issues of concern to Town Camp residents. Aside from myself, all employees of the Research Hub are Indigenous people with strong connections to the Town Camps and Arrernte language and culture.

In recent times, the Arrernte researchers have become concerned that the research they are asked to undertake has often been framed and specified according to Western ways of collecting and producing evidence. They have spoken of themselves as simply 'clip-boards for hire', required only to collect data without the opportunity to undertake the sorts of collaborations between funding bodies, governments and people on the ground that reflect their own traditional agreement-making practices. They note that this may produce changed understandings and practices that could contribute to what constitutes 'good' research in this context through engagements with governments, universities, NGOs and Town Camp residents.

In seeking to make a difference, we are interested in how our research is understood within the Town Camps and by those who provide funding to undertake projects. To achieve this, we are exploring the notion of 'accountability' as we believe this will help us to make visible the criteria that people use for evaluating our work (Campbell et al., 2014). Looking at accountability will help us and others to understand the ends to which different parties aspire through our research work.

Several issues have emerged, particularly in relation to the conduct of research work and its outcomes. On the one hand, paying attention to accountability helps us to do meaningful and productive work because we are consciously working to ensure that our research delivers benefit to Town Camp residents. Our ability to do this is increased because all the researchers are known and trusted and know how to work respectfully in the Town Camp context. In addition, every researcher is also part of the complex governance of the Town Camps; they are part of families, thus they are aligned in ways determined not only by themselves but by the community, meaning that they could not do 'arms-length' research even if they wanted to. Finally, we are contracted by various GOs and NGOs to undertake research through the Tangentyere Council. Working to understand these multiple and complex accountabilities has the potential to change the way research is done and alters the way accountability might be understood.

We are exploring how we might conceptualise and make visible our accountability story so that we might involve a diverse range of Town Camp residents (and other participants) in helping us to do work that works for them. In this way, we are seeking to better understand how we might make the complex politics of Town Camps and their governance systems visible, both internally, so that it can be more effectively engaged with, and externally, so that agencies we partner with can understand what we are doing and why taking our accountabilities seriously is the right and proper thing to do.

## Conclusion

Emergent in our descriptions is a figure of an academic researcher involved in a wide range of projects in various remote places, drawing on a diverse repertoire of personal expertise and relationships. Sometimes characterising this work as 'ground up', we have previously recognised ourselves as working with and within both traditions of Western European and Aboriginal knowledge and governance practices, face to face in very local contexts, where both traditions must adapt. This work entails starting with and accepting difference and negotiating ways of making connections. It involves resisting the usual role that academics are cast in, as 'removed judging observers', and instead seeing ourselves as particular sorts of participants in the collective action of generating sustainable and transparent governance practices when cooperating across linguistic, cultural and epistemic boundaries (Addelson, 2002). Located within the Northern Institute, we see ourselves as having and changing roles, and those roles as themselves emerging from collective action of those struggling to coexist due to differences in knowledge and governance practices.

However, these accounts also show that we are now increasingly finding our role to be one of not just brokering and translating across differences between differing knowledge and governance traditions, but of also grappling with how differences in knowledge and governance traditions might remain visible as something we are all accountable to, within the practices and processes of new forms of governance. Working within this new and multiply implicated positioning, while visibly holding tensions associated with difference, we have begun to explore possibilities for making connections that have a chance of generating futures that do not merely reproduce pasts.

# References

Addelson, K. P. (2002). The emergence of the fetus. In C. L. Mui & J. S. Murphy (Eds), *Gender struggles: Practical approaches to contemporary feminism* (pp. 118–136). New York, NY: Rowman & Littlefield.

Bow, C. & Hepworth, P. (2019). Observing and respecting diverse knowledge traditions in a digital archive of Indigenous language materials. *Journal of Copyright in Education and Librarianship*, *3*(1), 1–36. doi.org/10.17161/jcel.v3i1.7485

Bow, C., Christie, M. & Devlin, B. (2014). Developing a living archive of Aboriginal languages. *Language Documentation & Conservation*, *8*, 345–360. hdl.handle.net/10125/24612

Campbell, M., Foster, D. & Davis, V. (2014). Looking back, moving forward: The place of evaluation at the Tangentyere Council Research Hub. *Learning Communities Journal*, *14*, 144–153. doi.org/10.18793/LCJ2014.14.10

Christie, M. J. (1993, June). Yolngu linguistics. *Ngoonjook*, (8), 58–77.

Christie, M., Devlin, B. & Bow. C. (2014, October). The birth of the living archive: An emerging archive of Australian Aboriginal languages and literature. *Archifacts*, 48–63.

Christie, M. & Perrett, B. (1996). Negotiating resources: Language, knowledge and the search for 'Secret English' in northeast Arnhem Land. In R. Howitt, R. Connell & P. Hirsch (Eds), *Resources, nations and Indigenous peoples* (pp. 57–65). Melbourne, Vic.: Oxford University Press.

Ford, P. L. (2010). *Aboriginal knowledge, narratives & country: marri kunkimba putj putj marrideyan*. Brisbane, Qld: Post Pressed.

Ford, P. L., Barwick, L. & Marett, A. (2014). Collaborative Ethnomusicology: Caring about ceremony: Indigenous knowledge across boundaries of time, space and society. In K. Barney (Ed.), *Collaborative ethnomusicology: New approaches to music research between Indigenous and non-Indigenous Australians*. Melbourne, Vic.: Lyrebird Press.

Miller, P. & Rose, N. (1990). *Governing the present*. Cambridge, England: Polity.

Verran, H. & Christie, M. (2015, March). Editorial. *Learning Communities Journal*, (15), 4–7.

# 23

# Local Knowledge and the Challenge of Regional Governance

Paul Carter

This chapter considers the challenge of research capability building from the point of view of 'Ocean Connections', an interdisciplinary project convened as part of the Cooperative Research Network (CRN) program. Ocean Connections aimed to develop a new methodology of regional governance that allowed 'fragile environments' often lying outside governmental definition to be recognised and cared for. A three-sided dialogue between Indigenous knowledge systems, eco-scientific environmentalism and urban design and creative arts discourses was brokered to offer planners and planning authorities a new way of understanding planned place making. This chapter offers a critical view of the terms 'building' and 'capability'. It describes an unfulfilled collaboration with the Northern Territory (NT) Government to establish a Strategic Planning Suite, discussing the place-making concepts and principles that informed its conceptualisation. Key concepts that we interpreted in new ways were local knowledge and regional governance. Proposing the idea of a 'creative region' that was self-organising and extra-territorial, we suggested this term contributed to a paradigm shift in contemporary master planning ideology. Such a shift, when it occurs, will question the identification of regional development with building and will associate capability with socially and environmentally sustaining attitudes of holding.

# The Idea of Building Research Capability

The CRN initiative underlying the present collection of essays had as its goal 'capability building'. The etymologies informing this phrase suggest a confusion of ideas. To be capable means to be receptive, to be able to grasp with two hands. The physical gesture associated with this idea, a cupping of hands, shapes a holding place—one that is roomy, ample and fitted for what will occupy it. The cultural (and geographical) analogue of capability is the harbour, a naturally capacious coastal zone whose human potential has been grasped. In this derivation of the word's meaning, a two-way moulding occurs. New research capability (in our context across the human, social and environmental sciences) reaches out to an environment in such a way that a new spaciousness, or room to live, is grasped or comprehended. Evidently, this poetic logic is different from the core associations of building, the act of house construction usually imagined as an act of resistance, enclosure and exclusion. To build new structures implies a natural deficiency or environmental hostility. Whether taken metaphorically or literally, it identifies being in the world with clearly circumscribed foundations and (logical) building blocks whose cumulative effect is to redefine the environment territorially and to assert control over the new divisions.

At the same time, particularly in a Northern Australian context, the notion of building capability translates into research programming a deeply entrenched historical and cultural identification of regional capability with development. Research that is useful to government, for example, will assist in clearing away obstacles to progress, define and consolidate structural and functional relations and, in general, provide the reason for planning. In this narrowed approach, better understandings of local environments and their cultures—which the bio- and ethno-sciences can respectively be expected to deliver—will improve regional capability. While regional capability is rarely defined, governments at least understand it quantitatively. Increased economic activity, improved social relations and opportunities and their mediation through improved communications enable politicians to reassure their constituencies that the region is, paradoxically, resilient to change and ready for it. However, the politico-cultural logic informing this discourse depends on not questioning the building metaphor—the instrumentalist construction of knowledge in the interests of physically building the region is tacitly accepted by all parties. Other ways of conceiving the region—in terms, for example, of reciprocity, commensurability, integration and receptiveness—may be dismissed, even though these demonstrably lead to improved planning and public policy outcomes. In short, governments better equipped to build may have little grasp of, or capacity to deliver, good governance.

## The Strategic Planning Suite

A significant illustration of this last statement was afforded by the Strategic Planning Suite, a joint proposal of the NT Government's Department of Infrastructure (formerly Department of Lands, Planning and Environment) and Charles Darwin University's Faculty of Law, Education, Business and Arts. Taken forward with support from the CRN research initiative Ocean Connections, the Suite was conceived as a new forum where planning priorities could be placed in a larger regional context. In bringing together representatives from different government departments charged with societal and infrastructural development and professional leaders in the study and exercise of alternative approaches to environmental management and governance, the expectation was that the rhetoric of region building could be loosened and diversified. In particular, by thinking between projects, the capability for growth and self-transformation already active in community and environment could be taken into account. In the context of the traditional neglect of expertise found in the broader place making, Indigenous and ecological knowledge communities, this would have represented an important innovation.

As I noted in my August 2013 vision statement:

> Planning for development in the Northern Territory has traditionally been handled by the Department of Lands Planning and the Environment, and its predecessors, through a number of Divisions and also through other Northern Territory Government agencies and local government councils; more often than not in a sequential silo environment which is time-consuming, expensive and does not tend to capture more than the 'sum of the parts'. (Carter, 2013a, p. 2)

In promoting the Suite to the new CLP administration, we stated:

> the object is to enable the Government to take advantage of the evolution occurring nationally and internationally from narrowly-defined master planning to holistic place making, from a narrowly functionalist practice of built environment planning and design to

> one that builds resilience and prosperity through the incorporation of environmental, cultural, social and creative resources into the planning and visioning process. (Carter, 2013a, p. 2)

The context of this offer was the growth in research capability occurring through the CRN programs. The purpose of the Ocean Connections program, for example, which I led, was to strengthen cross-disciplinary dialogue between the eco-sciences, Indigenous knowledge systems and sea/land management practices and environmental design, with a view to expanding our capability to understand better what might be meant by 'Northern Australia', what narratives and techniques might distinctively belong to its constitution and what environmental planning and management approaches might flow from these understandings. Translated into the language of planners, we urged 'holistic place making' against master planning. The point here, though, is that the proposed dialogue was across levels and disciplines. It sought to translate between place-based knowledges of different kinds and policy and planning. Our proposition was that the 'strange attractor' in this vertical translation between localised communities and their regional government was design, understood here as a multidisciplinary, bottom-up approach to place making. The object was not primarily to add to the quantity of information available, rather a qualitative shift was proposed, focused on recognising the capability of these different disciplines. What are the values to which they are receptive, and how, we asked, could these values inform 'the evolution of democratically-based governance systems' (Carter, 2013b, p. 8).

Ocean Connections proposed a connection between assumptions about spatial organisation and the premises of efficient administration. What, for example, is the relationship between the administrative region known as the NT and the domain referred to as 'Northern Australia'? What, further, is the operational value of either in the context of cultural histories that link parts of the northern coasts of Australia more strongly to what Frederickson and Walters (2001, p. ix) refer to as the 'Arafura region' than to the continental land mass of Australia itself? Frederickson and Walters (2001, p. ix) 'illustrate some of the many forms of cultural iteration objects undergo through their passage within and between cultures of the Arafura region'. This is a theme congenial to Ocean Connections, which, as described in Chapter 16 of this volume, aims to replace a 'continentalist' or 'dry thinking' approach to the historical imagination of places with one that is 'fluid', relational and interactive. In the present context, the concept of the 'Arafura region' not only displaces land-based definitions of region but redefines region itself as a network of displacements. As objects travel and acquire new meanings, so a region of new interests emerges. Translated into the rhetoric of regional development, Darwin, for example, begins to be the gateway or front door to Asia when its administrative and political cultures develop and exercise a capability for inter-regional exchange. Such a region has a different geography—its imaginary coastlines (see Carter, 2008a) are not hard and fast frontiers but irriguous, estuarine and receptive, like the harbour.

The proposed Strategic Planning Suite advocated the value of place making in informing government policy and planning. As a cross-department forum for integrated planning, it sought to integrate different understandings of place and to reflect these in the planning of planning—attention would be given to the synergies of interest across different portfolios and, if possible, the traditional specialisations and exclusions of the different departmental interests would be relaxed and strategically blurred. The role of research, and of the research dialogue convened through the Suite, would be to provide expert understandings of places, their cultural, environmental and territorial characteristics and, no less important, new notions of place more adequate to the present globalised state of communications. In a way, the successful functioning of the Suite would create a new hybrid public region, one where administrative and research cultures could think holistically between projects. One of the functions of the Suite was to model:

> future options for key locations, situations, and scenarios. In the first instance these options are strategic preferences, not prescriptive master plans. One of their key functions is to present complex datasets drawn from a variety of sources in visual, graphic and interactive forms that facilitate informed, engaged and creative discussion. (Carter, 2013b, p. 6)

## Local Knowledge

One contribution of Ocean Connections to this discussion was to explore the knowledge peculiar to places. Local knowledge is conventionally defined oppositionally and defensively—long residence and an implicitly anti-developmentalist attitude are associated with it. For these reasons, local knowledge is, paradoxically, invaluable and discountable in the context of regional capability building—its authenticity is inversely proportional to its general utility (Carter, 2014, pp. 11–14). In the context of building capability, the object was not to propose and defend a new operational definition of place, but to show how variably places can be imagined, narrated and inhabited. An awareness of this in policy and planning circles would, presumably, improve government-auspiced exercises in place making. We approached this issue of definition through the lens of local knowledge—that is, the interdisciplinary domain of place-based experience and study jointly constituting 'sense of place'. This is not without difficulties:

> Local or traditional ecological knowledge, for example, is very different from what planners understand local knowledge to mean in the context of 'place making'; in the biosciences, local knowledge is something different again, being, approximately, a local demonstration of general principles. (Carter, 2014, p. 2)

There are other vulnerabilities:

> A detailed familiarity with one locality produces a unique experience of place; it is the basis of asserting that a locality has a character that is special. The value of the local resides in its particularity. There can be endless debate about the physical limits of the local but the human claim is clear: this place matters because it is different from anywhere else. Evidently, this claim is two-edged: local knowledge may enjoy a privileged authority but if it cannot generate senses of place that are applicable elsewhere, it is defenceless against 'general knowledge,' whose principles (whether ecological, political, cultural or strategic) are deemed valid precisely because they *can* apply anywhere. (Carter, 2014, p. 2)

A familiar paradox resulting from these vulnerabilities is what might be called a 'Xerox' approach to planned urban redevelopment (see Pratt, 2009). Invariably, master plans assert that one of their objectives is to build a sense of place. The zone earmarked for redevelopment or revitalisation (whether it is a downtown shopping mall, bayside suburb or an entirely new item of public/private infrastructure) will, it is asserted, enjoy or has enjoyed a unique cultural identity, one that the new plan aims to support. However, the terms of reference are entirely generic—high-quality urban design, heritage protection, public art and cultural activities are recommended without any indication that local knowledges might exist, making these measures of success supererogatory or, at worst, actively destructive. Given that in these schemes it usually falls to public art to give 'sense of place' values symbolic expression, it is even more astonishing to observe how public art strategies across all jurisdictions are essentially identical. Invariably, the public art will celebrate local stories and act as 'place makers' (or 'markers', as it is sometimes difficult to tell which is meant). But no generative power is ascribed to these symbolic narratives. What Lyotard (1984, p. 25) calls 'narrative knowledge' is firmly subordinated to the 'pragmatics of scientific knowledge', represented here by the efficiency of the master plan in producing a 'solution' legitimated not by any sensory resurgence ('sense of place') but by the simple operational criterion that the outcome corresponds to the plan.

To counter any devaluation of the local, Ocean Connections proposed a regional approach to local knowledge, one that defines the local non-territorially but in terms of common interests (Carter, 2014, p. 3). This had a number of aspects. It was strategic or pragmatic but also conceptual or political. With the geographical dispersion of communities along Australia's northern coastlines (and, more broadly, the Arafura region) in mind, I wrote:

> In the context of the challenges to cultural and environmental biodiversity presented by development of all kinds, it is strategic that local knowledges make common cause. When a large scale mining project and its associated coastal infrastructure will affect a ribbon of communities across many hundreds of kilometres, a *regional* response, where different local knowledges are coordinated and integrated, carries more political weight than submissions from individual communities that are likely to differ in detail and in priorities. (Carter, 2014, p. 4)

I also made the point that:

> when it is suggested that local knowledge can or should be 'scaled up' so that its principles can alter the way decisions are made at a regional level, it is often assumed that a head-to-head struggle with state or federal administrations is anticipated. However, the object of filtering different local knowledges for their common principles is not to create a case for greater powers being delegated to local or regional governments in their present form. The aim is to influence regional *governance,* that is, to redefine the way in which regions are conceptualized; when this happens, the change implied is not regulatory or fiscal but constitutional. (Carter, 2014, p. 4)

## Creative Regions

In a useful critique of *Developing local knowledge*, Davis indicated that the isolation I had attributed to place-based cultures and their knowledge systems might have been overdrawn. He cited a number of cases where 'local Aboriginal groups, whether clan based, language based or other community entities … embed into various regional agreements and charters, statements regarding their local ecological knowledge and practices' (Davis, 2014, p. 6). These include the promotion of Indigenous 'water rights' in the Murray-Darling Basin through the formation of the Murray Lower Darling Rivers Indigenous Nations alliance, the establishment in the Dubba-Ga clan of the Wiradjuri people of 'networks among knowledge holders that transcend the specifics of a local place', the agreement between the Commonwealth Government's Wet Tropics Management Authority and the Aboriginal Forest Council to develop joint management strategies for 'a natural biological region, as well as a large and important Aboriginal cultural region', and the charters and statements of principles of the (former) Desert Knowledge Cooperative Research Centre (Alice Springs) (Davis, 2014, pp. 6–8). However, three of the four cases cited here accept terms of reference established by non-Indigenous legal or administrative/managerial fiat. This implies no criticism of the initiatives, which, as Davis (2014) emphasised, may stimulate the very debate about the commensurability of different local knowledges that I am keen to encourage. But the motivation of these regional agreements remains pragmatic—differences do not extend to a re-evaluation of the region as such.

The 'creative region' advocated in Ocean Connections negotiates the subtle relationship between administrative and geographical cultures in a different way. While it is extra-territorial in the same sense that the Dubba-Ga knowledge holders live apart from the country from which their knowledge springs, its authority does not spring from actual or ancestral long residence in a particular place. Neither extra- nor intra-territorial, it is, rather, inter-territorial. The example is given in Ocean Connections of coastal zones. Although of defining importance in the colonial territorialisation of the word, they lack most of the formal properties of regions. As I noted:

> Considered as a land/water ribbon, a linear zone stretching from Broome in the west to the Torres Strait in the east, Australia's northern coastline is a region between regions. It belongs neither to sea nor land: in the spatial discourse of the nation state it therefore

counts for nothing. Even if the coast is where all the action is historically, commercially and strategically, no intermediate identity or distinctive topology is accorded it. (Carter, 2014, p. 5)

The argument for maintaining that the coast is a region is not, however, a purely cultural one. It reflects the broader human experience of living next to and with the sea. We have no difficulty in grasping the concept of a 'Mediterranean culture', where geographically scattered communities are connected by a shared maritime experience. A similar situation prevails across the Arafura and Timor seas, where Australian Aboriginal and Indonesian fishing communities live with the sea in similar ways. Ocean connections exist historically between Arnhem Land communities and Macassar. Many Macassan loanwords are found in northern coastal Aboriginal languages. A comparable cultural diaspora, differently motivated geo-politically, was promoted in the late eighteenth and early nineteenth centuries when British commercial interests mediated through the East India Company established trading headquarters in Calcutta, the Malacca Straits, Singapore and (intermittently and unsuccessfully) at Port Essington. The literature of coastal survey represents a continuum of style, content and interests reflective of a distinctively imperial interest, although in the aftermath of colonisation, this is marginalised. In any case, as a ribbon culture, the interests of the coast typically extend into and across the adjacent seas and, via rivers, inland as far as natural borders (catchments or escarpments) suggest (see Carter, 2015).

If, though, coasts can be regions, they immediately and dramatically bring into question the definition of region. Any region is a collection of parts, a multiplicity of shared interests. Its identity in difference is the key to its scale—constitutionally many, an aggregate of many localities, it yet possesses a recognisable identity. Conventionally, a region is a closed figure, a piece of the nation-state jigsaw. Alternatively, it is an international arrangement, an association of nations drawn together by geographical, economic or shared strategic interests. In every permutation, though, the problem of self-determination arises. The members of a regional arrangement do not meet on behalf of the region—the region is a rhetorical device that allows members to pursue their local interests collectively. Inside the nation-state, where the interests of local communities are supposed to map to the national interest, regional governance structures and mechanisms are correspondingly weak. In any case, regions are not established to operate inter-regionally, rather, they are constituted either top down, to mediate the devolution of centralised power, or bottom up, to find and protect common ground between local interests. In this doubly-disabling situation, the ribbon region of the coast is not an anomaly as it dramatises a political-administrative reality. Apart from the local communities that stake them out, regions have no powers, voices or distinctive responsibilities. The care they extend to the cultures and environments they share is not recognised in law or politically represented.

The consequences of this vacuum in cultural and environmental care are obvious. In our study region, the Arafura and Timor seas are treated as extensions of their bordering nation-states. No regional interest inhibits or benefits from the exploitation of their natural resources—which either occurs in 'international waters' or within the nation's 'territorial waters'. In general, the public and private promoters of large-scale natural resource projects (and the coastal infrastructure associated with servicing them) deal with objections to development on a case-by-case basis. Any resistance to the environmental and cultural impact of their operations is presumed to be local. The corollary—that local communities can be bought off if sufficient economic benefits can be shown locally—is also generally true. In this dialogue between inter/national and local, the regional has no voice. This can lead to a characteristic paradox. Where a proposed development is offshore, it is assumed that the developer is responsible to no local community—a local community's interests only come into play when the development of port facilities in their locality is mooted. In another version of this de-regionalisation of development, local communities are granted a voice solely on the basis that they are directly affected by the proposed change—a local community belonging to the same coastal region, but located a thousand kilometres away from the site of the contested development, would not be recognised as having a legitimate interest in minimising the impact of industrialisation on the local culture and environment.

This exclusion from governance issues of legitimate interest to local communities is not overcome by the kind of regional arrangements described by Davis (2014)—in these, a consolidation of common interests occurs but only on condition that the impact of these is experienced by each contributing community locally. The constitution of the region remains unchanged. In Ocean Connections, we proposed a different mechanism for the regionalisation of local interests. Invoking the idea of a 'creative region', one predicated on exchange across interests, borders and disciplines, we described a region that emerged through the conversation itself. The medium of exchange is narrative—the mediation of sense of place through symbolic forms that exercise the imagination and supplying the terms of reference for future innovation. Despite the unusual vocabulary deployed here (at least from a planning perspective), there is nothing strikingly novel about this proposal. It simply extends the 'language' of public art to every aspect of public domain planning. In this process, public art ceases to be a separate category of public infrastructure. Instead, new places are described, inhabited and cared for through a process of re-narrativisation. The inherited place myths are examined for their creative mechanisms—their explanations of coming-into-being—and the common ground found between them opens the way to forms of development that incorporate place memory into the place-making design. In this way, objectives treated separately in master plans can be thought together—enhanced environmental integrity, heritage protection, social inclusiveness and so forth are secured through a prior constitution of the place as a 'creative region', one capable of generating its own best governance practices.

As we noted:

> A recognition of the role poetic thinking plays in making sense of place redefines local knowledge as a mode of knowing that renders the abstract concrete. This aligns local knowledge with the material thinking characteristic of the creative arts. It is argued that key to building regional governance models responsive to local interests is the formation of creative communities. The region they envisage is archipelagic rather than territorialized; its governance is performative rather than procedural. (Carter, 2014, p. 1)

A 'creative region' is not simply a fragile environment, it embodies a different way of thinking about the biases of present governmental arrangements (and priorities) and provokes the possibility of alternative governance models. Such a region is essentially infinite, uncontainable, fluid and difficult to possess. Between territories, it defines the region of the 'commons'. Such a 'region' opens a new dialogue between place-based knowledges and the placeless axioms of regional planning. It is not amalgamated local knowledge—an up-scaling that simply defers the problem of authority, as any region can also be up-scaled without discernible impact on the abstraction of administrative categories and operational procedures—instead, it is a way of thinking about the different discourses of 'local knowledge' together through the conceptualisation of new places where, precisely, they talk to one another.

## Master Planning

The obvious situation where reconfigured local knowledge finds its application is in master planning. To redefine place making as the promotion of creative regions overcomes the technicist bias of current administrative specialisations, allowing (in principle) different departments and a widened community partnership to collaborate in an act of collective re-narrativisation. After uniplex and multiplex models of master planning urban design and infrastructure development, Healey (2005) discerned the emergence in the last couple of decades of a softened mode of planning—the one we have referred to as 'place making'. She characterised this as involving a new institutionalism, associated with environmentalism and driven by questions of sustainability, which emphasises the importance of a politics of place making, and which focuses on 'the active social construction of place-focused frameworks and efforts to cultivate strategic imagination through which key attributes of place can become identified and "owned" by many stakeholders, and "permanences" created in the "dynamic relational dialectics of urban life"' (Healey, 2005, p. 261). In other words, the proposal to engage planners in cross-disciplinary dialogue about the establishment of integrated, regional templates for the identification, design and management of individual projects is not novel. It simply seeks to shift the responsibility for the ideation of new places from the abstract lexicon of planning to the concrete, symbolic narratives characteristic of creative communities and their regions.

One of the start-up research collaborations proposed for the Strategic Planning Suite was a review of the industrial development occurring at East Arm in Darwin Harbour. From a neo-liberalist or capitalistic point of view, the provision of new peri-urban infrastructure that enables the region to benefit from foreign investment is exemplary regional capacity building. However, the development had not been thought of regionally— even its impact on the local environment had been confined to an arbitrary circuit of water in the immediate lee of the development. In the context of reconceptualising regions as archipelagoes of local knowledges, the object of the review was not to counter the localist bias of the East Arm cultural and environmental impact statements with, for example, a holistic description of the harbour as a whole. Such a description would certainly be an improvement on the fragmentary, project-by-project impact literature currently available, but it would not overcome the tendency to conceptualise the harbour as a territory for building. It would not measure important qualities of capaciousness, receptiveness and ocean connectedness that constitute it as both fragile and creative.

To bring these qualities into play would be, as I wrote of another project (a public spaces strategy for Victoria Harbour, Melbourne), to recognise the place

> as a legacy of appearances and disappearances, in short, as a history of change. In this way attention shifts from static objects to mobile processes. It becomes possible to see the space as a dynamic, self-reinventing network of tracks, outlines, shadows, edges, sightlines and wakes—to see it as if it were reflected in the ever-changing face of the water. (Carter, 2008b, p. 186)

These insights might inform the cultural programming of the adjacent Darwin waterfront—they might be part of a discourse that reoriented Darwin to its maritime environment. To translate such poetic perspectives into a regional economy, it is necessary to relate the harbours to other harbours and recognise that they belong to a distinctive geographical taxonomy of 'half places' and doubled places. Defined by their receptiveness, harbours exist in relation to one another. As distinctive places of exchange, they model the potential of coastlines as a whole, to materialise the existence of a shared region of care. The cultural self-confidence evident in this analysis translates into planning. It becomes possible to narrate major infrastructural developments contextually, for which the case of the proposed Glyde Point Industrial estate and the adjoining Muttamujuk Residential development was cited. In the context of a fly-in, fly-out employment pattern, with associated social isolation and communal stress, the insertion of new development opportunities into planning strategies that take account of regional care and governance expectations makes obvious sense.

Other agendas overtook the Strategic Planning Suite. Handed to Telstra, in return for the promotion of government programs, its link with the research sector was severed. In the wake of this, a pilot Australian Research Council Linkage–style research partnership was brokered with the NT Government's Department of Infrastructure and the Parks and Wildlife Commission. The invitation was to establish the brief for a full study into the options, timelines and costs for a complete 're-invigoration' of the Parks and Wildlife Commission, with a closer and more attractive alignment with eco-tourism and university-based research. 'Local knowledge'—

defined in Ocean Connections as a multidisciplinary place-based discourse able to generate regional governance principles—was to underwrite the study. As we noted:

> Successful place making builds on sound local knowledge. Local knowledge of critical value to PWCNT comes in three main forms: planning (awareness of local conditions), ecological sciences (understanding of biodiversity principles), Indigenous knowledge systems (traditional management of land and water). However, research shows that successful place making occurs when these three kinds of local knowledge are combined to produce place-based knowledge. Place based knowledge is the foundation of building a PWCNT vision that optimizes the individual visitor experience while communicating a Territory wide sense of place. It is the key to biodiversity conservation techniques that preserve local ecologies, at the same time understanding them as components of a regional mosaic of refuges. Place-based knowledge mediates between local knowledge and regional values. (Material Thinking, p. 4)

In the few days that we were permitted to work on this study, we produced impressive results. A new model of park management was proposed for investigation:

> Networked (looped local knowledge is shared across the network to protect and promote regional values; qualitative data exchange and participatory management practices). The latter model factors in the value of the parks that exceeds the parts—the potential for the individual holdings to form an 'archipelago' of biodiverse 'refuges'. It also factors in the condition of the environment immediately adjoining key reserves. In this way it builds an awareness of the inter-connectedness of one of North Australia's primary assets and sources of social wellbeing. (Material Thinking, pp. 5–6)

A new interpretation strategy was proposed based on the 'Three circle park experience':

> Multisensory experience of a natural environment (circle 1) is nested within narrative expectations of the place (the expectations the visitor brings, the memories they take away (circle 2). Both these experiences are themselves framed by the symbols (NT Tourism imagery, private transport operator imagery, internet information) used to communicate the park values (circle 3). The design, integration and interpretation of these different levels can transform the visitor experience: producing emotional identifications that foster further curiosity and interest,

this investment in producing authentic stories about the place directly contributes to the challenge of maintaining biodiversity. (Material Thinking, p. 8)

In addition, and in consultation with local park rangers, we developed a new approach to the physical function and design of on-site interpretation facilities. Under the aegis of regionally appropriate and innovative design, the new 'meeting places' reconfigured the specialist knowledge from traditional and Western ecological sources as provocations to conversation and action incubating new creative communities. Perhaps it was a case of too much, too soon, as immediately after these first proposals were shared the study was closed down. In the absence of any further communication, the reasons behind the Parks and Wildlife Commission's decision to abort the partnership remain a matter of speculation. In a way, the curtailment of this attempt to broaden the definition of region-based research capability building to incorporate creative place making, management and governance practices already resident in the community illustrates the challenge that still remains. A new dialogue between government and research sectors is inevitable, but its cultivation will evidently depend on a careful mix of good communication, cross-sectoral trust and bold leadership.

# References

Carter, P. (2008a). Dark with excess of bright: Mapping the coastlines of knowledge. In P. Carter, *Dark writing, geography, performance, design* (pp. 49–78). Honolulu, HI: University of Hawai'i Press.

Carter, P. (2008b). Solutions: Storyboarding a Humid zone. In P. Carter, *Dark writing, geography, performance, design* (pp. 173–202). Honolulu, HI: University of Hawai'i Press.

Carter, P. (2013a, 23 April). *Ocean Connections, a new region leadership, care and design project, located at The Northern Institute, Charles Darwin University, 2013–2015*. Paper delivered at Northern Institute, Charles Darwin University (pp. 1–23). Obtainable on request from author.

Carter, P. (2013b, 6 August). *Proposal to develop a Strategic Planning Suite*. Australia: Land Development Division, Department of Lands, Planning and the Environment, Northern Territory Government and Charles Darwin University. Obtainable on request from author.

Carter, P. (2014, March). *Developing local knowledge: What translates?* Paper delivered at Northern Institute, Charles Darwin University (pp. 1–32). Obtainable on request from author.

Carter, P. (2015). Australindia: The geography of imperial desire. *Postcolonial Studies*, *18*(2), 1–12.

Davis, M. (2014, October). *Critical response to Paul Carter 'Developing Local Knowledge: What translates?'*. Paper commissioned by Paul Carter on behalf of 'Ocean Connections' project. Obtainable on request from author.

Frederickson, C. & Walters, I. (2001). Introduction. In C. Frederickson & I. Walters (Eds), *Altered states: Material culture transformations in the Arafura Region* (pp. i–xii). Darwin, NT: Northern Territory University Press.

Healey, P. (2005). Planning in relational space and time: Responding to new urban realities. In A. Ballantyne (Ed.), *Architecture theory: A reader in philosophy and culture* (pp. 259–271). London, England: Continuum.

Lyotard, Jean-François. (1984). *The postmodern condition: A report on knowledge* (Geoffrey Bennington and Brian Massumi trans.). Manchester: Manchester University Press.

Material Thinking. (2014, December). *Parks and Wildlife Commission of the Northern Territory: An integrated management vision based on a review and assessment of PWCNT's two exemplar parks: Litchfield National Park and Casuarina Coastal Reserve*. Obtainable on request from author.

Pratt, A. (2009). Policy transfer and the field of the culture and CCIs: What can be learned from Europe? In L. Kong & J. O'Conner (Eds), *Creative economics, creative cities*. Dordrecht, The Netherlands: Springer.

# 24

# Revisiting Governance Systems Analysis in Northern Australia: Exploring Critical Systems Thinking as a Framework for Engaging with Multiplicity and Incommensurability

Anne Stephens, Elspeth Oppermann
and Allan P. Dale

## Introduction

Northern Australia, the region of Australia north of the Tropic of Capricorn, is characterised by profound difference and complexity in cultures, worldviews and ways of being. An array of diverse governance responses to the way this complexity and difference manifests itself has been discussed elsewhere (Stephens et al., 2014). This chapter reflects, in particular, on the use of Governance Systems Analysis (GSA) in Northern Australia in improving governance outcomes in this complex world. GSA is an analytical tool deployed to support deliberative dialogue among those involved in complex governance systems and contexts in the north. To date, its most common use has been in the mobilisation of the dominant norms of governmental practice to resolve complex problems at a landscape scale. In the context of multiplicity and incommensurability of different ways of being, this chapter seeks to enhance GSA's ability to engage explicitly and ethically with genuine cultural difference embedded within Northern Australian society. It uses Critical Systems Thinking (CST) to revisit, through systems thinking, GSA's structural-functionalist foundations. The chapter's objective is to enhance an approach to complex problem solving that is already used in Northern Australia to support practical policy engagements.

GSA has been developed to analyse complex problems of governance in socio-environmental contexts in Northern Australia (Dale, 2013, 2014). As a broad analytical method, it was first published and developed by Dale, Vella and Potts (2013). Its earlier conceptual origins emerged from methods used to explore complex policy failures in Indigenous affairs and later in social impact assessment methods (Dale, 1993; Dale & Lane, 1993). Its most significant application is its use to facilitate deliberative dialogue between government agents and stakeholders responsible for the protection of the Great Barrier Reef. In this case, it explores the deficiencies of the present governance arrangements in attaining desired ecological, social and economic outcomes (Dale, Vella, Pressey et al., 2013). Latent within this approach is a concern to give voice to disempowered populations who are intimately connected in complex ways to various geographies and landscapes.

In engaging with the question of governance in Northern Australia, GSA wades into the profound question of 'what is governance', comprising the questions of how to govern ethically and, indeed, how to ethically develop governance systems per se. In contrast to other parts of Australia, Northern Australia is notable in that, when considering the wider governance system, it must be accepted that, alongside a Western system of governance, there is an array of active Indigenous systems of governance (Christie, 2014; Prout & Howitt, 2009) that have remained strong despite colonisation. These Indigenous governance systems are often unknown, unrecognised or misunderstood by dominant Australian society, and there are long-running, tragic policy failures emerging from one form of governance attempting to ignore or co-opt the other and positive and creative generative adaptations and co-productions of integrated governance practices (McMullen, 2013; Trudgen, 2012; Verran, 2011). These multiple accounts of government, but also the state, land and country, and the fabric of reality itself are embedded in, and come into conflict through, a highly contested socio-ecological landscape (Woinarski, 2014). Further, rather than just seeking to govern society as if it were an extant and immutable object, forms of governance actively produce our wider northern society (Stephens et al., 2014). As such, not only 'what' is governed but how that governance occurs is a deeply significant question for determining what ways of life, identity and ecology are (re)produced in Northern Australia.

Destructive and productive encounters between governance systems and the forms of life they produce are not confined to the intersections of Indigenous and non-Indigenous worlds (Stephens et al., 2014). However, Northern Australia demonstrates the profound implications of multiplicity and incommensurability of ways of being, challenging Western assumptions of an 'ideal' system of governance and governance practices based on consensus. These assumptions authorise the occlusion or absorption of other ways of life into the dominant governance system and its attendant identity of the neoliberal subject (Peck & Tickell, 2002). The devastating impact of such agendas on Indigenous identity, wellbeing and health is well known (Trudgen, 2012). Yet the region continues to be subject to ever more intensive forms of political intervention with transformational objectives (Anderson, 2015), such as through the Northern Territory Emergency Response and, more recently, the Indigenous Advancement Strategy. Policy approaches, including those that embed corporate governance, are some of the carriers of these transformational agendas, precursors to complex encounters with Indigenous forms of governance and ecological governance (Christie, 2006). This makes Northern Australia an excellent case study for exploring governance and difference that is not so clear elsewhere. It also provokes GSA to consider its own inherent assumptions about the nature of governance, enabling the explicit development of an ethical practice for its intervention into governance systems that is cognisant of the multiplicity of governance systems and ways of being.

On the basis of GSA's ontological foundation in systems thinking and because of our concern to develop and address GSA's ability to engage with questions of multiplicity and incommensurability, we propose CST as an appropriate framework to engage with GSA, as it has emerged from a similar ontological foundation (Jackson, 1991; Midgley, 1996). This chapter uses CST's core commitments or principles of practice to enable ongoing critical reflexivity during the analysis of, and intervention in, each stage of governance activity described in the GSA process. The objective is to develop GSA into a more nuanced analysis and intervention tool for governance systems, capable of acknowledging and engaging with its own contingency and the contingency of the systems it is analysing. Doing so allows multiplicity and incommensurability to be acknowledged, which enables the explicit political and ethical consideration of practice. The next section introduces GSA itself, followed by an account of why incommensurability and multiplicity, which characterise Northern Australia, pose a challenge to GSA's current form. CST is then put forward as a useful way to render GSA more capable of supporting different ways of being in Northern Australia.

# Origin and Use of Governance Systems Analysis

GSA has been used, primarily in Northern Australia, as a way to seek systemic reform in government-driven interventions. In Australia, a number of empirically and theoretically grounded frameworks have been developed to analyse and evaluate natural resource governance systems and other complex systems, including their constituent plans, programs, strategies and institutions (Althaus et al., 2007; Bellamy et al., 2001; Connick & Innes, 2003; Curtis et al., 1998; Hajkowicz, 2009; Turnbull, 2005; Vogel, 2011). While it is widely recognised that governance systems operate in a non-linear, systemic fashion, they are not always analysed in this way (Abrahams, 2005; Carman, 2007; Hoggarth, 2010; Plummer & Armitage, 2007; Rauschmayer et al., 2009). Thus, GSA was developed to deal with the management of complex governance contexts such as complex landscape management and natural resource management (NRM) (see Dale, Vella & Potts, 2013).

The GSA framework is grounded in structural-functionalism to help analyse real-world governance systems. Accordingly, it attempts to bring into focus the interactions of governance system structures, functions and their impact on the likelihood of the system delivering its desired outcomes (Dale, Vella & Potts, 2013). Structures tend to be the more static elements of systems and include networks and alliances of individuals and institutions that contribute independently and collectively towards the delivery of key system outputs, such as plans, strategies, research, implementation and monitoring and, consequently, outcomes such as improved water quality and human health outcomes. Functions, on the other hand, are the characteristics that emerge as a property of the relationship between structural components in the system. The functionality of the system includes system connectivity, while the agency of key players and the role of knowledge are also crucial. While we cannot assume that functions are always deliberate, they can be planned for and viewed as a measure of how governance systems deliver desired outcomes.

Dale, Vella and Potts (2013) developed GSA to apply structural-functionalist concepts to support deliberative dialogue within society about securing continuous improvement in extant governance systems. It is, to some extent, assumed that structural aspects of any governance system can be enabled by defined concepts of rationality that are commonly inherent on Western processes of policy development. Hence, structural components of governance processes are broadly considered to cover by the following (but non-linear) activities:

- vision and objective setting
- strengths, weaknesses, opportunities and threats analysis and research
- strategy development (within various structural elements of the system)
- implementation
- monitoring, evaluation and review.

The GSA framework seeks dialogue among all participants in a governance system, but particularly decision-makers, to identify which structural and functional components of a governance system are limiting the success of governance activities. The process builds evidence to support reforms, decisions and actions and then focuses attention on supporting improvement and reform in those areas. Governance processes that reduce losses of goodwill, capacity and partnerships, for example, are more likely to enhance governance systems. In Northern Australia, the multiple, overlapping and different jurisdictional and human worldviews add complexity and fragmentation of governance systems within an already contested landscape. This means good policy development and the nurturing of the sound functional integration of structural and functional activities across the governance system needs to be attended to explicitly through overtly collaborative mechanisms. GSA does this effectively within the parameters of a Western policy development norms, but in past applications it has tended to underplay the need to implicitly and explicitly allow different ways of being to coexist, including different ways of doing governance and redefining the different objectives of governance itself (Springer, 2010). Hence, the next section explores why this is of importance in theorising governance and how GSA might learn from CST as a mode of engagement with difference that shares its basic systems ontology.

## Governance and Difference: Ethical Engagement with Multiplicity and Incommensurability

In accounting for governance as systemic, we begin by noting the distinction between 'governance' and 'government'. Government refers to the formal institutions of political power and formal policy practices of the nation-state, while governance refers to the broader intentional shaping of the flow of events to realise desired public good (Parker & Braithwaite, 2003) within a wider governance context. The two are not mutually exclusive. The institution of government crosses over and negotiates the multiple other institutions involved in our societal system of governance, leading to a complex and emergent array of peoples, practices and rationales of governance, including different accounts of the public good (or indeed the 'good public'). The wider notion of the term governance has become more familiar as concepts of network society (Castells, 2000). Globalisation, complexity, liberal governance and advanced liberal governmentality have redefined political practice and analysis (see, for example, Dean & Hindess, 1998; Lefèvre, 1998). This changing ontology has accounted for politics no longer just being considered as the domain of governments, but, rather, as underpinning the broader practices of societal governance operated by and affecting a much more diverse network of interests and societal problems. Policies and programs that govern are no longer solely designed, implemented or evaluated by government or government agencies alone or a dominant role. Here, governance is understood as inherently systemic. Epistemological approaches to this new ontology have lessened their focus on the structure and form of relatively defined institutions to the nature of relationships between elements that contingently produce an emergent system.

The account of the political context and emancipation also changes in light of this new ontology. Without finite, pre-defined institutions, roles, responsibilities and rights, systemic approaches to governance (including where it is exercised by government) has reopened the meaning of democracy, emancipation and participation (Midgley & Richardson,

2007). This shift dovetails with, and in part arises from, post-colonial and post-modern accounts of multiplicity and diversity that reject the notion of universal values and universalising ideals. Having accepted the ontological challenge, debates rage over whether consensus is possible or desirable and how to engage with diversity and plurality and with the people, communities and organisations affected by policy interventions (see Forester, 1999; Lane, 2005; Muro & Jeffrey, 2008; Parkins & Mitchell, 2005). The key question is, can we create consensual systems of governance, or is this ideal not only practically unachievable, but ethically fraught? This question is valid and visible in Northern Australia with its diversity and contested/competing post-colonial worlds.

Approaches to these questions vary, but for CST, two main bodies of thought have been central. These are often both termed 'critical theory', but encompass a range of thought, perhaps best epitomised in the thought of critical theorist Jurgen Habermas and the post-structuralist thinker Michel Foucault. Habermas' 'free speech ideal' denotes the conditions free from domination that he argued will permit communicative rationality to produce consensus and a collective way of being that enables improved equality (Ashenden & Owen, 1999). However, post-structuralists, such as Michel Foucault, argue that the differences and multiplicity of identities, cultures, worldviews and values in society are 'irreducible'—that is, agreement between people in matters of contested social issues may be unlikely, even impossible, due to the incommensurability of worldviews and values and ways of living (Gregory, 1996). From this perspective, efforts to resolve such differences into consensus can be seen as violent, however implicitly, as opting for a single, shared view necessitates the exclusion of elements of other worldviews that are dismantled to reject their validity and integrity. In the context of Northern Australia, for example, one may consider Australia's 'Closing the Gap' policy and program agenda, regarding Indigenous Australians, as being more akin to an assimilationist versus self-determinationist policy divide. Striving for consensus, while recognising worldview differences, might seem like a pragmatic strategy for long-term governance reform.

The consensus–incommensurability divide has major implications for how governance systems are intervened in, by whom and for what purpose. For Habermas, governance systems are ideally the result of, and enable, consensus building through communicative rationality (Bausch, 2001; Beaumont & Nicholls, 2008; Brocklesby & Cummings, 1996). Whereas for Foucault, Western forms of governance systems enable a particular *governmentality*—a particular set of technologies and practices that produce a particular form of public good, which, far from being universal, must produce a 'good public' that conforms to this way of life, necessarily at a cost to other ways of being and particular social groups' or individuals' ability to engage in emancipatory practices (Bevir, 2010; Lemke, 2002).

Although it has not explicitly engaged with this debate, GSA, in its use to date, has been aligned more closely to a Habermasian account of communicative rationality. While recognising differing worldviews, the GSA framework has systematically applied a process to derive shared understandings and consensus between the stakeholders of large and complex socio-environmental systems towards their sustainable and planned futures (Dale, Vella & Potts, 2013; Potts et al., 2014). GSA has traditionally addressed itself to the problem of how to make an extant system more effective in achieving its objectives. It has focused on the pragmatic problem that multilayered systems of governance are not always functionally optimised (Potts et al., 2014). Systems and their objectives can be discordant, redundant or corrupting of the overall system objective and, therefore, require reform. As a practice founded in structural-functionalism, however, GSA does recognise the problem of governance as systemic and diverse. Its focus has been to take a more pragmatic approach to reform, which does not seriously challenge a single coherent system as ideal. It has not, therefore, been used to facilitate a radical questioning of systemic goals. Although it has emancipatory concerns, these have not, to date, been fully developed into actionable principles.

CST stands in contrast to this ontology of coherent, knowable and consensual systems. While its literature and practice is heavily influenced by Habermasian thinking, CST practitioners have also been influenced by the post-structural critiques of Habermasian practice and methodologies with approaches such as systemic intervention developed to engage in the politics and ethics of governance systems per se (Brocklesby & Cummings, 1996; Gregory, 1996; Midgley, 2000; Valero-Silva, 1996). CST responds to the concern that post-structuralists avoid intervention or change for fear of becoming a dominating force that avoids a thorough engagement with what a practice of emancipation might look like itself. Boundaries must be questioned to ensure any practices aimed at making an extant system more effective minimise harmfulness to difference or subjectification. To do this, it is essential that all system participants are engaged in the analysis to open up the boundaries as a mode of critique in the first- and second-order modes. Participants question the objectives, goals, functions and structures of the system and the nature of the system, even the paradigms that shape these governance systems themselves. Both GSA and CST practice entail making judgments concerning the boundaries of the systems in question. We argue that, within a more critical theoretical framework, there is a place for both first- and second-order boundary judgment practices.

The remainder of this chapter advances a methodology that recognises that participants in governance systems are inescapably connected into one or more systems of governance embedded in a wider systemic context and they have agency within that wider system. It endeavours to show how the practical considerations and decisions in a particular empirical context (in this case, the deployment of a GSA-based approach in Northern Australia) may make the resolution of irreducible difference an active political act. This methodological approach acknowledges deliberative ethical practice and, in doing this, we hope to respond to the challenge GSA sets—that is to work with, recognise and identify the extant governance agencies and their interconnections as systems. We hope to develop a method that sees all the analysis and interventions of GSA as inherently supporting political and ethical practices, thereby enabling much deeper engagement with critique and explicit engagement with power and emancipatory actions in conditions of incommensurability and irreducible multiplicities.

## Critical Systems Thinking: A Critique of Governance Systems Analysis

Both GSA and CST have their origins in systems thinking. The fundamental idea of systems thinking is that cause and effect linearity is insufficient to describe complex, changing phenomena that are recognisable and characterised by both the inter-relatedness of their parts and the emergence of properties that cannot be fully comprehended by the system's constituent parts (Flood, 2010; Maani & Cavana, 2000). There are two systems thinking applications that can be traced back to an ontological shift demarcating a first and second wave of systems thinking, which also map onto realist and post-structural ontologies. Realist systems describe hierarchies of systems that contain 'nested' subsystems, not unlike a Russian matryoshka doll (Midgley, 2000). This metaphor assumes the objective reality of systems, however, as valid and extant social institutions and functions.

Several questions have been posed of structural-functionalism, GSA's ontological foundation, by the systems thinking community. Can we assume that complex systems behave predictably? Are healthy systems stable? Are stable systems 'just'? At the root of such questions is the concern that structural-functionalism, and in this case GSA, could become oblivious to the contingency of a particular governance system itself. This contingency is as much practical as it is ethical. First, the system is a product of an incalculable multitude of relationships and interactions that keep it constantly changing. The uncertainty of integrated systems outcomes is due to the systems property known as 'emergence'—the revelation of a new phenomenon arising through interactions in the system, but which may not resemble the system or subsystems of its origin (Ison, 2008). Second, if the system is contingent, partial and likely to change, on what ethical and political basis is using this model appropriate for decisions (Valero-Silva, 1996)?

This realist notion of the systems and their structures is contested by the post-structuralist approaches of CST thinkers such as Taket & White (1993), Valero-Silva (1996), Brocklesby and Cummings (1996) and Midgley (2000). The alternative account of 'systemic' thinking is grounded in the proposition that reality, or realities, are in fact subjective and/or historically contingent and that a particular reality or way of being may be named or otherwise established by boundaries constituting a 'knowledge generating system' for the knower or the subject (Midgley, 2000, p. 76). Such boundaries, therefore, have profound ethical and political implications as they establish what elements of being and existence fall on which side of binaries such as true/false and right/wrong.

To respond to these concerns in terms of systems thinking, a distinction has been made between adopting a systematic or systemic perspective as exclusivist and inclusive connotations. Systematic practice can be characterised as goal-oriented behaviour that seeks to describe or discover an extant system that it takes to be natural, where what is considered to be relevant knowledge (true and right) is unquestioned, even though it may in practice emanate from an exclusive group of people (Ison, 2008). In contrast, systemic practice actively facilitates learning and change to accommodate a plurality of interests (Ison, 2008), which is responsive to post-structuralist concerns. GSA has its roots in structural-functionalism, which is closely related to realist and systematic approaches, yet it also adopts deliberative, even emancipatory practices (Potts et al., 2014). Thus, GSA attempts to operate within both systemic and systematic methodologies, but without explicit consideration of the philosophical distinctions between realist approaches and post-structural ones or the constraining effects of systematic practice on systemic modes of engagement with questions of power and emancipation. As such, there is a currently a gap between GSA's participatory aspirations and its practical approach to systemic thinking.

GSA does see itself as enabling greater visibility and effectiveness of actors as part of a system that is to make explicit a boundary definition. However, its current failure to theorise multiplicity, difference and irreducibility is a limitation. Systems thinking that places emphasis on structure and function does not see the assumed legitimacy of extant actors as contingent on particular power relations. As such, the emancipatory implications of power struggles can be underdeveloped. Peoples' values, knowledges, paradigms and cultural interpretations of governance are rendered less visible by GSA's theoretical framework and practical toolkit, as is the possibility that these can always change and that previously visible and legitimate actors may come to be contested by an array of alterative bodies and positions. GSA attempts to build a more consensus-oriented representational tool to be used to make co-constructed meaning. However, because complexity also occurs at an ontological and epistemological level through different worldviews, governmental rationales and organisational narratives, such a representative tool is likely to be controversial and interpreted in multiple ways as 'people come to appreciate a quite different systemic quality to their existence' (Flood, 2010, p. 275). In this regard, GSA's structural-functionalist ontology and epistemology becomes harder to marry with its participatory and deliberative intent as the implicitly realist approach potentially hides from view those agents who work beyond the realist account of modernity's political institutions and functions.

## Using Critical Systems Thinking to Refine Governance Systems Analysis

CST is a framework that brings critical theory's broad ontological and epistemological influences into a systemic mode of thinking about social complexity (Flood, 2010; Fuchs & Hofkirchner, 2009; Jackson, 1991, 2010; Midgley, 2000; Valero-Silva, 1996). CST is framed through core values, themed around critique that is often expressed as systemic boundary reflection, pluralism or a manner of allowing for a multiplicity of theories and methodologies, or ontologies and epistemologies, and emancipation as some way of allowing for social improvement or the freedom to change. These core values are expressed by Flood (2010) as six commitments—the systems thinking idea, critical awareness, theoretical pluralism, methodological pluralism, social awareness and human emancipation. After a brief introduction to CST as a whole, these commitments are discussed below. To demonstrate the significance of this theoretical framework for an intervention tool such as GSA, the following sections also draw on Midgley's (2000) methodology for practice grounded in CST.

The starting point of a CST analysis is to assume that everything in the universe is directly or indirectly connected, but that a 'God's eye' view of that interconnectedness is impossible (Midgley, 2000). To combat the inevitable limits to understanding and to enable discussion, we apply 'boundaries' around knowledge. Systemic intervention seeks to explore these boundaries proceeding on the principle that a boundary indicates not only what is included but also that something is excluded (Midgley & Richardson, 2007). These elements, be they people, objects, or values, are distinguished from that which they are not, which comes to be distinguished in turn with reference to another boundary (Midgley, 2000). Thus, in post-structuralist terms, we could say that meaning and reality are produced through the (re)articulation of boundaries which are inherently political (Laclau & Mouffe, 2001). With this in mind, boundary critique and boundary judgment are not just innocuous forms of examining the limits of the system but are inevitably political processes for bounding systemic intervention practice.

Midgley (2000) makes the system and its contingency explicit by making 'first and second boundary judgments' explicit. Making judgments about primary boundaries, their placement and content of its system can be made when looking 'outward' from within the system towards the world. This is called making a first-order judgment. When looking 'back' at the knowledge system that produced the outward judgment, we are engaged in second-order judgments (Midgley, 2000). Second-order boundary judgments denote the system's identity and the contingency of this identity on first-order judgments. Second-order judgments are dependent on there being a first-order judgment; however, second-order judgments do not automatically proceed from the first and must be a deliberate practice of critiquing one's own knowledge.

We propose that this process of first and second boundary judgments can be applied to the use of GSA and systemic intervention. GSA is capable of making first-order boundary judgments, but is limited in its capacity for second-order judgments or critique of the system it takes for granted. Electing to use systemic intervention enables practitioners to come to know the systems themselves and, therefore, question the ontologies and epistemologies on which the account of the system is based, and the way that system is governed based on these knowledges and ways of knowing. The process of constant iteration and reflection between the first- and second-order judgments are analytically essential as it is this process that contributes to the growth of knowledge and emancipatory potential by highlighting the contingency of the system, thus allowing other ways of being to be entertained within the system. The following sections use CST's six core commitments to organise GSA and CST's sets of reflective practices. We highlight occasions where GSA expresses a similar account of emancipation to those expressed by CST scholars and practitioners. However, we also note differences in accounting for power, knowledge and emancipation. In some cases, these sections also reflect on the rift within CST that reflects the breadth of critical theory, including the debate between consensus and incommensurability that we have chosen to represent through Habermas and Foucault. Within each commitment, implications for GSA as a practical tool are explored through a comparison with systemic intervention, as a praxis methodology for CST.

## Systems Thinking Idea

The first of CST's core commitments is the systems thinking idea—the idea that valid knowledge and meaningful understanding comes from building up whole pictures of phenomena, not by breaking them into parts (Flood, 2010). This core understanding is present in the GSA framework. GSA attempts to benchmark systems to determine how the 'Systemic functionality (i.e. how parts of the system work) across and within structures serves to reinforce and maintain the stability of the system's structures' in the context of an ever-changing, complex and unpredictable environment (Dale, Vella, Pressey et al., 2013, p. 10). These are examples of first-order boundary judgments, concerned with questions of the system's core characteristics and attributes. However, GSA makes the ontological and epistemological assumption that these can be known, by all, at a given point in time. The framework draws on functions to describe the way in which structures are produced and operated and related to subsystems. For governance systems, three 'cornerstone functional elements' are identified (Dale & Bellamy, 1998) as knowledge application to improve governance systems, connection of effort within governance systems and decision-making capacity of players within the system (agency).

It is through these three functional and across different structural elements that GSA analysis is organised throughout each stage of its analysis. 'Knowledge application' to improve governance systems implies the presence of several CST core commitments—critical awareness, theoretical plurality and methodological plurality. The 'connection of effort' within governance systems entails both the systems idea and social awareness. The decision-making capacity of players within the system engages with the emancipatory, critical awareness and social awareness commitments, each of which are discussed in detail in the relevant following sections.

Despite GSA's grounding in structural-functionalism, it recognises that systems are complex, may transform and 'consist of many component parts that contribute towards the overall operability of the system' (Potts et al., 2014, p. 2), and it references concerns with agency and processes to achieve a more ethical and efficacious outcome involving multiple stakeholders in complex problems. However, functions themselves do little work to analyse these relationships, as they tend to refer to what the relationship achieves, rather than how it is constituted—namely through particular power relations mediated and produced by knowledge and its communication (Foucault, 2000). It is relations of power and communication (described in post-structuralist literatures as power and knowledge) that produce emergence (Foucault, 2000) and are, therefore, central concepts to a systemic analysis of governance (Brocklesby & Cummings, 1996; Valero-Silva, 1996) or to an analysis of governance as emerging from and harnessing systemic emergence (Dillon, 2000,

2007; Dillon & Reid, 2009). The remainder of CST's core commitments enable engagement with the contingency of the particular system that the systems thinking idea makes space for, which are developed below in terms of GSA to help it move beyond first order boundary critique.

## Critical Awareness

The second CST commitment is critical awareness, demonstrated when the underlying assumptions of a system are made explicit and open to questioning, which we have argued is currently limited in GSA. Critical awareness is an applied second-order boundary critique that encourages an exploration of the ontology, epistemology, methods and techniques used in governance analysis. However, it is important to understand what is meant by the term 'critical'. As previously mentioned, critical theory, loosely used, often obscures the differences between Habermasian critical theorists and post-structuralist thinkers such as Foucault. While CST has been largely dominated by Habermasian accounts, we seek to explore a more critical Foucauldian account here. A Habermasian approach to CST understands that human liberation can be achieved by changing the material conditions in which people live, work and socialise. Therefore, CST practitioners would be more likely to promote expert-led interventions into problematic situations in which some improvement is sought, meaning that critical thinking can be of an instrumental nature (Valero-Silva, 1996). This is similar to the current approach of GSA. However, for post-structuralist thinkers, liberation is enabled through 'The provision of tools for thinking critically, so as to enable individuals to gain control for themselves [of] a greater sense of self "unfettered-ness"' (Brocklesby & Cummings, 1996, p. 751). To make the ethical stakes of this distinction clear, Valero-Silva (1996, p. 74) noted:

> we should concentrate our efforts on understanding the relationship between the different methodologies and the shared cultural practices that have shaped what we are. In this sense, the systems methodologies are not only disciplinary techniques for the normalisation of individuals within organisations according to a particular rationality, but also expressions of wider disciplinary mechanisms in contemporary society.

Critical awareness enables us to observe that the values or practices that might be understood as emancipatory actions to some may be seen as 'problems' or 'weaknesses' of the system to others. The issue, therefore, is the unquestioned use of universalising concepts by practitioners—concepts such as 'emancipation', 'improvement' and 'participation' can assume the validity of the extant system. Post-structuralists do not doubt that 'improvements' are achievable and meaningful, but they see these as defined by their particular knowledge systems, rather than as necessarily universally good (Hewlett, 2007; Rancière, 2007; Rancière et al., 2001). What is rejected here is not emancipation per se, but the binding of emancipation to the assumed developmental march of human progress and to a single account of the good society. This also has implications for the practice of intervention, as Valero-Silva (1996, p. 77) stated:

> the practitioner must realise that his/her intervention would be framed within the unchallenged acceptance of certain boundaries and rationalities—unchallenged assumptions that made possible the very existence of management sciences and the organisations s/he is helping, the same ones that make possible his/her intervention in the first place.

The commitment of critical awareness in both systemic intervention and GSA practitioners can start with a rigorous first-order boundary critique, an effort to articulate 'who' and 'what' is to be included, but then to move beyond this to a second-order critique that seeks to reveal the power/knowledge relations that are perhaps more hidden or presented as unavoidable and logical in the constitution of the system (Valero-Silva, 1996). GSA's grounding in structural-functional thinking has a pragmatic intention to demonstrate critical awareness through opening dialogue to identify the components of a system and the work that each does towards building a holistic model. GSA's authors contend that systemic components may be broadly inclusive of government agencies or civil society groups, or, at a different scale, Indigenous governance systems, local organisations, communities or individuals, and provide the example of individual parents, teachers and students in a school system (Potts et al., 2014). GSA assumes each of these have some degree of decision-making capacity, connectivity and use knowledge within the system.

If we are to honour the spirit of CST's core commitments, the question of knowledge extends from what knowledge is present and whether it is used to how knowledge is produced and by whom in the process of making boundary decisions—that is, the active (re)articulation of the system. If, in analysing this, we only focus on the content of an established body of knowledge, we assume that its particular perspective is unquestionable. Second-order boundary critique examines the contingency of knowledge itself that within the systems paradigm is the product of emergent relations of knowledge and power. Identifying knowledges, questioning the 'changes, and the processes that lead to them' (Valero-Silva, 1996, p. 76) and their agents as participants and interventionists, in a contingent space of knowledge production, is essential in considering the ethics and politics of different possible actions. Building on GSA's good intentions then, systemic intervention provides a model for how these concerns can be addressed by asking who is accounting for good and bad here? What knowledges and ways of knowing are included or excluded and why or how? For this reason, applied CST methodology is participatory in practice and concerned with actively preventing power abuses through research and consequent decision-making. Individual and social knowledge is generated by the process facilitating generative, rather than linear or normative change, which is a potential outcome of GSA unless practices that enable critical awareness are explicitly adopted.

Within CST, there is an explicit commitment to always engage at the level of the individual regardless of scale. This disrupts the assumed validity of more established, larger institutions and structures. It also enables practitioners and participants to make sense of the actual operation of power in performing particular functions. Clearly, a critical attitude necessary for second-order boundary critique is present here, and with the adaptation of a boundary critique process, practitioners and participants are enabled to decide which boundaries are to change and the change processes that are to occur.

## Theoretical Pluralism

The third commitment is theoretical pluralism, which is based on the avoidance of establishing a single theoretical approach or an exclusive ontology and epistemology. This commitment asks us not to work with one single account of the world as if it is the only one. Neither does it seek to establish a particular account of the world as the only one. Rather, an acceptance of the incommensurability of ways of knowing and ways of being allows for all paradigms that have existed to exist simultaneously and continue to exist and change (Flood, 2010). This commitment has significant philosophical implications for the status of systemic approaches themselves, as necessarily partial. It also suggests that emancipation is not necessarily a single or shared state and that it might occur in a multitude of different ways. As such, practitioners need not (indeed, should not) appropriate the uniqueness of others in the name of a single theory to explain the whole world or system. They should also accept that emancipation can be multiple and irreducible, such that no single, universal account of what is 'right' or 'good' will ever be sufficient (Brocklesby & Cummings, 1996), and that such an assumption could in fact do violence to these other ways of being.

In practical terms, theoretical pluralism enables context-driven, open engagement with multiple theoretical approaches (Gregory, 1996). Its goal is to allow alternative, incommensurate, epistemologies and ontologies to engage with each other in a 'localised' practice of making boundary judgments and generating new knowledge. Different approaches, while equally present, provide space to explore the irreducibility of ways of knowing and being through the differences between and distinctiveness of each.

All players within the system, from elected legislatures to street-level bureaucrats (Lipsky & Hill, 1993) and activists, can choose to accept paradigms as multiple, discordant and incommensurable. A second-order critique reveals differences and exclusions. Competing and conflicting perspectives may appear to be localised, contingent and historically situated, but nonetheless embody tensions and ambiguities. An acceptance, or even critical appreciation of difference, has the potential to enrich our understanding of the complex governance problem. The value to systemic intervention practice and the GSA framework is that the discordant pluralism or theoretical pluralism perspective provides an ethical foundation for decision-making that denies the need for an 'either/or' reduction, as the juxtaposition of oppositional viewpoints are supported as a both/and position (Gregory, 1996).

## Methodological Pluralism

Methodological pluralism, the fourth commitment, is closely related to theoretical pluralism. It shares the principle that there is no universal theory and that adopting one would necessarily preclude the full realisation of others (Midgley, 1996, 2000). Thus, we are left with a variety of methods and the knowledge that each privileges particular ontologies and epistemologies over others (Midgley, 2000), and that we need to be attentive to this in when and how we use such methods. Pluralism can then be a methodological tool for choosing between different methods that bring differing and perhaps incompatible philosophical foundations to the table while committing to a broad repertoire of methods that nonetheless affect particular kinds of change or analysis in particular ways. Through the practical application of second-order boundary critique we can draw on, learn from and purposefully mix methods (Midgley, 2000). Doing so allows participants to bring alternative knowledge to the table and bring new knowledge into being—they learn from critical reflection and build shared understandings in an ongoing cyclical application of philosophy to methodology, leading to generative and original responses to particular problems, the boundaries of which are also critically engaged with. An ethical model of learning uses theoretical and methodological pluralism to activate one another by building the methodological skills and repertoires of the practitioners, asking penetrating questions of the theoretical assumptions underlying a method or the intervention and critically reflecting on the practitioner's practice and finding gaps between the espoused methodology of the practitioner and stakeholders' interpretations of the methodology in use (Midgley, 2000).

If choices are made by experts with regard to the most suitable and appropriate methods for the intended purpose of a project, they do not open themselves up to this methodological pluralism and, therefore, may allow implicit and explicit assumptions to remain unexamined. Systemic intervention requires that practitioners acknowledge these. Making such theoretical and methodological decisions in an open context is the practice of emancipation itself, as it allows space for the emergence of knowledge and being. As such, we are enslaved and emancipated in relation to the methods for understanding and accounting for our internalised and extant rationalities and their technologies (Brocklesby & Cummings, 1996). GSA is intended as a framework methodology within which multiple sub-methodologies might be applied to enhance analysis. In this sense, it strongly recognises multiple methodology principles. GSA as a framework method, however, could better acknowledge the role of methodology in both emancipating and enslaving, which will enable it to acknowledge that its methodological accounting for governance is partial and can be situated in a more open approach to framework methods for reforming governance.

## Social Awareness

The fifth commitment, social awareness, seeks to identify the power relations at work in society that implicitly and explicitly work to legitimise or delegitimise particular practices. Both GSA and the systemic intervention approach are intended to deal with complex social relations. In the GSA literature, Potts et al. (2014) drew on Buchy and Race (2001) to acknowledge that public participation can result in challenges to existing power structures, the outcome of which may result in empowering stakeholders. Without an explicit secondary boundary analysis of the social nature of the system, it seems that the emancipatory outcomes of using GSA are less likely to be the outcome of methodological design than they are the unexpected product of emergence. In the absence of a clear commitment to emancipatory outcomes, it is conceivable that participatory methods in GSA are constrained by implicit assumptions about who should participate and how governance should be 'known' and 'done'.

However, social awareness extends much further. For the GSA framework, which relies heavily on an expert-facilitated approach to governance analysis, the associated power of the expert must be critically reviewed through self-reflexivity and being open to critique from others. There has been a longstanding critique of such expert roles (Taket & White, 1994) and whether and how stakeholders may or may not agree with the expert's priorities (Ferreyra, 2006). The actions of experts and researchers need to be considered in terms of the effects they might have on participants during the course of the intervention. The very act of an intervention into any system assumes both the necessity and validity of questioning the extant system and, as such, is political as it could reinforce or challenge power relations and dynamics. Thus, any agent of intervention needs to be as aware as possible of extant power relations to avoid unintended consequences and cause the least amount of unauthorised disruption possible. In this analytical exercise, it should also be made explicit, and considered at the ethical and political level, as to what implications (non-) intervention might have. GSA needs to better consider how it will be imbricated in an array of power relations, how any intervention might affect this system, and proceed with appropriate sensitivity to the wider society that may not be commensurable with the Western norms of governance and the Western form of life these modes of governance often seek to produce.

## Human Emancipation

The sixth commitment, human emancipation, is the overriding commitment to which all the other commitments are geared. Human emancipation cannot be achieved unless the explicit role of power relations in the shaping of individuals as subjects is articulated. Through systems of power relations, human emancipation is inherently related to the operation of power. Crucially, for both CST and GSA, the ontological distinctions in how power and knowledge are accounted for has major implications for how emancipation is conceptualised. A Habermasian view regards power as exerted 'over' people and a relatively 'equal' power situation is assumed to enable collective emancipation (Brocklesby & Cummings, 1996; Ashenden & Owen, 1999; Valero-Silva, 1996). A Foucauldian account, however, states that power is 'always already' and 'everywhere'—power is the connection or 'strategic web' between people and things and that this is productive and inhibitive (Foucault, 2000). Power is not inherently bad or good, but it can be modulated and changed within and between particular power relationships. If power is always contingent and present only in its enactment between the people and the things of complex systems (Foucault, 2000), resistance is just as particular and momentary. Emancipation, by this account, is the ability of individuals and collectives to self-order their identities and practices, rather than being altered by someone or something else from one relation or systemic state to another specified form of relation or state. In Midgley's (2000) terms, emancipation is 'improvement', but one that is temporally and locally defined and will be viewed differently between agents with differing ontological worldviews, applying their own boundary judgments, values and ethics from their particularly situated position.

These distinctions have enormous implications for our practice and the role of first- and second-order boundary critique. Taking the GSA, which sits closer to a Habermasian approach in so far as it strives towards consensus making, experts may be seen to be able to emancipate, or improve, situations through the force of a better argument. Yet, the Foucauldian view notes the contingency of knowledge and identity and, therefore, that the designation of an expert to intervene may be a dangerous proposition as their knowledge, while it may not be 'wrong', is also not universally 'right'. As Levin (1994, pp. 26–27) stated, '[Practitioners] can [either] support a micro-emancipation process or they can act as suppressors'. So while individual emancipatory actions could come together in either collaboration or a collective endeavour, its realisation may not be universal or collective. Everyone's emancipation will be partly the product of their situatedness.

Clearly, the choice to extend the analysis to involve a second-order critique, in keeping with systemic intervention, resides in the degree of recognised incommensurability within the problem situation. The awareness of self-emancipation must be able to be developed, practised and opted out of as openly as possible. That is, no system or form of system should be assumed to be valid or invalid—the 'natural order' of things is questionable and the situation we find ourselves in can be reordered. The objective is not the development of a 'better' argument that will provide a 'better' system for all, but an ethos for the development of an undefined, open outcome that will be particular and contingent for its place and time, and for the people who developed it. In terms of collective emancipation, and the transformation of institutions, the trick here is to not to assume or enforce institutions or their rulings as universal in space and time. Emancipation is in the practice of the journey, rather than the arrival at a destination. For GSA, in its structural-functionalism-informed approach, emancipation as a practice is not highly visible and instead is assumed to reside in the perfection of the system, potentially disallowing emancipation itself.

So, what is the role of the academic, policy officer, activist or consultant if the better argument is not 'better' but just useful, absorbable or believable in particular ways to particular people, in a particular place and time, with particular power relations in play? For systemic interventionists, no particular system is 'right' per se, rather, it is the processes through which systems are constituted, emerge and change that are the places and moments of emancipation:

> The contradiction and real challenge in this process is how to integrate professional skill and knowledge in the participants' struggle to develop control over their own situation. Accordingly, emancipation is linked to and cannot be separated from the process by which it is acquired. (Levin, 1994, p. 28)

Does this prevent any system-wide social emancipation? Less hierarchical systems allow more flexibility and the potential for emancipatory change for both the system as a whole and individuals within it, but the system itself is not emancipated per se. Indeed, based on principles of irreducible difference, it cannot be. Emancipation is a practice and the nature of people's participation in change practices, including of governance systems, is crucial and enabled by second-order boundary critique of those systems (Midgley, 2000). Participation in the process is initiated by a dialogue that should make explicit what is included in the first- and second-order boundary critique. Systemic intervention might explore contingency, forms of power, relations of power and inherent limitations—fallibility and practicalities—in the here and now. However, such openness itself enables emergence and the ability for each and every participant to 'emancipate from where they are' situated in the system at that moment.

## Discussion

The previous sections have identified CST's six commitments and how the systemic intervention approach would supplement GSA's own processes to enable more attention to, and allowance of, the multiplicity and irreducibility of ways of knowing and being. Repositioning GSA in this way allows it to be a more nuanced analytical and intervention tool, with several implications for practice. First, it is important to note that use of the second-order boundary critique for governance analysis is inherently political in that it questions the nature of the social order and, in so doing, allows for other ways of being and for the possibility of change. As such, it does not assume that norms of governance, their institutions or their agents are necessary or right, nor does it inherently assume that they should or will remain the only approaches to governance. For Northern Australia, Indigenous governance and ways of being are grounded in its incommensurability with Western norms of governance, and even Western modes of governance are fragmented and conflicting as a result of state, territory and federal political structures (Stephens et al., 2014). In this context, second-order boundary critique allows for acknowledgement of these differences and crucially respect for them to remain different, rather than assuming they must be subsumed into a coherent single system, particularly one predicated on the dominant Western model.

A deeply nuanced, critical and emancipatory stance matters because governance practices profoundly shape the lives of the population and landscape. GSA is, of course, just one of many approaches for looking at broader governance systems, but as GSA is a tool that is being used in practice in Northern Australia and as emancipation is itself a practice, it is essential that where it is used it enables, rather than shuts down, difference. In Northern Australia, the tool is currently being used in relation to NRM and social policy. In such cases, second-order boundary critique and consideration of CST's six commitments gives space to a broader pool of stakeholders, ontologies, epistemologies and outcomes. GSA could more explicitly apply these considerations to better identify its own role in these deeply political and ethical engagements with difference and identify how its own practice may or may not enable emancipatory action. There is also a challenge here for CST in its engagement with questions of governance and systems of governance as to whether a more systemic approach to these can be developed. There has been limited engagement from the CST literature with governance in terms of Foucauldian thought, particularly on liberal governmentality and bio-politics, while the last decade or so has seen much more engagement from post-structuralist scholars with complexity (Cilliers, 1998; Dillon, 2007; Olssen, 2008; Urry, 2005). As such, much of the groundwork is now laid for CST to re-engage with post-structuralist approaches once more, particularly in relation to questions of ethics, the political and practice.

Governance is no longer understood as being solely located in the institutions of formal government and its implications for emancipation are often more difficult to discern as the power and knowledge relationships are less readily identifiable but nonetheless powerful. As such, rather than large-scale shifts in overall system structure determined by a universal and singular account of the 'good life' and the 'public good', there has been a shift to a focus on localised and relational practices as the places or moments where governance occurs and where they can be critiqued or changed. CST and systemic intervention provide GSA with an enhanced set of conceptual and practice tools to support its goal of participatory approaches in this context. In Northern Australia, where divergences between governance systems are wide and where accounts of what is a 'good' life also vary immensely, there is a particular need to engage with gradual 'ground up approaches' to 'going on together' (Christie, 2006; Stephens et al., 2014). CST and systemic intervention provide a route for GSA into considering and engaging with such alternative methodologies and theories through allowing for pluralism.

The lessons for GSA and mainstream governance approaches come amid a growing concern, nationally and internationally, about ongoing harm to people, cultures and the environment in Northern Australia (Dale, 2014). The failure to resolve ongoing social inequality concerning Indigenous Australians, treatment of people seeking political and economic asylum in Australia and the threatened extinction and destruction of ecological systems of global significance such as the Great Barrier Reef all belie a deeper ontological form of 'inequality' where existing ontological and epistemological difference is obfuscated while the repercussions of this denial are magnified. By taking these challenges seriously, this political moment could also enable the rethinking of Northern Australia and its governance systems, not only for national, state and territory governments, but for local populations and their diverse worlds. A supplemented approach to GSA could help engage with mainstream government practices to find (re)solutions—not necessarily as in 'closure', but as 'agreements' of processes that move us onwards in an ethical fashion. One clear example of boundary critique is that to create 'new' agreements and ways of being, individuals and groups must be courageous enough to recognise different accounts of the social body, past and present. Reconciliation (as opposed to reparation, retribution or retaliation) is a generative process that allows new ways of being to emerge yet accepts multiplicities, incommensurability and the irresolvability of different ways of being (Hewlett, 2010; McDonough, 2009; Rancière et al., 2001).

Such a radically political democratisation of GSA and decision-making changes the emphasis of interventions to processes and relationships and focuses less on the proposed outcome. It changes our understanding and expectations of the analysis process; in this case, shifting GSA from a systematic procedure to a systemic practice where primacy is granted to knowledge creation, from the nature of a 'knowledge generating system' or institution itself to the process of generating that knowledge (Bawden, 2003; Midgley, 2000). As such, the question becomes not 'what is the system?', but 'how do we know the system?' and 'how do we "do" or "perform" this system?' The intellectual capacity to question the foundational rules of the system (its ontology and epistemology) is the highest level of understanding and critique of a system (Meadows, 1999) and the most profound point at which to make space for systemic change.

# Conclusion

This chapter has demonstrated how CST can supplement GSA to enable an awareness of multiplicity and incommensurability that enables the perusal of emancipation as a practice that is not predicated on the perfection of a Western system of governance and government, while also acknowledging that such institutions play a significant role in the production of the wider social and ecological system. As such, GSA is able to adopt a systemic rather than systematic approach. For practical reasons, GSA had intentionally established its framework internally within the norms of Western governance practices, rather than engaging externally with them. By doing so, it adopted an implicitly foundationalist and universalist ontology and epistemology that could co-opt or exclude different ways of being. For the purpose of critical engagement with GSA, we drew on an account of CST that takes seriously post-structuralist and anti-foundationalist belief in the irreducibility of ways of being, acknowledges multiplicity and its loss through foundationalist practices, adopts Foucauldian analyses of power and knowledge and attempts to deliberately conduct boundary critique of systems to achieve a critical stance.

In particular, this chapter has outlined the value of undertaking a secondary boundary critique through the lens of CST's six core commitments that, when applied, can assist GSA in making ethical interventions in governance systems sensitive to power, knowledge and emancipation. This does not make it relativist. Rather, the theoretical and methodological pluralism proposed, premised on multiplicity and irreducibility of different ways of being and knowing, makes sure that questions of intervention are seen as properly ethical and political in their most fundamental and profound sense and are engaged with in that fashion. As Brocklesby and Cummings (1996, p. 751) stated, this does not mean that '*anything goes*, rather [that] *everything depends*' (emphasis original). Therefore, rather than seeking a consensus, this repositioned account of GSA seeks a '*consent to act*' (Brocklesby & Cummings, 1996, p. 751 [emphasis original]) for a limited period and fashion, with recognition of its situatedness, limitations and assumptions to enhance its utility and validity in Northern Australia, or indeed anywhere else where difference plays such a profound role in the tensions over the shaping of people's lives and the landscape.

# References

Abrahams, H. (2005). Devolution enhances integration. *Australasian Journal of Environmental Management*, *12*(suppl), 57–61.

Althaus, C., Bridgman, P. & Davis, G. (2007). *The Australian policy handbook* (4th ed.). Crows Nest, NSW: Allen & Unwin.

Anderson, I. (2015). The crisis of Australia's Indigenous policy. *Meanjin, 74*(3), 54–59.

Ashenden, S. & Owen, D. (1999). *Foucault contra Habermas*. London, England: SAGE.

Bausch, K. C. (2001). *The emerging consensus in social systems theory*. Springer.

Bawden, R. (2003). Book review. Systemic intervention: Philosophy, methodology, and practice. Contemporary systems thinking. *Systemic Practice and Action Research, 16*(5), 369–372.

Beaumont, J. & Nicholls, W. (2008). Plural governance, participation and democracy in cities. *International Journal of Urban and Regional Research, 32*(1), 87–94.

Bellamy, J., Walker, D., McDonald, G. & Syme, G. (2001). A systems approach to the evaluation of natural resource management initiatives. *Journal of Environmental Management, 63*, 407–423.

Bevir, M. (2010). Rethinking governmentality: Towards genealogies of governance. *European Journal of Social Theory, 13*(4), 423–441.

Brocklesby, J. & Cummings, S. (1996). Foucault plays Habermas: An alternative philosophical underpinning for critical systems thinking. *Journal of the Operational Research Society, 47*, 741–754.

Buchy, M. & Race, D. (2001). The twists and turns of community participation in natural resource management in Australia: What is missing? *Journal of Environmental Planning and Management, 44*(3), 293–308.

Carman, J. G. (2007). Evaluation practice among community-based organizations research into the reality. *American Journal of Evaluation, 28*(1), 60–75.

Castells, M. (2000). *The rise of network society* (vol. 1). Malden, MA: Blackwell.

Christie, M. (2006). Transdisciplinary research and Aboriginal knowledge. *The Australian Journal of Indigenous Education, 35*, 78.

Christie, M. (2014). Decolonizing methodology in an Arnhem Land Garden. In B. N. K. Schaffer (Ed.), *Decolonizing the landscape: Indigenous cultures in Australia* (pp. 57–69). Amsterdam, The Netherlands; New York, NY: Rodopi.

Cilliers, P. (1998). *Complexity and postmodernism: Understanding complex systems*. London, England: Routledge.

Connick, S. & Innes, J. (2003). Outcomes of collaborative water policy making: Applying complexity thinking to evaluation. *Journal of Environmental Planning and Management, 46*(2), 177–197.

Curtis, A., Robertson, A. & Race, D. (1998). Lessons from recent evaluations of natural resource management programs in Australia. *Journal of Environmental Management, 5*(2), 109–119.

Dale, A. P. (1993). An assessment of planning for government-funded land-use development projects for Aboriginal communities in Eastern Australia (unpublished doctoral thesis). Griffith University, Qld.

Dale, A. P. (2013). *Governance challenges for Northern Australia*. Cairns, Qld: Cairns Institute, James Cook University.

Dale, A. P. (2014). *Beyond the north-south culture wars: Reconciling Northern Australia's recent past with its future*. Springer.

Dale, A. & Bellamy, J. (1998). *Regional resource use planning: An Australian review* (LWRRDC Occasional Paper 9/98). Canberra, ACT: Land and Water Resources Research and Development Corporation.

Dale, A. P. & Lane, M. B. (1993). Strategic perspective analysis: A procedure for participatory and political social impact assessment. *Society and Natural Resources, 7*(3), 253–267.

Dale, A. P., Vella, K. & Potts, R. (2013). Governance Systems Analysis (GSA): A framework for reforming governance systems. *Journal of Public Administration and Governance, 3*(3), 162–182. doi.org/10.5296/jpag.v3i3.4385

Dale, A. P., Vella, K., Pressey, R. L., Brodie, J., Yorkston, H. & Potts, R. (2013). A method for risk analysis across governance systems: A Great Barrier Reef case study. *Environmental Research Letters, 8*(1), 1–16.

Dean, M. & Hindess, B. (1998). *Governing Australia: Studies in contemporary rationalities of government*. Cambridge University Press.

Dillon, M. (2000). Poststructuralism, complexity and poetics. *Theory, Culture & Society, 17*(5), 1–26.

Dillon, M. (2007). Governing through contingency: The security of biopolitical governance. *Political Geography, 26*(1), 41–47.

Dillon, M. & Reid, J. (2009). *The liberal way of war: Killing to make life live*. London, England: Routledge.

Ferreyra, C. (2006). Practicality, positionality, and emancipation: Reflections on participatory action research with a watershed partnership. *Systemic Practice and Action Research, 19*(6), 577–598.

Flood, R. L. (2010). The relationship of 'systems thinking' to action research. *Systemic Practice and Action Research, 23*(4), 269–284. doi.org/10.1007/s11213-010-9169-1

Forester, J. (1999). *The deliberative practitioner: Encouraging participatory planning processes*. MIT Press.

Foucault, M. (2000). *Essential works of Foucault 1954-1984. Volume 3: Power*. New York, NY: New Press.

Fuchs, C. & Hofkirchner, W. (2009). Autopoiesis and critical social systems theory. In R. Magalhães & R. Sanchez (Eds), *Autopoiesis in organization theory and practice* (pp. 111–129). Bingley, England: Emerald.

Gregory, W. (1996). Dealing with diversity. In R. L. Flood & N. R. A. Romm (Eds), *Critical systems thinking, current research and practice* (pp. 37–59). London, England: Plenum.

Hajkowicz, S. (2009). The evolution of Australia's natural resource management programs: Towards improved targeting and evaluation of investments. *Land Use Policy, 26*, 471–478.

Hewlett, N. (2007). *Badiou, Balibar, Rancière: Re-thinking emancipation*. London, England: Continuum.

Hewlett, N. (2010). *Badiou, Balibar, Rancière: Re-thinking emancipation*. A&C Black.

Hoggarth, L. (2010). *A practical guide to outcome evaluation*. Jessica Kingsley Publishers.

Ison, R. L. (2008). Systems thinking and practice for action research. In P. Reason & H. Bradbury (Eds), *The Sage handbook of action research participative inquiry and practice* (2nd ed.) (pp. 139–158). London, England: SAGE.

Jackson, M. C. (1991). The origins and nature of critical systems thinking. *Systems Practice, 4*(2), 131–149. doi.org/10.1007/BF01068246

Jackson, M. C. (2010). Reflections on the development and contribution of critical systems thinking and practice. *Systems Research and Behavioral Science, 27*(2), 133–139. doi.org/10.1002/sres.1020

Laclau, E. & Mouffe, C. (2001). *Hegemony and socialist strategy: Towards a radical democratic politics*. London, England: Verso.

Lane, M. B. (2005). Public participation in planning: An intellectual history. *Australian Geographer, 36*(3), 283–299.

Lefèvre, C. (1998). Metropolitan government and governance in western countries: A critical review. *International Journal of Urban and Regional Research, 22*(1), 9–25. doi.org/10.1111/1468-2427.00120

Lemke, T. (2002). Foucault, governmentality, and critique. *Rethinking Marxism, 14*(3), 49–64.

Levin, M. (1994). Action research and critical systems thinking: Two icons carved out of the same log? *Systems Practice, 7*(1), 25–41.

Lipsky, M. & Hill, M. (1993). Street-level bureaucracy: An introduction. In M. Hill (Ed.), *The policy process: A reader* (pp. 381–385). London, England: Harvester Wheatsheaf.

Maani, K. & Cavana, R. (2000). *Systems thinking and modelling: Understanding change and complexity*. Auckland, New Zealand: Prentice Hall.

McDonough, T. (2009). The hypothesis of incommensurability and multicultural education. *Journal of Philosophy of Education, 43*(2), 203–221.

McMullen, J. (2013). Dispossession neo-liberalism and the struggle for Aboriginal land and rights in the 21st century. In R. Craven, A. Dilton & N. Parbury (Eds), *Black & white: Australians all at the crossroads* (pp. 105–126). Ballan, Vic.: Connor Court.

Meadows, H. D. (1999). *Leverage points: Places to intervene in a system*. Retrieved from donellameadows.org/archives/leverage-points-places-to-intervene-in-a-system/

Midgley, G. (1996). What is this thing called CST? In L. R. Flood & N. R. A. Romm (Eds), *Critical systems thinking: Current research and practice* (pp. 11–22). New York, NY: Plenum Press.

Midgley, G. (2000). *Systemic intervention: Philosophy, methodology, and practice*. New York, NY: Kluwer Academic.

Midgley, G. & Richardson, K. A. (2007). Systems thinking for community involvement in policy analysis. *Emergence: Complexity and Organization, 9*(1–2), 167–183.

Muro, M. & Jeffrey, P. (2008). A critical review of the theory and application of social learning in participatory natural resource management processes. *Journal of Environmental Planning and Management, 51*(3), 325–344.

Olssen, M. (2008). Foucault as complexity theorist: Overcoming the problems of classical philosophical analysis. *Educational Philosophy and Theory*, *40*(1), 96–117.

Parker, C. & Braithwaite, J. (2003). Regulation. In P. Cane & M. Tushnet (Eds), *The Oxford handbook of legal studies*. Oxford, England: Oxford University Press.

Parkins, J. R. & Mitchell, R. E. (2005). Public participation as public debate: A deliberative turn in natural resource management. *Society and Natural Resources*, *18*(6), 529–540.

Peck, J. & Tickell, A. (2002). Neoliberalizing space. *Antipode*, *34*(3), 380–404.

Plummer, R. & Armitage, D. (2007). Charting the new territory of adaptive co-management: A Delphi study. *Ecology and Society*, *12*(2), 10.

Potts, R., Vella, K., Dale, A. & Sipe, N. (2014). Exploring the usefulness of structural-functional approaches to analyse governance of planning systems. *Planning Theory*, *15*(2), 162–189. doi.org/10.1177/1473095214553519

Prout, S. & Howitt, R. (2009). Frontier imaginings and subversive Indigenous spatialities. *Journal of Rural Studies*, *25*(4), 396–403.

Rancière, J. (2007). *On the shores of politics*. London, England: Verso.

Rancière, J., Bowlby, R. & Panagia, D. (2001). Ten theses on politics. *Theory & Event*, *5*(3). doi.org/10.1353/tae.2001.0028

Rauschmayer, F., Berghöfer, A., Omann, I. & Zikos, D. (2009). Examining processes or/and outcomes? Evaluation concepts in European governance of natural resources. *Environmental Policy and Governance*, *19*(3), 159–173.

Springer, S. (2010). Neoliberalism and geography: Expansions, variegations, formations. *Geography Compass*, *4*, 1025–1038. doi.org/10.1111/j.1749-8198.2010.00358.x

Stephens, A., Oppermann, E., Turnour, J., Brewer, T., O'Brien, C., Rayner, T., Blackwood, G. & Dale, A. P. (2014). Identifying tensions in the development of Northern Australia: Implications for governance. *Journal of Economic and Social Policy*, *17*(1), Article 5.

Taket, A. & White, L. (1993). After OR: An agenda for postmodernism and poststructuralism in OR. *Journal of the Operational Research Society*, *44*(9), 867–881.

Taket, A. & White, L. (1994). The death of the expert. *The Journal of the Operational Research Society*, *45*(7), 733–748.

Trudgen, R. (2012). *Why warriors lie down and die: Towards an understanding of why the aboriginal people of Arnhem Land face the greatest crisis in health and education since European contact*. Why Warriors Pty Ltd.

Turnbull, W. (2005). *Evaluation of current governance arrangements to support regional investment under the NHT and NAP*. Canberra, ACT: Department of the Environment, Water, Heritage and the Arts and Department of Agriculture, Forestry and Fisheries.

Urry, J. (2005). The complexity turn. *Theory Culture and Society, 22*(1), 1–14.

Valero-Silva, N. (1996). *A Foucauldian reflection on critical systems thinking*. New York, NY: Plenum Press.

Verran, H. (2011). Imagining nature politics in the era of Australia's emerging market in environmental services interventions. *The Sociological Review, 59*(3), 411–431.

Vogel, N. (2011). *Analysis of performance excellence evaluations of regional natural resource management organisations*. Australian Knowledge Management Group.

Woinarski, J. C. (2014). The illusion of nature: Perception and the reality of natural landscapes, as illustrated by vertebrate fauna in the Northern Territory, Australia. *Ecological Management & Restoration, 15*(1), 30–33.

# 25

# Building Regional Research Capacity: The Northern Research Futures Collaborative Research Network

Lawrence Cram

## Introduction

Australia's Collaborative Research Networks (CRNs) are a modest program (A$81.1 million for 15 projects each over three to five years) of publicly funded research, development and extension (RD&E) designed to support relatively youthful universities with rapidly developing research capacity (Department of Education and Training, 2015). For socio-historical reasons, many youthful Australian universities are located in Australian regional settings (including 60 per cent of CRN-eligible universities). This chapter features the Northern Research Futures CRN (NRF-CRN) to show how the CRN program has supported RD&E capacity building in regional settings.

We propose that the CRN program fortuitously positioned Charles Darwin University as a well-qualified and well-prepared provider of RD&E capabilities that can support the re-invigorated government agenda to attend to the development of Australia's north. The chapter argues that these capabilities have matured as the result of 1) an application of well-established policy drivers for public funding of RD&E that has been 2) applied to university-based RD&E and 3) aimed towards the needs of regional socioeconomic development of Australia's north through 4) social science using a diverse menu of methods, team formation and rich networking.

Public funding of research—how much and to what ends—emerged as a preoccupation of policymakers and research communities some half a century ago owing to the confluence of 1) clear opportunities to promote the protection and/or welfare of people and communities through the application of de-militarised scientific and project management methods forged in war and 2) advances in public financial systems that generated budgets and released funds for research and related activities (Bush, 1945; Snow, 1962). Since that time, many studies have explored the links between RD&E and prosperity in firms, industries, regions and nations (Aghion & Howitt, 2008; Geisler, 2000). Although the linkages are many and complex, the evidence for their potency is compelling. Accordingly, many national and supra-national governments now establish aspirational targets for the proportion of gross domestic product that is allocated to research and development, targets for the public and private funding components of this proportion and, in many cases, priorities for selecting fields and modalities of research focus. Public funding of research in relation to *regional research capacity* is often viewed as a particularly important part of this policy arena.

In his foreword to the Productivity Commission's (2007) report *Public support for science and innovation* (the PC report), Chairman Gary Banks observed that the benefits arising from public funding of science and innovation[1] are 'not just the gains that end up in gross domestic product or other statistical measures of economic performance, but the social and environmental benefits as well' (p. v). The report itself presents one of the most comprehensive accounts of the public policy considerations that come into play when the Australian Government is designing (and refreshing) the institutions and programs tasked with delivering benefits from public funding of research to the Australian community.

---

1   The term 'research, development and extension' (RD&E) is used in this chapter to describe the cluster of activities implied by the phrase 'science and innovation' used in the PC report. The term RD&E is not code for the narrow notion of discovery of new knowledge in the natural sciences or for the creation of private economic advantage. It is intended that the term RD&E refers to the systematic creation of generalisable knowledge of any kind and the gamut of processes that enable that knowledge to be used. For example, *Ancient history* is RD&E because it involves research, as is *I'm having a rainbow for dinner* because it represents an extension of nutrition research.

The recent *White paper on developing Northern Australia* (Australian Government, 2015) sustained these considerations, emphasising, for example, that the role of government is to create successful business environments, not successful businesses. This policy objective will be pursued through the implementation of the White Paper as a range of activities including 'the basic research necessary for business to identify opportunities in the north' (p. 2). The White Paper concludes that the case for further public investment in RD&E in the north arises, for example, because private agricultural businesses typically underinvest in RD&E because the benefits tend not to be exclusively captured by the investor. Similar investor behaviour also justifies government-funded RD&E that can increase the competitiveness and productivity of industry in the north by supporting collaboration between specific industry and research organisations to improve commercialisation outcomes and returns. Not all of this public investment must be made in the region, but few if any of the intended policy outcomes of the white paper could be achieved by a strategy that fails to provide for public investment in RD&E specifically conducted in and for the focal regions (Walker et al., 2012). So, the government is committed to subsidising industry RD&E?

Compelling reasons for providing public money to fund certain categories of RD&E do not automatically establish the optimal means of undertaking that RD&E. Instead, they raise consequential questions for innovation policy such as 'Into what kinds of institutions is the public investment in RD&E best made?' Despite the intense attention that has been applied to policy issues relating to innovation systems in Australia and elsewhere, options for answering such questions remain controversial and incomplete. Indeed, few if any stakeholders anywhere in the world express satisfaction with the architecture and operation of any specific national or regional innovation system, leading to a perennial, heroic and never-ending quest for change or improvement akin to the Quixotic search of the holy grail or a cult of cargo (Hughes, 2008).

Symptomatic of this peculiar situation is the great number of fundamental concepts and issues in innovation policy that remain poorly understood or controversial despite a notable level of careful, scholarly attention. One of these is the point made by Derek John de Solla Price (1984) more than 35 years ago concerning the importance of advances in what he called instrumentalities[2] for stimulating and enabling in parallel both radical theoretical advances in fundamental science and radical innovations in practical application. Through case studies and historical analysis, Price showed how public funding provided to discover and apply new instrumentalities will provide extraordinary returns on RD&E investments compared with other kinds of programs. We shall also explain how instrumentalities for research in the social sciences often rely on novel ways to organise research teams, including teams working in regional settings, using NRF-CRN as an exemplar.

A second area of innovation policy that seems persistently out of focus—at least in Australia—is the role of people and their social behaviour, contrasted with the roles of technologies or services or structural/functional considerations. Despite many sharp questions being raised about its empirical validity (Blaug, 1976)—but see also Quiggin (1999)—human capital theory remains an oft-quoted but rarely examined cornerstone of innovation policies (e.g. Hodgson, 2014). By contrast, Allott (2006) explained how a more people-centric approach can bring those who perform publicly funded RD&E together with those who use the results. When blended with the recognition of the value of institutional perspectives on regional development (Amin, 1999), a people-centric view offers rich policy options for spaces of innovation (Healy & Morgan, 2012).

This chapter explores the formation and usefulness of university-based regional RD&E capacity within the public policy context for publicly funding of RD&E that has been shaped by the PC report and the White Paper. The chapter starts by summarising some of the rationales for public funding of RD&E and the Productivity Commission's findings regarding benefits and impediments. This approach exhibits what may be taken to be the important components and linkages of a well-functioning RD&E and innovation system, including measures to develop RD&E capability within the regions themselves. The chapter then turns to consider the importance of novel research instrumentalities and people-centric approaches to RD&E, particularly in the context of the delivery of RD&E

---

2   Price argued that advances in instrumentation and experimental techniques—instrumentalities—in physical, biological and social sciences are potent sources of discovery in both pure and applied settings, so that policy should pay attention to financing progress in instrumentalities. It is apparent from his writings that Price would have regarded NRF-CRN as an instrumentality of the social sciences (Price, 1963, 1984).

for remote regions such as Australia's north. It is then explained how the NRF-CRN sustains specific components and linkages in the context of the challenges and opportunities for Northern Australia development.

## Rationales for Public Funding of Research

The PC report identified two strong contenders for a reasoned approach to public funding of RD&E. First, is the need for a government to fund the RD&E required by that government itself as it discharges its functions. There are abundant examples of government requirements for RD&E including such diverse fields as defence technology and the formation of public opinion—and the Australian Government spends approximately 20 per cent (A$1.8 billion in 2014) of its entire expenditure on RD&E for its own needs. Within the context of this chapter, there are many government RD&E requirements that are consequential to the policy intent of the White Paper. They include, for example, RD&E to explore and promulgate better ways to use and plan infrastructure, improved information about land title and use, comprehensive water resource assessment, development of business-friendly policies, engagement with international development in the region and formation of capable and sustainable local institutions.

As the PC report noted, the major public policy questions regarding RD&E required by government arise in relation to procurement issues such as quality and track record, institutional location and organisation of RD&E providers. The questions include whether the RD&E should be outsourced (domestically or internationally) or conducted in house, whether outsourced RD&E should be conducted by the public or the private sector, whether it is better procured by commission or by competition and so forth. We return to some of these questions below.

The second credible rationale for public funding of RD&E relates to the existence of knowledge spillovers that at the margin reduce the incentive for private investment and necessitating public intervention if the research is to be undertaken. The effect is particularly evident in relation to basic research, where the PC report concludes that private agents simply do not have the right incentives to develop an optimal system for undertaking basic research. Whenever—and it occurs frequently—private interests avoid certain kinds of important RD&E because they cannot capture the full benefits of their investment, governments are asked or led to call on alternative institutional forms for conducting that RD&E. The publicly funded research university[3] is such an institutional form. Research universities have been almost universally sponsored by national governments (Crow & Tucker, 2001) to achieve two different but usefully aligned purposes: 1) juxtaposition of creative researchers in many disciplines in settings that favour the cumulative generation and dissemination of many kinds of knowledge, together with 2) responsibility for tertiary educational processes, professional networks and a system of higher qualifications.

As explained in the PC report, when RD&E is publicly funded in institutions such as universities, the challenge for the government as investor switches from the private focus on fully capturing the benefits of the RD&E to the public benefits derived by ensuring the highest possible levels of spillover. Optimal spillover requires ancillary mechanisms such as procedures for weeding out mediocre research (the PC report estimated that mediocre research entails an economic loss of around A$1.30 for each A$1 invested), sound RD&E governance to ensure that public funding for RD&E is used efficiently and effectively (e.g. that creative researchers have access to the equipment and facilities that their work requires) and efficient knowledge diffusion systems including those directed at business. As this chapter illustrates, the CRN program is an effective and efficient way to promote spillover from publicly funded RD&E.

The PC report identified other rationales for public funding of RD&E that go beyond the cost–benefit perspectives that underlie the two contenders listed above. There are, for example, three separate intangible grounds on which public funding of RD&E might be justified: 1) as a cultural statement about the kind of society we have created, 2) to increase national prestige, and 3) to meet moral obligations. These values are hard to relate to the question of the desirable quantum of public funding, but nevertheless they do have validity as rationales for providing some public funding of RD&E, provided that they reflect the public's preferences, not just those of the funder or funded.

Public intervention to vary the risk profile of private investment is sometimes presented as a rationale for public funding of private RD&E. For example, it is often argued that capital investment that is related to

---

3   While a research university may be publicly or privately owned, for-profit universities are quite rare and normally do not conduct RD&E.

private RD&E is so difficult to obtain that attractive business opportunities are being missed. Barriers to such investment might arise, for example, from unfavourable taxation of RD&E risk (cf. capital investment in property), or from the specialist nature of knowledge required to assess the risk of investment in RD&E, or from excessive focus on near-term shareholder value at the expense of future business growth. While there are elements of special pleading, neoliberal techniques for self-serving (Peck & Tickell, 2002) and perhaps the occasional naive dismissal of potent and beneficial market mechanisms for pricing and funding business risk, it seems clear that these and similar issues are all relevant considerations in the design of a national innovation system. The White Paper specifically identifies a large number of publicly funded programs with RD&E elements of relevance to the development of Northern Australia, including the reduction of investment uncertainty (Australian Government, 2015, pp. 152–170).

The PC report mentioned an alternative view of public funding of RD&E that arises from theories of innovation economics based on analogies with biological evolution. The PC report observed that public policies derived from an evolutionary perspective will emphasise experimentation, variety, competitive approaches and continual change. They will relish complexity as a measure of healthiness. As the PC report correctly concluded, complexity itself can hardly be a compelling public policy end in itself—once this is recognised, the differences between the goals of evolutionary and those of conventional economic perspectives tend to evaporate. This conclusion is consistent with the influential and relevant work of Boschma and Frenken (2006) on evolutionary economic geography, conducted around the same time as the PC report was being prepared and offering valuable alternative perspectives on many of the issues raised in this chapter.

## Benefits from RD&E

It has been appreciated for more than 70 years that economy-wide productivity improvement is linked with advances in RD&E, although the specific mechanisms of the linkages are elusive. The PC report set out careful criticisms of much previous work on the specific contribution of RD&E to productivity in Australia and presented a set of general models that have been designed to avoid many of these pitfalls. Considered as a set spanning the likely range of contributions to productivity, the models reveal just how difficult it is to establish quantitative descriptions of the econometrics of the contemporary Australian innovation system (Shanks & Zheng, 2006). Nevertheless, the econometric models do suggest that there is a positive productivity return for public funding of RD&E and a positive contribution to growth in GDP.[4] Cost–benefit studies based on specific case studies or RD&E portfolios also reveal positive returns.

The PC report considered benefits produced by public funding of RD&E that extend beyond those found in the market economy. For example, RD&E relating to environmental matters may produce benefits to the environment (or to people who are active in the environment) as well as benefits in the market economy. Examples include RD&E on salinity, pesticide use, bio-security, energy and water resource management, bushfires, Australian coasts and the urban fringes. Readers will recognise both the importance of this RD&E and the high levels of uncertainty that surround attempts to estimate the economic and environmental value of RD&E in these areas. However, it is important to recognise that this uncertainty has two edges. While it makes it hard to give precision to, for example, a cost–benefit analysis, the overt uncertainty also helps to support the estimation of the risk-related value of actions that are designed to cope with uncertainty, such as investing to be prepared (e.g. building a cyclone shelter) and deliberately delaying a costly but uncertain decision about long-lived infrastructure (such as constructing a dam).

## Public Funding of RD&E for Regional Development

Amin (1999) presented a contemporary overview of approaches to the broad issue of regional economic development, contrasting the Keynesian legacy focused on redistribution, welfare and state incentives with neoliberal faith in markets, deregulation and support for entrepreneurialism. Characterising the implications as choice between 'dependent development or no development' (p. 365), Amin (1999) developed an alternative institutionalist perspective that would aim to build clusters of inter-related businesses, promote a learning culture,

---

4   It is important to acknowledge that the PC report concluded that it is impossible to give accurate estimates of the beneficial effects of RD&E stimulated by public funding (Shanks & Zheng, 2006).

broaden local institutions and mobilise the social economy. The 'learning culture' component of Amin's alternative perspective bring us closer to issues of public funding of RD&E in regions, a topic explored by Healy and Morgan (2012) who reverberate with Amin in concluding that:

> After more than a decade and a half of research it does seem that geographical proximity (and so territorial space) remains important to learning (and to the exploitation of the resultant knowledge). The evidence suggests that it is within the territorial space that knowledge (from near and far) is combined most effectively, but only if efficient inter-organizational relations are constructed. Therefore, the question for policy-makers is what happens if those relations are not present either internally for the spread of knowledge or externally for the influx of knowledge? It is clear that a Learning Region needs to be more than the sum of its parts, but how are the parts best brought together and combined? In the context of LFRs [Less Favoured Regions] in particular, there is clearly a role here for the public sector to act as a more robust facilitator. One of the key questions for future research is whether the state, and the wider public sector, has the competence and the confidence to play such a demanding role. (p. 1051)

An earlier exploration of controversies surrounding education and regional development by Neave (1979) framed these issues and opportunities in similar terms, drawing on the Okun-Richardson typography of regional development: Low-Stagnant, Low-Growing, High-Stagnant and High-Growing. Northern Australia is, by this typography, clearly a High-Growing region, albeit coextensive with prominent and ubiquitous Indigenous people and communities that defy categorisation in these terms, thereby revealing the poverty of conventional policy perspectives. Neave's (1979) study suggested that in High-Growing regions there is likely to be many fruitful opportunities for linking universities and industry, a thirst for non-formal and second-chance education to upskill existing community members to avoid being overrun by inwards migration and a need for patience as the region's university develops over a considerable amount of time. Unusually for academic literature on this topic, Neave (1979) also situated in his study a cultural perspective of regions, noting the importance of the role of a university in cultural mobilisation orientated both to maintenance and to operating as an instrument of adaption. Neave's (1979) study was published some 40 years ago, yet his findings remain essentially unchanged and at the forefront of the current role and development plans of Charles Darwin University, which is the sole university in the 'High-Growing' area of Northern Australia. An important conclusion emphasised by Neave (1979) is that a regional university is an instrument of consolidation 'amplifying and broadening trends which emerge from initiatives taken from other sectors in the economic and social system' (p. 266). To ask more of a university might be essentially pointless, but to expect anything less might be to sell a university short.

## Linear Models for Innovation and the Importance of Instrumentalities

The idea that commercially or socially beneficial technologies are created from discoveries made initially through basic research (i.e. research conducted to make discoveries as academic knowledge projected onto a featureless 'blue sky') was cultivated by Vannevar Bush and his colleagues in the context of the postwar economic recovery of the United States (US) and the battle to form the US National Science Foundation (Bush, 1945). Although there are important truths in the model (Balconi et al., 2010), it is not the way that most beneficial technologies have been created, nor is it a fertile source of the innovations in services that have done so much to produce commercial and social value over the past century. Yet our experience is that deliberate human action and enquiry clearly does play an important role in RD&E—alongside sleepwalking (Koestler & Butterfield, 1968), serendipity (Roberts, 1989), luck (Smith, 2012) and the co-evolved capacities of humans to improve on cultural artefacts (Richerson & Boyd, 2008). If the linear model of innovation based on scientific discoveries is not usually in operation, it becomes an important issue to determine the mechanisms whereby deliberate human activity in RD&E does lead to benefits.

Price (1984) proposed that one answer may be found in a reading of the history of science and technology that tells us both science and technology advance through the discovery and application of new instrumentalities.[5] Science, Price (1984) suggested, appears superficially to be driven for utilitarian gains, but in practice is an internally shaped activity where problems, as they are solved, are assembled in a kind of knowledge jigsaw puzzle, re-orientated through paradigm shifts on those occasions when

---

5   Price included the instrumentalities of social science in this proposal, listing the national census, opinion polls and personal tests as examples.

its scientist-creators get into serious difficulties. Conversely, technology is not the descendent of science, but rather the fruits of revolutionary changes wrought from the wellspring of human inventiveness, tested and shaped in markets. Both fundamental science and technology develop from a foundation comprising the 'the discovery of new techniques for doing something or producing some new effect, then perfecting and extending the technique and using it on everything in sight' (p. 12). These new techniques consist of instruments such as telescopes, effects such as voltaic electricity, processes such as recombinant DNA, new raw material for social analysis derived from polls and personal tests, and a suite of mathematical methods—together comprising what Price (1984) calls instrumentalities. The term is useful as a way to refer to activities extending well beyond the ideas of 'methods' as used, for example, in the social sciences.

Insofar as instrumentalities are a dominant source for innovation, Price (1984) argued that their development and application should become a public policy priority over the other expenses of RD&E. Price (1984) noted a number of implications of this insight that could usefully inform contemporary public policy for RD&E. First is the need to disaggregate and treat differently research and development. He argued:

> Development[6] should be regarded as part of the expense of production, an overhead on innovative industries rather than an investment, and it should be taxed and funded on that basis, leaving policy to be dictated by the market and by government procurement … anything that can be done to shift government funding away from D and into R will automatically cause more innovation and less production of the thing already innovated. (p. 19)

Even more controversially, Price (1984) went on to argue for a partial retreat to conditions wherein 'academics and physicians earn their keep by teaching and giving health service and require(ing) them to do research in order to have something to teach and deliver' (p. 19). This would cut the umbilical cord linking institutional welfare to public funding for researcher salary costs, potentially increasing the relative amount of resources made available for apparatus, technicians and hardware, thereby accelerating progress in science and in technology.

---

6   'Development' here refers to the 'D' in RD&E.

Finally, and importantly for this account of the NRF-CRC, Price (1984, p. 19) pointed out the importance of doing whatever we can to promote 'interactions between all places where a craft of experimental science is practiced', be they universities, government laboratories or industry. It is highly desirable that all of these sectors have the opportunity to access an abundance of new instruments, materials, effects and methods in case new instrumentalities will yield on the one side novel scientific advances and on the other side unforeseen technological innovation.

The institutional design of the NRF-CRN addresses the challenges and opportunities revealed in Price's (1984) study. For example, the original concept of CRNs included the idea of 'hub-and-spoke' arrangements,[7] whereby a research-intensive university would collaborate with a developing university to facilitate researchers' access to advanced facilities and experienced technicians. Social science researchers in the NRF-CRN collaborate with colleagues at The Australian National University and James Cook University to access advanced social science instrumentalities including research methods and data, providing to them in return in situ tests and applications that reflexively improve methods and models. In another example, the NRF-CRN delivers a range of knowledge-transfer programs ('extension') to government and north Australian communities, helping to ensure that the new instrumentalities of social science (such as new ways of approaching the design of institutional governance) become available to those who might be able to exploit them in innovative ways.

## People-Centric Innovation

Just as Price (1984) identified instrumentalities as an overlooked but important feature of sound innovation policy, so Allott (2006) identified people as an overlooked but central component of public policy designed to create wealth from RD&E conducted in universities. Allott's (2006) point is not that public funding of university RD&E is misplaced, but rather that when the purpose of the funding is technology transfer (broadly defined) grounded on a linear model of innovation, the funding

---

7   'Hub-and-spoke alliances will ensure that all researchers get access to the best colleagues and the best infrastructure. They will ensure that all research students get access to the best supervision and the best learning aids' (Senator Kim Carr speaking at Charles Darwin University, 9 November 2009, retrieved from web.archive.org/web/20160402185435/http://archive.industry.gov.au/minister archive2011/carr/Speeches/Pages/CHARLESDARWINCHANCELLERY.html).

is targeted in the wrong place. He advocated knowledge transfer that is not idea centric but people centric. This, Allott (2006) stated, has two aspects: 1) contact with the researchers in universities who can answer the questions being asked, and 2) university graduates meeting the potential employers who have the jobs they want.

At first sight, an emphasis on people seems like a hollow motherhood statement. The sharp edge of a people-centric approach to public policy becomes clearer when Allott (2006) highlights the role of PhDs from his standpoint—namely, looking things up when they are needed, thereby accessing 100 per cent of the world's publicly available knowledge in relevant domains, rather than inventing things after long and unpredictable work. To PhD candidates and universities alike, this position would generally represent a major shift in the perceived place of highly skilled knowledge workers in an advanced economy. It is, of course, consistent with the observation by Neave (1979) mentioned above, that the dominant contribution of regional universities is to broaden and amplify trends emerging from other sectors.

While Allott's (2006) perspective is that of an 'industrial Visitor' to Cambridge University, scholars more centrally involved in studying the question of people centric learning and innovation policy express similar ideas. For example, in a carefully constructed and highly regarded theoretical overview, Asheim, Coenen and Vang (2007) pointed to the need for innovation scholars to address a people-centric view of innovation and creativity, untangling conflated ideas of face-to-face and buzz as modes of personal interaction, of interindustry differences and the consequent exaggeration of cities as the sites of creativity and innovation. According to this analysis, buzz is the concoction of rumours, recommendation, folk lore and information, transmissible electronically or directly and, therefore, both local and global. It is the mode of knowledge transfer that is particularly important for symbolic goods, such as film, theatre and publishing where time-limited projects tend to dominate. Face-to-face interaction, on the other hand, is important for activities resting on an analytic knowledge base (e.g. in biotech and nanotech) that can benefit from direct access to expert researchers working at the forefront of knowledge generation. It is often important also for industries that rely on a synthetic knowledge base (e.g. plant engineering and production systems) resting on access and transmission of tacit know-how and diverse skills. Asheim et al. (2007) argued that if these ideas were better understood, policymakers should be in a position to implement customised support into different regions and sectors, assisting the competitiveness of regions in a globalising world.

As revealed in other chapters of this book, the NRF-CRN has adopted a wide range of people-centric approaches to knowledge transfer, including the appointment of Indigenous leaders as visiting fellows, frequent face-to-face briefings that take place in various geographical settings, fostering 'buzz' in social media and the development of social science approaches that engage researchers directly in community-led and industry-led activities.

## Discussion

One of the most important and difficult challenges for governments in relation to the public policy for funding research universities is to strike a sound balance between concentration and selectivity.[8] In the US system, this challenge is addressed by a number of programs including the long-running Experimental Program to Stimulate Competitive Research (EPSCoR), founded in 1979. EPSCoR provides funding to research universities in US states that are traditionally underfunded through federal RD&E programs (Feller, 2000; Institute of Medicine, 2013). In the United Kingdom (UK), the discovery through peer-review processes that research excellence is widespread (Adams & Gurney, 2010, 2014) prompted expressions of concern by leaders of universities large with research portfolios. This lead to a funding settlement that protected these universities while recognising dispersed excellence. The CRN program in Australia shares some of the policy objectives of the US EPSCoR program, and faces some of the UK's challenges created when powerful research universities mobilise to protect their funding base against relatively small proposals to distribute it more broadly.

The White Paper and other studies (e.g. Allison & Eversole, 2008) reveal just how important it is for Australia that public funding for RD&E conducted within regional universities be an embedded component of Australia's research and innovation system. The CRN program is such a program, and evaluations of its implementation (e.g. ACIL Allen

---

8   Concentration is the policy of building research scale in selected institutions, while selectivity is the policy of supporting research excellence wherever it arises (see Adams & Gurney, 2010).

Consulting, 2015) provide an opportunity to improve the design and delivery of such programs. Some of the principal alignments between public policy drivers and the NRF-CRN design features are shown in Table 25.1, illustrating how straightforward it can be to deliver on national priorities through a funding program like the CRN.

Table 25.1: Alignment of public policy drivers and NRF-CRN design features.

| Area of public policy relevance | NRF-CRN design features |
| --- | --- |
| Public funding for RD&E to provide for the requirements of government. | Capability to deploy research teams with distributed disciplinary expertise to address government RD&E needs in an integrated and situated manner (e.g. demography and its implications for business and communities). |
| Public funding for RD&E when private interests cannot capture the full return; findings to be widely disseminated. | Baseline studies of emerging problems in northern development, including better designs for liveability; improved approaches to negotiation of land use; improved approaches to shared governance. |
| Public funding for regional RD&E situated in the specific region of interest. | Field work and stakeholder networks with an enduring footprint in the region, attached to conduits connecting to the leading research groups in Australia and overseas. |
| Instrumentalities enabling both fundamental research and applied research. | Access to a diverse range of qualitative and quantitative research methods; innovative approaches to research organisation and leadership. |
| People-centric innovation policy with attention to regional issues. | Higher degree research students working in team-based approaches to community and societal issues and problems. |

There is a compelling case for a continuing program of public RD&E funding by the Australian Government for institutional arrangements similar to the CRNs. The NRF-CRN or a descendent of it provides an exemplary vehicle to undertake, absorb and diffuse the RD&E required to shape, inform and sustain critically important agendas in the development of Northern Australia.

# Acknowledgements

Many of the ideas presented here were developed during and after workshops conducted with the members of NRF-CRN. I thank the participants and in particular acknowledge discussions with CRN Director Professor Ruth Wallace. Professor Robin Stanton of The Australian National University also provided a number of deep insights into the concepts behind this chapter.

# References

ACIL Allen Consulting. (2015). *Mid-term program evaluation: Collaborative Research Networks*. Canberra, ACT: Department of Education and Training.

Adams, J. & Gurney, K. (2010). *Funding selectivity, concentration and excellence—How good is the UK's research?* Oxford, England: Higher Education Policy Institute.

Adams, J. & Gurney, K. A. (2014). *Evidence for excellence: Has the signal overtaken the substance?* Digital Science.

Aghion, P. & Howitt, P. (2008). *The economics of growth*. MIT Press.

Allison, J. & Eversole, R. (2008). A new direction for regional university campuses: Catalyzing innovation in place. *Innovation: The European Journal of Social Science Research, 21*(2), 95–109.

Allott, S. (2006). *From science to growth: What exactly is the mechanism by which scientific research turns into economic growth?* Cambridge, England: Hughes Hall, Cambridge University.

Amin, Ash. (1999). An institutionalist perspective on regional economic development. *International Journal of Urban and Regional Research, 23*(2), 365–378.

Asheim, B., Coenen, L. & Vang, J. (2007). Face-to-face, buzz, and knowledge bases: Sociospatial implications for learning, innovation, and innovation policy. *Environment and Planning C, 25*(5), 655–670. doi.org/10.1068/c0648

Australian Government. (2015). *Our north, our future: White paper on developing Northern Australia*. Retrieved from www.industry.gov.au/data-and-publications/our-north-our-future-white-paper-on-developing-northern-australia

Balconi, M., Brusoni, S. & Orsenigo, L. (2010). In defence of the linear model: An essay. *Research Policy, 39*(1), 1–13.

Blaug, M. (1976). The empirical status of human capital theory: A slightly jaundiced survey. *Journal of Economic Literature, 14*(3), 827–855.

Boschma, R. A. & Frenken, K. (2006). Why is economic geography not an evolutionary science? Towards an evolutionary economic geography. *Journal of Economic Geography, 6*(3), 273–302.

Bush, V. (1945). Science: The endless frontier. *Transactions of the Kansas Academy of Science (1903), 8*(3), 231–264.

Crow, M. M. & Tucker, C. (2001). The American research university system as America's de facto technology policy. *Science and Public Policy, 28*(1), 2–10.

Department of Education and Training. (2015). *Collaborative Research Networks*. Retrieved from web.archive.org/web/20150711064003/https://www.education.gov.au/collaborative-research-networks-crn

Feller, I. (2000). Strategic options to enhance the research competitiveness of EPSCoR Universities. In Albert H. Link, Stephen D. Nelson, Celia McEnaney & Stephen L. Lita (Eds), *AAAS science and technology policy yearbook* (pp. 341–363). Washington, DC: American Association for the Advancement of Science.

Geisler, E. (2000). *The metrics of science and technology*. Greenwood Publishing Group.

Healy, A. & Morgan, K. (2012). Spaces of innovation: Learning, proximity and the ecological turn. *Regional Studies, 46*(8), 1041–1053.

Hodgson, Geoffrey M. (2014). What is capital? Economists and sociologists have changed its meaning: Should it be changed back? *Cambridge Journal of Economics, 38*(5), 1063–1086.

Hughes, A. (2008). Innovation policy as cargo cult: Myth and reality in knowledge-led productivity growth In J. Bessant & T. Venables (Eds), *Creating wealth from knowledge: Meeting the innovation challenge* (pp. 80–104). Cheltenham, England: Edward Elgar.

Institute of Medicine. (2013). *The experimental program to stimulate competitive research*. Washington, DC: The National Academies Press. doi.org/10.17226/18384

Koestler, A. & Butterfield, H. (1968). *The sleepwalkers*. London, England: Hutchinson.

Neave, G. (1979). Education and regional development: An overview of a growing controversy. *European Journal of Education, 4*(3), 207–231.

Peck, J. & Tickell, A. (2002). Neoliberalizing space. *Antipode, 34*(3), 380–404.

Price, D. J. de Solla (1963). *Big science, little science*. New York, NY: Columbia University.

Price, D. J. de Solla (1984). The science/technology relationship, the craft of experimental science, and policy for the improvement of high technology innovation. *Research Policy, 13*(1), 3–20.

Productivity Commission. (2007, March). *Public support for science and innovation* (Research report). Canberra, ACT: Productivity Commission.

Quiggin, J. (1999). Human capital theory and education policy in Australia. *Australian Economic Review, 32*(2), 130–144.

Richerson, P. J. & Boyd, R. (2008). *Not by genes alone: How culture transformed human evolution.* University of Chicago Press.

Roberts, R. M. (1989). *Serendipity: Accidental discoveries in science.* Wiley.

Shanks, S. & Zheng, S. (2006). *Econometric modelling of R&D and Australia's productivity* (Productivity Commission staff working paper).

Smith, E. (2012). *Luck: What it means and why it matters.* Bloomsbury.

Snow, C. P. (1962). *Science and government: The Godkin lectures at Harvard University, 1960.* New English Library.

Walker, B. W., Porter, D. J. & Marsh, I. (2012). *Fixing the hole in Australia's heartland: How government needs to work in remote Australia.* Alice Springs, NT: Desert Knowledge Australia.

www.ingramcontent.com/pod-product-compliance
Lightning Source LLC
Chambersburg PA
CBHW041223030426
42334CB00037B/3137